A HISTORY OF THE MODERN BRITISH ISLES, 1603–1707

A HISTORY OF THE MODERN BRITISH ISLES

Founding Editor: Sir Geoffrey Elton
General Editor: John Stevenson

This series will cover the history of the British Isles from 1529 to the present. The books will combine the results of the latest scholarship and research with clear, accessible writing.

Published

A History of the Modern British Isles, 1603–1707:
The Double Crown
David L. Smith

In Preparation

A History of the Modern British Isles, 1529–1603:
The Two Kingdoms
Mark Nicholls

A History of the Modern British Isles, 1707–1815:
The Age of Wars
John Stevenson

A History of the Modern British Isles, 1815–1914:
Liberal Britain
James Webster

A History of the Modern British Isles, 1914–present:
The Age of Missed Opportunities
Arthur Marwick

The British Empire, 1500–1955
T. N. Harper

In association with the series:

A History of Ireland, 1778–1972
Alvin Jackson

A HISTORY OF THE MODERN BRITISH ISLES, 1603–1707

The Double Crown

David L. Smith

BLACKWELL Publishers

Editorial Offices:
108 Cowley Road, Oxford OX4 1JF, UK
    Tel: +44 (0)1865 791100
Osney Mead, Oxford OX2 0EL, UK
    Tel: +44 (0)1865 206206
Blackwell Publishing USA, 350 Main Street, Malden, MA 02148-5018, USA
    Tel: +1 781 388 8250
Iowa State University Press, a Blackwell Publishing company, 2121 S. State Avenue, Ames, Iowa
    50014-8300, USA
    Tel: +1 515 292 0140
Blackwell Munksgaard, Nørre Søgade 35, PO Box 2148, Copenhagen, DK-1016, Denmark
    Tel: +45 77 33 33 33
Blackwell Publishing Asia, 54 University Street, Carlton, Victoria 3053, Australia
    Tel: +61 (0)3 9347 0300
Blackwell Verlag, Kurfürstendamm 57, 10707 Berlin, Germany
    Tel: +49 (0)30 32 79 060
Blackwell Publishing, 10, rue Casimir Delavigne, 75006 Paris, France
    Tel: +331 53 10 3310

First published 1998 by Blackwell Publishers Ltd
Reprinted 2000, 2002

Library of Congress Cataloging-in-Publication Data
Smith, David L. (David Lawrence), 1963–
   A history of the modern British Isles: 1603–1707 / David L. Smith.
      p.   cm.– (A history of the modern British Isles)
   Includes bibliographical references and index.
   ISBN 0–631–19401–0. — ISBN 0–631–19402–9 (pbk.)
   1.   Great Britain–Politics and government–1603–1714.
   2.   Scotland–Politics and government–1371–1707. 3. Scotland–History
   –Stuarts, to the Union, 1371–1707. 4. Monarchy–Great Britain–History
   –17th century. 5. Great Britain–History–Stuarts, 1603–1714. 6. Great
   Britain–Constitutional history. 7. Great Britain–Kings and rulers.
   8. Scotland–Kings and rulers. 9. Stuart, House of. I. Title. II. Series
DA375.S63   1998   97-29541
941.06–dc21   CIP

A catalogue record for this title is available from the British Library.

Set by Grahame & Grahame Editorial, Brighton, East Sussex
Printed and bound in Great Britain by T. J. International Ltd, Padstow, Cornwall

For further information on
Blackwell Publishers visit our website:
www.blackwellpublishers.co.uk

Contents

Plates

Maps

Preface

Ever since I first began teaching undergraduates nearly ten years ago, I have regularly commented in lectures and supervisions how difficult it has now become to write a single-volume introductory survey of seventeenth-century Britain. The complexity of the period and the remarkable scale and diversity of the historiography make this an exceptionally hard subject to capture in an 'overview'; and the problem becomes ever more acute. It was therefore with a mixture of delight and trepidation that I accepted the late Sir Geoffrey Elton's invitation to write this volume. It is a source of particular sadness to me that I only had the benefit of his wise advice on the chapter structure and the first two chapters. But the contents and approach of the book clearly bear the stamp of the guidelines that he established for this series: that is to say, the book seeks to offer an analytical and interpretative narrative the backbone of which is mainly political, and into which social, economic and cultural themes are interwoven. Such a book inevitably has a strong element of the personal in it: I could see no way of giving every theme or problem equal priority without rendering the treatment of everything skimpy and superficial. As a result, the primary – but not exclusive – focus of the volume is political and constitutional history, and some areas of current scholarly activity (especially those related to social and economic history) receive less attention than others.

The scholarly literature on this period is vast and complex, and I offer some guidance to how it may be approached further in the endnotes and the Bibliographical Essay. The text itself frequently engages with current debates between historians and consciously tries to integrate the fruits of recent research into a general account. It is not, however, constructed around the historiography, partly because that would lead it to date extremely quickly, and partly to avoid the loss of coherence that would unavoidably arise from any attempt to summarize such a diffuse body of writing.

The title, *A History of the Modern British Isles, 1603–1707: The Double Crown*, captures two themes that are especially central to this book. It covers a very particular period in British history, that of the regal union of England and Scotland. The fact that between 1603 and 1707 the Crowns – but not the kingdoms – of England and Scotland were united constituted the basis of a highly distinctive polity, with structures and problems characteristically its own. Throughout this book I examine how successive rulers handled a composite monarchy that included Ireland and Wales as well as Scotland and England, and how the course of events in each nation was shaped by being part of a multiple kingdom as well as by their own internal dynamics. The first and last chapters offer 'snapshots' of Britain and Ireland in the years which saw the Union of the Crowns and the Union of the Kingdoms respectively, thus allowing an assessment of change and continuity during the intervening period.

If my first theme explores the ramifications of a *double* Crown, the second takes up the importance of the *Crown* itself. In one sense the centrality of individual monarchs within a personal monarchy seems a very obvious and tautological point. However, much current research is drawing out the influence of the personalities of successive kings on political, constitutional and cultural developments with a greater sophistication than ever before. Some of this research is also pointing to profound underlying patterns in the nature of kingship during the period as a whole. My account tries to overcome the artificial divide of 1660 by emphasizing the parallels between James I and Charles II in their (mainly) successful handling of government. Conversely, it also highlights the disastrous parallels between Charles I and James II, both of whom emerge in much recent literature as personalities ill-suited to rule seventeenth-century Britain and Ireland. The last two chapters suggest that during the years 1689–1707 a very different political system began to emerge which pointed decisively away from personal monarchy towards constitutional monarchy. The changes concentrated in those years ushered in a genuinely new era, and in this, as in so many other ways that will be explored during the course of this book, the seventeenth century proved of seminal importance.

For the sake of clarity and accessibility in a volume intended primarily for undergraduates and the proverbial 'general reader', I have modernized spelling and punctuation in all quotations from primary sources. All dates are given in the 'Old Style' then used in Britain and Ireland (which in this period was ten days behind the 'New Style' employed in continental Europe), except that I have regarded the year as beginning on 1 January rather than 25 March. The date charts at the beginning of each chapter are necessarily selective and are designed – together with the maps, glossary and appendices – to provide specific information about individuals, events and issues referred to in the text.

The debts that I have incurred while researching and writing this book are many and pervasive: it is impossible to acknowledge all of them here, but the greatest must certainly be recorded. My debt to John Morrill, both personal and academic, is so immense and extends over so many years that it is difficult to put into words. The origins of a book such as this go back a very long way, right back to the undergraduate days when he first introduced me to the period. Typically, amidst his exceptionally busy schedule he found time to read the entire book in draft and to produce seventeen pages of detailed suggestions and corrections. Those notes have greatly improved the final product; and without his friendship, inspiration and example over the years I doubt it would exist at all.

I have already written of my debt to the late Sir Geoffrey Elton. It was a great privilege to discuss this project with him at various times during the last eighteen months of his life, and to have such a warmly supportive and encouraging editor. Since his death, the role of series editor has been admirably fulfilled by John Stevenson, who has given me a great deal of helpful advice and practical guidance on many aspects of this project. I am very grateful to Jon Parkin for reading and commenting on the book in draft, and for his willingness to debate and challenge its arguments in numerous stimulating conversations. I have also benefited greatly from extensive discussions of the draft with Graham Seel, and from his sharp eye for errors and infelicities. Between them, those who read the typescript saved me from innumerable mistakes and misjudgements; but I cannot believe that even they have managed to weed out every lapse, and responsibility for those that remain must lie with me.

Many other scholars have helped me by offering advice, or by answering specific queries, or just by talking about the seventeenth century with me. It is invidious to single out names, but I particularly wish to thank Ian Atherton, Andrew Barclay, John Coffey, Sir Alan Cook, Nicholas Cranfield, Patrick Higgins, Clare Jackson, Mark Kishlansky, John McCafferty, Anthony Milton, Mića Panić and Neil Reynolds. The Master and Fellows of Selwyn College, Cambridge, have not only continued to provide a splendidly collegial and conducive working environment, but also granted me two terms of sabbatical leave away from teaching and administrative duties during which this book was completed. I must also thank the two commissioning editors at Blackwell Publishers with whom I have worked, John Davey and latterly Tessa Harvey, for their efficiency, professional expertise and unfailing helpfulness.

It is something of a truism to record that one has learned from pupils, but in the case of this book I feel the debt even more acutely than usual. I have had ideal opportunities to try out many of my main themes and arguments in Cambridge undergraduate lectures and also in a Special Subject class for the Cambridge Board of Continuing Education's international summer programme. The feedback that I have received has been invaluable in shaping and refining my view of the period. I have also gained an immense amount from supervising my research students, Tim Amos and Harry Bowcott. Above all, since 1988 I have had the highly rewarding experience of supervising undergraduates individually for the outline paper on early modern British political and constitutional history, and/or the final year paper on 'The British Problem, 1534–1707'. I have taught over 250 students in this way, and they have contributed far more to the making of this book than they can possibly realize. I dedicate it to all of them, with gratitude, affection and respect. It could not have been written without them.

D. L. S.
Selwyn College, Cambridge
May 1997

Abbreviations

EcHR	*Economic History Review*
EHR	*English Historical Review*
HJ	*Historical Journal*
HR	*Historical Research*
IHS	*Irish Historical Studies*
JBS	*Journal of British Studies*
JEH	*Journal of Ecclesiastical History*
JMH	*Journal of Modern History*
PP	*Past and Present*
ScHR	*Scottish Historical Review*
TRHS	*Transactions of the Royal Historical Society*

Table 1   The House of Stuart and the line of succession.

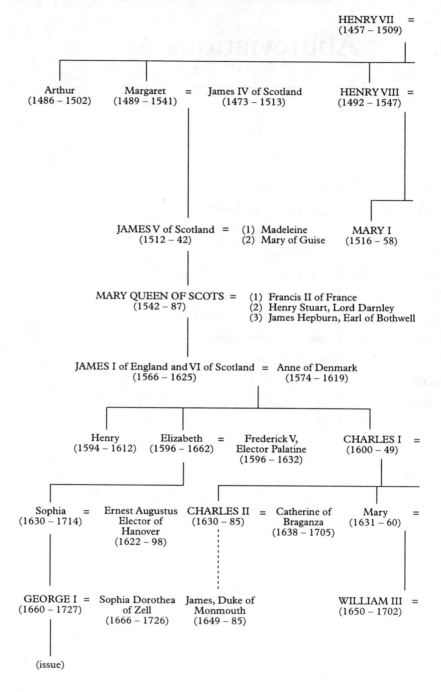

HENRY VII   =
(1457 – 1509)

Arthur   Margaret   =   James IV of Scotland   HENRY VIII   =
(1486 – 1502)   (1489 – 1541)   (1473 – 1513)   (1492 – 1547)

JAMES V of Scotland   =   (1) Madeleine   MARY I
(1512 – 42)   (2) Mary of Guise   (1516 – 58)

MARY QUEEN OF SCOTS   =   (1) Francis II of France
(1542 – 87)   (2) Henry Stuart, Lord Darnley
(3) James Hepburn, Earl of Bothwell

JAMES I of England and VI of Scotland   =   Anne of Denmark
(1566 – 1625)   (1574 – 1619)

Henry   Elizabeth   =   Frederick V,   CHARLES I   =
(1594 – 1612)   (1596 – 1662)   Elector Palatine   (1600 – 49)
(1596 – 1632)

Sophia   =   Ernest Augustus   CHARLES II   =   Catherine of   Mary   =
(1630 – 1714)   Elector of   (1630 – 85)   Braganza   (1631 – 60)
Hanover   (1638 – 1705)
(1622 – 98)

GEORGE I   =   Sophia Dorothea   James, Duke of   WILLIAM III   =
(1660 – 1727)   of Zell   Monmouth   (1650 – 1702)
(1666 – 1726)   (1649 – 85)

(issue)

Source: John Wroughton, *The Longman Companion to the Stuart Age, 1603–1714* (Harlow, 1997)

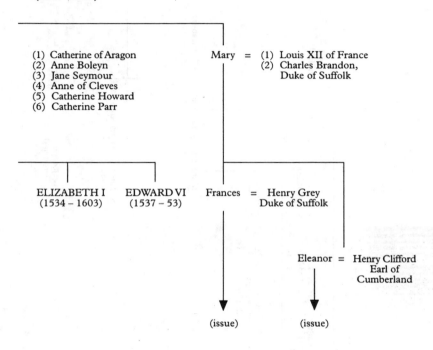

Elizabeth of York
(1466 – 1503)

(1) Catherine of Aragon
(2) Anne Boleyn
(3) Jane Seymour
(4) Anne of Cleves
(5) Catherine Howard
(6) Catherine Parr

Mary = (1) Louis XII of France
       (2) Charles Brandon,
           Duke of Suffolk

ELIZABETH I   EDWARD VI   Frances = Henry Grey
(1534 – 1603)   (1537 – 53)   Duke of Suffolk

Eleanor = Henry Clifford
          Earl of
          Cumberland

(issue)   (issue)

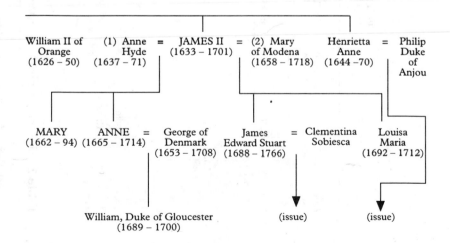

Henrietta Maria of France
(1609 – 69)

William II of   (1) Anne = JAMES II = (2) Mary   Henrietta = Philip
Orange   Hyde   (1633 – 1701) of Modena   Anne   Duke
(1626 – 50)   (1637 – 71)   (1658 – 1718) (1644 –70)   of
                                                                       Anjou

MARY   ANNE   = George of   James   = Clementina   Louisa
(1662 – 94)   (1665 – 1714) Denmark   Edward Stuart Sobiesca   Maria
                            (1653 – 1708)   (1688 – 1766)   (1692 – 1712)

William, Duke of Gloucester
(1689 – 1700)

(issue)   (issue)

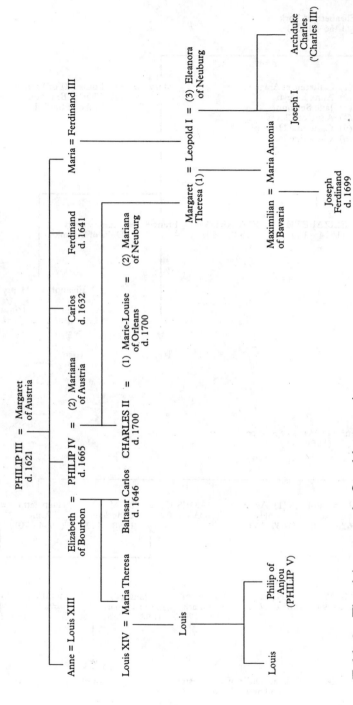

Table 2 The claimants to the Spanish succession.

Source: Barry Coward, *The Stuart Age: England, 1603–1714* (2nd edition, Harlow, 1994)

1   1603: Union of the Crowns

	5 November– 27 May 1606	Second session of James's first Parliament
1606	January	Two penal laws passed against recusants
	12 April	James proclaims a single 'Union Flag' for England and Scotland
	11 July	Scottish act restoring 'the Estate of Bishops'
	July	Visit by Christian IV of Denmark
	18 November– 4 July 1607	Third session of James's first Parliament: union of the kingdoms debated but not approved
	November	Judges find for James in Bate's Case, upholding the King's right to levy impositions
1607	2 May	Abolition of the 'hostile laws' limiting trade, aid and communication across the Anglo-Scottish border
	May	Midlands Rising against enclosure of common fields
	4 September	Flight of Tyrconnell and other leading Ulster lords to Continent
1608	January/ February	Court of King's Bench declares tanistry illegal
	4 May	Robert Cecil, Earl of Salisbury, appointed Lord Treasurer
	June	Calvin's Case gives English legal rights to Scots born after the Union of the Crowns
	July	Salisbury introduces new Book of Rates
	July–October	Lord Ochiltree's expedition to Western Isles to bring certain chiefs to Edinburgh
	First Gaelic translation of Prayer Book published	
1609	30 March	Truce of Antwerp between Spain and the Dutch (until 1621)
	24 June	Establishment of Justices of the Peace in Scotland
	21 July	Appointment of commissioners to oversee plantation of Ulster
	August	Statutes of Iona: leading chiefs from Western Isles submit to royal authority

1610	9 February–23 July	Fourth session of James's first Parliament: debates over Great Contract
	July	James agrees to levy no new impositions without Parliament's consent
	16 October–6 December	Fifth session of James's first Parliament: discussions over Great Contract break down
	21 October	Three Scottish bishops consecrated at Westminster
	2 November	Death of Archbishop Bancroft
1611	4 March	George Abbot nominated as Archbishop of Canterbury
	May	Creation of order of baronets, for sale at £1,095 each
		Authorized Version of the Bible published
1612	24 May	Death of Salisbury; beginning of ascendancy of Howards
	23 October	Scottish Parliament acknowledges James as Supreme Governor of the Scottish Church
	6 November	Death of Prince Henry; Prince Charles becomes heir to the throne
		Publication of Sir John Davies' *Discovery of the True Causes why Ireland was never entirely subdued*
1613	14 February	Marriage of Princess Elizabeth and Frederick V, Elector Palatine
	15 September	Death in the Tower of Sir Thomas Overbury
	26 December	Marriage of Earl of Somerset and Countess of Essex
1614	5 April–7 June	Addled Parliament: disputes over impositions
	11 July	Thomas Howard, Earl of Suffolk, appointed Lord Treasurer
	December	Alderman Cockayne's Project: export of unfinished cloth prohibited; causes crisis in cloth industry for the next three years

1615	23 April	George Villiers appointed a gentleman of the bedchamber; beginning to emerge as new royal favourite
	April	Irish Convocation adopts new Articles of Faith
	18 October	Earl and Countess of Somerset arrested on charges of involvement in Overbury's murder
1616	May	Trial of Earl and Countess of Somerset for involvement in Overbury murder; death sentence commuted to imprisonment
	August–September	Weavers riot in Wiltshire and Gloucestershire due to depression in the cloth industry caused by Cockayne Project
	15 November	Sir Edward Coke dismissed as Lord Chief Justice of King's Bench
1617	5 January	George Villiers created Earl of Buckingham
	May–August	James visits Scotland
	28 September	James re-admits Sir Edward Coke to the Privy Council

1 James's Accession

Early in the morning of 24 March 1603, Elizabeth I, Queen of England and Ireland, died peacefully at Richmond. Barely eight hours later, James VI of Scotland was proclaimed her successor in London. The proclamation asserted James's 'undoubted right' to 'the imperial crown of these realms' and rehearsed his descent from Margaret Tudor, the elder sister of Henry VIII. The fact that Henry VIII had excluded Margaret's descendants from the succession by act of Parliament in 1543 was completely ignored, and instead the principle of indefeasible hereditary right was resoundingly affirmed. This proclamation had been drafted in advance by Elizabeth's Secretary of State Robert Cecil and shown to James, who enthusiastically approved it. Cecil's secret contacts with James since the spring of 1601 prepared the way for a remarkably smooth accession which united the Scottish Crown with that of England and Ireland. There was, noted one observer, 'no tumult, no contradiction, no disorder'. The 'union of the crowns' was achieved with deceptive ease; yet over a century elapsed before it was followed by a full-scale 'union of the kingdoms'.

Within three days of Elizabeth's death a despatch rider, Sir Robert Carey, conveyed the news to Edinburgh. The King who greeted him was, at nearly thirty-seven, already a figure of impressive accomplishments. He had stamped his authority on the decentralized and sometimes turbulent Scottish polity with notable success. Through a combination of careful manipulation of faction and the development of a party of loyal officials, he had raised respect for the Crown to an unprecedented level. He had restrained the more radical leaders of the Presbyterian Kirk. An intellectual of European importance, he was the author of poetry and biblical commentary as well as two major works of political theory, *The True Law of Free Monarchies* (1598) and the *Basilikon Doron* (1599). Shrewd, intelligent and determined, James also possessed considerable political skill. These qualities and achievements, together with the fact that he was a confirmed Protestant and already had two male heirs, ensured an enthusiastic reception from his new English subjects. He never forgot his first encounters with them as he journeyed south and saw 'their eyes flaming nothing but sparkles of affection'.

The multiple kingdoms over which James now ruled were far more diverse and contrasted than their relatively limited geographical area might suggest. In terms of political traditions, institutions of government, legal systems, and economic and social structures, the three kingdoms of England, Scotland and Ireland and the principality of Wales not only differed from each other but often displayed significant internal variations from region to region. But in the long term, the greatest source of instability was probably religion. The experience of multiple kingdoms on the Continent, especially the French and Spanish monarchies, suggested that for one monarch to rule over more than one religion was a recipe for trouble. In 1603, not only did James's three kingdoms each possess their own distinctive religions; they were themselves divided over religion. We must look more closely at each part of his inheritance in turn.

2 England: Politics and Government

As regards political and legal institutions, much the most centralized of these kingdoms was England. The Norman Conquest had allowed the machinery of government to be reshaped and moulded by successive medieval monarchs to a degree unparalleled elsewhere in Western Europe. During the course of the Middle Ages, a single common law had developed, a unique amalgam of ancient custom, Roman law and case-law dispensed by the judicial officers of the Crown. The thirteenth century saw the emergence of a bicameral Parliament comprising the Houses of Lords and Commons. Parliament combined the functions of a court of law and of the monarch's Great Council (as opposed to the Privy Council). Its central purposes were to advise the monarch of happenings in the localities, to collaborate with the Crown in the passing of acts of Parliament (statutes) and to vote taxes (the so-called 'extra-ordinary revenue' of the Crown). It was far more powerful than its Scottish and Irish counterparts, and increasingly perceived itself as the 'representative of the whole realm' of England.

These developments were consolidated and greatly extended under the Tudors, and in particular during the 1530s. That decade saw the emergence of a genuinely unitary State. The famous preamble to the Act of Appeals (1533) declared England to be 'an empire', free from the intrusions of any external authority. The Franchises Act of 1536 abolished those few remaining pockets of jurisdiction (such as the palatinate of Durham) where the monarch's writ did not run. The fact that these measures were enshrined in statute was itself highly significant. The period of the Reformation Parliament (1529–36) established the King-in-Parliament as the supreme legislative authority in England, jointly enacting statutes which were omnicompetent. There was no matter, no area of life, which statute could not regulate. This principle, clearly borne out through the remainder of the sixteenth century, gave reality to the view of the English polity as a 'dominium politicum et regale' (constitutional monarchy) which Sir John Fortescue had advanced in the fifteenth century.

All this meant that by 1603 English monarchs were far more powerful when they acted in collaboration with Parliament and the law, and when they governed with the consent of their subjects (or at least of the political elite) than if they tried to rule alone. Although the Crown possessed certain discretionary powers known generically as the 'royal prerogative', it was widely thought that such powers were granted and defined by the common law. The proclamations which the Crown could issue unilaterally were regarded as inferior to the common law and to the statutes passed by King-in-Parliament: proclamations could deal with administrative, economic and social matters, but they could not touch life, limb or common law rights of property. Moreover, the Crown had no police force to impose its will, and the total number of paid government officials was fewer than two thousand. As a result, the government was entirely dependent on the voluntary co-operation of local nobles and gentry for the collection of taxes, the training of the militia, the enforcement of all manner of laws, and the trial of most criminals. Such co-operation was essential to both

parties: the local elites held office (such as justice of the peace, deputy lieutenant, lord lieutenant) on royal commissions, and their status and influence
depended upon the Crown's support; but equally without their loyalty and
effectiveness throughout England the Crown's claims about the obedience and
docility of its subjects would have been empty rhetoric. Government – at both
national and local levels – rested upon the co-operation of the monarch with
the leading subjects; and if this harmonious collaboration did not occur naturally the constitution possessed absolutely no formal mechanisms to bring it
about.

In another sense too the English Crown was dependent on the support of the
political elite. Historically, royal revenues had been divided into two categories,
'ordinary' and 'extraordinary'. The first came from Crown lands, customs
duties, excise duties, feudal revenues, the profits of justice and (after 1534)
from the Church. These sources were generating a total income of around
£350,000 a year at the time of James's accession, a figure which, if maintained,
would enable the Crown to finance its activities during peacetime. However,
the effects of war and inflation were making the Crown more and more reliant
on its 'extraordinary' revenue, and especially on the direct taxation which could
only be levied with Parliament's consent. By the last decade of Elizabeth's
reign, these direct taxes were becoming a regular part of royal income.
Elizabeth requested such taxes in twelve of her thirteen parliamentary sessions.
Although in the early seventeenth century barely 10 per cent of royal revenues
came from direct taxation, the Crown was quite unable to wage war without
it. That the Stuarts depended on Parliaments to balance their wartime budget
in a period which saw Europe engulfed by successive conflicts was to have a
major impact on the course of English politics during the seventeenth century.

This situation was complicated by the fact that the continental wars stemmed
in large measure from profound religious divisions. Under the Tudors England
had first repudiated papal jurisdiction and then embarked on a Protestant
Reformation. After a brief attempt under Mary to reintroduce Catholicism,
Elizabeth had established a Church of England which was reformed in doctrine
but traditional in structure. The result was a Church that, in Conrad Russell's
words, 'looked Catholic but sounded Protestant'. The Elizabethan Church was
deliberately designed to appeal to as many different tastes as possible, but in
the process it also incurred criticism from a number of quarters. The most
vociferous and consistent attacks came from those 'hotter sort of Protestants'
often loosely called 'Puritans'. Such people thought the Church 'but halfly
reformed': they loathed the legacies of Catholicism in the form of bishops, vestments and a Prayer Book 'culled from that popish dunghill, the mass'. They
sought 'further reformation' which would sweep away the remnants of popery
and bring the structure of the Church into closer accord with its doctrine. For
inspiration they looked to 'the example of the best reformed Churches',
especially Geneva and the Presbyterian Kirk which had developed in Scotland
since 1560.

Yet very few hated the Elizabethan Church enough to separate from it
completely. The few sectarians who did, most notably the Brownists and the
Barrowists, were largely rooted out by persecution during Elizabeth's later

years; and thereafter sects such as the Family of Love led a passive, underground existence which historians have only just begun to reconstruct.[1] These separatists cannot be classed as 'Puritans'. The term 'Puritan' should rather be applied to those who remained within the Church but wished to purify it of all remnants of the old religion. They felt that there was enough that was godly about the Church – that there was still 'much piety in Babylon' – to make it worth trying to reform it from within. They longed for a new Constantine, a godly Prince who would remodel the Church; we shall see that in 1603 they had high hopes that James, with his Presbyterian upbringing, would fulfil this ideal. In the meantime, they preferred to supplement the official worship according to the Prayer Book with additional services, sermons and prayer meetings of their own. Elizabeth was always happy to allow these distinctive practices as long as they did not promote debate over the nature of a Church which she wished to preserve unchanged. At the other end of the religious spectrum, the English Catholic community settled for loss of status and office as the price for minimal persecution. By the end of the sixteenth century the Church of England was firmly established, and it received systematic and eloquent justification in Richard Hooker's *The Laws of Ecclesiastical Polity* (1593–1600). Yet the long-term stability of the Church depended on the monarch's ability to balance the different strands of opinion within it, to make all shades of belief feel welcome and to avoid becoming identified with any one position. As Supreme Governor of the Church, the monarch played a vital part in maintaining its equilibrium and broad appeal.

3 England: Society and Economy

The monarch was thus the apex of both Church and State, or to use a common contemporary metaphor, the head of the 'body politic'. The Crown also stood at the summit of the social order, which was highly stratified and hierarchical. Inequality of wealth and status was everywhere apparent. Yet English society was certainly not ossified, and new wealth enabled individuals to gain social status just as poverty could bring social ruin. Since the mid-sixteenth century, there had been a growing redistribution of wealth towards the middle ranks of society; and those who prospered, especially from farming or trade or the law, were able to rise into the upper social echelons. It is probably fair to say that England offered greater scope for upward (and downward) social mobility than most of its continental neighbours.

Immediately below the Crown stood the peerage, a hereditary nobility which in 1603 comprised only fifty-five peers. They appear to have maintained their position among the Crown's wealthiest subjects, and recent research has cast doubt on the theory that the later sixteenth and early seventeenth centuries witnessed a financial 'crisis of the aristocracy'.[2] Their influence in local and national affairs originally derived from their role as the Crown's senior military leaders who raised and commanded troops in wartime. In their counties, peers continued to occupy military offices such as lord lieutenant. At the national level, they were automatically members of the House of Lords, which (as we shall see) retained more political importance in this period than was once supposed. If English nobles lacked the legal and financial privileges of many of their continental counterparts, they often held senior offices at Court and usually dominated the King's Privy Council.

Below the peers stood the gentry, who made up no more than 5 per cent of heads of households but were increasing rapidly at the time of James's accession. It is likely that the total number of English gentry grew from around 5,000 in 1540 to about 15,000 by 1640. They were defined not by title but by lifestyle. According to Sir Thomas Smith, whoever 'can live idly and without manual labour, and will bear the port, charge, and countenance of a gentleman ... shall be taken for a gentleman'. Gentry were those whose landed income freed them from labour or dependence on others and gave them the leisure to become involved in government. They served as deputy lieutenants, lords of manors and militia captains; above all, as justices of the peace they enforced the King's laws and dispensed justice at the quarter sessions. In addition, the gentry were expected to behave charitably and hospitably towards their tenants and neighbours. Whereas in France or Spain commercial activity precluded gentility, in England any successful merchant could buy land and adopt the lifestyle of a gentleman, prompting Sir Thomas Smith to conclude that 'gentlemen be made good cheap in England'.

Beneath the nobility and gentry were those who worked for a living and whose status was determined by their economic function. The minor gentry shaded into the yeomanry, who had a similar income, owned up to about a hundred acres, and discharged the lesser local offices such as constable, elder and juryman at the quarter sessions. The evidence of their homes and probate inventories suggests that yeomen were prospering and increasing at the end of the sixteenth century, and some of them ultimately entered the ranks of the gentry. Below them stood the husbandmen, who farmed less than fifty acres; and finally the cottagers and labourers. These last three groups formed the majority of the rural population, and at the time of Elizabeth's death they were becoming both poorer and more numerous.

Contemporary anatomies of the social structure were couched in heavily masculine terms, and this reflected the fact that women could legally hold neither land nor title in their own right. The conventional (male) ideal of womanhood emphasized the qualities of submission, deference and obedience. In 1590 William Perkins defined a husband as 'he that hath authority over the wife': the latter, 'being subject to her husband, yieldeth obedience to him'. Yet, if women were the 'weaker vessel', in need of guidance from their husbands, men also had a duty to provide maintenance and protection. In reality, the relationships between wives and husbands varied greatly from marriage to marriage. Some outstanding women – such as Lady Joan Barrington, or Lady Anne Clifford, successively Countess of Dorset and of Pembroke – defied the stereotype of subservience and assumed a vitally important role in the running of large households and estates. Married couples often formed an economic partnership, especially among the small farmers and independent craftsmen or tradesmen. Plentiful evidence survives, particularly among diaries and wills, to suggest that genuinely affectionate marital relationships were far from uncommon, and that 'companionate' marriage was certainly not a discovery of the later seventeenth century. On the other hand, male dominance was pervasive, and it was often only as widows that women could attain a significant measure of independence by gaining control over their husbands' property or trade. Mocking rituals such as 'charivaris' or 'skimmingtons' often derided households where the woman was thought to rule the roost, and served to reinforce a double standard that penalized female sexual misdemeanours far more severely than male. Such conventions and assumptions help to explain the shock and hostility that greeted the increased prominence and freedom that many women were able to achieve during the disruption of the 1640s.[3]

As the yeomanry and gentry expanded and prospered, so the divide between them and the lower orders of rural society widened. A number of recent local studies have shown that one of the most marked social trends of this period was a growing polarization of the 'haves' and the 'have-nots'. This gulf was very often reflected also in contrasting religious and cultural attitudes. Those who thrived commonly embraced an individualistic outlook which contrasted with the more traditional, paternal, cohesive view of the community held by their poorer neighbours. Nor was this process of polarization confined to the countryside. There is plentiful evidence that urban society was filling out at the bottom as people migrated from the countryside into the towns in search of work. During Elizabeth's reign the population of London increased from about 120,000 to nearly 200,000; and observers noted with alarm the proliferation of apprentices as well as of 'beggars and other loose persons, swarming about the City'. No other town expanded at anything like the rate of the capital. London was larger than the next fifty English towns put together, and even the biggest – such as York, Bristol, Exeter, Norwich and Newcastle – only had between 10,000 and 20,000 inhabitants each. Yet everywhere similar social patterns were replicated: while many merchants, lawyers, tradesmen and shopkeepers found new opportunities and wealth, artisans, apprentices and labourers often lived on or below the subsistence level.

These developments had their roots in demographic growth. England's population had risen from about 2.5 million in the 1520s to around 4.1 million by 1600. This trend would continue for another fifty years, reaching a peak of just over 5.2 million by 1650. Such steady growth was sustained despite the occasional setbacks of famine and disease (especially in 1594–7), and ensured that the population was growing faster than food resources. This produced long-term price inflation: food prices increased sevenfold between 1500 and 1640, whereas wages increased only threefold. The majority of the population who did not grow their own food therefore found that a growing proportion of their income went on food purchases, and this in turn meant that their living standards declined markedly. The first two decades of the seventeenth century saw periodical subsistence crises which caused hunger and even starvation. Thereafter, famine ceased to pose a serious threat, but the continued rise in the population led to growing pressure on land and jobs, and widespread hardship.

The English economy at the end of the sixteenth century remained predominantly agrarian. In an attempt to increase the food supply marginal lands were pressed into service and existing lands were cultivated more intensively.

More efficient production involved the enclosing of many arable, woodland and fenland areas, but often at the expense of the smaller landholders and labourers who lived there. Enclosure, together with the seasonal nature of much agricultural work, thus contributed to a dramatic increase in vagrancy and underemployment. The burgeoning poor either migrated to towns, or tried to eke out a living in the countryside from an 'economy of makeshifts'. They sought additional wages from non-agrarian sources. Such industry as existed in England at this time was mostly 'cottage industry': with a few important exceptions – notably coal-mining in the northeast – production of commodities such as textiles, leather goods, small iron articles, and pottery was 'put out' to workers in their cottages. This valuable income was supplemented by scavenging food and fuel from waste lands, and by recourse to local charities and to the national system of poor relief recently codified by statutes of 1597 and 1601.

These general trends should not obscure the fact that England's agrarian economy was both highly localized and very diverse. The harsher climate and poorer soils of the northeast and southwest encouraged the raising of sheep rather than the production of cereals, whereas the lighter soils of East Anglia lent themselves to the cultivation of fodder crops. By the end of the seventeenth century such regional specialization would become much more marked, yielding surplus crops and goods which could then be exchanged for other products from elsewhere. But in 1603 most localities still attempted to be self-sufficient and internal trade, although on the increase, was circumscribed by the relatively limited network of roads and navigable waterways. In the coming years the expansion of towns, and above all of London, greatly stimulated inland trade. The capital's insatiable demand for food, fuel and consumer products did much to encourage economic growth and specialization, such as coal shipments from Newcastle or the development of market gardening in Kent and the Thames Valley. London also enjoyed a virtual stranglehold on England's export trade. During the second half of the sixteenth century it handled over 90 per cent of England's total exports, of which cloth exports constituted no less than 80 per cent. As Antwerp declined due to famine and war, London gradually assumed its role as Europe's leading commercial entrepôt and money market. The seventeenth century was to see a dramatic increase in England's overseas trade which would ultimately place it at the centre of a world-wide market.

Taken as a whole, these economic trends enabled England to avoid major subsistence crises after the opening decades of the seventeenth century. The agrarian crises of the late 1590s, 1607 and 1629–31 caused unrest rather than actual rebellion. Food riots were very much a last resort, and recent research has shown that they were remarkably orderly and controlled. In Keith Wrightson's words, 'there was order in this disorder'. Such riots were designed to rectify specific grievances, most commonly the inequitable provisioning and distribution of foodstuffs, and presented no fundamental threat to the social order or the institutions of government. They were directed against particular individuals – aggressive landlords, hoarders, those who exported grain or sold it at inflated prices – and they attacked such people in order to defend traditional rights and customs. Rioters did not run out of control or abandon all respect for authority; and by the same token the authorities usually treated them leniently and actively tried to redress the grievances which provoked them.

The restrained nature of riots was symptomatic of a nation which appeared in 1603 to be moving steadily away from the danger of civil war or revolution. Lawlessness, violence and disorder were decreasing, and the pervasive assumption was that most problems could be remedied through existing channels and institutions. The fact that the business of the law courts had expanded throughout the Tudor period reflected less an increase in criminality than a litigiousness born of the conviction that the arbitration of the courts offered more authoritative and enforceable solutions than could be achieved by taking the law into one's own hands. By 1603 the English were one of the most litigious peoples of Europe. The same belief in the power of established institutions to reflect diverse opinions and to solve all manner of problems explains why so few decided to opt out of the Church of England, and also why most Parliaments were widely welcomed as opportunities to remedy the ills of the commonwealth. As long as Court, Privy Council and Parliament continued to operate effectively as 'points of contact' between monarchs and their subjects, the underlying stability of the polity would be preserved. The smoothness of James's accession both demonstrated the essential soundness of England's government and further reinforced it by establishing what had never existed under Elizabeth: a well-nigh unchallengeable title and an indisputable line of succession.

4 Scotland

The northern kingdom which James left early in April 1603 presented a striking contrast with its southern neighbour. At the close of the sixteenth century Scotland's population was steadily expanding but remained well below one million. The impact of inflation was felt later than in England but no less severely: prices increased at least fourfold between 1550 and 1625. This, together with the Crown's relentless depreciation of the coinage, meant that the pound Scots was worth only one twelfth of the pound sterling by 1603. Scotland was still, as Bruce Galloway has written, 'a poor and in some ways primitive society', with a much smaller economic base than England. Scotland remained overwhelmingly agrarian: four in every five people continued to make their living from the land. The most characteristic form of settlement was the hamlet built around a notional 'farm', and such communities often achieved a high level of self-sufficiency. Even more than in England, there was no single national economy but rather a series of local economies. Large areas remained barren and grain yields were comparatively low. James had tried to encourage native industry and manufactures, but these were limited by lack of natural resources and by vested interests such as the craft guilds. He did succeed in reducing the autonomy of the burghs and casting the tax net more widely over their inhabitants, but Scottish burghs remained mostly small and medieval in

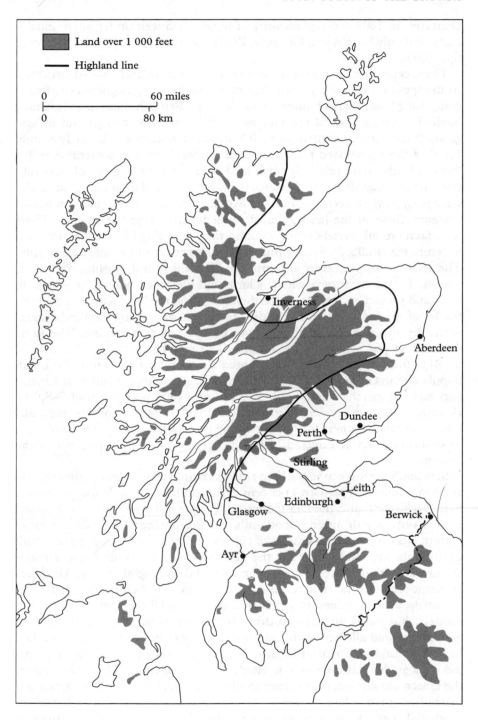

Map 1 Scotland.

character. In 1603 the vast majority of burghs had well under 3,000 inhabitants, and only Edinburgh, Glasgow, Perth, Aberdeen and Dundee had more than 5,000.

These economic facts were in turn reflected in Scotland's social structure. At the apex of rural society stood the nobility and leading Highland chieftains, comprising fewer than a hundred great families. Beneath them, the remaining landholders were classed together as 'lairds'. This was a large and diverse group that embraced as many as 10,000 heads of households, but only around 1,500 of these possessed really extensive estates. The rest, sometimes called 'bonnet lairds', were relatively small landowners who were generally less substantial than English gentry. Many of them were more akin to the yeomen who were prospering all over England, but Scotland had no exact equivalent to that category. Beneath the lairds, almost immediately, came the tenants. These were far more subservient to the landlord than their English counterparts, and in return the landlord offered protection, jurisdiction and military leadership. The relationship was seen in terms of paternalism and kinship, and many 'bonds of manrent' survive whereby lords and their men bound themselves to serve and protect each other. Nevertheless, during the later sixteenth century, the lot of the rural peasantry steadily deteriorated as many landlords aggravated the effects of population growth by ruthless rack-renting. The same polarization was evident in the burghs. The merchants and craftsmen who together formed the burgesses accounted for a tiny proportion of the urban population: in Glasgow in 1604 the fourteen craft guilds contained 361 members and the merchant guild only 213 out of a total population of 7–8,000. Beneath them, journeymen, domestic servants, hawkers, labourers, vagrants, thieves and many others formed a growing proletariat which often lived close to destitution. As in England, urban society was rapidly filling out at the bottom.

Scotland's narrow economic base also meant that its overseas commerce was small in volume and perhaps 4 per cent of England's in value. It was conducted mainly with the Baltic, the Low Countries, France and Spain, whereas England ranked only fourth among Scotland's trading partners. Exactly the same pattern was evident in the spheres of culture and politics. During the sixteenth century, the art and literature of the Scottish Court established it as a major cultural centre influenced more by continental than English trends. The characteristic architectural style of this era, often known as 'Scottish baronial', was essentially a native achievement which drew eclectically on Dutch and French models, but owed virtually nothing to buildings in England. Similarly, Scotland's 'auld alliance' with France retained its importance and continued to pose a standing threat to English security. Nevertheless, Elizabeth's reign did see a gradual improvement in Anglo-Scottish relations. Unlike her father, the Queen did not assert any claim to suzerainty over the Scottish Crown and instead adopted a largely non-interventionist approach. This allowed an Anglophile party to grow up in Scotland free from the stigma of abetting an intrusive foreign power. By 1603 it seemed that the long period of wars between the two kingdoms was finally over.

The Union of the Crowns, and subsequently of the kingdoms, has often led

English historians to underestimate the distinctive and highly successful nature of the Scottish polity. Certainly the machinery of government and the law was much more diffuse and less centralized than in England. But when the Scottish monarchy is judged on its own terms rather than condemned for failing to emulate English models, the scale of its achievements becomes clear. Scotland's often difficult terrain and poor communications ensured that local government remained very much in the hands of individual chieftains. The Crown was therefore even more dependent on magnates than in England, but precisely because it posed less of a threat to regional power it was more likely to obtain their co-operation. During the later Middle Ages and the sixteenth century, the Stuarts developed a remarkably stable and resilient relationship with their leading subjects. The strength of this rapport was most clearly revealed by the monarchy's ability to survive an extraordinary sequence of dynastic disasters: between 1406 and 1625 only two of the seven monarchs died in their beds, and for no fewer than seventy-seven of these years Scotland was ruled by a minor. Yet as successive monarchs attained the age of majority they found that their powers remained largely intact and that Crown lands alienated to the nobility during their minority could be easily 'revoked'. Through it all, the monarchy was able to portray itself as the embodiment of Scottish identity and a focal point for a highly localized nation.

The stability of such a polity clearly rested to a large extent on personal contact between the monarch and the leading subjects. The monarch's personality was crucial, particularly because the institutional 'points of contact' were much less formally defined than in England. The Privy Council was a large body, comprising many of the leading nobility, but with a regular attendance which often barely reached double figures. Under James it became increasingly dominated by professional administrators, lawyers and churchmen. Some councillors were also nominated by the Scottish Parliament, which was strikingly different from its English equivalent. It consisted of a single chamber containing the most important landowners, clergy and burgesses. The Crown managed Parliament through an inner committee of trusted advisers known as the Lords of the Articles, and was able to exercise rather firmer control than in England. But whereas English statutes once passed could be easily enforced through very tight legal and administrative structures, in Scotland chieftains could render them a dead letter in the localities. Government was highly informal, and its effectiveness ultimately depended on the personal relationship which individual monarchs forged with their 'natural counsellors'. Political relations could display a roughness unknown in England: in 1582 the sixteen-year-old James had been kidnapped by a group of Protestant nobles and held in Ruthven Castle for over a year to ensure that their counsels held sway. For a band of nobles to seize the monarch's person was far from unprecedented in Scottish history, and was accepted as a legitimate, if extreme, political tactic. But, like other forms of personal contact, it was impossible to achieve with an absentee monarch, a fact which was to have profound implications once James moved to London.

By 1603, the nature of Scottish government was beginning to change. From 1587, when James attained his majority and assumed personal control of affairs, he steadily created a much closer relationship between the centre and the localities. Increasingly, the Crown intervened directly to resolve blood-feuds, with the result that these ceased to be widespread. New officials were sent to the localities, making government more visible and less dependent on the caprices of individual magnates. Parliamentary commissioners were appointed to enforce all manner of statutes, to regulate poor relief and to secure payment of more and more regular taxation. Yet James consistently avoided offending the greater nobility: with political agility and a shrewd awareness of personalities, he won their co-operation by giving them offices and responsibilities. Highland chieftains who had hitherto shunned the Court were attracted by the lure of patronage and found they could work with the easy-going King. Without seriously disrupting the polity, James managed to strike a balance between noble factions and to raise the effective authority of the Crown to new heights.

The same increased centralization was also evident in Scotland's legal system. Here again the contrast with England was very marked. There was no single body of law but rather a complex blend of Roman law, feudal bonds and customary law partly derived from English models. Records were few and there was little reliance on precedent. The Highlands in particular were a patchwork of different jurisdictions and legal codes; while in the Northern Isles justice even showed traces of Nordic influence. In much of Scotland, local baron's courts operated with little interference from royal justice. From the early 1580s, however, local autonomy was gradually curtailed by the extension of judicial eyres and the introduction of royal commissions to deal with petty crimes and social abuses. One of James's most striking successes was to insist that the Highlands paid the same respect to the law as other parts of Scotland. In 1597, all Highland landowners were ordered to produce titles for their land and to provide sureties for good behaviour. The last quarter of the sixteenth century also saw a considerable expansion in the business of the central courts – especially the Court of Session – and a growing readiness to submit to their jurisdiction. But, for all these moves towards regulation and standardization, the law remained one of the most important structural differences between England and Scotland.

Another, scarcely less dramatic, lay in religion. Assisted by very limited English military expeditions in 1560 and 1573, the Scottish Reformation took root astonishingly quickly. The two particular characteristics of the reformed Kirk, established by Parliament in 1560, were its emphatically Calvinist doctrine and its aggressive assertion of autonomy from the State. Both traits stemmed from the fact that the Kirk grew up under a Catholic, Mary Queen of Scots, who yet did virtually nothing to stifle Protestantism. The Kirk therefore repudiated any notion of royal supremacy, abolished episcopacy and developed instead a classically Calvinist structure of regional assemblies (presbyteries) run by ministers and lay elders. James VI thought that the Kirk's doctrine of the 'two kingdoms' (religious and secular) posed a threat to royal authority: he regarded bishops as the Crown's natural supporters and had their existence confirmed by the 'Black Acts' of 1584. Eight years later, however, he was forced to accept the 'Golden Acts' which deprived bishops of effective power. But thereafter James continued to search for ways to enhance episcopal authority and restrain militant presbyterianism. He was supported by a minority of episcopalian clerics, led by Archbishop Patrick Adamson of St Andrews, who looked to the Church of England as a model. Throughout the 1590s, James exploited his right to summon General Assemblies of the Kirk by calling them infrequently, at short notice, and away from the Presbyterian strongholds of Lothian and Fife. Hostility between Kirk and State led to some fiery debates, as in 1596 when Scotland's most famous Presbyterian reformer Andrew Melville tugged the King's sleeve and called him 'God's silly [= weak] vassal'. Yet, characteristically, James always tried to preserve good personal relations even with his strongest opponents. It was a technique which would stand him in very good stead when he found himself Supreme Governor of the Church of England.

As with so many other aspects of Scottish life, the social impact of the Kirk varied considerably from region to region. It enjoyed its greatest success in the Lowlands, where godly discipline and regular Church attendance became the norm. Elsewhere, adherence was more patchy. Despite its proscription, significant pockets of Catholicism survived, especially in the Highlands, although these soon ceased to pose a major threat to the Kirk. A more serious and widespread problem was friction with local magnates. Many nobles resented the Kirk's demands for the restitution of ecclesiastical lands alienated prior to the Reformation, and also saw the Church courts, known as kirk-sessions, as an encroachment on their own baron's courts. By the end of the sixteenth century, antagonism between Kirk and nobility had become an established feature of the Scottish scene. It would take a singularly inept monarch to reunite them against himself.

All of this meant that, while they were both Protestant in doctrine, the Scottish and English Churches displayed fundamental structural differences. Exactly the same was true of the institutions of law and government. For most Scots, their distinctive polity and Kirk were sources of considerable pride and important ingredients of national consciousness. An even more potent symbol of Scottish identity was the monarchy itself. The English had always had to treat their northern neighbour rather differently from other parts of what John Pocock has called the 'Atlantic archipelago' because the kingdom of Scotland possessed its own ruling dynasty. Throughout the centuries of conflict, English monarchs had sought overlordship or suzerainty over the Scots rather than sovereignty and annexation. But such claims were successfully resisted. The House of Stuart provided a rallying point for the entire nation; and whatever Scotland's comparative poverty in 1603, it could savour the irony that its own King now wore the crown of England.

5 Wales

The absence of a native dynasty helps to explain why another Celtic nation, the principality of Wales, developed in very different ways from Scotland. England had conquered Wales in the later thirteenth century, but did not actually annex it until the so-called 'Acts of Union' of 1536 and 1543. Then, the lack of a Welsh monarchy allowed its easy absorption into the unitary State envisaged by Thomas Cromwell. This was moreover accomplished with the active co-operation of the Welsh elite. England never had either need or desire to uproot the natural leaders of Welsh society or to suppress their language. The Acts of Union consolidated effective central control over Wales and remodelled the old Council of the Marches as a delegative body of the English Privy Council with wide-ranging judicial and administrative responsibilities throughout the region. Wales's 'sinister usages and customs' were replaced by the common law of England. Welsh gave way to English as the language of law and administration, and Wales was to send twenty-four members to Westminster. English patterns of local government and justice were introduced: Wales was divided into shires, administered by justices of the peace, sheriffs and (from the 1580s) by lords lieutenant and deputy lieutenants. All this was successfully accomplished largely because the Welsh gentry secured many of these offices and welcomed the status and power gained by working with the English authorities. The Tudors' Welsh origins no doubt smoothed their feelings: one Welsh poet, Lodowicke Lloyd, praised Elizabeth I as a ruler sprung from 'Cambria's soil'. Overwhelmingly, the new style of government remained in the hands of gentry families with a tradition of local responsibility, and this combination proved highly stable and effective. One of those who gained office, the author George Owen who became vice-admiral of Pembroke and Cardigan and sheriff of Cardigan, described Wales in 1594 as 'a perfect well-governed commonwealth'. Certainly vagabonds, 'masterless men' and even pirates continued to defy the law, especially in South Wales. But the rule of law steadily became established, particularly through the Courts of Great Sessions which sat twice a year in each shire. Feuds still occurred but were more and more likely to be resolved by law suits. During the course of the sixteenth century, the Welsh increasingly looked to Westminster as the ultimate seat of legal and political authority.

Another institution which served as a bulwark of order, unity and good government was the Church. Henry VIII's break with Rome had encountered virtually no serious resistance in Wales: the old Church inspired little loyalty and the dissolution of the monasteries had only minimal impact on religious and economic life. Protestantism made very rapid headway under Edward VI, and Mary failed to re-establish Catholicism as signally in Wales as she did in England. The 1559 Acts of Supremacy and Uniformity applied also to Wales and during the course of Elizabeth's reign at least formal adherence to the established Church became general. Pockets of Catholicism survived, especially in the northeast and southeast, but never posed any serious threat; Puritanism was much weaker than in England and John Penry was almost alone in separating from the Church completely. Yet, as in England, it proved more difficult to instil really enthusiastic commitment to the Church. In general, Elizabethan Wales found bishops of unusually high calibre, but they faced an uphill struggle against the ignorance and superstition of the peasantry, the lack of effective preaching, and the twin evils of clerical pluralism and absenteeism caused by the poverty of the Church. Ironically, the translation of the Bible and

Prayer Book into Welsh in the 1580s, designed to foster religious devotion and uniformity of practice, actually encouraged the Welsh language and sparked something of a renaissance in Welsh poetry and prose during Elizabeth's final years.

This paradox was typical of the way in which Tudor Wales was 'Englished' in structure and institutions without the complete destruction of her own identity or culture. The social order adapted very easily to the new demands placed upon it. Traditional ideas of hierarchy and gentility survived and were reworked. The Welsh concept of a gentleman (*uchelwyr*), with its emphasis on status conferred by ancestry, gradually blended with the English idea of gentility determined by lifestyle. The poetic tributes paid to Welsh gentry throughout the sixteenth century revealed the continued vitality of bardic culture. Many Welsh gentlemen continued to act as patrons to writers, topographers and antiquaries, and stoutly defended the reputation of the medieval Welsh chronicler Geoffrey of Monmouth.[4] This distinctive identity survived despite the growing numbers of Welsh gentry educated in England, especially at Oxford, and the increasing English influence on their way of life. For many of the disadvantaged in Wales – such as younger sons or those of humble birth – the Union greatly extended the opportunities to migrate to England and pursue careers in government, commerce or the professions. While the Welsh remained proud of their national identity, the elites of the two countries became gradually assimilated.

Wales was thus much more firmly bound to England in 1603 than was Scotland. Wales's trade was predominantly with England, and its terrain in many ways resembled the less hospitable parts of the English landscape. The two economies were becoming ever more closely aligned. As Wales's population grew – from less than 200,000 in 1536 to perhaps 290,000 in 1603 – inflation reached a similar rate to England, social mobility in both directions increased, and the gulf between rich and poor widened. Although there was as yet no real breakthrough in agricultural production, as in England a prosperous yeomanry began to emerge. English visitors to Wales in the opening years of the seventeenth century were far less struck by unfamiliarity and 'otherness' than they were in Scotland or Ireland. As Glanmor Williams has written, in the decades following the Union the English came to regard the Welsh as 'the closest and most familiar of foreigners, and also the most distant and outlandish of provincials'.

6 Ireland

A peaceful union founded on co-operation with the native elite and respect for their property, language and culture: all this offers a profound contrast with the experience of the final component of the 'Atlantic archipelago', Ireland. During the sixteenth century, English policy in Ireland moved decisively away from delegating authority to the Anglo-Irish nobility towards conquest and colonization. Medieval English monarchs claimed overlordship or suzerainty over the whole of Ireland, but in practice their control was restricted to the 'Pale', a small area abutting the coast between Dundalk and Dublin and extending about twenty to forty miles inland. The English Crown's hold on the country beyond remained much more tenuous, and power was in practice wielded either by Gaelic lords, or by Anglo-Irish nobles such as the Fitzgerald Earls of Kildare or the Butler Earls of Ormond. These Anglo-Irish, or 'Old English', were descended from the first wave of English colonists who had migrated to Ireland in the wake of the conquests of the later twelfth century. Outside the Pale, most of these Old English families had to a large extent become Gaelicized by the early sixteenth century. Although the King's writ technically ran throughout the country, beyond the Pale its impact was quite limited, and the primary loyalty of most people was to their lord rather than to the Crown.

Indeed, it was only in the wake of the Kildare Rebellion of 1534 that a serious attempt was made to settle the whole of the country. The first stage in this process was an Act passed by the Irish Parliament in 1541 creating the kingdom of Ireland. English monarchs henceforth held the title of King or Queen of Ireland rather than being overlords: Ireland thus became a dependent kingdom, 'united and knit to the imperial crown of the realm of England'. Yet its constitutional relationship with England remained complex and ambiguous. Instead of delegating authority to an Old English noble such as Kildare, Henry VIII and his successors entrusted the government of Ireland to an English-born Lord Deputy (sometimes a Lord Lieutenant) who ruled on the monarch's behalf. The Lord Deputy's powers were comparable to those of the monarch on the mainland, except that executive and judicial appointments were reserved to the Crown, as was the power to summon and dissolve Parliament. There continued to be a separate Irish Council, whose members, like the principal officers of state, were English-born Protestants. However, the English Council was entitled to hear petitions or disputes directed to it from Ireland without reference to the Council in Dublin.

From time to time, English Parliaments still passed legislation that was applicable to Ireland as well. Nevertheless, Ireland retained its own Parliament, modelled on that of England and traditionally dominated by the Old English lords and gentry. Its relationship with England was defined in 1494 by Poynings' Law, which stipulated that no Irish Parliament could legally meet without a licence from the monarch, and that all measures submitted to the Irish Parliament had first to be approved by the King and Council in England. Although Poynings' Law curtailed Ireland's constitutional autonomy, the Old English generally valued it as a safeguard against Lord Deputies who tried to introduce legislation hostile to their interests. If necessary, they could appeal over the head of a Lord Deputy directly to the Crown. A similar ambivalence characterized the judicial system. Within the Pale, Anglo-Norman institutions had taken fairly deep root, and the central law courts of King's Bench, Common Pleas, Chancery and Exchequer were very similar to those in England. Like the Irish Council and Parliament, the judiciary was semi-independent in that the English courts asserted their right to hear appeals against judgements made in Ireland.

Outside the Pale, Anglo-Norman institutions had only been very partially superimposed upon Gaelic customs and structures during the Middle Ages, and the Gaels' way of life, sustained by their own distinctive form of law and bardic culture, proved remarkably resilient. The English system of shiring was no more than loosely operational, and the Gaelic and Old English lords retained considerable control over the administration of justice within their lordships. Gaelic *brehon* law, a highly fluid and pragmatic system practised by a hereditary caste of jurists, remained widespread and presented a powerful obstacle to the spread of English law. Gaelic society was based on a unit called the *tuath*, an area of land belonging to a tribal or kinship group that could encompass as much as 300 or 400 square miles. Within the *tuath* patterns of landholding varied considerably, and there was no uniform law of inheritance. Unlike English law, where the principle of primogeniture was well established, Gaeldom operated a system known as 'tanistry', whereby the dead lord's land was conferred by election upon the 'eldest and worthiest' of his surviving kinsmen. In practice, this tended to assume diverse forms in different lordships: frequently it led to partible inheritance or collective landholding. There were few fixed tenancies, and only gradually did the common law system based on legally recognized titles to land begin to gain ground. To many English observers 'tanistry' looked utterly anarchic, and it was finally declared illegal in 1608, yet it was well suited to the mobile methods of pasture-farming and strong sense of family characteristic of Gaeldom.

The creation of the kingdom of Ireland in 1541 was accompanied by the concerted attempts of a new Lord Deputy, Sir Anthony St Leger, to transform Gaelic lords into Anglicized nobles by the policy of 'surrender and regrant'. A lord would surrender his lands to the Crown; then, in return for his swearing allegiance to the English monarch, they would be regranted to him with a recognized title in English common law. At the same time, the lord would agree to renounce his Gaelic title in return for an English one, and to accept primogeniture as the principle of inheritance rather than tanistry. Unfortunately, this policy, which offered a chance of absorbing the natural leaders of Gaelic society into a power structure controlled from London, was not given sufficient time and was pursued less systematically after 1543. A great opportunity was missed, and instead after Henry VIII's death renewed waves of colonization brought further English settlers (the 'New English'), who steadily displaced Gaelic and Old English and established major new plantations in Munster, Leix, Offaly and later Ulster. In 1603 these Protestant colonists probably comprised about 2 per cent of a total population that has been estimated at approximately 1.4 million. But their impact was disproportionate to their numbers, and this colonialism provoked a series of Gaelic revolts culminating in the Nine Years' War (1594–1603), which was finally resolved by a decisive English conquest. The rebel leader Tyrone surrendered shortly after Elizabeth died, leaving to her successor the task of achieving a settlement.

Religious divisions added to James's difficulties. By the end of the sixteenth century it was clear that the overwhelming majority of the Old English would join the Gaelic population in adhering to Catholicism. They insisted that this was compatible with loyalty to the Crown and the adoption of English legal and political institutions. The Old English were increasingly drawn to the continental Counter-Reformation, and many of them preferred to send their sons to European seminaries rather than to English universities. When they returned to Ireland, these Old English priests were crucial in propagating Catholic doctrine as redefined by the Council of Trent. Yet the impact of the Counter-Reformation on the Gaelic Irish was much more limited. The Jesuits did not begin to arrive until the latter stages of the Nine Years' War, and they found it difficult to reform many aspects of Gaelic Catholicism. Gaeldom lacked the parish structure that played so central a role in the Counter-Reformation, and many Gaelic attitudes and social customs, especially regarding the conduct of baptisms, marriages and funerals, diverged considerably from the decrees of the Council of Trent. Within Gaeldom the priesthood tended to be hereditary within certain families, and priests, bishops and abbots were usually clients or kinsmen of local lords. There was thus a marked contrast between Gaelic Catholicism and the Counter-Reformation Catholicism embraced by most of the Old English, and serious rifts also opened up between the secular and regular clergy. Nevertheless, the fact that the vast majority of the population adhered to Catholicism was of immense significance for Ireland's subsequent history, for it ensured that Catholicism gradually superseded Gaelic language and law as the crucial hallmark of Irish identity.

By contrast, English attempts to establish a Protestant Reformation in Ireland proved a spectacular failure. Beset by problems of poverty, insufficient numbers of able Protestant clergy, and the ineffectiveness of attempts to enforce conformity, the Church of Ireland made little headway against the entrenched Catholicism of the majority. The spread of Protestantism was further stymied by the fact that the 1559 Irish Act of Uniformity stipulated that the services of the English Prayer Book should be provided in English or, in Gaelic areas, in Latin, but not in Gaelic. In 1596, William Lyon, Bishop of Cork, Cloyne and Ross lamented the 'miserable state' of the Church of Ireland and concluded that 'a great part of the people of this kingdom are no better than mere infidels, having but a bare name of Christians'. Eight years later, he complained that his dioceses were 'overwhelmed with the palpable darkness of idolatry', and claimed that no Protestant christenings, marriages or funerals had taken place within them for the previous eleven years. In 1603 the proportion of families in Ireland that had adopted Protestantism was less (probably much less) than one in ten.

Officially a kingdom but in reality more and more like a colony, Ireland presented a fascinating and distinctive landscape utterly unlike that of the mainland. In 1603 woodland still covered over an eighth of the land. The vast majority of people lived directly off the land and there was virtually no industry except that associated with woollen goods. Towns were sparse and small. The capital, Dublin, had a population of barely 5,000 at the end of the sixteenth century, and there were only eighteen other towns with more than 2,000 inhabitants in the whole of Ireland. The limited nature of communications, together with the territoriality of many Gaelic lords, hampered internal trade, and the towns – many of which were controlled by Old English oligarchies – were largely self-contained. Such overseas trade as there was involved the exchange of hides, tallow and above all wool and cloth in return for wine, salt and manufactured goods, and trading links existed with the Continent as well as the mainland. For most people, dairy products and grain (especially oats) were the staple diet: relatively little meat was eaten, and the large herds of sheep and cattle were valued more for their milk, skins and wool than for their meat. In most of the country housing was fairly primitive and transitory, and clothing, consisting mainly of linen and woollens, was practical and basic.

Such a way of life was quite alien to English experience, and the deep-rooted Catholicism of the majority of the population reinforced the widespread English perception of the Irish as savages and pagans. Ireland was viewed as a truly foreign country, as barbarous as the Dark Ages and as unfamiliar as the Orient. It was, in English eyes, a land of meagre diet and squalid living conditions where uncivilized practices such as tying a plough to the tail of an ox still survived. This perception was nowhere more compellingly expressed than in Edmund Spenser's *A View of the Present State of Ireland*, written in 1596 but not published until 1633. Spenser advocated a war of conquest as the necessary precondition for a general reformation. Without use of the sword, he argued, the Irish would remain ungovernable and the benefits of the English polity could not be extended to them. Other English writers echoed Spenser's view of Ireland and her people: to Fynes Moryson the Irish were a 'rude and barbarous people', while John Derricke complained of their 'wild shamrock manners'. Such attitudes lay behind generations of English colonial activity in Ireland. The profound differences between Ireland and the rest of the archipelago meant that James in effect ruled two kingdoms and a colony.

7 Union of the Kingdoms Defeated

The British monarchies in 1603 thus contained an extraordinary variety of political, religious, economic and social structures. Yet they all displayed two common characteristics which will emerge as fundamental themes throughout this book. First, England, Scotland, Wales and Ireland were all part of a composite monarchy, and their own individual histories can only be fully understood within the context of the larger entity which they collectively formed. Historians are only just beginning to explore the challenges and implications of a genuinely 'British' history. What is clear is that, although the nature and extent of the interaction between the kingdoms varied through time, the historical experience of the Stuarts and their subjects during the seventeenth century was profoundly affected by the fact that multiple kingdoms were ruled by a single monarch. That the Stuarts ruled rather than merely reigned brings us to the second common characteristic. Notwithstanding the very different institutions and political traditions of each kingdom, throughout the archipelago the personalities and priorities of individual monarchs had a crucial impact on the style of government and the formulation of policy. The monarch remained the ultimate source of patronage and all public offices were held on commissions from the Crown. Personal access to the monarch still conferred immense influence, and for this reason the Court remained a vital centre of political discussion and decision. Time and again, the nature of political life and the course of events were shaped by particular royal attitudes and characteristics.

The intertwining of these two themes was strikingly illustrated soon after James's accession. Now that he held the titles to the kingdoms of England and Ireland as well as Scotland, James attempted to secure the full-scale union of his kingdoms. He determined to use all his influence as a personal monarch to adapt the multiple kingdoms of Scotland and England into a united kingdom. Yet his hopes that the union of the crowns of England and Scotland would lead naturally to a union of the two nations were quickly dashed.

The general direction of James's thinking was immediately clear from his farewell speech as he left Edinburgh early in April 1603: 'think not of me as of a king going from one part to another, but of a king lawfully called going from one part of the isle to another that so your comfort be the greater'. On his arrival in London, James issued a 'proclamation for the uniting of England and Scotland' (19 May 1603) which declared that 'all the best disposed subjects of both the realms' felt 'a most earnest desire that the said happy Union should be perfected . . . and the inhabitants of both the realms to be the subjects of one kingdom'. James promised that he would 'with all convenient diligence with the advice of the Estates and Parliament of both the kingdoms make the same to be perfected'. In the meantime, all his subjects were to regard 'the two realms as presently united, and as one realm and kingdom, and the subjects of both the realms as one people'.

This last phrase helps to illuminate what James meant by a 'perfect union'. He wanted a 'union of hearts and minds' which would merge his peoples into one and pave the way for a full institutional union. As James told his first English Parliament on 19 March 1604, any other course seemed utterly un-natural:

> I am the husband, and the whole isle is my lawful wife; I am the head and it is my body; I am the shepherd and it is my flock: I hope therefore no man will be so unreasonable as to think that I, that am a Christian King under the Gospel, should be a polygamist and husband to two wives; that I, being the head, should have a divided and monstrous body; or that being the shepherd to so fair a flock . . . should have my flock parted in two.

Parliament's cool response should have warned James of the entrenched resistance his ideas would face. At first the Houses stalled for time by appointing commissioners to meet with Scottish counterparts to investigate the issue. Four weeks later, when a full-scale debate took place, English hostility instantly became clear. When James requested a statute declaring him King of Great Britain, Sir Edwin Sandys, perhaps the most vociferous opponent of union, retorted that 'by this name' of Britain 'the kingdom of England is dissolved'. James's hopes suffered a further blow when the judges insisted that such a change of title would involve 'the utter extinction of all the laws now in force'. By the time Parliament was prorogued on 7 July, it was obvious that a union of the kingdoms could not be straightforwardly achieved.

James nevertheless pressed ahead without Parliament, and on 20 October issued a proclamation assuming the 'name and style of King of Great Britain'.[5] He argued that in view of 'the blessed union, or rather reuniting of these two mighty, famous and ancient kingdoms of England and Scotland under one imperial crown', and 'seeing there is undoubtedly but one head to both peoples', he had therefore 'thought good to discontinue the divided names of England and Scotland out of our regal style'. Beyond this, however, James was not very precise about exactly what sort of union he wanted. It is possible, as Jenny Wormald has argued, that his vagueness was a conscious ploy designed to allow him greater room for manoeuvre than a more detailed and fully developed programme would have done.[6] Certainly there is evidence that in private, as James began to recognize the level of parliamentary hostility towards a 'perfect union', his thoughts turned towards a more gradualist strategy. In a letter to Cecil in November 1604 he wrote that 'the full accomplishment of the Union ... should be left to the maturity of time, which must piece and piece take away the distinction of nations as it hath already done here between England and Wales'. His wish to emulate the Tudor union led him to adopt the motto *Henricus rosas regna Jacobus* ('Henry [VII] united the roses, but James united the kingdoms'). He embarked on a series of largely symbolic reforms, including the introduction of a common coinage and the design of a new British flag, the Union Jack (see plate 1). His ultimate goal remained 'the uniting of both laws and parliaments of both the nations' (but it is interesting that he omitted the Churches from this list). In the shorter term, however, a more piecemeal approach seemed to offer the most appropriate way forward.

The full extent of English hostility to the union became apparent during the parliamentary session of November 1606–July 1607. When the commissioners of both nations recommended the abolition of mutually hostile laws and the freeing of trade between the two kingdoms, prolonged and bitter debate ensued. The reasons for English hostility can be divided into three categories. First, there was a widespread fear that James's aim of 'community of commerce' would in practice mean that Scottish poverty undermined English prosperity. Perhaps the most eloquent expression of such anxieties was voiced by Nicholas Fuller:

> One man is owner of two pastures, with one hedge to divide them; the one pasture bare, the other fertile and good. A wise owner will not pull down the hedge quite, but make gates, and let them in and out etc. If he do, the cattle will rush in in multitudes, and much against their will return.

These economic concerns were closely linked to the second issue, naturalization.

James not only wanted those born in either England or Scotland after his accession to the English throne (the so-called *post-nati*) to be granted legal rights in both kingdoms; he also wished those born before March 1603 (the *ante-nati*) to be naturalized by statute. Again, many feared that these measures would encourage an influx of Scots into England. This was already a very sensitive issue because of the large number of Scots who had received offices at

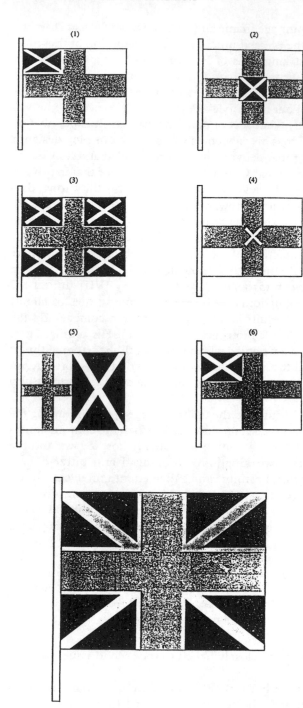

Plate 1 Designs for the Union Jack, 1606. As part of his gradualist approach to securing a union of hearts and minds between the peoples of England and Scotland, James issued a proclamation on 12 April 1606 establishing a single 'Union Flag'. But it proved extraordinarily difficult to design a flag that combined England's (vertical) St George's cross with Scotland's (diagonal) St Andrew's cross in a way that gave them complete equality. These were some of the designs that were considered before, after prolonged wrangling, the first Union Jack was finally agreed on. This flag remained in use until 1801 when, following the union with Ireland, it was adapted into its present form.
Source: Courtesy of the National Library of Scotland

Court when James came south. Sir John Holles complained that 'the Scottish monopolise his princely person, standing like mountains betwixt the beams of his grace and us'. To naturalize the Scots – whom Sandys thought 'better than aliens, but not equal with natural subjects' – promised only to intensify the competition for offices and honours.

The question of legal rights in turn brings us to the third sticking-point, which concerned the integrity of England's constitution and common law. To many English these were as distinctive a national blessing as was their Kirk to many Scots. The common lawyers in particular believed their law to be an immutable part of England's 'ancient constitution'. They were alarmed to hear James's call for 'such a general union of laws as may reduce the whole island, that as they live already under one monarch, so they may all be governed by one law'. The majority in Parliament were only willing to contemplate such a 'perfect union' of the legal systems if this meant the subordination of Scottish laws to English: those, such as Francis Bacon, who advocated an assimilation of the two bodies of law were massively outnumbered. James lamented that these three considerations persuaded Parliament to move 'with leaden feet', adding 'delay unto delay, searching out as it were the very bowels of curiosity', and he admitted ruefully that he knew his 'own end but not others' fears'.

Accounts of the resistance to James's proposals have generally stressed the concerted opposition of the English Parliament, but it is worth noting that there was also much scepticism north of the border. The Scots, too, wished to protect the integrity of their own institutions. Furthermore, the contemptuous language used at Westminster only served to fuel centuries of resentment against the English. They viewed their southern neighbours rather as the Catalans or Aragonese viewed the Castilians within the Spanish composite kingdom. Scottish opposition focused particularly on any suggestion of an 'incorporative union': this was the one type of union which commanded some measure of support in England, but it would have been tantamount to annexation. The Scots were however happy to call James King of Great Britain because they thought this title would help them to resist dominance by England. Indeed, in so far as there was any support for further union north of the border it was as a means to safeguard Scotland's position within a composite monarchy and to offset the problems created by absentee kingship.

What finally wrecked the union proposals in the parliamentary session of 1606–7 was Sandys' alternative scheme for a 'perfect union'. By this phrase he meant not what James meant but rather an incorporative union in which 'the Scottish nation [should] be ruled by our laws'. James saw this for the wrecking tactic it almost certainly was. In despair, he fell back on the idea that a full union might be achieved gradually, and told Parliament on 2 May 1607:

[The Union] is no more unperfect, as now it is projected, than a child, that is born without a beard . . . The Union is perfect in me; that is, it is a Union in my blood and title; yet but *in embrione* perfect. Upon the late Queen's death, the child was first brought to light; but to make it a perfect man, to bring it to an accomplished Union, it must have time and means; and if it be not at the first, blame not me; blame time; blame the order of nature.

In the end, James realized that there was no way round an English Parliament which he regarded as 'barren by preconceived opinions'. When he prorogued the session two months later, the only one of his proposals to have been enacted by statute was the repeal of all laws in each kingdom hostile to the other. Plans for free trade were rejected. Although in June 1608 a test case, known as 'Calvin's Case', established the legal rights of the *post-nati* in both England and Scotland, the naturalization of the *ante-nati* was quietly forgotten. Serious proposals for union in effect came to an end with the parliamentary session in July 1607. When one member, Sir William Morris, tried to re-open the question in the Parliament of 1610, he met with howls of derision. James very sensibly decided to cut his losses and drop the matter. Indeed, the fact that his original proposals had been couched in fairly vague terms probably enabled him to do this with less difficulty than if he had committed himself to a clearer, more detailed programme. Thereafter, as we shall see, he continued to pursue changes 'piece and piece' which pointed towards a 'gradual union', but he never raised the wider issue in Parliament again. His failure to achieve his ideal of 'one king, one people, one law' signalled the beginning of over a century in which England and Scotland remained separate kingdoms while living under a 'double crown'.

James's surrender over the union undoubtedly showed political sense. If he had badly misjudged the outlook of the English Parliament, he was at least able to recognize when to make a tactical retreat and to adopt a more gradual, long-term strategy. Contemporaries were beginning to acknowledge James's political instincts. In the autumn of 1604, just after the proclamation declaring James King of Great Britain, John Gordon, recently appointed Dean of Salisbury, preached a florid sermon in which he thanked God for the union of the realms and likened the King to Great Britain's Solomon. This identification with Solomon was to enjoy wide currency in sermons, prayers and visual representations of James, and it reflected a contemporary perception of his wisdom and political skill. Such qualities were to become more and more evident during the fifteen years following the Union of the Crowns, years which saw the heyday of James's kingship.

2 Great Britain's Solomon

1 James's Kingship

The historical reputation of James I is currently undergoing a remarkable rehabilitation. For centuries, James VI of Scotland attracted very favourable
assessments, whereas James I of England was derided both as a public and a
private personality. This discrepancy bedevilled accounts of his reign and
prompted Jenny Wormald to ask whether James VI and I was 'two kings or
one?'[1] How could James's evident success in governing the Scottish polity be
reconciled with the received view of him in England as a would-be absolutist,
a slobbering drunkard, a coward, a lazy debauchee who preferred hunting,
extravagance and homosexual affairs to the business of ruling? Wormald and
others have cleared the way for a radical reassessment of James's abilities by
showing how much of this image is based on hostile contemporary descriptions,
of which the most famous is that by Sir Anthony Weldon. A minor Court
official, Weldon accompanied James on his visit to Scotland in 1617 and then
wrote a contemptuous account of the Scots and their country. Unfortunately
for Weldon, this fell into James's hands and he was expelled from the Court.
Thereafter, he poured out his bitterness in a memorably vitriolic character
sketch of the King which influenced how James was perceived for generations.

Weldon's deeply biased portrait undoubtedly exaggerated the King's moral
and physical shortcomings, but it did contain a grain of truth. James certainly
cut an undignified and unprepossessing figure. His demeanour was scruffy,
unkempt and slovenly. He shambled around and had little regard for personal
hygiene. His new English subjects found his Scottish accent difficult to understand, and this probably fuelled rumours of him dribbling because his tongue
was too big for his mouth. He could also be very earthy, and once grew so exasperated at the constant presence of onlookers that he cried out 'God's wounds!
I will pull down my breeches and they shall also see my arse'. Yet there was
much more to James than this physical description suggests. The latest research
indicates that he was a shrewd and highly effective governor of both Church
and State, with a political style well suited to managing the delicate machinery
of England's constitution. Far from misunderstanding his new kingdom, he
seems to have grasped its essentials quickly, and to have applied with notable

success the lessons he had learnt in Scotland. As both King of England and King of Scotland, James emerges in recent writings as a figure of sense, intelligence and flexibility who exerted a powerful force towards political stability and international peace. At last, James VI and James I have become recognizable as the same monarch.

Before we look at James's rule in practice, we must first examine his views on kingship and the art of politics. These were far more subtle and perceptive than the traditional stereotype of an aspiring absolutist wedded to the divine right of kings suggests. Of all his extensive writings, James's most practical discussion of what he called 'kingcraft' was *Basilikon Doron*, his manual of advice for his eldest son Prince Henry, originally printed for private circulation in 1599. Early in 1603 he decided to issue a revised public edition in Edinburgh, which by chance appeared within days of Elizabeth I's death. A further eight editions (an estimated 16,000 copies) were then reprinted in London during the first three weeks of James's reign. The treatise greatly enhanced James's reputation in his new kingdom, and it expresses many of the principles and attitudes which made him a successful ruler of England as well as Scotland.

Throughout *Basilikon Doron*, the King's respect for the rule of law is very striking. He distinguished carefully between 'a lawful good king' and a 'tyrant', and argued that the former saw his highest honour as 'the making and execution of good laws' to promote 'the welfare and peace of his people'. This in turn led him to praise Parliament as the highest court of law and the Crown's partner in the making of legislation. It was crucial for the monarch to work harmoniously with Parliament. Proclaiming himself 'ever for the medium in every thing', James wished to achieve a similar equilibrium in the Church. His principal concern was to quell the unrest caused by 'turbulent spirits' and he warned his son to 'cherish no man more than a good pastor, hate no man more than a proud Puritan'. Above all, James realized the value of personal contact with the political elite. He thought it vital that the nobility and gentry felt able to voice their grievances directly to the king, provided that they never transgressed the law. He advised his son to

> acquaint yourself so with all the honest men of your barons and gentlemen, and be in your giving access so open and affable to every rank of honest persons, as may make them . . . make their own suits to you themselves . . . beating ever in their ears, that one of the principal points of service that you crave of them is in their persons to practise, and by their power to procure due obedience to the law.

Although composed while James was in Scotland, these precepts translated much more elegantly to English circumstances than is often realized. Indeed, James explicitly urged his son to remember them if ever 'it please God to provide you to all these three kingdoms'. Faced after 1603 by a constitution which required close co-operation with leading subjects, especially through the 'points of contact' of Court, Council and Parliament, and by a Church that embraced an exceptional diversity of opinion, James's ideas about 'kingcraft' made him eminently suitable to tackle the challenges of ruling England.

Another excellent insight into James's views on monarchy is afforded by his speech to Parliament on 21 March 1610. None of his utterances has suffered so badly over the centuries from selective quotation. The most frequently cited passage is James's famous claim that 'the state of monarchy is the supremest thing upon earth: for kings are not only God's lieutenants upon earth, and sit upon God's throne, but even by God himself they are called Gods'. However, he then went on to make a fundamental distinction between 'the state of kings in their first original' and 'the state of settled kings and monarchs that do at this time govern in civil kingdoms'. In the latter, the king was bound by his coronation oath to 'the observation of the fundamental laws of his kingdom'. As soon as these laws were broken the monarch became a tyrant, whereas 'all kings that are not tyrants . . . will be glad to bound themselves within the limits of their laws'. James promised to 'rule my actions according to my laws'. He recognized that the law could only be changed 'by the advice of Parliament', and that the King-in-Parliament was the supreme legislative authority. He accepted that his 'ordinary' prerogative was exercised through Parliament and the common law. When James also argued that in national emergencies he could wield an 'extraordinary' (or absolute) prerogative which could supplement (but not contravene) the law in order to defend the nation's interests, he was not claiming a power which his subjects would have denied him. It was widely accepted that in that sense the monarch was both absolute and limited. Indeed, this whole speech appealed to an ideological framework which commanded a remarkable level of agreement in Jacobean England. It demonstrated a much more instinctive engagement with the constitutional nuances of his southern kingdom than is often supposed. Nor was it simply a collection of pious platitudes: we shall see that James actually lived up to these ideals in practice.

Before we turn to explore how he did so, one further aspect of James's political thought deserves mention. His vain attempt to achieve a union of the kingdoms of England and Scotland has already been recounted. But it is important to remember that he regarded such a union as only the first stage in a broader process of international reconciliation. His aversion to war sprang not from alleged cowardice but from a genuine wish to foster peace throughout Christendom and to become known as the 'peacemaker king' ('rex pacificus'). Addressing Parliament in March 1604, he listed 'outward peace' as the first of the 'blessings' arising from the Union of the Crowns. James's desire for peace produced a major success the following August when the Treaty of London ended the war with Spain after nearly twenty years. Without abandoning her alliance with the Dutch, England felt immediate benefits: trade prospered and a massive drain on the Exchequer was removed. Shortly afterwards, a new commercial treaty was signed with France. Throughout the early modern period, England's strategic and economic interests were always best served by peaceful co-existence with her two great Catholic neighbours, and this was precisely what James had achieved after barely a year as King. How far, then, was he able to translate his ideals into reality in other areas of policy?

2 James and his Early Parliaments

We have seen that on general points of political theory a very high level of agreement existed between James and his subjects. Almost everybody spoke a common language and subscribed to the same basic principles about the 'ancient constitution'. The disagreements arose over the application of those principles in practice. It was possible to accept shared constitutional ideals while differing over how far specific policies were compatible with them. In particular, the lack of definition in the constitution left considerable scope for disagreement about the practical relationships between Crown and Parliament and between the prerogative and the common law. It was for this reason, rather than because James harboured absolutist ambitions, that he had disputes with several of his Parliaments. But because these tussles concerned specifics and took place within an agreed framework, their political effects were usually transient. Early on, perhaps, James triggered debate about the nature and origins of royal power, parliamentary privilege and the common law where this might have been avoided. But against a certain tactlessness must be set his marked ability to reconcile and to restore harmony within the political nation.

The Buckinghamshire Election Case which dominated the session of 1604 illustrates these points very well. The Lord Chancellor had excluded Sir Francis Goodwin on the customary grounds that he was an outlaw and declared Sir John Fortescue elected in his place. The Commons insisted that they were the sole judge of the validity of election returns, reversed this decision and ordered Goodwin to take his seat. James then intervened, stating that the Commons 'derived all matters of privilege from him and by his grant'. When the Commons balked at such a claim, he ordered them 'as an absolute king' to attend a conference with the judges. This 'thunderbolt' alarmed many members, but James then defused the situation by insisting that he 'carried as great a respect to [Parliament's] privileges as any prince ever did' and thought that their 'privileges [were] his strength'. This conciliatory gesture smoothed the way for a compromise whereby both candidates stood down and a fresh election was held. Henceforth, a parliamentary standing committee would resolve election disputes. It seems likely that the Commons' stand was in part engineered by Fortescue's enemies at Court. Although a minority of members drew up the *Form of Apology and Satisfaction,* in which they rehearsed their privileges and liberties at length, this document was not passed by the Commons as a whole and was never presented to the King. The episode blew over and does not mark any step along a supposed 'high road to civil war'.[2]

Rather more intractable were the problems relating to royal finances. Here controversy focused on the Crown's 'ordinary' revenue, and especially on those feudal rights which Elizabeth had exploited increasingly vigorously in her later years. The most unpopular of these were wardship (the right to receive income from estates whose heirs were minors) and especially purveyance (whereby food and transport for the Court could be purchased at greatly reduced prices). James and his advisers were far from unwilling to consider some alternative arrangement. The problem was that inflation had caused the Crown's income to decline by 40 per cent in real terms during the sixteenth century, and James had inherited a royal debt of over £400,000 from Elizabeth. The Crown therefore needed adequate financial compensation if it were to surrender these prerogative rights. This was all the more necessary because James's family made his household at least £80,000 a year more expensive than that of the Virgin Queen, and because of his own (somewhat exaggerated) extravagance.[3] But while the Commons acknowledged the legality of wardship, they denied that of purveyance and were therefore reluctant to offer any compensation for it. In 1604 they rejected the Lords' proposal for an annual tax in lieu of purveyance, and discussions reached deadlock.

There the matter rested until 1606, when relations between Crown and Parliament were particularly friendly in the wake of the Gunpowder Plot.[4] James declared that had he been blown up with them, his 'end should have been with the most honourable and best company, and in that most honourable and fittest place for a king to be in, for doing the turns most proper to his office'. During the session of 1606–7, the Houses voted the Crown no fewer than three subsidies and six fifteenths (a total of £453,000 over four years), but this did not solve the underlying problem. The royal debt had by now soared to £735,000, with an annual deficit of around £180,000, prompting James to lament 'this eating canker of want'. The Commons also submitted a lengthy statement of grievances in which a further issue was added to the existing list of feudal dues: impositions. The Tudors had claimed the right to levy these duties on imports, but had always kept them – including those on currants introduced in 1601 – on a fairly small scale. However, in 1606 John Bate, a prominent member of the Levant Company, refused to pay impositions on currants imported from the eastern Mediterranean, claiming that they had never received Parliament's consent. After the end of the parliamentary session, at the instigation of Robert Cecil, now Earl of Salisbury,[5] and the Lord Treasurer, the Earl of Dorset, Bate was sued in the Court of Exchequer. In November, the judges upheld the King's right to levy impositions on the grounds that this fell within his 'absolute' prerogative (which operated outside but not contrary to the law) rather than his 'legal' prerogative. The regulation of trade was thus classed among those emergency powers through which the Crown controlled foreign policy and national defence. It is worth noting that this verdict was reached without any hint of coercion or intimidation on the King's part: James was apparently not even consulted about the original decision to sue Bate, and there was no question of his ever challenging judicial independence or trying to subvert due process of law. The key issue was to which category of royal powers impositions belonged, for this in turn determined whether or not they were deemed illegal.

Although many in the Commons – especially the merchants – were unhappy with this verdict, the subject was not raised in the session of 1606–7, which was devoted almost entirely to the projected Anglo-Scottish Union. But impositions became a key issue when Parliament reassembled in 1610, thanks to the robust policies of Salisbury, who had been appointed Lord Treasurer in May 1608 following Dorset's death. Salisbury saw how the verdict in Bate's Case could be applied to generate considerable extra revenue for the Crown. Like other sources of royal income, impositions were not protected against inflation. They were charged at specific rates, such as 'three pence per tonne' of a certain commodity, laid down in the Book of Rates drawn up in 1558 and not significantly revised since. In July 1608 Salisbury introduced a new Book of Rates which levied impositions on a total of 1,400 items, bringing around an extra £70,000 a year into the Exchequer. But this was only the first stage in Salisbury's financial reforms. He perceived that the whole structure of feudal and prerogative levies was too limited, too diffuse and too contentious to solve the Crown's escalating fiscal problems. He therefore proposed a radical solution which would replace this system completely. Known as the Great Contract, Salisbury's plan envisaged the replacement of feudal dues by a fixed annual sum. It was a highly imaginative solution to a complex problem, and might have prevented many subsequent crises. But when the Contract was brought before Parliament in February 1610, the atmosphere was so poisoned by the issue of impositions that negotiations broke down.

Salisbury proposed that in return for abolishing wardship, purveyance and other dues, the Commons would grant James £200,000 a year. He also requested a supply of £600,000 to pay off existing debts, strengthen the navy and provide a financial reserve. Discussions proceeded smoothly until the Commons requested the abolition of impositions as well. When James defended his right to levy impositions and forbade further discussion of the matter, the Commons drew up a Petition of Right asserting the 'ancient, general and undoubted right of Parliament to debate freely all matters which do properly concern the subject and his right or state'. James had unwittingly revived memories of Elizabethan disputes over parliamentary freedom of speech. However, he quickly smoothed Parliament's ruffled feathers by removing this ban and urging members to discuss their anxieties personally with him, 'without using ceremonies and compliments'. The grievance of impositions was finally removed early in July when James agreed in principle not to levy any new impositions without Parliament's consent. Parliament then rose for its summer recess, but by the time it reassembled in October both sides had had time to reflect and had become much more nervous about the Contract. Salisbury's enemies warned James that he would sacrifice a great deal of patronage and lose flexible sources of revenue in a period of high inflation. Sir Julius Caesar called the Contract 'the most unprofitable bargain that ever king made'. When members returned to their counties, they encountered stiff resistance to the proposal that the sum of £200,000 should be raised by a land tax. Some also disliked the idea of funding the King's extravagance or his Scottish courtiers: Thomas Wentworth questioned the point of drawing 'a silver stream out of the country into the royal cistern if it shall daily run out by private cocks'. As a result, both King and Parliament raised their terms and discussions reached an impasse. The failure of the Contract ensured the dissolution of Parliament in February 1611 and the collapse of Salisbury's influence with James.

The Crown was thereafter forced to find expedients within the framework of the existing rickety fiscal system. A Forced Loan of £116,000 was raised in

1611. More damaging in the long run was the sale of honours. That same year the order of baronets was created for the express purpose of raising revenue. Baronetcies could be bought for £1,095 each and their sale raised about £90,000 by 1614. After that, profits declined as the honour became devalued. Salisbury, broken by illness and the incessant sniping of his enemies at Court, died in May 1612 and James never found another servant of comparable administrative ability. The King's woes were compounded by the death of his eldest son, Prince Henry, probably from typhoid fever, the following November. Although his true qualities did not have time to become apparent, Henry was known to be a strong Protestant with a dynamic personality; the new heir apparent, the future Charles I, had lived in his elder brother's shadow and was thought a poor substitute. James's one consolation was the marriage in February 1613 of his daughter Elizabeth to Frederick V, Elector Palatine, an alliance with Germany's leading Protestant prince which greatly advanced the King's strategy for international peace. Unfortunately, the wedding costs of £60,000, on top of £16,000 for Prince Henry's funeral, brought the Crown to the verge of bankruptcy. Faced by an overall debt in excess of £680,000, James decided to call another Parliament for April 1614.

This turned out to be by far the least successful of James's Parliaments. It was dissolved after only eight weeks without passing any legislation and hence acquired the nickname 'the Addled Parliament'. Some contemporaries even questioned whether a meeting which had failed to enact a single statute could legitimately be called a Parliament. The problems apparently stemmed less from any inherent antagonism between James and the two Houses than from factional politics at Court which spilled over into Parliament. Many of those who had risen to prominence after Salisbury's death, especially the Howards and James's new favourite, Robert Carr,[6] were impatient with what they regarded as parliamentary troublemakers. They deliberately fostered (false) rumours that the Commons was being packed and managed by 'undertakers', and also encouraged fears that the Crown might henceforth reduce Parliament's role by increasing use of impositions. Many members believed that it was only a short step from the King's raising taxes without Parliament's consent to his making laws unilaterally as well, and feared that Parliament would then become redundant. Sir Edwin Sandys, as ever one of James's most outspoken critics, declared: 'Nay, so do our impositions increase in England as it is come to be almost a tyrannical government in England'. The Commons offered to grant two subsidies (about £140,000 in all), but only if James would cancel impositions (by then worth £70,000 a year). The King could hardly be blamed for refusing such a deal. When Bishop Richard Neile accused the Commons of sedition for bickering over the royal prerogative, many members were incensed. During the prolonged and chaotic scenes which ensued, James concluded that there was no longer any hope of supply and – to the delight of the Howards – dissolved Parliament on 7 June.

The King was understandably exasperated with Parliament's behaviour, yet it would be quite untrue to say that he wished henceforth to rule without it. He poured out his anger to the Spanish ambassador, Gondomar, complaining bitterly that 'members [of the Commons] give their opinions in a disorderly manner. At their meetings nothing is heard but cries, shouts, and confusion. I am surprised that my ancestors should ever have permitted such an institution to come into existence.' However, he then added: 'I am obliged to put up with what I cannot get rid of'. This is a highly revealing comment. It was simply not on James's agenda to try to rule without Parliaments. Over the next few years, the possibility of summoning another Parliament was often given serious consideration. The fact that Parliament did not in fact meet again until 1621 does not reflect any conscious decision on James's part to establish personal rule, but rather the Crown's ability to muddle through financially in a period of international peace. The Dutch–Spanish truce of 1609–21, which had been secured in part by James's mediation, meant that Parliaments became less vital than in wartime. At no time did James stubbornly resist pressure to call a Parliament; and we shall see that when the international situation deteriorated after 1618 he quickly turned to Parliament for advice and supply.

Throughout these years, James's attachment to Parliament, so eloquently expressed in theory, was sustained also in practice. He displayed a resilient willingness to keep calling Parliaments and to work with them. The fact that calls for regular or triennial Parliaments remained very muted indicates the political elite's recognition of this. Except for the knotty problem of impositions, there was no recurrent issue, no continuity of opposition and no cumulative build-up of grievances during these Parliaments. Criticisms of James's handling of his Parliaments very often underestimate the problems which confronted him, especially in matters financial. Certainly his predilection for philosophizing could open up areas of fundamental constitutional uncertainty which would have been better left concealed. Equally notable, however, was his ability to conciliate touchy members by appealing to shared attitudes and beliefs. At home, no less than abroad, he was a peacemaker. Discord sometimes arose because Court politics spilled over into Parliament, or because James was not always well served by advisers who were less committed to Parliaments than he was. But his own instincts all pointed towards harmony and the preservation of broad lines of agreement; and at his best, he showed a deft capacity to reconcile and to foster political stability. This approach also characterized his policies as Supreme Governor of the Church.

3 The Jacobean Church

The recent revision of James's achievements has been nowhere more marked than in the area of ecclesiastical policy. The older view that James alienated Catholics and Puritans alike, and contributed to growing unrest within the Church, has been replaced by a picture of a King dedicated to religious unity who pursued an ecumenical policy which tolerated diverse opinions within a broad national Church. This policy hinged on a fundamental distinction between moderates and radicals: James successfully wooed both moderate Catholics and moderate Puritans, while expelling or repressing radicals of any hue. As a result, although he disappointed small minorities of extremists, he generally pleased the moderate majority, and his conciliatory policies proved remarkably adept at defusing religious conflict. They were in fact just what the Church needed.

In 1603, all those who had been alienated from the Elizabethan Church, of whatever persuasion, pinned their hopes for reform on James. The most eloquent expression of Puritan aspirations was the Millenary Petition, ostensibly supported by a thousand ministers, and presented to James on his journey south. Insisting that they were neither 'factious men affecting a popular parity in the Church' nor 'schismatics aiming at the dissolution of the state ecclesiastical', the petitioners made a number of fairly moderate requests, including that ministers be free not to wear surplices, that the sign of the cross be no longer used in baptism, and that new steps be taken to ensure an effective clergy and to prevent non-residence. James, whom the petitioners called 'our physician to heal these diseases', was not unsympathetic to these desires and summoned a delegation of leading reformers, together with selected bishops, to a conference at Hampton Court in January 1604. Reliance on the biased account of this conference by the conservative Bishop Barlow of Lincoln gave rise to a long-held view that James did little but harangue the Puritans. We now know that while he affirmed his commitment to episcopacy ('no bishop, no king'), James was by no means uncritical of the bishops and accepted several of the Puritans' key demands, including the reform of the Court of High Commission, some revisions of the Book of Common Prayer, and a series of measures intended to limit pluralism and non-residence and promote a learned, preaching ministry. Most important of all, he agreed to a new translation of the Bible, which appeared as the Authorised Version of 1611. The learning, language and broad appeal of this version have been justly praised, and it is worth noting that James himself drew up detailed instructions to the translators.[7]

In return for these concessions to moderate Puritan opinion, James made it clear that he expected conformity to the established Church. To that end, he commissioned Convocation to draw up new Canons for the discipline and government of the Church. These in fact upheld several practices – such as the use of surplices and the sign of the cross in baptism – which had been condemned at Hampton Court. Following Whitgift's death in February 1604, James appointed Richard Bancroft Archbishop of Canterbury. Bancroft took up James's distinction between radicals and moderates and vigorously enforced conformity to the new Canons, with the effect that about ninety beneficed clergy (about 1 per cent of the total) were deprived early in 1605. But this was very much a temporary campaign, and thereafter action was only taken against those intransigent nonconformists who openly defied royal authority. Indeed, between 1610 and 1625 only two ministers were deprived for nonconformity. James wanted to accommodate moderate Puritans inside the fold provided that their reservations about the worship and discipline of the Church did not threaten its stability. He was, as Kenneth Fincham and Peter Lake have written, 'much more interested in extracting proof of loyalty and obedience than in the small print of regular conformity'.

The King's attitude undoubtedly encouraged Puritans to remain within the Church. Reluctant conformists were won over and those who called for a

Presbyterian system of Church government became fewer and fewer. The godly sort drew comfort from St John's letter to the true believers of Laodicea, in which he encouraged those who lived under a church pure in doctrine but corrupt in worship to work for reform from within. Very few, if any, doubted that James was a Calvinist ruler, and if a significant number felt that the pace of reform was too slow, they conceded that it was at least in the right direction. James firmly supported a preaching ministry and even encouraged the 'exercises' or 'prophesyings' (meetings of clergy, often before a lay audience, to preach and expound Scripture) which Elizabeth had always forbidden. In 1629, the godly John Pym even tried to include James in a list of 'Fathers of the Church'. Puritan willingness to conform to the Church was further strengthened by a feeling that all shades of Protestants should unite against the common threat of popery – horror of which was dramatically confirmed by events early in James's reign.

The King's ideal of a 'general Christian union in religion' extended also to Catholics. He was less unequivocally hostile towards papists than were many of his subjects, and he wished to apply to them the same distinction between moderates and radicals as to Puritans. While he was inveterately hostile to 'factious stirrers of sedition and perturbers of the commonwealth', he promised to be 'a friend' to Catholics 'if they be good subjects'. As with Puritans, he was anxious to secure outward conformity, and enforced fines for recusancy (non-attendance at church) with renewed vigour. Most Catholics willingly complied, but a fringe group, frustrated in their hope that peace with Spain would bring a greater measure of religious freedom, and probably also driven by hatred of a Scottish king and his proposals for an Anglo-Scottish union, hatched the Gunpowder Plot of November 1605.[8] This attempt to blow up the King and both Houses of Parliament greatly reinforced the widespread fear of Catholics as potential traitors, and in January 1606 two penal laws were passed against recusants. The first forbade them to live near London or to hold public office, while the second empowered the King to seize their property as well as impose fines, and obliged them to take an oath of allegiance repudiating the pope's claim to depose kings. Here again, James's guiding principle was to separate moderates from radicals: he wanted to distinguish between those Catholics who respected their 'natural duty to their sovereign' and those who used their religion as 'a safe pretext for all kind of treasons and rebellions against their sovereign'. In practice, however, these penal statutes were never implemented very energetically. The result was a healthy and stable compromise: Catholics continued to worship in private, while English anti-popery was placated by the new penal laws.

James's willingness to embrace a range of moderate opinions within a broad Church was also evident in his clerical appointments. A wide spectrum of theological positions was represented on the Jacobean bench of bishops. At one end were those dedicated above all to evangelism and the promotion of a preaching ministry, such as Toby Matthew (York), John King (London) and Arthur Lake (Bath and Wells). At the other, stood a number of anti-Calvinist divines who objected to the emphasis on preaching and complained that ceremonies and sacraments were being unduly neglected. They disliked concessions to moderate Puritans and wanted ceremonial conformity to be enforced more rigorously. They also wished to see the clergy play a more active political role. Among the leading exponents of this outlook were Bishops Lancelot Andrewes (Winchester), John Buckeridge (Rochester), Richard Neile (Rochester, Lichfield, Durham and York), and later on William Laud. In between these two extremes, the majority were mainstream, orthodox Calvinists, and in this respect George Abbot, who became Archbishop of Canterbury in 1611, was a much more typical figure than his anti-Puritan predecessor, Bancroft. Such a richly diverse episcopate helped to foster a pastoral ministry of exceptional quality, prompting Joseph Hall, later Bishop of Exeter and of Norwich, to remark in 1624 that 'the clergy of Britain is the wonder of the world'. The King's readiness to tolerate a plurality of opinions and his flexibility in the enforcement of conformity surely deserves much of the credit for this achievement. James was always prepared to listen to – and commonly debate with – any point of view, provided it did not actually subvert the established Church. It is significant that Lancelot Andrewes and John Buckeridge were regular preachers at Court, even though their views were (in this period) *avant-garde* and the King disagreed with many of them. This epitomized not only his style as Supreme Governor of the Church but also the atmosphere of the Jacobean Court, a subject to which we now turn.

4 The Jacobean Court

For many years, it was fashionable to dismiss James's Court as a place of decadence, immorality and corruption. It was argued that the King, fatally given to extravagance and to affairs with male courtiers, presided over a Court in which standards of behaviour and morality deteriorated as the reign progressed. In this tale of debauchery, certain lurid episodes loomed especially large, such as the drunken entertainment held at Theobalds in honour of Christian IV of Denmark in 1606, or the murder of Sir Thomas Overbury in 1613. This picture finds support among the reflections of a number of contemporaries, including Sir Walter Raleigh who wrote that the Court 'glows and shines like rotten wood'. Only recently has the Jacobean Court been subjected to more serious scrutiny, with the result that the established interpretation has been not so much superseded as qualified and supplemented. We shall see that the seamier side of James's Court was very real and cannot be overlooked; but it was not the whole story, and the Court's very important political and cultural achievements are at last receiving due recognition.

The Court did not exist solely to provide a ceremonial setting for the monarch: it was also a nerve-centre of political activity and a 'point of contact' between the king and his most powerful subjects. During the early sixteenth century, all alternative centres of political loyalty and preferment had gradually been eliminated, leaving the royal Court as a unique focus of honour and patronage. Personal access to the sovereign became a vital source of political influence, and the extent to which the monarch participated in Court life or held aloof from it therefore had a direct effect upon the making of policy.

Elizabeth had always remained quite distant from her courtiers, and her legendary parsimony held in check the patronage she bestowed upon them. In this respect, James was very different from his predecessor. His extrovert, gregarious nature led him to participate fully in Court life to a degree not seen since the days of Henry VIII. As *Basilikon Doron* shows, he appreciated the crucial political role of close personal relations with the nobility and gentry at Court. Once again, experience gained in Scotland proved extremely helpful in an English context.

The King's enjoyment of personal contact went along with exactly the same willingness to listen to diverse opinions as he showed in religious affairs. As in the Church, he carefully avoided becoming associated with one particular faction, and instead remained accessible to a wide range of views. Francis Bacon wrote that the King 'giveth easy audience', and James clearly relished the lively exchange of ideas and arguments. John Hacket described the 'King's table' as 'a trial of wits', and such openness meant that nobody felt excluded. James's one lapse in English eyes was the overwhelming preponderance of Scots among his inner entourage, the Gentlemen of the Bedchamber: this caused great resentment among his English subjects, although it did have the advantage of ensuring that at least some Scots retained direct access to their absentee king. In the outer circles of the Court, by contrast, James displayed his characteristic desire for balance, dividing his Privy Chamber evenly between English and Scots and even attempting (not always successfully) to have both an English and a Scottish favourite at any given moment. What really galled English Parliaments was the fact that the Scots gained disproportionately from the King's bounty: between 1603 and 1610, Scottish beneficiaries in all gained on average £40,000 a year in gifts or pensions, whereas the English received only an annual average of £10,000. It is worth remembering that behind the repeated parliamentary complaints about James's extravagance often lay a xenophobic hostility towards his Scottish followers.

The harmful effects of that extravagance cannot be denied. During the first four years of his reign, James handed out monetary gifts of about £68,153 and pensions worth nearly £30,000 a year. This generosity possibly owed something to the fact that the pound Scots was worth only one twelfth of the pound sterling, which made it difficult for the King to adjust his sense of the value of money. James also seems to have needed to buy affection, and once remarked that 'my heart is greater than my rent'. Whatever the explanation, such expenditure could only add to the Crown's financial difficulties, yet the King's largess raises far more complex and subtle issues than was once supposed. The monarch was after all expected to be a fount of patronage. Elizabeth had definitely erred on the side of stinginess, and created only 878 knights during the whole of her forty-five year reign. James on the other hand dubbed 906 in his first four months alone. Although James's lavish dispensing of knighthoods, baronetcies and other honours tended to devalue them, it was in some ways a welcome change from the previous reign. As Salisbury reminded Parliament during the Great Contract debates, 'for a King not to be bountiful were a fault'. Furthermore, there was an assumption among European states in this period that a royal court should present a magnificent spectacle to the world. An impoverished Court would bring dishonour on the whole nation. Few begrudged expenditure on the ceremonial aspects of the Court, but there were many who felt that James was spending money on the wrong things – on favourites who had not earned rewards through public service, and on sheer self-indulgence.

Some contemporaries were also sceptical about the frequent Court entertainments, yet several recent studies have suggested that James's munificence greatly enriched the cultural life of the Court. Particularly in the areas of drama, music and architecture, the Court stimulated important innovations that engaged with continental trends while retaining a distinctively English flavour. If the truly great works of Jacobean drama were performed in the popular theatre – especially the later plays of Shakespeare (d. 1616) – James's Court did spawn an entirely new genre, the masque. A ritualized blend of dance, drama and fantasy, the Jacobean masque was developed by the remarkable partnership of Ben Jonson and Inigo Jones. In masques such as *Masque of Blacknesse* (1605), *The Masque of Twelve Months* (1612) and *Masque of Gypsies* (1621), Jonson's texts were produced with scenery, props and costumes by Jones. Jones was appointed Surveyor-General of Works in 1615, and his designs included the Queen's House at Greenwich (1617) and the Banqueting House at Whitehall (1619). He had travelled widely on the Continent, and his buildings introduced Italianate proportions and motifs into English architecture in the style known as Palladianism. That the famous ceiling of the Banqueting House depicting the apotheosis of James VI and I was later painted by Peter Paul Rubens, a native of Flanders, is further testimony to the increasingly international culture of the Court. Continental influences were also apparent in the music of the Court, where English composers like Anthony Holborne worked alongside Italians such as Alfonso Ferrabosco. It became fashionable among Jacobean courtiers to collect works of Renaissance and Baroque art. Although some in the 'country' were suspicious of these foreign imports, they did give the Court a cultural vitality which bore comparison with those of other European monarchs. All in all, as befitted a King dedicated to reconciliation between Christian nations, James's Court presented an incomparably more cosmopolitan spectacle than its somewhat insular Elizabethan predecessor.

These very real achievements nevertheless coexisted with much less attractive developments, especially in the wake of Salisbury's death. From 1612, the Howards – led by Henry Howard, Earl of Northampton and his nephew Thomas Howard, Earl of Suffolk – became the dominant faction at Court. At the same time, they and their allies emerged as a powerful force in the Privy Council. James had doubled the number of councillors from thirteen at Elizabeth's death to around twenty-five. In characteristic style, he ensured that a variety of opinions were represented within the Council, and the Howards were counter-balanced by an influential faction which included Archbishop Abbot, the Earls of Pembroke, Southampton and Montgomery, Sir Edward Coke and Sir Ralph Winwood. In general, these men advocated a 'Protestant', anti-Spanish foreign policy and co-operation with Parliament, as opposed to the Howards who mistrusted Parliament and sought closer relations with Spain

Plate 2 *Oberon's Palace*, by Inigo Jones, 1611. This formed part of the scenery that Jones designed for Ben Jonson's masque *Oberon, the Fairy Prince*. Jonson wrote this masque for Prince Henry, and it was performed on 1 January 1611 (the year before Henry's death), with the Prince playing the part of Oberon.

In this and other masques, Jones's elaborate settings led the spectators on from scene to scene, and his introduction of the proscenium arch and perspective scenery made a lasting contribution to the history of English theatre.
Source: Devonshire Collection, Chatsworth. Reproduced by permission of the Chatsworth Settlement Trustees/Courtauld Institute

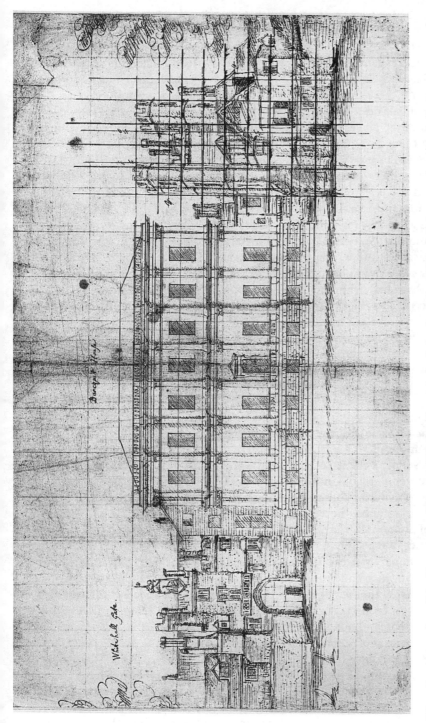

Plate 3 A drawing of the Banqueting House in Whitehall, made by Inigo Jones in 1623 while he was planning some stage scenery for a Twelfth Night masque. This drawing also shows some other parts of Whitehall Palace, including the Holbein Gate (on the right). In buildings such as the Banqueting House, built between 1619 and 1622, Jones derived inspiration from the designs of the sixteenth-century Italian architect Andrea Palladio. The Banqueting House was envisaged as a splendid setting for Court masques, and during Charles I's reign its ceiling was adorned by the Flemish painter Peter Paul Rubens. On 30 January 1649 Charles I was beheaded on a scaffold erected outside the windows on the first floor.

Source: Pierpont Morgan Library

along with better treatment of English Catholics. James carefully appointed members of each faction to senior offices: Winwood became Secretary of State in March 1614, while four months later Suffolk took over as Lord Treasurer. However, the expansion of the Council made it less efficient as an executive body, and as a result the making of policy tended to take place more and more at Court; and there the Howards became ever more powerful until two sensational scandals destroyed their charmed life.

The Howards' power was dramatically enhanced by the King's attachment to the first of his two great favourites, Robert Carr, who was created Viscount Rochester (1611) and later Earl of Somerset (1613). Somerset fell in love with Suffolk's daughter, Lady Frances Howard, and with James's support she was granted a divorce from her husband the Earl of Essex on the grounds of his alleged impotency. In December 1613, Somerset and Lady Frances were married at a spectacular wedding paid for entirely by the King. Over the next eighteen months, Somerset and the Howards seemed impregnable, secure in the King's favour and wielding great influence. Then, in the autumn of 1615, Lady Frances was implicated in the secret murder two years earlier of Sir Thomas Overbury, who had strongly opposed her divorce from Essex and claimed to possess information which might have impeded it. In May 1616, she and Somerset were tried, convicted and sentenced to death, although this was commuted to imprisonment in the Tower.[9] Somerset was ruined and the Howards were badly shaken. Their final destruction came two years later when Lord Treasurer Suffolk and his wife were convicted of embezzlement of funds on a truly heroic scale. Suffolk was fined and imprisoned in 1619, and the Howards' ascendancy came to an end.

Such scandals involving people so closely connected to the King were bound to bring the Court into disrepute. Nor were these isolated incidents. By the end of 1619, Suffolk and the Earl and Countess of Somerset had been joined in the Tower by Suffolk's client Secretary Lake and by his son Lord Walden, both of them convicted of sexual or financial offences. The public image of the Court fell to a low ebb during these years. To make matters worse, the Overbury case helped to bring James into open conflict with Sir Edward Coke, the most eminent of the common law judges. The King had long distrusted Coke's vehement defence of the supremacy of the common law and his reservations about royal discretionary powers; he also resented Coke's zealous exposure of dirty linen at Court which had brought the Earl and Countess of Somerset to justice. Coke had made another powerful enemy in Lord Chancellor Ellesmere by issuing writs of prohibition to prevent Chancery proceedings in cases which could be tried at common law. Finally, when Coke refused in 1616 to consult the Crown in cases of ecclesiastical patronage involving the prerogative, James seized the opportunity to dismiss him as Chief Justice of King's Bench and suspend him from the Privy Council.[10] However, it was typical of James's style of government that he recalled Coke to the Council the following year. This willingness to hear all points of view, so that not even his most trenchant critics were left out, characterized James's management of Council, Parliament and Church as well as the Court. Such an accessible style was extremely well suited to the English constitution because it enabled these essential 'points of contact' to operate very effectively. This was evident not only in England but also elsewhere in the British monarchies.

5 Ireland and Scotland

James's reign was a pivotal period in Irish history. In general, his policies there served to enhance his reputation as a peacemaker, but they also laid the foundations of the modern 'Irish Problem'. James inherited a kingdom conquered but not yet pacified. Although Tyrone had surrendered in March 1603, his power was not totally destroyed. However, the English relentlessly undermined his economic and social status in an attempt to reduce him to the level of any other subject. After the Treaty of London removed any hope of Spanish assistance he became increasingly demoralized and, together with Tyrconnell and several other leading Ulster lords, fled to the Continent in September 1607. This finally put an end to Irish resistance to English rule and greatly enlarged the government's freedom of action. The flight of the earls allowed the Crown to annex the most recalcitrant parts of Ireland, including almost all of Armagh, Cavan, Coleraine, Donegal, Fermanagh and Tyrone. In 1609, James appointed commissioners to oversee the systematic plantation of Ulster by Scottish and English settlers who were to be granted units of 1–2,000 acres each. This policy was dictated primarily by strategic considerations and conditions of military service were attached to these grants. Often the removal of lawless elements from Scotland to Ireland also helped to pacify James's northern kingdom. The native Irish – whom we have seen the English regarded as savage barbarians – were to be transplanted from these areas to the West of Ireland.

The guiding spirit behind this process of segregation was Sir John Davies, who served as Ireland's Solicitor-General (1603–6) and then Attorney-General (1606–19). Using the argument that conquest gave the Crown a free hand, Davies sought to replace the Gaelic system of law with the English common law. By 1613, all but two of Ireland's judges were English. English patterns of tenure and inheritance were to supplant the Gaelic practice of communal landholding, and the Irish were also encouraged to adopt arable farming. In his *Discovery of the true causes why Ireland was never entirely subdued until the beginning of His Majesty's reign* (1612), Davies explained that the underlying purpose of these reforms was to make the Irish 'become English'.

In Ulster, however, this policy of 'Anglicization' was more akin to colonization. James was liberal in granting units of land to courtiers and their clients, with the result that the area of plantation was gradually extended to strategically important regions outside Ulster, including Longford and Wexford (see map 2). Much of the actual work of colonization was left to private enterprise, such as the City of London joint-stock company which settled the town and county of Londonderry. Very often, the Gaelic Irish were not displaced to the West but submerged as tenant farmers beneath New English settlers. At the same time, the Old English were increasingly identified with the native Irish, both politically and economically. Although Old English figures like Richard

Hadsor begged James to recognize their shared ethnicity with the English of the mainland, the imposition of English property law affected them as adversely as the Gaelic Irish. The Parliament of 1613–15 revealed the growing marginalization of the Old English, for it comprised 132 Protestants but only 100 Catholics, nearly all of them Old English. The Irish Parliament, once the traditional mouthpiece of the Old English, was rapidly becoming an instrument for extending the direct rule of the Crown through the aggrandizement of the New English.

This process of differentiation was powerfully reinforced by the religious gulf between Protestant New English on the one hand and Catholic Old English and native Irish on the other. Protestantism was very much the religion of conquest, and while the majority of the population embraced Catholicism, the Church of Ireland formed an embattled Calvinist minority. It made little attempt to convert the Catholic majority, and in effect served only the Protestant colony. Most of its manpower and inspiration derived from England. The Prayer Book of 1604 and Archbishop Daniel's Gaelic translation of that Prayer Book (1608) adopted many of the changes which Puritans desired in England (and which also appealed to the preferences of Scottish settlers in Ulster). Similarly, the Irish Articles of 1615 were closely modelled on the Calvinist Lambeth Articles of 1595. As we shall see in relation to the Scottish Church, James wanted to bring the Churches of his three kingdoms into closer accord (but not uniformity) with each other. Equally, all his instincts were towards tolerance and liberty of conscience, and although the Crown's official aim was to proscribe Catholicism and enforce conformity to the Church of Ireland, in practice the Irish recusancy laws remained a dead letter.

It was thus during James's reign that we catch the first glimpse of the 'Irish problem' which has persisted to the present day. The creation of a Protestant colony in Ulster – distanced in political, cultural, religious and economic terms from the Catholic majority – was the product of the Jacobean plantations. Yet the King cannot be blamed for what happened after his death, and although Ireland remained unreconciled to English rule, it was at least pacified and even showed some signs of prosperity. James took a close personal interest in the Irish Church, in legal reforms and in the plantations, and he regarded his Irish policy as one of his 'masterpieces'. For, as he told the Lord Deputy Sir Arthur Chichester in 1612, he esteemed 'the settling of religion, the introducing [of] civility, order, and government amongst a barbarous and unsubdued people, to be acts of piety and glory, and worthy always of a Christian prince to endeavour'.

James faced a very different pattern of problems north of the border. Whereas the Irish had long been ruled (at least nominally) from London, in Scotland a highly personalized political system had suddenly to adjust to the novel experience of absentee kingship. In his farewell speech of April 1603, James had promised to return to his native land every three years; yet he soon became so preoccupied in England that he in fact went back only once, in 1617. However, he insisted that his absence did not make him any less effective as King of Scotland, and boasted memorably in 1607: 'This I must say for Scotland, here I sit and govern it with my pen, I write and it is done, and by a clerk of the

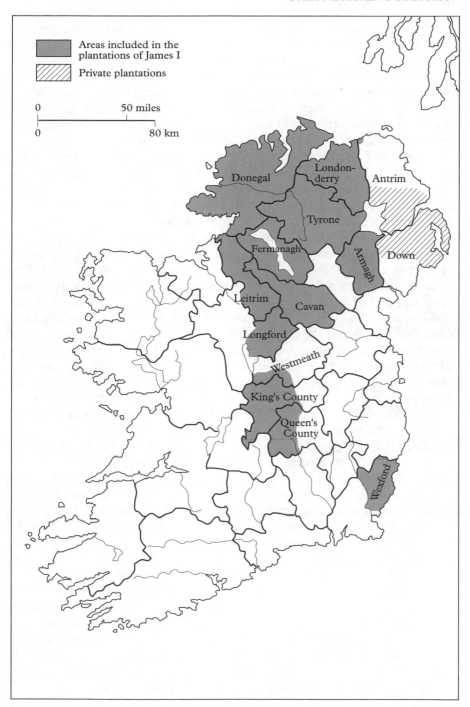

Map 2   Plantations in Ireland during the reign of James VI and I.

Council I govern Scotland now, which others could not do by the sword'. He realized that the Scottish Privy Council formed the linchpin of this system. It gained increased authority and efficiency by being reduced in size to a hard core of royal officials. As the Council's *Register* shows, James took a very active interest in its business and kept himself closely informed about Scottish affairs. He established a very efficient postal service between Edinburgh and London, and sent a constant stream of letters to the Council carefully explaining policies and decisions. Communications were further improved by the Lord High Treasurer, the Earl of Dunbar, who journeyed endlessly between the two kingdoms from 1605 until his death in 1611. As important as this gathering of information was the fact that James knew how to interpret it and take appropriate action: except perhaps in his last years, his instinctive understanding of Scottish politics and society remained undiminished.

All this meant that absentee kingship proved remarkably successful, and the Crown continued to extend its control over Scotland after 1603. The presence of growing numbers of Privy Councillors among the Lords of the Articles ensured even tighter management of Parliament. The borders – which James called 'the middle shires' – were pacified by an Anglo-Scottish border commission created in 1605. In the Highlands, a bloody raid by the MacGregors on Glen Fruin prompted the Crown to issue a commission of 'fire and sword' aimed at extirpating that troublesome clan completely. A different strategy was adopted towards the Western Isles, where Lord Ochiltree led an expedition in 1608 to capture a number of leading chiefs and bring them to Edinburgh. There they were obliged to submit to the Statutes of Iona (1609), drawn up by Andrew Knox, Bishop of the Isles, which made them responsible for the conduct of their own clan and outlawed vagrants and masterless men. As a consequence, law and order immediately began to improve, while the plantation of Ulster deprived the Islemen of possible assistance from Northern Ireland. Throughout Scotland, James's policy was to reward those nobles who co-operated with the Crown – for example, by granting lordships of erection created in 1606 from former monastic lands – and to punish those who defied the law, such as Lord Maxwell, executed for murder in 1613. The King also began to emulate English models of local government: justices of the peace were introduced in 1609, and although this innovation had only limited success it did further strengthen the Crown's hold on the localities.

This drawing together of English and Scottish institutions had marked affinities with James's ecclesiastical policies. John Morrill has argued that his aim was not to make the Churches of his three kingdoms uniform, let alone Anglicized, but to make them 'congruent'.[11] Just as he sought the repeal of the 'hostile laws' as the first step towards a 'union of hearts and minds', so he wanted to remove those elements in each Church which created friction with the other in order to improve mutual respect and co-operation between the English and the Scots. He wanted to make preaching as effective in England as it was in (at least Lowland) Scotland, and he encouraged many Scottish ministers to come south. By the same token, he wished to restore episcopacy and an apostolic succession in Scotland, and to use bishops to reassert royal supremacy within the Kirk. In 1606 a Scottish Act of Parliament restored 'the

Estate of Bishops', and three years later they regained jurisdictions lost at the Reformation. The climax of this enhancement of the episcopate came when three Scottish bishops were brought to Westminster to be consecrated by English bishops in 1610. The same year, the General Assembly at last conceded that the power to summon assemblies of the Kirk belonged to the King, while in 1612 James secured an Act of Parliament which acknowledged him as 'Supreme Governor'.

Although James's goal was 'congruity' of the two Churches, it must be admitted that over the course of his reign he required the Scottish Kirk to adapt rather more than the Church of England. In 1606–7, he allowed four English bishops to become involved in the disciplining of dissident Scottish ministers. Likewise, Archbishop Abbot was permitted to release the Marquis of Huntly from a sentence of excommunication which had been confirmed by the Scottish Court of High Commission. There was never any comparable Scottish interference south of the border. In England preachers were encouraged to follow the Scottish example, but there were no systematic changes in patterns of worship. Indeed, James became increasingly drawn to the order and formality of the English Church, and felt the lack of a 'form of divine worship' in the Kirk. When he visited Scotland during the summer of 1617, he introduced the English service in the Chapel Royal at Holyrood. Over the next four years he pressed for major liturgical reforms, of which the Five Articles of Perth were the centrepiece. The most contentious of these required kneeling at communion and the observance of Holy Days. Many Scottish Presbyterians were horrified at what they regarded as the intrusion of popery. In the face of considerable resistance, James eventually secured the adoption of the Articles by the General Assembly (1618) and the Scottish Parliament (1621). Once again, his objective was less to establish conformity with England than to discourage the Scots from thinking these English practices idolatrous. It was also highly characteristic of James that once the Articles were safely on the statute book he was fairly relaxed about enforcing them: as in so many other areas of policy, he was much more concerned to assert his authority in theory than in practice.

Overall, James's gradual reform of the English and Scottish Churches constituted one of his greatest successes. Nevertheless, the furore over the Five Articles of Perth illustrated the weaknesses of absentee kingship which became apparent during James's final years. He misjudged the prevailing mood in Scotland during his visit in 1617. Although the trip was in many ways a public relations success – especially when James told the delighted Scots of the 'salmonlike instinct' which had brought him back to the land of his birth – he failed to anticipate the antagonism his liturgical reforms would provoke. More and more, he was growing away from Scotland and losing touch with opinion on the ground. Because of the Five Articles controversy, the Scottish Parliament of 1621 was by far the stormiest since 1603, and James was very nearly denied a vast grant of taxation (1,200,000 pounds Scots over four years). The gulf between Scotland and the world of the Court was again revealed the following year when courtiers in London proposed that Scottish wool exports be restricted to England alone. Only furious resistance from Privy Councillors in Edinburgh caused the scheme to be rejected. The drawbacks of 'government by pen' were by now becoming plain, although it was surely remarkable that such a system had operated so smoothly for so long in a constitution which was so dependent upon personal contact between the monarch and the political elite.

There were also other, more sinister clouds looming on the horizon in 1617. James had recently become hopelessly embroiled in an affair with the most notorious of all his favourites, George Villiers, later Duke of Buckingham. The public influence of Buckingham was to prove utterly disastrous, and would ultimately destroy the delicate political stability at home which James had so carefully nurtured. On the Continent, the international climate was about to deteriorate dramatically with the outbreak of the Thirty Years' War in 1618. This conflict shattered James's vision of peace and reunion between Christian nations, and would further destabilize Britain's political and religious affairs over the coming decades. The last seven years of James's life were dogged by crisis, upheaval and unhappiness, all against a background of growing weariness and declining health. Although he could not have known it, as he journeyed back to London in the late summer of 1617, his sun had already passed its zenith.

3 The Ascendancy of Buckingham

Inigo Jones designs Banqueting House in Whitehall (completed 1622)

1620	August	Habsburg forces occupy the Rhenish Palatinate
	29 October	Battle of the White Mountain: Habsburg forces rout Elector Palatine and invade Palatinate
	13 November	James summons Parliament for January 1621
1621	30 January–4 June	First session of James's third Parliament: impeachment revived for use against monopolists and Lord Chancellor Bacon
	April	Hostilities resume between Spain and Dutch Republic
	June–July	Arrest of Sir Edwin Sandys and the Earls of Southampton and Oxford (released in July)
	10 July	James issues proclamation cancelling eighteen monopolies
	4 August	Scottish Parliament ratifies the Five Articles of Perth
	29 September	Cranfield appointed Lord Treasurer
	18 November	William Laud consecrated as Bishop of St David's
	20 November–18 December	Second session of James's third Parliament: debate on foreign policy
	30 December	James tears Protestation out of Commons' Journal
1622	6 January	James's third Parliament dissolved
	June	Imperial troops expel Elector Palatine from the Palatinate
	16 September	Cranfield created Earl of Middlesex
1623	23 February	Buckingham and Prince Charles set off for Spain in attempt to secure marriage alliance
	18 May	Buckingham created a Duke
	5 October	Buckingham and Prince Charles return from Spain to public rejoicing

1624	19 February–29 May	James's fourth Parliament: Monopolies Act; impeachment and dismissal of Cranfield; complaint against Richard Montagu's *A New Gag for an Old Goose*
	6 April	Dissolution of treaties with Spain
	20 November	Anglo-French marriage treaty signed
1625	January	Mansfeld's expedition sets out to recapture the Palatinate; it gets as far as Flushing, where the forces waste away because of severe weather, disease and inadequate supplies
	27 March	Death of James VI and I; accession of Charles I
	Spring	Publication of Richard Montagu's *Appello Caesarem*
	3 May	Charles marries Henrietta Maria of France by proxy
	5 May	Funeral of James VI and I in Westminster Abbey
	18 June–11 July	First session of Charles's first Parliament: debates over tonnage and poundage; Montagu attacked for 'Arminian' views
	July	Charles appoints Montagu a royal chaplain
	1–12 August	Second session of Charles's first Parliament (adjourned to Oxford because of plague in London): attacks on Buckingham
	September–November	Buckingham organizes unsuccessful expedition to Cadiz
	12 October	Charles issues Act of Revocation, revoking all Crown gifts of royal and Kirk property made in Scotland since 1542
1626	6 February–15 June	Charles's second Parliament: attempted impeachment of Buckingham
	11, 17 February	York House Conference: Buckingham upholds anti-Calvinists
	20 June	William Laud nominated as Bishop of Bath and Wells
	July–August	Benevolence fails to generate much revenue

	September	Charles orders collection of Forced Loan to raise money for war against Spain
1627	January	England declares war on France
	February	Robert Sibthorpe preaches sermon in defence of the Forced Loan
	June	Buckingham leads expeditionary force to island of Rhé off La Rochelle; an attempted assault goes disastrously wrong and the much-depleted force limps home in November
	July	Roger Manwaring preaches two sermons in defence of the Forced Loan
	November	Five Knights are tried in King's Bench for refusal to pay Forced Loan; Charles subsequently amends judges' decision to make it appear that they had upheld his general right to imprison without trial
1628	17 March–26 June	First session of Charles's third Parliament: Petition of Right; impeachment of Manwaring; Remonstrances attacking collection of tonnage and poundage without Parliament's consent, and Buckingham's conduct of war
	4 July	William Laud nominated as Bishop of London
	5 July	Richard Montagu nominated as Bishop of Chichester
	July	Confiscation of goods of London merchants, including John Rolle, who refused to pay tonnage and poundage
	23 August	John Felton assassinates Buckingham at Portsmouth
	15 December	Thomas Wentworth appointed President of the Council of the North
1629	20 January–10 March	Second session of Charles's third Parliament

2 March	Speaker of Commons held in his chair to forestall a dissolution while House passes three resolutions against religious innovation and collection and payment of tonnage and poundage; nine members are later charged with sedition and imprisoned
27 March	Charles issues proclamation stating that he will not recall Parliament until 'our people shall see more clearly into our intents and actions'

1 The Rise of Buckingham

George Villiers' seemingly inexorable ascent to royal favour and political dominance had its origins in the factional politics of the Jacobean Court. In 1614, the enemies of Somerset and the Howards, led by Archbishop Abbot and the Earl of Pembroke, introduced James to Villiers, the twenty-two year-old son of a minor Leicestershire gentleman. Villiers had recently arrived at Court and was reputed to be 'the handsomest bodied man in England': his patrons hoped that the King would find him attractive and that they could influence James through him. The first part of this strategy proved a spectacular success, the second a dismal failure. James immediately took a liking to Villiers and as Somerset's position crumbled he rapidly became the King's new favourite. Over the next decade James showered 'marks of extraordinary affection' upon him: Villiers was knighted and made a gentleman of the bedchamber in 1615, appointed Master of the Horse the following year, created Earl of Buckingham in 1617, Marquis of Buckingham in 1618, Lord High Admiral in 1619, and finally in 1623 Duke of Buckingham, the first non-royal duke to be created since 1551. Yet he also turned out to have canny political instincts and much more independence of mind than his backers had anticipated: he refused to become their mere cipher and soon realized that he could use the King's favour to his own advantage. From the final disgrace of the Howards in 1619 until his assassination nine years later, Buckingham exploited the confidence and affections of both James and Charles to achieve a remarkable hold over patronage and the formation of policy.

Although precisely how far James's relationship with Buckingham was actively physical will probably never be known, the King was clearly infatuated with his new favourite. For the first time in his life, his personal feelings impaired his political judgement and blinded him to warnings that he was becoming unhealthily dependent on Buckingham. Some observers began to draw disturbing parallels with Edward II and his notorious friend Piers Gaveston. But those who criticized Buckingham were ignored or brushed aside. In 1617 James told the Privy Council that

> he loved the Earl of Buckingham more than any other man, and more than all those who were here present. They should not think of this as a defect in him, for Jesus Christ had done just what he was doing. There could therefore be nothing reprehensible about it, and just as Christ had his John, so he, James, had his George.

This intense attachment is dramatically illustrated by their private correspondence, in which James and Buckingham addressed each other as 'Dear Dad and Gossip' and 'Steenie' respectively. James often also called Buckingham his 'only sweet and dear child', a sentiment which initially made the young Prince Charles jealous and led to a number of tantrums, including one where he turned on a water fountain in Buckingham's face. By 1620, however, Charles had grown to like Buckingham, and gradually became as dependent upon him as his father, although he certainly never shared James's infatuation. This growing friendship with the Prince of Wales further strengthened Buckingham's position and later allowed him to perform the feat – almost unique among royal favourites in early modern Europe – of maintaining his political ascendancy into the following reign.

In the end, however, the nature of James's affections is less significant than the immense power and patronage which they enabled Buckingham to acquire. In this respect he was vastly more ambitious – and vastly more dangerous – than earlier favourites such as Somerset. His dispensing of patronage was, according to Clarendon, 'guided more by the rules of appetite than of judgement', and he expected total loyalty and obedience from his clients. His large family gained quite unfairly in the distribution of honours, pensions and Court perquisites. As the years passed, Buckingham became less and less tolerant of opposition or even disagreement, and by the mid-1620s his virtual monopoly over patronage was bitterly resented. Yet, ironically, in the early years his influence did produce some benefits, especially in the area of fiscal reform. He shrewdly persuaded James that an able London merchant, Lionel Cranfield, could remedy the financial ills caused by Suffolk's speculation. Surveyor-General of the Customs since 1613, Cranfield became Master of the Court of Wards in 1619 and Lord Treasurer two years later; and from 1618 he began to take the royal accounts in hand and to introduce measures designed to curb waste and corruption at Court. By 1621 he had reduced the annual cost of the Wardrobe[1] from £42,000 to £20,000, while that of the Ordnance Office had fallen from £34,000 to £14,000. At the same time, Cranfield increased the Crown's revenue by revising the customs farms and extending impositions. These policies were widely disliked – especially among the courtiers who lost many of their benefits in kind – and Cranfield would ultimately pay the price of alienating so many vested interests. Nevertheless, his policies brought short-term financial gain and in 1620 government income came closer to matching expenditure than at any time in James's reign.

Yet, these successful reforms apart, Buckingham lacked the political judgement and ability needed to tackle the major crises that were emerging both at home and abroad. The positive effects of Cranfield's reforms were soon dissipated by a severe economic slump. Many blamed this recession on the King's excessive grants of monopolies and above all on his ill-advised interference in the wool trade. Since the fifteenth century, England's principal export had been woollen cloth, which was shipped out in an unfinished state for dyeing and finishing in the Netherlands. In 1614, an unscrupulous London alderman, Sir William Cockayne, persuaded the King that it would encourage English manufacturing industry and generate employment if the cloth could be finished at home. Lured also by the promise of an additional revenue of £40,000 a year from increased customs, James revoked the Merchant Adventurers' charter to export unfinished cloth and allowed Cockayne to form the so-called New Company which would supervise the dyeing and finishing of cloth in England, and then buy up and export the finished products. The scheme turned out to be a disaster. The Dutch reacted by imposing an embargo on the import of all English cloth. This disrupted England's embryonic finishing industry and caused widespread unemployment and hardship. In 1616 weavers rioted in Wiltshire and Gloucestershire, and in December of that year James decided to abandon Cockayne and restore the Merchant Adventurers to their original privileges. This resolved the immediate crisis in the cloth industry, but its long-term recovery was greatly delayed by a gradual shift in fashion away from the 'Old Draperies', the heavy woollens which had long been England's particular speciality, towards the 'New Draperies', a lighter, cheaper and more easily tailored cloth which was steadily spreading northwards from the Mediterranean countries. It took time for English manufacturers to adjust to this change in taste. By 1620, notwithstanding the end of the Cockayne Project, the cloth industry remained in a state of deep depression.

England's recovery from this economic recession was further hampered by the collapse of the European export market due to the outbreak of war on the Continent. The conflict, which came to be known as the Thirty Years' War, began in 1618 when Bohemia refused to accept the Catholic Habsburg Emperor, Ferdinand II, as its king and tried to set up a Protestant government in Prague. The crown of Bohemia was offered to James's son-in-law, Frederick, Elector Palatine who – against James's advice – accepted in September 1619. This precipitated a confrontation between the Catholic and Protestant powers of Europe: the Austrian Habsburgs looked for help to the Spanish branch of the family and to Bavaria; while England inevitably became involved not only because of James's family ties with Frederick and Elizabeth but also because public opinion was deeply sympathetic to the royal couple. When, in August 1620, Habsburg forces occupied the Rhenish Palatinate and then in October routed Frederick at the Battle of the White Mountain, just outside Prague, he and his wife fled to The Hague. In England there were cries, especially from the more zealous Protestants, for James to intervene and send a military expedition to restore Frederick to the Palatinate. Such demands placed the King in a cruel dilemma. He instinctively wished to avoid war, and initially tried to negotiate with the Habsburgs through the Spanish ambassador, Gondomar. He was most reluctant to sacrifice the international peace he had coveted for so long, and even explored the possibility of a marriage alliance between Prince Charles and the King of Spain's daughter. Cranfield, always keen to avoid unnecessary expenditure, encouraged James's peace talks. Buckingham and Prince Charles, on the other hand, strongly supported the advocates of war. They persuaded the King to threaten military action on Frederick's behalf unless Habsburg troops were withdrawn from the Palatinate by the spring of 1621. The fact that the twelve-year Dutch–Spanish truce was also due to expire in 1621 made an international conflict all the more likely. Such a war was bound to involve heavy costs. Buckingham initially advised prerogative taxation in the form of a benevolence, but when this raised a mere £35,000 it became clear that only parliamentary subsidies could provide the necessary revenue. So, on 13 November 1620, James summoned another Parliament which assembled on 30 January the following year.

2 James's Later Parliaments

The new Parliament found both the King and the members in a conciliatory mood, anxious to co-operate and to avoid the ugly scenes of the Addled Parliament. James made a generous opening speech in which he acknowledged previous errors, emphasized his commitment to reform and to reducing expenditure at Court, and pledged to maintain peace if at all possible. He argued that in the meantime, however, it was necessary to make contingency plans for war. Only three weeks later, Parliament voted the King two subsidies (about £140,000) which were insufficient to fund a war but left open the possibility of a further grant. Then, following the lead of Cranfield and Sir Edward Coke, the Houses turned to investigate the royal grants of patents and monopolies which many blamed for the current economic crisis. John Chamberlain's lament that 'the world doth even groan under the burden of these perpetual patents' typified the prevailing mood. This issue dominated the first session of the Parliament, which lasted until 4 June.

The Commons' enquiries soon led them onto delicate ground. They focused on two particularly unpopular monopolies: the right to license inns and alehouses, and the patent for the manufacture of gold and silver thread. Their investigations identified the two entrepreneurs who had gained most from these grants, Sir Francis Michell and above all Sir Giles Mompesson. To complicate matters, Buckingham's brother Christopher Villiers and his half-brother Sir Edward Villiers were both heavily involved in various monopolies, and Mompesson himself was Sir Edward Villiers' brother-in-law. Led by the Earls of Southampton and Oxford, Buckingham's enemies in the Lords encouraged their friends in the Commons, such as Sir Edwin Sandys, to revive the medieval process of impeachment, a form of trial where the Lower House acted as prosecutors and the Upper as judge and jury.[2] In the event, a formal trial was hardly needed because Michell's guilt was plainly evident and Mompesson fled abroad. However, the Commons wanted to condemn the original grant of these monopolies as well as the way in which they were implemented. Since they accepted the maxim that 'the king could do no wrong', they turned their attention to the 'referees', those officers of state who had authorized the grants in the first place.

At this point, as on several earlier occasions, political wrangles within Court and Council spilled over into Parliament's proceedings. In encouraging the attack on patents and monopolies, Coke and Cranfield were motivated in part by their dislike of the Lord Chancellor, Sir Francis Bacon, the most prominent of the referees. They accused Bacon of corruption, alleging that he had accepted bribes from litigants whose cases were pending in Chancery. There was no evidence to suggest that these 'gifts' had affected his legal judgement, and they were often difficult to distinguish from the monetary fees paid to an officer of state which in the early modern period were regarded as totally above board. Nevertheless, Bacon was impeached, fined £40,000 and deprived of office. Aware that impeachment gave Parliament a potent new weapon, James gently warned the Houses not to 'abridge the authority of courts, nor my prerogative'; but he then let justice take its course and allowed Bacon to be sacrificed.

The attack on monopolists had clearly threatened Buckingham and some of his relatives, and during the summer Sandys and the Earls of Southampton and Oxford were arrested as a warning to other parliamentary critics. However, James was generally keen to conciliate Parliament, and they were released within a few weeks. The King's desire for reconciliation was further illustrated on 10 July when he issued a proclamation which 'fully and absolutely' cancelled eighteen monopolies and promised that seventeen others could henceforth be challenged at common law. James also established a standing committee of the Privy Council to investigate the 'decay of trade', a subject which Parliament had begun to explore after it concluded proceedings against the monopolists. But there was other, less encouraging news. Hostilities between Spain and the Dutch Republic had resumed in April, while during the summer the King's special envoy John Digby found the Habsburg Emperor intransigent about any withdrawal of Imperial troops from the Palatinate. As a result, when Parliament reassembled on 20 November, the question of England's response to the continental war was once again at the top of the agenda.

The second session of the 1621 Parliament lasted barely four weeks and culminated in perhaps the most famous of James's confrontations with the Commons. Members were under the impression that the King wanted their advice on military affairs and on Prince Charles's marriage. Yet they were uncertain about what sort of war to support: both in Parliament and the Privy Council, opinion was divided over whether to send an expedition over land to the Palatinate or to launch a naval campaign against Spain. On the suggestion of Buckingham's client Sir George Goring, the House drew up a petition on 3 December which exhorted James 'speedily and effectually to take the sword into your hand' on behalf of the Elector Palatine – if necessary by declaring war on Spain – and also to ensure that 'our most noble Prince [Charles] may be timely and happily married to one of our own religion'. In return for this they offered one subsidy. James responded the same day by forbidding members to 'meddle with anything concerning our government or deep matters of state, and namely not to deal with our dearest son's match with the daughter of Spain, nor to touch the honour of that King or any other our friends and confederates'. The last phrase was hardly calculated to mollify a growingly anti-Spanish House, and the Commons replied with another petition on 9 December complaining that the King 'doth seem to abridge us of the ancient liberty of Parliament for freedom of speech ... a liberty which we assure ourselves so wise and so just a king will not infringe, the same being our ancient and undoubted right, and an inheritance received from our ancestors'. Two days later James replied rather loftily that he was 'an old and experienced king needing no such lessons'. Then, in an almost exact replay of his exchanges with the Commons in 1604, he asserted that Parliament's privileges were 'derived from the grace and permission of our ancestors and us'. This caused uproar in the Commons and prompted members to compose a Protestation (18 December) in which they claimed that parliamentary privileges were 'the ancient and undoubted birthright and inheritance of the subjects of England'. James immediately ordered Parliament to adjourn, and on 30 December in front of the Privy Council tore the Protestation out of the Commons' Journal with his own hands.

One week later James issued a proclamation dissolving Parliament. At the same time he briefly imprisoned several of the most outspoken members whom he branded 'fiery and popular spirits', including Coke, Sir Robert Phelips, William Mallory and John Pym. Yet he had not lost his capacity to appease parliamentary opinion. In this proclamation he went out of his way to emphasize that the first session of the Parliament had seen 'such harmony between us and our people as cannot be paralleled by any former time', and to stress his 'intent and full resolution . . . to govern our people in the same manner as our progenitors and predecessors'. He concluded with the hope that it would 'not be long' before he could summon another Parliament 'with confidence of the true and hearty love and affection of our subjects'.

It was a sad end to a Parliament which had begun so promisingly, and its precipitate dissolution deprived James of further supply. The breakdown stemmed partly from a misunderstanding over whether the King actually wanted members to debate foreign policy and Prince Charles's marriage. He later claimed that he wished them to discuss a campaign to relieve the Palatinate but to avoid the subjects of a war against Spain and the Prince's marriage. However, neither the Privy Councillors nor Buckingham's clients in the Commons ever made this clear and members were therefore astonished at the King's reaction.[3] There is also evidence that the Spanish ambassador was goading James to take a firm stand against the Commons. By 1621 Gondomar's influence over James was at its height, and this probably explains the King's hostility to any parliamentary debate about a Spanish war. In December Gondomar told James that Spain would not negotiate further while so unruly a Parliament remained in existence. This advice – which was vigorously supported by Buckingham – was crucial in driving James to tear the Protestation out of the Commons' Journal and then dissolve Parliament. But such a violent outburst was highly uncharacteristic and, perhaps for that reason, it seems to have left no lasting scars. Indeed, the next Parliament of 1624 saw a remarkable reconciliation between James and the Houses.

It is likely that the King's intemperate behaviour was also partly caused by deteriorating health. A number of his symptoms – including insomnia, recurrent fevers, increasingly violent mood swings and general debility – have been plausibly attributed to porphyria. Whatever the truth of this theory, during 1622–3 James's health began visibly to fail and observers noted that his grasp on affairs was weakening. Early in 1623 the Venetian ambassador described the 'weak state of his health' and his 'infirmity of mind'. To the dismay of many of his subjects, he continued to pursue negotiations for a Spanish marriage and was attracted by the large dowry which the Infanta[4] might bring. But as the talks dragged on without any agreement Buckingham and Prince Charles grew impatient and finally decided to take direct action. In February 1623, wearing false beards and calling themselves Thomas and John Smith, they set off on horseback for Madrid.

James soon regretted allowing his 'sweet boys and venturous knights' to undertake the expedition. Torn with anxiety that they would be killed or imprisoned, he sent letter after letter urging them to take care, warning Charles not to catch fever from jousting, and praying that God would grant them 'a happy success' and 'a comfortable and happy return to their sweet and dear dad'. James's subjects shared his concern about the Prince's safety, and many were also very fearful of a Spanish match. One pamphlet written in the summer of 1623 warned that such an alliance would be neither 'safe for the King's person nor good for the Church and Commonwealth'. In the event, the trip turned out to be a fiasco. The Spaniards spun out the negotiations in order to forestall any English military action over the Palatinate. As the price for a marriage treaty they demanded more and more concessions, including the suspension of penal laws against English Catholics. Charles was repeatedly denied access to the Infanta and his attempt to meet her by climbing over a wall into a private garden offended the Spanish Court's sense of protocol. All the Prince's romantic dreams gradually disintegrated and in the autumn, bitterly disappointed and humiliated, he and Buckingham left Spain. Their return to England early in October was greeted with an extraordinary outburst of popular rejoicing. Bells were rung and services of thanksgiving held all over the country. Bonfires were lit in the streets of London and the choir of St Paul's Cathedral sang a special anthem: 'When Israel came out of Egypt, and the house of Jacob from amongst the barbarous people'. The Bishop of St David's, William Laud, recorded 'the greatest expression of joy by all sorts of people that ever I saw'.

This popular euphoria owed as much to the collapse of talks for a Spanish match as to the safe return of Charles and Buckingham. The experience altered their attitudes dramatically and convinced them that there was no alternative to a naval war against Spain, modelled on Elizabethan precedents. Once back in England, they immediately began to exert pressure on James to call a new Parliament for the express purpose of financing a Spanish war. They organized a 'patriot' coalition which included several peers who were usually hostile to Buckingham, such as the Earls of Essex, Southampton, Oxford, Pembroke and Warwick, together with traditionally outspoken members of the Commons like Digges, Coke and Sandys. They thus won over many of the 'fiery and popular spirits' of the 1621 Parliament and created a broad-based political alliance committed to an anti-Habsburg war. James was extremely reluctant to sacrifice his pursuit of peace but, with the powerful support of the 'patriot' coalition, Buckingham and Charles finally persuaded him to summon another Parliament for February 1624.

James's opening speech on 19 February was a masterpiece of conciliation. He declared that as a 'proof of my love and my trust', he had called Parliament to 'give me your advices in matters of greatest weight and importance'. He insisted that he had no wish to alter Parliament's liberties 'in any thing', and hoped that the Houses would reciprocate by not being 'over-curious' on 'matters of privileges, liberties and customs'. He thus very cleverly removed the principal source of friction in 1621 and laid the foundation for fruitful co-operation between the Crown and the Houses. This was reflected in the

Parliament's legislative achievement: seventy-three statutes were passed in just over three months, as compared with two in 1621, none in 1614, and 237 in the much longer Parliament of 1604–10. Much of the legislation left unfinished in 1621 was now enacted: a Monopolies Act finally declared grants of monopolies to individuals illegal, while a range of other acts regulated trade and manufacture, reformed the administration of the land law, limited the activities of common informers, and repealed many obsolete statutes.

These important domestic reforms were all the more impressive given that the Parliament was inevitably dominated by issues of foreign policy. Throughout, Charles and Buckingham collaborated closely with their allies in the two Houses to maintain pressure on the ailing King. James still hankered after an expedition over land to relieve the Palatinate and desperately wanted to avoid an open breach with Spain. However, the 'Prince's party' persuaded him to accept the direct taxes worth approximately £300,000 which the Houses had voted on the understanding that Spanish negotiations would be broken off and the money administered by a Council of War accountable to Parliament. Charles and Buckingham also co-operated with Parliament to remove another major obstacle to war: Lord Treasurer Cranfield, who constantly offered gloomy prophecies about how much the conflict would cost. Cranfield's relentless economies had made so many enemies that it proved easy for Buckingham to orchestrate a campaign against him, and in May the Lord Treasurer was impeached on (almost certainly false) charges of 'bribery, extortion, oppression, wrong and deceit'. The King lamented that all good Treasurers 'must be generally hated' but allowed Cranfield to be fined £50,000 and deprived of public office.[5] Yet James accurately perceived the dangers of the strategy adopted by the 'Prince's party': he warned Buckingham that by encouraging another impeachment he was 'making a rod with which you will be scourged yourself', and predicted that Charles would 'live to have his belly-full of Parliaments'. Even in his declining years, James had lost none of his shrewd political insight.

That insight was equally evident in religious matters. Perhaps the most ominous moment of the 1624 Parliament came when the Houses lodged a formal complaint against an Essex rector, Richard Montagu, who had written a tract, *A New Gag for an Old Goose*, which denied that the Church of England was essentially Calvinist and played down the differences between it and the Church of Rome. Pym thought the pamphlet 'full fraught with dangerous opinions of Arminius'.[6] James referred the matter to Archbishop Abbot, who told Montagu to 'review' his work. However, when Montagu explained his views to the King, James exclaimed 'By God, if this be popery, I am a papist!' Convinced that the King was sympathetic to his arguments, Montagu wrote another tract, *Appello Caesarem*, in which he presented his case even more forcefully. The controversy blew up violently in the opening years of the next reign, and is sometimes taken to indicate that towards the end of his life James's sympathies were inclining away from Calvinism. In fact the evidence for this is slight. James had sent a Calvinist delegation to the Synod of Dort in 1619 which condemned Arminius's beliefs. Although anti-Calvinist divines such as Laud, Matthew Wren and John Cosin were first accepted at Court in the early 1620s, this reflected the growing influence of Charles and Buckingham rather than any change of attitude on James's part. As always, the King sought to include a spectrum of opinion on the episcopal bench, and there was room for 'ceremonialist' clerics as much as for moderate Puritans. He wanted a broad national Church, and he had a canny ability to spot those who might threaten this ideal. Only with great reluctance was he persuaded to appoint Laud Bishop of St David's in 1621, and he warned Buckingham 'take him to you, but on my soul you will repent it'. It was another characteristically perceptive and prophetic statement. In the context of the Thirty Years' War, religious issues had to be handled with particular care. The furores over the Spanish match and over Montagu's tracts clearly showed that religious tempers were becoming frayed as confessional strife engulfed the Continent and as the forces of the Catholic Counter-Reformation won a series of notable victories. Yet James was temperamentally well suited to calm those tempers, and had he lived a little longer it seems unlikely that religious opinion in England would have become polarized as quickly or as dramatically as it did after 1625.

James displayed the same deft touch when he prorogued Parliament on 29 May 1624. He praised 'the obedience and good respect of the Commons in all things this Parliament' which would 'make this the happiest Parliament that ever was', and promised to meet them again 'towards the winter'. At the very end of proceedings, as he was giving the royal assent to the lengthy list of bills, he recalled 'the breaking up of three former Parliaments' and compared those acrimonious occasions with 'the happy conclusion of this session'. James's words provided an elegant and touching epitaph for what had been by far the most successful Parliament of his reign.

During the summer of 1624, as England slid towards war against Spain, negotiations were opened with Europe's leading anti-Habsburg power, France. Unfortunately, Louis XIII refused to offer his sister, Henrietta Maria, as Prince Charles's bride without religious concessions as sweeping as the Spaniards had demanded. Despite a solemn undertaking to Parliament never to make such concessions, Buckingham eventually persuaded James that they were the necessary price of a military alliance. When an Anglo-French marriage treaty was signed in November, James had to undertake to suspend the recusancy laws in England and to promise naval help against the colony of French Huguenots (Protestants) at La Rochelle who had rebelled in order to defend their freedom of worship. Ashamed of these concessions, James preferred not to face Parliament again late in 1624, as he had originally planned. As France's side of the bargain, Louis's chief minister Cardinal Richelieu agreed to join forces with England in sending troops to the Palatinate under the leadership of a ruthless German mercenary, Count Ernest von Mansfeld. Unfortunately, the Huguenot revolt forced Richelieu to concentrate his resources at home, while Parliament's three subsidies proved wholly inadequate to finance a force of English conscripts. When Mansfeld's army set out in January 1625 it got as far as Flushing but there, hit by severe weather, starved of pay and supplies, and decimated by disease, it rapidly wasted away. Against this background of military disaster and financial bankruptcy, the King lapsed into his final illness and died at Theobalds on 27 March 1625.

James's funeral was held on 5 May in Westminster Abbey. It cost over £50,000 and was performed, according to John Chamberlain, 'with great magnificence, but the order was very confused and disorderly'. This extravagant and disorganized spectacle was somehow highly appropriate for a king who had always lived beyond his means and never attended to appearances, least of all his own. Yet, for all his faults, James was undoubtedly a successful king of Britain. He coped very creditably with the new demands of ruling multiple kingdoms. Although his initial proposals for a 'perfect union' of England and Scotland were thwarted, he gradually achieved a greater measure of 'congruity' between his three kingdoms, and especially their Churches. He avoided conflict at home and abroad for twenty years and thus presided over the longest period of unbroken peace enjoyed by Britain during the seventeenth century. At his funeral, Bishop John Williams of Lincoln preached a sermon in which he praised James's wisdom and ability as a peacemaker, and laid such emphasis upon the familiar comparison with 'Great Britain's Solomon' that the sermon was later published under that title. In England, James's sound judgement and political skill proved eminently well suited to preserve the delicate balances in Church and State which he had inherited from Elizabeth. Precisely because he could live with untidiness, and did not try to tie up loose ends or define blurred edges, he evolved an effective style of government which appealed to a broadly agreed ideological framework and promoted political and religious stability. His free and easy manner made for good personal relations with his leading subjects and allowed the 'points of contact' between ruler and ruled to operate efficiently. The occasional moments of tactlessness, especially in his speeches to Parliament, stood out all the more because James's approach was generally so conciliatory. Apart from his dangerous dependence upon Buckingham, he remained a shrewd judge of character until the end of his life. Some of his subjects viewed him with distaste or yearned for more systematic reforms, but very few of them actually disliked him. Those who looked back nostalgically during the 1640s often spoke of the reigns of Elizabeth and James in the same breath, while men of such diverse political persuasions as John Pym and Edward Hyde saw no need to trace the origins of the Civil War back earlier than Charles I's accession. In the end, the continuities between James and Elizabeth are more striking than the contrasts, and in the political and constitutional history of Britain, 1603 marks a much less crucial turning-point than 1625.

3 The Accession of Charles I

The reasons for this lay in the personality and political style of the king who now succeeded to the throne. Seldom has the contrast between two monarchs been sharper than that between James VI and I and Charles I. In place of a gregarious, affectionate and loquacious king came one who was painfully shy, aloof, taciturn and cold. Charles suffered from a pronounced stammer and therefore tried to make his public utterances as brief as possible: he informed his first Parliament that it did not 'stand with [his] nature to spend much time

Plate 4 *James VI and I as Solomon,* by William van de Passe, from the title page of *A Thankfull Remembrance of Gods Mercie,* by George Carleton, 1624. Throughout his reign, James was regularly likened to Solomon, both in words and images. This page celebrates England's deliverance from the evils of Catholicism ('Ecclesia Malignantium') during the reigns of Elizabeth and James. On the right, James is portrayed as Solomon, holding a shield bearing his motto, 'Beati Pacifici' ('Blessed are the Peacemakers'), together with an olive-branch. Opposite him stands Elizabeth I, in a design that neatly highlights the perceived continuities between their two reigns.
Source: Cambridge University Library

in words'. He had grown up in the shadow of his glamorous elder brother, and this experience seems to have left him with a profound lack of self-confidence. All his life, he tended to latch on to stronger, more powerful personalities – Buckingham, Laud, Wentworth, Henrietta Maria – while yet always remaining strangely detached and self-contained. As if to compensate for his own insecurity, Charles developed an inflated sense of the dignity of kingship and an obsessive concern with order, symmetry and uniformity. Where his father had been untidy and promiscuous but politically adroit, Charles was austere and chaste, a man of impeccable private morals but far too brittle, inflexible and authoritarian to be a successful ruler. A deeply reserved man, he was much less accessible to his subjects than James had been, and preferred to withdraw from the rough-and-tumble of political life into a private world surrounded by his family, art collections and Court masques. He invited misunderstanding because, convinced of his own rectitude, he made little effort to explain his actions. This self-righteousness also blinded him to the sincere beliefs of others, and led him to assume that his critics acted from base and treacherous motives. Because he found personal contact awkward, he asserted his authority by deeds rather than words, and thereby acquired a reputation for duplicity and underhand dealings. All his life he remained unpredictable and difficult to advise, and so introverted was he that even his closest intimates never felt they really knew him.

Had these traits been confined to regulating and reforming the royal Court, their effects might have been less damaging. But in a personal monarchy the character of an individual ruler was bound to have profound political implications, and Charles soon showed himself poorly suited to governing the three kingdoms he had inherited. As John Reeve has recently observed, he lacked 'political sense' and 'had no conception of the art of the possible'. In particular, Charles's lack of self-confidence led him to try to define the many grey areas which existed within the constitution and the Church. Nothing could have been more disastrous. For in defining his own position so uncompromisingly, Charles forced others to define theirs, and in a polity so full of complexities and latent contradictions agreement was virtually impossible to restore once the conventional maxims about peaceful harmony had started to crumble. In the Church, Charles made the fatal mistake of becoming identified with one particular outlook and allowed Laud and his allies to gain a stranglehold on patronage and preferment. His speech impediment and lack of self-confidence meant that he intensely disliked the cut-and-thrust of debate in which his father had revelled: as a result, Charles preferred to fill the 'points of contact' with those who either agreed with him or were too docile to offer any resistance. He ruthlessly excluded those who advanced opinions contrary to his own, and persisted in believing that they comprised only a small minority of 'discontented, seditious persons'. Yet his attempts to root out those he branded 'ill-affected' alienated more and more people, with the consequence that his fears about disloyalty became self-fulfilling.

Although the problems created by Charles's personality and policies only gradually became apparent, contemporaries soon realized that he was a very different man from his father. Charles's accession was the smoothest since that of Henry VIII in 1509 (and possibly since that of Henry V in 1413), yet the 'honeymoon period' at the beginning of the new reign did not last long. Charles had become something of a popular hero in the wake of his trip to Spain, but it is astonishing how quickly this goodwill evaporated. Barely a fortnight after Charles came to the throne, John Chamberlain wrote that 'the King shows himself every way very gracious and affable, but the Court is kept more straight and private than in the former time'; while the Venetian ambassador reported that 'the King observes a rule of great decorum'. As early as 26 July the Earl of Kellie informed the Earl of Mar that 'you cannot believe the alteration in the opinion of the world touching His Majesty'. Within only a few weeks of his accession, some contemporaries already had an uneasy sense that Charles was not going to be a success as king. Their fears were borne out all too plainly by his dealings with successive Parliaments during the first four years of his reign.

4 Wartime Parliaments

Charles's first Parliament met on 18 June 1625 in decidedly unpropitious circumstances. A severe outbreak of bubonic plague was raging in London, while at Portsmouth an army of ten thousand men was being assembled. Unfortunately, the terms of the French alliance obliged Charles to use these troops to mount an over-land expedition to the Palatinate or to help suppress the Huguenots of La Rochelle rather than launch the naval campaign against Spain which Parliament sought. The recent arrival of Henrietta Maria, whom the King had married by proxy in May, reinforced fears that Charles was becoming a puppet of Catholic France. The temper of the Houses was not improved when Charles, in a curt opening address, reminded them that hostilities had been commenced because of their 'engagements' and 'entreaties', and urged them to provide the necessary financial support as expeditiously as possible. Uncertain of what sort of war it was being asked to underwrite, Parliament voted a mere two subsidies (about £140,000). The Commons granted Charles tonnage and poundage – which had been bestowed for life on every monarch since 1485 – for one year only, in the hope that this would pave the way for a thorough reform of the customs system, and especially the abolition of impositions. But the bill for tonnage and poundage had not passed the Lords by the time the Parliament was dissolved, and Charles's military commitments left him no choice but to collect the money without parliamentary consent.

The 1625 Parliament also saw a serious escalation of religious differences. The issues raised by Montagu's tracts ranked second only to the war in terms of the amount of time that the Houses devoted to them. John Pym led the Commons' attack on Montagu, arguing that his writings 'tended to the disturbance of church and state'. Members were shocked when, early in July, Charles suddenly announced that he had appointed Montagu a royal chaplain and ordered the Commons to drop the matter. This was welcome news to those 'ceremonialist' divines, such as Laud, John Buckeridge and John Howson, who protested that Montagu had not asserted anything contrary to 'the resolved doctrine of the Church of England'. But the royal protection and promotion of Montagu left many members anxious about the new King's religious sympathies. Shortly afterwards, Charles adjourned Parliament to Oxford in order to avoid the plague. This second session lasted barely ten days. The Houses refused to grant any further supply without clarification about what kind of military action was envisaged. They also demanded enforcement of the recusancy laws and a full-scale enquiry into the sale of offices and honours. As their hostility became focused more and more explicitly on Buckingham, Charles quickly lost patience with Parliament and dissolved it on 12 August.

In a bid to redeem his public image, the Duke decided to mount the naval campaign against Spain demanded by Parliament. Using the Crown's credit and his own jewels as security, Buckingham borrowed money from the Dutch which, together with Henrietta Maria's dowry of £120,000, enabled him to send a fleet to Cadiz in September 1625. He hoped to emulate Elizabethan victories by seizing the Spanish galleons which brought bullion from the New World. Unfortunately, the expedition turned into an ignominious failure. The troops were landed without food or weapons, and many more died from starvation, disease and too much local wine than from Spanish gunfire. When the remains of the fleet limped home in November, in a 'miserable condition', all the blame was heaped on Buckingham's mismanagement as Lord High Admiral. Charles, however, stood by the Duke and instead attacked the previous Parliament for not voting sufficient revenue to finance the expedition properly. Further military operations clearly depended on obtaining such supply, and to that end the King summoned another Parliament to meet on 6 February 1626.

It was highly characteristic of Charles that he tried to remove several of Buckingham's most outspoken critics from the new Parliament before it met. Coke, Sir Thomas Wentworth, Sir Robert Phelips, Sir Francis Seymour and two others were appointed sheriffs, which obliged them to remain in their counties and thus rendered them ineligible to sit in Parliament. Yet this manoeuvre only made the Commons more determined to pursue Buckingham. Their hostility increased when, early in the Parliament, Buckingham chaired a theological conference of selected divines and Privy Councillors at his London residence, York House. Following the King's lead, Buckingham aligned himself with the anti-Calvinists and defended the orthodoxy of Montagu's opinions. This was a great disappointment to ardent Calvinists such as Warwick and Viscount Saye and Sele, who had hoped to see Montagu convicted of Arminian heresy. The conference further reinforced members' fears about the direction of official religious policy. The Commons voted four subsidies (nearly £300,000) but made these conditional upon the redress of grievances. Then, led by Sir John Eliot and Sir Dudley Digges, they embarked on a detailed investigation of their pre-eminent grievance, Buckingham.

Charles initially tried to ward off the Commons with dark threats. On 29 March he warned them to 'remember that Parliaments are altogether in my power for their calling, sitting and continuance; therefore as I find the fruits of them good or evil, they are to continue or not to be'. But the Commons refused to be deflected and drew up articles of impeachment against the Duke. He was accused of a lengthy list of 'misdemeanours, misprisions, offences [and] crimes' including persistent abuse of his offices, wasting the King's estate, negligence of the nation's defences and of the navy in particular, the corrupt procurement and sale of honours, and even the hastening of James's death by means of a 'drink or potion'. Buckingham refuted these charges and denied that he was guilty of any criminal behaviour. Throughout, Eliot insisted that the Commons' intention was not 'to reflect the least ill odour on His Majesty or his most blessed father of happy memory', but rather to protect the King's honour from an evil counsellor who threatened it. But Eliot overstepped the mark when he compared Buckingham with Sejanus, the hated adviser to Tiberius, which implicitly likened Charles to that tyrannical emperor. The King imprisoned Digges and Eliot, violating the Commons' privilege of freedom from arrest while Parliament was sitting, but he was forced to release them when the House refused to do any more business until they were set free. A similar confrontation occurred in the Lords when Charles attempted to imprison two of Buckingham's fiercest enemies, the Earls of Bristol and Arundel. This breach of privilege so enraged the peers that Charles could not rely on them to reject the impeachment articles. When it became clear that the Commons would never vote any subsidies until Buckingham was 'removed from intermeddling with the great affairs of state', Charles dissolved Parliament on 15 June in order to protect his favourite. Shortly afterwards, he issued a declaration in which he characteristically blamed all the difficulties with both his Parliaments on the 'violent and ill advised passions of a few members'.

Back in May, the King's spokesman Sir Dudley Carleton had warned the Commons that if they stirred up a 'tumultuary liberty', Charles might be 'enforced to use new counsels'. That is precisely what happened. In the wake of Parliament's dissolution, many of those who had defended Buckingham – including the Earls of Rutland, Holland, Dorset, Bridgewater, Suffolk and Exeter, Viscount Savage, Viscount Mansfield, and Sir George Goring – were appointed to senior Court offices, to Lord Lieutenancies or to the Privy Council. The Duke's opponents were either dismissed from the Council (like Arundel) or deliberately marginalized (like Pembroke). The King allowed Buckingham's stranglehold on patronage to become tighter than ever, prompting the Venetian ambassador to report that many could not 'endure that one born a simple gentleman ... should be the sole access to the Court, the sole means of favour, in fact one might say the King himself'. The result was that the Privy Council became dominated by those least sympathetic to calling another Parliament and most willing to contemplate non-parliamentary ways of raising money. It was thus gravely weakened as a 'point of contact' which ought to reflect all shades of opinion.

Spurred on by these 'new counsels', Charles ordered the continued collection of tonnage and poundage, and the imprisonment of those who refused to pay. The attempt to raise a 'benevolence' (or free gift) during the summer of 1626 proved an abject failure, and so in September, after a lengthy debate in Council, Charles authorized the levying of a Forced Loan to raise the equivalent of five subsidies.[7] Whereas the 'benevolence' had been voluntary, special royal commissioners pressed individual subsidy-payers to contribute to the

Forced Loan. Privy Councillors also toured the country urging payment. Charles argued that in a national emergency he was entitled to raise taxes 'for the common defence' without Parliament's agreement. This claim was strongly supported in a series of sermons preached between February and July 1627 by clerics such as Matthew Wren, Isaac Bargrave, Roger Manwaring and Robert Sibthorpe. These sermons argued that since the King's power was divinely ordained, he could only be judged and condemned by God. Subjects therefore had a duty to obey royal commands. As Sibthorpe put it: 'If a prince impose an immoderate, yea an unjust tax, yet the subject may not thereupon withdraw his obedience and duty. Nay, he is bound in conscience to submit, as under the scourge of sin.' To refuse the Loan was, according to Wren and Bargrave, tantamount to rebellion. All these sermons developed a theme originally suggested by Laud, and he and Charles took great care to ensure that those by Sibthorpe and Manwaring were printed. In adopting 'new counsels', the King thus found vociferous allies among Laud's followers in the Church.

Fiscally, the Loan was a considerable success. Within a year, more than £240,000 of the £300,000 Charles demanded had been raised.[8] Yet the political cost was severe. Many of those who paid up were nevertheless deeply aggrieved, and public opinion became polarized to an unprecedented degree. The root of the controversy lay in a fundamental ambiguity within the constitution. It was generally accepted that the monarch could raise prerogative taxation in an emergency. But who determined whether there was an emergency? And if the King declared an emergency, could that assertion be tested at law? Those who opposed the Loan did not deny that the King could raise such taxes in emergencies, but they did assert that no such emergency existed and that it was therefore illegal to raise the Loan without Parliament's consent. They believed that Charles was abusing his emergency powers of taxation by employing them in a non-emergency situation. The most bitter critics of the Loan, like Thomas Scott, the member of Parliament for Canterbury, argued that royal powers which existed for the good of the commonwealth (*pro bono publico*) were now being used for the King's own benefit (*pro bono suo*) and that of his favourite.

In the end, however, relatively few people actually refused the Loan, and the Council was divided over how to treat those who did. With the backing of the more hard-line councillors, Charles began to billet soldiers on the poorer refusers and to imprison the more prominent 'by His Majesty's special commandment'. Five knights challenged the legality of their imprisonment by seeking a writ of *habeas corpus* which required them to be granted bail unless a reason was given for their detention. Charles was determined that their trial before the Court of King's Bench in November 1627 should uphold his general right to imprison at will without giving a cause where he alleged reasons of state security. The judges felt very uneasy about this claim and therefore entered only an interim 'rule of court', which was useless for Charles's purposes because unlike a full judgement it could not be cited as a precedent. The King then took the extraordinary step of ordering the Attorney-General, Sir Robert Heath, to change the judges' ruling into a firm precedent. When Buckingham revealed this the following year, there was widespread consternation at

Charles's authoritarian methods and his readiness to use royal powers to override the proceedings of the common law.[9] Many of his subjects began to fear that the common law no longer offered adequate protection of their lives, liberties and property. Brought up on the principle that royal powers and due process of law operated in symbiosis, contemporaries were appalled by the mounting evidence that they were coming into conflict.

These anxieties were reinforced by other wartime policies, including the billeting of troops on the civilian population and the imposition of martial law over large parts of the country. Such measures escalated as the international situation deteriorated. Early in 1627, Buckingham's clumsy diplomacy had precipitated a wholly unnecessary war against France. He had thus led England into the worst possible scenario of having to fight both her great Catholic neighbours simultaneously. Determined to retrieve his reputation, the Duke launched a campaign to assist the Huguenots of La Rochelle, who were fighting to protect their freedom of worship. In June 1627 Buckingham personally led an expeditionary force which landed just off La Rochelle, on the island of Rhé. He advanced no further. The French troops withdrew into the citadel of St Martin, and Buckingham's men were forced to begin a long siege for which they were totally unprepared. After sixteen weeks, Buckingham tried to break the deadlock by a direct assault on the citadel, but the scaling-ladders proved too short for the walls: the English were easily repelled and suffered heavy losses. When the remains of the expeditionary force struggled home in November Buckingham was more universally hated than ever. One observer commented mordantly that 'since England was England, it received not so dishonourable a blow'.

This disastrous campaign had largely exhausted the proceeds of the Forced Loan, and Charles therefore had no option but to summon another Parliament for March 1628. The members – twenty-seven of whom had been imprisoned for refusing the Loan – assembled in a mood of grave anxiety, aware that if the Parliament failed to grant supply Charles would probably dissolve it and reintroduce prerogative taxation. As Sir Benjamin Rudyerd put it: 'This is the crisis of parliaments: we shall know by this if parliaments live or die'. Members were determined not to vote five subsidies until their grievances received a full hearing, but in order to minimize the risk of an early dissolution they studiously avoided attacking Buckingham or raising the issues of tonnage and poundage or impositions. Instead, they drew up a Petition of Right which sought the King's agreement not to raise taxation without Parliament's consent, imprison any of his subjects without showing cause, billet troops on civilians without their consent, nor impose martial law on civilians. Although they explicitly denied any wish to tamper with royal discretionary powers, the fact that members sought to define the law so exactly indicated their mistrust of Charles's use of those powers. The Petition stated the law with novel precision in an attempt to safeguard the liberties of the subject; but to save Charles's face, Magna Carta and a range of medieval statutes were cited to create the impression that it was simply declaring existing law. The King initially gave a qualified and evasive answer (2 June) but then five days later accepted the Petition in full. Believing that the Petition would now have statutory force, a delighted

House of Commons promptly passed a bill for five subsidies and sent it up to the Lords.

Charles's subsequent behaviour greatly increased his reputation for duplicity and subterfuge. When the Petition came to be printed, Charles instructed the royal printer to include his unsatisfactory first answer as well as the second. He also ordered the statute number originally assigned to the Petition to be effaced with a pumice stone, thereby making its authority as a statute much less certain. These underhand dealings all came to light in 1629, and were strongly reminiscent of Charles's secret instructions to Attorney-General Heath in the Five Knights' Case. They created the impression that he was trying to renegue on his concessions to Parliament as soon as he had gained the supply he so urgently needed.

In the wake of the Petition, Charles's relations with Parliament quickly turned sour over other issues. Led by Pym, the Commons impeached Manwaring for his public support of the Forced Loan. Eliot resumed his attack on Buckingham, whom Coke now termed 'the cause of all our miseries' and 'the grievance of grievances', and on 17 June the House presented a Remonstrance which severely criticized the Duke's conduct of the war. Charles had meanwhile continued to collect tonnage and poundage on the grounds that this was not explicitly forbidden in the Petition of Right. The Commons responded on 25 June with a Remonstrance which declared that tonnage and poundage was contrary to the Petition and 'a breach of the fundamental liberties of this kingdom'. The next day, Charles prorogued Parliament with a brief speech in which he confirmed his acceptance of the Petition but again denied that it extended to tonnage and poundage. He concluded, ominously, with the assertion that he owed 'the account of [his] actions to God alone'.

Less than two months later, on 23 August, the political landscape was suddenly and dramatically transformed. Buckingham was at Portsmouth making preparations for another expedition to La Rochelle when he was stabbed to death by a demobbed soldier, John Felton, who claimed to have been inspired by Parliament's Remonstrance of 17 June. Although Charles displayed characteristic self-control in public, in private he was grief-stricken, and all the more so because of the overt rejoicing which greeted the assassination. People drank to Felton's health in the streets and the Duke's funeral had to be held at night to avoid hostile demonstrations. Few public figures have been so widely loathed in their own lifetime as Buckingham, for reasons which are not difficult to find. For all his energy and flamboyance, he was a hopeless administrator who embroiled England in a war against both France and Spain. This placed an intolerable strain on England's rickety fiscal machinery, which in turn destabilized the Crown's relations with the Parliaments of the later 1620s. Buckingham's overweening ambition led him to monopolize patronage and the management of policy to a point where he was held personally responsible for all the nation's ills. Many therefore hoped that his removal would open the way for a much better understanding between the King and his subjects.

They were soon disappointed. Buckingham was never replaced as favourite, with the unfortunate result that the King became more closely identified with the conduct of government. Charles blithely chose to continue the policies which had already proved so unpopular. In the Church, the dominance of Laud and his allies was greatly strengthened by a series of promotions during the second half of 1628. Laud became Bishop of London, while Samuel Harsnet went to York, John Howson to Durham, and Francis White to Norwich. Most provocatively, Charles appointed Richard Montagu Bishop of Chichester. The King's patronage ensured that by the start of 1629 the majority of English sees were occupied by bishops of a Laudian persuasion. Similarly, although he agreed to suppress Manwaring's writings, he granted him a full pardon from his impeachment and secured a lucrative benefice for him in Essex. In November, Charles reissued the Thirty-Nine Articles together with a proclamation stating that any dispute over their interpretation should be settled by Convocation, and then only with his permission. The same authoritarian approach was evident in the secular sphere. Charles continued to collect tonnage and poundage, and during the summer and autumn of 1628 he ordered those merchants who refused payment to be imprisoned. The Privy Council instructed the customs officers to confiscate the goods of several London merchants, including a member of Parliament, John Rolle. This order was subsequently upheld by the Court of Exchequer. When Parliament investigated Rolle's case the following year, it became clear that Charles had personally authorized the confiscation. With the end of Buckingham's ascendancy, such high-handed behaviour could not so easily be blamed on 'evil counsellors'.

All these grievances came to a head early in 1629 when the Parliament reassembled for its second session. The King's first priority was to obtain an act legitimating the collection of tonnage and poundage, but instead the Commons insisted on a full investigation of the printing of the Petition of Right, the recent developments in the Church, and the punishment of Rolle. Charles's patience rapidly wore thin. He especially resented the Resolutions on Religion prepared by a Commons sub-committee and presented to the House on 24 February. These condemned 'the subtle and pernicious spreading of the Arminian faction' and urged the King to 'confer bishoprics and other ecclesiastical preferments . . . upon learned, pious and orthodox men'. The next day, Charles adjourned Parliament for a week while he vainly tried to reach a settlement with its leaders, and when the Houses reconvened on 2 March there were rumours of an imminent prorogation or dissolution. In a dramatic bid to forestall the end of the session, two of Eliot's allies, Denzil Holles and Benjamin Valentine, physically restrained the Speaker, Sir John Finch, in his chair until the Commons had passed a Protestation. This consisted of three resolutions: that whoever brought in 'innovation in religion' or introduced 'popery or Arminianism' was 'a capital enemy to this kingdom and commonwealth'; that whoever advised the King to collect tonnage and poundage without Parliament's consent was likewise a 'capital enemy'; and that anyone who voluntarily paid tonnage and poundage was an enemy to 'the liberties of England'. This unruly behaviour dispelled any doubt about the Parliament's fate, and Charles announced its dissolution on 10 March.

That same day he issued a lengthy declaration justifying his conduct. He acknowledged 'the merit and good intentions of those wise and moderate men' in both Houses, and blamed all his problems with Parliaments since his accession on the 'causeless jealousies stirred up by' a minority of 'ill-affected' members. He insisted that their complaints were groundless, and pledged to maintain 'the true religion and doctrine established in the Church of England', and 'the ancient and just rights and liberties of our subjects'. In the belief that harmony would be restored if he could only remove those few 'ill-affected' individuals, Charles imprisoned nine members, including Eliot, Valentine and Holles, for their part in the events of 2 March. He overrode the procedures of the common law yet again by moving the prisoners to different gaols in order to give the law officers time to devise charges against them which would not allow them to claim parliamentary privilege. They were eventually charged with conspiring to 'raise sedition and discord between the King, his peers, and people'. Some, including Selden and Holles, were freed in due course, but the King detained Eliot – whom he regarded as the real ringleader – until his death in November 1632.[10]

Eleven years would elapse before Charles faced another Parliament. By 1629 the political climate had already changed considerably in the four years since his accession. Charles's policies and style of government had alienated a significant number of his subjects and raised fundamental legal, constitutional and religious issues. Unlike his father, Charles's behaviour tended to divide rather than unite the political elite, with the result that he and many of his subjects increasingly mistrusted each other. The later 1620s saw the gradual emergence of two competing conspiracy theories based on diametrically opposed views of the political situation. Whereas Charles attributed all his problems to a minority of 'ill-affected' individuals pursuing their own 'private interests', his leading critics blamed all their grievances on the 'new counsels' which encouraged Charles to govern *pro bono suo* rather than *pro bono publico*. These mutual fears were reflected in Charles's deteriorating relations with his first three Parliaments. Gradually, the delicate balances which preserved constitutional equilibrium were being upset. As the relationships between Crown and Parliament and between the royal prerogative and the common law became increasingly contested, tensions sprang up within the shared ideological framework which James had carefully maintained. A similar process was visible in the Church. By promoting one strand of opinion above all others, Charles undermined the broad national Church which his father had nurtured. As Laud and his allies tightened their hold on senior clerical appointments, even moderate Puritans ceased to feel welcome within the Church. Whereas the subtle political and religious compromises achieved by Elizabeth and James had concealed the potential for these developments, Charles's personality and policies brought them into the open. In the end, he must bear the principal blame for the resurgence of ideological conflict and for the collapse of a common framework in both Church and State. Yet it is important not to exaggerate the extent of this collapse by 1629, and nobody at that time anticipated the outbreak of civil war thirteen years later. With the dissolution of Parliament the King clearly held the initiative, and in his hands lay the choice of which paths to take in the future. His subjects waited anxiously to see what his next move would be. But, as ever, Charles remained utterly inscrutable. All he said, in a proclamation issued on 27 March 1629, was that he would not recall Parliament until 'our people shall see more clearly into our intents and actions'. Then, in a strangely sinister conclusion, he expressed the hope that 'when such as have bred this interruption shall have received their condign punishment', those who had been 'misled by them' would 'come to a better understanding of us and themselves'.

4 The Personal Rule of Charles I

	20 June	Proclamation commanding nobility and gentry to return to their counties within forty days
	November	William Palmer fined £1,000 for remaining in London without permission
1633	February	At Laud's instigation, Exchequer abolishes the Feoffees for Impropriations because of their Puritan sympathies
	February	William Prynne sent to the Tower for publishing *Histriomastix*: his denunciation of stage-plays and 'female actors' was seen as an attack on the Queen's participation in Court masques
	June–July	Charles visits Scotland; crowned at Holyrood on 18 June
	23 July	Wentworth arrives in Dublin
	4 August	Death of Archbishop Abbot
	6 August	William Laud nominated as Archbishop of Canterbury
	14 October	Birth of Prince James, the future James VII and II
	18 October	Charles reissues the Book of Sports
	October–November	Menteith disgraced
	November	St Gregory's Case: King and Privy Council rule that the bishop should have the right to decide the position of communion tables within each diocese

Charles and Laud issue instructions that only ministers of parishes can preach sermons

1634	9 May	John Bramhall nominated Bishop of Londonderry
	May	Prynne's first trial: sentenced to lose his ears
	14 July	Irish Parliament meets: Wentworth blocks statutory confirmation of the 'graces'
	Summer	Beginning of systematic exploitation of forest fines to raise revenue
	October	Ship Money levied on coastal towns and counties

	10 December	Irish Convocation adopts Thirty-Nine Articles
	12 December	Charles admits Gregorio Panzani to Court: first papal agent at the English Court since 1558
1635	13 March	Death of Lord Treasurer Richard Weston, Earl of Portland
	March	Lord Balmerino convicted of treason and sentenced to death for opposing religious changes, but later pardoned (July)
	April	New Book of Rates issued, increasing customs duties
	August	Ship Money extended to inland counties: levied annually until 1639
1636	January	Scottish Canons promulgated
	6 March	Bishop Juxon of London appointed Lord Treasurer: first clerical Lord Treasurer appointed since 1469
	April	George Con succeeds Panzani as papal agent at Court
1637	June	Trial of William Prynne, Henry Burton and John Bastwick for criticizing Laudian innovations: sentenced to be fined, imprisoned and to lose their ears (the stumps in the case of Prynne)
	11 July	Bishop Williams of Lincoln fined and imprisoned for attacking Laudian altar policy in *The Holy Table, Name and Thing*
	23 July	Introduction of the new Scottish Prayer Book provokes riots in Edinburgh
1638	February	Trial of John Lilburne for circulating Puritan literature: sentenced to be whipped; National Covenant drawn up in Scotland to maintain the 'true religion, liberties and laws of the kingdom'
	June	John Hampden's Case: judges rule in favour of the King's right to levy Ship Money by seven votes to five

1 The Road to Personal Rule

The controversy surrounding the years 1629–40 is reflected in the different labels that historians have applied to them. To the Whig historians these were the 'eleven years' tyranny', a period of royal autocracy in which England moved rapidly down the 'high road to civil war'. Recent historians have preferred the more neutral term 'Personal Rule' as a straightforwardly factual description of an epoch when the Crown governed without Parliament.[1] Although most scholars would now accept that there was no inexorable advance towards conflict, they remain divided over the nature and significance of these years. Kevin Sharpe, in the most detailed account of the Personal Rule yet published, sees it as a time of stability and peace at home and abroad.[2] He stresses not only the viability of Charles's attempt to establish non-parliamentary government but also the creative reforms in both Church and State which it fostered. In 1637 England appeared to be nowhere near a civil war.[3] However, there are other historians who argue that Charles's policies flouted the most deeply held convictions of many of his subjects. His programme thus proved intensely divisive and generated debate over fundamental constitutional and religious issues. Recent research has shown that although such debate was usually covert and seldom voiced in public, it undeniably took place.[4] It therefore seems likely that the calm of the Personal Rule – upon which many contemporaries remarked – was deceptive, and that while Charles's three kingdoms appeared quiet enough on the surface, underneath there lurked deep-rooted tensions and grievances.[5] In assessing these contrasting interpretations, we should perhaps remember the Earl of Clarendon's perceptive comment that the 'outward visible prosperity' of the Personal Rule concealed 'the inward reserved disposition of the people to murmur and unquietness'. To many observers – and not only those who looked back with hindsight after the outbreak of civil war – the 1630s were indeed a halcyon idyll of peace and calm. Yet the same decade prompted widespread unease about Charles's kingship and generated a climate of mistrust without which the rapid breakdown of 1640–2 is impossible to explain.

It is unclear exactly when Charles's decision to rule without Parliament hardened into a firm resolve not to recall it except in extreme necessity. The possibility of another Parliament continued to be debated in the Privy Council until about 1632, and John Reeve has argued that it was only in that year that Charles decisively aligned himself with the pro-Spanish faction which opposed Parliament's recall. The dominant figures in this faction were Laud, Wentworth, the Earl of Arundel, Lord Treasurer Weston, the Chancellor of the Exchequer Sir Francis Cottington, and Sir Francis Windebank (Secretary of State from June 1632). Against them stood a pro-French, pro-Dutch group – led by the Queen, the Earls of Holland and Northumberland, the other Secretary of State Sir John Coke, and the diplomat Sir Thomas Roe – which was much less hostile to international Protestantism and more amenable to the idea of another Parliament. Reeve suggests that Charles retained political links with both these factions during the early years of the Personal Rule, and only in 1632 did he firmly commit himself to the pro-Spanish policy which precluded the summons of a Parliament for the foreseeable future. It is nevertheless clear that from March 1629 onwards his own inclinations were very much towards rule without Parliament. He was by then so suspicious of Parliaments that whenever the possibility of one was mooted in 1629–32 he rejected it. At the same time, he took immediate steps to ensure the long-term financial viability of non-parliamentary government by seeking peace with France and Spain. Since he could not continue to fight both these continental powers without parliamentary supply, Charles quickly concluded the Treaty of Susa with France (April 1629) and the Treaty of Madrid with Spain (November 1630). From the spring of 1629, he began to cut his foreign policy to suit the cloth of non-parliamentary government. This strategy presents a striking contrast with James, whose eleven years without a statute being passed (1610–21) were largely the result of a period of international peace during which the need for Parliaments became less urgent.[6] With Charles, on the other hand, a wish to avoid further Parliaments preceded and necessitated a withdrawal from the continental conflict. He was consciously opposed to risking another Parliament in a way that his father had never been.

The Personal Rule was thus a natural expression of Charles's personality and attitudes. Even more than was usual in a personal monarchy, during these years the formulation of policies lay firmly in Charles's hands. Happiest when governing alone, he preferred to have as little consultation as possible; and although he was not impervious to advice, he remained distinctly selective in his adoption of it. Above all, his temperament was not that of an instinctive politician. His rigid convictions and almost obsessive concern for order led him to try to organize his kingdoms as though they were a gigantic Court masque. But in attempting to turn government into an art form he failed to learn the art of the possible. Surrounded by his paintings and sculptures, his close-knit family, and a Court which rigorously excluded his noisiest critics, Charles grew more and more cut off from the state of opinion in his three kingdoms. One anecdote of late 1631 beautifully captures his personality and priorities. That autumn, as the Swedish King Gustavus Adolphus carried all before him in Northern Germany, the possibility at last emerged that the Protestants might regain the Palatinate. At the height of these events, Charles's Secretary of State, Viscount Dorchester, needed to see the King urgently to discuss possible courses of action. After searching all over the palace of Whitehall, he eventually found Charles in the picture gallery arranging his busts of the Roman emperors in chronological order. In the end, England failed to capitalize on the Swedish victories and the moment of opportunity passed, never to return. Nothing could show more clearly the King's aestheticism, his orderliness and his detachment from political reality. Out of these characteristics grew Charles's Personal Rule; and nowhere were they more apparent than in the Court which formed the centre of his monarchy.

2 The Caroline Court

The Court of Charles I was quite unlike the relaxed, permissive and readily accessible milieu which James had created. Within days of his accession, Charles began to regulate the Court to establish formality, dignity and what the Venetian ambassador called 'a rule of great decorum'. In large parchment books of ordinances which bore his signature on every page, the King stipulated in minute detail the routines and procedures of the Court and royal household. These often harked back to practices which had lapsed into disuse since Henry VIII's Eltham Ordinances, but their long neglect made their restoration appear innovatory. A determined campaign was launched to curb waste and corruption: the overall number of servants was reduced, efficient accounting was introduced, household officers were made responsible for arrears in their particular departments, all provisions were to be carefully monitored, and utensils which might previously have been discarded were ordered to be repaired. Although some pilfering and peculation did continue, these reforms were undoubtedly a qualified success.

The books of ordinances also affirmed the hierarchy of the Court by stating very precisely who could enter which sections of the royal apartments. Charles's concern for privacy ensured that access to his person was restricted to a select few. The Privy Chamber was closed to all but nobility, Privy Councillors and the Gentlemen of the Privy Chamber, while leave to enter the innermost apartment, the Bedchamber, could be granted only by the King or by the Groom of the Stool – an official who now regained a degree of influence and intimacy with the monarch not seen since the days of Henry VIII. Access to the King was permitted solely via the state apartments: alternative entry via back stairs or privy galleries was henceforth strictly forbidden. In 1626 and again in 1636–7, all the locks were changed at the palace of Whitehall to restrict the 'freedom of access' caused by 'undue procurement of keys', and Charles gave meticulous instructions about who was to be issued with the new keys. Furthermore, in those sections of the palace to which they were admitted, courtiers and servants were expected to conduct themselves with proper decorum. Charles wanted the Court to be 'a place of civility and honour', and any servant who was 'so vicious and unmannerly that he be unfit to live in virtuous and civil company' was immediately dismissed. To enforce these exacting standards of behaviour, Charles re-established the Court of the Marshal of the Household in 1630. To contemporaries the difference from the previous reign was dramatic: Lucy Hutchinson observed that 'the face of the Court was much changed in the change of the king, for King Charles was temperate, chaste and serious; so that the fools and bawds, mimics and catamites of the former Court grew out of fashion'.

In their place came an emphasis on formality, deference and ceremonial reminiscent of the French and Spanish Courts. In contrast to James's earthy spontaneity, every stage of Charles's day was carefully regulated and attended by ritual. His getting up and going to bed, his mealtimes and his procession to chapel all became ceremonial occasions. A heightened formality marked festive days and special events such as the receipt of ambassadors. Closest of all to Charles's heart were the annual ceremonies of the Order of the Garter, which had declined since the mid-sixteenth century. To Charles, the Order – originally founded by Edward III in 1348 – symbolized an ethos of chivalry, piety, honour and hierarchy. In 1629, he revived the ancient custom of the monarch processing to Windsor Castle on the eve of St George's Day for the annual Garter feast. When his eldest son was installed as a Knight of the Garter in 1638, the King planned a spectacular cavalcade from Somerset House to Windsor. To commemorate the occasion, he commissioned Van Dyck to design a painting or series of tapestries of the procession for the Banqueting House, although only the sketch was ever completed. As Kevin Sharpe has written, the Garter procession was 'the public vaunting of the order, dignity and spirituality of the new royal Court'.

These developments inside the Court were accompanied by a series of measures designed to distance it from the outside world. Whereas under James petitioners had been able to enter the palace and present their grievances personally to the King on his way to and from chapel, Charles imposed tight restrictions on this practice. This contravened his subjects' longstanding expectation that they could if necessary petition their monarch in person. Even more offensive to many people was Charles's drastic limitation of the ceremony of touching for the King's Evil[7] – which James had performed throughout the year except during the summer months – to Easter and Michaelmas. Between 1625 and 1640, Charles issued over a dozen proclamations forbidding his subjects to seek help at other times of the year and insisting that 'in this as in all other things, order is to be observed'. Although he was as anxious as any of his predecessors to assert his curative powers, and ensured that the ritual of royal healing was included in the Book of Common Prayer from 1634, Charles caused widespread disappointment by his refusal to use them more frequently. It was surely unwise to spurn customs which offered the King such excellent opportunities to meet informally with a cross-section of his people. Here was yet another area where 'distant' kingship replaced the much more 'intimate' style of James, and where Charles's behaviour was at odds with what many of his subjects expected of their king.

Charles's concern for order, dignity and distance profoundly influenced the cultural life of the Court. He embarked on grandiose plans to transform the rambling complex of buildings which formed the royal residence at Whitehall into a vast classical palace. The designs by Inigo Jones's collaborator and pupil John Webb envisaged a palace comparable in size to the Escorial near Madrid, incorporating Jones's earlier Banqueting House (1619). Inside the Banqueting House, Charles commissioned the Flemish artist Peter Paul Rubens to paint a series of magnificent panels depicting James VI and I ruling as Solomon and ultimately ascending into Heaven. These paintings, which were finished in 1635 at a cost of £3,000, were not only a magnificent achievement of Baroque art; they also conveyed an important political message which asserted the power of monarchy to impose order upon chaos. This same theme is visible in the remarkable equestrian portraits which another Flemish artist, Sir Anthony Van Dyck, painted of Charles I, as well as in the work of the French sculptor Hubert

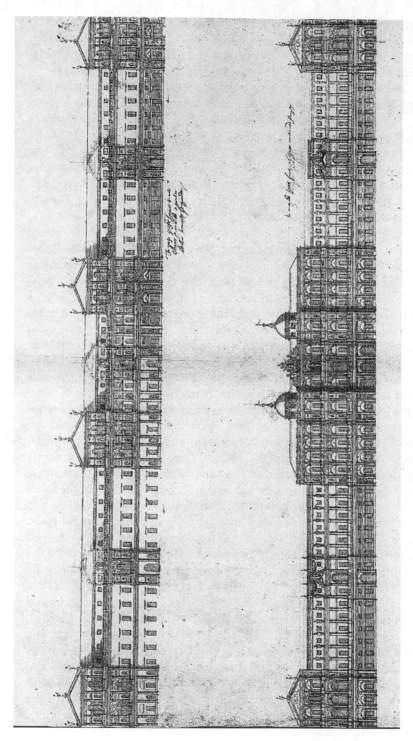

Plate 5 *Design for a New Palace at Whitehall*, by Inigo Jones's pupil and collaborator John Webb, *c.* 1637–9. The upper elevation would have faced onto the park, the lower onto the River Thames; and the scale and magnificence of the palace would have rivalled the Escorial near Madrid or the Louvre in Paris. The designs epitomized Charles's desire to emulate the great palaces associated with the continental monarchies, but to many of his subjects such Baroque splendour seemed tainted by Catholicism and royal authoritarianism.
Source: The Provost and Fellows of Worcester College, Oxford/Courtauld Institute

Plate 6 *King Charles I Equestrian*, by Hubert Le Sueur, 1633. This statue was commissioned by Richard Weston, Earl of Portland, for the garden of his house in Mortlake Park at Roehampton. It now stands in Trafalgar Square. Born in France, Le Sueur came to England in the mid-1620s and worked extensively for Charles I and a range of private patrons. He was especially active between 1625 and 1635. Although commissioned by Portland, this statue epitomizes the image that Charles wished to project of himself: of a chivalric figure, wearing the armour of a tournament-knight, and commanding all he surveyed. Yet at the same time, the statue just faintly hints at the diminutive stature of the King.
Source: Conway Library, Courtauld Institute

Le Sueur. The King appears as a heroic figure ruling over a landscape of Arcadian peace and tranquillity. These works of art were very close to the heart of a king whom Rubens described as 'the greatest amateur [= lover] of painting among the princes of the world'. Yet to many of Charles's subjects these developments were profoundly unwelcome: they feared that beneath the cosmopolitan cultural milieu of the Court there lurked the insidious influence of the Catholic monarchies of the Continent; and they strongly disapproved of the immense sums which the King spent as a patron of the arts. When, in 1627, he bought the vast collection of the Gonzaga Dukes of Mantua for a sum of around £18,000, one contemporary complained that he was squandering money on 'old rotten pictures and broken-nosed marbles' at a time when war had brought the Crown to the verge of bankruptcy.[8]

Yet Charles was oblivious to such criticism. As the 1630s wore on he became more and more engrossed in the culture of the Court, cocooned in an environment that was increasingly detached from the wider world. Nowhere was this trend more apparent than in the many masques written for the Caroline Court by such writers as Thomas Carew, Aurelian Townshend and Sir William Davenant. The texts of these masques – and the elaborate scenery which Inigo Jones designed for them – reveal much about Charles's vision of kingship. He was closely associated with the composition of many of the masques, and he and Henrietta Maria often took part in them, usually in roles which portrayed them replacing turmoil and discord with order, harmony and peace. This Neoplatonist theme is explored, for example, in *Britannia Triumphans* (Davenant), *Albion's Triumph* (Townshend), *Coelum Britannicum* (Carew) and most ironically of all in Davenant's *Salmacida Spolia*. This last masque was performed in January 1640, just as the Personal Rule teetered on the brink of collapse, yet in it the King 'out of his mercy and clemency . . . seeks by all means to reduce tempestuous and turbulent natures into a sweet calm of civil concord'. These words perfectly capture the ideal which Charles hankered after in his meticulous regulation of Court life; and it was this same ideal that he sought to extend to the government of all three of his kingdoms.

3 Caroline Government

During the Personal Rule the Privy Council formed the hub of government to an even greater degree than at other times. In the absence of Parliaments, it handled an ever-increasing volume and variety of business. The full Council met over a thousand times between March 1629 and April 1640. In addition, a growing number of specialist standing committees were convened to advise on such subjects as trade, foreign affairs, ordnance and Ireland, while a plethora of other sub-committees were created to advise on a wide range of more specific problems. The overall membership of the Council grew to more than thirty in these years, although only about a dozen councillors were in regular attendance. Charles I presided over Council meetings far more frequently than his father had done, especially during the later 1630s. For example, his attendance at over forty of the 131 Council meetings held in 1637 almost equalled James's total for his entire lifetime. Often Charles was also present when the committees of the Council met. There is plentiful evidence that he prepared very carefully for all these meetings, and that he participated fully in the discussions.

Charles's close involvement stemmed from his wish to use the Council to implement a far-reaching reformation of government. He was single-minded in the pursuit of this goal, and impatient of any debate or dissent. As the decade progressed, his management of the Council revealed his essentially authoritarian temperament. Increasingly, the King turned to an inner circle of trusted advisers – led by figures such as Archbishop Laud, Lord Treasurer Weston, Secretary Windebank and Cottington – who could be relied upon not to challenge his preferred lines of policy. Very often it was this coterie rather than the full Council which took the crucial decisions: in June 1637 one Councillor, the Earl of Dorset, lamented that the 'mysteries' of public affairs were 'not divulged to us that are of the Common not the Cabinet Council'. This closed style of government was a natural reflection of Charles's secretive nature. His love of order was likewise reflected in the much more sophisticated record-keeping which characterized the Council during the Personal Rule. Charles gave instructions that the registers of the Council's proceedings were to be carefully indexed, and that a record should be kept of those decisions which created precedents for future action. The records of the Council during the 1630s reveal a highly organized and efficient institution which handled a growing range of business promptly and effectively. There is surely much justice in Kevin Sharpe's suggestion that in administration and government these years saw 'the winning of the initiative by the Privy Council'.

A similar pattern of reform was also applied to local government. A series of harvest failures, combined with the privations of war, a slump in trade and a severe outbreak of plague, led to a number of disturbances in 1629–31 which affected counties as far apart as Somerset, Wiltshire, Berkshire, Sussex, Kent, Hertfordshire, Suffolk and Essex. In response, the Council issued two Books of Orders, sets of instructions which were despatched periodically to enable Justices of the Peace to resolve a specific and immediate problem. The government's reforming ambitions once again became plain when these routine books were followed up in January 1631 by a new kind of Book of Orders which introduced the principle of continual reporting by the Justices to the Council about a wide range of local business for the indefinite future. This was an attempt to 'quicken' local magistrates into a more vigorous enforcement of statutes relating to such matters as the regulation of alehouses, the apprehension of vagrants, the maintenance of highways and the relief of the poor. However, its implementation depended entirely on the co-operation of local officials, and this varied considerably from region to region. There is evidence that in some areas the central government's agenda struck a chord with local Justices; but elsewhere, particularly in the northern and western shires, the Book appears to have been resented as an encroachment on the autonomy of local communities which had evolved methods of government that suited their local needs but did not always follow statute law to the letter. Once again, Charles's pursuit of order and his love of minutely detailed regulation produced division and polarization rather than the harmony and unity that he craved.

Even greater suspicion greeted Charles's attempts to reform the militia. The wars of 1625–30 had highlighted the woeful inadequacy of the existing arrangements for raising and maintaining the militia. The Arms Act passed under Mary I had been repealed in 1604, and thereafter Lords Lieutenant and Deputy Lieutenants derived their authority to muster troops directly from the Crown. Critics of the conduct of the war were quick to point out that the militia had no foundation in statute. Charles responded with a series of measures designed to create an 'exact militia'. Central to this programme was the appointment of a muster master in each county, responsible for ordering and training the militia. Deputy Lieutenants were instructed to maintain beacons and magazines, and the Council appointed commissioners to undertake regular inspections of arms, armour and ordnance. These initiatives were widely perceived as another example of central interference. Muster masters were often especially disliked as outsiders, and some counties – such as Shropshire in the mid-1630s – refused to pay their fees. Charles's bid for an 'exact militia' met with at best very patchy success, as became all too clear when he tried to mobilize troops against the Scots at the end of the 1630s.

These military reforms, like the Book of Orders, were intended to make the nobility and gentry discharge their local responsibilities more energetically, a goal which was particularly close to Charles's heart. In 1626 and again in 1627, 1630 and 1632, he issued proclamations commanding the nobility and gentry to leave London within forty days and to 'resort to the several counties where they usually resided and there keep their habitations and hospitality'. There was nothing new about such orders in this period: similar instructions had been issued at regular intervals since 1596. What was innovatory was Charles's characteristic determination to ensure that they were strictly observed. Any doubts about how serious he was were dispelled when, in November 1632, William Palmer was fined £1,000 in Star Chamber for remaining in London without permission. Those who claimed to have a compelling reason for staying in the capital had to secure a special licence from the Attorney-General, Sir John Bankes: over 200 such dispensations survive in Bankes's papers for the years 1632–40. The large numbers of gentry summoned before Star Chamber for being in London without a licence (248 in February 1633 alone), together with the fact that the proclamation had to be reissued several times, suggest that Charles's campaign enjoyed only limited success. There is evidence in contemporary diaries and newsletters that it generated considerable ill will, and in so far as it did achieve its desired effect it only served to make the Court even more isolated from the wider world.

Local duties and responsibilities were not the only area in which the government made increased demands on the gentry and nobility. Many found that they were also having to pay more in taxes and other duties. By 1629, the royal debt stood at approximately £2,000,000. The absence of Parliament did not in itself signal financial disaster, because scarcely one tenth of royal revenues came from parliamentary supply during the early seventeenth century. The Crown could not wage war without the taxes voted by Parliament, but it could manage without them in a period of peace. Charles nevertheless established a number of commissions to try to curtail the expenditure of official departments. He also devised a series of fiscal expedients to increase his annual income, reduce the royal debt and balance the peacetime budget. The most important of these expedients were higher customs duties, the sale of new monopolies and projects, knighthood fines, forest fines and – most profitable of all – Ship Money.

The customs had long been a staple part of the Crown's 'ordinary' revenue. In 1635 a new Book of Rates raised the duties on a wide range of commodities, with the result that customs revenue increased from an average of £270,000 a year in 1631–5 to about £425,000 a year in the second half of the decade. By raising new impositions and increasing existing ones, the Crown exploited the verdict in Bate's Case and was thus able to take full advantage of the expansion in trade that accompanied a period of peace. The Crown also gained from the sale of various projects, patents and monopolies, of which the most notable were the patent for the drainage of the Fens and the monopoly for the manufacture of soap.[9] Both of these schemes soon ran into difficulties. Fen drainage was strongly opposed by local vested interests whose livelihood and whole way of life were threatened. Yet, despite numerous acts of sabotage, extensive areas of fenland were drained – especially in Lincolnshire, Cambridgeshire and Nottinghamshire – and the economic benefits were certainly felt later in the century. The soap monopoly was granted in 1632 to a syndicate including several prominent Catholics who claimed to have discovered a superior method for making soap which lathered better and washed whiter. This grant brought the Crown about £30,000 a year, but was abandoned in 1637 following consumer complaints that the 'popish soap' did not live up to the lavish claims made on its behalf. Nevertheless, considering the bitter debates which impositions and monopolies had aroused earlier in the century, it is perhaps surprising that there was not more overt hostility to these policies.

Rather more discontent greeted Charles's use of ancient and largely forgotten laws to yield additional revenue. Among the most lucrative examples of this 'fiscal feudalism' was distraint of knighthood. In January 1630, Charles appointed a commission to fine those who owned freehold land worth £40 a year, and were thus eligible for knighthood, but who had ignored the sixteenth-century precedents requiring them to present themselves to be knighted at the King's coronation. These fines varied from £10 (the most common rate) to as much as £70, and by the end of the 1630s they had raised a total of £174,284 from 9,280 individuals. There was some quiet evasion, but in general the policy was successful, not least because it enabled the Crown to tap the growing wealth of those London merchants who were prospering in the trade boom. Another instance of the King's use of antiquarian research to augment his revenue was his revival of the forest laws. Legal records in the Tower were scoured to determine the medieval boundaries of the royal forests, and landowners whose estates had inadvertently encroached upon them were fined. From the summer of 1634 onwards, long-dormant forest courts were revived to adjudicate disputed boundaries and administer fines. Yet the modest financial gains from this campaign hardly justified the resentment that it caused. In all, it produced a total of barely £40,000; but, by questioning the validity of titles to land, it struck the nobility and gentry on an extremely sensitive nerve and left many of them anxious and mistrustful of the King.

It was another product of this fiscal antiquarianism, Ship Money, that proved to be the most contentious of all Charles's additional sources of revenue during the Personal Rule. Since the reign of Edward III, the Crown had claimed the right to levy money from coastal towns and counties during national emergencies in order to build a fleet. Such levies were normally imposed every few decades, but between 1634 and 1639 Charles raised them every year. Furthermore, from 1635 onwards he took the radical step of extending Ship Money from coastal regions to cover the whole of England and Wales. Ship Money was a county rate rather than a tax, and the sheriff of each shire was therefore made responsible for collecting it. On average, a total of about £200,000 was demanded each year, roughly the equivalent of three parliamentary subsidies, and the rates of payment were remarkably high. Between 1634 and the autumn of 1638, more than 90 per cent of the assessments were paid, generating a total of over £800,000, all of which was spent on building and equipping a sizeable fleet. Only in 1639, as Charles's financial demands on his English subjects escalated in order to fund a war against the Scots, did the willingness to pay Ship Money evaporate. At least initially, such active resistance as there was arose less from principled constitutional objections than from disputes over the way in which individual sheriffs distributed the rate among the various parts of their shires. Those who refused to pay, such as Lord Saye and Sele, were distrained rather than arrested or imprisoned, and this restrained approach further contributed to the fiscal success of Ship Money. By 1637, Charles's financial expedients were bringing in an annual revenue of over £1 million – 50 per cent higher in real terms than it had been on his accession – and enabled him to balance the peacetime budget.

Yet that same year also saw the first major constitutional challenge to the legality of Ship Money. In an attempt to clarify his right to levy Ship Money on a permanent basis, Charles decided to prosecute a Buckinghamshire squire, John Hampden, for refusing payment. But, once again, a bid to define the extent of his powers only led the King into deep constitutional waters. The case dragged on in the Exchequer from November 1637 until June 1638, when the judges finally pronounced in favour of the King by the narrowest possible margin (seven to five), giving Charles a legal victory but a moral defeat. The critical issue was that Charles sought a judgement allowing him to raise through his legal ('ordinary') prerogative a rate which most of his subjects – and predecessors – thought he could only levy under the emergency powers conferred by his absolute ('extraordinary') prerogative. As with the Forced Loan, Charles's claims infringed Jacobean conceptions of the prerogative and unleashed a conflict between divergent interpretations of that agreed framework. That in turn raised the murky questions of who determined whether or not a state of emergency existed, and of whether or not the King's assertion of such an emergency could be challenged at law. The King's policy presented the judges with a cruel dilemma. How could they uphold his claim without weakening the ordinary prerogative as a safeguard of lawful royal action (which included the defence of property rights) and thus subordinating it to the absolute prerogative? But equally, how could they find against the King without restricting *all* acts of prerogative to legal forms and thus eroding the absolute prerogative? That was in effect what Hampden's counsel, Oliver St John, had done; and he was supported by a minority of the judges, including Sir Richard Hutton, who argued that 'the people of England are subjects, not slaves; ... and are not to be taxed ... at will, but according to the laws of this kingdom'. In desperation, the judges who supported Charles argued that Ship Money was not a tax but a form of conscription: this allowed them to defend the legality of Ship Money while still preserving the principle of taxation by consent.

Despite this clever attempt to square the circle, Hampden's Case had raised the profound issue of whether the royal prerogative could really be both absolute and limited. James had taken great care to maintain this paradigm, but his son's policies caused it to break down. Perhaps the most dangerous aspect of Charles's behaviour was that in a political culture which revered consensus, it stimulated debate. A good example of this was the discussion about Ship Money among the Kentish gentry in February 1637. Some thought that 'the King had full right to impose it'. Others, by contrast, argued that it breached 'the known maxims of law, of which they held this to be the chief, that a King of England could lay no tax but by Parliament'. They invoked Sir John Fortescue to show that 'the King had not an absolute power ... [and] hath no prerogative but that which the law of the land doth give and allow'. This last point – that the King's authority was not absolute precisely because it was legally limited – reveals how far the paradigm of a monarchy that was both absolute and limited was already breaking down. This Kentish debate was recorded in the commonplace book of the antiquarian Sir Roger Twysden, and such private sources allow us to glimpse the constitutional division and disagreement behind the peaceful façade of Charles I's Personal Rule. On the surface everything appeared to be tranquil enough. In October 1637, for example, the courtier John Burghe informed his patron Viscount Scudamore that 'all things are at this instant here in that calmness that there is very little matter of novelty to write'. He even thought that the 'great tax of Ship Money is so well digested ... I suppose [it] will become perpetual'. Yet, as the divided reactions of the Kentish gentry illustrate, there was more disagreement, more silent unease and dissent, than was ever expressed in public. Reactions to Ship Money surely demonstrate that quietness on the surface does not necessarily indicate the existence of stability and consensus. This point can be applied with even greater force to religious affairs in this period.

4 Laudianism and the Church

In Church, as in State, Charles I pursued a vigorous and authoritarian programme of reform during the 1630s. The key figure in implementing his religious policies was William Laud, whom Charles appointed Bishop of

London in 1628 and then, on Abbot's death in 1633, Archbishop of Canterbury. Laud has often been branded – by both contemporaries and historians – as an 'Arminian', yet there is no evidence that he had read, let alone been influenced by, the writings of the Dutch theologian Jacobus Arminius. It probably makes more sense to see Laud as an exponent of that 'ceremonialist' position which had formed one strand of opinion within the Church of England since 1559. Like earlier divines such as Hooker, Whitgift, Andrewes, Howson and Buckeridge, Laud played down the significance of the sermon and advocated instead a greater emphasis on the sacraments, allied to a beautification of church fabric and an enhancement of the status of the clergy. Laud always claimed that he was simply enforcing neglected aspects of the existing canons and statutes of the Church. What was so new in the 1630s was not Laud's outlook as such but the fact that, with the King's strong support, he launched a systematic attempt to secure conformity with his preferred style of worship through a strict policy of episcopal visitations. By the mid-1630s, Laud and his allies had acquired a virtual monopoly over senior Church offices, prompting Dr George Morley, when asked 'what the Arminians held', to quip that 'they held all the best bishoprics and deaneries in England'. The delicate 'Jacobethan' balance, which tolerated diverse beliefs and practices within a broad national framework, was overturned by the ascendancy of one particular group who insisted that they were the only legitimate members of the Church.

Exactly what Laud did hold has remained the subject of debate: he was not a major theologian and his work reveals little of what he actually believed about such questions as salvation. Charles banned public discussion of the contentious doctrine of predestination, and as a result during the Personal Rule, controversy focused less on doctrinal issues than on what Peter Lake has called the 'Laudian style', the physical changes in patterns of worship designed to foster the 'beauty of holiness'. As Laud explained in a letter to Charles I, he believed that ceremonies were 'the hedge that fences the substance of religion from all the indignities which profaneness and sacrilege too commonly put upon it'. He regretted 'the want of uniform and decent order in too many churches of the kingdom', and urged the need 'for decency and an orderly settlement of the external worship of God in the church'. In particular, Laud preferred that in most churches the altar should stand against the east wall of the chancel, that it should be railed in, and that communicants should kneel when they received the bread and wine. He had a horror of desecration and was appalled by reports of dogs defiling unrailed altars or running off with communion bread. Yet the Elizabethan injunctions had permitted the eucharist to be celebrated round a plain 'communion table' set in the middle of the church, and this was the arrangement in most parishes until the 1630s. To many people, a railed-in altar at the east end of the chancel (and even the word 'altar') reeked of popery, and such feelings were not confined to radical Puritans. In 1633, the parishioners of St Gregory's Church, near St Paul's Cathedral, challenged the removal of their communion table to the east end on the instructions of the Cathedral's Dean and Chapter. Charles decided to use this as a test case, brought it before the Privy Council, and ruled that the bishop should have the right to decide the position of communion tables within each diocese. As the majority of bishops were of a Laudian persuasion, the St Gregory's Case marked a crucial victory for the new altar policy. Yet the controversy rumbled on, and in 1637 Bishop John Williams of Lincoln was fined and imprisoned for publishing *The Holy Table, Name and Thing*, in which he argued that the correct interpretation of the Elizabethan injunctions was that the communion table should stand lengthways in the chancel and only be moved to the east end for the communion. It is difficult to assess how successful the altar policy was. There is evidence that by 1640, around 80 per cent of English parishes had their altars railed in at the east end.[10] However, in 1641, in response to an invitation from the House of Commons, the vast majority of these were removed. Perhaps we can conclude from this that outward conformity to the altar policy did not necessarily indicate that inward change in attitudes which Laud so keenly desired.

The altar policy grew out of Laud's conviction that under Elizabeth and James the sacraments had been unduly neglected in favour of lengthy sermons. He was anxious to redress the balance, and in particular to reaffirm the importance of the eucharist. In 1637 he described the altar as 'the greatest place of God's residence upon earth', adding:

> I say the greatest, yea, greater than the pulpit; for there 'tis *hoc est corpus meum*, 'this is my body': but in the pulpit 'tis at most but *hoc est verbum meum*, 'this is my word'. And a greater reverence, no doubt, is due to the body than to the word of our Lord.

To many of Laud's contemporaries, such words came dangerously near to the Catholic doctrine of transubstantiation. There was also unhappiness at the instructions issued by Charles and Laud in 1633 stipulating that only ministers of parishes could preach sermons, and that 'the afternoon sermons be turned into catechising'. Many of the godly accepted the need to attend official Church services but wished to supplement these by 'gadding' often considerable distances to hear afternoon sermons given by nonconformist lecturers. Laud further undermined such lecturers in February 1633 by securing the abolition of the Feoffees for Impropriations, a group of laity and clergy established in 1625 to buy back impropriated tithes and use them to augment the stipends of lecturers. Laud regarded the Feoffees as a Puritan 'plot', but to his critics their suppression seemed another instance of his desire to deprive the populace of adequate spiritual guidance through sermons. One contemporary even accused the Archbishop of seeking 'to keep the people in darkness and blind superstition'. A similar reaction greeted Charles's reissue of the Book of Sports in October 1633 licensing archery, dancing and other recreations on Sundays. Originally published uncontroversially by James in 1618, it now – in the very different context of Laudian reforms – provoked an outcry from those who saw it as yet another affront to sabbatarian opinion.

Laud's emphasis on the sacraments and his regulation of lecturers have often been cited as evidence of his anti-Calvinism. Certainly, his policies appear to have had some theological basis. He abominated the Calvinist doctrine of predestination, in which the majority of human beings were predestined to be damned regardless of the sort of lives they led, declaring that 'it makes the God of all mercies to be the most fierce and unreasonable tyrant in the world'. Against this, his reforms implied a belief that the sacraments offered a channel for God's grace that was available to all. But, once again, such a view struck many of his contemporaries as far too reminiscent of the Catholic doctrines of universal grace and the free will of all people to obtain salvation.

There were many other aspects of Laudian policy which in the charged atmosphere of the 1630s – with the Catholic powers winning victory after victory on the Continent in the Thirty Years' War – seemed frighteningly close to popery. The restoration and beautification of church fabric, epitomized by the refurbishment of St Paul's Cathedral, may often have brought much-needed repairs, but they also caused widespread dismay that so much money should be spent on stained-glass windows and other symbols of 'idolatry'. Similarly, under Charles's patronage Church music in this period developed the polyphonic forms widely associated with the Catholic Counter-Reformation on the Continent. The King led the way in commissioning composers such as Thomas Tomkins, organist of the Chapel Royal, to write sacred works which abandoned the plainer Jacobean style perfected by Orlando Gibbons and William Byrd in favour of greater intricacy and elaboration. Later, in the 1640s, Tomkins' compositions were denounced as 'sprouts of popery'. That such music was performed in the Chapel Royal was widely perceived as part of a more sinister problem: the insidious growth of Catholicism at Court. In 1634, the King admitted a papal agent, Gregorio Panzani, to Court for the first time since 1558. Panzani was succeeded by George Con in 1636. Many also feared the influence of the Catholic services held in the Queen's chapel, and the Personal Rule saw a number of spectacular conversions among highly placed courtiers such as Lord Boteler, Lady Newport and Lady Hamilton.

Fears of a resurgence of 'popery' were strengthened by Laud's aggressive clericalism. He believed that the authority of bishops and archbishops existed by divine right, and he saw them as not just another 'degree' of clergy but as an entirely separate 'order'. He wanted to claw back clerical lands alienated to the laity since the Reformation, restrict lay control over tithes and over clerical appointments, and enhance the status of the clergy in both Church and State. At local and national levels alike, clergy were appointed to secular office on an unprecedented scale: many gentry and nobility were disconcerted to find themselves joined by clergy on the commission of the peace, and in March 1636 Bishop Juxon of London became the first clerical Lord Treasurer since the reign of Edward IV. Laud also insisted on the autonomy of the Church courts, above all the Court of High Commission, and with Charles's powerful backing he tried to prevent the writs of prohibition whereby common law courts could transfer to themselves cases triable at common law. Laud's exalted view of the clerical estate logically undercut the idea of the royal supremacy – he was later accused of dishonouring the Crown – and only Charles's strong commitment to Laudian reforms prevented this fundamental conflict of interests from becoming apparent during the Personal Rule.

All these policies help to explain why so many people shared the Earl of Bedford's perception of Laud as 'the little thief put into the window of the church to unlock the door to popery'. There is no reason to doubt his consistent denials of Catholicism, or the sincerity of his repudiations of Catholic doctrine in writings such as his *Conference with Fisher the Jesuit*. Yet it remains true that he viewed the Church of Rome in a different light from many of his contemporaries. Far from sharing the Puritan perception of Rome as 'the whore of Babylon' or the 'horn of the Beast', Laud regarded it as '*a* true Church but not *the* true Church'. He believed that the Church of England had far more in common with that of Rome – with which it shared an apostolic tradition – than it did with what he termed 'Calvin's new fangled device at Geneva'. He saw the Reformation as a necessary separation from the abuses and worldliness which had infected Rome by the early sixteenth century, but he did not regard either the separation or the abuses which prompted it as necessarily irrevocable. In 1639 he declared that:

> The Protestants did not get that name by protesting against the Church of Rome, but by protesting ... against her errors and superstitions. Do you but remove them from the Church of Rome, and our Protestation is ended, and the separation too.

He was thus able to envisage a hypothetical scenario in which the Churches of England and Rome might be reunited. That time had not yet come, but it was not (as it was for the Puritans) utterly unthinkable that it one day might. Indeed, when Laud was twice offered a Cardinal's hat – and the fact the offers were made is itself telling – he declined in very moderate, lukewarm terms, remarking in his diary that 'somewhat dwelt within me which would not suffer that till Rome were other than it is'. That entry was later used at Laud's trial to support the charge that 'he hath traitorously and wickedly endeavoured to reconcile the Church of England with the Church of Rome'.

The charge that Laud was a 'traitor' was problematic because his policies were carried out with the King's enthusiastic approval. Charles and Laud appear to have been in agreement on all fundamental questions of religious policy. The surviving evidence suggests a close collaboration between them, rather than a relationship in which one consistently led and the other followed. Each year, Laud submitted minutely detailed reports on the state of the Church, and the equally meticulous King worked carefully through them making comments in the margins. These annotations often gave promises of support or advice about how to handle specific problems. It is clear that the uniformity, formality and ceremonies of Laudianism were highly attractive to Charles, and formed the ecclesiastical counterpart of the order and decorum which he promoted at Court.

Hence, when Laud's policies were strongly criticized, Charles was prepared to use the full power of the State against the culprits, whom he regarded as 'seditious'. The 1630s saw a series of show-trials in the Court of Star Chamber (the Privy Council sitting as a judicial body) of those who voiced overt hostility to Laudian reforms. The earliest was that of Alexander

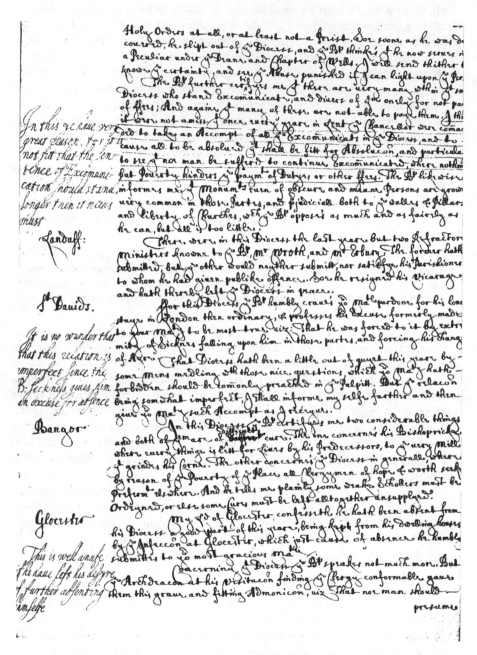

Plate 7 Report by William Laud as Archbishop of Canterbury to Charles I on the state of the Church of England, 1638, together with the King's annotations. Charles and Laud worked closely together to reform the Church, and the King's annotations reveal a deep interest in, and support for, all aspects of Laudian policies. Such documents suggest that they were like-minded collaborators, rather than that one consistently dominated the other.

Source: The Archbishop of Canterbury and the Trustees of Lambeth Palace Library

Leighton who, in a treatise entitled *Sion's Plea against Prelacy*, had denounced bishops as the 'trumpery of Antichrist' and 'knobs and wens and bunchy popish flesh'. In 1630 the Star Chamber fined him £10,000, and sentenced him to have one ear cut off, his nose slit, and his face branded. In 1638, John Lilburne was sentenced to be whipped through the streets of London for circulating Puritan literature. The most spectacular of these trials was that of three Puritan pamphleteers, William Prynne, Henry Burton and John Bastwick. In bitter polemic, they accused the Laudians of introducing innovations in the Church in order to prepare the way for popery. Bastwick, for example, complained that 'the substance of religion is thrust out' and that 'the Church is now full of ceremonies, as a dog is full of fleas'. In June 1637 all three were brought before Star Chamber charged with libel: they were convicted, fined £5,000 each, imprisoned for life and condemned to have their ears cropped. Prynne had already had his ears cropped in 1634 for an implied attack on the Queen in *Histriomastix*, and now lost the stumps as well. He was also sentenced to be branded on each cheek with the letters 'S.L.' meaning 'seditious libeller', but which he claimed stood for *stigmata Laudis* ('the scars of Laud'). Such savage penalties, like those imposed on Leighton and Lilburne, provoked demonstrations of sympathy with the victims and a widespread sense of revulsion which left the reputation of Star Chamber permanently tarnished.

In assessing the wider significance of these *causes célèbres*, it is important to distinguish between the punishments inflicted on Prynne, Burton, Bastwick, Leighton and Lilburne (which were exceptional) and the opinions they had expressed (which were not). There is a growing body of evidence to suggest that many people felt profound reservations about the religious policies of the Personal Rule, but thought it best not to air them in public. In recent years, our understanding of the 1630s has been illuminated by studies of individuals such as the Kentish gentleman Sir Edward Dering, who deplored what he called, with biting sarcasm, 'the piety of the times'; or the Warwick schoolmaster Thomas Dugard, who found solace and support in the household of Lord Brooke at Warwick Castle, which provided a secluded haven for a circle of godly ministers and laity. But there were others, like Robert Woodford the steward of Northampton, who lacked such patrons and who therefore poured out their misery into private diaries. Woodford outwardly conformed; only in his diary did he denounce 'bishops and their hierarchy' and all 'promoters of superstition and idolatry'. These sentiments led others – perhaps 15,000 during the whole decade – to emigrate to New England to begin a fresh life.[11]

The surviving evidence does not allow us to assess precisely how common such feelings were. What is clear is that far more people disliked the nature of Laudian reforms than ever chose to say so openly. Outward compliance often concealed inner anger which was to burst into the open in 1640 – what John Morrill has termed 'the coiled spring effect'. Whether or not we follow Patrick Collinson in seeing Laud as 'the greatest calamity ever visited upon the Church of England', it would be hard to dissent from Peter Lake's conclusion that Laudianism 'did exist as a coherent, distinctive and polemically aggressive vision of the Church'. All over England, that vision polarized opinion and disrupted the stable 'Jacobethan' Church. It was Laud's refusal to leave well alone that led James to lament his 'restless spirit' and the Headmaster of Westminster School to call him a 'meddling little hocus-pocus'. Laud collaborated with the King in a programme which generated passionate antipathy among many laity as well as clergy. Whereas under James I it had seemed to many that the Church was moving in the right direction, albeit too slowly, under Charles I it appeared to be moving rapidly in the wrong direction. As with Ship Money, the real problem was not that the government faced a solid wall of opposition, but rather that it divided people and provoked heated debate. Only a few paid the price for voicing their anger publicly. But unless we recognize the silent alienation caused by the religious policies of the Personal Rule we cannot hope to understand why Laud was so virulently denounced in 1640. No matter how 'halcyon' the 1630s appeared on the surface, only years of pent-up hostility among more than a Puritan fringe can explain rhetoric like that of Harbottle Grimston, for whom Laud represented 'the sty of all pestilential filth that hath infested the state and government of this commonwealth'.

5 Ireland under Wentworth

Charles's authoritarian style of government was even more marked outside England. In his other kingdoms he was less inclined to acknowledge any limitations upon his power and he became even more out of touch with local opinion. His government of Ireland during the Personal Rule is indelibly associated with the name of Thomas Wentworth, later Earl of Strafford, who was appointed Lord Deputy in 1632. Wentworth has justly been called 'the ultimate in poachers turned gamekeeper'. Although he had been one of the most outspoken critics of Buckingham and the policies of the 1620s, Wentworth had long sought to secure a foothold at Court, and from 1628 he proved himself a loyal servant of the Crown as President of the Council of the North. A blunt, ambitious and energetic Yorkshireman, he possessed a forceful personality, outstanding administrative ability and considerable political skill. His principal weaknesses were a lack of subtlety and tact, a tendency to oversimplify and a total incapacity either to compromise or to understand alternative points of view. In Ireland he committed himself to governing 'thoroughly' and, with Charles's staunch support, set about harnessing royal powers which were much less hedged about by law and custom than in England. The King's backing made it difficult for the Irish to appeal – as they had in the past – over the head of the Lord Deputy directly to the Crown. As in Charles's other kingdoms, it proved very hard to voice opposition legitimately. The result was that by 1640 Wentworth's behaviour had alienated all sections of Irish society and fuelled tensions which would ultimately explode in the rebellion of 1641.

When Wentworth arrived in Dublin in July 1633, he flatly refused to grant the concessions sought by the political elite in return for their co-operation. England's wars against France and Spain during the later 1620s had made it essential to defend Ireland from invasion by a foreign Catholic power. In the interests of security, Wentworth's predecessor, Viscount Falkland, had opened negotiations with the Old English and New English landowners. These talks produced a settlement in 1628 whereby the landowners agreed to pay subsidies totalling £120,000 over three years in return for a relaxation of the use of the oath of supremacy as a test for public office, the non-imposition of recusancy fines, and a guarantee of the security of titles for all those who had held lands for over sixty years. These concessions, known as the 'graces', represented a particular success for the Old English. Unfortunately, although the subsidies were paid in full, Wentworth aroused lasting resentment by ensuring that the 'graces' were never enshrined in statute.

Wentworth's overriding objective was to ensure that Ireland became financially self-sufficient and ceased to be a drain on the English Exchequer. He was determined to extend the Jacobean plantations in Connacht and Munster, and to impose the heaviest fiscal burdens on the New English settlers, such as Richard Boyle, Earl of Cork, who were least likely to rebel. Insisting that the King's needs had to come first, he refused to bargain away royal authority by granting concessions to particular interest groups. This intransigence became brutally clear in the 1634 Parliament when he brusquely rejected the 'graces', denied security of tenure to those who had held estates for more than sixty years, and refused to recognize Catholic office-holders. He thus alienated New and Old English alike, with the result that the latter gradually came to forge a common identity with the Gaelic Irish based upon their shared Catholicism. This developing identity was memorably expressed by the Old English writer Geoffrey Keating, whose *Foras Feasa ar Éirinn* (A History of Ireland) of *c.* 1634 conflated the traditional categories of *Gaeil* (Gaelic Irish) and *Gaill* (Old English) into a single group known as *Éireannaigh* (Irish) which embraced the whole of the Irish Catholic community.

In practice, during the 1630s Irish Catholics enjoyed a greater measure of religious freedom than at any time in living memory. Wentworth's first priority in religious policy was not to persecute Catholicism but to impose Laudian-style reforms on the Church of Ireland. His voluminous correspondence with Laud testifies to the mutual respect and strong personal rapport that existed between the two men. They did not seek to make the Irish Church uniform with the Church of England, but rather to bring both (and the Scottish Kirk as well)[12] into closer 'conformity . . . with the whole Catholic Church of Christ'. Laud took a great interest in the Irish Church, and John Bramhall, who was appointed Bishop of Londonderry in 1634 with instructions to reform the Church, soon introduced new ceremonies and liturgical practices reminiscent of Laud's programme in England. The influence of Laud and Wentworth ensured the displacement of the Irish Articles of 1615 in favour of the much less Calvinist Thirty-Nine Articles, which were formally adopted by the Irish Convocation in 1634. However, these policies achieved only limited success among Irish Protestants, and Wentworth lamented to Laud that 'as for bowing at the name of Jesus, it will not down with them yet; they have no more joints in their knees for that than an elephant'. A new Irish Court of High Commission was established by royal prerogative to enforce ecclesiastical reforms, but it failed to secure anything like universal compliance. Even more unpopular was the use of other prerogative institutions, notably the Court of Castle Chamber, the Court of Wards and the Commission for Defective Titles, to bypass common law defences of property rights and reclaim former Church lands and tithes. This use of royal authority to uphold clerical claims was profoundly threatening to all landowners, and especially to the New English. Wentworth never missed an opportunity to rub salt into their wounds, as when he ordered the tomb of the Earl of Cork's wife to be moved from the east wall of St Patrick's Cathedral in Dublin in order to make way for a railed-in altar.

Wentworth's rule in Ireland undoubtedly had its successes: he expanded Irish revenues to about £80,000 a year, above all by introducing a new customs farm, and he greatly improved administrative efficiency. Yet these were small compensations for the damage caused by his policies. In England and Scotland, many suspected that Ireland was being used as a laboratory to test reforms which would then be introduced on the mainland. In particular, there were growing fears that the concerted attempt to undermine property rights and break down the defences of the common law – particularly in order to reclaim former Church lands – might be implemented in Charles's other kingdoms as well.[13] Yet, despite such fears, 'Thorough' remained essentially a colonial policy, informed by a perception of the Irish that can be traced back to Edmund Spenser and Sir John Davies,[14] and sanctioned by a king who was largely ignorant of Irish conditions and opinions. In the long term, by eroding the wealth and status of both the New and Old English settlers, the years of Wentworth's ascendancy served to affirm Ireland's status as a colony. In the short term, the consequences of his actions were even more catastrophic: not only did his brutality and insensitivity earn him countless personal enemies; he achieved the remarkable feat of uniting against himself hitherto mutually hostile sections of Irish society. Worst of all, by tolerating Catholicism and imposing Laudian reforms on the Church of Ireland, Wentworth left the Protestants of Ulster and the Pale feeling more and more insecure. They reacted by demanding much tougher measures against Catholics; and it was in an attempt to forestall such measures that the Catholics rebelled in the autumn of 1641. The rebellion's ferocity reflected tensions and grievances which had been building up over several decades. But in order to understand why Irish Catholics chose that moment to launch this pre-emptive strike, we must locate the rebellion in a wider British context – a context crucially shaped by events in Scotland.

6 Scotland during the Personal Rule

Charles's government of Scotland demonstrated the same authoritarianism and the same propensity to unite previously antagonistic groups as in England and Ireland. In so far as he had a 'British' policy, it was designed less to Anglicize or unite the three kingdoms than to assert his authority in each of them. In Scotland, as in Ireland, Charles grew woefully out of touch with grassroots opinion and made little attempt to understand the limitations which local laws and customs imposed on his authority. Although he had been born in Scotland and all his life retained a Scots accent, he always behaved towards his northern kingdom like an English monarch. He emulated the aggressive approach of medieval English kings rather than the more pacific and genuinely 'British' ideals of his father, with the result that in Scotland, as in his other kingdoms, 1625 marked a watershed of real significance.

Charles's relations with the Scottish elite began badly when, in October 1625, he issued an Act of Revocation rescinding all Crown grants of royal and kirk property since the death of James V in 1542. Characteristically, this measure twisted an established custom into a radical innovation. It was a long-accepted tradition that on attaining the age of majority Scottish monarchs could revoke any grants of Crown lands made during their minority. But Charles had never reigned as a minor, and his revocation was extended to ecclesiastical property and back-dated to 1542. As in Ireland and (to a lesser extent) England, the security of titles to land was undermined. The sweeping terms of the act allowed for the surrender and regrant of all lands secularized during the Scottish Reformation, and thus affected all Scottish nobles and the majority of lairds. The King was so ill-informed that he expressed amazement at the bitter protests which greeted the revocation. As unpopular as the act's contents was the way it was implemented by direct royal fiat, without any consultation of either the Scottish Council or Parliament. The policy was eventually defeated by the collective non-co-operation of Scottish landowners; but it left a legacy of mistrust which led the contemporary historian Sir James Balfour to call the Act of Revocation 'the groundstone of all the mischief that followed after'.

The atmosphere of mistrust was intensified by Charles's disastrous visit to Scotland in June–July 1633. This visit was in every way a striking contrast with James's triumphant return of 1617. The Scots were deeply hurt that Charles had been king eight years before he was crowned in Scotland; and when he finally did journey north the manner of his coronation could not have been more offensive. Royal authority was emphasized by the choice of Holyrood Palace rather than the traditional locations of Scone or Stirling. The coronation ceremony on 18 June was consciously modelled on the English one and incorporated part of the English coronation oath, while the service was conducted before a raised altar in front of a tapestry into which was woven a crucifix. The historian John Spalding recorded that such a spectacle 'bred great fear of inbringing of popery'. The coronation exemplified Charles's insensitivity to the feelings of his Scottish subjects, and his lack of respect for their traditions and laws.

A similar insensitivity and lack of respect lay behind Charles's shabby treatment of the Scottish elite. During the later 1620s and 1630s, the Scottish Privy Council became more and more a cipher used to implement policies decided in England. No Scots were consulted except for those – like the Duke of Lennox or the Marquis of Hamilton – who, by holding lands and offices in both Scotland and England, were gradually emerging as 'British' peers. Between 1628 and 1633, Charles found a loyal servant in the Earl of Menteith, who was prepared to commute between London and Edinburgh and keep the King in touch with developments north of the border as Dunbar had done for James. But Charles grew suspicious that Menteith harboured an ancient claim to the Scottish throne, and these (probably unjustified) fears led him to place the best Scottish servant he ever possessed under house arrest. After Menteith's disgrace, Charles became ever more seriously out of touch with Scottish affairs. In 1634 he summarily rejected a supplication of the lords against religious innovations, and when Baron Balmerino tried to revive this he was tried, convicted of treason and sentenced to death. Only an outcry from the nobility persuaded the King to grant Balmerino a full pardon, but the episode was another dramatic illustration of the extreme difficulty – encountered time and again during the Personal Rule – of expressing grievances in a way that Charles would accept as legitimate.

All these tensions came to a head in Charles's most disastrous Scottish policy: his attempted reform of the Church. As in Ireland, his aim was not to make the Scottish Kirk uniform with the Church of England, but rather to bring all three Churches into 'conformity with the whole Catholic Church of Christ'. That meant chipping away – despite the abandonment of the revocation – at those landowners who had appropriated clerical lands and teinds (tithes). Above all, it meant introducing radical liturgical change in the form of new Canons and a new Prayer Book. The Canons, promulgated in 1636, stipulated that the altar must be placed against the east wall of the chancel, required ministers to wear a surplice when they celebrated communion, and placed a ban on extempore prayer. These reforms were imposed by royal prerogative, with no attempt to secure the agreement of either the General Assembly of the Kirk or the Scottish Parliament. The same was true of the Scottish Prayer Book which Charles issued by royal proclamation the following year. It is important to note that he was not trying to introduce the English Prayer Book north of the border. The new Prayer Book had been specially written for Scotland and it revealed much about Charles and Laud's vision of an ideal Church. It was in some ways more offensive to Scottish consciences than the English Prayer Book would have been, for example in its visual depiction of angels. Once again, the way the Prayer Book was introduced was as unpopular as its contents: Charles and Laud canvassed some of the Scottish Bishops, who were hardly representative of the clergy as a whole, and never consulted the General Assembly or Parliament. Such a dictatorial approach – so different from James's handling of the Five Articles of Perth – provoked protests in churches all over Scotland when the Prayer Book was first used in July 1637.

In the wake of these initial demonstrations, the Scots adopted the time-honoured strategy of bonding themselves together in a solemn oath refusing to comply with royal policy. In February 1638, the vast majority of nobles, lairds, ministers and others signed the National Covenant pledging to 'maintain the true worship of God' and the 'true religion, liberties and laws of the kingdom', and to disobey any orders which contravened them. It was a restrained and conservative document, committed to the defence of 'our dread sovereign, the King's Majesty, his person and authority', and to the preservation of the purity of Scottish religion as defined in such documents as the Second Book of Discipline (1578), the Negative Confession (1580–1) and the Golden Acts

(1592). The authors of the Covenant did not (at least publicly) confront the possibility that allegiance to the Crown and the defence of their concept of true religion might become incompatible. It was not their intention to incite rebellion or the taking up of arms. Rather, they wished to address a peaceful and distinctively Scottish form of complaint to Charles as King of Scotland. Unfortunately, Charles chose to react like a King of England: he regarded the Covenant as a direct challenge to his authority and decided to use military force to bring the Scots into line. The resulting conflict bankrupted the Crown, obliged the King to recall Parliament, and so brought the Personal Rule to an end.

Some historians have suggested that Charles's attempt to rule without Parliaments might have been viable in the long term, and they have speculated that it could have survived but for the outbreak of rebellion in Scotland. Certainly, once he had succeeded in balancing his peacetime budget, only a war could oblige Charles to recall Parliament. Yet such counterfactual arguments may in the end be academic. After all, the rebellion in Scotland was not a *deus ex machina*: it was the direct consequence of Charles's own initiative to impose religious reforms and of his own decision to suppress Scottish passive resistance by force. The conflict with the Scots was thus the outcome of the reforming policies and authoritarian style of government that were the very essence of the regime. It is possible that the Personal Rule might have survived had Charles not launched a campaign against his Scottish subjects. But the issue is more apparent than real because the conflict was caused by precisely the same attitudes and objectives that had encouraged Charles to abandon ruling with Parliaments in the first place. In other words, the King's outlook, which was shared by Laud and Wentworth and which underpinned the establishment of the Personal Rule, was also the cause of the regime's downfall.

We shall see in the next chapter how that collapse of royal authority led to war in all three of Charles's kingdoms. Does it follow that the crisis was therefore a natural result of the early Stuarts' attempt to govern multiple kingdoms? Certainly, the continental instances of what J. H. Elliott has called 'composite monarchies' – most notably France and Spain – indicate that such States were prone to instability. This was especially true where, as in the Stuart kingdoms, one monarch ruled over more than one religion. The conflicts that broke out in Scotland, Ireland and England in part reflected potential sources of stress that can be traced back over several decades, and they were profoundly affected by the fact that each kingdom was part of a composite monarchy. Such long-term, structural problems help to explain why a crisis of some kind befell the early Stuart monarchies. Yet they cannot tell the whole story. It is an obvious but highly significant point that the crisis did not come under James VI and I but under Charles I. Unlike James, his son upset delicate balances and enflamed areas of tension. We have seen that in so far as Charles had a 'British' policy, he sought not to unify his three kingdoms but to assert his personal authority in each of them. In the end, it was primarily his policies and his authoritarian style of government that brought about the 'fall of the British monarchies'. Although the stresses inherent in composite monarchies may have made a crisis of royal authority probable eventually, the particular crisis that engulfed Charles's three kingdoms at the end of the 1630s was determined above all by the destabilizing effects of the King's personality and policies. In the end, the term 'Personal Rule' is not just a straightforward description of a period of non-parliamentary government: it is also a deeply appropriate label for a regime devised and ultimately destroyed by the visions of one king.

5 The Collapse of Multiple Monarchies

	13 April–5 May	Short Parliament: Charles fails to secure supply for another campaign against the Scots; he nevertheless prepares to attack Scotland
	May	Convocation passes seventeen Canons
	11 June	Scottish Triennial Act
	August	Montrose and seventeen other Scottish Lords sign Cumbernauld Band against the Covenanters
	20 August	Second Bishops' War begins: Leslie leads Scottish army into England
	28 August	Scots rout English forces at Newburn and gain control of northeast of England; twelve Peers submit Petition to Charles condemning recent royal policies and requesting the recall of Parliament
	24 September	Charles convenes Great Council of Peers at York
	21 October	Truce of Ripon: Scots to receive £850 a day and to remain in northeast of England until a settlement is agreed and confirmed by English Parliament
	3 November	Long Parliament assembles
	November	Strafford imprisoned and impeachment articles drawn up
	11 December	London Root and Branch Petition calling for the abolition of episcopacy submitted to Parliament
	16 December	Commons votes 1640 Canons illegal because Convocation passed them after dissolution of Parliament
	18 December	Laud impeached
	December	Impeachment of Lord Keeper Finch and other judges who had upheld Ship Money; Finch, Windebank and others flee to Continent
1641	23 January	Commons passes order for destruction of images
	25 January	Charles promises to defend 'the true Protestant religion by law established'

8–9 February	Commons debates London Root and Branch Petition
15 February	Triennial Act: Parliament to be summoned at least every three years
22 March	Trial of Strafford begins
Spring–summer	Sporadic outbreaks of enclosure riots and iconoclasm
3 May	Commons draws up Protestation Oath against popery; first Army Plot revealed
9 May	Death of Earl of Bedford: effectively ends attempts to create 'bridge-appointments'
10 May	Charles assents to Strafford's attainder, and to Bill against the dissolution of Parliament without its own consent
12 May	Strafford executed on Tower Hill
18 May	Charles announces intention of visiting Scotland to conclude final peace treaty
Late May–early August	Parliamentary debates over abolition of episcopacy
22 June	Abolition of tonnage and poundage
24 June	Commons agrees Ten Propositions as basis for negotiations with Charles; Lords agrees, with minor amendments, on 26 June
5 July	Abolition of Courts of High Commission and Star Chamber; judicial powers of Privy Council, Council in the North and Council in the Marches suppressed
7 August	Ship Money declared illegal; boundaries of royal forests limited
10 August	Knighthood fines declared illegal
13 August	Charles leaves for Scotland
August	Charles agrees settlement with Scots, who withdraw their troops from England
1 September	Commons passes resolution for destruction of altar rails, candlesticks and crucifixes
9 September	Parliament begins six-week recess (until 20 October)
11–12 October	Scottish 'Incident': Charles's bungled attempt to arrest Argyll and Hamilton

	22 October	Outbreak of Catholic rebellion in Ireland: massacres of Protestants; first reports reach London on 1 November
	30 October	Second Army Plot revealed
	8 November	Pym brings Grand Remonstrance before the Commons
	22–23 November	Commons passes Grand Remonstrance by 159 votes to 148, after lengthy debate
	25 November	Charles returns to London
	21 December	City of London elects new Common Council much more sympathetic towards Pym and his allies
	23 December	Charles rejects Grand Remonstrance
	27 December	Crowds outside Palace of Westminster prevent bishops from taking their seats in the Lords
	30 December	Excluded bishops petition for Lords' proceedings in their absence to be declared null and void; they are impeached
1642	2 January	Charles offers Pym the Chancellorship of the Exchequer; when he refuses Sir John Culpepper is appointed instead
	4 January	Charles's attempted arrest of five members of the Commons and one member of the Lords
	5 January	Commons adjourns to the Guildhall; London Common Council refuses to surrender five members to Charles
	8 January	Falkland appointed Secretary of State
	10 January	Charles and his family retreat to Hampton Court
	14 January	Oliver Cromwell moves for a committee 'to put the kingdom in a posture of defence'
	12 February	Houses of Parliament submit list of approved Lords Lieutenant to Charles, who refuses to give up control of the armed forces
	13 February	Bishops' Exclusion Act excludes bishops from the House of Lords
	23 February	Henrietta Maria leaves England; on the Continent she begins to raise money for troops

5 March	Houses of Parliament pass the Militia Ordinance
23 April	Sir John Hotham denies the King entry to arsenal at Hull
2 June	Houses of Parliament present the *Nineteen Propositions* to Charles
11 June	Charles issues commissions of array to raise troops
18 June	Charles's *Answer to the XIX Propositions*
9 July	Houses of Parliament vote to raise an army of 10,000 volunteers
12 July	Houses of Parliament appoint Earl of Essex Lord General
15 July	Skirmish at Manchester: first bloodshed of the English Civil War
18 August	Houses of Parliament declare Charles's supporters 'traitors'
22 August	Charles raises standard at Nottingham against Parliamentarian 'rebels': this marks the formal outbreak of the English Civil War

1 The Bishops' Wars and the Short Parliament

In the summer of 1638, as the Covenanting movement grew from strength to strength, Charles I had two choices open to him: either he could abandon the Scottish Prayer Book, or he could try to suppress the Scots by force. It was characteristic of him that he chose to pursue both strategies simultaneously. He despatched the Marquis of Hamilton, one of the few Scots he trusted, to negotiate with the Covenanters, and authorized him to grant such important concessions as the calling of a Scottish Parliament and the withdrawal of the Prayer Book. He also permitted a General Assembly to meet at Glasgow the following November, and was galled when this body annulled the Canons of 1636 and proclaimed the abolition of episcopacy in Scotland. In his private letters to Hamilton, however, Charles made it clear that any conciliatory gestures to the Covenanters were only 'to win time ... until I be ready to suppress them', and admitted that he would 'rather die than yield' to their 'impertinent and damnable demands'. Typically, he blamed the Covenant on a small circle of 'traitors', and was determined to 'suppress rebellion'.

As soon as Charles set about recruiting an army to fight the Scots, the woeful inadequacy of England's military organization and finance became glaringly apparent. It took him until April 1639 to assemble an army of around 15,000 troops from the English militia, financed mainly from loans. Not since 1323 had an English monarch undertaken a major war without calling Parliament. Charles's demands for military dues, such as coat-and-conduct money, provoked (for the first time) a widespread refusal to pay Ship Money and eventually led to a nationwide taxpayers' strike. Charles had hoped to deploy the resources of all three of his kingdoms against the Covenanters: the Earl of Antrim – the greatest Catholic landowner in the north of Ireland, and heir to an ancient lordship in the western Highlands and Islands – was to lead an army of 5,000 Irish troops into Western Scotland and link up with the King's potential supporters among the Catholic Highlanders. Yet these projected campaigns came to nothing and Charles ended up with the worst of both worlds. His military preparations antagonized the Scots and made them suspicious of any concessions; while the endless delays in mobilization and Charles's failure to co-ordinate his campaign adequately gave them ample opportunity to raise an army. By the time that Charles's forces finally confronted a Scottish army of roughly equal size at Kelso near Berwick in June 1639, many of his troops and their noble commanders were so disaffected that they promptly sued for peace without firing a shot. So ended the First Bishops' War. Under the terms of the Pacification of Berwick, Charles agreed to call another Scottish Parliament and a General Assembly at Edinburgh, which to his chagrin subsequently ratified the abolition of Scottish episcopacy.

From Charles's point of view, perhaps the most disturbing aspect of the First Bishops' War was the mistrust and discontent which it revealed among his own soldiers and their officers. Many sympathized with the Scots and some were even prepared to collude with them. The recent research of Peter Donald and Conrad Russell has shown that by the summer of 1639 secret contacts existed between the Covenanter leaders and several of Charles's most outspoken critics in England, most notably Lord Brooke, Viscount Saye and Sele, and Saye's son Nathaniel Fiennes.[1] These links also extended to Ulster Protestants such as Sir John Clotworthy. Charles was desperately keen to stamp out such contacts: although keen to use the military resources of all his kingdoms against the Scots, he wanted to isolate his critics and to prevent opposition from becoming a 'British' phenomenon. But in vain. During the Personal Rule the style of Charles's government in England, Scotland and Ireland had displayed a similar authoritarianism, especially in the field of religious reform, with the result that his critics in all three kingdoms had similar grievances and felt able to co-operate with each other. Charles's behaviour during the First Bishops' War only served to reinforce their anxieties about a 'popish plot' to subvert lawful government and 'true religion' throughout the archipelago. Not only was the King quite willing to employ Catholic officers in his army; he was even prepared to ask Spain and the Papacy for aid against the Scots. When, in the summer of 1639, he also permitted Spanish coin to be minted in England and allowed Spanish troops to march across southern England prior to launching an assault on the Dutch Republic, there were complaints that he was endangering the cause of European Protantism. Such decisions strengthened anti-popish paranoia, and there were even fears in some quarters that Spain might send another Armada against England.

In this tense atmosphere, Charles felt the need for strong counsel and therefore asked Wentworth to return to England. On his arrival in September Wentworth immediately became one of the King's inner circle of advisers, and joined Laud and Hamilton among the leading members of a sub-committee of the Council charged with reviewing Scottish affairs. Wentworth regarded the Scots as rebels: he argued bluntly that Scotland should be conquered and henceforth ruled as a direct dependency of the English Crown. In his view there was no alternative 'but the way of an effectual war', and he felt that no war could 'be made effectually but such a one as should grow and be assisted from the high counsel of a Parliament'. Charles accepted this advice and in February 1640 writs were issued summoning a new Parliament to assemble on 13 April.

Charles had one purpose only in calling what became known as the Short Parliament: to secure enough revenue to wage a successful war against the Scots. However, he soon found that a minority of the Lords and a majority of the Commons were unwilling to grant the twelve subsidies he requested until their religious, legal and constitutional grievances had received a thorough hearing. Some members of both Houses – especially those most vehemently hostile to Laudianism – clearly sympathized with the Covenanters and wished to defeat supply in order to encourage Scottish resistance. Faced with this deadlock, Charles had three alternatives: he could dissolve Parliament and make concessions to the Scots; or he could make concessions to Parliament, gain supply and then launch a further campaign against the Scots; or he could dissolve Parliament and embark on another war without proper resources. Although the first two strategies were in different ways painful for Charles, both were perfectly viable; the third was not, and unfortunately that was the one he chose. Egged on by Wentworth (now Earl of Strafford), who advised the King that he was 'loose and absolved from all rules of government', Charles dissolved Parliament on 5 May – a fateful decision that led him, for the first time, to lose control of events.

The Short Parliament's rapid demise fuelled the growing mistrust of Charles. To make matters worse, the King breached custom by instructing Convocation to continue sitting after the dissolution of Parliament. This extension enabled Convocation to pass seventeen Canons, ostensibly designed to disabuse those misled into believing that the King intended 'to bring in some alteration of the religion here established'. In fact, many of the Canons proved highly controversial, including those which explained the divine right of kings and imposed sweeping penalties on all those branded 'sectaries'. But by far the most contentious Canon – inserted on Charles's personal orders – was that enforcing an oath to uphold 'the government of this church by arch-bishops, bishops, deans and archdeacons, etc., as it now stands established'. This notorious '*et cetera* oath', intended to detect Presbyterian sympathizers, provoked a bitter outcry. Many petitions, pamphlets and satires circulated in protest at the Canons, and by the autumn Charles had been forced to abandon the oath.

The Canons unwittingly played right into the hands of the Scots. During the spring and summer of 1640, Scottish propaganda focused constantly on the common threat to 'true religion' in both kingdoms. Whereas in 1638–9 the Scots had sought nothing more than the protection of their own Kirk, by 1640 many Covenanters thought it essential to bring Charles's other kingdoms 'to our happiness'. A lasting settlement could not be achieved without the destruction of what Robert Baillie called (in April 1640) 'the prelacy in England, the fountain whence all the Babylonish streams issued unto us'. Galvanized by this radical agenda, the Scots did not wait for Charles to launch another campaign against them; instead, they seized the initiative and on 20 August the Earl of Leslie led an army of about 18,000 across the Tweed into England. Charles had only belatedly been able to raise an army, and the 9,000 Irish troops which Strafford had promised never materialized. The English army was badly demoralized and manifested what Strafford called 'a general disaffection to the King's service': they proved no match for the Scots, who routed them at Newburn on 28 August and then occupied the northeast of England as far as Newcastle.

That same day saw further evidence of covert Anglo-Scottish contacts. Twelve of Charles's most consistent critics among the English peerage, including Saye, Brooke, Essex and Warwick, signed a Petition lamenting 'the sundry innovations in matters of religion', 'the great increase of popery' and 'the great grief of your subjects by the long intermission of Parliaments'. They urged the King to summon a Parliament to redress 'these and other great grievances', and hoped that it would also facilitate 'the uniting of both of your realms against the common enemies of the reformed religion'.[2] The Petition was probably drafted by John Pym and Oliver St John, and some of those involved with it were clearly working in collusion with the Covenanter leaders. A letter informing the Scots of the Petition, almost certainly by Saye's son Nathaniel Fiennes, communicated plentiful intelligence and asked for information about

Scottish plans so that they could co-ordinate their future efforts. This letter – which surely constituted treason – showed that the Privy Council's fears about the 'tribe of the Covenant' in England were fully justified.

Charles responded to the Petition by summoning a Great Council of Peers to York. When they met on 24 September he immediately announced the summoning of a Parliament for 3 November. In the meantime, he continued to negotiate with the Scots and on 21 October concluded the Truce of Ripon whereby they would remain in Newcastle and receive £850 a day from Charles until satisfactory terms were agreed and guaranteed by the English Parliament. That costly settlement ensured that the Parliament which met in November could not be dismissed as easily as the Short Parliament. Indeed, it was not finally dissolved until March 1660.

2 The Long Parliament: The First Year

The ceremonial that attended the opening of the new Parliament was traditional enough, but its context was wholly unprecedented. Never before had an English Parliament's existence been secured by 18,000 Scottish troops occupying northeastern England. Members assembled in a mood of tense expectation, conscious, as Sir Henry Slingsby remarked, that 'the subject' now had a unique opportunity to secure 'a total redress of all his grievances'. The first week saw an extraordinary outpouring of bitterness against recent royal policies in Church and State. John Pym condemned a design to 'alter the kingdom both in religion and government'; while Sir Benjamin Rudyerd attacked those 'destructive counsels' that rang 'a doleful, deadly knell over the whole kingdom'. The intemperate language of these future Parliamentarians was matched by that of future Royalists, such as Sir Francis Seymour, who complained of the King's 'ill counsel', or Sir John Culpepper who presented a lengthy statement of the 'grievances of the Church and Commonwealth'. Although their political paths would subsequently diverge dramatically, in November 1640 most members of both Lords and Commons were able to unite in denouncing the policies and personnel associated with the Personal Rule.

That shared hostility sustained the Houses for the next six months. This period did not see significant constitutional legislation: the only major reform was the Triennial Act (15 February 1641). Inspired by a Scottish act of June 1640, this required the King to summon Parliament at least every third year and set up elaborate machinery to ensure that Parliament would meet even if he failed to issue the necessary writs. Otherwise, the Houses concentrated their energies on removing and punishing the 'evil counsellors' of the Personal Rule. Laud was arrested, impeached as 'an actor in the great design of the subversion of the laws ... and of religion', and imprisoned pending a full trial. The Houses were happy to leave him languishing in the Tower and he was not finally executed until 1645. Lord Keeper Finch and the six other judges who had upheld Ship Money were also impeached; and Finch joined a number of highly placed Catholics, like Secretary Windebank, in fleeing to the Continent. But the adviser that the Houses were most anxious to destroy was Strafford. He was the figure they really feared because of his notorious ruthlessness and suspected willingness to deploy Irish troops on the mainland. But he proved exceptionally difficult to get rid of.

In November 1640 impeachment articles were drawn up accusing Strafford of 'endeavouring to subvert the ancient and fundamental laws and government of England and Ireland', of erecting an 'arbitrary and tyrannical government' in Ireland, and of provoking war against the Scots. The charges were thus genuinely British in scope and were assembled by men from all three kingdoms. However, when Strafford's trial opened the following March it was impossible to make the charge of treason stick because he had clearly been acting on the King's instructions. The attempt to formulate a doctrine of 'cumulative treason' – whereby his actions were deemed to constitute treason collectively even though none did individually – collapsed in disarray. After prolonged wrangles, the Houses therefore decided to use a bill of attainder, which would simply declare Strafford's guilt already proven. In the end, 204 members of the Commons voted in favour of attainder and only 59 'Straffordians' against. The bill then passed a thinly attended Upper House, and finally the King – intimidated by angry demonstrations outside Whitehall Palace and fearing for the safety of his wife and children – gave the royal assent on 10 May. Strafford was beheaded on Tower Hill two days later.

What ultimately sealed the fate of 'Black Tom Tyrant' was the revelation on 3 May of a plot by a group of army officers to capture the Tower, release Strafford and threaten Parliament with dissolution, possibly with the assistance of French or Dutch troops. Conrad Russell has shown the extent of the King's complicity in this 'first Army Plot', but nothing could be proved at the time.[3] Instead, the terrified Houses passed a bill against the dissolution of the Parliament without its own consent, to which Charles also assented on 10 May. In addition, the Commons took the radical step of drawing up the Protestation Oath, an oath of association to be taken by all MPs. The preamble to this oath warned of continued 'endeavours to subvert the fundamental laws of England and Ireland, and to introduce the exercise of an arbitrary and tyrannical government by most pernicious and wicked counsels, practices, plots and conspiracies'. Those who took the oath pledged their allegiance to 'the true reformed Protestant religion . . . against all popery and popish innovation', and swore to defend 'His Majesty's royal person and estate' and the 'power and privilege of Parliaments'. Pym and his allies regarded the Protestation Oath as 'a shibboleth to discover a true Israelite' and recommended that it be adopted throughout the whole nation.

The Houses' high level of unity behind the Protestation Oath and against the 'evil counsellors' of the Personal Rule is in marked contrast with the serious disagreements which opened up over Church reform. During its first six months the Parliament collected plentiful criticisms of Laudian policies and received numerous petitions calling for the abolition of episcopacy. The earliest and most famous of these was the so-called Root and Branch Petition, allegedly signed by 15,000 Londoners and submitted in December 1640. Probably drafted with the help of Presbyterian Scots, such as Robert Baillie, this Petition

5

A
DECADE
OF
GRIEVANCES,

Prefented and approved to the Right
Honourable and High Court of Parliament,
againft the Hierarchy or government of the
Lord Bifhops, and their dependant offices,
by a multitude of people,

Who are fenfible of the ruine of Religion, the finking
of the State, and of the plots and infultations of
enemies againft both.

The tottering Prelates, with their trumpery all,
Shall moulder downe, like Elder from the wall.

Printed in the yeare, 1641.

Plate 8   From the end of 1640, there were growing calls for the abolition of bishops.
During the following year, nearly twenty counties submitted anti-episcopal petitions
to Parliament. In this pamphlet of mid-1641, Alexander Leighton, who had been
severely punished for attacking bishops in 1630, listed grievances dating back over the
previous decade. His work provides a good illustration of how such hostility towards
episcopacy did not develop overnight. He blamed bishops for 'the ruin of religion and
the sinking of the state', and this picture shows them being shaken down from the
branches of a tree, together with mitre, crook, bell and other episcopal 'trumpery'.
Source: British Library

described episcopacy as 'a main cause and occasion of many foul evils, pressures and grievances', and demanded its abolition along 'with all its dependencies, roots and branches'. It argued that the 'very dangerous' effects of episcopacy extended beyond the Church into the 'consciences, liberties and estates' of the King's subjects. This foreshadowed a wave of similar anti-episcopal petitions from nearly twenty counties all over England during the course of 1641.

When the Commons debated the Root and Branch Petition on 8–9 February 1641, opinion was bitterly divided. The supporters of the Petition, of whom the most eloquent was Nathaniel Fiennes, denounced the 'evils and inconveniences' of episcopacy. Only its outright abolition, they argued, could protect the Church from the likes of Laud and allow the creation of a godly commonwealth. The members most bitterly opposed to episcopacy were generally those, like Fiennes, who sympathized with the Covenanters. By contrast other speakers, who had usually been less well disposed towards the Scots, wanted to reform rather than abolish bishops. Lord Digby urged the Commons not 'to root up a good tree because there is a canker in the branches', and declared: 'Let us not destroy bishops, but make bishops such as they were in primitive times'. This desire to preserve episcopacy was inseparable from a wish to defend the rule of law and the existing social and political hierarchies. Sir John Strangways warned that 'if we made a parity in the Church we must at last come to a parity in the Commonwealth'. This division was highly significant because it forecast allegiance in the Civil War much earlier than views on any other issue. Those who advocated a reformed episcopacy, such as Strangways, Culpepper, Viscount Falkland, Edward Hyde and Lord Digby, virtually all joined the King in 1642; whereas the supporters of root and branch reform, including Nathaniel Fiennes, Denzil Holles and Oliver Cromwell, all became Parliamentarians. No other debate so accurately prefigured subsequent political allegiance at so early a date.

This contrast between a relatively high degree of unity on purely legal or constitutional issues and growing disagreement focused on Church government became even plainer between May and September 1641. By mid-May over half of Charles's Privy Councillors of November 1640 had been imprisoned, exiled or disgraced. The Houses now embarked upon structural reforms to obliterate the institutional machinery that had made non-parliamentary government possible. On 22 June the abolition of tonnage and poundage without Parliament's consent removed a long-standing grievance. On 5 July, the Courts of High Commission and Star Chamber were abolished, while the judicial powers of the Privy Council, the Council in the North and the Council in the Marches were suppressed. The following month, prerogative finance followed the prerogative courts into oblivion. Ship Money was declared illegal, knighthood fines were prohibited, and the boundaries of the royal forests were clearly defined. These bills passed both Houses with enormous majorities, and Charles assented to them, albeit with obvious displeasure. Members were still able to rally behind a negative programme of legal and constitutional reform. But these same months also saw increasing divisions between and within the Lords and Commons over the Crown's financial settlement, over whether further limitations should be placed on the King's powers, and above all over the future of the Church.

Charles had originally summoned the Long Parliament to resolve the desperate financial problems caused by his agreement to pay the Scots £850 a day until a satisfactory settlement was achieved. He soon found that several of his most important critics were willing to suggest constructive reforms of the royal finances, in return for their own elevation to senior office. The most important of these 'bridge-appointments' were those of the Earl of Bedford as Lord Treasurer, of Pym as Chancellor of the Exchequer, and of Oliver St John as Solicitor-General. In return for preferment, they proposed a radical scheme whereby Parliament would pay the King's existing debts, and parliamentary subsidies would in future be replaced by the payment of a fixed sum from each county divided among the taxpayers at the discretion of county commissioners. This principle of a lump sum in place of subsidies was reminiscent of the Great Contract of 1610, and it offered an imaginative solution to the Crown's long-term fiscal difficulties. But it did not find universal favour in the Houses – one member even accused Pym of seeking to introduce a 'Turkish despotism' – and it was linked to a highly controversial plan to confiscate and lease the lands of Deans and Chapters.[4] Any hopes of a financial settlement associated with strategic 'bridge-appointments' were dashed by Bedford's sudden death from smallpox on 9 May 1641. Thereafter, although the Houses produced a new Book of Rates, any fundamental overhaul of royal finances was prevented by their inability to reach agreement over what constitutional guarantees (if any) Charles should offer in return.

Behind the quest for such guarantees lurked the issue of royal counsel. Despite the assault on the 'evil counsellors' of the Personal Rule, many members still had nagging doubts about whether Charles really could be trusted to choose what they regarded as reliable advisers. The level of parliamentary mistrust became plain when, in late May, the King announced his intention of journeying to Scotland in order to conclude a final peace settlement. With memories of the first Army Plot still fresh, some members were fearful that he might try to deploy both the English and Scottish armies against Parliament. This edginess enabled Pym to secure the consent of both Houses to the Ten Propositions, the most contentious of which called for the delaying of the King's journey to Scotland, the removal of Catholic priests from the Queen's service, the dismissal of advisers who stirred up division between the King and his people, and the appointment of 'such officers and counsellors as his people and Parliament may have just cause to confide in'. Such an encroachment on the King's discretionary power to choose his own advisers was quite unprecedented, and Charles predictably rejected it outright. Instead, he insisted that he 'knew of no ill counsellors' and – after appointing a regency commission to exercise royal authority during his absence – departed for Scotland on 13 August.

It was, however, the question of Church reform that generated the most heated debates in Parliament during the summer of 1641. Despite the reservations of members such as Hyde, on 1 May the Commons passed a bill removing bishops from secular employment. When the Lords subsequently deleted the clause which excluded the bishops from the Upper House, the advocates of root and branch reform in the Commons retaliated by introducing a bill for the abolition of episcopacy. The extreme divisiveness of this bill is indicated by the fact that on 27 May the Commons only agreed to a second reading by 139 votes to 108, and after heated discussion. Parallel proposals for the reallocation of Dean and Chapter property to the Crown, and for the use of episcopal lands to promote education and augment poor livings, proved equally controversial. From late May until early August, members engaged in a series of long and bitter debates during which opinion became starkly polarized around two irreconcilable positions. On one side stood those like Sir Henry Vane the younger, who argued that the Commons would flout 'divine providence' if they did not immediately destroy Church government by bishops. On the other were the defenders of a moderate, non-Laudian episcopacy, such as Culpepper, who insisted that 'the grievances had grown from the abuse of the government and not from the government itself'.

Although focused on the issue of episcopacy, these debates quickly embraced more secular concerns as well. Those who upheld bishops not only praised their ministry within the Church over many centuries; they also regarded episcopacy as a vital bastion of stable government, social order and the rule of law. For the poet Edmund Waller, episcopacy formed a 'counter-scarp or outwork' protecting hierarchy and property; while the Cheshire gentleman Sir Thomas Aston feared that the 'true aim' of the exponents of root and branch reform was 'to shake off the yoke of all obedience, either to ecclesiastical, civil, common, statute or customary laws of the kingdom and to introduce a mere arbitrary government'. Such anxieties were deepened by news from the provinces suggesting that property was under attack and public order on the verge of collapse. There were sporadic enclosure riots during the spring and summer of 1641, especially in the midlands and the north, and these months also witnessed outbreaks of popular iconoclasm all over England. While many county communities drew up petitions calling for root and branch reform, some people took the law into their own hands, smashing stained glass windows, burning altar rails, and tearing down any images associated with 'popery' and 'idolatry'. Parliament's deliberations did not take place in a vacuum, and lurid accounts of provincial developments soon reached Westminster. For many members these weeks marked a crucial turning-point. Sir Edward Dering, who had originally introduced the root and branch bill in the Commons, 'defected' from the cause when he received reports of popular 'disorder' in his native Kent. During the course of the summer, more and more members became uneasy about the Commons' order of 23 January 1641 for the destruction of 'images' and 'ornaments and relics of idolatry'; and they condemned as utterly irresponsible the sweeping resolution against altar rails, 'scandalous pictures', candlesticks and crucifixes which Pym and his allies pushed through the Commons on 1 September. They were disturbed by Pym's leniency towards 'mechanical' lay preachers and 'schismatics', and his willingness to tolerate unlawful religious assemblies. They were equally alarmed by the vehement calls for radical reformation made in Fast Sermons to Parliament by preachers such as Stephen Marshall, Edmund Calamy and Thomas

Goodwin, and vigorously echoed by Scottish ministers in London. If people were allowed to 'speak and preach what they would' against the Prayer Book, warned Culpepper, they might ultimately come 'to open force and blows'. An attachment to episcopacy and the Prayer Book thus became inseparable from a wider commitment to the rule of law and to established patterns of government.

This backlash against religious radicalism had dangerous political implications because its natural leader was none other than Charles I. In his speech of 25 January 1641, the King had pledged his commitment to 'the true Protestant religion by law established without any connivance of popery or innovation'. He stated his intention to 'reduce all matters of religion and government to what they were in the purest times of Queen Elizabeth's days', and he promised to defend episcopacy as 'one of the fundamental institutions of this kingdom'. Charles made no attempt to prevent Laud's imprisonment and instead began appointing bishops who were mainstream Calvinists in the mould of Archbishop Abbot. By committing himself to non-Laudian episcopacy and to the rule of law, as well as by accepting the constitutional reforms of 1640–1, he reassured those who were primarily exercised by his earlier breaches of the rule of law. For the many – including Hyde, Falkland, Strangways and Culpepper – who had opposed Laudianism because it was authoritarian and violated custom, but who wished to preserve the institution of episcopacy, Charles increasingly appeared less threatening than the radical opponents of bishops. This reaction gathered pace, both at Westminster and in the provinces, during the summer of 1641. Its critical role in the formation of a Royalist 'party' was not lost on Nathaniel Fiennes, who remarked that 'if the King resolved to defend the bishops, it would cause the kingdom much blood'.

Charles, meanwhile, had reached a settlement with the Scots. By August enough revenue had been raised, or security obtained on future taxes and loans, to pay off the Scottish army. In return for Charles's acceptance of their reforms to date, including the abolition of episcopacy, and a guarantee that English or Irish troops would not be deployed against the Scots without the consent of the English Parliament, the Covenanters agreed to withdraw their troops from England. In the long term they still hoped for further reformation south of the border, and they also sought a greater degree of legal, administrative and political union with England. But they were prepared to pursue those goals from a distance. In September Charles agreed in principle that his nominations of Scottish officers of state, judges and councillors should be confirmed by the Scottish Parliament, and by November most of the leading Covenanters had been appointed to key offices. Yet, as so often with Charles, these concessions were made too late and too grudgingly for him to reap as much benefit as he might have done. There were signs of growing disaffection among the Covenanters' ranks, and as early as August 1640 the Earl of Montrose and seventeen other Lords had signed the Cumbernauld Band pledging to defend the King and resist 'the particular and indirect practicking of a few'. Gradually nobles emerged, led by Montrose and his brother-in-law Lord Napier, who wished to preserve the powers of the Scottish Crown and who resented the Covenanter leaders such as the Earl of Argyll. Considerable sympathy for the King existed, especially among the Highlanders and the Catholic nobility. Characteristically, however, Charles would not wait for this support to develop and take root in its own time. Instead, in early October he overreached himself by conspiring in the so-called 'Incident', a bungled attempt to arrest and possibly murder Argyll and Hamilton, whom he now suspected of treason. Recent research has demonstrated the full extent of Charles's complicity, and the 'Incident' further strengthened suspicions that he was willing to sanction force against his opponents and violate due process of law.[5] It played into the hands of the King's English critics and undoubtedly impeded the resurgence of loyalism to him in Scotland.

Although Charles signally failed to maximize his potential support in Scotland, he had at least achieved his main objective: to get the Scots off English soil and remove the obligation to pay them £850 a day. The crisis which had forced him to summon the Long Parliament was thus resolved. Charles was no longer financially dependent upon Parliament, and his leading English critics had lost the vital security afforded by the Scottish troops. True, Parliament could only be dissolved with its own consent, but by the autumn of 1641 that was no longer an impossibility. Fatigue and fear of a new plague epidemic made members so desperate to leave Westminster that the Houses decided to begin a six weeks recess on 9 September. English opinion was gradually turning in the King's favour, and it seemed possible that he might be able to secure a majority in favour of dissolution when Parliament reassembled. Small wonder that between mid-August and late October there was evidence of growing optimism among Charles's advisers. On 12 October, Sir Edward Nicholas informed the King that although Pym and 'those of his junto' were prepared to 'sit here at Westminster and die here together', there were 'few . . . [others] of that opinion'. Time appeared to be on the King's side, and he began to look forward to his return to England.

3 The Irish Rebellion and the Grand Remonstrance

This situation was suddenly and dramatically transformed in the last week of October by the outbreak of rebellion in Ireland. The origins of this rebellion lay in the fears of the Old English and Gaelic Irish that the Scottish Covenanters, in alliance with leading Puritans within the English Parliament, wished to suppress Catholicism in Ireland. Irish Catholics were profoundly alarmed by utterances such as the Petition of the Twelve Peers, which had urged the King to pursue 'the uniting of *both* your realms against the common enemies of the reformed religion',[6] and the Scottish demands for 'one form of church government in all the Churches of His Majesty's dominions'. Fearing that 'the puritans of England, Scotland and Ireland intended the utter extirpation and destruction of the Catholic religion', they decided to launch a pre-emptive strike against the Protestant inhabitants of Ulster. The rebellion was initially intended to disarm the Protestants, but it quickly got out of control and resulted in the massacre of perhaps 3,000 Protestants and the flight of many more to England. The first reports of the rebellion reached London on

Plate 9 The outbreak of the Irish Rebellion appeared to confirm all the worst fears of English Protestants about a 'popish plot'. Rumours circulated of the horrific atrocities committed by Catholics on Protestants. Images such as these depicted in gruesome detail the torture and slaughter of men, women and children. Later, in 1649, the memory of these alleged crimes prompted Cromwell to exact 'vengeance' on the people of Drogheda and Wexford whom he claimed had 'imbrued their hands in so much innocent blood' (as in the picture marked W here).
Source: The Fotomas Index

1 November. Over the next few weeks rumours began to circulate which described horrific atrocities against Protestants and put the death toll as high as 20,000.

The impact of these reports in England was devastating. Parliament had reassembled on 20 October, and Pym had spent the following ten days trying to unravel the King's suspected complicity in the Incident. On 30 October, Pym revealed the existence of a second Army Plot, hatched the previous June. But it proved impossible to establish Charles's involvement in these episodes and Pym's investigations quickly lost momentum. Then, suddenly, the Irish rebellion transformed the political landscape by presenting what appeared to be the terrifying reality of a 'popish plot'. All the worst fears of Pym and his 'junto' were confirmed when the rebels, led by Sir Phelim O'Neill, claimed that Charles had sent them a commission authorizing them to take up arms. The commission itself was almost certainly a forgery; but whether the King really was secretly trying to mobilize Irish Catholic troops under the Earl of Antrim during the summer and autumn of 1641 remains the subject of fierce controversy.[7] Although conclusive *proof* of his involvement has yet to be adduced – and may well not exist – it is none the less true that Charles's habitual use of underhand tactics and his willingness on other occasions to recruit Irish troops for use against his enemies on the mainland do lend plausibility to his alleged role in the 'Antrim plot'. In a sense, the question of his actual guilt or innocence is less important than the fact that to the likes of Pym it seemed all too believable that Charles had helped to foment the rebellion. How, they argued, could such a King be trusted to lead an army against the rebels? Whatever the extent of Charles's personal responsibility, the Irish rebellion was thus a genuine watershed. For by posing with such acute urgency the question of the King's military authority, it raised the issue over which the English Civil War broke out the following year.

Pym's immediate reaction was to try to strengthen the case against entrusting Charles with an army by presenting a comprehensive indictment of his misgovernment since 1625. On 8 November, Pym brought before the Commons a document that had been drafted and redrafted by several different committees over the previous year. This 'Remonstrance of the state of the kingdom' – or the Grand Remonstrance, as it came to be known – attributed all England's 'evils' to 'a malignant and pernicious design of subverting the fundamental laws and principles of government, upon which the religion and justice of this kingdom are firmly established'. The principal 'actors and promoters' of this 'design' were the 'Jesuited Papists' and 'Jesuited counsels'. The Remonstrance castigated the 'multiplied evils and corruption *of fifteen years*': none of the grievances listed in it preceded the accession of Charles I. However, although the Remonstrance was very much a denunciation of one monarch's misgovernment, its authors did not consider that such ills could be remedied simply by turning the clock back to 1625. It was necessary once and for all to curtail the 'exorbitant power' of 'prelates' and to establish 'a general synod of the most grave, pious, learned and judicious divines' to 'effect reformation' of religion. Further constitutional innovations were needed to root out 'evil counsellors' and to prevent any more being appointed in future. The framers of the

Remonstrance insisted that they intended nothing 'that should weaken the Crown either in just profit or useful power'. But to ensure that the King was rightfully advised, he was requested to 'employ such counsellors, ambassadors and other ministers in managing his business at home and abroad as the Parliament may have cause to confide in'. As in the Ten Propositions, the King's discretionary right to choose his own advisers was coming under direct attack. This was a demand to which he had already acquiesced in Scotland, but he was not prepared to make a similar concession south of the border.

Over the next fortnight, the opponents of the Remonstrance secured the softening of some of its more extreme statements but not of its main demands. As a result, when the final text was tabled in the Commons on 22 November it provoked a furious debate which lasted twelve hours. The supporters of the Remonstrance insisted that it was their duty to tell Charles 'all necessary truths' about his subjects' grievances. Against this, future Royalists such as Hyde and Culpepper were appalled that the Lords had not been involved in discussing the Remonstrance and that it was not addressed directly to the King. Dering 'did not dream that we should remonstrate downwards, tell stories to the people, and talk of the king as of a third person'. Eventually, at about 2 a.m. on 23 November, the Remonstrance was passed, but only by 159 votes to 148. For many MPs it was a critical test: Cromwell allegedly said that he would have emigrated to New England had it been defeated; but for others, like Hyde, it seemed to confirm that Pym's proposals formed a greater threat to constitutional equilibrium than the evils they were intended to remedy. Such people were reassured when, on 23 December, Charles bluntly rejected the Remonstrance, pledged to defend the 'purity of doctrine' of the Church, and asserted that the free choice of advisers was 'the undoubted right of the Crown of England'.

This polarization of opinion was not restricted to the political elite. Throughout November and December 1641, many Londoners became increasingly restive as horror stories circulated about the massacres in Ulster. A worsening economic recession within the city, exacerbated by political uncertainty, added an extra bitterness to their resentment. Large crowds of apprentices and 'poor artificers' began to assemble outside Parliament, calling in particular for the exclusion of bishops from the Lords. On 27 December bishops were forcibly prevented from taking their seats, and several demonstrators were injured in a violent clash with the London militia. Meanwhile, on 21 December, the City of London had elected a new Common Council (governing body) much more favourably disposed towards Pym and very willing to organize further demonstrations in support of his policies. By the end of the year, Charles was clearly losing control of London.

At this point, in a bid to regain the initiative, he made a terrible blunder. On 30 December, twelve bishops submitted a petition demanding that all the Lords' proceedings conducted in their absence should be declared null and void. The Lords regarded this as a breach of their privileges and accepted a Commons vote impeaching the bishops for high treason. At the same time, rumours surfaced that Henrietta Maria was about to be impeached as a key protagonist in the 'popish plot'. On 2 January, in a final attempt to win over

Pym, Charles offered him the Chancellorship of the Exchequer. When Pym refused, Charles swung decisively towards those moderates who were increasingly in sympathy with him: he appointed Culpepper as Chancellor of the Exchequer and Falkland as Secretary of State. From then until the outbreak of civil war these men, together with Hyde, became very influential within the King's counsels and skilfully fostered the perception of Charles as a law-abiding constitutional monarch. Unfortunately, in constructing this image, they constantly had to contend with Charles's readiness – encouraged by hardliners such as Henrietta Maria and Lord George Digby – to use violence against his opponents. On 3 January, the King issued articles of high treason against Pym, Holles, Sir Arthur Hesilrige, John Hampden, William Strode and Lord Mandeville, accusing them of seeking 'to subvert the fundamental laws and government' of England, of endangering 'the rights and the very being of Parliaments', of casting 'foul aspersions' upon the King, and of encouraging the Scots to invade England. In view of what is now known about Anglo-Scottish contacts during the Bishops' Wars, the last charge clearly did not lack foundation. Yet the King's next move lost him any advantage that he might have derived from the strength of his legal case. It was highly characteristic of Charles to believe that if he could only root out a small circle of ringleaders all his problems would be solved. On the afternoon of 4 January, in a flagrant breach of parliamentary privilege, he led a sizeable body of armed men to Westminster to arrest the five members of the Commons. But they had been tipped off and had already sought refuge in the City. Snarling that 'the birds are flown', Charles withdrew from the House amid cries of 'Privilege! Privilege!' The attempt to seize the five members backfired badly, and few thereafter could ever forget such an unconstitutional show of force against Parliament. Charles's behaviour appeared to confirm what many had already suspected in the light of the Army Plots and the Incident.

On 5 January, in search of a more secure location, the Commons adjourned to the Guildhall. Later that day, Charles entered the City of London and demanded that the Common Council hand over the five members so that they could stand trial. The Council refused, and the visit was a singularly uncomfortable experience for Charles: a hostile mob gathered around his carriage, and he was left in no doubt that he had alienated the majority of Londoners. Fearful for the safety of his wife and children, and hoping to rally support in the country at large, Charles and his family retreated from the capital to Hampton Court on 10 January. The next day, MPs – including the five members – returned to Westminster amid cheering crowds. Charles's withdrawal from London was surely another critical error. For by thus creating a physical separation between monarch and Parliament, civil war at last became an immediate possibility.

4 The Outbreak of Civil War

Nevertheless, nearly eight months passed before the King raised his standard at Nottingham, thus marking the formal beginning of the English Civil War. That it took so long for England to slide into conflict reflected the fact that, to a greater degree than in Scotland and Ireland, the political elite continued to believe in the possibility of a settlement through established constitutional channels. Throughout the spring and summer of 1642 the vast majority still sought an 'accommodation' between Crown and Parliament, and very few could conceive of a war between them. Conflict was all the more difficult to contemplate because early Stuart England was a remarkably demilitarized society. Members of the nobility had far fewer armed men at their disposal than in earlier centuries, and the weapons in their private arsenals often belonged in a museum rather than on a battlefield. Despite Charles's attempted reforms, the local militia was poorly equipped and reluctant to accept commitments outside their own community. But this only makes it harder to answer the crucial question: if all these circumstances were working against a civil war, what forces ultimately overcame them and propelled the nation into conflict?

The central theme of the period between January and August 1642 was the gradual emergence of two sides associated with two competing conspiracy theories. On one side was what might be called the Puritan–Parliamentarian theory, which attributed England's troubles to a 'popish' plot to subvert Church and State. This theory was most eloquently set out in the Grand Remonstrance, and it gained renewed credibility from the Irish Rebellion and the attempted arrest of the five members. On the other side stood what can be termed the Anglican–Royalist theory. This pinned all the blame on religious radicals or 'schismatics' who, it was claimed, sought to overthrow hierarchy and order in Church, constitution and society. The regional outbreaks of icon-oclasm during 1641 and the mass demonstrations outside Parliament at the end of the year served to fuel such fears. These two theories were symmetrical and within their own terms entirely coherent. They were self-sustaining and ultimately self-fulfilling. For every step that each side took to cow the other into submission only confirmed the other side's worst suspicions and persuaded it to raise its own demands. The crisis thus steadily escalated, and the really remarkable feature of these months is why the progressively higher demands and tougher threats made by each side failed to achieve their desired effect of persuading the other to back down.

The Houses' behaviour in the wake of the King's withdrawal from London set the pattern for the events that followed. Horrified by the attempt on the five members, Cromwell moved on 14 January for a committee to be established 'to put the kingdom in a posture of defence'. This committee revived earlier proposals for a militia bill, first mooted the previous year, and drew up a bill by which military authority would be transferred from the Crown to Lords Lieutenant in whom Parliament had confidence. On 12 February the Houses submitted a list of Lords Lieutenant to the King, who bluntly refused to surrender control of the armed forces and retreated north to York. The Houses decided to press ahead on their own, and on 5 March took the unprecedented step of unilaterally passing the bill as the Militia Ordinance. They claimed that in 'this time of imminent danger' the two Houses could wrest authority from the King and pass ordinances which had the force of statute even though they lacked the royal assent.

Parliament's claim to legislate without the King was soon put to a practical test. At the end of the wars against the Scots, most of Charles's arms and ammunition had been stockpiled in Hull. In a bid to gain control of these vital military supplies and so flout the Militia Ordinance, Charles journeyed to Hull in the last week of April, only to find the town's gates shut against him. Parliament had sent the MP for Beverley, Sir John Hotham, to serve as governor of the town and to deny the King access. Charles insisted that such a move was totally illegal and demanded by what right he, as King, could be refused entry to an English town. The Houses responded by claiming that the King's powers were only 'entrusted to him for the good and safety and best advantage ... of the kingdom', and that it would have been utterly irresponsible to allow the magazine of Hull to fall into the hands of those 'few ill-affected persons' about the King who might expose the kingdom to 'hazard or danger'.

Having thus gained the initiative, on 2 June the Houses presented Charles with far-reaching demands in the form of the *Nineteen Propositions*. All Privy Councillors had henceforth to be approved by the two Houses; those not approved were to be immediately removed. Another clause, modelled on the Scottish settlement of September 1641, demanded that sixteen of the most senior officers of state be likewise 'chosen with the approbation of both Houses'. The King was required to accept the Triennial Act and the Militia Ordinance; to enforce more rigorously the existing laws against 'Jesuits, priests and popish recusants'; and to grant a full pardon to the five members. He was also requested to consent to 'such a reformation' of 'Church government and liturgy' as the two Houses 'shall advise'. If Charles accepted these terms, the Houses promised to settle his revenue and to deliver Hull to those whom the King appointed – 'with the consent and approbation of Parliament'. The King's *Answer to the XIX Propositions*, drafted for him by Falkland and Culpepper and published on 18 June, was a masterpiece of moderate propaganda. It argued that the Houses' terms would involve a 'total subversion of the fundamental laws and [the] excellent constitution of this kingdom'. That 'ancient, equal, happy, well-poised' constitution rested on a delicate balance of powers between the three estates of Crown, Lords and Commons which would be destroyed if the King accepted the *Nineteen Propositions*. Charles pledged to defend this system of 'regulated monarchy', to uphold the rule of law, and thus prevent the 'dark, equal chaos of confusion' into which Parliament's demands threatened to plunge the nation.

But, typically, Charles combined such temperate words with the threat of further use of force. Convinced that a hard core of 'malignant spirits' were responsible for Parliament's demands, he retaliated on 11 June by issuing commissions of array to nobility and gentry whom he trusted in every county of England and Wales. The commission of array was an expedient originally devised by Edward I and later enshrined in a statute of 1405. It had fallen into disuse during the sixteenth century, but Charles I – with his penchant for reviving moribund legal precedents – now employed it because it enabled him to raise troops by royal prerogative and had the added advantage that such forces could legally be moved around the country in a way impossible under the lieutenancy. But the commissions backfired on Charles: they were widely perceived as dangerously innovatory and could be portrayed by the Houses as another act of provocation. Parliament could also point to the fact that in the summer of 1642 Henrietta Maria, who had left England on 23 February, was known to be selling or pawning royal jewels in Amsterdam in order to buy arms and pay troops.

The two Houses were by now so mistrustful of Charles that instead of bowing to his threat of force they thought it essential to negotiate from a position of strength. They therefore voted on 9 July to raise an army of 10,000 volunteers, and three days later to appoint the Earl of Essex Lord General. On 15 July the first blood was shed in a skirmish when the Royalist Lord Strange attempted to gain control of the county magazine at Manchester. A succession of similar incidents occurred all over the country in late July and early August as local activists moved to take up arms and implement either the commission of array or the Militia Ordinance. Such activists were only a small minority of the total population, but they emerged in sufficient numbers to persuade each side that it had enough support to win a war.

By the second half of August both King and Parliament were convinced that a further threat of force would make the other capitulate; but – lethally – they also believed that they could win a civil war if their bluff was called. By this stage each side had shown itself so willing to raise troops that the trust of the other had been permanently eroded. Each could use the other's military preparations to justify its own. The stakes could not have been higher: it seemed to Crown and Parliament alike that at issue was nothing less than the future of England's Church and constitution, and the preservation of her 'fundamental laws'. In the eyes of Charles no less than of Pym's 'junto', to capitulate in August 1642 would have been to surrender not just to tyranny and arbitrary rule in the State, but also to error and superstition in the Church. Only the conviction that the alternative was an evil more terrible than civil war can explain the intransigence of the two sides. On 18 August the Houses issued a declaration condemning all those who supported Charles as 'traitors'. Four days later, in a gesture that symbolized the formal commencement of hostilities, the King raised his standard at Nottingham against the Parliamentarian 'rebels'.

The following month there was an exchange of declarations that revealed how the two conspiracy theories had ultimately become self-confirming and driven the two sides into war. On 6 September the Houses insisted that they had to take up arms against the 'delinquents and other malignant and disaffected persons' who supported the King in order to ensure 'the preservation of the parliament, religion, the laws and liberties of the kingdom'. Two weeks later, Charles informed those who rallied to him: 'You shall meet with no enemies but traitors, most of them Brownists, Anabaptists and Atheists; such who desire to destroy both Church and State, and who have already condemned you to ruin for being loyal to us'.

The fact that the two sides were using such similar language and claiming to defend the same things only made the choice between them more agonizing. Lady Sussex lamented that 'both sides promise so fair, that I cannot see what it is they should fight for'; while the Wiltshire MP William Pleydell declared that 'we have to steer the bark of state betwixt Scylla and Charybdis, popery on the one side, and I know not what to call it on the other'. The prevailing mood of divided loyalties was powerfully expressed by the Devon gentry in a petition to the King on 16 August: 'How unhappy are we here, made judges in apparent contraries! In how hard a condition are we, whilst a twofold obedience, like twins in the womb, strives to be borne to both!' The vast majority of the population wished to stay out of the war and tried desperately to avoid taking sides. John Morrill has found evidence of 'attempted neutrality pacts' in twenty-two counties which sought to keep the two sides out of the shire completely, or to reach a demilitarization agreement between them.[8] The localism that was so characteristic of early Stuart England ensured that 'neutralism' was the predominant reaction to the approaching conflict. Unfortunately, the moderate majority in the provinces was usually disorganized and indecisive, and it was this paralysis of will that in most counties allowed the minority of activists to seize the initiative.

The thrust of recent research has been to suggest that these activists were those who felt most strongly about religion. In general, this is more obviously true of Parliamentarians than of Royalists. Time and again, we find that the people who pushed the Houses into making a tougher stand against the King, or who enacted the Militia Ordinance in the localities, were those who had a long-standing commitment to a strict Calvinist theology and to further reformation of the Church.[9] Peers such as Lord Saye and Sele, Lord Brooke and the Earls of Warwick and Northumberland, and MPs like John Pym, Francis Rous, Nathaniel Fiennes and Sir Robert Harley are just some of the leading examples of this type. In the counties, men of similar outlook thrust themselves forward to organize troops on Parliament's behalf, including Oliver Cromwell in Cambridgeshire, John Pyne in Somerset, Sir William Brereton in Cheshire or John Hutchinson in Nottinghamshire. The case of Sir Simonds D'Ewes illustrates how for some Parliamentarians these godly convictions could override other loyalties: a Suffolk antiquarian of essentially conservative attitudes, he none the less sided with Parliament out of a belief that Elizabeth I had 'rather settled a beginning of a reformation than a reformation'. That belief was, in Conrad Russell's words, 'the diagnostic sign of a Parliamentarian'.

It is much harder to single out a religious motive when we turn to the Royalists. Certainly the majority of those who rallied to Charles in 1642 wished to preserve the existing structures and practices of the Church of England. In many cases they were responsible for promoting the petitions in favour of episcopacy and the Prayer Book that were circulated in twenty-eight counties in England and Wales between September 1641 and May 1642. But this was often only one aspect of a wider attachment to established forms of government in both Church and State. Many joined the King out of an almost feudal sense of honour and an abhorrence of 'rebellion'. Charles's standard-bearer Sir Edmund Verney exclaimed that 'my conscience is only concerned in honour and gratitude to follow my master', while Henrietta Maria's Lord Chamberlain the Earl of Dorset wrote that 'honour, duty, piety and gratitude' obliged him to follow 'my King, my master, my benefactor'. The importance of honour was strikingly expressed by Lord Spencer, who wrote from the King's headquarters in September 1642 that he had 'daily handsome occasion to retire, were it not

for gaining honour . . . If there could be an expedient found to salve the punc-
tilio of honour, I would not continue here an hour'. For others, a sense of
honour and personal loyalty to the King was less important than a belief that
he was a far more convincing guardian of the constitution and the rule of law
than his opponents. Such 'Constitutional Royalists' – of whom the most
notable were Hyde, Falkland and Culpepper – wished to protect constitutional
balance, the lawful powers of the Crown, and the 'Church by law established'.
Their defence of the Church was inseparable from their commitment to the
rule of law, and this explains why these people had frequently been among the
critics of Charles's previous policies. Many of those who became
'Constitutional Royalists' had earlier denounced the Forced Loan and Ship
Money as illegal, but in 1642 they rallied to Charles because Pym's 'junto' now
seemed to present a greater threat to the rule of law. Thus, when the Cheshire
Royalist Sir Thomas Aston, who had campaigned against Ship Money and for
episcopacy, joined the King it was not because religious convictions had over-
ridden secular; rather, a consistent belief in constitutional propriety and in the
rule of law explains his stance on both issues and his subsequent allegiance to
the Crown.[10]

Of course, as the conflict gradually engulfed the nation, many chose sides on
the basis of pragmatic, materialist, non-ideological considerations: they took
the line of least resistance, or calculated how their property and family might
be best protected, or did the opposite of their local arch-enemies. In some
counties, a long-standing antagonism between two leading families is crucial
in accounting for the pattern of allegiance: notable examples include the
ancient rivalries between the Greys and the Hastings in Leicestershire, or
between the Herberts and the Seymours in Wiltshire. Faced by such feuds,
many lesser folk simply did as they were ordered and joined the noble or gentry
family to which they had been attached for decades. But what is really striking
about the English Civil War, as distinct from earlier conflicts, is the degree to
which people were able to make free political choices. A striking illustration of
this freedom is the way in which the tenants of the Cheshire gentleman William
Davenport blithely ignored his request for assistance on the King's behalf in
September 1642 and enlisted for Parliament instead.[11] Men and women of all
social classes were able to follow their consciences and to make informed political choices of their own.

The war divided all classes equally, and it is therefore inappropriate to label
it a class conflict. The social profiles of the two sides were remarkably similar.
The nobility was almost evenly split (with a slight majority in favour of the
King), while the gentry divided with roughly 4,000 on each side and perhaps
another 10,000 who sought to avoid making a clear allegiance. The 'middling
sorts' – yeomen, craftsmen, tradesmen – have sometimes been seen as the
driving force behind the Parliamentarian war effort, but in fact they were just
as likely to become Royalists as Parliamentarians. On both sides there were
more 'middling sorts' than gentry or nobility: they were simply a larger social
category. Other groups, such as lawyers, clergy and merchants, can also be
found in similar numbers on both sides. Certainly social tensions fed into the
conflict: so complete a breakdown of the existing order, with such a profound

fracture of the governing elite, was bound to bring latent resentments and frustrations to the surface. David Underdown and Brian Manning in particular have shown how enclosure riots and other attacks on property escalated during the summer and autumn of 1642. But it is important to note that such attacks were not motivated solely by class antagonism: the victims were often chosen for other reasons, most commonly – as in the case of the Countess of Rivers at Melford Hall – because they were Catholics. Social tensions undoubtedly fed into the Civil War, but they did not cause it.[12]

An analysis of members of the Long Parliament reveals no significant social differences between those who sided with Crown or Parliament except for the fact that the Royalists were on average ten years younger. This absence of marked social contrasts between the two sides brings us back to the question of why the moderates – especially those at Westminster or at Charles's headquarters – were unable to form a united middle ground. They were, after all, very much in the majority. There were also striking similarities of outlook and temperament between moderate Royalists, such as Hyde, Falkland and Culpepper, and moderate Parliamentarians like John Selden, Bulstrode Whitelocke and Sir Benjamin Rudyerd. On both sides, these figures can be found trying to calm tempers and to promote an 'accommodation' between Crown and Parliament. They all desperately wished to avoid a conflict, and in choosing sides they opted for what they saw as the lesser of two evils. None of these moderates, or the many others like them, regarded their own side as blameless. But they were crucially divided over who they perceived as the greater threat to constitutional balance, the rule of law and true religion – Charles or Pym's 'junto'. In the end, moderate Royalists and moderate Parliamentarians could not unite during the summer of 1642 because the former mistrusted Pym more than Charles, whereas the latter mistrusted Charles more than Pym. As a result, they were unable to agree on what minimum terms were essential for any settlement, and what guarantees needed to be secured from the other side. While the moderate majority dithered and failed to reach a settlement, a minority of activists on both sides were able to push the country into civil war. As we shall see, this fragmentation of moderate opinion was in sharp contrast with the Glorious Revolution of 1688–9, when bloodshed was averted precisely because the middle ground held firm.[13] But in 1642 it disintegrated, with catastrophic consequences for all three of the British monarchies.

6 War in Three Kingdoms

Chronology

1642	April	10,000-strong Scottish army led by Monro arrives in Ireland
	10–13 May	Leading Irish Catholic laity and clergy meet at Kilkenny
	4 July	Committee of Safety established
	2 September	Parliament orders the closing of all theatres (ban continues until 1660)
	23 October	Indecisive Battle of Edgehill
	24 October–21 November	General assembly of Confederate Catholics meets at Kilkenny (meets annually until 1648)
	13 November	King's advance towards London halted at Turnham Green; Charles retreats and establishes his headquarters at Oxford
	26 November	Committee for the Advance of Money established
1643	1 February–14 April	Treaty of Oxford: unsuccessful peace talks
	22 February	Henrietta Maria arrives back in England
	24 February	Parliament introduces weekly (later monthly) assessment
	27 March	Committee for Sequestrations established
	30 June	Newcastle defeats Fairfax at Adwalton Moor
	1 July	Westminster Assembly opens, established by Parliament to plan reform of English Church along Presbyterian lines

	5 July	Hopton defeats Waller at Lansdown
	13 July	Prince Maurice and Wilmot defeat Waller at Roundway Down
	22 July	Parliament introduces excise on certain commodities
	26 July	Prince Rupert captures Bristol
	8 September	Essex relieves Gloucester from Royalist siege
	15 September	Ormond concludes 'cessation' with Irish Confederates on Charles's behalf
	20 September	Essex halts King's advance towards London at first Battle of Newbury
	25 September	Parliament signs the Solemn League and Covenant with the Scottish Covenanters
	8 December	Death of John Pym
1644	19 January	Earl of Leven leads Scottish army of 21,000 troops into England
	22 January–16 April	Oxford Parliament meets
	25 January	Fairfax routs Royalist forces at Nantwich
	16 February	Committee of Both Kingdoms established
	29 March	Waller defeats Charles's western army at Cheriton
	29 June	Royalists defeat Waller at Cropredy Bridge
	2 July	Parliamentarian/Scottish victory at Marston Moor near York: Royalists lose control of North of England
	1 September	Montrose defeats Covenanter forces at Tippermuir
	2 September	Royalist victory at Lostwithiel
	27 October	Indecisive second Battle of Newbury
	November–December	Major public quarrel between Cromwell and Manchester over conduct of the war
	9 December	Zouch Tate moves proposal for 'self-denial' in the Commons
1645	2 January	King appoints Earl of Glamorgan as his special envoy to negotiate with the Irish Confederates

4 January	Parliament authorizes new Directory of Public Worship drawn up by the Westminster Assembly
6 January	Committee of Both Kingdoms recommends creation of New Model Army
10 January	Execution of Laud
30 January–22 February	Treaty of Uxbridge: unsuccessful peace talks
2 February	Montrose defeats Argyll at Inverlochy
17 February	Ordinance creating New Model Army commanded by Sir Thomas Fairfax
3 April	Self-Denying Ordinance: members of both Houses to resign all military commands and civil offices; Cromwell subsequently receives a series of short-term exemptions
9 May	Montrose defeats Covenanter forces at Auldearn
14 June	New Model Army defeats Royalist forces at Naseby
2 July	Montrose defeats Covenanter forces at Alford
10 July	New Model Army defeats King's western armies at Langport
15 August	Montrose defeats Covenanter forces at Kilsyth
19, 26 August	Parliament passes ordinances proscribing use of the Prayer Book and establishing a national Presbyterian Church
25 August	Glamorgan concludes second 'cessation' with the Irish Confederates: concessions promised to Catholics in return for troops to assist Charles on the mainland
10 September	Bristol falls to Parliamentarians: Royalists lose control of the West Country
13 September	Covenanter forces led by David Leslie crush Montrose at Philiphaugh
24 September	Royalist defeat at Rowton Heath, near Chester
12 October	Papal nuncio Cardinal Rinuccini arrives in Ireland

1646	24 February	Abolition of the Court of Wards and Liveries
	February	New Model Army easily defeats Royalist rising in Glamorganshire
	February, May, December	Publication in three parts of Thomas Edwards's *Gangraena*, attacking radical religious sects
	28 March	Ormond signs peace with the Confederates
	5 May	Charles surrenders to Scots at Newark
	5 June	Confederates led by Owen Roe O'Neill defeat Monro's Scottish forces at Benburb: power of Rinuccini and Gaelic Irish strengthened within Confederation
	24 June	Oxford surrenders: end of the First Civil War
	13 July	Newcastle Propositions presented to Charles
	16 September	Death of the Earl of Essex
	9 October	Parliament passes ordinances abolishing episcopacy and authorizing sale of bishops' lands
1647	30 January	Scots hand Charles over to Parliament; he is taken to Holdenby House in Northamptonshire; the Scottish army subsequently returns to Scotland
	March	Army petitions against proposed disbandment; Parliament issues Declaration of Dislike against petitioning by soldiers
	April–May	Army regiments elect representatives ('agitators')
	25–27 May	Both Houses vote to disband large sections of the Army
	3 June	Cornet Joyce arrives at Holdenby House; the next day he takes Charles to army headquarters at Newmarket
	14 June	General Council of the Army issues *Declaration* protesting against disbandment
	17 July	General Council of the Army discusses the *Heads of the Proposals*
	23 July	*Heads of the Proposals* presented to Charles
	26 July	Rioters invade Commons in support of Presbyterian leaders; Independent minority flee to Army

	2 August	*Heads of the Proposals* published
	6 August	Army occupies London and reinstates Independents
	24 August	Charles moved to Hampton Court
	15 October	'Agitators' from five regiments draw up *The Case of the Army Truly Stated*
	28 October–5 November	Putney Debates; *Agreement of the People* tabled on the first day
	11 November	Charles escapes from Hampton Court; arrives at Carisbrooke Castle on the Isle of Wight on 13 November
	15 November	Cromwell prevents near mutiny at Corkbush Field near Ware
	24 December	Parliament presents *Four Bills* to Charles
	25 December	Riots in London, Norwich and Canterbury against Parliament's suppression of Christmas festivities
	26 December	Charles concludes Engagement with Scots
	28 December	Charles rejects the *Four Bills*
1648	3 January	Commons passes Vote of No Addresses forbidding further negotiations with Charles (passed by Lords on 17 January)
	March–July	Rising in South Wales (Pembroke surrenders on 11 July)
	29 April	Army prayer meeting at Windsor Castle: officers vow to bring 'Charles Stuart, that man of blood' to account
	April–August	Rising in East Anglia (Colchester surrenders on 27 August)
	May–June	Rising in Kent
	June–December	Rising in Yorkshire
	8 July	Hamilton invades England in support of Charles
	17–19 August	Cromwell defeats Hamilton at Preston: effectively ends Second Civil War
	24 August	Vote of No Addresses repealed
	18 September	Treaty of Newport begins

	September	Covenanters' Whiggamore raid in support of anti-Engagers
	4–7 October	Cromwell in Edinburgh: reaches agreement with anti-Engagers, led by Argyll
	20 November	*Remonstrance of the Army* presented to Parliament
	30 November	*Declaration of the Army*
	2 December	Army re-enters London
	5 December	Commons votes by 129 to 83 to continue negotiations with Charles
	6 December	Pride's Purge
	23 December	Charles brought to Windsor
1649	4 January	Rump of the Commons assumes supreme legislative power
	6 January	Rump establishes High Court of Justice to try Charles
	20 January	Charles's trial opens in Westminster Hall
	27 January	Charles sentenced to death
	30 January	Charles executed
	8 February	First of thirty-six editions of the *Eikon Basilike* published

1 The First Civil War

When the English Parliament finally resolved to take up arms against Charles I, nobody foresaw – let alone hoped – that the ensuing conflict would ultimately lead to his trial and execution. Regicide was not on anyone's political agenda in the summer of 1642. Indeed, the Houses were only able to justify their actions by forging a subtle distinction between the office of King and the person of Charles I. Far from articulating any theory of resistance, they fell back on the medieval concept of the monarch's two bodies, the human and the official. They argued that if the King failed to discharge the 'duty and trust' reposed in him, or was incapacitated from doing so by wicked advice, then the two Houses could if necessary perform the functions of his office 'after a more eminent and obligatory manner than it can be by personal act or resolution of his own'. This doctrine lay behind all the peace terms that the Houses presented to Charles during the first Civil War. Their aim was not to destroy the monarchy but to restrain one particular king who they believed was 'seduced by evil counsel'. Their military campaigns were designed to achieve sufficient strategic superiority to persuade Charles to accept their terms – to reduce him, in Lord Brooke's phrase, 'to a necessity of granting'. Yet such limited objectives only make it more difficult to explain the eventual outcome of the conflict: why was Charles I executed, and why was his death accompanied by the abolition of the monarchy and the House of Lords, and the dismantling of the Church of England?

Initially, the advantage lay with the King. During the late summer and autumn of 1642, both sides raised armies consisting mainly of regiments recruited personally by officers at their own expense. Most of the rank and file were volunteers, and many on both sides were reluctant to fight outside their own counties. Nevertheless, Charles was able to advance towards London, and on 23 October, in the first major engagement of the Civil War, clashed with the Earl of Essex's army at Edgehill. The battle was indecisive, but left the road to London open to the King. However, Essex mobilized the London trained bands, assisted by a large turn-out of apprentices and other volunteers, and halted Charles's advance at Turnham Green on 13 November. The King withdrew to Oxford, where he established his headquarters. In the long run his failure to capture London and to win a quick victory at the start of the Civil War was crucial because, for reasons that will be examined below, during a more protracted conflict the odds gradually shifted in favour of Parliament.

In Ireland, meanwhile, the rebellion had spread rapidly but unevenly during the first half of 1642, as many of the Gaelic Irish and Old English of the southern towns joined the rebels. Only a few towns held out in Ulster, while in the Pale the Protestant forces were commanded by a royal ward, the Earl of Ormond. He begged both King and Parliament to send additional forces, but the gathering crisis in England meant that, apart from around 3,000 reinforcements early in 1642, he was left to fend for himself. However, the Protestants of Ulster were assisted from April 1642 onwards by a Scottish army

Map 3   Major battles and sieges in Britain and Ireland, 1639–51.

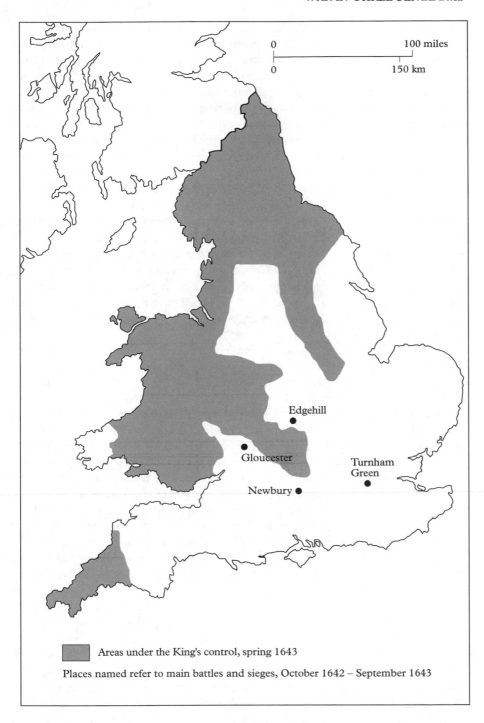

0   100 miles

0   150 km

Edgehill

Gloucester

Turnham
Green

Newbury

Areas under the King's control, spring 1643

Places named refer to main battles and sieges, October 1642 – September 1643

Map 4   Areas of England controlled by the Royalists in the spring of 1643.

of over 10,000 men led by Major-General Robert Monro and paid (but poorly supplied) by the English Parliament. The Scots were keen to defend Protestantism as well as their own strategic interests in the Ulster plantations, and by the end of the year they had succeeded in pushing the rebel forces out of Counties Antrim and Down, and parts of Armagh.

Among the rebels, the Catholic clergy wielded a growing influence, and in May 1642 lay and clerical leaders met at the rebels' headquarters at Kilkenny. There they took an oath of association establishing the 'Confederate Catholics of Ireland'. The Confederates pledged their loyalty to the King, denounced 'the puritans' as their 'enemies', and swore to fight 'pro fide, pro rege, pro patria' ('for the [Catholic] faith, for the King, for the fatherland'). This Confederation was especially notable for the way in which Gaelic Irish and Old English affirmed their common Irish, Catholic identity and insisted that there should be 'no distinction at all' between them. An executive council and a representative assembly, which met for the first time the following October, were soon established as the institutions of a Confederate 'government'. By January 1643, the Confederation controlled most of Ireland apart from significant areas of resistance in Ulster and the Pale, and Charles, who now badly needed reinforcements on the mainland, instructed Ormond to open negotiations with the rebels.

In February 1643, the Houses sent commissioners to Oxford to present peace terms to the King. The Oxford Propositions requested that Charles disband his armies, accept the Triennial Act, agree to the abolition of episcopacy, 'settle' Church government and the militia on the Houses' advice, and make various named appointments to the judiciary. The King was also to grant a full pardon for all offences committed before 10 January 1642 (which would thus have exonerated the five members and also the secret Scottish contacts developed by some of Pym's 'junto'). In the event, the talks never got beyond the first clause. Charles made the disbandment of his forces conditional upon the restoration of all his 'own revenue, magazines, towns, forts and ships'. The Parliamentarian commissioners replied that they would only agree if these resources were placed in the hands of officers they trusted, and when the King flatly refused the Treaty of Oxford collapsed on 14 April. Shortly afterwards Royalist forces began a three-pronged advance on London, led by the Earl of Newcastle from the North, Sir Ralph Hopton from the Southwest, and by the King and his nephew Prince Rupert from Oxford. These campaigns were at first highly successful. Newcastle defeated Sir Thomas Fairfax's Parliamentarian army at Adwalton Moor (30 June), thus bringing Yorkshire under Royalist control, and then marched on towards the army of the Eastern Association led by the Earl of Manchester. In the meantime, Sir William Waller's forces were crushed at Lansdown (5 July) and Roundway Down (13 July); and, most important of all, on 26 July Bristol fell to Rupert's troops. The Houses were thoroughly dispirited by the loss of England's second port and Royalist morale soared. Parliament's only comfort came in the autumn when Essex succeeded in relieving Gloucester from the Royalists' siege and then halting the King's advance at the first battle of Newbury on 20 September.

Five days earlier, Ormond had concluded a one-year truce with the Irish Confederates. This 'cessation' was very much a mixed blessing for both parties. The rebels gained nothing, because Charles refused their demand for redress of grievances and would offer no guarantees against the confiscation of their lands. For the King, the 'cessation' was a propaganda disaster because it reinforced the perception that he was willing to do a deal with Catholics. It also strengthened English fears that an army of Irish papists might be brought to the mainland to assist the Royalist war effort. Between October 1643 and June 1644, a series of convoys transported a total of around 22,000 troops from Ireland to England, Scotland and Wales. These included some returning English soldiers, but the majority were native Irish. However, they proved of little benefit to the King. For example, when 2,500 Irish soldiers were sent to England in January 1644 they were easily overwhelmed by Fairfax at the battle of Nantwich: most of them either fled or were captured, and some subsequently defected to the Parliamentarians. The bulk of the King's other Irish troops were absorbed into existing Royalist armies, and their military contribution totally failed to compensate for the bad publicity which their very presence brought upon him.

But in the autumn of 1643 the Houses could not have known this, and in the wake of their recent setbacks they became even more desperate to exploit their contacts with the Scottish Covenanters in the hope of securing military assistance from them. On 10 September 1642 they had told the Scottish General Assembly that 'their chiefest aim' in fighting the King was to defend 'the truth and purity of the reformed religion'. But it took another year for terms to be agreed in the form of the Solemn League and Covenant (25 September 1643). Like the English, the Scots feared the deployment of Irish troops on the mainland, especially after it was revealed in May 1643 that the Earl of Antrim was again plotting with Charles to raise an army which would link up with the King's supporters in the Scottish Highlands and Islands and in the process reclaim Antrim's ancient patrimony, the 'Lordship of the Isles'. The main target of such an expedition would have been the Marquis of Argyll, leader of the Campbell clan and a prominent Covenanter. However, before they joined forces with the Houses, the Scots wanted assurances of money for their troops; more problematically, they sought the imposition of Presbyterianism throughout the archipelago. Eventually, the most radical of the Parliamentarian negotiators, Sir Henry Vane the younger, devised a form of words that satisfied both English and Scots. The two sides agreed to pursue 'the reformation of religion' in England and Ireland '*according to the word of God*, and the example of the best reformed Churches' (my emphasis). This phrase – which appeared merely tautologous to the Scots – allowed the English to avoid the literal introduction of Scottish models of worship and Church government throughout the three kingdoms.

The Solemn League and Covenant – unlike the earlier Scottish National Covenant – was very much a 'British' document in its objectives. Issued in the name of the nobility, gentry and ministers of England, Scotland and Ireland, it pledged to 'bring the Churches of God in the three kingdoms to the nearest conjunction and uniformity in religion', and also to protect the rights of

Parliaments and the King's 'just power' and authority throughout all three kingdoms. The reform of the English Church was entrusted to the Westminster Assembly, a body of 125 ministers, thirty laymen and eight Scots observers. The English were pleased with Scottish promises of military assistance, but to the Scots the treaty had a much more profound religious significance than it did for most English Parliamentarians. To them it was literally 'solemn', in the sense of 'sacred' or 'holy', and one leading Covenanter, Archibald Johnston of Wariston, called it 'God's dishcloth' – a means to cleanse the three kingdoms of popery and superstition. During the years that followed, this difference in priorities between the English Parliamentarians and the Scottish leaders would place their alliance under increasing strain; but in 1643 it represented the culmination of the links between them that had developed since 1639, if not earlier.

Not all Scots, however, viewed the English Parliament as their natural allies. The Solemn League and Covenant was a much more divisive document than the National Covenant, and many Scots nobles found themselves increasingly out of sympathy with the more radical aims of the Covenanter movement. In particular, many were highly suspicious of what they saw as the overweening ambitions of Argyll. This allowed Montrose to rally the growing number of Royalist sympathizers, especially in the Highlands, and during 1644–5 to stir up a full-scale civil war in Scotland.

The principal architect of the Solemn League and Covenant had been John Pym, and after his death in December 1643 the leadership of the Commons increasingly passed to more radical figures, such as Vane, St John and Cromwell. In February 1644 a Committee of Both Kingdoms, comprising English and Scots representatives, was established to direct their joint war effort. Charles, meanwhile, in an attempt to appease moderate opinion, had accepted Hyde's suggestion that he summon an alternative Parliament to Oxford. About forty peers and over 120 members of the Commons met there in January 1644. Those at Westminster regarded this assembly as 'a mock Parliament', and Charles grew increasingly impatient with its incessant requests that he resume peace talks with the Houses. He brushed aside the 'base and mutinous motions' of the Oxford Parliament, and preferred instead to embark on renewed military campaigns.

However, during the course of 1644 the war began to turn against him. An army of 21,000 Scottish troops led by Alexander Leslie, Earl of Leven crossed the border into England in January, and quickly pushed Newcastle's army back towards York. Charles's western army was virtually destroyed by Waller at Cheriton (29 March). Then, during the early summer, the largest armies on both sides converged near York. Prince Rupert marched rapidly through the Northwest of England and across the Pennines to assist Newcastle, while Fairfax together with the Eastern Association Army under Manchester and Cromwell joined forces with their Scottish allies. On 2 July, at Marston Moor outside York, the Parliamentarians won a major victory that effectively ended Royalist control of the North. To Cromwell – whose brilliance as a cavalry commander was plainly demonstrated during the battle – this success was evidence of 'the Lord's blessing upon the godly party'. He wrote immediately afterwards that God had made the Royalists 'as stubble to our swords'. But his mood quickly turned to frustration as the Parliamentarians failed to follow up their victory. The Scots felt that they were given insufficient credit for their contribution at Marston Moor and grew bitter and resentful. As Montrose's campaigns against the Covenanters in Scotland gathered momentum,[1] they became more and more distracted by developments at home and less willing to get involved in England. Even worse in Cromwell's eyes was the fact that Manchester, instead of capitalizing on his victory or marching south to assist Waller (who had been badly defeated on 29 June at Cropredy Bridge in Oxfordshire), insisted on taking the Eastern Association Army back to East Anglia. When the Royalists in the West Country rallied and inflicted a serious defeat on Essex at Lostwithiel (2 September) it seemed that Parliament was throwing away the advantage it had gained at Marston Moor.

The growing tension between Cromwell and Manchester came to a head at the indecisive second battle of Newbury on 27 October. In a famous confrontation over whether to pursue the battle into a second day, Manchester declared that 'if we beat the King ninety and nine times, yet he is King still, and so will his posterity be after him, and we subjects still; but if the King beat us once, we shall all be hanged, and our posterity made slaves'. Cromwell retorted by asking 'if this be so, why did we ever take up arms at first?' On 25 November he lodged a formal complaint in the Commons alleging that behind Manchester's 'backwardness to all action' lay a conscious desire to avoid defeating Charles conclusively. Manchester issued counter-charges accusing Cromwell of trying to subvert the nobility and gentry, of promoting only Independents, and of being hostile to the Scottish Presbyterians.[2] Out of this bitter quarrel emerged a proposal for 'self-denial' – first moved by Zouch Tate on 9 December and supported by Cromwell and his allies – whereby all members of the two Houses would resign their military commands and civil offices. The Self-Denying Ordinance was eventually passed on 3 April 1645, but with a proviso that the Houses could grant exemptions to specific individuals at their discretion. Cromwell was to receive a series of such exemptions, permitting him to remain a Parliamentarian officer throughout the rest of the war.

The removal of Essex and Manchester under the terms of the Self-Denying Ordinance was accompanied by a full-scale reshaping of Parliament's high command and the formation of the New Model Army. Unlike the earlier regional armies, this was a national, centralized army, controlled and paid from Westminster rather than the counties. It was commanded by Sir Thomas Fairfax, with Cromwell precariously appointed for forty days at a time as second-in-command and lieutenant-general of the horse in defiance of the Self-Denying Ordinance, and until the Houses decided who else could do the job. The army was not at first the hotbed of radicalism that historians once imagined: it was essentially an amalgamation of three existing armies (previously commanded by Manchester. Essex and Waller), and the majority of its officers – at least initially – came from the gentry. Nevertheless, over the years that followed exposure to godly preaching, fasting, prayer meetings and Bible study became normative for troops in the army, and its extraordinary military successes owed much to religious zeal as well as to regular pay.[3]

The 'new modelling' of the Parliamentarian army gained extra impetus from the King's rejection of fresh peace terms early in 1645. The Uxbridge Propositions were significantly tougher than Parliament's earlier proposals, and clearly reflected the influence of the Scots on the Committee of Both Kingdoms. The King was requested to sign the Solemn League and Covenant, to pass a bill for the abolition of episcopacy, and 'to endeavour the nearest conjunction and uniformity in matters of religion' between England and Scotland 'according to the Covenant'. The Irish 'cessation' of September 1643 was to be declared void, and fifty-eight named Royalists were to be excluded from any pardon. All military officers were to be 'persons of known integrity, and such as both kingdoms may confide in', and a number of civilian officers of state were to 'be nominated by both Houses of Parliament'. At the Treaty of Uxbridge (30 January–22 February 1645) the two sides discussed the three issues of the Church, the militia and the Irish 'cessation' for three days in rotation. But on each issue they soon reached deadlock. Charles flatly refused to compromise with 'rebels' and 'Presbyterians', to surrender his 'lawful powers' of military command, or to desert his friends and supporters. The negotiations broke down after barely three weeks, and both sides made ready for another campaigning season.

In the spring of 1645, Charles had two military options open to him, and characteristically he attempted to pursue both at once. The first was to win a lightening victory over the New Model Army, which the Royalists derided as the 'New Noddle', before it got properly organized. But he had seriously underestimated his enemy, and on 14 June the New Model scored a decisive victory over the Royalist forces at Naseby near Leicester. In fact, the battle was remarkably close, despite the fact that Parliamentarians outnumbered Royalists by 14,000 to 8,000. It was finally settled when Cromwell, having put one wing of Royalist cavalry to flight, succeeded in re-forming his own cavalry and returning to the main battle with devastating effect. Cromwell perceived this triumph as 'none other but the hand of God', and although the war dragged on for another year, Naseby proved to be the crucial turning-point. It opened the way to the West Country, and the New Model quickly capitalized on its success by routing the King's western armies at Langport in Somerset on 10 July. With the fall of Bristol to Parliament on 10 September, the Royalists finally lost control of the West Country.

During the summer of 1645, Royalist forces were weakened by Charles's simultaneous pursuit of a second option: the attempt to link up with Montrose, who was winning a sequence of brilliant victories against the Covenanters in Scotland. The previous summer, Antrim had despatched a force of about 2,000 Irish troops to assist Montrose's Highlanders. The close cultural and ethnic links between the inhabitants of the Western Highlands and Northern Ireland helped to weld the army into a highly effective pan-Gaelic force: in particular, Irish Macdonnells led by Alasdair MacColla welcomed the opportunity to unite with their Macdonald kinsmen in Scotland. Dislike of Argyll and Catholic resentment of the Covenanter movement swelled the ranks of Montrose's followers, and enabled him to overwhelm the Covenanter forces at Tippermuir

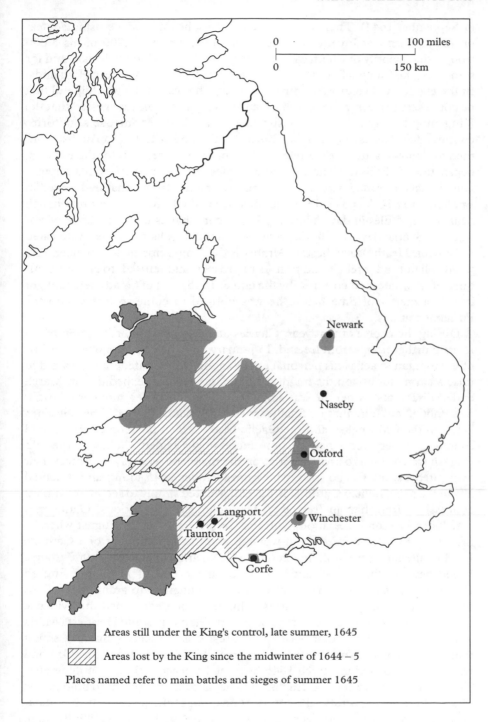

Map 5   Areas of England controlled by the Royalists in the late summer of 1645.

(1 September 1644). Then, on 2 February 1645, he inflicted a crushing defeat on Argyll's army at Inverlochy. Argyll lost no fewer that 1,700 of his 3,000 troops, the majority of whom were members of his own Campbell clan, and for some time the Campbells ceased to be a major power in the Western Highlands. In the euphoria of victory, Montrose assured Charles that he was hopeful that he could secure a complete Royalist victory in Scotland, and suggested that the King might march north to assist in this process. Montrose's victories continued at Auldearn (9 May), Alford (2 July) and Kilsyth (15 August); but then his followers, disillusioned by the lack of material rewards for their efforts, began to drift back to their Highland homes. At this point Leven's nephew David Leslie returned with 6,000 of the Covenanter troops that had served in England in 1644–5 and on 13 September he crushed Montrose at Philiphaugh near Selkirk.[4] Eleven days later, any hope that Charles could advance north-wards to Scotland was finally destroyed when the Royalists were badly defeated at Rowton Heath near Chester. Although the King remained convinced that 'God will not suffer rebels and traitors to prosper' and refused 'to give over this quarrel . . . whatever it cost me', by the end of 1645 most of his advisers thought it only a matter of time before he was obliged to come to terms with the Parliamentarians.

During the course of that year, Charles had also made abortive attempts to recruit further troops from Ireland. In January 1645 he commissioned the Earl of Glamorgan to act as his personal envoy to the Irish Confederates in a bid to raise an army for use on the mainland. Glamorgan's first expedition in March ended disastrously when he was shipwrecked on the Lancashire coast, and it was only in late June that he finally arrived in Ireland. By that time, divisions between the Old English and the Gaelic Irish – which the Confederation had sought to paper over – had become increasingly evident. Whereas the Old English were willing to assist Charles on the mainland as a way to protect their own interests, the Gaelic Irish, who from October 1645 found an influential ally in the papal nuncio Cardinal Rinuccini, wanted simply to secure maximum concessions from him in Ireland. After prolonged negotiations, Glamorgan concluded a second 'cessation' with the Confederates on 25 August whereby promises of Catholic freedom of worship and the appointment of a Catholic Lord Lieutenant were proffered in return for an army of at least 10,000 troops. When news of this agreement leaked out at the end of 1645, the English Parliamentarians were horrified at Charles's willingness to grant concessions to Catholics in order to secure arms. This revelation confirmed the evidence of his private correspondence – especially with Glamorgan and Henrietta Maria – that had been captured at Naseby. So great was the King's embarrassment that he publicly disowned all that Glamorgan had done in his name. Ormond was left isolated, and in March 1646 he signed a peace with the Confederates. This treaty benefited the Old English by safeguarding their right to hold public office and reversing Strafford's confiscations, but at the price of further alien-ating the Gaelic Irish and deepening the divisions within the Confederation. These rifts became even wider after Owen Roe O'Neill defeated Monro's Scottish forces at Benburb in June, thereby strengthening the power of Rinuccini and the Gaelic Irish within the Confederation. As a result, any hope of a common front between Irish Confederates and Royalists against Parliament's forces receded, and with it the possibility that intervention from Ireland on Charles's behalf might decisively affect the course of the English Civil War.

During the opening months of 1646, the King's position in England crumbled further. In February a Royalist rising in Glamorganshire was easily put down by the New Model Army. By March Charles had despaired of victory and decided to send the Prince of Wales abroad, first to the Scilly Isles and then to Jersey. Believing that he was likely to secure better terms from the Scots than from the English Parliament, the King slipped out of Oxford in late April, and on 5 May gave himself up to the Scottish forces besieging Newark. The remaining Royalists in Oxford surrendered on 24 June, so concluding the first Civil War.

2 The Impact of War

In the end, the Parliamentarians were victorious because they had won the most important battles, especially Marston Moor and Naseby. But those victories rested less on purely military considerations than on the fact that Parliament commanded superior resources and mobilized those resources much better than the King. The Houses' control of London throughout the war provided them with a source of revenue and other supplies unmatched within Royalist areas. It also gave them command of vital trade routes and of prosperous economic areas in the south and east of England. As the war engulfed all three kingdoms, Parliament benefited far more from Scottish assistance than Charles did from Irish. Above all, the Parliamentarian war effort was more organized, more systematic and more ruthless than its Royalist counterpart. All these factors meant that the longer the war dragged on, the more likely a Parliamentarian victory became.

The impact of the war was horribly destructive at all levels of society. At any given moment in the summers of 1643, 1644 and 1645 between 120,000 and 140,000 adult males (roughly one in eight) were in arms in England. The total throughout the three kingdoms as a whole was probably in the region of 200,000. In all, perhaps one in four or five Englishmen (about 300,000) bore arms at some time between 1642 and 1648, and approximately 190,000 died either in combat or from disease. In other words, about 3.7 per cent of England's population of around five million perished, a higher proportion than in either of the two world wars. In Scotland the dead numbered roughly 60,000 (6 per cent of the population) and in Ireland as many as 618,000 (41 per cent). Few, if any, could escape the effects of war. The Midlands and West of England, Ulster and the Western Highlands of Scotland were the regions that suffered most directly from the military campaigns. But innocent people elsewhere were liable to be sucked into the war as troops marched to and fro, seizing food, livestock or horses, requisitioning property and demanding free quarter (the billeting of troops on civilians). The war was very fluid, and involved many skirmishes and sieges – over one hundred towns were besieged for a month or longer – as well as the set-piece battles. As a result, virtually every borough was garrisoned as a potential stronghold and hastily defended by earthworks that often involved razing some of the suburbs. However, it was the financial demands made by both sides to maintain their armies that fell most heavily and indiscriminately on all areas within their control.

At the beginning of the war, the two sides had to raise money quickly and to establish their own executive institutions. This was easier for the King, who was able to take some members of existing bodies, such as the Privy Council and the central legal and financial courts, with him to Oxford. There he set up a Council of War, but all too often this was internally divided and proved unable to mediate between the local commanders on which the Royalist war effort depended. The Royalist chain of command was poorly defined and as a result, several commanders became locked in jurisdictional disputes. The same lack of co-ordination was evident in financial administration. Just as the King raised troops by the ancient device of the commissions of array, so Royalist fiscal expedients remained essentially conservative in form. As the war progressed, a 'contribution' was levied using traditional rating lists and collected by existing local officials. But by 1645, very little of this money was finding its way back to Oxford, with the consequence that during the latter stages of the war Royalist troops were very poorly paid. As discipline deteriorated, their officers grew more likely to take the law into their own hands by arbitrarily plundering civilians than did their better-paid Parliamentarian counterparts.

Unlike the King, the Houses had to construct an executive machinery from scratch, and their solution was to create a series of committees consisting mainly of members of both Houses. The war effort was directed initially by the Committee of Safety (July 1642), but this was replaced in February 1644, after Scotland's entry into the war, by the Committee of Both Kingdoms (later called the Derby House Committee). A number of other committees were designed to raise money and to impose fiscal penalties on Parliament's enemies. The Committee for the Advance of Money was established in November 1642 to raise loans and impose assessments on those who did not subscribe voluntarily. More draconian was the Committee for Sequestrations (March 1643) appointed to confiscate and administer the estates of Catholics and Royalists. In all, nearly 5,000 people suffered the loss of their estates in this way. When the yield from sequestrations proved disappointing, the less active Royalists ('delinquents') were allowed to regain their estates in return for taking oaths of loyalty and for paying heavy fines ('compositions'); but a minority of hardline 'malignants' were exempted from any form of redress. However, the bulk of Parliament's revenues came from taxation on a massive scale. In February 1643, the Houses introduced a weekly (later monthly) assessment, a land tax roughly equivalent to a parliamentary subsidy every fortnight. The following July, Parliament imposed an excise on vital commodities such as beer, meat and salt. These taxes were undoubtedly effective and help to explain why the New Model Army was so much better paid than the Royalist forces. But as the years passed Parliament's financial burdens produced enormous resentment among the civilian population. By 1645–6, for example, Kent was paying more each month in assessments than it had for an entire year of Ship Money, and understandably there was bitter hostility towards these 'illegal taxes'.

Such feelings were aggravated by the many other violations of the law that Parliament committed in order to win the war. The Houses granted both their national committees and their network of county committees extensive powers to work outside the framework of the common law. Parliamentarian officials were authorized to seize property and distrain goods without any redress, and to imprison without trial or cause shown. Rights of *habeas corpus* and trial by jury were swept aside, and conscription and martial law were widely enforced. In order to secure victory, Parliament did many of the things for which it had denounced Charles I in the Petition of Right. Furthermore, its members felt able to justify such acts on grounds of necessity: as Lord Wharton declared in 1643, 'they were not tied to a law for these were times of necessity and imminent danger'. The Parliamentarian writer Henry Parker insisted that in an emergency the Houses could exercise sovereign powers, and that, if the common good so required, they could flout the laws of the land. Small wonder, then, that by 1646 more and more people were beginning to feel that Parliament was behaving more tyrannically than the King had ever done.

This impression was reinforced by the Royalists' striking respect for legal propriety. Unlike that of the Houses, Charles's sequestration policy rested on the principle that his opponents should whenever possible be formally indicted for treason by a jury at common law. If they had been sequestrated without such an indictment they were generally allowed to appeal to the next assize. Similarly, the King consistently sought local approval, usually from grand juries, for all financial contributions and forced loans. Whereas the Houses tried to suppress the traditional local courts of assizes and quarter sessions, the Royalists supported their continuation. Such policies enabled the moderate Dorset Royalist Sir John Strangways to claim with some justice that 'we maintain that no man should be imprisoned, put out of his lands, but by due process of law, and no man ought to be adjudged to death, but by the laws established in the land ... [The Parliamentarians] practise the contrary'. During the first Civil War a number of Constitutional Royalist writers, including Dudley Digges the younger, Henry Ferne and Sir John Spelman, developed a theoretical justification for this position which saw the Crown's powers as limited by the rule of law and presented the King as the natural defender of the laws and liberties of his people.

Whatever the respective merits of the two sides, by 1645 the vast majority of people yearned for peace rather than victory by either Royalists or Parliamentarians. During the course of that year, some even decided to use force in order to drive the armies out of their counties and to promote a settlement based on a return to known ways of government. There is evidence that Clubmen Associations – mainly consisting of farmers and rural craftsmen – were formed for this purpose as far apart as Shropshire, Worcestershire, Herefordshire, Wiltshire, Dorset, Somerset, Hampshire, Berkshire, Sussex and South Wales. The Sussex Clubmen were typical in their condemnation of 'the insufferable, insolent, arbitrary power that hath been used amongst us, contrary to all our ancient known laws, or ordinances of Parliament, upon our persons and estates'. Although the Clubmen were genuinely neutralist, and preferred peace to either side, they were prepared to make tactical alliances with Royalists or Parliamentarians in order to clear their counties of troops. But because by this stage Royalist discipline had disintegrated more severely, in practice Clubman activities tended to benefit Parliament more often than the King.

This yearning for a return to the known ways was evident also in religious affairs. Between 1643 and 1646 the Houses overturned the existing Church of England, abolishing episcopacy, cathedrals, church courts, the Prayer Book and the Kalendar (including the festivals of Christmas and Easter). During the summer of 1644, in response to repeated Scottish demands, Laud was finally brought to trial: he was convicted of treason and executed in January 1645. These measures coincided with renewed iconoclasm, organized by Parliamentarian commissioners such as William Dowsing and directed against 'monuments of idolatry and superstition'. In place of the old Church, the Houses tried to establish a Presbyterian Church, modelled on the Scottish Kirk, in which ministers and lay 'elders' from a group of parishes formed 'classes' which in turn sent representatives to a provincial assembly (one for each county). A national synod would co-ordinate this structure in close association with Parliament. A new service book, the Directory of Public Worship, was drawn up, introducing a more austerely Calvinist pattern of worship based on the sermon and extempore prayer.

However, this ambitious system never took hold in more than about ten counties. The Scots thought it a pale shadow of their own Kirk, far too dependent on Parliament, 'a lame Erastian presbytery' as the minister Robert Baillie put it. A growing number of 'Independents' deplored so rigid a national structure and demanded autonomy for congregations and liberty of conscience for individuals. But the majority of people simply wanted a return to the old Church, to the Prayer Book services, and to the traditional celebrations of Christmas and Easter. Many parishioners secretly reinstated clergy ejected by Parliament's Committee for Scandalous Ministers and persuaded them to continue using the old liturgies. This persistence of what has been termed 'folk Anglicanism' further strengthened the growing dislike of Parliament's authoritarian policies.

These years also saw the emergence of various religious sects who took advantage of the collapse of ecclesiastical authority and the abolition of the Church courts to form 'gathered' churches of 'visible saints' outside any national structure. These sects often challenged traditional doctrines including the Trinity and the existence of Hell, while some practised adult baptism or even 'blasphemies' such as the baptism of horses. Wild rumours spread about the sectaries, alleging that they represented a fundamental threat to the social fabric because of their heretical beliefs and sexual delinquency. In February, May and December 1646, the Presbyterian minister Thomas Edwards published the three parts of *Gangraena*, 'a catalogue ... of the errors, heresies, blasphemies and pernicious practices of the sectaries of this time broached and acted in England in these last four years'. To people like Edwards, the sects

150

THE
220

Parliament of VVomen.

With the merrie Lawes by them newly

Enacted. To live in more Eafe, Pompe, Pride,
and wantonneffe : but efpecially that they might have fu-
periority and domineere over their husbands ; with a new way
found out by them to cure any old or new Cuckolds, and
how both parties may recover their credit
and honefty againe

London, Printed for *W. Wilfon* and are to be fold by him in
Will-yard in Little Saint *Bartholomewes*. 1646.

Aug: 14 . London 1646

Plate 10 *The Parliament of Women*, 1646. The dislocation of civil war brought many
changes to the lives of women, not least a proliferation of sects in which women often
played a prominent part. Male fears about an inversion of traditional gender roles
were expressed in satires such as this, lampooning women for seeking a political voice
as well as superiority over their husbands.
Source: British Library

seemed not only to propagate abhorrent religious beliefs: their activities also challenged the patriarchal nature of society, the authority of husbands and fathers, and the integrity of the family.

This horrified reaction was undoubtedly aggravated by the fact that women commonly outnumbered men in the sects. A fear of the inversion of traditional society was closely linked to male fears of an inversion of gender roles. Women found that within the sects they were accepted as free members, able to debate religious issues, to prophesy and even to preach. One contemporary was appalled by the sight of 'bold impudent housewives, without all womanly modesty' preaching 'after a narrative or discoursing manner, an hour and more, and that most directly contrary to the Apostle's inhibition'. There were, as we shall see, limits to the civil and political equality accorded to women among even the most radical sects,[5] but in the religious sphere their spirits were respected on the same footing as men.

The prominence of women in the sects was one aspect of wider changes in their lives caused by the dislocation of civil war. Women had always played a central role in households and in the local economy in diverse ways that belied the conventional early modern 'ideal' of the submissive wife. But in wartime conditions, with so many men absent in arms, women frequently took over the administration of estates and the running of workshops. On both sides, women can be found leading the defence of their besieged homes, such as the Royalist Lady Mary Bankes at Corfe Castle or the Parliamentarian Lady Brilliana Harley at Brampton Bryan. Royalist women, such as Lady Mary Verney, also undertook negotiations with the Parliamentarian committees for the return of sequestrated estates, a particularly difficult task that involved discussing the values and rental incomes of lands and haggling over the level of the composition fine. At all levels of society, the conflict extended the independence and responsibilities of women, while also making many aspects of their lives harder and more burdensome. In particular, pregnancy and childbirth were even more hazardous in wartime conditions than at other times, and stories of miscarriages or deformed births were rife.

There were numerous other ways in which the war seriously disrupted family life. Some families were torn apart by conflicting political allegiances – literally 'by the sword divided' – while others were weakened by the influence of new ideologies that encouraged certain individuals to place sectarian loyalties ahead of family ties. Many families suffered severe hardship because of the death, maiming, exile or imprisonment of relatives. Yet the latest detailed study of the family during the English Revolution suggests that the experience of war could often strengthen the family unit as well as weaken it.[6] Amidst the terrifying uncertainties of war, with the disintegration of so many established institutional and social landmarks, many families naturally closed ranks as people drew strength and security from their own relatives. During these turbulent years, most men and women looked instinctively to their families for private solace and safety, just as in public life their reflex response to the end of the first Civil War was to seek a return to the familiar, to the 'known ways' of government.

3 The Search for Settlement

The Houses had won the war, but they faced a bewildering array of problems as they set about trying to win the peace. Many felt that until a settlement was reached with Charles they needed to maintain their army, but that only perpetuated the crushing tax burden on the civilian population. There were about 22,000 troops in the New Model, plus another 40,000 in Parliament's various provincial armies, and as their pay became more erratic so discipline deteriorated. Parliamentarian soldiers mutinied in at least twenty English counties during 1646, and in seventeen the following year. By the end of 1646, the Houses owed over three million pounds to their soldiers in arrears. Wartime disruption of the economy had led to a deepening trade recession, aggravated by a series of harvest failures during the later 1640s. Unable to raise taxation any further, Parliament was left quite incapable of paying its troops.

These problems were rendered even more intractable by the growing divisions within Parliament. Confusingly, the religious terms Presbyterian and Independent were also used to denote the two main political groups, which operated as bi-cameral 'parties' in both Houses. The Presbyterians, who commanded a narrow majority at the end of the first Civil War, were led by Denzil Holles, William Strode and Sir Philip Stapleton in the Commons; and in the Lords by Essex (until his death in September 1646), Manchester, Warwick, Middlesex and Lord Willoughby of Parham. They favoured a close alliance with the Scots and supported the immediate implementation of the Presbyterian church structure devised by the Westminster Assembly. They also wanted a negotiated settlement with the King, and during 1646–7 became increasingly keen to see the New Model Army disbanded. The Independents, on the other hand, opposed a national church structure and were suspicious of the authoritarianism and intolerance of Scottish Presbyterians. Instead, they advocated liberty of conscience and allied readily with like-minded army officers. They robustly defended the army's interests and supported a purely English campaign of conquest and colonization along Spenserian lines to subjugate Ireland.[7] Although they had originally sought a vigorous prosecution of the Civil War, in 1647 they made a remarkable attempt to negotiate their own settlement with the King. The most prominent Independents included peers like Saye and Sele, Northumberland and Lord Wharton, and MPs such as Cromwell, St John, Sir Henry Vane the younger, William Pierrepont and Sir John Evelyn.

The Presbyterian ascendancy in both Houses in 1646 was reflected in the Newcastle Propositions, presented to Charles on 13 July. These were much the most stringent terms that Parliament had so far offered. The King was required to swear the Solemn League and Covenant, to accept the 'reformation of religion, according to the Covenant', and 'to endeavour the nearest conjunction and uniformity in matters of religion' between England and Scotland. One-third of the lands of bishops and clergy were to be sold. For the next twenty years – equivalent to Charles's presumed life-span – the Houses were to have absolute control over all armed forces. There was to be a general pardon, but fifty-eight named Royalists would be exempted from it. The King's response was to prevaricate. He refused to grant any concessions 'destructive to the regal power', but instead of rejecting the terms outright preferred to wait either for the Houses to moderate their demands or for the Scots to offer more attractive proposals.

In the meantime, Holles strengthened his position by negotiating a loan of £230,000 from the City of London that enabled him to pay off the Scottish army. In February 1647, the Scots delivered the King into parliamentary custody and then returned home. With the Scots gone, the Presbyterians decided to press ahead with the disbandment of the army, which they saw as the principal obstacle to a stable settlement. They envisaged a small standing force of 6,400 horse and dragoons, but the remainder of the 22,000-strong New Model Army was given a straight choice between disbandment and enlistment to serve in Ireland. Those who chose the former were initially offered no guarantees of pay at a time when payment was forty-three weeks in arrears for cavalry and eighteen weeks for infantry. Most of Parliament's provincial armies were disbanded without any fuss, but the rank and file of the New Model were so enraged that they submitted a petition to Fairfax. Holles and his allies enflamed this situation by passing a Declaration of Dislike that branded any troops who persisted with petitioning as 'enemies to the state and disturbers of the public peace'. Incensed, during April and May the regiments began electing representatives ('agitators')[8] to present their demands to Parliament through their officers, but during the last week of May Holles succeeded in securing votes in both Houses in favour of disbandment with eight weeks' pay. Then the political situation was transformed on 4 June when a junior officer, Cornet George Joyce, possibly with Cromwell's collusion, seized the King from Holdenby House and brought him to army headquarters at Newmarket. By capturing the King's person, the army had suddenly gained the political initiative.

On 14 June the newly formed General Council of the Army issued a *Declaration* that revealed how far the army's material grievances had developed into a fully-fledged political platform. Denying that they were 'a mere mercenary army', the troops claimed to protect 'our own and the people's just rights and liberties' against the tyranny of Parliament and especially of the Presbyterian leaders. In words that suggested the influence of Leveller ideas, they upheld petitioning as the right of all 'free-born people'.[9] The *Declaration* also demanded that the Houses publish their accounts and pay off all arrears, that 'a provision of tender consciences' be established, that an Act of Oblivion be passed to provide a general indemnity for actions committed during the Civil War, that all members hostile to the army be removed, and that the Parliament then be dissolved and fresh elections held. Holles tried to brush these demands aside, but soon found himself dramatically overtaken by events. On 26 July a violent mob, probably encouraged by Holles, invaded the Commons in support of the Presbyterian leaders, whereupon over fifty of the Independent members fled to the New Model encamped at St Albans appealing for help. On 6 August the army occupied London and reinstated its

Independent allies: now it was the turn of Holles and ten of his supporters to flee the capital.

The destruction of the Presbyterian ascendancy cleared the way for the Independent 'party' in both Houses, together with their friends among the army officers, to promote a settlement with the King on their own terms. The *Heads of the Proposals* had been discussed by the General Council of the Army on 17 July, presented to Charles on 23 July, and published on 2 August. Supported by an Independent coalition that included members of both Houses as well as army officers, the *Heads* stood in marked contrast to every other set of terms presented to the King. Whereas earlier propositions had all worked on the principle of transferring power from the Crown to the two Houses, the *Heads* sought to clip Parliament's wings by repealing the Triennial Act, establishing biennial Parliaments and redistributing seats so as to make the Commons 'an equal representative of the whole'. The Houses were to gain control of the militia for ten years (rather than twenty) and also approve appointments to 'the great offices for ten years'. Above all, the religious clauses were radically different from earlier propositions. Episcopacy was to be preserved, although shorn of 'all coercive power, authority, and jurisdiction', while the Prayer Book was allowed to be used but on a voluntary basis. No Presbyterian structures were to be created, nor was the Covenant to be enforced. Charles's followers would also be treated more leniently than under earlier terms: only five named Royalists were exempted from pardon. On all the key issues the *Heads* were much the most generous terms ever presented to Charles, and they represented a masterly attempt to enshrine the Independents' programme while also mitigating the Houses' assault on royal powers and accommodating the King's commitment to episcopacy. However Charles, who had been moved to Hampton Court in August, rejected moderate advice to accept the *Heads* and instead tried to use them as a bargaining counter to encourage the Houses to moderate the Newcastle Propositions. When this strategy failed, in another bid to divide and rule, he opened negotiations with the Scots.

Radical influences were meanwhile gaining ground within the army. During the summer and autumn of 1647, Leveller ideas became increasingly widespread among both officers and rank and file. The Levellers were an organized group of polemicists, led by John Lilburne, Richard Overton and William Walwyn. In all, these three men published nearly 250 pamphlets between 1645 and 1649. They began by advocating religious toleration, but moved beyond that to demand fundamental political and social reform. They denounced the tyranny of existing institutions and sought the abolition of the monarchy and the House of Lords. They wanted a unicameral Parliament elected by universal male suffrage (there was no question of votes for women), annual or biennial Parliaments, disestablishment of the Church, the drastic reduction of taxation, and radical reform of the legal system. To soldiers aggrieved by what they saw as Parliament's betrayal and by the King's refusal to agree terms, these ideas had an instant appeal. Leveller influence in the army reached its zenith in mid-October when new, more radical 'agitators' from five regiments drew up *The Case of the Army Truly Stated*, which attacked the General Council for backsliding on the army's earlier *Declaration* and advanced the principle that 'all power is originally and essentially in the whole body of the people of this nation'. The Council agreed to debate this document, with civilian Levellers present, in Putney Church at the end of October. The generals, including Cromwell, were increasingly wary of Leveller ideas, and they were deeply alarmed when at the meeting the Levellers tabled a much more revolutionary document, a draft republican constitution entitled *The Agreement of the People*.

The celebrated Putney Debates between the General Council, the agitators and Leveller representatives opened under Cromwell's chairmanship on 28 October. Cromwell and his son-in-law Henry Ireton began by establishing the need to continue negotiations with the King. There was then a long discussion that revealed a fundamental divergence of opinion over the franchise. Colonel Thomas Rainsborough, strongly supported by the agitator Edward Sexby, advocated universal male suffrage on the grounds that 'the poorest he that is in England hath a life to live as the greatest he; and therefore ... every man that is to live under a government ought first by his own consent to put himself under that government'. Against this, Ireton argued that the franchise should be restricted to those with 'a permanent fixed interest in the kingdom', and opposed making 'a disturbance to a good constitution of a kingdom'. The debates continued until 5 November, but in the end were inconclusive. Significantly, however, they did reveal the profound ambivalence of Cromwell's own position. In part a socially conservative gentleman who feared that Leveller ideas 'must end in anarchy', Cromwell was also a religious radical who professed himself not 'wedded and glued to forms of government' for they were 'but dross and dung in comparison of Christ'. The tension between these attitudes was to haunt Cromwell for the rest of his life. But his immediate priority was to head off the demands of the Levellers and agitators and to reaffirm the authority of the General Council. In an attempt to reunite the army, it was agreed that three rendezvous of various regiments would be held over the following weeks. At the first rendezvous, at Corkbush Field near Ware on 15 November, Cromwell faced a near mutiny when one regiment appeared wearing copies of *The Agreement of the People* in their hats. Cromwell and several other officers rode through the ranks plucking the document from each hat, and one of the ringleaders was then summarily tried, sentenced and shot. The other rendezvous passed off without incident, and thereafter Leveller influence within the army began to decline. The troops became quiescent, and during January and February 1648 18,000 men were peacefully disbanded.

It was against this background that Charles launched a bold new strategy to break the political deadlock. The army unrest during the autumn of 1647 made him fear for his life, and on 11 November he fled from Hampton Court to Carisbrooke Castle on the Isle of Wight. Although still a prisoner, he continued negotiations with three Scottish commissioners, Lanark, Loudoun and Lauderdale, who claimed to represent mainstream opinion north of the border. Many Scots were deeply disillusioned with the English Parliament's failure to implement the Covenant and were receptive to Hamilton's suggestion that they might secure a better deal from the King. They were also unnerved by the willingness of English Independents to contemplate a purely English campaign to conquer Ireland in the spring of 1647: might not such a strategy, the Scots wondered, subsequently be directed against them as well? Charles, for his part, was willing to offer concessions to Scottish Presbyterians in return for military assistance. So, on 26 December, he concluded a secret Engagement with the Scots whereby he agreed to establish 'Presbyterial government' in England for three years in return for guarantees of his military authority, his right to appoint advisers, and his 'honour, safety and freedom'. Most Scots still wanted not to break the union but to make it work more effectively. They wanted a closer legal and administrative union with England,[10] and Charles therefore promised to 'endeavour a complete union of the kingdoms', to allow one-third of his Privy Councillors and officers of state to be Scots, and to visit Scotland regularly. If the English Parliament refused to accept these terms and disband its army, the Scots 'engaged' to send forces to England to liberate the King and implement the Covenant.

The Engagement was part of a wider strategy whereby Charles hoped to deploy the resources of all three kingdoms against the English Parliament. His negotiations with the Scots were accompanied by renewed talks with Ormond about the possibility of Irish intervention on the mainland. As Rinuccini and O'Neill came to dominate the Confederation in 1646–7, and as the Independents who advocated conquest of Ireland held sway in England during the second half of 1647, Ormond was increasingly confirmed in his view that Charles was the natural ally of the Old English. He also found that he could make common cause with the Protestant Lord President of Munster, Inchiquin, who had hitherto been pro-Parliamentarian but who resented the Independents and their adherent Viscount Lisle, Lord Lieutenant of Ireland since January 1646. In the summer and autumn of 1647, while the Independents appeared set on an anti-Scottish, anti-Irish policy that would re-establish English dominance within the three kingdoms, Ormond made several visits to the King at Hampton Court. The outcome of these secret talks was clearly apparent in the pan-archipelagic nature of the Engagement: if necessary, the Scots agreed to send troops who would join up with Irish and English Royalists to defend the King's authority in England and Ireland as well as Scotland. In the event, divisions between the Old English and Gaelic Irish became so deep that these Irish forces were never to materialize. None the less, at the end of 1647 Charles seemed well on the way to harnessing the resources of his three kingdoms to renew the fight against Parliament. It was a high-risk strategy: if it worked, Charles would be able to impose a settlement on the Houses; but if it did not he would find himself at their mercy.

With his new-found allies in Ireland and Scotland, the King felt emboldened to take a tougher stand against the English Parliament. On 24 December the Houses had presented him with minimum terms in the form of *Four Bills* requiring him to accept parliamentary control of all armed forces in England, Ireland and Wales for twenty years, the voiding of all Royalist declarations against the two Houses, the cancellation of all peerages granted since May 1642 without Parliament's consent, and the confirmation of Parliament's right to adjourn wherever it thought desirable. After signing the Engagement Charles saw little point in even discussing these terms, and on 28 December he rejected the *Four Bills* claiming that they would divest 'himself of all sovereignty' and give 'an arbitrary and unlimited power to the two Houses for ever'. To add to the Houses' woes, on Christmas Day riots had broken out in London, Norwich and Canterbury in protest against the attempted suppression of Christmas festivities. This disorder was symptomatic of a widespread revulsion in the English provinces against Parliament's 'tyranny' which, in conjunction with the Scottish army, enabled Charles to spark off a second Civil War the following year.

4 The Second Civil War

To the army and Parliament alike, Charles's Engagement with the Scots appeared an act of duplicity and treachery. In disgust, the Commons passed a Vote of No Addresses on 3 January 1648[11] which forbade any more negotiations with the King and declared that the Houses would not accept further messages from him. During the debate that preceded the Vote, Cromwell warned the Commons not to break its trust to 'the honest party of the kingdom', or else the godly – especially within the army – 'might take such courses as nature dictates to them'. The meaning behind these sinister words became clearer when the army withdrew from London and its officers assembled for a prayer meeting at Windsor Castle at the end of April. By that time, a Royalist rising had already broken out in South Wales, heralding the outbreak of the second Civil War. In an atmosphere of high emotion, the officers considered whether any of their previous actions could have contributed to this renewal of hostilities, and concluded that the blame lay in 'those cursed carnal conferences' that they had held 'with the King and his party' the previous year. They therefore decided 'that it was our duty, if ever the Lord brought us back again in peace, to call Charles Stuart, that man of blood, to an account for that blood he had shed, and mischief he had done to his utmost, against the Lord's cause and people in these poor nations.'

It would be difficult to exaggerate the significance of the Windsor prayer meeting, for it marked a crucial shift in the army's objectives and self-perception that would eventually lead to the Regicide. When it had first intervened on the political scene in 1647, the army's official utterances presented it as the bulwark of popular liberties, in particular against the high-handedness of Parliament. At that time, many of its officers still hoped to achieve a settlement with the King. But following the Engagement and the outbreak of the second Civil War the army's outlook changed dramatically. It now believed that by seeking to overturn God's verdict in the first Civil War, Charles was committing nothing less than sacrilege. The troops saw themselves as God's instrument, called to affirm that earlier verdict and then bring Charles to account. To them he was no longer 'King Charles' but 'Charles Stuart', a 'man of blood' stripped of his regality and indelibly tainted by blood-guilt. They were inspired by Old Testament texts such as Numbers 35. 33: 'Blood it defileth the land: and the land cannot be cleansed of the blood that is shed therein, but by the blood of him that shed it'. Over the following months, these ideas enabled the army to cut through existing laws and customs, and to sweep aside the instinctive reverence which most people in all three kingdoms still felt towards 'God's anointed'. Deference towards the 'powers that be' was over-ridden by a deeper, more violent religious imperative that branded Charles 'a man against whom the Lord hath witnessed', and could ultimately be used to justify his trial and execution.[12]

These beliefs determined the mood of the army as it fought the second Civil War. The spring and summer of 1648 saw a series of provincial uprisings that were often initially directed as much against Parliamentarian centralization and military rule as in favour of the King; but they were undoubtedly stirred up by the Royalists. The principal areas affected were South Wales (March–July), Kent (May–June), East Anglia (April–August), and the West and North Ridings of Yorkshire (June–December). This 'revolt of the provinces' was neither co-ordinated nor simultaneous and the New Model Army was there-fore able to move around the country suppressing the risings one by one. The second Civil War was much shorter than the first, but also nastier. Convinced that they were defending God's cause against evil, the army court-martialled and executed the Royalist commanders after the sieges of Pembroke and Colchester. Such savage punishments following the surrender of enemy officers had no precedents in the earlier conflict for, as Cromwell put it, 'their fault who hath appeared in this summer's business is certainly double theirs who were in the first, because it is the repetition of the same offence against all the witnesses that God has borne'.

Cromwell was also bitterly angry at what he saw as Charles's attempt 'to vassalize us to a foreign nation'. In Scotland there was considerable support for the 'Engagers', but a widespread reluctance actually to fight for Charles until he took the Covenant. Argyll and the leaders of the Kirk strongly opposed Hamilton's campaign and he encountered some difficulty in raising an army. But in the end he led about 10,000 troops into England on 8 July, while another 6,000 arrived shortly afterwards. Northern Royalists, led by Sir Marmaduke Langdale, joined him with a further 4,000 soldiers. By July, however, the provincial uprisings had already been largely suppressed and it was far too late to stem the tide. Ill-disciplined and poorly supplied, Hamilton's army was destroyed by Cromwell with a much smaller force of 9,000 troops in a spec-tacular running battle near Preston on 17–19 August. Once again, Cromwell regarded his victory as 'nothing but the hand of God'. Hamilton himself surren-dered at Uttoxeter a few days later, and when news of his defeat reached Edinburgh the opponents of the Engagement soon regained control. Six thou-sand Covenanters from southwest Scotland mounted the so-called 'Whiggamore Raid' on Edinburgh and staged a coup that returned Argyll and the anti-Engagers (or 'Protesters') to power and excluded the Engagers from public office. In October Cromwell visited Scotland and concluded an agree-ment with the anti-Engagers to oppose all forms of Royalist 'malignancy'. But this alliance, though convenient, was not to last long.

Having secured God's 'mandate' by defeating the King a second time, the army hoped and expected that he would shortly be brought to justice. However, most members of both Houses – and the vast majority of Charles's subjects – were quite unable to contemplate any settlement without the King and hence could see no alternative but to resume talks with him. On 24 August Parliament therefore repealed the Vote of No Addresses, and on 18 September opened negotiations at Newport on the basis of the Newcastle Propositions. Charles agreed in October to parliamentary control of the militia for twenty years. But he categorically refused to abolish bishops: at most he offered to suspend episcopacy for three years, while letting it be known that he was only making this concession in order to facilitate his escape and intended to revoke it at the first opportunity.

The army regarded these talks as a betrayal of all that it had fought for. On 20 November it presented to Parliament a *Remonstrance*, drafted by Ireton, demanding that Charles, 'the capital and grand author of all our troubles', be brought to justice. Only in this way could all the bloodshed throughout the three kingdoms be 'avenged or expiated'. The *Remonstrance* went on to demand that the Long Parliament be dissolved and that in future supreme power be vested in annual or biennial Parliaments, elected on a wide franchise and with the power to elect a new king if they so wished. There could be no compromise with the King, just as there could be no reconciliation of 'light with darkness, of good with evil'. When Parliament simply ignored the *Remonstrance*, the army re-entered London on 2 December; and when, three days later, the Commons voted by 129 to 83 that Charles's answers at Newport constituted satisfactory grounds to continue with further negotiations, the officers decided to act.

On the morning of 6 December, troops led by Colonel Thomas Pride were positioned at the entrance to the Commons. There they arrested 45 MPs and secluded 186 others, while a further 86 withdrew in protest. This was a violation of parliamentary privilege far more drastic than the King's attempt on the five members, or the army's earlier 'purge' in August 1647. Pride's Purge was in fact a last-minute compromise agreed between the army commanders and a group of radical MPs in an effort to head off demands for an immediate dissolution of Parliament and the establishment of absolute military rule.[13] Instead, the purge preserved some semblance of parliamentary government while reducing the Commons to a 'Rump' of about 150 members who were willing to collaborate with the army in bringing the King to trial. Cromwell's failure to return from Yorkshire in time for the purge, and 'with all convenient speed' as he had been ordered, might indicate that he was reluctant to be associated with an unconstitutional use of force against Parliament. Alternatively, it may be that he supported the army's actions, but preferred to wait on political events without taking the lead in so bold a move. At any rate, when he did reach London on the evening of 6 December, the purge was complete and the army had decisively seized the initiative.

5 Regicide

The Treaty of Newport was immediately terminated, and Charles was brought to Windsor on 23 December. There, Cromwell allegedly made a final attempt to agree a compromise through the mediation of the Earl of Denbigh. If the Denbigh mission did take place, it is likely that Cromwell sought a providential sign of whether there was any alternative to bringing Charles to justice. Such an eleventh-hour settlement might at least have saved the King's life and throne, but when Charles remained intransigent Cromwell vowed to 'cut off his head with the Crown upon it'. On 1 January the Commons approved an ordinance setting up a special High Court of Justice to try the King. The Lords refused to accept this ordinance, whereupon the Commons resolved on 4 January that:

> The people are, under God, the original of all just power; . . . that the Commons of England in Parliament assembled, being chosen by and representing the people, have the supreme power in this nation; and . . . that whatsoever is enacted and declared for law by the Commons in Parliament assembled has the force of law . . . although the consent and concurrence of the King and House of Lords be not had thereunto.

In a revolutionary constitutional step that reflected the influence of Leveller ideas, the Commons was thus empowered to govern and make laws unilaterally. Two days later, the Rump used this authority to establish a High Court of Justice comprising MPs, civilians and army officers, and presided over by John Bradshaw, an obscure provincial judge of known republican sympathies. Now nothing could prevent Charles from being brought to account, and on 20 January his trial opened in Westminster Hall.

The outcome was already a foregone conclusion, for the Rump and its allies in the army were determined to execute Charles as a 'man of blood'. The charge against the King was a rather awkward attempt to cover this doctrine of blood-guilt with a veneer of legality. Charles stood accused of harbouring 'a wicked design to erect and uphold in himself an unlimited and tyrannical power to rule according to his will and to overthrow the rights and liberties of the people', and of 'traitorously and maliciously [levying] war against Parliament, and the people therein represented'. He was therefore to be impeached as 'a tyrant, traitor and murderer, and a public and implacable enemy to the Commonwealth of England'.

Charles laughed aloud when he heard the last phrase, and he maintained this contemptuous attitude throughout the eight-day trial. His speech impediment deserted him and, speaking more calmly and effectively than ever before, he refused to plead on the grounds that the Court had no authority to try him. He maintained that it violated both God's law, 'for . . . obedience unto Kings is . . . strictly commanded in both the Old and New Testament', and the common law, which affirmed that 'the King could do no wrong'. Far from expressing the will of the people, as it claimed, the Court had 'never asked . . . the tenth

Plate 11 *The Execution of Charles I in 1649*, by Weesop (detail). The execution of Charles I was very much the act of a determined minority, and to most of the population it seemed like an upset of the natural order. Many were less convinced of Charles's 'blood-guilt' than they were of the army's guilt for shedding the blood of 'God's anointed'. It was widely believed that the monarch's blood possessed supernatural properties, and this scene shows horrified onlookers gathering drops of it on their handkerchiefs.
Source: Courtesy of the Earl of Rosebery/National Galleries of Scotland

man in the kingdom'. It thus threatened 'the true liberty' of the subject, which consisted 'not in the power of government, but in living under ... such a government as may give themselves the best assurance of their lives, and property of their goods'. Charles pledged 'to defend the fundamental laws of [the] kingdom', and argued that if the army might arbitrarily try the King, then no 'free-born subject of England' could 'call life or anything he possesseth his own'. By identifying himself so closely with 'the welfare and liberty of [his] people', and by conducting himself with such serene dignity, Charles won a massive propaganda victory which greatly enhanced the long-term strength of the Royalist cause.

But in the short term his own fate was sealed. Because Charles refused to plead, the High Court was able to deny him the right to speak further, and on 27 January it sentenced him to death as 'a tyrant, traitor, murderer and public enemy to the good people of this nation'. Behind this legal rhetoric lay the need to destroy a 'man of blood', an imperative that would brook no compromise, nor even a fair trial. As Bradshaw told the King just before he passed sentence, 'I will presume that you are so well read in Scripture as to know what God Himself hath said concerning the shedding of man's blood'. Only 59 of the 135 members of the High Court, including Bradshaw, Cromwell[14] and Ireton, signed the King's death warrant two days later. This small group of 'regicides' were implementing the wishes of a tiny minority – but a minority with the armed might to enforce their will.

Because the King's death was intended as an act of public expiation, it was decided that he should be ritually killed, as the regicide Thomas Scot put it, 'in the face of God, and of all men'. In the early afternoon of 30 January, Charles stepped through the second-floor windows of the Banqueting House onto a scaffold specially constructed in Whitehall. It is thus likely that one of his very last sights was of Rubens' magnificent painting of the Apotheosis of James VI and I, perhaps the supreme expression of Charles's vision of absolute monarchy. In his final speech on the scaffold, however, he wisely associated himself with the Constitutional Royalism eloquently advocated in the *Answer to the XIX Propositions*. He defended the 'liberty and freedom' of the people, condemned 'the power of the sword' and swore to 'die a Christian according to the profession of the Church of England'. Then, in a masterly peroration, Charles portrayed himself as 'the martyr of the people'.

These words struck a chord with many of his subjects. The deep reverence which the vast majority still felt for monarchy was hauntingly illustrated by the reaction of the onlookers in Whitehall. To them, the killing of the King seemed like an upset of the natural order. At the moment that the axe fell, one observer recorded, the crowd let out 'such a groan as I never heard before, and I desire I may never hear again'. Some fainted with shock, while others ran beneath the scaffold holding out their handkerchiefs to catch drops of the King's blood, believing it to possess supernatural curative properties. For many, such ancient beliefs about a monarch's blood were still far more potent than any doctrine of 'blood-guilt'. Over the following year, the posthumous (and probably in part ghosted) collection of Charles's speeches and meditations, the *Eikon Basilike*, ran into thirty-six editions, far more than the radical writings of the Levellers.

Even Parliamentarians such as Andrew Marvell found much to admire in the bearing of a King who 'nothing common did, or mean, upon that memorable scene'. Charles thus served the cause of monarchy far more effectively in death than he had in life, and his final commitment to a constitutional monarchy guarding popular liberties and the Church of England would ultimately provide the basis for the Restoration of his son eleven years later. In the meantime, however, as mounted troops rode in to disperse the stunned crowds after the King's execution, there could be no doubt that control of affairs lay with the Rump and the army leaders.

7 The British Republic

	10 May	Adultery Act: death penalty imposed for adultery
	21 May	Execution of Montrose
	26 May	Cromwell leaves Ireland
	June	Charles agrees to sign both Covenants; arrives in Scotland
	17 July	Treason Act
	22 July	Cromwell invades Scotland
	9 August	Blasphemy Act
	3 September	Cromwell defeats Royalist forces at Dunbar
	27 September	Toleration Act: compulsory attendance at parish churches abolished
1651	1 January	Charles's Scottish supporters have him crowned at Scone
	April–May	Publication of Thomas Hobbes's *Leviathan*
	July–August	Charles leads Scottish army into England
	3 September	Battle of Worcester: Cromwell defeats Charles, who escapes to the Continent (15 October)
	9 October	Navigation Act: introduces measures aimed against Dutch carrying trade
	28 October	Rump's declaration for incorporation of Scotland into a single Commonwealth with England
1652	January	Dalkeith Convention: cosmetic opportunity for Scottish representatives to consent to incorporative union
	24 February	Act of Pardon and Oblivion
	February	Publication of Gerrard Winstanley's *The Law of Freedom*
	19 May	First Anglo-Dutch War begins
	12 August	Act for the Settlement of Ireland
1653	January	Beginning of Glencairn's Rising; escalates from the spring onwards
	20 April	Cromwell dissolves the Rump Parliament
	4 July	Nominated Assembly convenes

	31 July	Battle of the Texel: Monck defeats Dutch
	12 December	Nominated Assembly surrenders power back to Cromwell
	15 December	Council of Army Officers adopts Instrument of Government
	16 December	Cromwell installed as Lord Protector
1654	20 March	'Triers' established: a national body to vet all new clergy
	5 April	Treaty of Westminster ends Anglo-Dutch War
	12 April	Ordinance for union of England and Scotland; ordinance of Pardon and Grace (proclaimed in Edinburgh on 5 May): Scottish landlords except those implicated in Glencairn's Rising permitted to retain estates
	27 June	Ordinances for elections in Scotland and Ireland
	June	Monck begins to quell Glencairn's Rising (complete by May 1655)
	28 August	'Ejectors' established: county commissioners to expel inadequate ministers and schoolmasters
	3 September– 22 January 1655	First Protectorate Parliament
	November– December	George Cony, a London merchant, fined and then imprisoned for refusing to pay customs duties that had not been approved by Parliament
	13 December	Commons votes to imprison John Biddle, a Socinian
	December	Western Design launched
1655	12–16 March	Penruddock's Rising: abortive Royalist uprising in Wiltshire
	April–May	Failure of Western Design: unsuccessful attempt to capture Hispaniola, although Jamaica is taken
	7 June	Resignation of Lord Chief Justice Rolle

	9 July	Henry Cromwell arrives as Major-General of the army in Ireland, and soon emerges as driving force in Irish Council
	9 August	Rule of Major-Generals established in England and Wales
	22 August	First instructions issued to the Major-Generals
	21 September	Decimation Tax on former Royalists established
	11 October	Further instructions issued to Major-Generals
	24 October	Anglo-French treaty
1656	17 September–26 June 1657	First session of second Protectorate Parliament
	October	James Nayler, a Quaker, re-enacts Christ's entry into Jerusalem
	November	Publication of James Harrington's *Oceana*
	5–17 December	Parliament debates Nayler's case: it convicts him of 'horrid blasphemy' and sentences him to savage mutilation
1657	28 January	Cromwell abandons the Major-Generals experiment and the Decimation Tax
	23 February	*The Humble Petition and Advice*: Cromwell offered the kingship
	13 March	Anglo-French treaty: offensive alliance against Spain
	8 May	Cromwell formally declines the kingship
	9–16 May	English troops begin campaign in Flanders
	12 May	Publication of Sir Henry Vane's *A Healing Question Propounded*: critical of Cromwell
	25 May	Cromwell accepts revised version of *The Humble Petition and Advice*: he is to remain Lord Protector
	26 June	Cromwell's second installation as Lord Protector
	17 November	Henry Cromwell appointed Lord Deputy of Ireland

1658	20 January– 4 February	Second session of second Protectorate Parliament
	28 March	Anglo-French alliance renewed
	14 June	Battle of the Dunes: Anglo-French force defeats Spanish; English troops occupy Dunkirk
	3 September	Death of Oliver Cromwell; Richard Cromwell becomes Lord Protector
1659	27 January– 22 April	Third Protectorate Parliament
	7 May	Rump reinstated
	19 May	Rump elects new Council of State
	24 May	Rump demands Richard Cromwell's resignation
	July–August	Booth's Rising: pro-Royalist uprising in Cheshire and Lancashire; put down by Lambert
	13 October	Army dissolves Rump
	20 October	Monck sends declaration from Scotland demanding return of the Rump
	25 October	Council of State ceases to sit
	26 October	Committee of Safety established
	Early December	Monck begins to march south
	17 December	Committee of Safety disperses: over a week with no government at all
	26 December	Three regiments reinstate Rump
1660	1 January	Monck's army enters England
	3 February	Monck's army arrives in London
	21 February	Monck secures readmission of those members 'purged' in December 1648
	16 March	Long Parliament calls 'free elections' and dissolves itself
	4 April	Charles II issues the Declaration of Breda expressing willingness to settle all disputed issues with Parliament
	25 April– 13 September	First session of Convention Parliament

8 May	Convention Parliament declares Charles II to have been King since 30 January 1649
25 May	Charles II lands at Dover
29 May	Charles II enters London

1 The Establishment of the Republic

Just as the Regicide had been the act of a determined minority, so the Interregnum regimes were built upon a narrow base of support. They never succeeded in winning more than the grudging co-operation of most people in England, Wales, Scotland and Ireland, nor in establishing the legitimacy of republican government. This meant that in the last resort they always depended upon the army for their survival. The army, however, had its own radical objectives and constantly exerted pressure on the civilian politicians to fulfil the revolution, especially by introducing religious toleration and promoting a godly commonwealth. While most people yearned for a return to the 'known ways', a minority saw the Regicide as an opportunity to cut loose from the past and build a new world. But because the army's aims were not in tune with the attitudes of most civilian politicians – let alone of the population at large – they further destabilized the republic. The army and the politicians thus found that they could neither work together, nor survive without each other. In this paradox lies the key to understanding the British Republic's failure to generate lasting stability.

Cromwell once remarked of Church government that he knew what he would not have, but not what he would have; and this is true in a broader sense of the revolution in general. Most of those who had demanded the execution of Charles I were motivated more by a wish to destroy a monarch tainted with 'blood-guilt' than by any preference for republican government as such. This helps to explain the curiously hesitant way in which the republic was formally created. On 7 February the Commons voted to abolish the monarchy in England and Ireland as 'unnecessary, burdensome and dangerous to the liberty, safety and public interest of the people'. The principal concern seems to have been a pragmatic one: to pre-empt any bid by Charles's son to regain the throne. Significantly, Ireland was simply assumed to be a direct dependency of England, whereas Scotland was still treated as a separate kingdom.[1] The previous day, the Commons had voted to abolish the House of Lords as 'useless and dangerous': 'useless' because attendances had by now dwindled to single figures; and 'dangerous' because the Upper House had attempted to impede the King's trial and could not be expected to co-operate in the trials of other leading Royalists.[2] But it was not until 17 and 19 March respectively that acts were passed abolishing the monarchy and the Lords, and only on 19 May was England declared to be 'a Commonwealth and Free State' in which 'supreme authority' henceforth lay with 'the representatives of the people in Parliament ... and that without any King or House of Lords'. In January 1650, acting more from fear than ideological enthusiasm, the Rump required all adult males to take an Engagement declaring that they would be 'true and faithful to the Commonwealth of England, as it is now established'. Finally, in July 1650, a new Treason Act made it 'high treason' to deny the 'supreme authority' of the Commons, and the transfer of sovereignty to the Rump Parliament was complete.

The Rump's caution was profoundly irksome to a zealous minority who saw the Regicide as a unique chance to break decisively with the existing order. As the established landmarks – Crown, Church, House of Lords – were swept away, there was an upsurge of sectarian activity that deeply unnerved property-owners. Among the earlier groups to emerge were the Diggers, or 'True Levellers', led by a failed London shopkeeper, Gerrard Winstanley. During the winter of 1648–9, Winstanley became convinced that individual freedom and social equality could only be achieved by means of the common ownership of property. He denounced private property as a legacy of the 'Norman Yoke', and in the wake of the Regicide he urged his followers to occupy waste or common land. The first Digger community was established by a group of poor labourers and cottagers on St George's Hill, Surrey, in April 1649. For four months they cultivated the wasteland and cut down timber until in August local landowners drove them away. By the spring of 1650, the Diggers had established colonies in Northamptonshire, Kent, Buckinghamshire, Hertfordshire, Middlesex, Bedfordshire, Leicestershire and Gloucestershire; but they never numbered more than a few hundred and their experiment in practical communism collapsed soon afterwards. Winstanley continued to write pamphlets, most notably *The Law of Freedom* (1652), a draft communist constitution for the Commonwealth; but his hopes for transforming society had been dashed and he died in obscurity in 1676.

Other groups perceived the Regicide as a prelude to the Second Coming of Christ. The most precisely formulated of these millenarian ideas were those of the Fifth Monarchists who, inspired by the Old Testament prophecies in the books of Revelation and Daniel, predicted that the four great empires of Babylon, Persia, Greece and Rome would shortly be followed by the Fifth Monarchy in which King Christ would rule on earth with his saints for one thousand years culminating in the Day of Judgement. The Fifth Monarchists strongly advocated reform of the legal system in order to bring it into accordance with the law of Moses. They never numbered more than ten thousand at the absolute outside, and drew their support mainly from labourers, servants, apprentices and journeymen in the urban areas of southern England, especially London. Their humble social background was stigmatized by many contemporaries, one of whom branded the Fifth Monarchists 'the worst of men, the scum and very froth of baseness'.

Another millenarian sect that emerged in the early 1650s took its name from Lodovick Muggleton, who claimed to be one of the two witnesses foretold in the Book of Revelation whose arrival would herald the end of the world. The Muggletonians were concentrated in London and the south, and much of their support was drawn from artisans and shopkeepers. There were probably several hundred of them, although the loose-knit nature of their organization makes it difficult to gauge numbers at all precisely. Like the Fifth Monarchists, they continued to lead an underground existence after the Restoration, and the last Muggletonian is thought to have died in 1979.

Far more numerous were the Quakers, another religious sect whose origins lay in the aftermath of the Regicide. They rejected the idea of a formal ministry and stressed instead the concept of the 'inner light', a manifestation of Christ's spirit working within people that would bring salvation to those who accepted its guidance. The conviction that this 'inner light' existed within all people who recognized it made them deeply hostile to every form of social hierarchy and civil authority. The pacifism so characteristic of modern Quakers only developed after 1660, and during the Interregnum they were known principally for their refusal to swear oaths, to pay tithes, and above all to take off their hats in the presence of anyone. They were widely seen as socially subversive, and by the later 1650s – when there were perhaps as many as 40,000 Quakers – they were widely feared among the gentry.

The concept of the 'inner light' was taken to its logical extreme by the Ranters. Recent research has demonstrated that the Ranters were never an organized group with a coherent ideology, and that the received view of them derives largely from the hostile writings of contemporary clergy and landowners. There was no single body of ideas advocated by those lumped together as Ranters – men such as Lawrence Clarkson, George Foster or Abiezer Coppe.[3] Yet, despite their different priorities and emphases, the direction of their writings clearly pointed towards antinomianism, the conviction that true believers could not sin and might therefore ignore all moral restraints. As Clarkson asserted, 'sin hath its conception only in the imagination'. Such views fostered lurid stories about the permissiveness and sexual promiscuity of the Ranters, prompting the Rump to pass acts against adultery (May 1650) and blasphemy (August 1650). The Ranters were undoubtedly among the most radical movements to surface at the end of the 1640s, and they appealed especially to the urban and rural poor; but as a result pamphlets about them – such as *The Ranters Religion, Or a Faithful and Infallible Narrative of their Diabolical Opinions* (1650) – often tell us more about the fears of property-owners in the early months of the Republic than about the Ranters themselves. Those fears eventually led to the arrest and imprisonment of most of the Ranter leaders, and by 1651 the movement had effectively been stamped out.

But the limits of the regime's willingness to tolerate sectarian radicalism had already become plain long before that, as the Levellers had discovered. At the time of the King's trial they had hoped that the *Agreement of the People* would form the basis of England's next constitution. They were horrified when the Council of Officers spent nearly two months discussing the document at the Whitehall Debates (December 1648–January 1649), only to set it aside. When the Rump failed to dissolve itself after the Regicide, and instead entrusted executive powers to a Council of State numbering forty, including Cromwell, the Leveller leaders felt utterly betrayed. In February and March, Lilburne published a two-part pamphlet entitled *England's New Chains Discovered* denouncing 'this new kind of liberty' imposed by the Rump. Another pamphlet, Overton's *The Hunting of the Foxes*, accused Cromwell of ruthless ambition and a hypocritical readiness to 'weep, howl and repent even while he doth smite you under the first rib'. More dangerously, Lilburne and Overton attempted to stir up the rank and file of the army to stage a coup against the grandees. The spring of 1649 saw a series of Leveller-inspired mutinies that were firmly suppressed by Cromwell and Fairfax. In May, mutineers from Salisbury were pursued to Burford, where they were easily defeated, and three of the ringleaders were then shot. Lilburne was subsequently tried for high treason and acquitted, but the crushing of the Burford mutiny marked the end of Leveller influence within the army. Although civilian Levellers continued to agitate in London, the movement ceased to be a serious political force. The troops were further pacified by the Rump's decision to issue debentures entitling them to purchase former Crown lands. As its material grievances diminished, the army became more docile. With his command over his men now unassailable, Cromwell turned to confront the regime's enemies in the rest of the archipelago.

2 The Conquest of Ireland and Scotland

The most immediate danger to the fledgling republic came from Ireland. In January 1649 Ormond had finally concluded a treaty with the Confederates whereby an Irish expeditionary force of 18,000 men would be despatched to England. This new alliance between Catholics and Protestants disgusted Rinuccini, who returned to Rome shortly afterwards, but it made Ireland a formidable springboard from which Charles II could launch an invasion. Cromwell shared the Rump's view that the conquest of Ireland was now the most urgent priority. As he told the Council of State in March 1649, 'I had rather be over-run with a Cavalierish interest than a Scotch interest; I had rather be over-run with a Scotch interest than an Irish interest; and I think of all, this is the most dangerous ... For all the world knows their barbarism'. The first wave of English reinforcements arrived in May and June, and on 2 August Colonel Michael Jones defeated Ormond's main army at Rathmines. Two weeks later, filled with a burning desire to smash the Royalist threat and to avenge the massacres of Protestants during the rebellion of 1641, Cromwell landed near Dublin at the head of 30,000 highly trained soldiers.

The notorious campaign that followed led to the complete military subjugation of Ireland. Cromwell clearly saw the Catholic Irish as tainted by a collective, racial 'blood-guilt' for the 1641 massacres. This belief led him to regard the infamous massacres of the civilian populations of Drogheda (11 September 1649) and Wexford (11 October 1649) – none of whom had been involved in the rebellion – as 'a righteous judgement of God upon these barbarous wretches, who have imbrued their hands in so much innocent blood'. In all, about 4,600 people were put to death in the two towns. Although Cromwell had summoned both garrisons, and was thus technically acting within the rules of seventeenth-century European warfare, these atrocities had no parallel on the mainland and the memory of them has remained seared into Irish national consciousness ever since. Cromwell's Protestant contemporaries approved of his behaviour, and were delighted as he advanced from victory to victory through southern and western Ireland. Despite brief setbacks at Waterford in late 1649 and Clonmel the following spring, by May 1650 Irish resistance had largely disintegrated, and although some pockets held out until 1652 Cromwell was able to return to England.

By the summer of 1650, the Scots had replaced the Irish as the principal threat to the Commonwealth. Many Scots had been appalled by England's unilateral execution of their king: when news of the Regicide reached Edinburgh on 5 February 1649, Charles II was immediately proclaimed King of Great Britain and Ireland. The vote two days later to abolish monarchy simply ignored Scotland: the Rump reasoned that now the Union of the Crowns had been severed, Scotland could be treated as a separate kingdom able to determine its own affairs. By contrast, the Scots believed that their future continued to lie not in secession but as part of a British State. By proclaiming Charles King of Great Britain, they posed a direct threat to the English Commonwealth that Charles was only too happy to exploit. An initial attempt by Montrose to rally Scottish Royalists in April 1650 went disastrously wrong and led to his execution in Edinburgh the following month. But in June, recognizing that his best hope of regaining his throne now lay in Scotland rather than in Ireland, Charles agreed to sign both Covenants and landed at the mouth of the Spey.

On 20 June the English Council of State decided to launch a pre-emptive strike against Scotland before Charles had time to complete his military preparations, and on 22 July Cromwell crossed the border with 16,000 men. He viewed the Scots very differently from the Irish, yet his perception of each was directly determined by his religious attitudes. The Scots he regarded as fellow Protestants who had been duped into forging a misguided political alliance with Charles: they were 'a people fearing [God's] name, though deceived'. He wrote to the Lieutenant-General of the Scottish army, David Leslie, on 14 August questioning whether 'the satisfaction of God's people in both kingdoms' was really advanced when 'a King should be taken in by you, to be imposed upon us'. To the General Assembly of the Scottish Kirk, he declared: 'I beseech you in the bowels of Christ, think it possible you may be mistaken'. On 3 September, although outnumbered by nearly two to one, Cromwell routed Leslie's forces at Dunbar. Four thousand Scots were killed and a further ten thousand taken prisoner. So complete a victory could only, Cromwell believed, be 'the great hand of the Lord', and it is alleged that after the battle he laughed uncontrollably with the release of tension and the absolute certainty that 'the Lord hath done this'.

Dunbar enabled Cromwell to occupy Edinburgh and the southeast of Scotland but, with his supply lines already overstretched, he dared advance no further into Scotland than Perth. Meanwhile, the Scots were further weakened by internal divisions. An influential group of Presbyterian ministers, together with the more hardline Covenanters of southwest Scotland, drew up a Remonstrance claiming that Dunbar was a clear sign of God's displeasure at the Scots' alliance with Charles. 'Our late proceedings with the King', declared the Remonstrants, had involved 'the backsliding breech of covenant and engagements unto the Lord'. However, a majority remained committed to supporting Charles: they issued a Resolution denouncing the Remonstrants, and on 1 January 1651 arranged for Charles to be crowned at Scone. During the ceremony, Charles took the Covenants as King of Great Britain and Ireland and swore to implement acts 'enjoining the same in my other dominions'. When Cromwell suffered a prolonged illness during the first half of 1651,

Charles determined to seize the opportunity and led a force of about 13,000 troops into England.

South of the border, he soon found that the lack of enthusiastic support for the Rump did not bring him vast numbers of recruits. Only about 2,000 English joined him, with the result that he was heavily outnumbered when Cromwell intercepted him at Worcester on 3 September. There, exactly one year after Dunbar, Cromwell scored a decisive victory that he later described as God's 'crowning mercy'. Heavily disguised, Charles made a dramatic escape to the south coast and then crossed to France. Scottish resistance quickly crumbled, and although some strongholds did not surrender until the following year, by September 1651 Cromwell was as firmly in control of Scotland as of Ireland. It now remained to settle and govern these two kingdoms.

Just as Cromwell viewed the Irish and the Scots very differently, so there was a dramatic contrast between the settlements implemented in each nation. In Ireland, Cromwell was strongly influenced by the Spenserian vision of a sweeping conquest favoured by his Independent allies and most recently expounded in Sir John Temple's *The Irish Rebellion* (1646). Cromwell believed that the conquest rendered Ireland 'as a clean paper' on which the English could write as they pleased. In a Declaration of January 1650, he explained that he came 'to break the power of a company of lawless rebels' and 'to hold forth and maintain the lustre and glory of English liberty in a nation where we have an undoubted right to do it; wherein the people of Ireland ... may equally participate in all benefits, to use liberty and fortune equally with Englishmen, if they keep out of arms'. Like Spenser, he believed that conquest opened the way for an English civilizing mission; and the combination of this arrogant self-righteousness with a thirst for vengeance and an urgent need to pay off those troops who had fought in Ireland produced truly revolutionary consequences.

In August 1652 the Rump passed an Act for the Settlement of Ireland that provided for nothing less than the dispossession of the native Irish elite. Old English and Gaelic Irish landowners alike were to be punished 'according to [their] respective demerits'. Irish and Catholic identities were thus conflated and taken to be synonymous. Only those who could demonstrate 'their constant good affection to the interest of the Commonwealth of England' since October 1641 escaped punishment altogether. Of the others, 109 named individuals and five categories of landowners were exempted from any pardon. A further five categories of those deemed less guilty would forfeit their estates and receive instead lands worth one-third or in some cases two-thirds of their value in Connacht, the least fertile part of Ireland. In the event, only a few hundred were executed rather than the hundred thousand or so who might have been liable under the act. But, far more significantly, the act led to the biggest transfer of land in Irish history until the Land Acts of the later nineteenth century. The proportion of Irish land owned by Catholics fell from 59 per cent in 1641 to 22 per cent in 1660. Vast areas were handed over to more than 600 Protestant 'Adventurers' – mostly absentee landowners who had loaned money to finance earlier Parliamentarian campaigns in Ireland – and to about 12,000 English soldiers. This expropriation of the political and economic elite of pre-civil war Ireland, and the imposition of a new landowning class, laid the foundations for the Protestant ascendancy of the eighteenth and nineteenth centuries.

From August 1652 Ireland was governed by a Council of parliamentary commissioners rather than a Lord Lieutenant. For the next three years this Council was dominated by English officers, many of whom were Independents. They were sympathetic to the various religious sects that began to thrive in Dublin and in the English garrison towns, but they were deeply hostile towards both the Scottish Presbyterians of Ulster and the New English (who were henceforth referred to as the 'Old Protestants'). Led on by these Independents, the Council savagely implemented the policy of transplantation. By the mid-1650s, however, the hardliners had become an embarrassment to Cromwell, who realized that their behaviour was alienating many people unnecessarily. In the summer of 1655, his younger son Henry arrived as Major-General of the army in Ireland: he rapidly became the driving force in the Irish Council and adopted more moderate policies. He achieved a *rapprochement* with the Presbyterians and Old Protestants, and even lessened the repression of Catholic worship. As a result, the population became less restive, and this permitted the original English army of 30,000 troops to be reduced to around 9,000 by 1657.

Yet the more positive aspects of Henry Cromwell's programme – especially in the fields of religion and education – were a dismal failure. The Church of Ireland had been dismantled at the end of the 1640s. Subsequent attempts to recreate an effective Protestant ministry that might woo the Irish away from Catholicism were hampered by shortage of funds and by the continuing feuds between Presbyterians, Independents and sectaries. As the influence of the Independents waned, Henry Cromwell concluded an agreement with Presbyterian ministers whereby they could receive government salaries, yet there were only 250 such ministers by 1658. The vast majority of the population remained resolutely loyal to Catholicism, all the more so because the old faith was now even more closely bound up with their national identity and their resentment of English rule. Parallel initiatives in education were similarly unsuccessful. Contrary to English rhetoric about using education to convert Irish children, only thirty-five State-supported schoolmasters were active in 1659, and most of these were working in English garrisons. By the end of the 1650s, as economic and agricultural prosperity gradually began to return to Ireland after nearly two decades of devastation, the die had been irrevocably cast: a Protestant, English elite of landowners ruled over a dispossessed native population firmly wedded to Catholicism. Such was the Cromwellian 'achievement' in Ireland.

It was otherwise in Scotland. Whereas the Rump assumed that Ireland was a dependency belonging to the English Commonwealth, Scotland was a free nation. The Great Seal of the Commonwealth, made in 1651, provides a graphic illustration of this distinction. Cromwell had originally conquered Scotland for strategic reasons – to defeat the Royalist threat – and there were no ready-made plans for the settlement to follow. Eventually, in October 1651, the Rump drew up a declaration stating that 'for the advancement of the glory of God, and the good and welfare of the whole island', Scotland was to be

Plate 12 The Great Seal of England, 1651. One side of the seal depicts the rulers of the Commonwealth, the Rump Parliament. The other shows graphically that whereas Ireland had been subjugated and was regarded as a dependent part of England, Scotland – although conquered in 1651 – was still seen as a separate kingdom. Not until 1652–4 was an incorporative union with Scotland formally enacted.
Source: The Fotomas Index

'incorporated into, and become one Commonwealth with this of England'. The administration of Scotland was entrusted to eight parliamentary commissioners. The estates of those in arms against the English Parliament since 1648 were to be confiscated, but all others who agreed to co-operate and place themselves under Parliament's protection would enjoy the same liberties as the people of England. Certain heritable jurisdictions were to be abolished, so freeing the Scots from 'their former slaveries, vassalage and oppressions', and enabling them to live 'like a free people'. Religious toleration was to be established throughout Scotland. As a separate nation, the Scots were given a nominal right to consent to this incorporative union, and in January 1652 representatives of the boroughs and shires were summoned to Dalkeith for this purpose. There they were presented with a *fait accompli*, and their ostensible consent was purely cosmetic. However, several representatives refused to accept the union, mainly because they felt that it would undermine the Scottish Kirk. The burghers of Lanark, for example, objected to the 'general and doubtsome terms of a vast toleration' that would open 'a door to many gross errors'. The English simply ignored such 'scruples' and went ahead with the union. The Scots accepted what they could not prevent, but remained deeply suspicious: as the minister Robert Blair put it, 'the embodying of Scotland with England . . . will be as when the poor bird is embodied in the hawk that hath eaten it up'.

Because of Cromwell's difficulties with successive Parliaments,[4] it was not until 12 April 1654 that the union was confirmed by an ordinance. This formally stated that, with its own 'assent', Scotland had been 'incorporated into, constituted, established, declared and confirmed one Commonwealth with England'. The Scots were absolved of any allegiance to Charles II or his offspring, the Stuarts were disabled from ever wearing the Scottish crown, and the office of king of Scotland was abolished. Following the enactment of the Instrument of Government the previous December, Cromwell would be Lord Protector of the 'Commonwealth of England, Scotland and Ireland', and would govern through one Parliament to which Scotland and Ireland would each send thirty members (out of 460). A single British Parliament was thus created in which Scottish and English representatives sat together.[5] In another ironic echo of James VI and I's scheme for a union of the kingdoms, there was to be a single coat of arms for the Commonwealth incorporating the arms of Scotland. Free trade was established between England and Scotland. Finally, and very importantly, the ordinance abolished all feudal dues, heritable tenures and jurisdictions, and hereditary sheriffdoms. Instead, all tenants were granted security of tenure on low rents, while justice would be dispensed by itinerant English judges, Justices of the Peace, and local courts baron manned by liberated peasants.

Although Scotland never saw the mass expropriation of landowners that occurred in Ireland, these provisions nevertheless heralded a systematic erosion of the wealth and status of the Scottish landed elite. This was a calculated policy: as Colonel John Jones had written the previous year, 'it is in the interest of the Commonwealth of England to break the interest of the great men of Scotland, and to settle the interest of the common people upon a different foot from the interests of their lords and masters'. Many Scottish landlords had already had their estates confiscated because of their involvement in waging war against England. Believing that they had nothing to lose, early in 1653 Glencairn and several other nobles launched a rebellion in the Highlands that was only finally crushed in May 1655 by General George Monck, who had been appointed commander-in-chief of the army in Scotland the year before. Glencairn's rising prompted Cromwell to issue an ordinance of Pardon and Grace (12 April 1654) permitting all but twenty-four named landlords – and all those implicated in the rising – to retain their estates. But this softening of the penalties for earlier war-guilt could not conceal the dramatic loss of legal, social and economic power suffered by the nobility of Cromwellian Scotland.

Later, in January 1658, Cromwell singled out these reforms as one of the Protectorate's most notable achievements. He praised the 'plentiful encouragement to the meaner sort' that ensured that their lords no longer 'made them work for their living no better than the peasants of France', and he insisted that the lives of the middle sort were 'comfortable, if not better than they were before'. Although there is little evidence of Scottish rejoicing at the abolition of feudal oppression, the English judges were more likely to be impartial than their predecessors, and did at least offer regular and efficient justice. Yet the majority of Scots were far more conscious of their poverty than of any new liberties. Robert Baillie complained that 'the English have all the money', and even

Cromwell was forced to acknowledge that Scotland was 'a very ruined nation'. With the suppression of Glencairn's rising, the army in Scotland could safely be reduced from 18,000 in 1654 to 10,500 in 1657, but even that imposed a formidable financial load. By 1659, many Scots were paying up to a quarter of their incomes in taxation, yet a subsidy of £164,000 – 53 per cent of public expenditure – was still required from England to make ends meet. Although a few signs of returning prosperity were discernible, especially in manufactures such as glass and stockings, there was no prospect of Scotland becoming financially self-sufficient as long as the army remained in being.

The government met with similar frustration in its religious policies. Throughout the 1650s the Scottish Kirk remained deeply divided between the minority of Remonstrants (or 'Protesters') and the majority of Resolutioners who had supported the King. Both groups accepted the Cromwellian regime, but neither ever actively supported it. They were deeply suspicious of the toleration accorded to separatist congregations, and yet the dynamic sectarian preachers may have spurred many of the Presbyterian ministers into more vigorous activity. Certainly, unlike in Ireland, a settled parish ministry existed throughout most of Scotland, and one Presbyterian could later write that 'there were more souls converted to Christ in that short period of time than in any season since the Reformation'. But, when a delegation of Scottish ministers visited Cromwell in London in 1657, he still found them entirely resistant to his ideas about toleration, and even contemplated 'an extraordinary remedy' to change their minds.

That response was typical of a regime that always remained dependent upon force and never achieved the enthusiastic support for which Cromwell yearned. In the end, the settlements in Ireland and Scotland were built upon conquest and ultimately rested on the threat of renewed coercion. However, it was not only among the Irish and the Scots that the impact of those conquests was felt. For Cromwell's remarkable victories – completing a run of success unbroken since 1642 – crucially shaped his sense of his own mission as well as his belief that the army was God's instrument; and those convictions were to have a profound influence on developments in England too.

3 The Rule of the Rump

On 4 September 1651, the day after his victory at Worcester, Cromwell wrote to the Speaker of the Rump, William Lenthall, expressing the hope that this 'crowning mercy' would 'provoke' Parliament to 'do the will of Him who hath done His will for it'. He trusted that 'the fatness of these continued mercies' would 'not occasion pride and wantonness, as formerly the like hath done to a chosen nation'. Yet, over the next eighteen months, Cromwell and the other army leaders became deeply disillusioned with the Rump's failure to live up to these high expectations. In the end, convinced that it had betrayed its 'trust' to God and to the godly, he saw no alternative but to dissolve the Rump and create a 'new representative'.

Cromwell's euphoria in the wake of Worcester was in marked contrast to the mood at Westminster. There the Rump lurched from crisis to crisis, reacting to events as they occurred, without the unity or vision or zeal to impose its own will. In the Republic's early years, as Cromwell was conquering Ireland and Scotland, the Rump's most urgent concerns were to quell the radical sects and to establish the legitimacy of its own rule. When, in January 1650, it imposed an Engagement requiring all adult males to pledge their loyalty to the Republic, there was widespread objection – led by Presbyterians such as William Prynne – to what was seen as an attempt to search men's consciences. Against this, a number of '*de facto* theorists', including John Dury, Anthony Ascham and Marchamont Nedham, asserted that the subjects were obliged to obey whatever sovereign wielded *de facto* powers and was able to offer them protection. It is within this ideological context that Thomas Hobbes's masterpiece *Leviathan* (1651) should be located. Building upon a model of man's political nature, Hobbes advanced a theory of absolute sovereignty in which authority was legitimated solely by its ability to afford protection to those living under it. He later boasted that *Leviathan* had 'framed the minds of a thousand gentlemen to a conscientious obedience to present government, which otherwise would have wavered in that point'. As the immediate threat to the Republic receded after 1651, Nedham, together with a group of other intellectuals led by John Milton, Algernon Sidney and Sir Henry Vane the younger, evolved a theory of classical republicanism. Drawing on Plato, Aristotle and Livy as well as Renaissance theorists such as Machiavelli, they developed a rationale for republican self-government based upon merit rather than birth. They were strongly anti-clerical and defended the role of 'reason' in government. They spurned monarchy and the ancient constitution and embraced instead an ideal of rule by an enlightened oligarchy whose closest contemporary parallels were the Regent Governors of the Dutch Republic and the Doge and Senate of Venice. By 1653, Milton was even speaking of the possibility of creating a 'new Rome in the West'. A few years later, classical republicanism was given a less elitist slant by James Harrington, whose *Oceana* (1656) offered an elaborate socio-economic explanation of the Civil Wars and argued that because the basis of political power lay in ownership of property, power should be vested in the people.[6]

To the army leaders, driven by religious zeal, these republican intellectuals only served to distract the Rump from its essential purpose of constructing a godly commonwealth. The officers were infuriated by the Rump's dwindling energy and by its failure to give priority to the advancement of God's 'cause'. Although 210 members sat at some stage between January 1649 and April 1653, only between sixty and seventy of these were at all active, and the average attendance was between fifty and sixty. The number of acts passed by the Rump steadily declined: 125 in 1649, seventy-eight in 1650, fifty-four in 1651, forty-four in 1652, and ten between 1 January and 20 April 1653. The number of committees appointed to draft new legislation registered an even steeper drop: 152 in 1649, ninety-eight in 1650, sixty-one in 1651, fifty-one in 1652, and twelve between 1 January and 20 April 1653.

There were a handful of radical reforms. In 1650 the Rump appointed a commission for the propagation of the gospel in Wales. That nation had been predominantly Royalist throughout the 1640s, and the Rump feared that an equation existed between political disloyalty and ungodliness. The commission had some success in improving education, and also in providing Welsh Bibles, augmenting poor livings and appointing Welsh-speaking preachers. It undoubtedly contributed to the long-term strength of nonconformity in Wales. The Rump's only major legislative concession to religious radicalism was the Toleration Act of September 1650, which abolished compulsory attendance at parish churches. Otherwise, it was too divided to agree on positive religious reforms and too conservative to abandon the parish system or the duty to pay tithes. In economic policy the only significant innovation was the Navigation Act of October 1651, which stipulated that goods imported into England should henceforth be carried either in English ships or in ships belonging to the country of origin. Clearly aimed at the Dutch Republic, this act was motivated less by economic rivalry than by a perception that the increasingly influential Orangists were hostile to radical Protestantism and harboured pro-Stuart sympathies. Such attitudes apparently branded them as natural enemies of the British Republic, and these tensions erupted in the first Anglo-Dutch War (1652–4). The Rump also introduced some reforms of the legal system, including the use of English in all common law proceedings, and new probate arrangements for the proving of wills. But the caucus of lawyers in the Rump strongly resisted the more far-reaching reorganization proposed in 1652 by a special Commission on Law Reform chaired by Sir Matthew Hale. The most common pattern in the Rump's deliberations was for urgent matters – usually relating to taxation, local government or the army – to take precedence over more fundamental issues. The nature of the Rump's legislative record makes this point very clearly. Of a representative sample of 131 acts passed in January–May 1649, January–May 1651 and 1 January–20 April 1653, seventy-four dealt with matters of security, finance or taxation, forty-three with local government or the army, and fourteen with social problems. Only five addressed religious issues, three law reform and six economic and social reform. By 1652–3, the Rump had completely lost any desire to pursue creative reforms.

To Cromwell and the army leaders this was exasperating. The Council of Officers had hoped that the Rump would 'proceed vigorously in reforming what was amiss in government, and to the settling of the Commonwealth upon a foundation of justice and righteousness'. Instead, Cromwell and his fellow-officers concluded that the Rump 'would never answer those ends which God, his people, and the whole nation expected from them'. To make matters worse, the Rump dragged its feet about setting a date for its own dissolution and holding elections for a new Parliament. In November 1651, Cromwell had finally secured its agreement to a dissolution not later than 3 November 1654. Between October 1652 and April 1653, he convened a series of meetings between leading MPs and army officers to discuss a bill for a 'new representative'. Eventually, on 19 April 1653, a compromise was agreed whereby the Rump would dissolve itself and transfer power to a temporary council of MPs and army officers who would oversee fresh elections. Candidates would be carefully vetted to ensure that they were 'pious and faithful to the interest of the Commonwealth'. However, the following day, Cromwell learnt that the Rump was planning instead to hold immediate elections, without any screening mechanism to exclude 'disaffected' candidates. He at once led a company of troops to Westminster and, after condemning the Rumpers as 'whoremasters' and 'drunkards', expelled them with the words: 'you have sat here too long for the good you do'. It is unlikely, as Cromwell later claimed, that the Rumpers were intending to 'perpetuate themselves'. Rather, his main fear was probably that free elections would return a Parliament full of 'Presbyters' and 'Neuters' who were even less sympathetic to the army's programme than the Rump. For this reason, he believed that 'the interest of all honest men and of this glorious cause had been in danger to be laid in the dust', and that 'necessity and providence' required him to dissolve an assembly that had ceased to be a 'Parliament for God's people'. As he put it a few months later, 'the dissolution of this Parliament was as necessary to be done as the preservation of this cause'. With the destruction of the last, truncated remnant of the Long Parliament, supreme power passed to Cromwell and the Council of Officers.

4 From Commonwealth to Protectorate

Cromwell has often been accused, both by his contemporaries and by historians, of being driven by ambition and self-interest. According to the Presbyterian minister Richard Baxter, for example, he never acted 'without an eye to himself'. Yet such critics could never explain Cromwell's behaviour following the dissolution of the Rump. For no sooner had he acquired 'boundless' powers than he sought to surrender them to a new assembly. Throughout his life, he remained committed to the idea that *a* Parliament was an essential part of any constitution. He insisted that he did not covet power but rather saw himself as 'a good constable set to keep the peace of the parish'. In the summer of 1653, he believed it would have been utterly irresponsible to call free elections, for they would almost certainly have produced a majority unsympathetic to the 'cause'. Instead, having dissolved the Rump because it had betrayed the godly, he decided to implement Major-General Thomas Harrison's scheme for a Parliament consisting exclusively of the godly.

The Nominated Assembly[7] was based on the ancient Jewish Sanhedrin or assembly of 'saints', and to the Fifth Monarchist Harrison it promised to usher in the Second Coming and the thousand-year 'rule of the saints'. The army officers, adopting and adding to nominations sent in by the separatist congregations, selected 139 'persons fearing God, and of approved fidelity and honesty': people, as Cromwell put it, with 'the root of the matter in them'.[8] He was not initially a member of the Assembly, and although he and four others were later co-opted he declined to take his seat. Despite this reticence, when the members first met on 4 July, Cromwell welcomed them in a mood of heady optimism. The Assembly was, he said, a 'door to usher in things that God hath promised and prophesied of': having been called to 'supreme authority' by a 'series of providences', it now had to 'own' its 'call' and 'win the people to the interest of Jesus Christ and the love of godliness'. Cromwell concluded with an assurance that he and the army would not interfere in the Assembly's deliberations, but would leave members to their 'own thoughts and to the guidance of God'.

His high hopes were soon dashed. Despite the unprecedented way in which the Nominated Assembly had been convened, the social profile of its members was not dramatically different from earlier Parliaments. At least four-fifths ranked as gentlemen, forty-four had some legal training, and no fewer than 119 had served as JPs at some time in their lives. The Assembly thus marked a shift of power within the gentry rather than away from the gentry. As a result, its religious radicalism was combined with an underlying social conservatism that would ultimately prove disastrous. The Assembly's achievements should not be overlooked. During its brief existence it set up fifteen committees to prepare legislation and passed a total of twenty-nine acts dealing with a broad range of social, administrative and financial matters. Its most important reforms included the legalization of civil marriages performed by a Justice of the Peace rather than a cleric; the compulsory registration of births, marriages and deaths; provision for the relief of impoverished creditors and debtors; protection for lunatics and their estates; and sterner measures against thieves and highwaymen. Unfortunately, deep divisions soon opened up. Those members with legal training were alarmed when the Assembly voted to abolish the Court of Chancery and to codify the common law into a pocket-sized digest. The moderates became increasingly nervous, and when members elected a new Council of State on 1 November there was a marked swing away from the radicals. Many members regarded the suppression of lay rights to nominate the ministers of particular parishes on 17 November as a direct assault upon property rights. Finally, on 10 December, when the Assembly voted by fifty-six to fifty-four to abolish tithes, many of which were paid to the laity, the moderates decided that they had had enough. Two days later, while the more radical members were attending a prayer meeting, about eighty moderates went early to Westminster and voted 'to deliver up unto the Lord General Cromwell the powers which they received from him'.

Cromwell later described this experiment with 'rule by the saints' as 'a story of my own weakness and folly', and believed that had it continued the Nominated Assembly would only have brought 'the confusion of all things'. He had been especially alarmed by growing evidence of the Assembly's hostility towards the army: the radicals had blocked the renewal of the excise and were even threatening the monthly assessment, the army's chief means of support. This antagonism had prompted Major-General John Lambert to draw up an alternative constitution, the Instrument of Government, during the autumn of 1653, and it was to this – Britain's first paper constitution – that Cromwell turned when the Nominated Assembly dissolved itself.

The Instrument of Government drew on the army's earlier plans for a limited monarchy in the *Heads of the Proposals*. It stipulated that the 'Commonwealth of England, Scotland and Ireland' should be governed by an elected Lord Protector advised by a Council of State numbering between thirteen and twenty-one. Lambert had initially hoped that Cromwell would accept the title of king, but he steadfastly refused. It was therefore decided instead that

Cromwell should be Lord Protector for life, and that the future Lord Protectors should be elected by the Council and confirmed by Parliament. Legislative authority was wielded by the Lord Protector together with triennial Parliaments sitting for a minimum of five months. These Parliaments would be genuinely British and consist of a single chamber of 400 English and Welsh MPs, plus thirty Scottish and thirty Irish. Senior public officials were to be 'chosen by the approbation of Parliament'. The Instrument named fifteen Councillors of State, and subsequent vacancies were to be filled by Parliament (or by co-option during the intervals between Parliaments). The first Parliament would meet on 3 September 1654, and until then the Lord Protector was authorized to issue ordinances with the force of law. The Lord Protector was granted 'a constant yearly revenue' to support an army of 30,000, plus a further £200,000 a year to cover the costs of civil government. The Instrument also sought to promote the army's vision of a godly commonwealth. MPs had to be 'persons of known integrity, fearing God, and of good conversation', and the Council of State was empowered to exclude those whom it judged to fail this requirement. A national Church would ensure the 'public profession' of 'sound doctrine', and outside it religious toleration was guaranteed to all those who 'profess faith in God by Jesus Christ', but not to 'popery', 'prelacy' and those who caused 'civil injury' to others or who disturbed 'the public peace'.

There is little doubt that Lambert and other leading officers were in collusion with the more moderate members of the Nominated Assembly and were waiting for the radicals to discredit themselves. However, the balance of probability is that Cromwell himself was genuinely surprised by the dissolution. But he needed little persuasion to accept the Instrument, and the Council of Officers voted to adopt it on 15 December. The following day, wearing a plain black suit and cloak, Cromwell was formally installed as Lord Protector in Westminster Hall.

5 The Lord Protector

At the age of fifty-four, Cromwell thus found himself Head of State of a united England, Scotland and Ireland. It was an extraordinary achievement for a man who had been born in Huntingdon on the fringes of the gentry and who until the age of forty was an obscure fenland farmer.[9] The source of his genius as a military commander is in the end mysterious, for certainly he had no experience as a soldier prior to 1642. But much of the almost manic energy that propelled him through an unbroken sequence of victories, and established him as a dominant figure on the political scene, can be traced back to a period of profound depression and religious introspection which he went through in his early thirties. This experience, which coincided with a bitter quarrel with the Huntingdon town council and his decision to move to St Ives, left him with a sense of having been found by God and rescued from his own sinfulness that was to colour the rest of his life. As he wrote to his cousin, Elizabeth St John, wife of Oliver St John, in October 1638: 'my soul is with the congregation of the firstborn, my body rests in hope, and if here I may honour my God either by doing or by suffering, I shall be most glad.'[10] Just as Cromwell believed that God had saved him, so he was convinced that God also had a mission for England, and that his own 'doing' had a crucial role to play.[11] That call could not be ignored, even though Cromwell admitted shortly before his death that he would rather 'have lived under a woodside, to have kept a flock of sheep'. But no: the fulfilment of God's purpose involved destroying the tyranny and popish menace associated with the Stuarts; and that was why, for Cromwell, the battles of the Civil Wars had immense religious significance. Yet they were only one dimension of the advancement of God's cause: military victory had to be accompanied by positive reform that would re-educate the nation and turn it from worldliness to the things of the spirit. Only in that way could England, an elect nation, enter the Promised Land. Although, as he had said in the Putney Debates, he was not 'wedded and glued to forms of government', he never ceased to be 'wedded and glued' to the fulfilment of God's 'cause' as the *end* of government.

As Cromwell's letter to Mrs St John had foreseen, this process involved 'suffering' as well as 'doing' – painful self-denial and self-discipline in addition to intense military and political activity. Cromwell was convinced that there was a direct parallel between England in the 1650s and the Israelites of the Old Testament. Just as the Israelites had been in bondage in Egypt, so England had suffered the tyrannical rule of the Stuarts. But by executing Charles I they had freed themselves and crossed the Red Sea. Now they were crossing the desert, led by Cromwell who fulfilled the role of Moses, and guided by a pillar of fire in the form of 'providences', those manifestations of God's will in the affairs of this world which Cromwell had discerned in the army's victories and which he endeavoured to follow throughout his career. Inevitably, that journey to the Promised Land was arduous. There could be no election without pain, and the English were as yet 'like the people newly under circumcision, but raw'.

However, these radical religious beliefs coexisted with much more conservative social and political attitudes. By the time of his 'spiritual conversion' in the early 1630s, Cromwell had already grown to maturity, become an established figure in Huntingdon, and served as its MP in the Parliament of 1628–9. During those early years he naturally acquired the outlook of a country gentleman, and he could never lose that even after his religious experience had given his life new direction and meaning. He was not a social egalitarian, but sought to reform people's spirits within the existing hierarchical framework. In September 1654 he promised to uphold 'the ranks and orders of men, whereby England hath been known for hundreds of years', and argued that 'a nobleman, a gentleman, a yeoman; the distinction of these, that is a good interest of the nation, and a great one'. The result was what Blair Worden has called 'ideological schizophrenia' – a constant and insoluble tension at the heart of a man who was at once 'inspired to spiritual radicalism' while yet remaining 'a conservative by social instinct and early political training'. That paradox helps to account for many of the apparent inconsistencies that litter Cromwell's career, and especially his years as Lord Protector.

It explains, first of all, why he remained committed to the principle of a Parliament but yet was unable to work effectively with individual Parliaments.

His political instincts told him that 'government by a single person and a Parliament' was 'a fundamental' and 'the essence', but his religious attitudes were not shared by most of the gentry and lawyers elected to Parliament. Unable to resolve – or even fully comprehend – that paradox, Cromwell persisted in calling successive Parliaments, hoping that perhaps next time they would 'be mindful of their duty to God' and God's people. But because the godly were not typical of the nation as a whole, Cromwell's repeated attempts to use Parliament, the 'representative of the whole realm', to advance a cause espoused only by a minority were bound to fail.

The first Protectorate Parliament followed much the same pattern as the Rump and the Nominated Assembly. When members gathered on 4 September 1654, Cromwell declared that they had upon their shoulders not only 'the interest of three great nations' but 'the interest of all the Christian people in the world', and that they were 'a door of hope opened by God to us'. Their 'great end', he asserted, should be 'healing and settling'. However, many of the MPs were Presbyterian gentry or lawyers, and during the first week they called for suppression of the sects and stubbornly refused to ratify the Instrument of Government on the grounds that it unduly curtailed the authority of Parliament. On 12 September Cromwell therefore made a long speech in defence of the Instrument and required members to take a Recognition pledging loyalty to the Lord Protector and to the principle of government by 'a single person and a Parliament'. About a hundred MPs, including leading republicans such as Thomas Scot and Sir Arthur Hesilrige, promptly withdrew from Parliament. Cromwell did not however find that it became any more co-operative after their departure. Nearly forty bills were introduced during the Parliament, but they addressed a great variety of problems – ranging from probate of wills to the management of saltpetre – rather than assigning priority to the process of settlement and moral regeneration.

Cromwell was incensed. He had hoped that Parliament would confirm and build on the eighty-two ordinances he had issued during the first nine months of the Protectorate. About twenty of these related to finance. Others dealt with such important matters as the union with Scotland and the treaty concluding the first Dutch War. The demise of the Nominated Assembly had removed many of the 'saints' who most vehemently supported the war. Furthermore, the merchant companies pleaded that the conflict was damaging Britain's economic interests and this, together with the eclipse of the pro-Stuart Orangists and a feeling that Spain was a more 'natural enemy', persuaded Cromwell that there was no point in continuing to fight the Dutch. Above all, a number of ordinances sought to improve ecclesiastical discipline. In partic-ular, in March 1654 a national body of 'triers' was set up to examine all new clergy before allowing them to preach. The following August, commissioners known as 'ejectors' were appointed in each county to expel 'scandalous, igno-rant and insufficient ministers and schoolmasters'. But instead of following Cromwell's lead, Parliament pursued its own legislative agenda and produced a long list of amendments to the Instrument of Government in the form of a 'constitutional bill'. To his annoyance, many members stressed the army's continued subordination to Parliament and attacked the provision for liberty of conscience. Finally, at the earliest possible constitutional opportunity, after five lunar (rather than calendar) months, he determined to be rid of the Parliament. On 22 January 1655, after denouncing members for 'throwing away precious opportunities committed to' them, he declared it his 'duty to God and the people of these nations, to their safety and good in every respect', to dissolve Parliament.

The failure of the first Protectorate Parliament to achieve 'healing and settling' brought the more authoritarian side of Cromwell's character to the fore. As early as 1647 he had argued that if necessary the people should be governed 'for their good, not what pleases them'. As Lord Protector, he was prepared to defend the arbitrary imprisonment of those whose actions 'tended to the disturbance of the peace of the nation'. He likewise condoned violations of the rule of law on the grounds that 'if nothing should be done but what is according to law, the throat of the nation may be cut while we send for some to make a law'. This was, of course, precisely the argument that Charles I had used to justify royal infringements of the law and non-parliamentary taxation such as Ship Money. The irony became glaring in November 1654 when a London silk merchant named George Cony refused to pay customs duties because they had not been approved by Parliament. Cromwell ordered that Cony and his lawyers should be imprisoned until they dropped their plea. Lord Chief Justice Rolle was so appalled by this high-handedness that he resigned in June 1655.[12]

Cromwell suffered other serious blows during the spring and summer of that year. In mid-March a Royalist rising in Wiltshire led by John Penruddock was easily crushed. But it revealed a disturbing apathy among the population as a whole: although only a few hundred rallied to Penruddock, hardly any took action against him. The regime's failure to win positive support was plainly evident. Even more disturbing was the failure of the so-called 'Western Design' in April. The previous December, Cromwell had despatched a fleet to protect the religious rights of English merchants in Spanish ports on the Caribbean. But the sailors were poorly trained and supplied: their attack on the island of Hispaniola was quickly repulsed and their only success was the capture of Jamaica. When Cromwell learnt of this defeat he was devastated, and wondered how he and the nation had 'provoked the Lord'. Spain had seemed a 'providential' enemy: why, then, had God 'smitten us'? In order to propitiate the Lord, he concluded, it was vital that 'all manner of vice may be thoroughly discountenanced and severely punished; and that such a form of government may be exercised that virtue and godliness may receive due encouragement'. It was this moral purpose, together with the need for heightened security against the Royalist threat, that led Cromwell to introduce the rule of the Major-Generals.

On 9 August 1655, England and Wales were divided into ten (later eleven) regions, each governed by a senior army officer. These Major-Generals received detailed instructions on 22 August and again on 11 October. They were authorized to raise new regional militias totalling 6,000 horse, paid for by the Decimation Tax. This was a 10 per cent income tax on all former Royalists, the legality of which was widely challenged as contrary to the Rump's 1652 Act of Oblivion. The Major-Generals were to use these forces to suppress 'unlawful assemblies', to arrest 'dangerous persons' and to disarm 'all papists and others who have been in arms against the Parliament'. In addition, they were to promote a 'reformation of manners' in the localities. They would 'encourage and promote godliness and virtue, and discourage and discountenance all profaneness and ungodliness'. Horse-races, cock-fights, bear-baiting and stage plays were all banned, and the laws against drunkenness, blaspheming and 'such like wickedness and abominations' were to be strictly enforced. The methods were new, but Cromwell's goal of morally re-educating a reluctant population was wholly consistent with his earlier policies.

Equally consistent, however, was the grudging acceptance that greeted this initiative. Cromwell later described the Major-Generals as 'justifiable as to necessity', and claimed that they had been 'more effectual towards the discountenancing of vice and settling religion than anything done these fifty years'. But it seems that their impact was actually quite limited. Because many of them came from outside the regions they ruled, county elites tended to close ranks against them. Some Major-Generals, such as William Goffe (Berkshire, Hampshire, Sussex), despaired of ever making much headway; while even the dynamic Charles Worsley (Cheshire, Lancashire, Staffordshire) – who closed nearly 200 alehouses in Chester alone and died from overwork aged thirty-four – did not leave a permanent mark on the attitudes of local society. Military rule and the Decimation Tax proved to be universally unpopular. When continuing campaigns in the West Indies, and the hope of joining with France in an attack on the Spanish in Flanders, forced Cromwell to summon a second Protectorate Parliament for 17 September 1656 the elections were dominated by the cry 'No swordsmen! No decimators!' The outcome was another assembly unsympathetic to the army's programme. On its very first day, the Council excluded nearly one hundred 'ungodly' MPs, while another fifty or sixty withdrew in protest.[13] But the remaining members were equally implacable in their hostility to the Major-Generals and the Decimation Tax, and Cromwell had no alternative but to abandon both on 28 January 1657 as the price for securing a parliamentary grant of £400,000 to finance the war against Spain.

The members of the new Parliament, like most of their predecessors, were also highly suspicious of Cromwell's commitment to religious toleration. In his providentialism, his sense of God's immanence in this world, and his assurance of his own salvation Cromwell was an orthodox Calvinist. Where he differed so strikingly from most of his contemporaries was in his belief that 'God's people' were not confined to one particular denomination but scattered among the different churches. He longed for 'a glorious union of the people of God, made to be of one spirit'. As he wrote to his cousin Robert Hammond in 1648: 'I profess to thee I desire it in my heart, I have prayed for it, I have waited for the day to see union and right understanding between the godly people (Scots, English, Jews, Gentiles, Presbyterians, Independents, Anabaptists, and all).' In 1655 Cromwell actively sought the readmission to England of the Jews (expelled by Edward I in 1290) in order to secure their conversion and thus promote the union of Gentile and Jew, although opposition within the Council ensured that their return was tacit rather than official. Corresponding to Cromwell's impatience with 'forms of government' was an anti-formalism in religion that led him to declare in September 1656: 'whoever has this [Christian] faith, let his form be what it will, [if] he [is] walking peaceably, without the prejudicing of others under another form, it is a debt due to God and Christ ... [that] that Christian may enjoy this liberty'. To deny liberty of conscience was to risk persecuting one of God's children, and only by assembling 'the several sorts of godliness in this nation' could a godly commonwealth be created. Cromwell did not, however, intend this as a licence for 'prodigious blasphemies' and 'heresies'. In December 1654 he did nothing to prevent Parliament's imprisonment of John Biddle, an exponent of the anti-Trinitarian heresy known as Socinianism;[14] and nearly two years later the limits of Cromwell's commitment to religious toleration were again tested by the case of James Nayler.

A former soldier, Nayler was a Quaker who in October 1656 re-enacted Christ's entry into Jerusalem on Palm Sunday by riding into Bristol on an ass, with women throwing palms at his feet. What Nayler and other Quakers saw as the working of the 'inner light' looked to local magistrates like a terrible blasphemy. Nayler was brought to London where he became a focus for conservative fears about the subversion and disorder caused by the radical sects. In December, Parliament convicted him of 'horrid blasphemy' and initially wanted to impose the death penalty. Cromwell then intervened, querying Parliament's jurisdiction over the case and urging clemency. He saved Nayler's life, but Parliament nevertheless voted to impose savage corporal punishments: Nayler was to be branded, bored through the tongue, flogged twice and then imprisoned for life. Cromwell, torn between his personal commitment to toleration and his public duty – as Lord Protector and as the 'good constable' – to preserve order, accepted these penalties. But he was haunted by the fear that such a fate might subsequently befall other sectaries and warned army officers that 'the case of James Nayler might happen to be your own case'. The episode provided yet another reminder of how far his own instincts diverged from those of most members of Parliament.

For their part, many of those in Parliament increasingly feared that the Lord Protector's powers were liable to be abused. Because it was a new office, unknown to the laws of England, adequate safeguards did not exist against arbitrary protectoral action. By contrast, the title of king was, as the lawyer Bulstrode Whitelocke put it, grounded 'in all the ancient foundations of the laws of England'. For this reason, a group of MPs sought 'an alteration of the present government': they drew up a new paper constitution, *The Humble Petition and Advice*, that would strengthen the powers of Parliament and restrain Cromwell by making him king.

The formal offer of the kingship, on 23 February 1657, presented Cromwell with the most painful dilemma of his career. As early as 1651 he had reflected that 'a settlement with somewhat of monarchical power in it would be very effectual', while a year later he asked Whitelocke 'what if a man should take upon him to be king?' Cromwell could see that a new royal house would secure the future and rule out a Stuart restoration. But in the end, after over two months of tormented indecision, Cromwell declined the kingship. He seems to have felt that he was freer to advance God's 'cause' and to protect the godly people as Lord Protector than he would be as king. It was not megalomania so much as an unwillingness to become constrained by the conservative gentry and lawyers in Parliament that made him balk at the kingship. The army officers' overt hostility to the proposal strengthened his resolve, not because he feared that they might depose him – although some threatened resignation there is no evidence that any coup was planned – but because he still regarded them as God's instrument. He interpreted their disapproval as a 'providence' indicating that God had set his face against the kingship. In addition, he seems to have been mortified by jibes suggesting that his own ambition was the cause of God's disapproval as manifested in the failure of the Western Design. In *A Healing Question Propounded* (1656), Vane had written that Cromwell since the Civil Wars, like Achan after the fall of Jericho, had 'brought not in the fruit and gain of the Lord's treasure, but covetously went about to convert it to his own use'. Horrified at the thought that by committing the 'sin of Achan' he might betray all that he and the army had fought for, Cromwell told MPs on 13 April: 'I will not seek to set up that, that providence hath destroyed and laid in the dust; and I would not build Jericho again'. Finally, on 8 May, he formally refused the kingship.

With 'this great and weighty business' settled, Cromwell accepted the remainder of *The Humble Petition and Advice* on 25 May. This established a parliamentary constitution in which the Lord Protector was obliged to govern 'according to the laws of these nations' and to call Parliament once every three years. Parliament would henceforth consist of a House of Commons and an 'Other House' of between forty and seventy persons nominated by the Lord Protector but approved by the Commons. Cromwell particularly welcomed the creation of a second chamber as a check on the Commons' religious intolerance so apparent in the Nayler case. Conscious of recent purges by the Council, Parliament insisted that its 'ancient and undoubted liberties and privileges' be 'preserved and maintained', and that freely elected MPs could only be excluded 'by judgement and consent' of Parliament. In another notable return towards earlier institutions, a 'Privy Council' of no more than twenty-one was to be chosen by the Lord Protector and 'approved' by Parliament. Cromwell gained the right to nominate his own successor, and he would receive a 'yearly revenue' of £1.3 million, none of which was to be raised by land taxes or without Parliament's consent. In the wake of the Nayler case, the religious settlement, although similar to that of 1653, introduced tougher measures against 'blasphemies'. Overall, the new constitution affirmed Cromwell's position as king in all but name. He was allowed to choose his own 'Other House' and his Privy Council; he signed official documents 'Oliver P'; and at the Protectoral Court he was increasingly surrounded by the trappings of monarchy. At his second installation as Lord Protector (26 June 1657) he wore a robe of purple velvet lined with ermine and carried a gold sceptre. He took an adapted form of the royal coronation oath, and then left Westminster Hall in a state coach amid cries of 'God save the Lord Protector'.

That ceremony symbolized the gradual drift back to 'known ways' that characterized the later 1650s. The republican regimes never won the enthusiastic backing of more than a minority of the population. By the final years of the Protectorate, perhaps a half of English parish churches were using at least parts of the old Prayer Book. There is evidence that the proscribed festivals of Christmas and Easter were being celebrated more and more widely. In provincial government, members of the traditional elite were steadily returning to the commission of the peace, and the ancient county courts, the quarter sessions and the assizes, began to revive. Many county communities were able slowly to knit together again as former enemies were brought together in administrative activity or on social occasions. Despite the abolition of the Lords, English peers retained much of their local status and influence, and by judicious manipulation of mortgages and legal protections many of them were able to rebuild their finances. Although the sectaries did send down roots (especially in urban areas and in Wales) that explain the strength of religious dissent after 1660, and although women did achieve and maintain a highly significant role within those sects, the collective change of consciousness – the 'reformation of manners' – which Cromwell hankered after proved elusive.

It is probable that by the last months of his life Cromwell realized this. Parliament adjourned on 26 June, and when it reassembled on 20 January 1658 he permitted those members excluded in September 1656 to return as well. The 'Other House' also met, although only forty-two of the sixty-three people Cromwell had summoned agreed to serve. He hoped that this session would promote 'peace and tranquillity' and safeguard 'the honest and religious interest of the nation'. He was appalled when the republicans, led by Hesilrige and Scot, questioned the legitimacy of the 'Other House', which they found far too like the old House of Lords. Enraged, Cromwell peremptorily dissolved Parliament on 4 February, concluding with the words: 'Let God be judge between you and me'. During the spring and summer, much of his declining energies were devoted to foreign policy. He signed a treaty with France in March, as a result of which a joint Anglo-French force defeated the Spanish off Dunkirk at the battle of the Dunes (14 June), enabling the English to occupy Dunkirk. Ten days later a Spanish attempt to recapture Jamaica was thwarted. But as the summer wore on Cromwell became increasingly exhausted and dispirited. His favourite daughter Elizabeth Claypole died of cancer on 6 August, and two weeks later Cromwell himself fell gravely ill, probably of a kidney infection. He died at Whitehall on 3 September, the anniversary of Dunbar and Worcester.

Cromwell's state funeral the following November was modelled on that of James VI and I in 1625. He was buried in Westminster Abbey, and the ceremonies, which cost £60,000, included a funeral effigy clad in royal robes of purple and ermine, holding an orb and sceptre, and wearing a crown. It was an ironic yet strangely appropriate end for the man whose fight against Stuart tyranny had brought him to the verge of the throne. To the last he remained full of paradoxes and embodied many of the contradictions of the revolution itself. The same religious zeal that carried him forward to become Head of State also prevented him from achieving his goal of 'healing and settling'. Unable to resolve the tension between his religious radicalism and his social and political conservatism, he repeatedly summoned Parliaments, and yet his godly programme ensured that he could never work harmoniously with them. He yearned for the whole nation to share the attitudes of 'God's people'. As he told the framers of *The Humble Petition and Advice*: 'I think you have provided for the liberty of the people of God and of the nation; and I say, he sings sweetly that sings a song of reconciliation betwixt these two interests, and it is a pitiful fancy and wild and ignorant, to think they are inconsistent'. 'Upon these two interests' Cromwell pledged to 'live and die'; and yet his whole life demonstrated their essential incompatibility. He alone straddled the worlds of the civilian politicians and the army officers and so enabled the republic to survive. Less than two years after his death, the regime was blown apart by its own contradictions.

6 The Fall of the Republic

Within hours of Cromwell's death, the Council announced that he had nominated his eldest son Richard as his successor.[15] Aged thirty-one, Richard proved wholly unsuited to fulfil the role of Lord Protector. He was mistrusted by both the army officers and the republicans, and so was unable to reconcile the conflicting interest groups on which the regime depended. He also inherited a rapidly deteriorating financial situation. By the end of 1658, England's annual deficit was over £500,000, while army arrears stood at £890,000. Overall, the State's debts had reached nearly £2.5 million, whereas its annual income was only £1.4 million. In an attempt to secure more revenue, Richard therefore summoned a third Protectorate Parliament which met on 27 January 1659. The republicans refused to recognize him as Lord Protector and called for the repeal of *The Humble Petition and Advice*, while the army officers were infuriated when Parliament voted to restrict their involvement in politics and to limit religious toleration. When Parliament began to debate settling the army as a militia, possibly under parliamentary control, the army forced Richard to dissolve Parliament on 22 April, and then to recall the Rump on 7 May. In fact, only forty-two of the seventy-eight eligible members actually reassembled. Shortly afterwards the Rump elected a new Council of State consisting of twenty-one MPs and ten others.

However, the Rump did not fulfil the army's expectations this time any more than it had during its previous existence. It refused to recognize the Protectorate, demanded Richard Cromwell's resignation on 24 May, and then re-established the Commonwealth. Relations with the army rapidly deteriorated as the Rump spent most of the summer in sterile constitutional bickering. Only the fact that the fall of the Protectorate encouraged a feeble pro-Royalist Presbyterian rising in Cheshire and Lancashire led by Sir George Booth served to maintain the uneasy alliance between the army and the Rump for a few months. But after Lambert had easily put down Booth's rising in August the mutual antipathy of Rumpers and officers became obvious. When the Rump declared illegal all acts and ordinances passed since its expulsion in April 1653, and tried to purge supporters of the Protectorate from both the army and local

Plate 13 Oliver Cromwell's funeral effigy, 1658. It was necessary to use this effigy for the lying in state and the funeral in November 1658 because the embalming of Cromwell's actual body was botched and the decomposing remains had to be quietly interred in Westminster Abbey in September. By presenting Cromwell clad in royal robes of purple and ermine, holding an orb and sceptre, and wearing a crown, the effigy dramatically illustrates that by the time of his death he was king in all but name. The effigy is now stored in the Jerusalem Chamber at Westminster Abbey. Too decayed and fragile to be on public view, it is also headless: possibly the effigy, like Cromwell's corpse, was beheaded at the Restoration.
Source: The Fotomas Index

government, the army once again dissolved it on 13 October. Some members of the Rump's Council of State continued to sit, but over the next two weeks the initiative gradually passed to the Army Council. The Council of State ceased to sit on 25 October, and the next day the army established a Committee of Safety of twenty-three 'to secure the people's liberties as men and Christians, reform the law, provide for a godly preaching ministry, and settle the constitution without a single person or a House of Lords'. This Committee, headed by General Charles Fleetwood, was a last desperate attempt to enshrine the 'cause' for which the army had fought, yet it wholly failed to maintain the loyalty of all the armed forces.

All along, the republican regimes had relied upon the army's support. They were, in Christopher Hill's memorable phrase, 'sitting on bayonets'. But now some of those bayonets turned decisively against the republic. In late October, General George Monck – leader of the army in Scotland and newly appointed commander-in-chief of the armed forces in all three kingdoms – demanded the return of the Rump; in early December he began to march south. Although the motives of the former Royalist Monck are difficult to reconstruct, his overriding concern was probably to achieve a stable settlement and so allay the threat of anarchy posed by the religious radicals, especially the Quakers. In a revealing letter to the theologian John Owen on 29 November, Monck denounced 'the fanatical and self-seeking party' and wrote that he 'dare not sit still and let our laws and liberties go to ruin'. The Committee of Safety could not possibly provide stability: it proved entirely unable to cope with mutiny in the north, unrest in the fleet, apprentice riots in London and a renewed trade depression. Amid widespread calls for a 'full and free' Parliament, together with a threatened taxpayers' strike, the Committee dispersed on 17 December, and for over a week England had literally no government at all. There was complete chaos until three regiments, following Monck's example, reinstated the Rump on 26 December. Monck's army entered England on 1 January: he easily swept aside a force that Lambert led against him, and reached London on 3 February. Later that month he secured the readmission of those MPs who had been 'purged' in December 1648. The restored Long Parliament bowed to the overwhelming popular pressure for 'free elections' and finally, unlamented, it dissolved itself on 16 March 1660.

Monck was meanwhile in touch with the exiled Court in the Low Countries, and at his suggestion Charles II issued the Declaration of Breda on 4 April. This proved to be a political masterstroke. Drawing on the ideas of moderate Royalists such as Hyde and Ormond, Charles set out a programme for a restored constitutional monarchy that would respect Parliament and the rule of law. He promised 'a free and general pardon' to all his subjects, except for a few individuals to be agreed with Parliament. He would collaborate with a free Parliament to ensure 'full satisfaction' of army arrears and to resolve disputed titles to property. Most controversially, on Hyde's advice he declared 'a liberty to tender consciences' – a promise that would return to haunt him. By reassuring his subjects that virtually none of them had anything to fear from him, Charles's declaration provided a manifesto for a Stuart restoration. It was warmly received in England, where the first free elections since 1640 produced the strongly pro-Royalist Convention Parliament. Throughout, Monck remained inscrutable and let events take their course.

The Convention assembled on 25 April, complete with the House of Lords, and on 8 May unanimously passed a declaration stating that 'it can no way be doubted but that His Majesty's right and title to his Crowns and kingdoms is and was [in] every way completed by the death of his most royal father, without the ceremony or solemnity of a proclamation'. Charles II was therefore affirmed to have been 'the most potent and undoubted King' of England, Scotland and Ireland ever since the moment of Charles I's execution. Officially the Interregnum had never existed, and Charles was deemed to be in the twelfth year of his reign. The way was now clear for the King's return: he landed at Dover on 25 May and began a triumphal progress to London, where he arrived four days later. He was greeted by tumultuous rejoicing, and the Royalist diarist John Evelyn recorded: 'I stood in the Strand, and beheld it, and blessed God: and all this without one drop of blood, and by that very army which rebelled against him'.

8 The Restoration of the British Monarchies

	28 March	Act Rescissory revokes all Scottish legislation since 1633; Act concerning Religion and Church government
	20 April	Sir Edward Hyde created Earl of Clarendon; Anthony Ashley Cooper created Baron Ashley
	April–July	Savoy House Conference on religious settlement ends in deadlock
	8 May–19 May 1662	First session of Cavalier Parliament: seeks more strongly Royalist and Anglican settlement
	13 May	Ashley appointed Chancellor of the Exchequer
	27 May	Execution of Argyll
	July	Militia Act gives Crown supreme control over armed forces and the militia
	November	Financial settlement grants Charles an annual revenue estimated at £1.2 million
	December	Corporation Act excludes non-Anglicans from borough corporations
1662	21 February	Ormond appointed Lord Lieutenant of Ireland
	April	Cavalier Parliament adopts revised Prayer Book
	20 May	Charles marries Catherine of Braganza
	May	Act of Uniformity requires use of new Prayer Book: 936 clergy deprived for failure to comply with its terms by 24 August 1662; Militia Act strengthens existing county militias; Quaker Act imposes harsh penalties on Quakers who refuse to swear oaths or attend meetings with five or more others; Hearth Tax introduced
	31 July	Irish Act of Settlement
	July	Charles establishes the Royal Society by royal charter
	9 September	Scottish Act of Indemnity and Oblivion
	27 October	Sale of Dunkirk to France for £300,000

	26 December	Charles's first Declaration of Indulgence: he seeks to use royal dispensing power to provide 'liberty for tender consciences'
1663	18 February–27 July	Second session of Cavalier Parliament: rejects Declaration of Indulgence and King's claim of a dispensing power in ecclesiastical matters
	April	Charles withdraws Declaration of Indulgence
	4 June	Death of Archbishop Juxon
	16 June	Gilbert Sheldon nominated as Archbishop of Canterbury
	18 June	Lords of the Articles restored in Scotland
	23 July	Execution of Archibald Johnston of Wariston
	27 July	First Cattle Act imposes limits on exports of Irish cattle to England
	23 September	Scottish Parliament authorizes Charles to raise an army of 22,000 troops
	October	Rising by radical dissenters in Yorkshire

Act for the Encouragement of Trade (Staple Act) requires colonies to import European goods only from England and only in English ships

1664	16 March–17 May	Third session of Cavalier Parliament
	April	Triennial Act: diluted version of 1641 Act; Conventicle Act prohibits religious assemblies of five or more people
	24 November–2 March 1665	Fourth session of Cavalier Parliament
1665	4 March	Charles declares war on the Dutch Republic: beginning of the second Anglo-Dutch War
	Summer–early autumn	Plague epidemic in London: perhaps as many as 100,000 (a quarter of the city's population) die
	3 June	Duke of York routs Dutch fleet off Lowestoft
	1 August	Bungled English assault on Dutch fleet at Bergen
	9–31 October	Fifth session of Cavalier Parliament

	October	Five Mile Act: ministers ejected under the Act of Uniformity and other unlicensed preachers forbidden to come within five miles of their former parish, or of any town or city
1666	1–4 June	Four Days' Battle: Dutch inflict heavy losses on English fleet
	18 June	Irish Act of Uniformity makes use of the Prayer Book obligatory
	25 July	St James's Day Battle: English defeat Dutch
	2–6 September	Great Fire of London
	18 September–8 February 1667	Sixth session of Cavalier Parliament: officers of navy and ordnance ordered to submit accounts for inspection
	November	Pentland Rising in southwest Scotland brutally suppressed
1667	18 January	Second Cattle Act prohibits Irish cattle and meat from sale in English or Scottish markets
	February	Appointment of commissioners for public accounts
	16 May	Death of Southampton; Treasury put into commission
	13 June	Dutch raid on English fleet in the Medway
	11 July	Treaty of Breda ends second Anglo-Dutch War
	25–29 July	Seventh session of Cavalier Parliament: many members call for Clarendon's resignation
	30 August	Clarendon resigns as Lord Chancellor
	10 October–1 March 1669	Eighth session of Cavalier Parliament: attempted impeachment of Clarendon
	29 November	Clarendon flees to France
	December	Accounts Commission established to investigate war finance

1 The Return of Charles II

The day of Charles II's entry into London, 29 May 1660, was also his thirtieth birthday. His life had already been remarkably full, and the events of his adolescence and early adulthood had stamped their mark clearly upon him. Aged twelve when the English Civil War broke out, eighteen when his father was executed, and twenty-one when his attempts to regain the throne were crushed and he fled for his life, he had then spent the rest of the Interregnum in France and (from 1656) the Spanish Netherlands. Throughout those years he was never sure whom he could trust: the exiled Court was infiltrated by Cromwellian spies and Charles lived in permanent fear of betrayal or even assassination. No wonder that these formative experiences made him the most worldly-wise and cynical of all the Stuart monarchs. Inevitably, he formed a very pessimistic view of human nature: as Bishop Gilbert Burnet later wrote, 'he had a very ill opinion of men and women, and so is infinitely distrustful; he thinks the world is governed wholly by interest'. This deep vein of mistrust gradually robbed Charles of the capacity to confide in others; instead, his personality became coated with a veneer of charm and *bonhomie* that made him extremely affable but ultimately concealed his true feelings. As extrovert as James VI and I, he yet remained as inscrutable as Charles I. These essential characteristics were already formed by 1660, and they decisively shaped Charles's style of kingship thereafter.

All those who knew Charles as king commented on his inexhaustible physical energy and vitality. Over six feet tall, and athletically built, he took exercise every day and enthusiastically pursued a variety of sports. He was also – contrary to the traditional image of an indolent pleasure-seeker – prepared to channel his energies into the activities of government. He assiduously attended meetings of the Privy Council and was always highly accessible to his subjects. It was easier to approach him in person than even James VI and I, and at times of national disaster – such as the Great Fire of London (1666) – he was quickly on the scene, personally directing safety measures. He was constantly in the public eye and really worked at playing the role of king, yet he detested paperwork. His mind was lively and vibrant, but somewhat superficial, so that he habitually sought to delegate more bureaucratic business to others. Samuel Pepys wrote that ministers had to 'administer business to him as doctors do physic, wrap it up in something to make it less unpleasant'. Charles was interested in a vast range of subjects, from the traditional royal pursuits of riding and hunting to works of art and architecture, and from the theatre to gardening. He was fascinated by the latest fashions and the newest discoveries: he took an active interest in science, especially mathematics and chemistry, and became a keen patron of the Royal Society, established by royal charter in 1660. However, his concentration span was limited and his interests were remarkable more for their breadth than their depth.

Not surprisingly, Charles's central political objective after the Restoration was 'not to go on his travels again'. Having spent the Interregnum consumed with a passionate desire to become king – an ambition that still seemed unattainable as late as 1659 – he then lacked the drive to pursue any systematic programme once on the throne. It was satisfaction enough for him to wake up each morning knowing that he was king and then to spend the day enjoying the exercise of power and his lifestyle as monarch. Unlike his grandfather and especially his father, he did not seek to implement a particular vision of Britain. Never a conviction politician, he pursued neither long-term strategies nor a coherent agenda. He did have preferred attitudes or lines of policy, most notably religious toleration and a *rapprochement* with France, but he would not push these beyond the limits of political expediency. Nor – again unlike Charles I – did he allow his own popularity to suffer by defending an unpopular minister. His ruthless discarding of Clarendon (1667) and Danby (1679) were without doubt ungrateful rejections of loyal servants; but politically they were very shrewd moves because they enabled the doctrine of 'evil counsellors' to deflect blame away from a monarch whom it was thought could do no wrong. Charles was supremely conscious that politics was the art of the possible, and he learnt from his father's disastrous fate not to allow his own intransigence to get him into corners. He knew how to make tactical concessions, and although he was never pro-active he reacted to changing political circumstances with singular adroitness.

The one principle on which he would brook no compromise was the maintenance of the legitimate succession and the dignity due to royalty. Precisely because he had been deprived of the throne for so long, he had a heightened sense of regality and its attendant trappings. His wish to reassert the distinctiveness and sanctity of monarchy in contrast to the republican regimes was most strikingly evident in his vigorous revival of touching for 'the King's Evil'.[1] He had already begun touching the scrofulous while in exile, and only a few days after arriving back in England he touched about 600 people in a single sitting. During the twenty years 1660–4 and 1667–83 he ministered to no fewer than 90,000 individuals, reaching a peak of 8,577 recorded in the King's Register of Healing between May 1682 and April 1683. This surge of activity coincided with the political reaction in favour of the Crown in the wake of the Exclusion Crisis, the most serious conflict of Charles's reign in which he insisted that James, Duke of York should remain the heir presumptive despite his recent conversion to Catholicism. As we shall see in chapter 10, Charles's refusal to compromise, allied to his accustomed political flexibility and opportunism, left him victorious over those who urged James's exclusion from the line of succession.

The same blend of joviality and inscrutability characterized Charles's relationships with his advisers. By expanding the Privy Council to over seventy he made it far too big for efficient executive action. Instead, he preferred to develop policies in liaison with inner circles of chosen counsellors whom he consulted privately and informally. These *ad hoc* groupings shifted constantly and were often unaware of the others' existence. The King has been likened to a spider at the centre of a web: he alone could see the whole picture and this enabled him to divide and rule. One leading Privy Councillor, the Marquis of Halifax, did 'not believe that ever he trusted any man or any set of men so entirely as not to have some secrets in which they had no share; as this might

The Manner of His Majesties Curing the Diseale,

CALLED THE

K I N G S - E V I L.

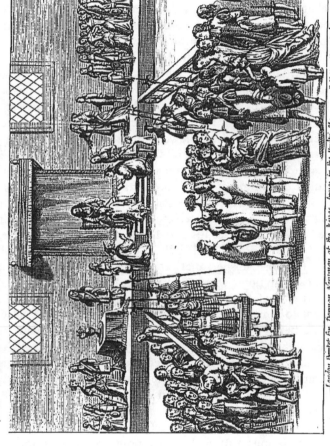

London Printed for Dorman Newman at the kings Armes in the Poultry 84;   F. H. Van Hove Sculp:

Plate 14 Charles II touching for the 'King's Evil', or scrofula. Charles made vigorous use of the healing powers ascribed to him as a way of affirming the sacred character of kingship following the Restoration. In striking contrast to his father, who had greatly curtailed the practice, Charles also saw it as an invaluable way of making direct personal contact with a broad cross-section of his subjects.
Source: The Fotomas Index

make him less well served, so in some degree it might make him the less imposed upon'. Usually, the full Council was only later informed of schemes that Charles had covertly hatched with trusted individuals. Throughout, his essential furtiveness was covered by a manner of consummate urbanity that left his advisers quite unable to judge whether or not he genuinely trusted them. According to Bishop Burnet, Charles had 'a strange command of himself . . . He [had] the greatest art of concealing himself of any man alive, so that those about him cannot tell when he is ill or well pleased'. His self-control ensured that he rarely lost his temper, but equally his geniality did not necessarily indicate real affection. Halifax wrote, mordantly, that 'he lived with his ministers as he did with his mistresses; he used them, but he was not in love with them.'

A similar enigma surrounds the nature of Charles's religious beliefs. There is some evidence – notably in his secret treaty with Louis XIV in 1670 and in his reception into the Catholic Church on his deathbed – that he had some sympathy for Catholicism. He was a worldly man who probably found the Catholic doctrine of grace attractive. The father of fourteen acknowledged bastards, he allegedly once remarked that 'all appetites are free and that God will never damn a man for allowing himself a little pleasure'. His mother, brother and favourite sister were all Catholics, and during the Civil Wars many Catholics had loyally served his father: they posed much less of a threat to the Crown than the 'hotter sort of Protestants'.[2] Charles undoubtedly wished to extend toleration as widely as possible, yet his motives appear to have been essentially political and self-interested. In the interests of reuniting the nation after the conflicts of the 1640s and 1650s he was happy to tolerate a range of religious opinions provided that their exponents did not challenge his own authority. Likewise, his personal beliefs were never imposed upon his subjects or pushed to the point where they caused divisions. As Ronald Hutton has written, 'he wished to have all confessional groups respectful of each other and subservient to himself'. He clearly sought a 'comprehensive' Church akin to that of Elizabeth I and James I, together with a broad measure of toleration for those 'tender consciences' who peacefully dissented from it. Although, as we shall see, the political nation thwarted these hopes, his ecclesiastical instincts were towards conciliation and the acceptance of diversity, in sharp contrast to his father's search for 'unity through uniformity'.

Charles's style of government was thus flexible and pragmatic. He regarded the restoration of stability as a higher priority than the pursuit of rigid ideologies. For all his abundant vitality, as a politician he was not, unlike Charles I but like James I, a monarch who 'suffered from energy'. In his preference for consensus over conviction, his readiness to govern with Parliament and within the rule of law, his moral permissiveness, his desire for a broad Church settlement, his natural gregariousness and his colourful private life, he resembled his grandfather far more closely than his father. While the parallels are not exact (he was more tactful than James and no less unfathomable than Charles) this comparison with the first two Stuarts provides an illuminating perspective on Charles II's political persona. By transcending the artificial divide of 1660 and placing him in the context of seventeenth-century British kingship as a whole we can appreciate fully why he became such an effective ruler. This is all the more true because the guiding principle of the Restoration settlement was to return as nearly as possible to the pre-war 'ancient constitution'. The contrasts between Charles II and his father, and the similarities with James VI and I, are a measure of how well suited he was to manage such a constitution.

2 The Restoration Settlement in England and Wales

In an attempt to re-establish constitutional legitimacy, the Restoration settlement consciously sought to turn the clock back to 1641 rather than 1640 or 1642. All those statutes to which Charles I had assented remained in force, but the thousand or more acts and ordinances passed by the Long Parliament and the republican regimes were declared null and void. This ensured that there could be no return to the policies of Charles I's Personal Rule: the constitutional reforms of 1641 – especially the destruction of Star Chamber and High Commission, the curtailment of the judicial powers of the Privy Council, and the abolition of the Crown's feudal revenues and prerogative taxes such as Ship Money – all stayed in place. The only measure of 1641 to be significantly modified was the Triennial Act, which was replaced in 1664 by a watered-down act that did not require fresh elections every three years but merely provided for a session of Parliament at least every third year. Otherwise, the status quo of mid-1641 was systematically reconstructed. Executive powers were again entrusted to the King and a Privy Council freely chosen by him, while supreme legislative authority was once more wielded by the Crown in conjunction with two Houses of Parliament identical in structure, membership and procedure with their pre-war counterparts.

This return to the situation of 1641 served to enshrine those reforms desired by Constitutional Royalists such as Hyde, but to jettison all the more far-reaching measures against Charles I which they had opposed. Nothing denounced by Hyde and his allies in 1640–1 was restored in 1660. In many ways the Restoration settlement – like the Declaration of Breda – reflected the advice that Constitutional Royalists had offered throughout the Civil Wars and Interregnum. Its principal architect was Hyde, who was confirmed as Lord Chancellor (an office he had held in exile since 1658) and created Earl of Clarendon in April 1661. His former ally Sir John Culpepper was appointed Chancellor of the Exchequer in June 1660, only to die the following month, while another old ally the Earl of Southampton became Lord Treasurer. The moderate royalism of these figures suited the prevailing mood in 1660 and, as Paul Seaward has written, 'in both religion and politics, if the government could have been said to have had a policy in the early 1660s, it was Clarendon's'. At its heart lay a conviction that royal powers and the liberties of the subject existed in symbiosis, and that the strength of each depended upon that of the other. This was a paradigm that Charles I had memorably advocated on the scaffold but only implemented erratically and unreliably during his lifetime. His elder son, on the other hand, exposed to Hyde's influence in exile, had come to embrace it much more firmly. Charles II possessed neither the inclination nor the application to develop consistently authoritarian policies. Rather, he wanted a settlement that would ensure strong royal govern-ment within the rule of law, an assured role for Parliaments, and a broad national Church. All but the last he achieved.

The widespread desire for a strong monarchy was immediately apparent in the financial settlement. To compensate for the loss of prerogative taxation and the Crown's feudal revenues, the Convention voted to grant Charles an annual income of approximately £1.2 million – higher than the sum that had enabled Charles I to avoid recalling Parliament during the 1630s. All the Crown lands appropriated during the Interregnum were restored, but these yielded little more than £100,000 per annum. It was estimated that the continuation of the excise would bring in about £400,000 a year, and customs duties a similar sum. Unfortunately, these figures proved far too optimistic, primarily because the economy remained in recession until the late 1660s. In an effort to boost royal income, the Hearth Tax (a levy of six pence on every hearth) was introduced in 1662 to raise another £300,000, but its yield seldom reached even half that amount. By the mid-1660s the King's annual revenue had fallen as low as £700,000, while his debts had soared to £1.25 million. Although the prerog-ative taxes that had so alienated Parliaments under Charles I had now been abolished, there was no evidence that his son's Parliaments had any clearer understanding of the monarch's financial predicament than their predecessors. This, aggravated by his own extravagance, meant that throughout his reign Charles II was constantly short of money. The old fiscal system, in which the King was expected to 'live of his own', was simply patched up and only in the 1690s did a fundamental overhaul belatedly take place.[3]

One central objective of the financial settlement was thus to transfer the prin-cipal source of Crown revenue from land taxes to duties on trade. Those who owned large estates found themselves far less burdened with direct taxation than before the Civil War. There was no attempt at the Restoration to unravel the extraordinarily tangled web of land transfers that had taken place during the Civil Wars and Interregnum. Over five thousand Royalists had lost their estates or been forced to pay swingeing fines to regain them. Although many had succeeded in recovering much of their property by the early 1660s, a size-able minority of ex-Royalists (generally comprising lesser gentry more than greater gentry or nobility) failed to get their lands back either wholly or in part. The King did not lift a finger to help such people. He had calculated – correctly – that it was safer to offend his erstwhile supporters, who could at least be relied upon not to rebel against him, than his former enemies, who just conceivably might. That meant letting the land settlement sort itself out by private trans-actions rather than pursuing the hazardous course of legislation to redress Royalist grievances. It also meant imposing the minimum of penalties on those who had fought against the King during the 1640s and 1650s. The Act of Free and General Pardon, Indemnity and Oblivion (August 1660) was extended to all except those responsible for the Irish Rebellion of 1641, those who had signed Charles I's death warrant, and a handful of other named individuals such as Sir Henry Vane the younger. Vane was executed, along with nine surviving regicides, and the corpses of Cromwell, Ireton and Bradshaw were exhumed, hanged and decapitated. Their heads were stuck on poles and displayed as traitors outside Westminster Hall, where they remained until the 1680s. But otherwise the Act was notable for its lack of vindictiveness. For three years it was made an offence to cast aspersions on anybody's conduct during the previous twenty years. Once again, Royalists lost more than their opponents: Church and Crown lands were to be returned, but those who had purchased all other estates were confirmed to have sound title, and there would be no compensation for those who had already paid heavy fines or mortgages to buy back their lands. Former Royalists were hardly going to rise up against a King whom they had just welcomed back with open arms; but many felt shabbily treated and their lasting bitterness was captured by a contemporary joke that the Act of Indemnity and Oblivion was really an 'act of indemnity to the King's enemies and of oblivion to his friends'.[4]

The same desire to reconcile as many old enemies as possible to the restored monarchy led Charles to appoint people from a very wide political spectrum to both national and local offices. No fewer than twelve of the twenty-seven Privy Councillors appointed in 1660 were former Parliamentarians. Among the officers of state, moderate Royalists like Hyde and Southampton rubbed shoulders with those who had supported Parliament such as the new Lord Chamberlain, the Earl of Manchester, or Anthony Ashley Cooper, who was created Baron Ashley and appointed Chancellor of the Exchequer soon afterwards. In most counties, no more than about 40 per cent of Justices of the Peace were ex-Royalists, and they found themselves working alongside many who had served the republican regimes. A similar range of opinion was represented on the majority of borough councils. Although, as with the land settlement, this policy of sharing power disappointed Royalist hopes, it did ensure that Charles's rule rested upon as broad a base of support as possible.

This base was further enlarged by the process of decentralization that characterized government during the 1660s. The collection of taxes and militia rates was entrusted to local commissioners. Although the Militia Acts of 1661 and 1662 stipulated that the 'sole right' of command over the militia lay with the King, day-to-day control and administration were delegated to Lords Lieutenant and Deputy Lieutenants in the shires. The Corporation Act (1661) authorized commissioners from the rural gentry to intervene in the affairs of boroughs and if necessary to remove members of corporations. The Restoration can thus be seen as a major victory for the county gentry, and it left the Crown even more reliant upon their co-operation than before the Civil Wars.

This decentralization was only possible because of wider changes in demographic and economic trends. After reaching a peak of just over 5.2 million during the 1650s, England's population fell back to below 5 million during the 1660s and did not exceed it again consistently until after 1700. The population of Wales likewise stabilized at approximately 350,000 after 1660. The end of over a century of sustained population growth had several causes, of which probably the most important were firstly a trend towards fewer and later marriages as mounting pressure on resources in earlier decades produced increasing economic hardship, and secondly higher mortality rates caused by the exceptionally frequent waves of epidemic disease, especially bubonic plague, that struck England and Wales between the late 1640s and the mid-1680s. The slump in population growth, together with generally good harvests after 1660, brought inflation to a halt and ensured that prices followed a plateau, or even fell slightly, until the middle of the eighteenth century. These developments fostered a more relaxed economic climate and meant that central government had less need to intervene in the localities to regulate the provision of scarce resources and to preserve order. Crown and Parliament could afford to stand back and leave local justice and administration to the provincial elites.

Ironically, it was the power of the gentry represented in Parliament that frustrated the final aspect of Charles's programme as set out in the Declaration of Breda, the establishment of 'a liberty to tender consciences'. Both Charles and Clarendon – and also a significant minority in the Lords – appear to have been genuinely committed to the idea of a broad, 'comprehensive' Church, with a generous measure of toleration for those whose consciences prevented their joining it.[5] This would have been the natural ecclesiastical counterpart to the conciliation and acceptance of diversity that characterized the secular aspects of the Restoration settlement. It would also have harked back to the easy-going ecumenicism of the Jacobean Church and thus perfectly coincided with the spirit of Charles II's regime. The King's moderate intentions were made plain in October 1660 when, following a conference between Anglicans and Cromwellian conformists held at Clarendon's London residence, Worcester House, Charles issued a declaration promising to curb bishops' powers by involving presbyters in the exercise of episcopal jurisdiction, and also offering a degree of latitude in the use of some of the more contentious ceremonies and phrases in the Prayer Book. During the autumn of 1660, the vast majority of those appointed to bishoprics were in the moderate Jacobean tradition, such as George Morley at Winchester,[6] or Gilbert Sheldon at London. Unfortunately, these months also revealed serious divisions within the Convention over religious issues which meant that attempts to translate the Worcester House Declaration into legislation were narrowly defeated. Paradoxically, it appears that Charles himself had opposed them, possibly because he was so attached to the royal supremacy that he did not as yet wish to see the Church establishment defined by Parliament. But this delay proved fatal, for once the Convention was dissolved (29 December 1660) and then succeeded on 8 May 1661 by the zealously Royalist and deeply unforgiving Cavalier Parliament, hopes of a comprehensive Church settlement rapidly evaporated.

The mood of the Cavalier Parliament was further hardened by an abortive Fifth Monarchist rising in London in January 1661 led by Thomas Venner. This confirmed the widespread perception that there was a direct equation between religious dissent and sedition, and reinforced the gathering reaction against nonconformity. Within ten days of its first meeting, the Cavalier Parliament had restored bishops to the House of Lords and ordered the Solemn League and Covenant to be burnt by the common hangman. Meanwhile, another conference of clergy held at Savoy House soon broke down amid bitter wrangling over revisions to the Prayer Book. The failure of the Savoy Conference was caused primarily by the obstinacy of Richard Baxter, whose rejection of the offer of a bishopric and steadfast refusal to accept anything less than a completely rewritten liturgy alienated more moderate comprehension-ists like Sheldon. The task of redrafting the Prayer Book then fell to Convocation which produced a text that – notwithstanding several hundred minor amendments – was at least as obnoxious to most dissenters as that of 1604. The Cavalier Parliament adopted this Prayer Book in April 1662, and the following month passed an Act of Uniformity requiring all ministers of religion to declare their 'unfeigned assent and consent' to everything contained in the new Prayer Book and making its use compulsory for all Church of England services. Those who failed to comply by 24 August 1662 would lose their livings. In all, out of approximately 9,000 parish clergy, nearly 700 had already been ejected since 1660, while a further 936 were deprived under the terms of the Act of Uniformity. About another 120 clergy were ejected in Wales.

Despite some resistance from a minority in the Lords who were sympathetic to Protestant dissenters, the Cavalier Parliament repudiated the principle of toleration along with that of comprehension. Having seen their old enemies do so well out of the secular settlement, Anglican Royalists were determined not to grant parallel concessions in the religious sphere. In December 1661, the Corporation Act excluded from borough corporations all those who would not swear oaths of allegiance and non-resistance, abjure the Solemn League and Covenant, and take the Anglican sacraments; while in May 1662 the Quaker Act imposed fines or even transportation on those who refused any oath legally tendered, or who attended a meeting with five or more other Quakers. After radical dissenters in Yorkshire tried to launch a rebellion in October 1663, all meetings of five or more people held 'under colour or pretence of any exercise of religion' were declared illegal by the Conventicle Act of 1664. The following year, the Five Mile Act prohibited all ministers ejected under the Act of Uniformity and other unlicensed preachers to come within five miles of their former parish, or of any city or borough.

These draconian measures against dissenters came to be known collectively as the 'Clarendon Code'. This was an ironic label, for Clarendon had tried hard to moderate the provisions of the Act of Uniformity. As late as the summer of 1663, he still hoped to extend 'such liberty as may be safe to men of peaceable spirits, though they differ in judgement'. However, he remained intensely committed to the rule of law and abominated any threat of sedition or public disorder. After the Yorkshire rising he advocated rigorous enforcement of the laws against dissenters, whom he ultimately came to regard as 'a pack of knaves'. He backed away from liberty of conscience as soon as it raised the spectre of lawlessness. In the end, despite his efforts to reconcile the two, his attachment to the rule of law proved stronger than his religious ecumenicism. Significantly, Clarendon also opposed the King's attempts to use his discretionary powers to grant dispensations from the Act of Uniformity. Throughout his reign, Charles II remained strongly attached to the principle of toleration for both Catholic and Protestant dissenters, and in December 1662 he issued a Declaration of Indulgence that would have allowed him to exempt certain individuals from the penal laws. Just as Clarendon had earlier attacked

Charles I's attempts to override the rule of law, so he opposed the bill to enact the Declaration of Indulgence on the grounds that it was 'a very unreasonable and unjust thing to commit such a trust to the King'. In a remarkable phrase that illustrated the fundamental consistency of his political thought, he declared that the bill 'was Ship Money in religion, that nobody could know the end of, or where it would rest'. He was thus opposing royal policy on exactly the same grounds as in 1640–1. By the summer of 1663 Charles II had wisely decided not to press the point, although he frequently resumed the fight for toleration during the years that followed, and found some allies within the House of Lords. Indeed, possibly because of his Catholic sympathies, he actually seems to have cared more deeply about toleration than about comprehension.

The effect of the Clarendon Code was not to extirpate religious dissent but to drive it underground.[7] Instead of accommodating 'tender consciences' inside the Church, or at least tolerating them outside it, the Restoration Church imposed rigid doctrinal requirements upon its members and persecuted an entrenched core of nonconformists comprising a few thousand ministers and perhaps 10 per cent of the laity. As a result, the religious settlement was utterly at odds with every other aspect of the Restoration settlement. Any hope of reconstructing a genuinely national Church had vanished, although nearly thirty years would pass before the fact of religious pluralism was officially recognized. The opportunity to revive the ecumenical traditions of the Jacobean Church that would so neatly have mirrored Charles II's secular programme was missed, and the consequent tension between political reconciliation and religious intolerance proved to be the greatest single weakness of the Restoration settlement and a major source of instability for several decades to come.

3 The Restoration in Scotland

On 14 May 1660, Charles II was proclaimed in Edinburgh as King of Great Britain and Ireland. The predominant mood was one of jubilation, for the return of the monarchy signalled the severance of the Cromwellian union and the liberation of Scotland from English rule. Once again, England and Scotland were only bound together by the fact that the same monarch happened to wear both crowns. Yet, as their use of the term Great Britain revealed, the Scots continued to see their future as part of a British state, and their newly regained independence was to prove a mixed blessing. During the later seventeenth century, the kingdoms of England, Scotland and Ireland were allowed to go their own ways. In stark contrast to the moves towards closer union under James VI and I and Charles I, and the incorporative union of the 1650s, Charles II preferred the freedom of action that came from ruling his three kingdoms as separate entities. As a result, there was no single British settlement at the Restoration: rather, Charles agreed different settlements with the political elites of each nation and then governed through them largely in isolation from the others.

Whereas in England the clock had been turned back to 1641, in Scotland it was turned back to 1633, the date of Charles I's Scottish coronation. The Act Rescissory (March 1661) revoked all legislation since that year, thus annulling at a stroke not only the Covenanter reforms of 1638–41 but also the hated religious innovations of 1633–7. As in England, the Scottish nobility and gentry realized that their interests were best served by collaborating with a strong monarchy. When Parliament met in January 1661, it promptly restored royal prerogative powers in full, including the right to appoint all officers of state and Privy Councillors. Every office-holder had to take an oath of allegiance recognizing the King as the 'only Supreme Governor of this kingdom' and denouncing the Covenants. The Lords of the Articles were restored in 1663, thereby enabling the King to control the business of Parliament, and the Crown was voted an annual revenue of £480,000 derived from customs duties and from the excise on ale and beer that had been introduced in 1644. A small standing army of about 2,000 soldiers was maintained under Middleton's command. Then, in 1663, the Crown was given sweeping powers to raise as many as 20,000 foot and 2,000 horse, and if necessary to deploy them in England or Ireland as well as Scotland. An Act concerning Religion left it up to the King to determine the future of Church government, but stated that he would settle it 'in such a frame as shall be most agreeable to the Word of God, most suitable to monarchical government and most complying with the public peace and quiet of the kingdom'.

In return for restoring the powers of the Crown, the landowners regained the private jurisdictions, hereditary influence and tight control over their tenants that they had lost during the Interregnum. They were happy to co-operate collectively with the Crown, but on the understanding that they were permitted to manage local affairs free from royal interference. Like James VI, Charles judged very shrewdly how far he could press central control into the provinces, and by respecting regional autonomy, especially in the Highlands, he avoided antagonizing the nobles and made them conscious of their common bond with the Crown. This was reinforced by the appointment of key nobles to senior offices of state. As in England, Charles was more anxious to win over former enemies than to reward old friends, and many of the most important appointments in 1660 went to ex-Covenanters: Middleton became the King's Commissioner to the Parliament, Glencairn Chancellor, Rothes Lord President of the Council, and Lauderdale Secretary of the Council. The people who came off worst were once again those who had been loyal to the Crown for longest, namely the pre-Engagement Royalists.

Having accommodated a number of leading ex-Covenanters within his administration, Charles was then happy to go along with their vindictive hounding of their old adversaries among the Protesters. In May 1661, Argyll was tried on charges of compliance with the Cromwellian regime and then beheaded. The following month, the most prominent Protester minister, James Guthrie, was executed for contriving the Remonstrance of 1650 and denying the King's ecclesiastical authority. Archibald Johnston of Wariston, by now half-deranged, was extradited from his exile in France and brought home for trial and execution in 1663. There were fewer executions than south of the border, but the terms of the Scottish Act of Indemnity and Oblivion of

September 1662 were harsher than its English equivalent: around 700 people were exempted from pardon and subjected to heavy fines.

Restoration Scotland remained very much poorer than England, and it took a long time for its economy to recover from the devastation of the 1640s and 1650s. The collapse of the republic brought free trade between the two kingdoms to an end, and the Navigation Act of 1660 rigorously excluded Scotland from England's colonial and continental trade. Three years later, new customs duties were imposed on Scottish goods imported into England, especially linen, cattle, salt and coal. Scotland's population in 1660 was possibly in the region of one million but it stagnated or even declined during the rest of the century. The Scots remained heavily dependent upon the land: four in every five either worked the land or lived on it, perhaps a third of them in the Highlands and islands. The landowners' recovery of their former status ensured that after 1660 Scotland remained very much a feudal country, dominated by a relatively small elite of around a hundred hereditary nobles and Highland chieftains who held their tenants in thrall. The development of Scotland's commerce and industry was hampered by Charles's refusal to develop an integrated British economy and by the effects of being dragged into the Anglo-Dutch wars. In economic terms, Restoration Scotland seemed to suffer all the drawbacks of being closely associated with her much wealthier southern neighbour without enjoying any of the benefits.

Although Charles deliberately tried to keep the settlements in each of his kingdoms as separate as possible, all three experienced a strong backlash in favour of episcopacy. In Scotland the most common attitude was anti-clericalism, directed especially against the Presbyterian ministers, and Charles therefore encountered little lay resistance when he decided not to recall the General Assembly of the Kirk and instead embarked upon an erastian settlement that restored the powers of lay patrons and bishops as they had been left by James VI. Led by James Sharp, who became Archbishop of St Andrews and Primate of Scotland, a system of episcopal government in which bishops acted as chairmen ('moderators') of synods and presbyteries within their dioceses was in place by the summer of 1662. That same year saw legislation declaring the Covenants unlawful, prohibiting conventicles and requiring all ministers appointed since 1649 to seek presentation from lay patrons and collation by bishops. This led by the end of 1663 to the deprivation of about 270 ministers – over one in four – mainly concentrated in the southwest of Scotland where attachment to the Covenants had always been strongest. While the settlement took root quite easily in most of Scotland, the southwest became increasingly restive and in November 1666 an uprising broke out.

The Pentland Rising was finally precipitated not only by religious grievances but also by the build-up of troops in the southwest following the outbreak of the second Dutch War in 1665.[8] Fearful of alleged contacts between Scottish Presbyterians and the Dutch, Rothes, who had replaced Middleton as the King's Commissioner in 1663, despatched a force led by Sir James Turner to suppress illegal conventicles. The troops soon began collecting fines that were still outstanding under the Act of Indemnity and pocketing the proceeds, and their heavy-handedness sparked off a spontaneous and ill-organised revolt. The rising never involved more than one thousand poorly equipped men who found no support among the nobility, but the government, believing that it confirmed the link between religious dissent and insurrection, reacted with ruthless brutality. Thirty-three rebels were hanged, two after being tortured, and many others were transported to Barbados. The savagery of these punishments provoked a reaction against Rothes and Sharp, whose repressive policies were widely blamed for causing the rising, and their influence waned considerably thereafter. The fall in 1667 of Clarendon, who had broadly supported their actions, further weakened their position. In 1669 Lauderdale, who aligned himself with Clarendon's opponents in advocating a more tolerant and conciliatory approach, was appointed Commissioner, and from then until 1680 he remained the pre-eminent figure in Scottish affairs.

4 The Restoration in Ireland

Whereas in England and Scotland the traditional elites regained their earlier status at the Restoration, in Ireland the Cromwellian land settlement was preserved largely intact. Although Charles and Clarendon may privately have hoped that some expropriated lands might be returned to their Catholic owners, in practice the solidarity of the Irish Protestant community precluded any significant reversal of the massive transfers of the 1650s. The Irish Parliament that assembled on 8 May 1661 included only one Catholic, and the following year it passed a strongly anti-Catholic Act of Settlement. The Cromwellian confiscations were to stand, but Catholics could submit claims to seven commissioners sitting in what was known as the 'court of claims', pleading to be declared 'innocent papists' and hence eligible to recover their lands. In the event, the court sat for less than eight months in 1662–3, during which time it issued nearly 600 decrees of innocence to Catholics but left several thousand claims unheard. Yet even these decrees were enough to antagonize the Protestant interest. To provide restitution for those designated 'innocent papists', most soldiers and adventurers were required to surrender one third of the lands they had gained during the Interregnum. In all, about 850,000 acres passed from Protestant to Catholic hands in this way. That was quite insufficient to appease the Catholics – who retained only about 22 per cent of Irish land – but enough to leave the Protestants feeling aggrieved. The fundamental tensions and antagonisms within Irish society remained unresolved.

Catholics were likewise systematically excluded from political life. Charles governed Ireland through members of the Protestant community, and appointed a series of Lords Lieutenant of whom by far the longest serving was Ormond (1662–9 and 1677–84). Paradoxically, Ormond himself came from the Catholic Old English Butler family, but his Protestant beliefs, his unflinching loyalty to the Crown during the 1640s and 1650s, and his friendship with Clarendon all commended him to Charles. Like his predecessors, the strength of his authority in Ireland depended heavily on his perceived status at Court, and Ormond exploited his office as Lord Steward of the Royal

Household to build up a circle of clients close to the King who could safeguard his interests during his absence. In Ireland, Ormond tried to pursue a moderate policy that would win over the conflicting groups but he merely ended up antagonizing all interests. The Catholics felt utterly marginalized both politically and economically, yet the Protestants chafed at the lack of even sterner measures against them. Despite the complaints from all sides, as long as Ormond possessed Charles's confidence he was secure, but this left him acutely vulnerable to the factionalism of English politics. It was no accident that only two years after the fall of his old friend and ally Clarendon in 1667, Ormond's enemies led by the Duke of Buckingham had stirred up intrigues against him and secured his dismissal. Yet, after a number of short-lived, ill-fated successors had failed in turn, and after his leading opponents had themselves fallen from favour, Ormond was reappointed Lord Lieutenant in 1677 and remained in office until nearly the end of the reign.

At the heart of Ireland's instability lay the religious issue: 80 per cent of the population still espoused Catholicism, while only 10 per cent were members of the established Church of Ireland. The remaining 10 per cent belonged to various Protestant sects, of which the largest were the Scottish Presbyterians and the Quakers. Although in theory only Church of Ireland services were legal, in practice this proved impossible to enforce and Ormond generally turned a blind eye to Catholic worship. By the end of the 1660s Catholics enjoyed a large measure of *de facto* religious toleration, provided that they demonstrated their political loyalty to the Crown. The Catholic hierarchy gradually found that it could co-operate with the administration in Dublin and in 1666, to the annoyance of Rome, the clergy acknowledged their duty of obedience to Charles. There is even evidence of some mixed marriages between Catholics and Protestants. At a local level, Catholic influence proved remarkably resilient, especially in the field of education: there was, for example, a Catholic schoolmaster working in every parish in Limerick by 1670. By contrast, the Church of Ireland's only real foothold lay in the towns, and it was estimated that at the end of the 1660s it had only about 50,000 adherents in rural areas. Although its wealth was swelled by endowments, tithe payments and government support, there was no disguising the fact that the Church of Ireland represented an embattled minority within an overwhelmingly Catholic population. Apart from the Protestant Trinity College, Dublin, which expanded considerably after 1660, the Church failed to make significant progress in education. In 1666 the Irish Act of Uniformity prescribed the revised English Prayer Book, required episcopal ordination of all clergy, and strengthened the hand of the bishops against Protestant dissenters. Concentrated mainly in Ulster, the nonconforming Protestants were vulnerable to legislation against conventicles and often suffered more severely from religious repression than the Catholics. Faced with persecution, the Presbyterians of Ulster increasingly sought to make common cause with their Scottish brethren, and the period after 1660 saw immigration from Scotland into Ulster on a growing scale.

In contrast to England and Scotland, the later seventeenth century was an era of sustained demographic growth in Ireland. The population, which had stood at approximately 2.1 million in 1641, had been so badly decimated by the mid-century conflicts that as late as 1672 it was probably no more than 1.7 million. However, mainly because of a marked trend towards early marriages, it had risen to perhaps 2.2 million by 1687. That population remained overwhelmingly dependent on the land, and despite the increase in numbers Ireland's rural economy was marked by low prices and low rents. Irish revenue, derived from customs, excise and the Hearth Tax, proved so inadequate that regular subventions from the English Exchequer were essential, and only in the later 1670s did prosperity begin to return. This coincided with a major readjustment of Irish trade in response to English policy. At the Restoration, three-quarters of Ireland's trade was with England, and involved the exchange of mainly pastoral products in return for finished goods. In 1665, sheep, cattle (and related products), fish and horses accounted for 80 per cent of Irish exports, while its principal imports were woollen cloth, tobacco, coal, haberdashery, grocery, ironware, silks, linen and hops. The English Navigation Act of 1660 had treated England and Ireland as a single entity, separate from Scotland. However, as Charles's reign progressed, the Irish also found themselves rigorously excluded from England's colonial and continental markets, and Irish imports were increasingly subject to prohibitions of which the most notorious were those imposed by the Cattle Acts of 1663 and 1667. Although recent research has suggested that the impact of these acts was somewhat exaggerated by contemporaries, they undoubtedly contributed to a marked shift in later seventeenth-century Ireland towards sheep-raising and butter production. By the early 1680s, wool and butter comprised 40 per cent of Ireland's exports, and only 30 per cent of its total exports went to England. Instead, the Irish steadily developed their own trading links with the Continent and with the colonies, particularly the West Indies, and as a consequence Ireland became less dependent upon her economic ties with the mainland.

This trend epitomized a period in which English policy towards Ireland was characterized less by aggression than by apathy. Following several decades of plantation and active colonization, the English became much less interested in Ireland after 1660. The Restoration settlement wholly failed to alleviate the basic problems of Irish society. A Protestant colonial elite continued to rule over a dispossessed Catholic majority that lacked both religious rights and political voice. The foundations were thus laid for the next two-and-a-half centuries of Irish history – for the Protestant ascendancy of the eighteenth century, and the subsequent rise of a nationalist movement committed to redressing the twin grievances of land and religion. The Restoration settlement in Ireland thus settled nothing: as Roy Foster has written, 'the vital thing about the Restoration "settlement" was its unsettled nature'.

5 Clarendon

Clarendon, whose commitment to a strong monarchy ruling with Parliament and within the rule of law had been a formative influence on the Restoration settlement, remained Lord Chancellor and the King's principal adviser until 1667. During these seven years, his remarkable attention to administrative detail and his possession of the King's trust combined to make him the pre-eminent figure in government. Yet, beneath the pomp with which he surrounded himself, Clarendon's position was essentially insecure. He lacked the vision and dynamism needed to be a creative administrator, and his stuffy, pompous, self-righteous personality ensured that he was never widely popular. Above all, he failed to understand the need to build up a network of clients at Court, in the Privy Council and in Parliament. In this he was a victim of his own profound loyalty to the Crown and his belief that the King should be in command of decision-making. Clarendon's reluctance to play the role of 'chief minister' deprived the Council of badly needed leadership, and by refusing to 'manage' Parliament he contributed to the growth of opposition in both Houses by the mid-1660s. Sufficiently passive to give his enemies a chance to mobilize their own supporters, yet sufficiently prominent to be easily blamed for unpopular policies, Clarendon provided a natural scapegoat once the initial euphoria that had greeted the Restoration wore off.

The list of misfortunes laid at Clarendon's door grew steadily longer. In May 1662 the King married Catherine of Braganza, a Portuguese princess, and when she turned out to be barren Clarendon was denounced for negotiating the treaty even though it had been supported by the whole Council. He was also criticized for selling Dunkirk to France for £300,000: although this decision made economic sense, to many it appeared an ignominious surrender of a symbolic bridgehead that had been gained under Cromwell. The Lord Chancellor was likewise held responsible, again somewhat unfairly, for the repressive body of religious legislation branded the 'Clarendon Code'.[9] His exalted position inspired considerable jealousy, and the marriage in 1660 of his daughter Anne to the heir presumptive, James, Duke of York, prompted snide comments that he was trying to worm his way into the royal family. To make matters worse, Clarendon played into his enemies' hands by seeming to feather his own nest, and the massive house that he built for himself in Piccadilly fuelled rumours of peculation. The supreme irony was that when Clarendon was finally dismissed, it was as a result of a war that he had tried hard to prevent and that had been forced upon him by his enemies.

Throughout the early 1660s relations between England and the Dutch Republic steadily deteriorated. The Navigation Act of 1660 was much more effective than the act of 1651 because it listed certain commodities that could only be imported in English ships and targeted the bulk cargoes that were the preserve of the Dutch carrying-trade. Furthermore, all imports from the developing colonies in West Africa, Asia and the West Indies had to be conveyed in English ships. In 1663 the Act for the Encouragement of Trade (Staple Act) struck another blow at Dutch colonial trade by requiring the colonists to import European goods only from England and only in English ships. These measures did not stem only from the fact that the Dutch were England's principal commercial rivals. At least as important was the hostility felt by Anglican Royalists towards a Calvinist republic whose values seemed antithetical to monarchical government and religious conformity. By 1664 many Anglican Royalists, including such younger figures as Lord Arlington and Sir Thomas Clifford, were clamouring for war, causing Charles to write:

'I never saw so great an appetite to a war as in both this town and country, especially in the parliament men'. Despite Clarendon's dark warnings of the financial implications, the King was attracted by the prospect of rich prizes from plundering the Dutch merchant fleet, and after a series of skirmishes between Dutch and English traders in West Africa during the summer of 1664 he formally declared war on the Dutch in March 1665.

The conflict began well for England. In June 1665 the Lord High Admiral, the Duke of York, routed the Dutch fleet off Lowestoft and killed the enemy admiral, Opdam. But this victory was not followed up. In August the English made a bungled assault on the Dutch fleet at Bergen. France and Denmark entered the war against England early the following year, and in June 1666 the Dutch sank about twenty English ships and killed 8,000 men including two admirals, in the Four Days' Battle in the Channel. An English success in the St James's Day Battle at the mouth of the Thames on 25 July could not hide the fact that by the summer of 1666 naval administration had disintegrated and the admiralty was in dire financial straits. The Parliament that in 1665 had voted a total of £3,750,000 towards the war was by now thoroughly alarmed at the growing evidence of corruption and misgovernment.

Amid this gathering crisis two natural disasters occurred which further weakened the Crown's finances and seriously undermined national self-confidence. During the summer and early autumn of 1665, London experienced by far the worst outbreak of bubonic plague of the century. The epidemic spread with terrible rapidity through the narrow, rat-infested streets of the city, and caused nearly 70,000 recorded deaths.[10] The Court fled first to Salisbury and then to Oxford, where Parliament met; but London's commerce was brought to a standstill for over six months. Even more serious in its economic implications was the Great Fire of London, which started on 2 September 1666 just as the capital was beginning to return to normal. Fanned by a strong wind, the fire raged for five days, laying waste 395 acres of the City and destroying 13,200 houses, St Paul's Cathedral, eighty-seven churches, four bridges and goods estimated at £3.2 million. Nearly a quarter of a million people were left homeless. In the long term, the fire provided an opportunity for the rebuilding of London with wider, more hygienic streets – a major reason why the plague did not recur – and with buildings of brick and stone rather than wood. But at the time it was a terrible psychological blow that led contemporaries to wonder whether this might be a popish plot or a divine punishment visited upon a sinful nation. The breezy confidence and optimism so apparent at the Restoration had given way by the mid-1660s to a mood of fear and uncertainty.

Exacerbated by the effects of these two catastrophes, royal revenue slumped from nearly £820,000 in 1665 to an annual average of £647,000 in 1666–7. Parliament blamed the Crown's financial difficulties on the incompetence and corruption of officials, and in the autumn of 1666 the Commons ordered the officers of the navy and ordnance to submit their accounts for inspection. The following February, a further parliamentary grant of £1,800,000 was accompanied by the appointment of commissioners to examine the public accounts. By this time, public opinion had turned decisively against the Dutch War. The trading companies complained that England's economic interests were suffering badly, and there was a growing feeling within the political nation that a far greater long-term danger lay in the Catholic authoritarianism of Louis XIV. During the spring of 1667 peace negotiations were therefore opened with the Dutch, and a large part of the English fleet was paid off and anchored in the Medway near Chatham. There, the following June, a Dutch raiding force under De Ruyter scored a spectacular success when it sailed straight up the river, sank three ships at their moorings and towed two others back to Holland, including the flagship, the *Royal Charles*.

This humiliating defeat sealed Clarendon's fate. His political isolation was increased by the death of his old ally Southampton in May 1667. Against Clarendon's wishes, the Treasury was entrusted to a commission that included several of his leading critics, such as Ashley, Clifford and Sir William Coventry. They immediately began to abandon Southampton's obsolete methods and vigorously attacked Clarendon as an obstacle to administrative innovation and efficiency. When the Treaty of Breda brought the Dutch War to an end in July, England's meagre gains hardly appeared to justify the ruinously high cost: the only significant acquisition was the Dutch colony of the New Netherlands, which included New York and New Jersey. The economic value of these colonies was not yet apparent, and they seemed to offer small compensation for the fact that royal debts now exceeded £2.5 million. When Parliament met briefly in late July there was a chorus of demands for Clarendon's resignation: for many he had come to symbolize all the failings of a corrupt and incompetent administration. By this time, even Charles regarded the Lord Chancellor as too great a political liability. He had never much liked Clarendon, and resented his prudish chiding of his private life and inattentiveness to paperwork; now, egged on by the likes of Buckingham, Arlington and Coventry, Charles decided that the only way to protect the Crown and defuse the political crisis was to dismiss him. On 30 August, in poor health and heartbroken by his wife's death earlier that month, Clarendon was required to tender his resignation.

But this was not enough for his enemies. Determined to destroy Clarendon permanently, Buckingham and some of his younger allies such as Edward Seymour launched impeachment proceedings in October. The charges of treason could not be substantiated, however, and the prosecution case soon broke down. When the Lords refused to commit Clarendon to the Tower, his enemies contemplated setting up a special court of twenty-four peers to try him. Realizing that the King would not move to prevent such a step, Clarendon sailed for France on 29 November. Parliament subsequently passed an act of perpetual banishment forbidding him ever to return. Clarendon spent the rest of his life in exile, completing his magnificent *History of the Rebellion and Civil Wars in England* and a much less distinguished, self-exculpatory autobiography. He died at Rouen in December 1674.

The fall of Clarendon undoubtedly made 1667 a watershed, for it marked, in Paul Seaward's words, 'the end of an administration and of a policy'. For all his austerity and stuffiness, in office Clarendon had constantly sought 'the Crown's military, constitutional and financial security within a respect for the law, liberty, and property', and pursued the 'restoration of stability and unity to the country by the reconstruction of a strong monarchy beside a powerful law'. His successors were less principled and less consistent. Certainly Clarendon's departure reduced the political temperature and facilitated the rise of a new group of advisers with whom the King was on much more convivial terms. The Crown's relations with Parliament became, for a time, more harmonious. Yet there remained underlying tensions within Church and State that would return to haunt Charles, notably the growing mistrust between Court and Country, the incessant friction between Anglicans and dissenters, and above all the spectre of popery. All these unresolved contradictions, that Clarendon had at least managed to contain, were ultimately to spell disaster for those thrusting younger figures who openly rejoiced at his downfall.

9 Court and Country

	21 December	*Traité simulé* between Charles and Louis XIV
1671	February	Auxiliary Excise Bill augments Crown revenue
1672	20 January	'Stop of the Exchequer': Crown suspends repayment of loans to its creditors
	February	Public version of the *traité simulé* between Charles and Louis XIV
	15 March	Charles issues second Declaration of Indulgence
	17 March	Charles declares war on the Dutch Republic: beginning of the third Anglo-Dutch War
	22 April	Arlington created an Earl
	23 April	Ashley created Earl of Shaftesbury
	21 May	Earl of Essex appointed Lord Lieutenant of Ireland
	28 May	Indecisive Anglo-Dutch naval engagement off Southwold Bay
	3 September	Charles issues second Letter of Indulgence in Scotland
	October	Charles grants royal stipend (*regium donum*) to Irish Presbyterian ministers
	17 November	Shaftesbury appointed Lord Chancellor
	28 November	Clifford appointed Lord Treasurer
1673	4 February– 20 October	Eleventh session of Cavalier Parliament
	14 February	Commons votes against royal suspending power in ecclesiastical matters
	February	Publication of Pierre du Moulin's *England's Appeal from the Private Cabal at Whitehall to the Great Council of the Nation*
	8 March	Charles withdraws second Declaration of Indulgence
	29 March	Charles assents to the first Test Act imposing oaths designed to exclude Catholics from public office

	30 March	Duke of York fails to take Anglican communion on Easter Day, thereby publicly confirming his conversion to Catholicism
	May–June	Indecisive Anglo-Dutch naval engagements off the Schonveld
	15 June	Duke of York resigns as Lord High Admiral under terms of Test Act
	18 June	Clifford resigns as Lord Treasurer under terms of Test Act
	19 June	Sir Thomas Osborne appointed Lord Treasurer
	11 August	Battle of the Texel: inconclusive Anglo-Dutch naval engagement
	Summer–autumn	Cabal gradually disintegrates
	30 September	Duke of York marries Mary of Modena, a Catholic
	17 October	Clifford commits suicide
	27 October–4 November	Twelfth session of Cavalier Parliament
	9 November	Shaftesbury dismissed from Lord Chancellorship
1674	7 January–24 February	Thirteenth session of Cavalier Parliament
	9 February	Treaty of Westminster ends third Anglo-Dutch War
	27 June	Sir Thomas Osborne created Earl of Danby
	11 September	Arlington resigns as Secretary of State

Lauderdale deploys troops in southwest Scotland to suppress illegal conventicles

1675	13 April–9 June	Fourteenth session of Cavalier Parliament: abortive attempt to impeach Danby
	17 August	Secret agreement between Charles and Louis: French subsidies promised in return for prorogation of Parliament
	13 October–22 November	Fifteenth session of Cavalier Parliament

	November	Publication of *A Letter from a Person of Quality to his Friend in the Country*, possibly by Shaftesbury and John Locke
1676	January	Bishop Compton of London instructed to organize a census to estimate the number of nonconformists in England and Wales
	16 February	Further secret agreement between Charles and Louis: promise of more subsidies if Parliament remains prorogued
1677	15 February–13 May 1678	Sixteenth session of Cavalier Parliament
	24 May	Ormond reappointed Lord Lieutenant of Ireland
	August	Danby colludes in secret negotiations by Ralph Montagu, the English ambassador in Paris, for further French subsidies
	4 November	Marriage of Princess Mary to William of Orange
	9 November	Death of Archbishop Sheldon
	29 December	William Sancroft nominated Archbishop of Canterbury
	31 December	Anglo-Dutch treaty: alliance against France
	December	Publication of Andrew Marvell's *An Account of the Growth of Popery and Arbitrary Government*
1678	January	'Highland host' billeted on southwest Scotland to quell dissenters
	17 May	Further secret agreement between Charles and Louis
	23 May–15 July	Seventeenth session of Cavalier Parliament
	31 July	Peace of Nijmwegen between France and Dutch Republic
	July	Ralph Montagu dismissed as ambassador to Paris because of affair with Charles's former mistress and her daughter
	Publication of John Bunyan's *The Pilgrim's Progress*	

1 The Cabal

With Clarendon's fall, Charles felt a sense of liberation and resolved to become less reliant upon one single minister. Instead, over the next six years he turned to a loose-knit group of five of Clarendon's principal enemies known, from the first letters of their names or titles, as the Cabal: Sir Thomas Clifford, who became Treasurer of the Household, Baron Ashley, Chancellor of the Exchequer, the Duke of Buckingham, Lord Arlington, one of the Secretaries of State, and Lauderdale, the King's Commissioner in Scotland. Contrary to the modern connotations of the word 'cabal', these ministers did not form a secret faction. In fact, they were united by little except a dislike of Clarendon's legacy, especially the narrow intolerance of the restored Church of England. They hoped to use the royal prerogative to extend religious toleration to both dissenters and Catholics, and their sympathy towards the latter led them to support an alliance with France. None of the Cabal could be described as an Anglican: Clifford was a concealed Catholic and Arlington a Catholic sympathizer; Lauderdale supported the Restoration Church in Scotland, with its blend of episcopacy and presbytery; while Ashley and Buckingham were both associated with freethinkers. They were never a coherent or co-ordinated group: although Clifford and Ashley worked closely together as Treasury Commissioners to overhaul the King's finances, Arlington and Buckingham detested each other, while Lauderdale spent most of his time in Scotland. The serious, industrious Arlington was probably the most politically influential of the five, while Buckingham – a debauched maverick of sparkling conversation and slender abilities – was personally the closest to the King. That left Charles with plenty of scope to divide and rule. Between 1667 and the collapse of the Cabal in 1673 – even more than at other times during his reign – Charles formulated different aspects of policy with individual ministers on a pragmatic basis, with the result that much of the reality of power was concentrated in his own hands.

These developments at Court were deeply alarming to many in the Cavalier Parliament. Although relatively few members had lamented Clarendon's departure, most remained deeply committed to the Church and abhorred anything that appeared to weaken the nation's defences against Catholicism. They also suspected that far more corruption persisted among courtiers and senior office-holders than had yet been brought to light. As a result, the years of the Cabal saw the gradual emergence of a Country opposition within the Commons, led by such members as Sir William Coventry, Sir Thomas Meres, Lord Cavendish, William Lord Russell and William Sacheverell. This was certainly not an organized 'party' in the modern sense; rather, these people shared a broadly similar outlook characterized by a wish to defend the rule of law and the rights of Parliament against any encroachment from the royal prerogative, a strong attachment to Protestantism both at home and abroad, a hostility towards any *rapprochement* with France, and above all an almost paranoid fear of the spread of 'popery'. The policies associated with the Cabal were hardly calculated to allay any of these anxieties.

Charles's desire to extend his freedom of manoeuvre was most clearly apparent in foreign policy. By 1667, the dominant figure on the Continent was his cousin, Louis XIV. Early that year, Louis claimed that his wife, Maria Theresa, was the rightful heiress to fourteen separate provinces in the Spanish Netherlands, and in the War of Devolution (1667–8) he launched a lightning campaign that secured most of his demands. In January 1668, England, the Dutch Republic and Sweden responded to this aggression by forming the Triple Alliance, a Protestant coalition against France that was warmly welcomed in Parliament. Alarmed, Louis despatched a special ambassador, Charles Albert de Croissy, to London to explore the possibility of an alliance with England. So began the negotiations that ultimately produced the celebrated pact between England and France in 1670.

There were three different versions of the terms. The first, the secret Treaty of Dover, was signed on 22 May 1670 and was known only to Charles, Arlington, Clifford and James, Duke of York. In it, Charles and Louis agreed 'to humble the pride of the States General' by launching a naval and military war against the Dutch, during which France would pay England £225,000 a year. Following such a war, parts of the Dutch Republic were to be ceded to England and France, while the remainder would become a hereditary principality ruled by Charles's nephew William of Orange. This secret version of the treaty included a further remarkable clause stating that Charles, 'being convinced of the truth of the Roman Catholic religion is resolved to declare it, and to reconcile himself with the Church of Rome as soon as his country's affairs permit'. In return, Louis promised to provide £150,000 and 6,000 troops to assist in 'the execution of this design'.

Such an important development in foreign policy, and the preparations for war against the Dutch that it entailed, necessarily had to be shared with Charles's other, Protestant, ministers. But he could not possibly tell them about the 'Catholicity' clause. For their benefit, and especially to flatter Buckingham's vanity, Charles therefore went through the elaborate ruse of concluding a second treaty, on 21 December 1670, known as the *traité simulé* (sometimes also called the secret Treaty of London). This was signed by all members of the Cabal, and by December 1671 the whole Privy Council was aware of it. The *traité simulé* omitted the clause relating to Charles's declaration of his Catholicism and Louis's military and financial assistance to him. Otherwise, it was identical with the secret Treaty of Dover except that it slightly enlarged the Dutch territory that England would receive after the conflict, and provisionally fixed the spring of 1672 for the declaration of war. Finally, as that season approached and preparations mounted, a public version of the *traité simulé* was signed in February 1672.

Had it become widely known, the secret Treaty of Dover would have been catastrophic for Charles, and his reasons for promoting it, despite Louis's reservations, remain highly controversial. Although he was constantly short of revenue, it seems unlikely that the relatively modest financial gain was his prime consideration. It is more probable that Charles genuinely admired Louis and that, while he had neither the energy nor the inclination to emulate his style of government, he welcomed the treaty as a chance to forge a closer alignment with him. Charles was also eager to secure vengeance on the Dutch following the humiliations of the second Dutch War. The treaty does not necessarily demonstrate that he was a closet Catholic: the fact that he never implemented the 'Catholicity' clause, and was only received into the Catholic Church on his deathbed, suggests rather that his motives were essentially secular, diplomatic and opportunistic.[1]

These negotiations took place against a background of growing parliamentary concern over the Crown's religious policies. In 1668 Charles allowed the Conventicle Act to expire without being renewed. This left nonconformists free to meet, and the next two years saw a growing number of reports of disorderly conventicles all over the country. The Anglican gentry in the Commons co-operated with the High Church bishops in the Lords to defend the Church 'by law established' and to oppose any move towards greater comprehension or toleration. Sir John Vaughan, for example, argued that comprehension would 'subvert the present government', while Samuel Sandys declared that he 'never knew a toleration without an army to keep all quiet'. In 1669 the Commons made its unhappiness plain by refusing to grant supply of more than £300,000. The following year Charles therefore assented to a second, more draconian, Conventicle Act in return for the most generous vote of extraordinary taxation of the entire reign, accompanied by grants of new duties on imported wines for eight years and additional excise for nine years.

If the English Parliament temporarily curbed Charles's desire for greater toleration, in Scotland he had a freer hand. As Lauderdale informed him, 'never was king so absolute as you are in poor old Scotland'. In June 1669 Charles issued a Letter of Indulgence that allowed Presbyterian ministers to take up vacant livings as long as they swore to 'live peaceably and orderly'. This was a conscious attempt to woo moderate Presbyterians while suppressing those who remained politically disaffected. The following November, an Act Assertory declared that 'His Majesty has supreme authority and supremacy over all persons and in all causes ecclesiastical within this kingdom; and that by virtue thereof the ordering and disposal of the external government and policy of the Church does properly belong to His Majesty ... as an inherent right to the Crown.' This was intended to give Charles scope to reshape the Scottish Church as he wished, and it was directed as much against the more extreme Episcopalians as against the Presbyterians. Such royal interference in the Church's affairs provoked howls of protest from many of the bishops, the most outspoken of whom, Archbishop Alexander Burnet of Glasgow, was compelled to resign his see. In Scotland, as in England, Charles was forced to introduce a new Conventicle Act in 1670 in return for badly needed supply: this so-called 'Clanking Act' forbade all unlicensed preachers from addressing conventicles and enacted the death sentence for any who defied that ban. However, his and Lauderdale's preference remained for toleration and conciliation, and in September 1672 a second Letter of Indulgence was issued. Although this was very much part of a specifically Scottish policy, designed to win over more Presbyterian ministers, its timing was strongly influenced by developments south of the border.

The situation in England had a similar impact on events in Ireland. The dismissal of Ormond in 1669 led to a period of greater religious toleration for nonconformists of all persuasions. He was replaced as Lord Lieutenant by Lord Robartes, who was sympathetic to dissent; while Robartes's successor from 1670, Berkeley, ensured that relations between the Crown and the Catholic hierarchy became noticeably less strained. In June 1670 a synod of Catholic bishops drew up a declaration pledging their 'true allegiance' to the King. Those administrators associated with a policy of coercion were removed, such as the President of Munster, the Earl of Orrery, who argued that 'Irish papists rebel every time the opportunity presents'. Restrictions on the Catholic Church were gradually relaxed and by January 1673 Irish Catholics were even being admitted to public office. These years also saw a growing presence, particularly in the east of Ulster, of young ministers from southwest Scotland. As on the mainland, the King's commitment to toleration caused alarm in the Cavalier Parliament, and in 1671 the two Houses complained to Charles about the 'great insolences of the papists in Ireland'. Charles, however, persisted in promoting toleration, and the following year issued the Declaration of Indulgence which applied to Ireland as well as England. In 1672 he also conferred semi-official legitimacy on Presbyterian ministers by granting them a royal stipend, the *regium donum*. As in Charles's other two kingdoms, this drive towards religious toleration was closely connected to an increasing *rapprochement* with France.

In the *traité simulé* Charles and Arlington deliberately ensured that the war against the Dutch was provisionally planned for the spring of 1672. The main reason for this interval was financial. Although the Treasury Commission established in 1667 had succeeded in reducing expenditure and improving the Crown's credit-worthiness by ordering the repayment of loans in the strict sequence in which they had been granted, royal finances remained insufficient to sustain a major war. At the beginning of 1672 it was calculated that further repayments would reduce the Crown's disposable income for that year to less than £400,000. Charles therefore decided to suspend repayment of all previous loans and on 20 January proclaimed the 'Stop of the Exchequer'. The most immediate victims of what was in effect a declaration of bankruptcy were the bankers who had advanced loans to the Crown; but in the longer term the Stop damaged the Crown's credit, making it less easy to secure future loans and thereby leaving Charles more dependent upon parliamentary supply.

In the short term, however, the Stop released about £1.2 million and thus opened the way to war. Possibly fearing that the 'Catholicity' clause in the secret Treaty of Dover left him vulnerable to blackmail by Louis, and egged on by all members of the Cabal, on 15 March 1672 Charles issued a Declaration of Indulgence. While promising to protect the Church of England as 'the basis, rule and standard of the general and public worship of God', the King invoked his 'supreme power in ecclesiastical matters' to suspend all penal laws against both Catholic and Protestant nonconformists. The latter were also permitted to worship in public provided that the gathering, and the minister who addressed it, received a royal licence. If Charles had hoped to unite Catholics and dissenters against the Anglican establishment, he failed. The two groups remained deeply suspicious of each other, and the main effect of the

Declaration was to frighten Protestants of all hues into closing ranks. Many in both Houses of Parliament, and especially the Commons, became even more dubious about Charles's religious sympathies and fearful that he was intent upon undermining the legal foundations of the Church.

The King's foreign policy seemed to point in exactly the same direction. Two days after he issued the Declaration, Charles declared war on the Dutch Republic. At the same time, he dignified several of his leading ministers with new titles, such as Arlington, who became an earl, and Ashley, who was created Earl of Shaftesbury. However, while Louis led 120,000 French troops into Dutch territory, Charles's naval campaign began very badly. An attempt in late March to capture the Dutch fleet returning from Smyrna was foiled, while on 28 May a naval engagement off Southwold Bay proved indecisive. The following month, French forces occupied Utrecht, a disastrous blow to the States General which precipitated the assassination of the Grand Pensionary Johan De Witt and the appointment of Charles's nephew William of Orange as Stadholder. In England, Protestant opinion swung decisively behind William, and by the end of 1672 the war was proving increasingly unpopular.

It was, however, against the Declaration of Indulgence that most hostility was initially directed when Parliament reassembled on 4 February 1673. Ten days later the Commons voted by 168 votes to 116 that 'penal statutes in matters ecclesiastical cannot be suspended but by an act of Parliament'. Charles initially tried to appease the Commons with a general pledge that he had no wish to suspend 'any laws wherein the properties, rights or liberties of any of his subjects are concerned; nor to alter anything in the established doctrine or discipline of the Church of England'. The House retorted that Charles had been 'very much misinformed', for 'no such power' to suspend statutes 'was ever claimed or exercised by any of' his predecessors. Early in March Charles was obliged to withdraw the Declaration and to accept a new Test Act as the price for securing parliamentary supply. The Test Act obliged all office-holders to swear the Oaths of Supremacy and Allegiance, to take a declaration repudiating the Catholic doctrine of transubstantiation, and to provide documentary proof that they had recently received communion according to the Church of England. By assenting to the Test Act, Charles dramatically curtailed his discretionary powers to appoint advisers of his own choosing. In return, Parliament voted the Crown a total of £1,126,000 in eighteen monthly assessments. Thus satisfied, Charles adjourned Parliament on 29 March.

The parliamentary session of February–March 1673 was remarkable principally for the profound anti-Catholicism that it revealed among Anglicans and dissenters alike. Many of the Protestant nonconformist members were just as hostile towards the Declaration of Indulgence as the Anglicans, and were prepared to co-operate against the common Catholic menace. These feelings deepened when James, Duke of York, the heir presumptive, publicly signalled his conversion to Catholicism (which had probably occurred secretly in 1668) by failing to take communion at Easter 1673. The following June, James resigned as Lord High Admiral under the terms of the Test Act, as did Clifford who had been Lord Treasurer since November 1672. Fears about Catholic influences close to the King were further enflamed by skilful Dutch propaganda, most notably in the form of a pamphlet probably written by Pierre du Moulin, William of Orange's agent in England, entitled *England's Appeal from the Private Cabal at Whitehall to the Great Council of the Nation*. Published in February 1673, and circulated widely throughout the spring and summer, this tract suggested that an inseparable link existed between 'France, popery and absolutism', and intimated that there was a conspiracy at Court to establish Catholicism and absolutism with French assistance. The conversion of the heir presumptive, followed in September 1673 by his marriage to a Catholic princess, Mary of Modena, whose family were clients of Louis XIV, could scarcely have come at a more embarrassing moment for the Crown.[2]

By the time of the next parliamentary session, in October–November 1673, the Cabal was beginning to disintegrate. That summer, two further naval engagements against the Dutch had again proved inconclusive, and in August Spain and the Empire had entered the war against England and France. During the autumn Shaftesbury, increasingly fearful of the popish threat, strongly urged Charles to divorce the barren Catherine of Braganza and to remarry in the hope of producing an heir. He also begged Charles to annul his brother's marriage. Infuriated at what he saw as gross impertinence, Charles dismissed Shaftesbury from the Lord Chancellorship on 9 November, and expelled him from the Privy Council the following spring. This drove Shaftesbury into outright opposition, and thereafter he waged an increasingly vociferous campaign to have James excluded from the succession. Clifford never recovered from his forced resignation from the Treasurership under the Test Act and committed suicide in October. Relations between Arlington and Buckingham deteriorated even further as each blamed the other for all the policies and failures of the previous six years. Never one to stand by unpopular ministers once they had outlived their political usefulness, Charles left them to be savaged by Parliament during the next session of January–February 1674. With his customary sang-froid, the King resolved to 'give the people an open field in order to curb them the better when they were tired with their gallop'. The result was that Buckingham was removed from all his offices, and although Arlington lingered on as Secretary until September, he was a spent force. Of the Cabal, only Lauderdale survived in office. When Parliament refused to vote supply, Charles was obliged to end the war and on 9 February signed the Treaty of Westminster with the Dutch. The central objectives of the Cabal era – religious toleration and an alliance with France – had thus been abandoned by the start of 1674, leaving the way clear for a radical change in the direction of government policy.

The legacy of the Cabal was essentially twofold. First, it was during this period that two groupings or platforms that can broadly be labelled 'Court' and 'Country' began to emerge in both Lords and Commons. In 1673, Sir Thomas Meres was able to speak of 'this side of the house, and that side' in a way that would have been impossible a few years earlier. By the beginning of 1674, a hard core of Country MPs existed, committed to a mixed monarchy in which power was shared equally between the three estates of Crown, Lords and Commons. They saw the powers of the Houses as an essential bulwark against misuse of royal powers, and they were deeply exercised by the apparent spread of popery in high circles. They opposed anything that smacked of royal authoritarianism or was reminiscent of the continental monarchies, such as a standing army. With the collapse of the Cabal, the Country members of the Lords gained two notable recruits in Buckingham and Shaftesbury. There is some evidence that before and during the sessions of 1673–4, some Country members met informally to co-ordinate their strategy in the two Houses of Parliament. It was no accident that 1674 saw the foundation of the Green Ribbon Club at the King's Head Tavern in Chancery Lane, which quickly became an important meeting place for opposition MPs and radical politicians.

This period also saw some tentative steps towards the development of a body of MPs sympathetic to the Court. Although the Cabal was too diffuse and disorganized to mobilize anything worthy of the name 'party', Clifford in particular did begin to use patronage to win over potentially hostile members. His efforts, which earned him the nickname 'Bribe Master General', were particularly effective in securing the co-operation of financially embarrassed former Royalists in return for minor offices and sinecures. This strategy proved so successful in 1670 that one disgruntled Country observer complained that 'the Courtiers now carry all before them in the House of Commons'. Such tactics laid a foundation of Crown influence in Parliament on which the Cabal's successors could build.

The second legacy of these years was that a horror of 'popery and arbitrary government' became ever more entrenched within Parliament and in the country at large. Sir Edward Dering recorded that from 1672 'the nation began to think the Court inclined to favour popery and France'. In November 1673, in the first of what became regular pope-burning processions, effigies of the pope and his cardinals were burnt in London. The following January, a manuscript libel addressed to Parliament denounced 'those who have at present the chief direction of affairs' for harbouring 'a wicked and treasonable design to subvert the fundamental laws of this kingdom by introducing popery and setting up an arbitrary government'. It then raised the possibility of 'settling the succession of the Crown so as may secure us and our posterities from those bloody massacres and inhuman Smithfield butcheries, the certain consequences of a Popish Government'. In February 1674 the Earl of Carlisle even proposed that any prince who married a Catholic without Parliament's consent should be excluded from the succession. Deep-rooted fears that the King and especially his brother wished to establish 'popery and arbitrary government' had become the most burning political issue of the day and would remain so for the next fifteen years.

2 Lord Treasurer Danby

Recognizing the need for a fundamental reorientation of policy, Charles turned to a figure whose reverence for Church and Crown struck a chord with most members of Parliament. Sir Thomas Osborne had become an MP in 1665, Treasurer of the Navy in 1668, a Privy Councillor in 1672, and Lord Treasurer in June 1673. He was created Earl of Danby in June 1674. Although Charles had little personal regard for him, he recognized the industry and political agility that led Sir Thomas Coventry to call Danby 'as experienced and crafty' as any of his enemies. Danby offered a three-pronged policy that marked a fundamental departure from the agenda associated with the Cabal. He was, first of all, vehemently committed to the Church of England and opposed to religious toleration for either Catholics or dissenters. Second, these religious attitudes led him to advocate a pro-Dutch, anti-French foreign policy. Third, and most appealingly from Charles's point of view, Danby was a staunch upholder of the monarchy and a great political 'fixer' for the Crown. In particular, he used the lure of offices and pensions derived from the excise revenue to build up a nucleus of members loyal towards the Crown. By the autumn of 1675, approximately thirty MPs were in receipt of pensions totalling £10,000 a year. Further support for the Court was mobilized by personal letters circulated to selected members of both Houses on the eve of parliamentary sessions. Danby was keen to secure Parliament's co-operation in making the King financially solvent, yet his managerial techniques fuelled fears that he was seeking to establish a 'Pension Parliament' subservient to the Crown, and even that he was secretly in league with France.

Unfortunately, these fears turned out to be self-fulfilling. Danby's position was weakened by the fact that he never possessed the King's unequivocal support. Although he was willing to go along with Danby's policies in the hope that they would make Parliament more emollient, Charles retained close links with Louis XIV as an insurance against the failure of this strategy, and even allowed French pensions to be paid to certain MPs. Suspicions of a design to establish a French-style authoritarian regime therefore persisted despite Danby's ostensible commitment to the Church. Among the most eloquent exponents of such fears were Shaftesbury and Buckingham, who from 1674–5 formed the core of Country opposition in the Lords and co-operated with like-minded members of the Commons in concerted efforts to dislodge Danby from power.

Danby's ascendancy soon led to a dramatic swing away from religious toleration in all three kingdoms. When the English Parliament assembled in April 1675, Charles pledged that he would 'leave nothing undone that may show any zeal to the Protestant religion, as it is established in the Church of England, from which I will never depart'. Shortly afterwards, a Test Bill was introduced requiring all office-holders and members of Parliament to declare the taking up of arms 'on any pretence whatsoever' to be unlawful, and to swear not to seek the alteration of government in Church or State. However, Shaftesbury, assisted by Arlington and Ormond, attacked this as part of a plot to make government 'absolute and arbitrary', and to impose rule by a standing army. After lengthy and acrimonious debate, the bill was defeated, and during April and May Arlington's clients in the Commons led an abortive attempt to impeach Danby. During the session of October–November 1675 the Houses became even less co-operative: they voted only a meagre supply of £300,000 for the navy, and in a further attempt to curtail the Crown added a clause appropriating all the customs revenues for the sole purpose of supporting the navy. November saw the publication of *A Letter from a Person of Quality to his Friend in the Country*, possibly written by Shaftesbury and John Locke, which portrayed Danby's Test Bill as symptomatic of a conspiracy by a 'distinct party' of the 'high episcopal man and the old cavalier' to establish arbitrary government, to maintain a standing army, and to render Parliament a mere 'instrument to raise money'. Had the authors known the extent of the King's contacts with Louis – which culminated in two secret agreements of August 1675 and February 1676 by which Louis promised Charles a subsidy of £112,000 in return for keeping Parliament prorogued – their fears would have seemed all the more justified. In November 1675, a bid by Shaftesbury and Buckingham to secure the dissolution of the Cavalier Parliament, in the hope that fresh elections might produce a Parliament more sympathetic to the Country interest and less compliant to the royal will, was defeated in the Lords by only 50 votes to 48. While he did not want a dissolution, Charles nevertheless registered his irritation with the Houses by proroguing them on 22 November and not recalling them until 15 February 1677.

Although he was the only member of the Cabal to remain in office, even Lauderdale found himself pushed onto the defensive by the Country opposition and by his enemies in Scotland, of whom the most outspoken was the Duke of Hamilton. Led by Burnet (who was now restored to his see of Glasgow) and Sharp, the bishops demanded tougher action against illegal conventicles, prompting Lauderdale to deploy troops in southwest Scotland in 1674. That same year, landowners were made responsible for the religious conformity of their tenants and servants. Unfortunately, such measures only confirmed Hamilton and his allies in their hatred of arbitrary government. Suspicions grew in England that Charles, like his father, was using his northern kingdom as a laboratory in which to try out authoritarian policies that could then be introduced south of the border. By 1677 Lauderdale's regime was firmly committed to the military repression of nonconformists throughout Scotland. During the following year, however, the limits of the government's control became glaringly apparent, especially in the Highlands and the southwest. There was simply no machinery to enforce conformity if local landowners refused to co-operate. When the 'Highland host', a militia force of about 9,000 Highlanders and Lowlanders, was billeted on the southwest in an attempt to crush dissent, Hamilton and his supporters denounced the troops' brutal behaviour and stirred up fears that Lauderdale was assembling an army for use in England. By 1678–9 the situation in Scotland was becoming increasingly volatile, and this in turn helped to destabilize English politics.

In Ireland, the nature of policy continued to be closely related to developments in England. The Earl of Essex,[3] who replaced Berkeley as Lord Lieutenant in May 1672, made every effort to govern Ireland as impartially as possible. However, he was subjected to unrelenting pressure from London, and above all from the English Parliament, to take a tougher stand against the nonconformists of Ulster. This became ever more of a problem after 1673–4, as Lauderdale's repression drove many Scottish nonconformists to settle in Ulster. In 1672 William Petty estimated that there were 300,000 Protestants in Ireland, of whom 100,000 were Scots Presbyterians, a figure that had increased markedly by the end of the decade. Although, as on the mainland, it was practically impossible to enforce conformity, the open existence of Presbyterian meeting houses was gradually restricted after 1673. The same fate befell the few Catholic schools that had begun to spring up during Berkeley's lord lieutenancy. As English anti-popery intensified during the course of the decade, fears grew that Ireland would provide the seedbed for a Catholic uprising, possibly fomented by the Jesuits. The MP Henry Powle warned of 'a general design to set up the popish and Irish interest, to out the Protestant and English'. Increasingly, the Country opposition denounced Essex as too relaxed in his approach to both Catholics and dissenters, and in 1677 they secured the reappointment of Ormond who was known to be far more sympathetic towards repression.

In England, meanwhile, Danby was making significant headway in his campaign to improve the Crown's financial position. His careful stewardship as Lord Treasurer, England's withdrawal from the third Dutch War, and a trading boom that boosted customs revenues, all combined to raise total royal income to an average of £1.4 million a year between 1674 and 1677. The customs revenues – which had been brought under direct royal control in 1671 – remained absolutely crucial for the Crown's solvency, yielding no less than £730,000 in 1674–5. The greatest problem that confronted Danby's fiscal policies was Charles's reckless extravagance, especially on mistresses, jewels and works of art: his expenses seemed to increase in direct proportion to the resources at his disposal. Danby initiated retrenchment schemes, with the King's approval, in 1675 and 1677, but these were constantly undermined by Charles's failure to keep his promises. In this respect, as in so many others, he resembled his grandfather far more than his father, and Danby's predicament closely paralleled that of Salisbury and Cranfield. As a result, the Crown's floating debt increased by £750,000 between 1674 and 1679.

Charles's excessive spending had the dual consequence of making him more dependent upon Parliament and Parliament less inclined to co-operate with him. When the Houses reassembled in February 1677, Shaftesbury, Buckingham, Salisbury and Wharton moved that the fifteen-month prorogation meant that the Parliament had legally been dissolved. This motion was defeated and its proponents sent to the Tower for five months. At the same time, however, Charles's position was weakened by a series of French military successes against the Dutch which provoked growing parliamentary pressure for a pro-Dutch, anti-French foreign policy. The Houses voted £600,000 for the navy and renewed the additional excise originally granted in 1671, but they made any further supply conditional upon an alliance against France. Charles retorted that 'should I suffer this fundamental power of making peace and war to be so invaded (though but once) as to have the manner and circumstances of leagues prescribed to me by Parliament, it is plain that no prince or state would any longer believe that the sovereignty of England rests in the crown.' Anxiety deepened about Charles's authoritarian inclinations and received memorable expression in December 1677 with the publication of Andrew Marvell's *An Account of the Growth of Popery and Arbitrary Government*. Marvell asserted that 'for divers years' a 'design' had been 'carried on to change the lawful government of England into an absolute tyranny, and to convert the established Protestant religion into downright Popery'. The architects of this 'design', he declared, sought to 'introduce French slavery and Roman idolatry'. The mid-1670s also saw a burgeoning of republican literature that was often circulated in manuscript through the taverns and coffee-houses of London and the provinces. This suggested less an ideological commitment to republican forms of government than a growing disillusionment with Charles. One poem of 1677, for example, stated that the gods had 'repented the King's Restoration'. Such views reflected a marked growth of opposition both in Parliament and more widely.

Danby nevertheless persisted in his hope that a Dutch alliance might still mollify Parliament. It was, he wrote, essential for the King to 'fall into the humour of the people'. To that end, during the summer and autumn of 1677, Danby engineered the betrothal of Mary, the elder of James's two Protestant daughters, to William of Orange. Their marriage in November was greeted with public rejoicing in London, and greatly boosted Danby's popularity. The following month, an Anglo-Dutch treaty was concluded whereby the two powers agreed to impose peace terms on Louis, if necessary by force. In January 1678, Parliament voted to raise an army of 30,000 troops and in principle to grant a war supply of £1 million for six months. In the event, however, the poll tax that it voted in March produced a mere £300,000. This shortfall may well have been intentional: as one MP bluntly informed the King, 'I am for keeping the revenue from being too big, for then you will need Parliaments'. Despite the Dutch alliance, many still feared that Charles would try to govern without Parliament given the chance.

Such anxieties reinforced – and were in turn reinforced by – the King's desire to retain close contacts with Louis. In August 1677, under severe pressure from Charles, Danby had colluded in secret negotiations by the English ambassador in Paris, Ralph Montagu, which culminated in a French grant of two million livres in return for Parliament remaining prorogued and an assurance that England would not use force against France. When the Dutch alliance was ratified, Charles tried to use it as a bargaining counter to secure further French payments, whereupon the French ambassador, Barillon, launched a campaign of bribes to seduce some of Danby's most outspoken critics, such as the republican Algernon Sidney, into opposing the Dutch and resisting the perceived threat of a standing army. In May 1678 Charles concluded another secret agreement with Louis by which he received further subsidies in return for disbanding his army and once again proroguing Parliament. In the end, this double game gave Charles the worst of both worlds, for the Dutch and the French alike came to mistrust him. In July those two States concluded an armistice, and then signed the Peace of Nijmwegen, but Charles refused to disband his army and instead prorogued Parliament. He thus reinforced all the Houses' worst fears that the 30,000 troops might be used to enforce non-parliamentary government.

By this time, Danby's attempt to woo popular opinion by cementing an alliance with the Dutch had gone irreparably wrong. Thanks to Charles's continued underhand dealings with France, Parliament's mistrust of the

Court's intentions had only increased. Many MPs blamed Danby for poisoning the King's mind and encouraging him to use a standing army to rule without Parliament. Such attacks were deeply ironic, for Danby's attitudes and priorities were naturally in tune with those of most members of Parliament. Although many resented his payments to MPs from secret service funds, and feared his interference in local affairs, his actions all served to strengthen the type of Anglican loyalist who dominated the Cavalier Parliament. As Bishop Gilbert Burnet later wrote, Danby wished to cast himself as 'the patron of the church party and of the old cavaliers'. Yet by 1677–8 he was widely perceived as an agent of 'popery and arbitrary government'. Danby's position ultimately disintegrated not because he harboured a design to do away with Parliament, but because the King never allowed him to pursue his policies to the exclusion of all others. When, finally, Danby accepted that he was unable to persuade Charles to abandon his links with Louis, and wearily resigned himself to going along with them, the results were disastrous. For when it became known that in 1677 the Lord Treasurer had accepted a secret treaty with Louis at exactly the same time as he was wooing the Dutch and seeking parliamentary grants ostensibly to raise troops against France, the outcome was a furore that swept Danby from power and signalled the onset of the greatest political crisis of Charles's reign.

3 Anglicans and Dissenters

Of all the issues that divided Restoration society, perhaps the most emotive concerned the nature of the Church. Alongside the Court–Country duality, and sometimes cutting across it, was a dichotomy between the advocates of greater toleration for both Catholics and Protestant dissenters, and those who staunchly defended the narrow, intolerant Church established in 1662. This difference of opinion was all the more liable to generate instability because of the mismatch between the broad, magnanimous political settlement of 1660–2, and the harsh, unforgiving nature of the restored Church. This produced a fundamental tension between those, including the King, who wished to see the Church comprehend (or at least tolerate) most of the former Parliamentarians who had already gained public office, and those Cavalier-Anglicans who felt that such secular concessions to the King's old enemies had already gone too far and should never be emulated in the religious sphere. After 1660, large-scale nonconformity became a fact of life, and the Church found itself unable to sustain its traditional claims to embrace the whole nation. As a result, relations between Anglicans and dissenters were characterized by deep mistrust and any attempt to mollify either group was likely to enflame the suspicions of the other.

The Restoration Church was a much weaker institution than its pre-Civil War counterpart. With the destruction of the High Commission and the decline of the diocesan courts following their suspension during the 1640s and 1650s, the Church lacked effective machinery to punish those who refused to conform. It therefore became more and more dependent upon local magistrates to enforce the Clarendon Code, but in practice their assiduity varied enormously from place to place. Some JPs and Deputy Lieutenants were more than happy to levy the maximum fine of £20 payable under the 1670 Conventicle Act for holding or addressing an illegal religious meeting, but many others lacked either the energy or the conviction to do so. In general, dissenters were more likely to find that they could worship openly in the towns than in the countryside, where the rural squirearchy were often intensely loyal to the established Church. Where there is evidence of rural dissent, it is usually in regions where industry was strong, or in the more dispersed villages of the forest, pastoral and upland regions where enforcement of conformity was more difficult. The resilience of urban dissent is illustrated by the fact that 28 per cent of those elected to civic office in Coventry between 1660 and 1687 were dissenters, as were 35 per cent of directors of the Levant, East India and Royal Africa Companies in London during the same period. This distinction between urban and rural areas should not however be overdrawn: dissenters could be found in most parts of the country and at all levels of society. Furthermore, the level of persecution varied considerably from time to time, with the peaks of severity coming in the early 1670s and the first half of the 1680s. It is also worth stressing that some nonconformist groups, such as the Quakers and Baptists, were treated much more harshly than others who were perceived as less of a threat to the social and political order.

It is extremely difficult to estimate the scale of dissent. In 1676, at the request of Danby, Archbishop Sheldon instructed Bishop Henry Compton of London to organize a census which concluded that of an adult population of 2.25 million in England and Wales, nearly 100,000 were nonconformists. Their geographical distribution varied considerably, from 10.5 per cent in the diocese of Canterbury to 0.8 per cent in the diocese of Bangor. But this figure is probably a drastic underestimate: it only counted those who 'either obstinately refuse, or wholly absent themselves from the communion of the Church of England' and thus did not include the many 'occasional conformists' who periodically attended services in their parish church while also supplementing them with 'nonconformist' activities.[4] Although the biblicism of Protestant nonconformity inevitably diminished its appeal to the illiterate, it is likely that the total number of dissenters at any given moment during Charles's reign was at least two or three times greater than that given in the Compton Census.

Despite the fears of the Anglican establishment, the mood of the majority of these nonconformists was very different from that of their Puritan predecessors. The collapse of the Republic and the disintegration of all their dreams of a godly commonwealth seemed like a divine judgement against their 'cause', and produced a deep sense of defeat and disillusionment. Instead of seeking further reform, they became much more passive and introspective. This change was even apparent in the case of the Quakers. Although Anglicans generally remained deeply suspicious of them, after 1660 most Quakers abandoned the militant rejection of authority that had made them so widely feared during the 1640s and 1650s, and instead followed their leader George Fox in adopting the pacifism and quietism for which they have been known ever since. The primary concern of most Restoration nonconformists lay with the private relationship between the individual conscience and God, rather than with the public and political duties dictated by godly principles. In John Spurr's words, 'personal dealings with the Lord were at the heart' of their piety. Perhaps the finest expression of this mental world was *The Pilgrim's Progress*, written by the preacher John Bunyan during his imprisonment for nonconformity in the 1660s and first published in 1678. This classic allegory of a soul's spiritual journey reflected a profound turning away from religious enthusiasm and a growing mistrust of zeal when applied to matters of public policy.

A similar tendency to look inwards can be discerned among the established clergy. Many felt that the experiences of the Civil Wars and Interregnum had been a punishment inflicted by God on a sinful people. They regarded the Restoration as a heaven-sent respite: to show itself worthy and to avoid further catastrophe, the nation had to demonstrate a capacity for 'holy living'. Establishment divines increasingly stressed the importance of 'morality' and 'solid and sincere piety' rather than the need for a conversion experience that had so preoccupied earlier Puritans. Devotional works such as *The Whole Duty of Man*, probably by Richard Allestree, or Jeremy Taylor's *Holy Living*, offered practical guidance on how to lead a sober and devout life. Here again, enthusiasm was rejected in favour of a commonsensical approach based on the private behaviour and morality of the individual.

This reaction against fervour and dogmatism, and a corresponding scepticism about the possibility of certainty in religious matters, was particularly associated with the so-called Latitudinarians. Those traditionally identified as leading exponents of this outlook included John Wilkins, Bishop of Chester (who had married Cromwell's daughter), Edward Stillingfleet, Bishop of Worcester, and John Tillotson, Dean of St Paul's and later Archbishop of Canterbury. John Spurr has recently argued persuasively that the Latitudinarians never formed a coherent party, that the label was often used as a term of abuse, and that many of their attitudes – most notably a rejection of Calvinist theology and a dislike of religious coercion – were widespread within the Restoration Church as a whole.[5] Characteristic also of the prevailing ethos of the Church was an acceptance that human reason could helpfully be applied to religion. As Joseph Glanvill, another divine commonly labelled a Latitudinarian, wrote: 'faith itself is an act of reason'. This idea would ultimately find classic expression in John Locke's *The Reasonableness of Christianity* (1695). Such a rational approach to religious experience was evident also in church architecture: Sir Christopher Wren's designs for the new St Paul's Cathedral and his replacements for over fifty other churches destroyed in the Great Fire of London combined classical models with a geometrical simplicity to produce an atmosphere of lightness and openness. Whereas prior to the Civil War the application of reason to religious matters had been denounced as the heresy of Socinianism, after the Restoration it was increasingly accepted that the principles of observation, deduction and reasoned proof associated with 'natural philosophy' (science) could help, in the words of Isaac Newton, to 'unfold the mechanism of the world'.

However, while the coherence of the Latitudinarians as a group has undoubtedly been exaggerated, it is important to note that many of the figures usually so labelled did hold some views that were far from universal among the

Restoration clergy. In particular, they often actively pursued an interest in science and many were among the earliest Fellows of the Royal Society. Their abhorrence of the 'fanatic enthusiasm' of the Puritans rested on a conviction that rational, scientific enquiry opened up the possibility of understanding and even improving the world that God had created. Yet any such improvement would be piecemeal, not integrated into any overarching vision such as the 'great instauration' – a wholly new moral, cultural and natural order – envisaged by pre-Civil War thinkers such as Samuel Hartlib. This interest in science led divines like Wilkins or Tillotson towards an idea of 'natural religion' which emphasized the moral duty of the individual and the need to present the fundamentals of Christianity in a straightforward manner to all mankind, irrespective of outward conformity. These views were articulated most strongly whenever the questions of toleration and comprehension were debated, especially in the late 1660s and early 1670s. At other times, and on other issues, these figures are difficult to distinguish from the mainstream of the Restoration Church. They were never a united group with a single, codified set of beliefs; yet they combined attitudes characteristic of the Church in general with other traits – most notably an intense interest in science and 'natural religion' – that remained the preserve of a minority.

In their scientific interests, their rejection of dogma and their desire for toleration these divines shared much common ground with the King. At the Restoration, Charles's preference was for as comprehensive a national Church as possible. When the Cavalier Parliament thwarted this goal, he persisted in seeking toleration for 'tender consciences', only to find that this too met with entrenched resistance. Yet, despite these defeats, Charles sought to foster an atmosphere of breadth and variety within the limits of the Church by promoting as diverse a range of clergy as he could. Like James I, he was keen that different opinions should be represented among senior clerical appointments. The Restoration episcopate encompassed figures as contrasted as the Laudian Matthew Wren of Ely and the former Presbyterian Edward Reynolds of Norwich. Charles's bishops held a range of views on such issues as the extent to which dissenters should be tolerated or the nature of episcopal authority, from the most rigorous exponents of divine right episcopacy, such as Jeremy Taylor of Down and Connor, to those, like John Gauden of Exeter, who advocated a 'reduced episcopacy'. As John Spurr has written, 'there was no typical Restoration bishop nor a typical episcopal style'. Notwithstanding the nearly two thousand clerics who were ejected in 1660–2 because of their nonconformity, the clergy of the Restoration Church included some who had served throughout the 1640s and 1650s (for example Ralph Josselin, vicar of Earls Colne) alongside others who during the same period had suffered for their 'Anglicanism'. An anonymous satire of 1673 jeered:

> Is any church more catholic than we?
> ... What a prodigious unity is here!
> Calvinist, Arminian, Roundhead, Cavalier,
> Protestant, Papist, atheist, devil and all,
> Tim, Tom and Tidy – isn't this catholical?

The following year, in a more serious and positive vein, Ralph Cudworth wrote that 'just as in Noah's Ark were all sorts of animals', so in the Church of England 'are all kinds of Protestants ... united with no apparent discord in one and the same communion'. It should also be stressed that the quality of the bishops and other clergy was in general very high, and that Archbishop Sheldon in particular proved a relentless campaigner against 'scandalous and faulty' clerics. In the end, what united these diverse elements was a fundamental belief in the need for a national, established Church and in the duty of Christian obedience to secular authority. This helped to make the Church, in the words of Clarendon's chaplain Dr Robert South, 'the truest friend to kings and to kingly government, of any other church in the world', although Charles's pursuit of greater toleration led some clergy to question how far he reciprocated the Church's friendship.

Certainly the diversity that Charles promoted – even within an institution whose confines were much narrower than he wished – helped to give the Restoration Church a distinctive ethos. These years saw the gradual emergence of an Anglican consciousness that praised the Church for combining the best elements of both 'Catholic' and 'reformed'. This partly reflected Charles's constant efforts to create something more along the lines of the 'Jacobethan' Church. Yet the result could only ever be stunted and incomplete. The settlement of 1662 had imposed such rigid limits on the comprehensiveness of the Church and the freedom that existed outside it that the opportunity to reconstruct anything resembling the broad national Church of Elizabeth and James was lost forever. Widespread dissent became ineradicable. The Church continued to claim that it embraced the whole nation while remaining edgily aware of the scale of nonconformity among clergy and laity alike. This helps to explain the almost neurotic horror that many churchmen felt for perceived 'enemies of the Church': whenever it seemed that toleration might be extended more widely, as in the years of the Cabal, anxious warnings were voiced about the spread of papists, sectarians or 'schismatics', or of darker heresies such as 'atheism' or 'Hobbism' (the belief that no religious idea had any authority except that which it derived from the civil power). These spectres were often more imagined than real, but they seemed to present a danger to the Church. The King's clear preference for toleration, the extensive concessions that had already been made to former Parliamentarians in the secular sphere, and the lack of any real means to coerce those who refused to conform only served to reinforce the embattled mindset of many Restoration clergy. Not until the Toleration Act of 1689 belatedly recognized that mass nonconformity was a permanent feature of the religious landscape, and that the Church could never again be a truly national institution, was some form of *modus vivendi* achieved between Anglicans and dissenters.

4 The Court of Charles II

Another area where there were pronounced parallels between Charles II and James VI and I, and a corresponding contrast with Charles I, was the life of the Court. Instead of the orderly, chaste and chivalric ethos of the Caroline Court, Charles II presided over a Court of notorious debauchery. As with James, these surroundings, together with Charles's own lack of sexual restraint, undoubtedly detracted from the dignity of the Crown. Yet precisely because it was such an open and easy-going environment, the Court functioned effectively as a political 'point of contact' in which different views could find a hearing. Charles II's Court, again like its Jacobean predecessor, was also accessible to the general public. The climate of the Court proved highly influential and did much to set the tone of the period as a whole: in particular, its air of vitality, earthiness, worldliness and cynicism also characterized much of Restoration drama.

Certainly the promiscuity and bawdiness of Charles's Court soon became proverbial. When the Great Plague of 1665 forced courtiers to flee to Oxford for safety, the antiquarian Anthony Wood observed that 'though they were neat and gay in their apparel, yet they were very nasty and beastly ... Rude, rough, whoremongers; vain, empty, careless'. Similarly, not long before Charles's death John Evelyn wrote:

> I can never forget the inexpressible luxury [= lasciviousness] and profaneness, gaming, and all dissoluteness, and as it were total forgetfulness of God (it being Sunday evening) ... the King sitting and toying with his concubines ... whilst about twenty of the great courtiers and other dissolute persons were at Basset[6] round a large table, a bank of at least 2000 in gold before them.

Charles's own sexual prowess was legendary. He was entirely open about his long succession of mistresses, from the Countess of Castlemaine to Nell Gwynn, and rewarded many of them with titles and pensions. Yet there was something brutal about the King's behaviour, prompting Halifax to remark that his inclinations as a lover had 'as little mixture of the seraphic part as ever man had'. Nothing could be more different from the ethereal chastity of his father's Court: a Platonic ideal of love was replaced by the physical reality of lust.

Charles's behaviour was emulated by his close companions at Court. He especially enjoyed the scintillating conversation of Buckingham, yet the Duke's self-indulgence and lack of principle ensured that his political career never fulfilled its initial promise. As Gilbert Burnet put it, 'he had no principles of religion, virtue, or friendship; no truth or honour ... Pleasure and frolic, and extravagant diversion were indeed all he minded.' Even more spectacular was the short life of John Wilmot, second Earl of Rochester (1647–80), who is often regarded as the emblematic figure of Charles's Court. He was, in John Miller's words, 'an extreme example of a recognisable type', a brilliant wit with a phenomenal capacity for pleasure, who died at the age of thirty-three from a mixture of alcoholism and syphilis. His poetry ranged from pungent satires to obscene and scurrilous verses – such as 'Signior Dildo', 'A Ramble in St James's Park' and 'The Maim'd Debauchee' – most of which were circulated clandestinely in manuscript and only published several decades after his death. This most famous of Court rakes summed up his royal master thus:

> Nor are his high desires above his strength;
> His sceptre and his prick are of a length . . .
> Restless he rolls from whore to whore,
> A merry monarch, scandalous and poor.

Yet Rochester seems increasingly to have felt a nagging dissatisfaction at his own pursuit of licentiousness and pleasure to the exclusion of any higher or more spiritual ideals. This mood of disillusionment was most savagely expressed in his *Satire against Mankind*. According to Gilbert Burnet, who ministered to Rochester at the end of his life, he finally expressed regret for the emptiness of his profligate lifestyle, and rejected the Hobbesian materialism and justification of sensual pleasure that he had previously found so attractive. But, despite this final repentance, Rochester none the less remains the epitome of a Restoration Court hedonist and libertine.

The behaviour of such courtiers clearly undermined the King's own image. When, in February 1669, Rochester struck the dramatist Thomas Killigrew in Charles's presence, Samuel Pepys wrote that it was 'to the King's everlasting shame to have so idle a rogue as his companion'. Other notorious courtiers included Sir Charles Sedley and Lord Buckhurst, who once caused a furore when they preached a mock sermon while standing naked on the balcony of an alehouse. As at the Jacobean Court, a series of scandals helped to reinforce the seamy atmosphere. These ranged from sexual offences, especially rapes, to accidental murders, as when Buckingham killed the Earl of Shrewsbury in a duel over Shrewsbury's wife. The presence of prominent Catholics at Court further alienated many of Charles's subjects: by the later 1660s his mother, wife, brother and heir, mistress and several of his leading ministers were all Catholics. Furthermore, many features of Charles's Court – from the adoption of French fashions in costumes and musical styles to the imitation of cere- monial forms employed at Versailles – strengthened anxieties that a *rapprochement* with France would be the first step towards the establishment of 'popery and arbitrary government'. In that sense, the Court reinforced all the Country's worst fears about the Crown's authoritarian ambitions.

Yet it is also worth stressing the more positive political role that the Court played. Charles's easy-going personality helped to create a remarkably open Court that was the antithesis of the closed world inhabited by Charles I during the 1630s. Although throughout his reign Charles II had favourite ministers who enjoyed privileged access to his private apartments, there was scope for a range of viewpoints to find a voice at Court. Charles disliked being too depen- dent upon one particular adviser, or group of advisers, and often preferred to play them off against each other in a manner that allowed him to arbitrate between different lines of policy. This approach ensured that the interplay of factions remained very fluid and that the Court never became ideologically monolithic. Charles was also remarkably accessible to his subjects at large. In particular, he enthusiastically revived the practice of touching for the King's Evil.[7] This ceremony – conducted in public every Friday throughout his reign – proved immensely popular and brought him into personal contact with a broad cross-section of the nation. John Evelyn recorded an incident in March

1684 where 'there was so great and eager a concourse of people with their children, to be touched of the Evil, that six or seven were crushed to death' in the scramble for tickets. This contrasted dramatically with Charles I's unpopular attempts to restrict the practice to Easter and Michaelmas, and instead resembled James VI and I's open and relaxed approach.

The Court of Charles II was a tolerant, promiscuous, worldly place, with few illusions or ideals, and a blend of energy, cynicism and humour that did much to define the atmosphere of the period as a whole. These qualities are also found in Restoration drama, and especially in the social comedies of manners, a genre – initially imported from Paris – that reached its apotheosis at the end of the century in the work of William Congreve and George Farquhar. With the reopening of the theatres in 1660, there was a powerful backlash against the Puritan restraints of the 1640s and 1650s. Charles was deeply interested in the theatre, and during his reign a number of playwrights – many of whom had links with the Court – gave Restoration comedy its distinctive flavour. The earliest of these was Sir George Etherege, whose greatest play, *The Man of Mode* (1676), explores the tension between genuine love and sexual appetite via the adventures of a rake, Dorimant, possibly modelled on Rochester. This play also contains a classic portrait of the 'prince of fops', Sir Fopling Flutter. A few years younger that Etherege was William Wycherley, best known for his satirical comedy *The Country Wife* (1675), in which Mr Pinchwife vainly tries to protect his new wife from the temptations of London society, and especially from the attentions of the hero, Horner, who feigns impotence as a cover for his amorous pursuits. In his final play, *The Plain Dealer* (1676), a version of Molière's *Le Misanthrope*, Wycherley traces the deceptions of love and friendship through the misanthropic central character, Manly. Many Restoration comedies also carried topical resonances: for instance, *The Virtuoso* (1676) by Thomas Shadwell was a biting satire on the scientific pretensions of the Royal Society. Another remarkable figure was Aphra Behn, probably the first Englishwoman to earn a (modest) living as a professional writer. Her seventeen plays included comedies such as *The Town Fop* (1676) and *Sir Patient Fancy* (1678). Behn's satires on contemporary social behaviour dwelt particularly on the miseries of mercenary, loveless marriages, and were significant for their portrayal of witty and independent heroines, and their advocacy of more mature relationships between the sexes. The work of all these playwrights shared the same general characteristics of comic virtuosity, razor-sharp verbal exchanges and mordant social satire. They were far more tolerant of affectation, promiscuity and deceit than of dullness and prudishness. Their plays have an unrestrained exuberance that vividly captures the ethos of Charles's Court and makes them appealing even today. The society they depict was secular, cynical and somewhat superficial, heavily materialistic and pleasure-seeking, lacking in ideals and generosity and any search for the things of the spirit. This dramatic achievement coincided with the rapid decline of other literary genres – such as religious poetry – and was another symptom of the widespread repudiation of religious enthusiasm and Puritan imperatives.

The close link between Restoration theatre and developments at Court was indicative of a gradual bridging of the gulf between elite and popular culture.

Charles II's Court was far less out of touch with the wider world than that of his father, and this interpenetration helped to prevent the sort of breakdown in communication that occurred under Charles I. But it did have the negative effect of ensuring that the behaviour of the Court was exposed to the public gaze. In terms of generating political instability, the Court's most dangerous failings were probably not so much moral as religious. The excesses of Charles's courtiers may have detracted from his dignity, but far more politically damaging were the fears that highly placed Catholics, influenced by the French model, might try to incline the King towards 'popery and arbitrary government'. The principal drawback of the Court was that some of its most prominent members aggravated the nagging doubts about Charles's commitment to the Church of England and to constitutional government. Just how hazardous that taint of popery could be was resoundingly demonstrated by the crisis that exploded in the autumn of 1678.

10 Exclusion and Reaction

	19 December	Ralph Montagu reveals Danby's collusion in negotiations for French subsidies; Commons votes to impeach Danby
	30 December	Charles prorogues Parliament
1679	24 January	Charles dissolves Cavalier Parliament
	6 March–27 May	First Exclusion Parliament
	26 March	Danby resigns as Lord Treasurer to avoid impeachment; he is imprisoned until February 1684
	20 April	Charles appoints leading critics, including Shaftesbury, to Privy Council
	27 April	Coleman's correspondence made public: it apparently implicates James in negotiations with France and Rome
	30 April	Charles proposes 'limitations' on any Catholic successor
	3 May	Archbishop Sharp of St Andrews murdered by Covenanters
	11 May	Thomas Pilkington proposes impeachment of James
	15 May	Exclusion Bill receives first reading in the Commons
	21 May	Exclusion Bill passes second reading in the Commons
	27 May	Habeas Corpus Amendment Act; Charles prorogues Parliament
	1 June	Covenanter rebels defeat royal troops led by John Graham of Claverhouse; rebellion spreads in western Lowlands
	22 June	Monmouth defeats Presbyterian rebels at Bothwell Bridge
	29 June	Charles issues third Letter of Indulgence in Scotland
	12 July	Charles dissolves first Exclusion Parliament
	September	Monmouth temporarily exiled to the Netherlands
	Autumn–spring 1680	Mass petitioning campaign calling for James's exclusion from the succession

	19 November	Laurence Hyde appointed First Lord of the Treasury
	November	James sent to Scotland as the King's Commissioner: launches harsh repression of Presbyterians
1680	Spring	Beginnings of loyalist backlash against exclusionists
	22 June	Radical Presbyterians ('Cameronians') issue Sanquhar Declaration declaring holy war on Charles
	26 June	Shaftesbury tries to bring charges that James is a recusant and the Duchess of Portsmouth (Charles's mistress) a French agent
	22 July	Cameronians defeated at Aird's Moss
	11 October	Lauderdale resigns as Secretary of the Scottish Council
	21 October–10 January 1681	Second Exclusion Parliament: Exclusion Bill passes Commons but is defeated in Lords

Publication of Sir Robert Filmer's *Patriarcha*

1681	18 January	Charles dissolves second Exclusion Parliament
	18 March	Secret treaty between Charles and Louis: Charles to gain further French subsidies in return for not summoning another Parliament for three years
	21–28 March	Third Exclusion Parliament meets at Oxford: decides to proceed with Exclusion Bill, and is dissolved after one week; effectively marks end of Exclusion Crisis
	8 April	Charles issues *Declaration Touching the Reasons that Moved Him to Dissolve the Two Last Parliaments*
	Summer	Beginning of purges of Whigs from commissions of the peace and lieutenancies
	2 July	Shaftesbury arrested on charge of treason; acquitted in November

	July	Irish finances to be managed by a commission directly responsible to the English Treasury
	13 August	Scottish Parliament recognizes James as heir to the throne
	31 August	Scottish Test Act
	December	Charles demands that London receive a new charter that can be used as a weapon against Whigs; many local Tories subsequently do likewise; fifty-one new borough charters are issued by February 1685

Publication of Sir George Mackenzie's *Jus Regium*

1682	1 May	Marquis of Queensberry appointed Treasurer of Scotland
	20 August	Death of Lauderdale
	29 September	Sir George Jeffreys appointed Lord Chief Justice
	28 November	Shaftesbury flees to Amsterdam
	29 November	Laurence Hyde created Earl of Rochester
1683	21 January	Death of Shaftesbury
	28 January	Earl of Sunderland appointed Secretary of State
	12 June	Discovery of Rye House Plot; Essex, William Lord Russell and Algernon Sidney subsequently arrested
	13 July	Essex found dead
	21 July	Execution of Russell
	4 October	Jeffreys appointed a Privy Councillor
	7 December	Execution of Sidney
1684	March	Charles violates Triennial Act by failing to call another Parliament after three-year interval: very little protest
	13 June	Earl of Perth appointed Chancellor of Scotland

	19 October	Charles informs Ormond that he will shortly be replaced as Lord Lieutenant of Ireland; but the King dies before a successor can be found
1685	2 February	Charles taken fatally ill
	6 February	Death of Charles II; accession of James VII and II

1 The Popish Plot

On the morning of 13 August 1678, Charles II was taking his customary stroll through Whitehall when he was accosted by one Christopher Kirby, an amateur scientist in whose chemical experiments the King had taken a keen interest. Kirby requested a private audience, at which he introduced Charles to Israel Tonge, a former Oxford don and obsessive anti-papist. Tonge presented Charles with a lengthy document of forty-three articles explaining how he had uncovered a conspiracy, masterminded by the Jesuits, to assassinate the King, place the Duke of York on the throne, and extirpate English Protestantism, possibly in conjunction with a rebellion in Ireland and an invasion from France. Charles did not initially take these claims seriously and referred the matter to the Privy Council. However, on 28 September, Tonge appeared before the Council armed with an even lengthier version of his story, consisting of eighty-one articles. The next day he produced his informant, an unsavoury drifter named Titus Oates who had briefly trained as a Jesuit and thereby gained enough inside knowledge to give his statements a thin veneer of credibility. 'Amazed' at the allegations, the Council immediately ordered a series of security measures, including the mobilization of the militia to search Catholic homes for arms.

Perhaps the most remarkable thing about these extraordinary – and utterly false – claims was that they were so widely believed. This was partly because they fitted in so well with the almost obsessive anti-Catholicism so characteristic of seventeenth-century England. Minds accustomed to regarding the papacy as the Antichrist, and popery as the embodiment of all evil and superstition, had no difficulty whatever in accepting the fantasies of Oates and Tonge as but the latest in a long line of Catholic conspiracies running from the Marian persecutions and the Gunpowder Plot through to the Irish Rebellion and (many suspected) the Great Fire of London. In fact, the Catholic community comprised less than 2 per cent of the population of England and Wales by 1680, and was notable more for its docility than for any involvement in plotting. But the long-standing fears of international Catholicism, reinforced by more recent anxieties about attempts to establish 'popery and arbitrary government', enabled Oates and Tonge to spark off a wave of anti-popish hysteria between the autumn of 1678 and the spring of 1679, during which time there were numerous reports that Catholics were secretly meeting and arming themselves, and possibly plotting to fire London. Chains were placed across major streets in the capital and the trained bands were put on constant alert.

Yet it is unlikely that this scare would have been as serious or lasted as long were it not for two coincidences. First, Sir Edmund Berry Godfrey, the London magistrate before whom Oates had originally sworn a deposition of his evidence, was found dead on 17 October. His body had apparently been strangled and run through with his own sword. The circumstances of his death have never been established, but the popular mood was such that it was widely assumed that Catholics had killed him in order to silence him. The second piece of chance was that Oates and Tonge had implicated Edward Coleman, formerly secretary to James and his wife. Although they had no information on which to base this accusation, when Coleman's house was searched a cache of letters to Jesuits – including Louis XIV's Jesuit confessor – was discovered. As a result, on 1–2 November, the two Houses of Parliament had no hesitation in voting unanimously that 'there hath been and still is a damnable and hellish plot contrived and carried on by the popish recusants for the assassinating and murdering the King, and for subverting the government, and rooting out and destroying the Protestant religion'.

The incrimination of his ex-secretary inevitably called James's own loyalties into question, and on 4 November it was proposed in the Commons that he be barred from the King's presence and counsels. Charles attempted to defuse this situation on 9 November by indicating that he would accept 'such reasonable bills as should be presented, to make them safe in the reign of any successor, so [long] as they tend not to impeach the right of succession, nor the descent of the crown in the true line'. To this end, he accepted a second Test Act excluding Catholics from both Houses of Parliament, but secured a special exemption for James, albeit by a majority of only 158 to 156. Charles also agreed to proclaim the more rigorous enforcement of existing laws against popish recusants and Jesuits. These measures were enough to deflect Parliament's attention away from James for the time being, and ensured that the issue of whether he should be excluded from the line of succession did not surface explicitly at this stage.

Ironically, the first major target of Parliament's attempts to quash the plot was not a papist at all but the Anglican loyalist Danby. The perceived symbiosis between 'popery and arbitrary government' was crucial here. It was almost universally believed that the two were inseparable, and that the presence of one was an infallible indication of the other as well. Marvell had written that Court papists sought 'to introduce a French slavery' as much as 'to establish the Roman idolatry'; or, in Shaftesbury's pithy phrase, 'popery and slavery, like two sisters, go hand in hand.' By the same token, it was assumed that to extirpate popery would prevent arbitrary government and vice versa: as Sir Henry Capel put it, 'lay popery flat and there is an end of arbitrary government'. Danby was a victim of this logic. For by the autumn of 1678 his attempts to manipulate Parliament, his hostility to religious toleration, and his reluctance to disband a standing army of 20,000 all smacked of arbitrary government. The ostensible reason for raising the army had been to fight France if she failed to make peace with the Dutch, but many feared that the troops might be used to impose authoritarian government and to dispense with Parliaments. When it was revealed that Danby had been involved in secret negotiations for French subsidies in return for the continued prorogation of Parliament, such fears were apparently confirmed and his fate was sealed.[1]

The instrument of his downfall was Ralph Montagu, who in July 1678 had been dismissed as ambassador to Paris for conducting an affair with both the Countess of Castlemaine (Charles's former mistress) and her daughter. Deeply resentful of Charles and Danby, Montagu successfully stood for Parliament and on 19 December presented the Commons with letters revealing Danby's collusion in requesting French subsidies during 1677–8. The House immediately voted to draw up impeachment articles against Danby, including the ridiculous claim that he was 'popishly affected'. Alarmed at the possibility of further embarrassing revelations, Charles prorogued Parliament on 30 December and then dissolved it on 24 January 1679.

In retrospect, this was possibly not one of Charles's wisest political moves. During the winter of 1678–9 Coleman and three others were executed for their involvement in the plot, while impeachment articles were brought against five Catholic peers implicated by Oates. Others jumped on the bandwagon, such as William Bedloe, an adventurer, swindler and confidence trickster who claimed that the Queen herself was complicit in the plot. As the nation became more and more hysterical, public opinion turned decisively against the Court. The result was that the Parliament which assembled on 6 March 1679 – known as the first Exclusion Parliament – contained an even larger anti-Court majority (approximately two to one) than its predecessor. Shaftesbury estimated that there were 302 'worthy men' in the Commons as against 158 loyal to the Court. Charles remarked sardonically that a dog would have been elected if it had stood against a courtier, and soon began to wish that he was still dealing with the Cavalier Parliament. As a precaution, Charles advised James to go to Brussels shortly before the Parliament met.

At first, the new Parliament, like the old, was primarily concerned with Danby. It proceeded with impeachment articles against him, but on 26 March Danby agreed to resign as Lord Treasurer in return for a full royal pardon. Furious that he should escape scot-free, MPs considered a Bill of Attainder, but Danby pre-empted this by surrendering to arrest and spent the next five years in the Tower. On 20 April, in another gesture intended to defuse the opposition, Charles remodelled his Privy Council by reducing its numbers from forty-six to thirty and incorporating such leading critics as Shaftesbury (who became Lord President), Halifax, Essex and Russell. The Houses meanwhile began to consider ways in which a future Catholic sovereign might be 'disabled to do any harm'. These included a grant of £200,000 for the disbandment of the standing army (which was finally carried out the following summer), and also the Habeas Corpus Amendment Act. The latter gave statutory recognition to what had long been regarded as a common law right by requiring that, except in cases of treason or felony, prisoners had to be brought to trial, and the cause of their imprisonment stated, within a specified period of time (usually three days). Above all, it was declared illegal to move prisoners from one prison to another or to detain them 'beyond the seas' – for example to Scotland or Ireland or the Channel Islands – in order to evade writs of *habeas corpus*. The overriding concern was to quash the popish plot and to ensure, as the full title of this act put it, 'the better securing [of] the liberty of the subject' in the event of a Catholic successor. As yet, the question of exclusion was not openly addressed.

This all changed dramatically when, on 27 April, part of Coleman's correspondence was disclosed which appeared to implicate James in negotiations with both France and Rome. The Commons immediately voted that James's Catholicism had 'given the greatest countenance and encouragement to the present conspiracies and designs of the papists against the King and the

Protestant religion'. Charles countered on 30 April by promising 'limitations' on any Catholic successor, including the renunciation of all ecclesiastical patronage and the transfer of the power of appointment to civil, legal and military offices to Parliament whenever a Catholic sat on the throne. Although such 'limitations' helped to allay the fears of some, like Halifax, they were not enough for the hardliners, vociferously led by Shaftesbury, who now demanded nothing less than James's exclusion from the line of succession. On 11 May Thomas Pilkington moved that James be impeached for high treason, and four days later an Exclusion Bill was read for the first time. The bill passed its second reading on 21 May by 207 to 128. Remarking bitterly that he 'would rather submit to anything than endure the gentlemen of the Commons any longer', the enraged King prorogued Parliament on 27 May.

2 The Exclusion Crisis

The period from the reading of the first Exclusion Bill in May 1679 until March 1681 has generally been known as the Exclusion Crisis, and for ease of recognition that customary label will be retained here. However, as Jonathan Scott and Mark Knights have recently argued, much more was at stake in this crisis than merely the issue of James's exclusion from the line of succession.[2] That issue was a symptom rather than the root cause of the crisis. The opposition to Charles was motivated primarily by fears of 'popery and arbitrary government' in the present rather than in the future. Shaftesbury wrote in a private memorandum of 1679 that James's 'interest and design are to introduce a military and arbitrary government in his brother's time, which only can secure a man of his religion a quiet possession of his beloved crown'. The memory of previous 'popish plots' only served to exacerbate these fears. As in the early 1640s, the King's critics between 1679 and 1681 feared that recent royal policies directly threatened the future of Parliaments and the survival of Protestantism. By the same token, the eventual resurgence of loyalism to the Crown in 1680–1 was prompted by horrific memories of what had happened the last time the Crown was resisted during the Civil Wars of the 1640s. As Scott has suggested, the Restoration Settlement proved almost too successful in that it restored not only the pre-war constitution but also pre-war fears and tensions. In that sense, the crisis of 1678–81 grew out of the very nature of the settlement itself: it was, in Scott's phrase, the 'Restoration crisis'.

The parallels with the earlier crisis were immediately apparent in the rebellion that engulfed Scotland during the summer of 1679. On 3 May, a group of Covenanters dragged Archbishop Sharp from his coach two miles outside St Andrews and, in full view of his horrified daughter, sang psalms as they stabbed him to death. Shortly afterwards, a troop of dragoons led by John Graham of Claverhouse was defeated while trying to suppress a large conventicle at Drumclog, whereupon nearly 6,000 Presbyterians in the western Lowlands rose in open revolt. The rebels issued a *Declaration* calling for the armed defence of the 'true Protestant religion', and 'the obtaining of a free and unlimited Parliament ... for preventing the imminent danger of popery, and

Plate 15 *A Prospect of a Popish Successor*, 1680. This was one of numerous items published during the Exclusion Crisis that consciously revived memories of earlier alleged 'popish plots' in order to reinforce the campaign for James's exclusion from the succession. The scenes depicted in this vivid representation include the Marian martyrs (bottom left), while at the top popish machinations are blamed for the Great Fire of London. Such memories exerted a crucial influence on the course of events. Ultimately, however, fears that the exclusionists' tactics might provoke another civil war led public opinion to rally strongly in support of the Crown.

Source: British Library

extirpating of prelacy from amongst us'. This was followed by several reprints of the National Covenant and the Solemn League and Covenant. Charles promptly sent an English expeditionary force, commanded by his eldest (illegitimate) son, James Scott, Duke of Monmouth, which routed the rebels at Bothwell Bridge on 22 June. Unlike the Covenanters of the late 1630s, the Presbyterian rebels were fatally weakened by their inability to make common cause with noble dissenters. This finally enabled Charles to drive a wedge between moderate and radical nonconformists by issuing a third Letter of Indulgence that legalized conventicles in private houses and pardoned most of the insurgents.

The effects of Monmouth's swift victory were immediately felt in England. For several months Monmouth had aligned himself with Shaftesbury in pressing for James's exclusion, and his supporters thought that his Protestant beliefs, good looks and personal charm made him a viable candidate for the throne despite his illegitimacy. Fearing that Monmouth's triumphal return to London would strengthen the exclusionists' hand, Charles dissolved Parliament on 12 July and summoned another for October. If he hoped to secure a more pliable assembly he was proved wrong, for the second Exclusion Parliament turned out to be just as wary of any sign of 'popery and arbitrary government' as its predecessor. In the meantime, Charles opened negotiations with both the French and the Dutch in the hope of securing funds that would free him from dependence upon Parliament: as he told the French ambassador, Barillon, his 'one and only interest was to subsist'.

In late August, however, even Charles's physical survival was briefly in doubt. He fell seriously ill, probably with pneumonia, and although the crisis passed quickly it took several months for him to regain his full strength. His brother's illness brought James rushing back to England, mainly to prevent the possibility of Monmouth's seizing the throne. In an attempt to deflect the increasingly urgent calls for exclusion provoked by his illness, Charles resolved to send both possible contenders out of the kingdom: Monmouth was exiled to the Netherlands in September, and in November James was sent to Scotland as the King's Commissioner to the Estates to supervise the re-establishment of order. But any possible benefit from these moves was precluded by the revelation of the 'Meal-Tub Plot', a hare-brained conspiracy by several leading Catholics to discredit Shaftesbury and his allies by trying to implicate them in a bid to seize power. Although this prompted a wave of sympathy towards Shaftesbury, Charles nevertheless proceeded not only to dismiss him from the Privy Council but also to prorogue Parliament, which had not yet met, until the following January. In protest, Halifax withdrew from the Court, and Essex resigned as head of the Treasury Commission. Their departures left Charles increasingly reliant on three new advisers: the wily Earl of Sunderland, Laurence Hyde (Clarendon's son) and Sidney Godolphin. This trio came to be known as 'the Triumvirate' or – more disparagingly – as 'the Chits' because of their relative youth.

Shaftesbury and his allies meanwhile organized a massive petitioning campaign, the central demand of which was not James's exclusion but the protection of Protestantism and the free meeting of Parliament without further prorogations. Furious at what he saw as an encroachment on his prerogative to summon, prorogue and dissolve Parliament whenever he chose, the King prorogued Parliament on 10 December; thereafter he issued a further six prorogations that prevented Parliament from sitting until October 1680.[3] Charles thus used his power of prorogation to great effect to stymie the opposition, but at the cost of reinforcing fears about his commitment to the existence of Parliament. Shaftesbury retaliated by stepping up the petitioning campaign, but to no avail: although during the winter of 1679–80 Charles was presented with a 'monster' petition from London, bearing 16,000 signatures, along with half a dozen county petitions, he brusquely denied the validity of such 'private' petitions and at the end of January 1680 calmly invited James back to England.

James's stay in Scotland had proved highly successful. Against his personal preference, he at first went along with Charles's third Letter of Indulgence. However, in April 1680 a number of Scottish Privy Councillors were invited to London where, with strong support from James and many of the English bishops, they persuaded Charles to abandon the policy of toleration. The King agreed to a savage campaign of repression against field conventicles, but this proved severely counter-productive. On 22 June a group of radical Presbyterians led by Richard Cameron issued the Sanquhar Declaration which claimed that Charles had 'forfeited several years since by his perjury and breach of covenant both to God and his kirk' any right to his subjects' obedience. These Cameronians, as they came to be known, declared 'a war with such a tyrant and usurper and the men of his practices, as enemies to our Lord Jesus Christ and his cause and covenants'. The Cameronians were savagely defeated at Aird's Moss on 22 July, but the survivors continued to wage a guerrilla war throughout the 1680s. Lauderdale, old and ailing, was increasingly eclipsed by James and by Hamilton, and he finally resigned as Secretary of the Council in October. Thereafter, his preference for toleration was replaced by vigorous persecution: on the advice of James and Hamilton, Charles embarked on a brutal campaign against Presbyterian dissenters that led the eighteenth-century historian Robert Wodrow to call the early 1680s in Scotland 'the Killing Times'.[4]

In England, meanwhile, public opinion was beginning to polarize. The circulation of petitions for mass subscription reminded many of the petitions that had preceded the outbreak of civil war: as the loyalist newswriter Henry Muddiman put it, petitioning was 'the old approved way of fomenting a new rebellion'. The memories of the 1640s thus cut both ways: Shaftesbury's campaign, stimulated by revived fears of 'popery and arbitrary government', in turn resurrected fears of a populist assault on the monarchy and established forms of government. Gilbert Burnet wrote that the petitioners 'alienated many sober and well-meaning men from all the counsels that were carried on in such a manner, for they began to think that the Protestant religion was under a pretence to alter the government, or to help the Duke of Monmouth into the throne after the King's death'. From the spring of 1680, a growing number of loyalists distanced themselves from the oppositionists and signed addresses of loyalty 'abhorring' the activities of Shaftesbury and the 'discontented'. These 'abhorrers' upheld the principles of divine right monarchy, the royal prerogative powers and patriarchalism, and insisted on the subject's duties of non-resistance and passive obedience. Small wonder that *Patriarcha*, Sir Robert Filmer's classic defence of these values, possibly written in about 1628–31, was published for the first time in 1680 as a refutation of the petitioners' arguments. At the same time, Shaftesbury's friend and employee John Locke began work on his *Two Treatises of Government*. These sought to rebut the loyalists' position, and Filmer in particular, by advancing an essentially contractual theory of government based on the ideas of the equality of man, popular sovereignty, the law of nature and the right of resistance. As we shall see, it was from these contrasting outlooks that the political ideologies associated with Whigs and Tories gradually emerged.[5]

Fearful that he was losing public support, and unnerved by James's success in Scotland, Shaftesbury tried to increase the pressure on the Crown during the summer of 1680. He announced first of all that he had evidence that a Catholic conspiracy was being hatched in Ireland. This was an entirely bogus claim, but he secured the support of Essex who hoped to discredit his old enemy Ormond. As with the revelations of Oates and Tonge, the idea of an 'Irish plot' coincided so well with English fears that it was widely believed, and in January 1681 the Lords resolved that there was a 'horrid and treasonable plot and conspiracy contrived and carried on by those of the papist religion in Ireland for massacring the English and subverting the Protestant religion'. Shaftesbury played on these fears and deliberately revived memories of the 1641 rebellion. In an even bolder move, on 26 June he brought charges before the Grand Jury of Middlesex that James was a Catholic recusant and the King's influential mistress Louise de Kéroualle, Duchess of Portsmouth, a common prostitute and a French popish agent. Charles immediately ordered the jury to disperse before it could pronounce, and Shaftesbury's extraordinary impudence only sharpened the King's hatred of him. It also confirmed the growing fears of loyalists that beneath the calls for exclusion lay a more fundamental hostility towards the monarchy itself. Such divisions of opinion did not bode well for the second Exclusion Parliament, which Charles finally agreed to meet on 21 October.

In his opening speech, the King promised to accept 'any remedies which shall be proposed that may consist with the preserving of the Crown in its due and legal course of descent'. However, as Halifax commented, 'the waves beat so high against [James] that [a] great part of the world will not hear of anything less than exclusion'. Shaftesbury, supported by such allies in the Commons as Sir John Maynard and Colonel Silius Titus, refused to be distracted by such issues as foreign policy or the King's requests for supply. Instead, another exclusion bill rapidly passed all three of its readings in the Commons and was sent up to the Lords on 15 November. There, however, Charles's personal presence, together with no fewer than sixteen eloquent interventions from Halifax, secured the bill's defeat by sixty-three votes to thirty. Halifax then sought to achieve a compromise by resurrecting the idea of limitations on a Catholic successor. Undeterred, the Commons hoped to lure Charles with the bait of supply, and on 20 December offered to grant £600,000 in return for exclusion. Charles repeated that he would not compromise on that issue, whereupon the Commons retaliated by resolving to grant him no money until he accepted exclusion. Furious at their intransigence, and emboldened by the growing evidence of a loyalist backlash against the opposition, Charles dissolved Parliament on 18 January 1681.

It is worth stressing that exclusion remained a symptom rather than a cause of the opposition to the Crown. The underlying menace was perceived as a threat to the very being of Parliaments and the survival of Protestantism, and lurking behind that the growth of popery. These dangers were seen as inseparably linked. As William Harbord told the Commons, 'ever since King James [VI and I]'s time popery has been increased when the Parliament was dissolved, and suppressed while they have been sitting'. Sir Henry Capel found that 'every session of Parliament we are still troubled with popery. In the descent of four Kings [sic], still the Parliaments have been troubled with popery.' It was this conviction that there was a direct link between the spread of popery and the eclipse of Parliaments that induced sixteen peers, led by Essex, to submit a petition to Charles shortly after the dissolution of Parliament lamenting the 'dangers that threaten the whole kingdom, from the mischievous and wicked plots of the papists', and expressing their 'unspeakable grief and sorrow, the [last] parliament . . . [was again] . . . prorogued and dissolved before it could perfect what was intended for our security'. Exclusion was only one aspect of a wider anxiety about the future of Parliaments and Protestantism.

Two days after dissolving Parliament, Charles summoned another to meet in Oxford the following March. This was a calculated blow to the opposition, which possessed considerable support in London. Oxford, by contrast, remained a centre of loyalism, and was also more easily guarded by troops. Simultaneously, Charles dismissed several of his leading critics from the Council, including Essex. He was probably encouraged to take these firm steps by the fact that his negotiations with the French were at last beginning to bear fruit. In late November 1680, Barillon had informed Charles that Louis XIV might be prepared to assist him financially. Towards the end of January, Louis offered a subsidy on condition that Charles abandoned the alliance with Spain that he had signed the previous summer, and also dispensed with Parliament. On 18 March a formal treaty was agreed whereby Charles accepted these terms in return for a sum of around £115,000 per annum over the next three years, together with a lump sum of £40,000 immediately. In return, he promised not to summon another Parliament for three years. It was no surprise, therefore, that when the Houses assembled in Oxford three days later, they found Charles in an uncompromising mood.

Charles held the initiative throughout the brief sitting of the Oxford Parliament. Nearly 700 troops were drafted into the city, and the local inhabitants were enthusiastically supportive, shouting slogans such as 'Let the King live and the Devil hang up all Roundheads!' On 21 March Charles opened Parliament with his final offer, that on his death, William and Mary would be appointed as regents while James became King in name only. However, the new Parliament was no more co-operative than its two predecessors: the Commons immediately began work on a new exclusion bill while in the Lords Shaftesbury proposed that Monmouth be named as Charles's successor.

Charles responded that he would rather die 'than ever part with any of [his] prerogative, or betray his place, the laws, or the religion, or alter the true succession of the Crown, it being repugnant both to conscience and law'. He insisted that he had 'law and reason and all right-thinking men on my side', and declared: 'Let there be no delusion: I will not yield, nor will I be bullied'. Equally, the advocates of exclusion privately admitted that 'they had engaged themselves so far in the exclusion, they could not recede; they should be ruined in their reputations and interests, if they should be guilty of such a change in their resolutions'. The result was a total impasse. On 26 March the Commons resolved, with only about twenty dissenting voices, to revive the exclusion bill. Two days later, Charles caught his opponents off guard with a dramatic surprise: he summoned the two Houses, announced that the Parliament was dissolved, and departed for Windsor.

Charles followed up this bold stroke with a direct appeal to the nation. On 8 April he issued a *Declaration Touching the Reasons that Moved Him to Dissolve the Two Last Parliaments*, a studiously moderate document that sought to win over as wide a range of opinion as possible. Charles castigated his opponents for trying to 'disable us' and reminded readers that the last time 'the monarchy was shaken off' 'religion, liberty and property were all lost and gone'. He promised henceforth to continue to rule according to law and to call Parliaments frequently. Archbishop Sancroft instructed all Anglican clergy to read the *Declaration* from their pulpits the following Sunday. Although it was not universally well received, the *Declaration* served to reinforce the growing loyalist reaction, and over two hundred loyal addresses were presented to Charles during the weeks that followed. One 'well-wisher to the King' spoke for many when he declared: 'If it be the undoubted prerogative of the King to call, adjourn, prorogue and dissolve Parliaments at his own will and pleasure, it is a high impudence in any subject, or assembly of men, to take upon them to advise him (unasked) how and when to execute his power.' With the tide of opinion flowing ever more strongly his way, Charles had successfully headed off the threat of exclusion: even if the events of March 1681 had demonstrated his failure to reach a settlement with Parliament and had reaffirmed his subservience to Louis XIV, they did at least ensure that Charles and the Tories were politically dominant for the rest of his reign.

By the spring of 1681, the terms 'Whig' and 'Tory' were becoming widely used to denote oppositionists and loyalists respectively. Both labels were employed pejoratively: 'Whig' was originally applied to Scottish Presbyterian rebels of the late 1640s, while 'Tory' was the name given to Irish (Catholic) cattle thieves. While it is important to avoid projecting modern standards of party membership, organization and coherence back onto the much looser and more fluid situation of the early 1680s, the latter stages of the Exclusion Crisis nevertheless saw the emergence of embryonic 'parties' characterized by identifiable ideological positions.[6] The Tories upheld the principle of divine right monarchy and insisted that civil authority derived directly from God. They argued that the people therefore had a duty of passive obedience and possessed no right of resistance even against a tyrant. As Sir Leoline Jenkins put it in November 1680: 'I am of opinion that Kings of England have their Right from

God alone, and that no power on earth can deprive them of it.' The Tories believed that the greatest danger of arbitrary government came instead from dissenters and republicans who sought to erect a 'tyrannous Parliament'. They vigorously defended the 'Church by law established' and found natural allies among the bishops and many other clergy who strongly opposed exclusion. The most eloquent Tory propagandist was Sir Roger L'Estrange, whose many pamphlets together with his newspaper *The Observator* were crucial in stimulating the loyalist reaction against exclusion.

The Whigs, by contrast, thought that civil authority derived from the people, and that if the ruler ceased to govern for the public good and thus betrayed the trust reposed in him then the people had a right of resistance. This contractual theory of government was most powerfully worked out in Locke's *Two Treatises of Government*, mainly written between early 1680 and the summer of 1683 but not published until 1690. To the Whigs, arbitrary government was inseparably linked to popery, and they feared its growth as much under Charles II as under a Catholic successor. They regarded Parliament not only as the representative of the people but as the essential safeguard of Protestantism, liberties and property. Most Whigs fiercely opposed Anglican intolerance: many were nonconformists, or at least sympathetic to dissent, and they disliked the bishops' stand against exclusion. By the early 1680s the political elite and many local communities were increasingly polarized along Whig/Tory lines. But the 'parties' remained relatively fluid and were by no means mutually exclusive. It was quite possible for individuals to combine elements of the two positions, or to move between them: in 1681 that movement was running inexorably towards the Tories.

In the end, Charles was able to deflect his opponents by standing back and waiting for public opinion to rally behind him. His financial position during the 1680s was more secure than at any time during his reign. The French treaty brought some extra income, but much more important was the fact that an economic boom increased revenues from customs duties and excise as well as from the hearth tax. The result was an ordinary revenue of over £1.3 million in 1681–2 that greatly reduced Charles's dependence upon Parliament. This favourable financial situation was at least as important in determining the outcome of the crisis as any political skill on Charles's part. His most courageous and effective act was to stand firm in defence of the legitimate succession; otherwise, much of his success stemmed from a willingness – perhaps less consciously calculated than has sometimes been claimed – to wait for his enemies to discredit themselves and frighten moderate opinion. The position of the Crown retained immense strength, the fundamental loyalism of most people ran very deep, and Charles's combination of passivity and refusal to compromise on the key point of principle ultimately encouraged loyalists to gather behind him. He was then able, with characteristic opportunism and good timing, to exploit this backlash to outflank his opponents. As we have seen, memories of 1640–2 remained very potent, and the course of events in 1680–1 resembled what might have happened in the earlier crisis had the reaction in favour of Charles I run its full course without being halted by the Irish Rebellion and the King's own misguided initiatives. The outcome of the

Exclusion Crisis owed much to the fact that the memory of 1641 ultimately worked to Charles's advantage rather than that of his opponents.

The crucial importance of memories of the build-up to civil war bears out Scott's arguments that the Restoration Settlement had in some ways proved too successful, in that it restored not only the pre-war constitution but also pre-war fears about the growth of 'popery and arbitrary government'. It consciously revived the early Stuart constitution complete with all its grey areas and stress points surrounding the nature of monarchy and the relationship between the Crown and Parliament. The inherent ambiguities of these constitutional arrangements were compounded by a Church settlement that institutionalized a bitter division between Anglicans and dissenters. The Whig/Tory divergence grew out of long-standing tensions and uncertainties about the nature of Church and State that had been left unresolved at the Restoration Settlement. The two 'parties' embodied contrasting attitudes not only to the issue of exclusion, but to the whole nature of Charles's kingship and the threat of 'popery and arbitrary government'. The King's tactical victory in the Exclusion Crisis prevented those issues from being resolved in 1681. Instead, the sources of instability persisted, until at the end of the decade an even greater crisis exploded that would finally necessitate the fundamental overhaul of this polity. But in the short term, Charles held the trump cards and for the remainder of his reign he presided over a period of relative political calm.

3 The Tory Reaction

Some historians have suggested that during the last four years of his life Charles made a systematic attempt to impose absolutism. It probably makes more sense, however, to see the years 1681–5 as the final phase of a career in which Charles had regularly adapted his policies and choice of advisers in order to harness changing currents in public opinion. He had always lacked the energy and single-mindedness needed to build an absolutist state: rather, in the period after 1681 he embraced the principles of his natural supporters, the Tory-Anglicans. That meant defending the established Church and abandoning any attempt to introduce religious toleration. It also meant abiding by the laws that governed both Church and State and espousing a legalist rhetoric that posed no threat to the Tory commitment to the rule of law. Often during these years, Charles did not so much initiate policy himself as encourage and exploit the activities of Tories at both national and local levels. He was able to sit back and ride a wave of enthusiastic support for Crown and Church that carried the majority of the nation along with it.

Following the dissolution of the Oxford Parliament, Charles pressed home his advantage against the Whigs. During the summer of 1681 many Whigs were purged from the commissions of the peace and the lieutenancies. Shaftesbury was arrested on a charge of treason in July and was only acquitted in November because the two Whig sheriffs of London had assembled a grand jury of like-minded people. The King retaliated in December by demanding that a new charter be issued to the City of London giving him the right to approve the

Lord Mayor, the sheriffs and all other major office-holders. Although the subsequent legal wrangle dragged on until June 1683, the Crown emerged victorious and local Tories all over the country followed this lead. They requested new borough charters and sought writs of *quo warranto* to enquire 'by what warrant' corporations were performing their functions. Lawyers could easily find technical flaws in many charters, necessitating the grant of a new charter that gave the King the right either to approve designated borough officers (usually those with judicial responsibilities) or – as was increasingly the case by 1684–5 – to remove any corporation member of whom he disapproved. Between 1681 and 1685, fifty-one new charters were issued (thirty-seven of them after 1683), and a further forty-seven were in the pipeline at the time of Charles's death. This should not be seen as evidence that Charles was pursuing a concerted policy; rather, as John Miller has written, 'throughout, the crown reacted, often cautiously, to initiatives from elsewhere'. In requesting new charters, local Tories were generally not seeking the total destruction of the Whigs, but they did want to secure dominance of local government and in particular to extend their influence over parliamentary elections and to ensure the stricter enforcement of the penal laws against dissenters.[7]

The Whigs became increasingly demoralized, and the desperate actions of some of their more radical leaders only served to discredit them further. During the summer and autumn of 1682, rumours circulated that the Duke of Monmouth was plotting with Whig peers such as Essex and William Lord Russell to launch a rising, and when Monmouth made a triumphant tour of the northwest of England Charles ordered him to be arrested. Shaftesbury, the target of mocking satires such as John Dryden's *Absalom and Achitophel* (1681–2) and *The Medal* (1682), was by now broken and ailing: he left for Amsterdam at the end of November and died there in January 1683. But what finally ended any hope of a Whig revival was the discovery in June 1683 of the so-called Rye House Plot. This was really two conspiracies: one, hatched by a group of former Cromwellians, planned to assassinate Charles and James at Rye House in Hertfordshire as they were returning to London from the races at Newmarket; the second was a scheme to seize the King's person and assume power, and those implicated included Essex, Russell and Algernon Sidney. These three Whig notables were promptly imprisoned. On 13 July Essex was found with his throat cut: he had probably committed suicide, but some Whigs claimed he had been murdered. Russell was executed on 21 July, as, on 7 December, was Sidney. The latter had been convicted of treason largely on the basis of his manuscript *Discourses concerning Government*, a brilliant anti-absolutist polemic that deployed classical republican ideas to justify both resistance and tyrannicide. By this time, even former exclusionists like the Wiltshire MP Lionel Ducket were disillusioned with many of the Whig leaders: as he put it, 'it is plainly evident that too many of them had at that time designs in hand more wicked than their malice could invent to accuse the papists of'. In the wake of the Rye House Plot support for the Crown and for Tory–Anglican values grew even stronger. A wave of loyal addresses congratulated Charles and James on their miraculous escape. The prevailing mood was well captured when, on the day of Russell's execution, the University of

Oxford denounced 'the machinations of traitorous heretics and schismatics', condemned doctrines such as that 'all civil authority is derived originally from the people', and insisted on the duty of 'passive obedience in all circumstances whatsoever'. This was a principle that would be sorely tested before the end of the decade.

Such a mood made people fairly relaxed when Charles on occasion pushed his prerogative powers to the very limit of what was legally permissible. It is worth stressing that the proceedings against Russell and Sidney were conducted with scrupulous respect for the rule of law: there was no question of Charles intervening or seeking to manipulate judicial proceedings. Nevertheless, from 1676 onwards he appointed judges *durante bene placito* (during the King's pleasure) rather than *quamdiu se bene gesserint* (for as long as they shall do good), thereby reasserting a power that Charles I had consistently claimed in theory but relinquished in practice after January 1641. Between 1676 and his death, Charles unilaterally removed eleven judges. Furthermore, in 1684 he calmly violated the Triennial Act by not calling a Parliament when one was due. Halifax vainly protested, but otherwise the lack of any public outcry was remarkable. Charles's annual revenue reached nearly £1.4 million by 1683–4, while the First Lord of the Treasury, the Earl of Rochester,[8] succeeded in curbing the King's extravagance and bringing expenditure down to less than £1,175,000 a year. This healthy financial situation meant that Charles simply did not need to face Parliament: as Sir Thomas Meres had perceived several years earlier, ''tis money that makes a Parliament considerable and nothing else'. The political nation, for its part, was prepared to support a monarch who was only intermittently authoritarian and whose Anglican credentials had never seemed less in question.

As the Tory Reaction gathered pace in 1684–5, the persecution of dissent became considerably harsher. The fate of dissenters had often depended on the vigour of individual local magistrates: in the 1680s the purging of many Whigs from office, together with the fact that the Exclusion Crisis had intensified Tory hostility towards dissent, ensured that the penal laws against nonconformists were implemented much more energetically. In January 1684, for example, over two hundred dissenters faced charges at Coventry for not attending church: nineteen of these were former Whig corporation members. The Quakers suffered most severely, and perhaps as many as four hundred of them died in prison between 1681 and 1685. This was in marked contrast to the relatively lenient enforcement of the penal laws against Catholics, which partly reflected the Duke of York's growing influence. In 1684 James was readmitted to the Privy Council and thereafter he and his associates – most notably Sunderland and a thrusting new Tory judge named Sir George Jeffreys[9] – formed an increasingly powerful reversionary interest. To the dismay of more moderate Tories, such as the Lord Keeper, Lord Guilford, whose primary commitment was to the rule of law, James and his allies pressed for the lifting of the recusancy laws and urged the even tougher use of writs of *quo warranto*. During the last months of the King's life, advisers like Halifax and Rochester found themselves gradually marginalized, although how far this trend would have continued had Charles lived longer remains uncertain.

James's increasing influence owed much to his remarkable successes as the King's Commissioner in Scotland, where he spent much of the period 1679–82. In August 1681 the Scottish Parliament recognized James as heir to the throne, declared the inviolability of divine, hereditary right, and affirmed its commitment to the suppression of dissent. A new Test Act required all office-holders in both Church and State to take an oath acknowledging the King as 'the only supreme governor of this realm, over all persons and in all causes as well ecclesiastical as civil'. Fifty ministers were promptly driven out of the Church for refusing to subscribe, and by 1683 anyone denying the royal supremacy was liable to be summarily executed. In all, about a hundred individuals were killed between 1681 and 1685, while many others suffered imprisonment, torture, maiming or the billeting of troops on their property. By 1684 the Cameronians were a miserable remnant detached from mainstream Presbyterian opinion. As in England, a loyalist reaction was in full swing, eloquently expressed in the Lord Advocate, Sir George Mackenzie's *Jus Regium* (1684), a robust defence of absolute monarchy. At the same time, a period of peace and a series of good harvests brought an upswing in the Scottish economy, and from the later 1670s the nobility and urban oligarchs became noticeably more prosperous and self-confident. Lauderdale had died in August 1682, and power increasingly lay with James's allies, especially William Douglas, Marquis of Queensberry, Treasurer from 1682, and James Drummond, Earl of Perth, who became Chancellor in 1684. By the mid-1680s James apparently possessed a very secure power-base north of the border.

Developments in Ireland followed a broadly similar pattern. In July 1681 Charles and the Privy Council decided that henceforth Irish public finances would be managed by a commission responsible directly to the English Treasury. This commission began work in 1683, and within a year had built up Irish revenue to a record level. The final years of Charles's reign saw rising prosperity in Ireland manifested in urban growth (especially Dublin) and in the building of some fine country houses for the more substantial gentry. In March 1684 another commission was appointed to investigate defects in the land settlement by checking titles and issuing new patents to all landowners. This proved largely successful and began to redress some long-standing grievances. As in Charles's other kingdoms, these years also saw a significant toughening of policy towards Protestant dissent, especially after the discovery of the Rye House Plot. All over Ireland conventicles were suppressed, meeting houses closed and ministers bound over, while the Presbyterian strongholds of Ulster were often singled out for the billeting of troops. At the same time – and here James's growing influence was again evident – life became easier for Irish Catholics, provided that they worshipped unobtrusively. Mass-houses were reopened and in some places religious orders even reappeared. James's allies, such as Richard Talbot, later Earl of Tyrconnell, began to form a reversionary interest, and Ormond's days as Lord Lieutenant were numbered. By now in his mid-seventies, he was gradually losing his grip, and Charles was alarmed by reports not only that corruption was widespread but also that Whig sympathizers still lurked in the army and the Dublin Privy Council. He therefore informed Ormond in October 1684 that Rochester would shortly replace him as Lord Lieutenant:[10] Ormond, grief-stricken by the death of his wife the previous summer, henceforth withdrew from public life and died in 1688.

It seemed by the beginning of 1685 that Charles was master of his three kingdoms to a greater degree than ever before. He had defeated his most bitter opponents and was ruling with the active support of the majority of his subjects. He appeared fit, energetic and in good spirits. Then, wholly unexpectedly, on the morning of 2 February, Charles was taken fatally ill.[11] It is a tribute to his immensely strong physical constitution that he survived the ministrations of his doctors – which included numerous bleedings and blisterings – for as long as four days. Death finally came on the morning of 6 February. The previous evening, with James's firm encouragement, Charles had been received into the Catholic Church; but whether this represented the fulfilment of a long-cherished wish, or the resigned gesture of a dying man too far gone to resist his brother's will, remains mysterious.

The final enigma surrounding Charles's religion was typical of a monarch who was both extrovert and accessible yet ultimately difficult to fathom. As a politician, Charles was flexible and pragmatic, wedded above all to survival and deeply reluctant to pursue rigid ideologies at the expense of stability. His canny instinct for knowing what was politically practical, together with his natural dislike of paperwork, ensured that he could never emulate the regime of his cousin, Louis XIV. Instead, his personality and political style – in many ways reminiscent of James VI and I – made him well equipped to preside over a Restoration Settlement that self-consciously tried to reconstruct the pre-civil war 'ancient constitution'. By the same token, he provided a welcome contrast to Charles I, the monarch whose policies had precipitated the downfall of that constitution. Unlike his father, Charles II was characterized, in John Morrill's words, by 'limited ambition and lazy pragmatism': as the Yorkshire Tory Sir John Reresby observed, he 'was not striving, nor ambitious, but easy, loved pleasures and seemed chiefly to desire quiet and security for his own time'. In the end, such a worldly and supple approach made him an effective and popular ruler. He was never more than mildly and erratically authoritarian, and only overtly espoused Catholicism on his deathbed. He became one of the best known and best remembered of British kings, the 'merry monarch', sufficiently well trusted to get away with flouting the Triennial Act in 1684. He was a king under whom most people in the three kingdoms were happy to live, perhaps above all because despite his periodic attempts to establish religious toleration he remained formally committed to the established Church. His final years demonstrated that the majority of his subjects were prepared to accept a *Protestant* authoritarianism; but, as his successor would soon discover, a *Catholic* authoritarianism was a very different matter.

11 A Glorious Revolution?

Chronology

1685	16 February	Rochester appointed Lord Treasurer
	April–May	Argyll launches unsuccessful rebellion in Western Scotland
	19 May–2 July	First session of James's first Parliament: generous financial grants to the Crown
	30 June	Execution of Argyll
	5–6 July	Battle of Sedgemoor: Monmouth's rebellion crushed
	15 July	Execution of Monmouth
	September	'Bloody Assizes': Jeffreys sentences 250 of Monmouth's rebels to death
	28 September	Jeffreys appointed Lord Chancellor
	8 October	Louis XIV revokes Edict of Nantes: 50,000–80,000 Huguenots flee to England by 1688
	9–20 November	Second session of James's first Parliament: protests at James's use of dispensing power to commission Catholic officers
1686	1 March	Earl of Tyrconnell appointed Lieutenant-General of the Irish Army
	5 March	James issues Directions to Preachers forbidding them to attack Church of Rome
	15 June	James dissolves Scottish Parliament when it rejects proposed concessions to Scottish Catholics

	16 June	Godden vs. Hales: judges uphold King's dispensing power (although James had dismissed six less sympathetic judges in advance)
	15 July	James establishes Commission for Ecclesiastical Causes under Lord Chancellor Jeffreys
	July	James appoints four Catholics to the Privy Council
	6 September	Commission for Ecclesiastical Causes suspends Bishop Compton of London
	November	James establishes Licensing Office where dissenters can buy certificates of dispensation from penal laws
	10 December	Rochester dismissed as Lord Treasurer
1687	5 January	Lord Belasyse, a Catholic, placed at head of new Treasury Commission
	8 January	Clarendon dismissed as Lord Lieutenant of Ireland; Tyrconnell appointed Lord Deputy
	12 February	James issues proclamation granting freedom of private worship to Catholics and Quakers in Scotland
	February	Dutch emissary Dykveldt establishes secret contacts with James's leading critics in England
	4 April	James issues Declaration of Indulgence for England and Ireland: suspends Test and Corporation Acts and penal laws
	April	James orders Fellows of Magdalen College, Oxford, to elect a Catholic President; they refuse
	28 June	James issues Scottish Declaration of Indulgence
	2 July	Dissolution of James's first Parliament
	Late summer	Publication of Halifax's *Letter to a Dissenter*
	October	Commission for Ecclesiastical Causes deprives Fellows of Magdalen College, Oxford, of their Fellowships

	Autumn	James begins campaign to pack Parliament: Lords Lieutenant sound out JPs and Deputy Lieutenants about Declaration of Indulgence and repeal of penal laws; only a minority are found to be positively in favour of James's policies; purges of local government officers are stepped up
1688	March	Bonaventure Gifford, a Catholic, imposed as President of Magdalen College, Oxford
	27 April	James reissues Declaration of Indulgence
	4 May	James instructs clergy to read Declaration of Indulgence from the pulpits on two successive Sundays
	18 May	Archbishop Sancroft and six bishops present petition claiming that use of suspending power is illegal; James decides to prosecute them for 'seditious libel'
	10 June	Mary of Modena gives birth to a son: opens up prospect of a Catholic dynasty
	29–30 June	Trial of Archbishop Sancroft and six bishops: their acquittal prompts public rejoicing
	30 June	'Immortal Seven' invite William of Orange into England to secure a free Parliament and investigate legitimacy of James's son
	Early July	William begins to assemble an expeditionary force
	14 September	Louis XIV launches attack on the Rhenish Palatinate
	29 September	States of Holland support William's plan to invade England
	30 September	William issues *Declaration of reasons for appearing in arms in the kingdom of England*
	Late September–early October	James grants a series of panic concessions
	5 November	William lands at Torbay; marches to Exeter
	19–23 November	James reaches Salisbury, but retreats back towards London as William advances from Exeter

	November	Peers sympathetic to William secure parts of North and Midlands
	8 December	James's commissioners meet William at Hungerford
	9 December	Queen and son flee to France
	11 December	James attempts to flee, but is intercepted; brought back to London on 16 December
	Mid-December	Assembly of Peers is called together to govern in King's absence
	18 December	William enters London
	23 December	James escapes to France; William summons irregular assembly
	24–26 December	Assembly of Peers and irregular assembly urge William to take control of government and to call a Convention
	28 December	William agrees, and the next day issues writs for elections to Convention
1689	22 January–20 August	First session of Convention Parliament: James declared to have 'abdicated' and left throne 'vacant'; Declaration of Rights drawn up
	13 February	William and Mary formally offered throne; Declaration of Rights read to them
	14 February	William and Mary proclaimed King and Queen
	12 March	James lands at Kinsale; lays siege to Londonderry in April
	20 March	Commons grants William a revenue of £1.2 million a year
	28 March	Mutiny Act: a standing army declared illegal in peacetime except with Parliament's consent
	11 April	Scottish Claim of Right; William and Mary crowned as King and Queen of England and Ireland
	7 May–18 July	James's 'Patriot Parliament' in Dublin: liberty of conscience proclaimed; 1662 Act of Settlement repealed; English Parliament can no longer pass laws binding on Ireland; but Protestantism is not proscribed

	11 May	William and Mary formally accept Scottish throne
	24 May	Toleration Act grants limited religious rights to dissenters, but not civil equality
	22 July	Scottish act abolishing 'prelacy'
	27 July	Jacobite rebels in Highlands defeat William's forces at Killiecrankie
	30 July	Williamite forces led by Percy Kirke relieve Londonderry
	21 August	Scottish Jacobite forces fail to take Dunkeld
	19 October–27 January 1690	Second session of Convention Parliament: Declaration of Rights enacted as the Bill of Rights
1690	February	Archbishop Sancroft and around 400 other 'non-jurors' are deprived for refusal to swear oath of allegiance to William
	20 March–23 May	First session of William's first Parliament
	25 April	Repeal of 1669 act asserting royal supremacy over the Scottish Church
	1 May	Scottish Jacobite forces finally defeated at Cromdale
	8 May	Lords of the Articles abolished
	7 June	Presbyterian government of the Scottish Church established
	14 June	William arrives in Ireland
	1 July	Battle of the Boyne: William inflicts heavy defeat on James; James flees to France on 4 July
	19 July	Abolition of lay patronage in the Scottish Church
	5 September	William leaves Ireland and returns to England
	2 October–5 January 1691	Second session of William's first Parliament
1691	22 April	John Tillotson nominated as Archbishop of Canterbury

12 July	Battle of Aughrim: Ginkel's Williamite forces decisively defeat Jacobites commanded by St Ruth
14 August	Death of Tyrconnell
3 October	Treaty of Limerick ends war in Ireland

1 The Accession of James VII and II

Few monarchs have inherited such an apparently strong position as James VII and II. His brother had died at the height of his power, his Whig opponents were defeated and discredited, and James's accession was warmly welcomed in all three kingdoms. The Earl of Peterborough captured the popular mood when he wrote in February 1685: 'Everything is very happy here. Never king was proclaimed with more applause than ... James II. He is courted by all men, and ... I doubt not but to see a happy reign.' James reinforced these feelings by announcing, within hours of Charles's death, his intention 'to preserve this government both in church and state as it is now by law established'. He laughed off his image as 'a man fond of arbitrary power', and declared: 'The laws of England are sufficient to make the King as great a monarch as I can wish, and as I shall never depart from the just rights and prerogative of the Crown, so I shall never invade any man's property'. His subjects were delighted.

The combination of popular loyalty to the Crown and the purges of borough corporations that had taken place since 1681 ensured that James's first English Parliament, which assembled on 19 May, was overwhelmingly Tory in complexion: only fifty-seven Whigs were elected in a House of Commons of 525 members for England and Wales. The atmosphere of solidarity behind James was further enhanced by the news that Monmouth was fomenting a rebellion in the West Country. The Duke always maintained that Charles II had secretly married his mother, and he traded on his Protestant credentials to assemble a poorly trained army of about 4,000 men drawn mainly from the dissenting farmers, tradesmen and clothworkers of Somerset, West Dorset and East Devon. He found virtually no supporters among the nobility or gentry. The rebels advanced as far as Sedgemoor protesting that Monmouth was the rightful king, but there, on 5–6 July, they were torn to shreds by the 8,000-strong standing army that James had inherited from Charles. The penalties were swift and savage. Monmouth was executed on 15 July, while in the space of nine days during September, Lord Chief Justice Jeffreys heard 1,336 cases in the so-called 'Bloody Assizes': he sentenced 250 rebels to death and a further 800 to be transported to the West Indies.[1] Monmouth's rebellion served to strengthen support for the King. In June, when Parliament learned that Monmouth was raising forces, it voted James not only all the revenues that his brother had enjoyed – which by 1688 yielded around £1.6 million a year – but also various extraordinary supplies for fixed periods which ensured that his annual income over the next three years exceeded £2 million. James was, as J. P. Kenyon has observed, the first English monarch since Henry VIII to be free of financial worries. The Houses also allowed James to expand the army, with the result that by December 1685 it comprised nearly 20,000 troops. In view of the perceived link between a standing army and 'arbitrary government', there could be no more telling sign of how deeply the political nation trusted James in the opening months of his reign.

That trust soon turned out to be misplaced. Whereas Charles II had in many ways resembled James I, James II was much more akin to Charles I. Not only did James immediately demand a high moral tone for the Court and curb the waste, drunkenness and promiscuity characteristic of his elder brother's reign. He also, like his father, was a conviction politician who displayed a restless energy, an inflexible commitment to principle and an inability to regard opposition as other than subversive. He was driven above all by an intense adherence to Catholicism, to which he had converted secretly as early as 1668, and openly in 1673. In his unshakeable belief that Rome was 'an infallible Church', James displayed all the passionate fervour of a convert. From the moment he became King, his overriding aim was to liberate his co-religionists in all three kingdoms. He was a bigot not in the sense that he wished to *impose* Catholicism on England, Scotland and Ireland but in his total incapacity to empathize with the profound anti-popery of the majority of his subjects, at any rate on the mainland. He informed the Spanish ambassador that he 'would force no man's conscience, but only aimed at the Roman Catholics being no worse treated than the rest, instead of being deprived of their liberties like traitors'. James assumed that as soon as the civil and religious disabilities on papists were lifted, there would be a surge of voluntary conversions as most people recognized the innate superiority and truth of the Catholic Church.

Contrary to what some historians have claimed, he did not systematically try to establish an absolutist State. We shall see that his legal and constitutional actions were entirely geared to the advancement of his religious policy: they were no more than means to an end. Nevertheless, his personality was naturally authoritarian, as was shown by his rule in Scotland and by a secret conversation with the French ambassador only two days after his accession in which he confided his hopes of securing a favourable financial settlement so that thereafter he could either 'put off the assembling of Parliament or ... maintain myself by other means which may appear more convenient for me'. Furthermore, most of his subjects assumed that 'popery and arbitrary government' were inseparable, and that the latter necessarily accompanied the former. Herein lay the roots of James's downfall. The enthusiastic support for the Crown during the Tory Reaction and Monmouth's Rebellion convinced James that the political nation would place loyalty to the legitimate succession above religious considerations. But he was wrong. The monarch's natural supporters, the Tory-Anglicans, were loyal to a package within which the Crown and the Church operated in symbiosis. They desperately wished to avoid having to choose between the two. As William Sherlock declared in a sermon to Parliament on 29 May 1685, 'to be true to our Prince, we must be true to our Church and to our Religion', for 'it would be no act of loyalty to accommodate or complement away our religion and its legal securities'.

James failed to heed such words of warning. He pressed ahead with policies that forced his subjects to choose between Church and Crown, and hence to explore the limits of their obedience to the monarch. He proved utterly inflexible in the pursuit of his goal, largely because he and his elder brother had drawn opposite lessons from Charles I's fate. If Charles II learnt that pragmatism, opportunism and compromise were the keys to political survival, James blamed his father's demise on such concessions as he had made, and felt a strong 'prepossession against the yielding temper which had proved so dangerous to his brother and so fatal to his father'. He was even less flexible than Charles I, and had even worse religious credentials. Unfortunately, the Restoration Settlement – just like the pre-war 'ancient constitution' – lacked any safeguards against a monarch who was perceived as an enemy to 'the Church by law established'. Nobody knew what to do if the royal supremacy were used to subvert the established Church. As a result, the same tensions surfaced as in Charles I's reign, prompting Jonathan Scott to label the Glorious Revolution the third 'crisis of popery and arbitrary government'. But, precisely because it came after the previous two crises, the outcome this time would be very different.

2 Towards Popery and Arbitrary Government?

In the long term, James wanted Parliament to repeal the penal laws against Catholics and dissenters along with the Test and Corporation Acts. He recognized that his Protestant daughter Mary was overwhelmingly likely to succeed him, and that only the statutory repeal of this legislation could ensure the permanent toleration of Catholicism. But in the meantime James intended to employ his prerogative powers to exempt named individuals from the force of these laws. When, in November, he informed Parliament that he had used this dispensing power to commission nearly ninety Catholic officers in the army, there were protests in both Houses that such commissions were illegal. Infuriated, James prorogued Parliament after a session of less than two weeks, and turned to the judges to uphold his power. In June 1686 the test case of Godden vs. Hales was heard before the judges of the common law courts. Shortly before the trial, James canvassed the judges and dismissed no less than six of them – including the Chief Justice of Common Pleas and the Chief Baron of the Exchequer – in order to ensure a favourable verdict. Eleven of the twelve judges then upheld the King's dispensing power on the grounds that 'the laws of England [were] the king's laws', and that it was therefore 'an inseparable prerogative in the kings of England to dispense with penal laws in particular cases'. Thus vindicated, James felt free to make ever-increasing use of the dispensing power, and promptly appointed four Catholics to the Privy Council in July.

Although his powers had been upheld in theory, in reality it was clear that James's hopes of winning over the Tory-Anglicans who had so warmly welcomed his accession had proved illusory. His open encouragement to his co-religionists to worship freely provoked a series of incidents in which Tory-Anglican magistrates, such as the Lord Mayor of Bristol in April 1686, attempted to prevent the celebration of mass. In London, the Tory Lord Mayor tried to prevent the construction of a Catholic chapel in Lime Street and refused to suppress the riots that erupted when it was opened. In March 1686 James had issued a set of Directions to Preachers that instructed them to avoid provocative subjects, and certainly not to make any attack on the Church of Rome. When John Sharp, Dean of Norwich and Rector of St Giles-in-the-Fields, London, disobeyed, James peremptorily ordered Bishop Compton of

London to suspend him from preaching. Compton refused, whereupon James created the Commission for Ecclesiastical Causes – a body widely thought reminiscent of the Court of High Commission – to enforce his orders. The Commission suspended Compton in September, sparking fears that the King wished to muzzle the clergy by preventing them from defending Protestantism. James was by now prepared to dismiss anyone who spoke out against him: when Rochester, who had become Lord Treasurer in 1685, stated that he would never become a Catholic, James removed him in December 1686 and placed a Catholic, Lord Belasyse, at the head of a new Treasury Commission in January 1687.

That same month also saw the dismissal of Rochester's elder brother Clarendon, who had succeeded Ormond as Lord Lieutenant of Ireland. In place of the English Protestant Clarendon, James's Irish favourite Richard Talbot, Earl of Tyrconnell, a Catholic of Old English ancestry, was appointed Lord Deputy. A forceful yet beguiling personality, the Earl found an invaluable ally at Court in Sunderland. Tyrconnell wanted the Old English Catholics to recover their former lands and power, and he persuaded James that this might be achieved without driving the Protestants into open opposition. As in England, one of James's earliest moves was to promote more Catholic army officers, and in April 1685 he instructed Tyrconnell to set about implementing this policy; he subsequently appointed Tyrconnell Lieutenant-General of the Irish Army in March 1686. The Earl acted with such energy in replacing the 'disaffected' Protestants who had effectively monopolized the army under Ormond that by September 1686 Catholics constituted 67 per cent of the army privates and 40 per cent of the officers. Earlier in 1686, Tyrconnell had persuaded James to appoint one Catholic judge to each of the four Irish law courts. These pro-Catholic policies accelerated after Tyrconnell became Lord Deputy in January 1687. Writs of *quo warranto* were extensively used to give Catholics a two-thirds majority in most corporations, ensuring that a future Irish House of Commons would be overwhelmingly Catholic, and by 1688 the bulk of Irish judges and Privy Councillors were Catholic. James steadily ran down the Church of Ireland and often left benefices vacant in order to use the revenues to subsidize Catholic clergy, schools and religious orders. Most controversially of all, Tyrconnell persuaded James to consider plans for a modified land settlement in which Protestants would hand over about half their lands to Catholics. Tyrconnell passionately wanted to redress the Protestant domination of land and power that had developed so dramatically during the seventeenth century, and he also sold his policies to James as part of a British programme in which Ireland formed the prototype for a Catholic ascendancy that could then be extended to England and Scotland. In the other two kingdoms, Ireland seemed – as in the 1630s – to provide a laboratory in which authoritarian policies could be tried out prior to their introduction on the mainland.

Many English people regarded Scotland, where James's reputation stood so high on his accession, as another testing-ground. Just as Monmouth's Rebellion deepened loyalty to the Crown in England, so a disastrous rising in the southwest Highlands led by the Earl of Argyll in April and May 1685

Plate 16 In April 1685, James VII and II instructed the Catholic Richard Talbot, Earl of Tyrconnell, to recruit more of his co-religionists as soldiers and officers into the Irish Army. James appointed him Lieutenant-General in March 1686 and by the following September, 40 per cent of Irish army officers were Catholics. English and Irish Protestants were horrified at this development, and blamed Tyrconnell for encouraging James to pursue strongly pro-Catholic policies. This English playing card of about 1689 depicts Tyrconnell as a knave placing arms in the hands of Irish papists.
Source: The Fotomas Index

strengthened James's hand and encouraged him to begin appointing Catholics to both civil and military office. He placed the Catholic Earl of Dunbarton in charge of commissioning more of his co-religionists as army officers. As in England, James hoped to obtain Parliament's consent to religious toleration. In May 1686 he attempted to strike a deal with Parliament whereby he would endeavour to secure 'a free trade with England' in return for Scottish Catholics being granted religious freedom and civil equality. When Parliament rejected this proposal, James brusquely dissolved it and, as in England, fell back on his prerogative powers. In February 1687 he issued a proclamation granting freedom of private worship to Catholics and Quakers, but not Presbyterians. This was followed in June by a Declaration of Indulgence that allowed complete toleration and admission to office for Catholics, and rights of private worship and a relaxation of the penal laws for Presbyterian conventiclers. James issued this Declaration by his 'absolute power, which all our subjects are to obey without reserve'. Presbyterians at once came back into the open, and in the west of Scotland in particular the established Church, robbed of its coercive powers, began to lose control. By the spring of 1688 the gradual breakdown of order seemed to present a terrible warning of what might happen in England.

In all three of his kingdoms, then, James's rule displayed a common authoritarian style based on policies that relentlessly favoured his co-religionists. Such an agenda could scarcely have come at a worse time. For in October 1685, Louis XIV revoked the Edict of Nantes which guaranteed the religious freedom and legal equality of France's one million or so Protestants (Huguenots). About 1,500 Huguenots were sent to serve as galley slaves, while over the next three years somewhere between 50,000 and 80,000 fled to England with horrific stories of their sufferings. Although James was not especially close to Louis, such stories made Protestant fears of 'popery and arbitrary government' even more intense.

During 1686 James therefore decided to abandon his attempts to woo the Tory-Anglicans and began instead to cultivate the dissenters as an alternative base of support. Hoping that the promise of toleration would win them over, James used his prerogative powers to issue pardons to imprisoned dissenters, especially Quakers, along with the remission of their fines. In November 1686 he established a Licensing Office where dissenters could buy certificates of dispensation from the penal laws. Then, on 4 April 1687, he issued a Declaration of Indulgence that suspended the Test and Corporation Acts as well as the penal laws against Catholics and dissenters. James promised to 'protect and maintain' the clergy and laity of the Church of England 'in the free exercise of their religion as by law established, and in the quiet and full enjoyment of all their possessions, without any molestation or disturbance whatsoever'. Most Anglicans thought that without an explicit guarantee of the Church as an institution, this pledge would be hollow rhetoric once the penal laws were suspended. Although some bishops – such as Samuel Parker of Oxford[2] – accepted the Declaration, most tried to dissuade their clergy from signing addresses of thanks for it, and the Archbishop of Canterbury, Sancroft, composed a lengthy list of 'Reasons against Subscription' condemning the

Indulgence for 'endeavouring to abrogate laws for their [the dissenters'] sake', laws which 'perhaps cannot be repealed'. Most ominously of all from James's point of view, although some dissenters were won over, such as the Quaker William Penn, the majority were profoundly suspicious of his motives and deeply reluctant to accept concessions from a papist king. Most believed Halifax's warning, in his *Letter to a Dissenter* published in the late summer of 1687, that they were 'to be hugged now, only that [they] may be the better squeezed at another time'. Such scepticism was well founded, for in 1685 James had remarked privately to a bishop that he 'would never give any sort of countenance to dissenters'. James's attempts to use the dissenters for his own ends misfired badly, and instead Anglicans and nonconformists became increasingly aware of what united them as Protestants and began to draw closer together against the common threat of popery. As the dissenter Roger Morrice wrote: 'It is plain to all mankind that a coalition between sober conformists and nonconformists is the only expedient that is within the reach of human prospect to save this nation'.

During 1687 James further antagonized Anglican opinion by trying to force the Universities of Oxford and Cambridge to treat Catholics on an equal basis. At the end of 1686 he pushed through the appointment of a Catholic, John Massey, as Dean of Christ Church, Oxford, while in January 1687 a Catholic became Master of Sidney Sussex College, Cambridge. But a furore broke out when, in April 1687, James ordered the Fellows of Magdalen College, Oxford, to elect a Catholic nonentity as their next President. The Fellows refused, and also rejected James's second suggestion of Samuel Parker. In October, the Commission for Ecclesiastical Causes deprived all twenty-five Fellows of their Fellowships; the following March a Catholic President, Bonaventure Gifford, was imposed on the College and mass was publicly celebrated in its chapel. This episode caused nationwide shock and anger, not least because College Fellowships were regarded as a form of legal freehold and the deprivation of tenured Fellows therefore seemed to presage a more general attack upon property rights. The King, for his part, snarled that he had 'no enemy but among those who call themselves Church of England men'. It was an extraordinary indictment of how far he had alienated those who only a few years before had championed his cause against the exclusionists.

James nevertheless pressed ahead with his aim of securing the repeal of the Test Acts and the penal laws. On 2 July 1687 he dissolved Parliament, and the following autumn set about engineering the return of another that would pass the repeal. In close consultation with Sunderland and Jeffreys, the King instructed Lords Lieutenant to ask JPs and Deputy Lieutenants three questions: would they, if elected, be 'for the taking off the penal laws and the tests'; would they assist the election of people who were; and did they support the Declaration of Indulgence? Only about a quarter (mainly Catholics and dissenters) replied positively: over a third answered definitely not, while the remainder – classified as 'doubtfuls' – were evasive but many expressed reservations. James responded by escalating the purges of local government officers that had begun in 1686. In an unprecedented bid to 'pack' Parliament, opponents of repeal were replaced by Catholics, dissenters and Whigs. By the spring of 1688, fourteen of the twenty-four Lords Lieutenant, three-quarters of all JPs, and over 1,200 members of town corporations had been dismissed. Such flagrant intervention by the Crown in provincial government was unparalleled. Tory-Anglicans were appalled by this assault on the status and influence of many long-established local families and their replacement by what John Evelyn called 'the meanest of the people'. In Lancashire, for example, the Earl of Derby, whose family had been Lords Lieutenant for generations, was displaced by a much less prominent Catholic, Viscount Molyneux. Similar purges took place at the centre. In less than three years James sacked a total of eighteen judges, in contrast to his brother's total of eleven during the last nine years of his reign. By 1688 none of the Tory ministers whom James had inherited from Charles remained in office. His principal advisers were the Catholic Lord Chancellor, Jeffreys, and the adroit Secretary of State, Sunderland, who converted to Catholicism in the summer of 1688. Virtually all James's appointments to the Privy Council were Catholics, such as Lords Arundel, Belasyse, Dover and Powys, and most notoriously of all, the Jesuit Father Petre.

Yet James's attempts to purge all levels of government and to pack Parliament were not inevitably doomed to failure. The instinctive response of Tory-Anglicans to these policies remained 'non-resistance and passive obedience', and the political elite was still remarkably deferential towards the Crown. Like the pre-Civil War gentry, they abhorred the idea of active resistance against the 'powers that be', and feared anarchy far more than tyranny. The memories of the 1640s that had recently surfaced so potently in the Exclusion Crisis only reinforced their belief that resistance to the sovereign could never be legitimate. This did not imply a slavish obedience to the subject's every command: in particular, it was widely held that the monarch's dispensing power did not extend to authorizing acts that were *malum in se* (wrong in themselves because contrary to divine and natural law) but only covered things which were *malum prohibitum* (wrongs prohibited by human positive law for some practical reason). But faced with a monarch who breached this principle, the most the subject could do was to engage in passive obedience or, as William Sherlock more accurately termed it, 'non-assistance'. Bridget Croft hoped that the people would 'passively suffer when they cannot with a clear conscience actually obey, having no thought of other weapons than prayers and tears'. These convictions ran very deep: as Halifax wrote in 1687, 'we are not to be laughed out of our doctrine of non-resistance and passive obedience on all occasions'. This passivity encouraged James and his advisers to believe that enough 'doubtfuls' could be won over or bullied into submission to produce a pliable Parliament. In April 1688 special government agents were sent into the localities to glean as much information as they could about the likely outcome of elections that were now being planned for the following autumn. The agents' preliminary reports, presented to James on 19 April, suggested that a two-thirds majority sympathetic to the Crown might be secured.

During the summer of 1688, however, two developments brought matters to a head. First, emboldened by the agents' reports, on 27 April James reissued the Declaration of Indulgence, adding that he intended to summon Parliament in November to enact it by statute. To give this news maximum publicity, on

4 May he ordered it to be read on two successive Sundays in late May and early June from the pulpits of all Anglican churches. On 18 May seven bishops, or – more precisely – the Archbishop of Canterbury and six bishops,[3] presented a petition to James asking him to withdraw this order on the grounds that 'the Declaration is founded upon such a dispensing power as hath been often declared illegal in Parliament', especially in 1663 and 1673. James was furious at what he regarded as 'a standard of rebellion', and prosecuted Sancroft and the others in the Court of King's Bench on a charge of seditious libel. The case generated intense public interest and reinforced the sense of Protestant solidarity. The bishops were hailed as martyrs, and on 10 June ten nonconformist ministers even visited them in the Tower, feeling that 'they could not but adhere to them as men constant in the Protestant faith'. When the seven were tried on 29 June, the judges of King's Bench disagreed over whether or not the petition was a libel. Such a question had hitherto been regarded as a matter of law, to be determined by the judges, but unprecedentedly they left it up to the jury to decide. Although it was not strictly speaking the subject of the trial, the legality of the royal suspending power was discussed at length and divided the judges: Sir Richard Alibone (a Catholic appointed to the bench the previous year) strongly defended it, but two of his colleagues, Sir Richard Holloway and Sir John Powell, argued forcefully against and were dismissed as a consequence. In the end, on 30 June, the jury acquitted the seven of seditious libel, amid much popular rejoicing. Notwithstanding this outcome, the case clearly revealed the limitations of the doctrine of 'non-resistance and passive obedience'. If the King was going to resort to legal prosecution when faced with a campaign of civil disobedience, how was he to be stopped?

The second crucial development occurred on 10 June, when Mary of Modena gave birth to a son. Until then, James's subjects had been able to console themselves that he would be succeeded by his Protestant daughter Mary, and that his policies would die with him. After all, if he lived to the same age as his brother, he would be due to die in 1688. But the birth of a Catholic heir transformed the situation because it raised the spectre of a Catholic dynasty stretching far into the future. Rumours circulated that the baby was not legitimate: that the Queen's pregnancy had been fabricated, or that the baby had been smuggled into the royal bed in a warming-pan. But no evidence was ever found to substantiate these claims, and they testified mainly to a desperation not to admit that there was now a Catholic heir apparent. Such desperation was especially characteristic of Tories, whose commitment to the legitimate succession meant that their only hope was to challenge the successor's legitimacy. Most importantly of all, the birth of a male heir, together with the bishops' trial, persuaded several leading figures from across the political spectrum that the time had come for drastic action. On 30 June seven Protestants – five Whigs, two Tories – wrote a carefully worded letter assuring William of Orange that the vast majority of people were 'generally dissatisfied with the present conduct of the government, in relation to their religion, liberties and properties', and pledging their support if he were to lead an expedition to England to secure a free Parliament and investigate the legitimacy of James's heir.[4] It was, in effect, an invitation to a foreign prince to invade England.

Plate 17 James's decision to prosecute Archbishop Sancroft and six bishops for seditious libel following their refusal to support the Declaration of Indulgence was a crucial turning-point for many of his subjects. It reinforced a sense of Protestant solidarity among both Anglicans and dissenters, and it also revealed the limitations of the strategy of 'non-resistance and passive obedience'. The acquittal of Sancroft and his colleagues was received with rapturous acclaim: this Dutch engraving shows them leaving the Tower of London amid scenes of public rejoicing.
Source: The Fotomas Index

3 The Dutch Invasion

This letter came as no surprise to William; indeed, he had been in contact with some of James's leading critics for over a year and had made a formal invitation a condition for intervening in England. His own relations with his father-in-law had steadily deteriorated over the previous three years, and by 1688 he was convinced that the protection of Dutch interests made an expedition to England essential. His primary concerns were strategic and economic. Since the early 1680s Louis XIV had been pursuing an increasingly aggressive policy along France's northeastern and eastern frontiers. This involved not only the annexation (*réunion*) of strongholds that he claimed were rightfully his, notably Strasbourg (1681) and Luxembourg (1684), but also a systematic attack on Dutch trade, shipping and fisheries. In the summer of 1686 William welcomed the anti-French League of Augsburg between the Emperor, the Kings of Spain and Sweden, and the Electors of Bavaria, Saxony and the Palatinate. James, by contrast, refused to countenance an international alliance against his cousin and thus prevented the encirclement of France. In February 1687 the Dutch emissary Dykveldt established secret contacts with such disaffected figures as Nottingham, Shrewsbury, Halifax and Bishop Compton. The following summer, despite James's cajoling, William refused to endorse the Declaration of Indulgence and strongly defended the Test Acts. By the spring of 1688, as French commercial warfare against the Dutch intensified and a military assault on the Empire or the Republic appeared imminent, William was convinced that he had at all costs to prevent James from joining Louis in a two-pronged campaign against him, and in April he informed the Whig Edward Russell that he was actively planning armed intervention in England. The birth of a Catholic heir provided the final catalyst, for it deprived Mary of her inheritance and William of such minimal influence as he still possessed over English foreign policy as husband of the heir presumptive. He promptly despatched an emissary, Zuylestein, ostensibly to convey his congratulations to James on the birth of his son but in reality to confer with opposition leaders and to secure a formal invitation. The letter composed by the 'Immortal Seven' was thus not a bolt from the blue: it was the product of lengthy consultations between William and James's critics that can only be fully understood in the light of developments in continental Europe. The Dutch invasion proved decisive in James's downfall, but his fate was sealed as much by decisions taken in Paris and The Hague as by events in England.

From early July William began to assemble a huge expeditionary force that ultimately comprised 463 ships, 5,000 horses and some 40,000 men.[5] By a skilful campaign of disinformation he managed to keep France and England guessing about his intentions, with the result that it was only in mid-September that James admitted the likelihood of a Dutch invasion. Louis XIV had made it plain that if William attacked England, France would invade the Dutch Republic, but thinking that William would not attempt a maritime expedition so late in the year, on 14 September Louis committed French forces to an all-out assault on the Rhenish Palatinate. This afforded the diversion that William needed. On 29 September the States of Holland passed a secret resolution supporting William's invasion plans, and the following day he issued a *Declaration of reasons for appearing in arms in the kingdom of England* – drafted in collaboration with Gilbert Burnet – in which he pledged to defend 'the Protestant religion and . . . the laws and liberties of those kingdoms', and insisted that the sole purpose of his expedition was 'to have a free and lawful Parliament assembled as soon as it is possible'. Although he wanted the legitimacy of James's son to be investigated, he made absolutely no mention of seeking to depose James or of coveting the Crown for himself. This may have been skilled political dissimulation, but equally there is no evidence that he sought to become King before December 1688. His immediate priority was to prevent an Anglo-French military alliance and to draw England into the coalition against Louis. This meant ensuring that James was guided by ministers and by a Parliament towards a Protestant, pro-Dutch, anti-French foreign policy. It meant dislodging those Catholic counsellors who had 'overturned the religion, laws and liberties of those realms', and defending Mary's rights as Protestant heir presumptive. But beyond that he kept his options open and reacted to events as they unfolded.

In England, meanwhile, the prospect of an invasion prompted James to make a series of panic concessions. In late September and early October, following several meetings with Sancroft and eight bishops, James dissolved the Commission for Ecclesiastical Causes; promised that the Church of England would be 'secured according to the Act of Uniformity'; reinstated the Fellows of Magdalen College, Oxford; permitted some corporations (including London) to regain their charters; and dismissed Sunderland. Apart from a free Parliament, these measures removed most of the grievances that had ostensibly provoked William's expedition, but they were made with obvious reluctance and came far too late to win James much support. During October William made several abortive attempts to set sail, but was repeatedly blown back into harbour. Then, at the end of the month, the wind direction changed and an eastward, 'Protestant wind' began to blow; this kept James's navy in port and enabled William to sail on 1 November. The spectacular success of the invasion testified not only to William's brilliant organization but also to the fact that he was, in W. A. Speck's words, 'incredibly lucky'. William landed at Torbay on 5 November and occupied Exeter four days later. From there he issued a declaration calling for a free Parliament.

Two things were remarkable and unforeseeable about the events that followed. First, the overwhelming response of the nation was to keep their heads down and not to get involved in a military show-down between James and William. The horrific memories of the 1640s ensured that people would go to very great lengths to avoid bloodshed. Peers sympathetic to William secured various parts of the country during the latter part of November: Lord Delamere in Cheshire, the Earl of Devonshire in Nottinghamshire, the Earl of Danby in Yorkshire. Otherwise, relatively few people rallied to William; but even fewer rallied to James. It was symptomatic of the extent to which he had alienated his subjects that so many people were not prepared to lift a finger to assist the reigning monarch. James's situation was actually far from hopeless.

Plate 18 *The Landing of William III and his Army at Torbay, 5 November 1688*, by Romeyn de Hooghe. William's invasion fleet was a gigantic operation: four times bigger than the Spanish Armada of 1588, it was by far the largest naval concentration that had been achieved in Atlantic waters to that date.

This engraving captures the sheer scale and excitement of the scene at Torbay as William's troops began to disembark, together with horses (pictured being brought ashore in the foreground) and large quantities of supplies.

Source: The Fotomas Index

He retained control of London and commanded a standing army of nearly 53,000. Furthermore, even his leading critics generally shied away from the idea of overthrowing him: Danby's son wrote later that neither he nor his father anticipated 'that the Prince of Orange's landing would end in deposing the King'. But James never provided a lead for loyalists and entirely failed to capitalize on the innate strengths of his position. He reached Salisbury on 19 November, but there his morale collapsed and he became listless and indecisive. All the signs are that he was suffering some kind of nervous breakdown. The religious zeal that had hitherto sustained and galvanized him suddenly turned against him as he became convinced that he had lost God's favour. His forces were diminished by a flood of desertions to William, including such high-ranking officers as John Churchill, Percy Kirke and the Duke of Grafton. James began to suffer from psychosomatic nosebleeds severe enough to incapacitate him for a day or two at a time. He received with resignation the news that on 21 November William had marched forth from Exeter in the direction of London, and two days later James retreated towards the capital.

Even then, all was not lost. After he returned to London, on Rochester's advice, James agreed to summon a free Parliament for 15 January 1689, thereby depriving William of his stated reason for intervening. The King then sent a delegation of commissioners led by Halifax to meet William at Hungerford on 8 December. William demanded the dismissal of Catholics from civil and military office, but he still made no mention of seeking the Crown. At this point, however, James finally lost his nerve. He was fearful for the safety of his wife and heir, and terrified lest he be put in custody like his father during the later 1640s. On 9 December, the Queen and her son were smuggled to France, and two days later James left London. As he crossed the Thames, possibly in a bid to preclude parliamentary elections and cause a breakdown in order that would necessitate his return on his own terms, he threw the Great Seal of England into the river.

To flee was the worst thing that James could have done because it deprived those who wished to maintain him as King of a leader to whom they could rally. In general, such people concluded that they had no alternative but to throw in their lot with William. On 11 December a group of bishops and peers led by Sancroft and Rochester met in the Guildhall and issued a declaration stating that since James had 'withdrawn himself . . . in order to his departure out of this kingdom', they had 'unanimously resolve[d] to apply' themselves to William. That evening, as London suffered the first of three consecutive nights of anti-Catholic rioting and looting, Rochester and Bishop Turner of Ely began to organize an Assembly of Peers who, acting as the King's natural counsellors (*consiliarii nati*), could govern the country in his absence. James, meanwhile, was intercepted by a group of fishermen on the beach at Faversham, who mistook him for a Jesuit and brought him back to London – where he was warmly received – on 16 December. Two days later, William entered the city. James briefly attempted to resume charge of government but, terrified of assassination, preferred to retreat to Rochester. William was only too pleased to see him go, and ensured that James was left so poorly guarded that he had no difficulty in escaping to France on 23 December. Later that day, William summoned an irregular assembly comprising all surviving MPs from Charles II's Parliaments, the Lord Mayor and Court of Aldermen of the City of London, and fifty representatives of the Common Council of London. He asked this body, about 400-strong, to give him 'speedy advice'. That was a shrewd move, because by choosing these individuals and excluding the members of James's Parliament William ensured a predominantly Whig body that was more likely to favour him. On 24 December the Assembly of Peers invited William to take over the reins of government. Two days later the irregular assembly reiterated this request and urged him to call elections for a Convention 'for the preservation of our religion, rights, laws, liberty and property', and 'the establishment of these things upon such sure and legal foundations that they may not be in danger of being again subverted'. William agreed on 28 December, and the writs ordering elections went out the next day.

William's acceptance marked the final extinction of James's reign, although it is often taken as having effectively ended with his first flight on 11 December. Such loyalists as remained in England felt utterly abandoned: as the Tory Lord Dartmouth exclaimed, 'O God, what could make our master desert his kingdoms and his friends?' At the request of peers, bishops and an irregular assembly of commoners, William now held the reins of government. As always during the seventeenth century, the key to government ultimately lay in the relationship between a ruler and the political elite. James had undermined his own position by his reckless pursuit of policies that alienated large sections of the nobility and gentry. But what finally precipitated his downfall was the fact that following William's intervention, James lost his nerve and created a power vacuum into which William could step. It is very unlikely that there would have been armed resistance to James in the absence of a Dutch invasion: so shrewd a politician as Sunderland could observe as late as 27 August that 'there never was in England less thought of rebellion'. James utterly failed to realize the terrible problems he could have created for his opponents had he stayed and fought. This would have forced them to confront the issue of whether or not they wished to depose him. As it was, he left his potential supporters leaderless and thereby enabled the disparate elements of the political nation to gather around William and co-operate with him. In essence, a Dutch coup had taken place. It now remained for William and the political elite to construct a settlement that would not only stabilize the situation but also enable people to make sense of what had happened.

4 The Revolution Settlement

As 1689 dawned William, in command of both his own forces and James's army that had deserted to him, was in a dominant position. His troops continued to occupy London until the spring of 1690, and the importance of this military presence in shaping the course of events should not be underestimated. By late December 1688 William seems to have had his eyes clearly set upon the Crown, and confided to Halifax 'with the strongest asseverations, that he would go if they went about to make him Regent'. However, when the Convention met on 22 January 1689 it soon became clear that opinion was sharply divided over the nature of the succession and whether William could become King. The assembly comprised approximately 319 Whigs and 232 Tories. The more hard-line Whigs, committed to a contractual theory of kingship, argued bluntly that James had 'broken the fundamental laws of the constitution' and thus forfeited his crown. Many Whigs and some Tories suggested that James had abdicated the throne. But most Tories, appalled by the prospect of a breach in the legitimate line of succession, clung to the idea that James was 'incapacitated' and argued either that William and Mary should act as regents on his behalf, or that Mary should rule with William as consort. Such differences notwithstanding, the predominant outlook was cautious and conservative, anxious above all to re-establish stable government. This mood enabled moderate Whigs and moderate Tories to form a strong middle ground that could agree on a compromise settlement, and the outcome thus presented a striking contrast to the events leading up to the Civil War. As John Morrill has written, 'in 1689, unlike 1642, the centre held and the fanatics on either side ... were stymied'.

The first attempt to formulate a common statement that embodied both Whig and Tory views came on 28 January when the Commons resolved, with only three Tory votes against, that

King James II, having endeavoured to subvert the constitution of the kingdom, by breaking the original contract between king and people; and by the advice of Jesuits and other wicked persons having violated the fundamental laws; and having withdrawn himself out of this kingdom; has abdicated the government; and that the throne is thereby vacant.

However, the Tories in the Lords resisted the idea that James had ceased to be King and that the throne was 'vacant'. On 29 January the Lords rejected (by fifty-one votes to forty-nine) a Tory proposal that James retain the nominal title of king while William and Mary became regents, while the following day they voted (by fifty-five to forty-one) to amend the Commons' resolution by replacing the word 'abdicated' by 'deserted' and deleting the final clause about the throne being vacant. These votes incensed the Whigs, and in the opening days of February hostile crowds began to demonstrate outside Parliament. It was William who broke the deadlock. He badly needed to resolve the crisis in England quickly in order to turn his attention back to the Continent. At a secret meeting with several leading peers on about 3 February, he made it clear that he 'could not think of holding anything by apron strings' and would never become 'his wife's gentleman usher'; if he were not made king, he informed the peers, he 'would go back to Holland and meddle no more in their affairs'. He did, however, offer two concessions to the hereditary principle: Mary would share the title (but not the power) of monarch jointly with him; and Anne would remain the next in line to the throne ahead of any offspring William might have by another wife in the event of Mary's death. Mary and Anne endorsed William's proposals, and most Tories concluded that it would be folly to hold out any longer. On 6 February the Lords accepted these arrangements, together with the use of the words 'abdicated' and 'vacant',[6] and the Commons agreed two days later.

Meanwhile, since late January a parliamentary committee comprising sixteen Whigs and six Tories had been drawing up the so-called Declaration of Rights. This document represented a more anodyne and conservative version of the 'Heads of Grievances' drafted in the opening days of the Convention. The more radical Whig demands – including the repeal of the militia acts as 'grievous to the subject', the appointment of judges 'during good behaviour', and guarantees of the 'frequent sitting' of Parliaments – were deleted after William indicated that 'he would not take the crown upon conditions'. The final Declaration provided the lowest common denominator on which most Tories and most Whigs could agree. After rehearsing the ways in which James had acted 'utterly and directly contrary to the known laws and statutes and freedom of this realm', the Declaration stated that he had 'abdicated the government' and left the throne vacant. Then followed a list of 'undoubted rights and liberties' which was in fact remarkably vague. The Crown's suspending power was declared illegal, but the dispensing power was only illegal 'as it hath been assumed and exercised of late'. It was stipulated that 'Parliaments ought to be held frequently', but no machinery was created to enforce this. The same was true of the requirement that Catholics 'shall be excluded, and be for ever incapable to inherit, possess or enjoy the crown'. Nowhere was it stated that James had broken a contract or been resisted, let alone been deposed: individuals were free to believe whatever they liked on these points. Furthermore, as a salve to Tory consciences the new oath of allegiance to William and Mary studiously avoided calling them 'rightful and lawful heirs' to the throne. It was thus possible to maintain that James remained King *de jure* and that William and Mary were only monarchs *de facto*. Some others – the Whig Gilbert Burnet as much as the Tory Edmund Bohun – could believe that William and Mary derived their title to the throne from the right of conquest (*ius gentium*) having defeated James in a just war. The moderates on both sides were happy to work together without imposing a single interpretation of events on each other. Similarly, although Whigs were perfectly free to believe that the Declaration constituted 'our original contract', in fact it had no binding force, nor was the offer of the throne to William and Mary conditional upon their accepting it. That offer was formally made at a ceremony in the Banqueting House on 13 February; only afterwards was the Declaration presented, and William and Mary were asked to do no more than to listen while it was read. They were proclaimed King and Queen the next day.

Later, in December 1689, a diluted version of the Declaration was passed as the Bill of Rights. This had the force of a statute, and was thus pleadable at law, but it was no more a fixed or binding contract between Crown and people than the Declaration. William and Mary had already been crowned on 11 April, and like any other statute, the Bill could easily be repealed by a subsequent Parliament. Possibly more significant was the fact that they took a heavily revised coronation oath. Unlike any of their predecessors, they swore not to 'confirm to the people of England the laws and customs to them granted by the Kings of England', but rather 'to govern the people of this kingdom of England,

and the dominions thereunto belonging, according to the statutes in Parliament agreed on, and the laws and customs of the same'. They also swore to 'maintain the laws of God, the true profession of the gospel, and the Protestant reformed religion established by law', and to defend the 'rights and privileges' of the Church, bishops and clergy. These changes marked a significant step towards ensuring that the monarch governed within the rule of law. As W. A. Speck has written, 'what triumphed in the Revolution Settlement was a version of the rule of law which saw the king as beneath and not above it'.

Two other important pieces of legislation were passed in 1689. In March, the Mutiny Act declared that 'the raising or keeping [of] a standing army within this kingdom in time of peace unless it be with consent of Parliament is against the law'. The act then set out the disciplinary measures that could be used to punish soldiers who mutinied or deserted. More controversial was the Toleration Act, which received the royal assent on 24 May. James's rule had served to improve relations between Anglicans and dissenters as they closed ranks against the common popish enemy. Believing the times propitious, in March 1689 the Tory Earl of Nottingham proposed a bill for comprehension that would have brought many dissenters within the fold of the Church. He also envisaged a bill for toleration of those (he hoped few) who still refused to conform. But Tory-Anglican fears were aroused when William – whose Calvinist background made him sympathetic to dissenters – proposed the repeal of the Test Acts for 'all Protestants that are willing and able to serve' in 'offices and places of trust'. As a result, the comprehension bill was referred to Convocation, where it was later rejected, while the toleration bill was only passed in a weakened form – far more limited, in fact, than James's Declarations of Indulgence. The Toleration Act exempted dissenters from the penal laws as long as they took the oath of allegiance and made a declaration against transubstantiation. They were not excepted from the Test and Corporation Acts and thus were still barred from public office: in that sense they remained second-class citizens. However, they were allowed to worship freely, provided that their meeting houses were licensed by the civil or ecclesiastical authorities, and the doors remained open. Over 900 such meeting houses were licensed during the first year of the act's operation. Only Catholics, Jews and Unitarians were excluded completely. For all its frustrating limitations, the Toleration Act did belatedly acknowledge that religious pluralism was now irreversible. The divide created in 1662 was not healed, but at least the rights of 'scrupulous consciences in the exercise of religion' received some statutory recognition.

Perhaps the most important aspect of the Revolution Settlement was the regulation of the Crown's finances. Many members of the Convention, Tories as well as Whigs, thought it essential not to vote William sufficient revenue for him to be able to govern without Parliament. As the Whig William Sacheverell urged the Commons on 29 January: 'Secure this House, that Parliaments be duly chosen and not kicked out at pleasure, which never could have been done without such an extravagant revenue that they might never stand in need of Parliaments'. The Tory Paul Foley echoed him: 'If you settle such a revenue as that the King should have no need of a Parliament, I think we do not our duty to them that sent us hither'. On 20 March the Commons therefore granted the King a revenue of £1.2 million a year. This figure – barely half what James had enjoyed for most of his reign – was determined without any proper investigation of the Crown's needs and proved quite inadequate even in peacetime. To make matters worse, the Commons stipulated that half of this sum was to be used for the civil administration and the other half for war. As a result, the Crown sank rapidly into debt, and William fumed that 'the Commons used him like a dog'. As we shall see in the next chapter, the long-term significance of the financial settlement was immense: in a period of almost incessant war, it imposed a genuine restraint on the Crown and secured for Parliament a permanent role in government in a way that the Bill of Rights never could.

The Revolution Settlement resembled the Elizabethan Church Settlement in the sense that it was a pragmatic compromise that sought to re-establish political stability by consciously appealing to as wide a range of opinion as possible. In general it achieved this aim very successfully and only the two extreme ends of the ideological spectrum were left alienated. On the one hand were those Tories who still regarded James as the rightful King and refused to recognize William and Mary. Archbishop Sancroft, seven bishops, several peers (including Clarendon) and nearly four hundred – or about one in twenty-five – clergy insisted that their oath to James precluded them from swearing the oath of allegiance to William and Mary and hence forfeited their offices. Ironically, these 'non-jurors' included five of the seven bishops whom James had prosecuted for seditious libel. Having suffered for defending the Church's rights against James, they now suffered again for defending James's rights against his successors: it was the supreme demonstration of a principled attachment to Church and Crown. The non-jurors overlapped with the Jacobites, a looser coalition of those who actively sought the restoration of the Stuarts. At the other extreme stood the commonwealthmen, or 'True Whigs', frustrated republicans like Henry Neville or John Wildman who lamented the failure of the Revolution Settlement to impose 'limitations' on the Crown. They felt that a great opportunity had been missed to change the nature of the constitution rather than just the ruler. In between, the moderate majority could live with a settlement that was, in John Morrill's phrase, 'a centrist compromise and constitutional blur'.

This settlement had the weaknesses of its own strengths in that while it resolved the crisis created by James's rule it also sowed the seeds of subsequent political divisions. It gained broad support by making it possible to believe different things about the events of 1688–9, especially about the extent to which James had been lawfully resisted and how far his successors were bound by a contract. But for precisely this reason, as in the Elizabethan Church, different people accepted the settlement for diverse reasons and wished to see it develop in contrasting directions thereafter. Rival interpretations of the Revolution – and alternative visions of Church and State – underpinned the Whig and Tory parties which, in various guises, would dominate political life for the next two centuries. If the Revolution changed the monarch without greatly changing the monarchy, it was the financial settlement above all that facilitated the major reforms of the Crown's relationship with Parliament enacted over the following decade. By a profound irony, those constitutional changes in turn owed much to the monarch's vulnerability during a war that William so badly wanted his new kingdoms to join.

5 The British Revolution

Whereas in Charles I's reign rebellions in Scotland and Ireland had helped to precipitate civil war in England, in 1688–90 events in England took their own course while the rest of the archipelago followed on behind. The revolutions in Scotland and Ireland were nevertheless significantly different from – and more bloody than – that in England. Although Scottish opinion was increasingly hostile towards James, there was no initiative towards revolution until after his second flight in December 1688. The following month, at the request of over a hundred Scottish peers and gentlemen who had journeyed to London, William summoned a Convention of Estates to meet in Edinburgh on 14 March 1689. Two days after it assembled, this Convention heard letters from both William and James. Whereas the former struck a conciliatory note and promised to defend Protestantism, the latter was completely uncompromising and threatened to punish all those who abandoned their 'natural allegiance' to him. Scottish Jacobites had refused to attend the Convention and on 4 April the members resolved, with only five votes against, that James had forfeited the throne. This unambiguously Whiggish idea was reiterated a week later in the Claim of Right which stated that James had attempted 'the subversion of the Protestant religion, and the violation of the laws and liberties of the kingdom, inverting all the ends of government'; he had thereby 'forfeited the right to the Crown, and the throne is become vacant'. Here, then, was the first key difference between the English and Scottish revolutions: whereas the English, in order to salve Tory consciences, insisted that James had simply vacated the throne, the Scottish Convention, boycotted by Tories, forthrightly claimed that he had violated 'the laws and liberties of the kingdom' and thus forfeited any right to the throne. The Scottish revolution thus rested on a far more explicitly contractual idea of kingship than the English.

Another important contrast lay in the demand for fundamental religious reform. The Claim of Right denounced prelacy as 'a great and insupportable grievance and trouble to this nation' and called for its abolition. This demand reflected the growing influence within the Convention of a powerful and organized Presbyterian grouping led by Sir James Montgomerie and known as 'the Club'. These members formed the nucleus of William's natural supporters in Scotland: as the Earl of Crawford observed, 'our King has no steady friends in this nation but such as are of the Presbyterian persuasion'. This political need, together with his own Calvinist convictions, secured William's assent to an act abolishing 'prelacy and all superiority of any office in the Church in this kingdom above presbyters' (22 July). However, he did not as yet agree to the formal establishment of Presbyterian government to replace prelacy.

William was entitled to develop his own policies for the offer of the Scottish throne had not – any more than in England – been predicated upon a binding contract. When William and Mary formally accepted the Crown of Scotland on 11 May, they took an oath to 'maintain the true religion of Christ Jesus' and the 'laws and constitutions received in this realm'. But they did not have to accept as a condition either the Claim of Right or the Articles of Grievances which listed grievances that were technically legal but considered highly undesirable. These included the management of Parliament through the Lords of the Articles, and the maintenance of a standing army, both of which soon became intensely controversial issues. On 4 July William refused to abolish the Lords of the Articles, while two days earlier, in a bid to placate James's erstwhile supporters, he vetoed an Incapacity Act against those 'who were grievous in the former government'. Relations between William and Parliament became more and more fractious and on 2 August he announced an adjournment without any supply being voted.

William's hopes of winning over the Jacobites proved vain. Whereas the Presbyterians of the Lowlands were overwhelmingly Williamite, Jacobitism remained strong in the Highlands. In the summer of 1689 several thousand Jacobite Highlanders led by Viscount Dundee (formerly John Graham of Claverhouse) rose up in support of James. The Jacobites defeated William's forces under General Mackay at Killiecrankie on 27 July, but this turned out to be a Pyrrhic victory: Dundee was killed and his army began to disintegrate after failing to take Dunkeld on 21 August. The Jacobite forces were finally trounced at Cromdale on 1 May 1690. However, the rebellion revealed the residual strength of Jacobite loyalties, not least among many of the episcopalian clergy, and thus pushed William into closer alliance with the Presbyterians.

As a result, when Parliament reconvened on 15 April 1690, William made every effort to be conciliatory. The 1669 act asserting royal supremacy over the Church was repealed on 25 April, and on 8 May William agreed to the abolition of the Lords of the Articles. On 7 June Parliament granted William supply for the next twenty-eight months in return for an act that established Presbyterian government in the Church on the model of the 1592 Golden Acts. This act also required the purging of 'all insufficient, negligent, scandalous and erroneous ministers', and by the end of the year 152 had been deprived. Over the next seven years more than 600 ministers (nearly half the total) were purged from their benefices. The Church Settlement was rounded off on 19 July by an act abolishing lay patronage and transferring the right to present ministers back to the kirk sessions. The settlement consciously avoided the more radical Presbyterian position: there was no mention of the Covenants, nor was any claim made that Presbyterianism existed by divine right. This displeased the Cameronian Covenanters, who remained outside the establishment, while at the other extreme the episcopalian clergy and nobility were mostly sympathetic towards Jacobitism. Unlike in England, no general toleration was introduced for fear of alienating mainstream Presbyterian opinion. As a result, the new Church was far from nationally representative, and when the General Assembly met in October 1690 it comprised only 180 ministers and elders, all from south of the Tay.

A crucial motive behind William's concessions was the desire to mollify Scottish Presbyterians while he turned to confront the much graver threat that had emerged in Ireland. The years 1688–91 were of critical importance for Ireland's subsequent history, and saw the country gradually drawn into the wider continental conflict. In the wake of James's flight, Tyrconnell mobilized Irish Catholics and by March 1689 controlled most of Ireland apart from Ulster, where the Protestants had sought refuge. With the encouragement and financial support of Louis XIV, who was anxious to distract William from the Continent, James landed at Kinsale on 12 March with about 3,000 French reinforcements to assist Tyrconnell in quelling the surviving pockets of Protestant resistance. This proved more difficult than he had anticipated, and in April he was forced to besiege Londonderry after being denied entry to the city.

Desperate for money to sustain his campaign, James summoned the so-called 'Patriot Parliament' to Dublin on 7 May. Only six of the 224 members were Protestants, and the Parliament's legislative programme reflected its over-whelmingly Old English complexion. This was something of an embarrassment to James, for he regarded Ireland as no more than a base from which to launch an assault on the mainland. He was not at all keen to alienate English opinion: as D'Avaux, the French ambassador at The Hague observed, James had 'a heart too English to take any step that would vex the English'. He therefore sought to restrain the Parliament's more hard-hitting measures. Although he proclaimed 'liberty of conscience' he refused to impose Catholicism or proscribe Protestantism. A Declaratory Act stipulated that the English Parliament could not pass laws binding on Ireland, but James vetoed the repeal of Poynings' Law.[7] He was embarrassed by an Act of Attainder which made over 2,000 Protestants liable to penalties for treason. He also opposed attempts to reopen the land question, but in the end was forced to back down: the Act of Settlement of 1662 was rescinded and those holding land in 1641 were permitted to take steps to recover their property. The Catholic members were anxious to exploit a unique opportunity to overturn the massive transfers of land to Protestants since the 1640s. Although they rallied to James, and granted him £20,000 a month for thirteen months, they were increasingly frustrated by his caution and reluctance to adopt more vigorously anti-Protestant policies. The Williamites, on the other hand, refused to recognize this 'pretended Parliament', summoned by a man they no longer regarded as king.

William meanwhile realized that he would be unable to participate effectively on the Continent until he had suppressed the Catholic danger in Ireland. At the end of July an English force led by Percy Kirke relieved Londonderry, and the following month Marshal Schomberg landed at the head of 10,000 troops who included Huguenot and Dutch infantry. Schomberg quickly took Carrickfergus but then made the disastrous mistake of camping on marshy ground just north of Dundalk, where his forces were decimated by fever, dysentery and insufficient supplies. These losses prompted William to intervene personally, and on 14 June 1690 he arrived with 15,000 troops, nearly half of them hired from King Christian V of Denmark. By the end of the month he had assembled a combined Protestant army of about 36,000 in which Irish and English troops served alongside Danes, Dutch and Huguenots. James's smaller army of around 25,000 was similarly international, and comprised a French

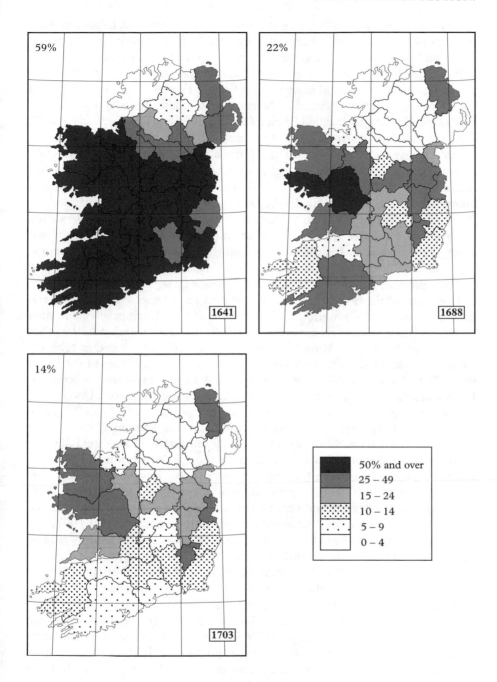

Map 6   The proportion of Irish land owned by Catholics in 1641, 1688 and 1703.

contingent of nearly 10,000 as well as Irish soldiers. In the end, larger numbers and superior training proved crucial, and on 1 July William inflicted a heavy defeat on James at the Battle of the Boyne. This victory has become enshrined in Protestant folklore, but its significance at the time was perhaps political and psychological more than military. James fled to France three days later and Catholic morale began to crumble. Nevertheless, a dashing, colourful (if none too bright) Gaelic officer called Patrick Sarsfield was able to rally nearly 20,000 Jacobites and form a stronghold at Limerick.

But his days were numbered. During the autumn of 1690 John Churchill, recently created Earl of Marlborough, captured the southern ports of Cork and Kinsale, thus blocking off the principal landing-points for French reinforcements. On 12 July 1691, Ginkel – the Dutch general who had commanded the Protestant forces since William's return to England in September 1690 – scored a decisive victory over the French commander St Ruth at Aughrim, the last great pitched battle in Irish history. Ginkel then marched towards Limerick. The death of Tyrconnell in August sapped Catholic morale still further, and on 23 September Sarsfield offered to begin peace talks.

The terms of the Treaty of Limerick, signed on 3 October, appeared relatively generous to the Jacobites. Catholics were allowed 'such privileges in their exercise of their religion as are consistent with the laws of Ireland, or as they did enjoy in the reign of King Charles II'. They were not obliged to take any oaths other than the oath of allegiance, and those who had fought for James were allowed to return home unmolested and with full restitution of property. In a successful bid to prevent further guerrilla resistance, Catholic troops were permitted to go abroad with their families and goods, and about 12,000 – known as the 'wild geese' – followed Sarsfield to France. But, for all its apparent leniency, the Treaty of Limerick was steadily undermined over the following two decades. A 'missing clause' that extended these terms to all Irish Catholics, not merely those in arms in Limerick and elsewhere, was left out of the final version. Whether this omission was deliberate or not remains mysterious, but it gave rise to uncertainty and bitter recrimination over exactly who benefited from the terms. The Irish Parliament did not ratify the treaty until 1697, and then only in a diluted form that omitted the key clause guaranteeing Catholic rights of worship. Over the years that followed a series of penal laws were passed that paved the way for the Protestant ascendancy of the eighteenth and nineteenth centuries. To Catholics, Limerick was the 'betrayed treaty', whereas to Protestants, such as William King or Anthony Dopping,[8] it was a sell-out belatedly remedied by subsequent penal legislation. Either way, the long-term outcome of the Williamite war of 1689–91 was to affirm Protestant domination and Catholic dispossession: the proportion of Irish land owned by Catholics fell still further, from 22 per cent in 1688 to 14 per cent in 1703 (see map 6). The war became embedded in the consciousness of both Catholics and Protestants and intensified the hatred between them over the centuries to come.

Ironically, the Irish war was not the primary concern of either William or James. William wanted to stamp out the Jacobite threat as quickly as possible in order to return to the continental war that was his main priority. James regarded Ireland only as a stepping-stone in his bid to regain the English crown, and Louis XIV's other military commitments ensured that he could offer only limited reinforcements. Thus, although Ireland assumed significance within the continental struggle, it remained a sideshow. James had initially been reluctant to intervene and only did so at Louis's request. As the months passed he became increasingly lethargic and by the Battle of the Boyne was gradually lapsing into pious apathy. The defeat of Irish Jacobitism ensured that thereafter the only hope for those who sought a Stuart restoration lay through Scotland.[9] For James personally it marked the end of the road. Granted the use of the palace of St Germain-en-Laye in Paris by Louis XIV, he became preoccupied with his religious devotions and died there in September 1701. Sometimes he received visits from French courtiers seeking momentary respite from the grinding routine of Versailles. These occasional visitors reached a unanimous verdict on James: 'when you listen to him talk, you realize why he has ended up here'.

12 Britain under William and Anne

	24 December	Members of Irish Parliament required to take oaths repudiating papal authority, transubstantiation and other Catholic doctrines
		Synod of Ulster Presbyterians established
1692	13 February	Massacre of Glencoe
	19–23 May	English and Dutch defeat French fleet in the Bay of La Hogue
	June	French capture Namur
	24 July	William defeated at Battle of Steenkirk
	4 November–14 March 1693	Fourth session of William's first Parliament
1693	January	Introduction of the land tax; funded National Debt established
	14 June	Scottish Act for Encouraging of Foreign Trade
	17 June	French destroy part of Anglo-Dutch merchant fleet off south coast of Portugal
	19 July	William defeated at Battle of Neerwinden
	July	French capture Huy
	October	French capture Charleroi
	7 November–25 April 1694	Fifth session of William's first Parliament
1694	April	Foundation of the Bank of England
	May	Whig 'Junto' gains political dominance (until 1699)
	12 November–3 May 1695	Sixth session of William's first Parliament
	22 November	Death of Archbishop Tillotson
	6 December	Thomas Tenison nominated as Archbishop of Canterbury
	22 December	Triennial Act
	28 December	Death of Queen Mary
1695	May	Press Licensing Act of 1662 expires

	May	Foundation of the Company of Scotland: subsequently makes disastrous attempts to establish trading colony at Darien in 1698–9
	22 August	William recaptures Namur
	7 September	Acts to restrain running of schools and keeping of arms by Irish Catholics
	22 November–27 April 1696	First session of William's second Parliament

Foundation of the Bank of Scotland

Publication of John Locke's *The Reasonableness of Christianity*

1696	January	Trial of Treasons Act strengthens position of the accused in treason trials
	February	Plot to assassinate William revealed; Whigs propose oath of association swearing loyalty to William as 'rightful and lawful' monarch; some Tories resign from Parliament and local government
	25 March	Introduction of the window tax
	20 October–16 April 1697	Second session of William's second Parliament
	November	Publication of Francis Atterbury's *A Letter to a Convocation Man*

1697	10 September	Treaty of Ryswick ends the Nine Years' War
	25 September	Marriage Act and Bishops' Banishment Act impose further constraints on Irish Catholic laity and clergy
	3 December–5 July 1698	Third session of William's second Parliament
	December	Parliament votes to disband most of armed forces

1698	April	Publication of William Molyneux's *Case of Ireland's being bound by Acts of Parliament in England, stated*: advocates Irish constitutional autonomy
	June	Civil List Act: costs of government and royal household to be met by annual parliamentary grant of tax revenues; end of old system of 'ordinary' and 'extraordinary' revenue

	5 July	Foundation of the New East India Company
	11 October	First Partition Treaty signed by France, Britain and the Dutch
	6 December–4 May 1699	First session of William's third Parliament

Scottish General Assembly reaffirms separation of Church and State and repudiates royal supremacy

1699	January	Death of Joseph Ferdinand of Bavaria: renders First Partition Treaty obsolete
	4 May	Woollen Act: export of Irish woollen cloth forbidden to any destination other than England
	16 November–11 April 1700	Second session of William's third Parliament

Foundation of the Society for the Promotion of Christian Knowledge

1700	3 March	Second Partition Treaty signed by France, Britain and the Dutch
	30 July	Death of Anne's last surviving child, William, Duke of Gloucester
	September	Carlos II of Spain makes will leaving Spanish inheritance to Louis's grandson, the Duke of Anjou
	21 October	Death of Carlos II; Louis subsequently backs his grandson's claim to the Spanish throne, in violation of the Second Partition Treaty
1701	6 February–24 June	William's fourth Parliament
	April–May	Kentish petition; Daniel Defoe's *Legion Memorial*; public opinion increasingly in favour of war against France
	12 June	Act of Settlement vests English succession in Protestant Electress of Hanover and her descendants, and stipulates that monarch must be in communion with the Church of England
	27 August	William concludes second Grand Alliance with the Emperor

	5 September	Death of James VII and II; Louis XIV recognizes his son as James VIII and III
	30 December–23 May 1702	William's fifth Parliament
1702	February	Abjuration Act: office-holders and members of Parliament to repudiate allegiance to descendants of James VII and II
	8 March	Death of William III; accession of Anne
	15 March	John Churchill, Earl of Marlborough, appointed Captain-General of the Forces
	4 May	Britain, Dutch Republic and the Empire declare war on France: beginning of the War of the Spanish Succession
	8 May	Lord Godolphin appointed Lord Treasurer
	20 October–27 February 1703	First session of Anne's first Parliament: first occasional conformity bill defeated
	14 December	Marlborough created a Duke
1703	April	Publication of Henry Maxwell's *Essay towards a Union of Ireland with England*: call for Anglo-Irish union
	May	Scottish Parliament meets: during the summer it passes laws in defiance of England, especially the Wine Act; Act Anent Peace and War; Act of Security
	15 May, 16 December	Methuen Treaties: Portugal joins the Grand Alliance
	9 November–3 April 1704	Second session of Anne's first Parliament: second occasional conformity bill defeated
	30 November	Isaac Newton elected President of the Royal Society
1704	February	Publication of Newton's *Optics*
	4 March	Act to prevent the further growth of popery in Ireland: effectively excludes entire Catholic population, together with Protestant dissenters, from public office
	23 July	Allies capture Gibraltar

	2 August	Allies, led by Marlborough, defeat French forces at Blenheim
	24 October–14 March 1705	Third session of Anne's first Parliament: third occasional conformity bill defeated
1705	14 March	Alien Act: Scotland to be treated as a foreign nation if it breaks regal union
	1 September	Hamilton urges appointment of Union commissioners; crucial change of front by Scottish opposition leader
	3 October	Allies capture Barcelona
	25 October–21 May 1706	First session of Anne's second Parliament
1706	16 April	Union commissioners convene at Whitehall
	12 May	Allies, led by Marlborough, defeat French forces at Ramillies
	16 June	Allies occupy Madrid
	22 July	Treaty uniting kingdoms of England and Scotland completed in draft
	3 October–16 January 1707	Scottish Parliament debates, and ultimately accepts, union of the kingdoms
	3 December–24 April 1707	Second session of Anne's second Parliament
1707	16 January	Scottish Parliament passes Act for securing the Protestant Religion and Presbyterian Church Government
	14 April	Allies defeated at Almanza
	1 May	Union of the Kingdoms of England and Scotland
	May	Publication of Edward Lhuyd's *Archaeologia Britannica*
	23 October–1 April 1708	Third session of Anne's second Parliament
	24 October	Irish national registry of deeds established in Ireland to prevent fraudulent land transactions by Catholics
		Jonathan Swift writes 'The Story of the Injured Lady': protests against Ireland's exclusion from the Anglo-Scottish union

1708	30 June	Allies, led by Marlborough, defeat French forces at Oudenarde
	16 November–21 April 1709	First session of Anne's third Parliament
1709	30 August	Irish Catholic clergy required to take oaths of abjuration and allegiance
	31 August	Allies, led by Marlborough, defeat French forces at Malplaquet
	5 November	Dr Henry Sacheverell preaches sermon denouncing Low Churchmen and occasional conformists; Whigs press for his impeachment
	15 November–5 April 1710	Second session of Anne's third Parliament
1710	27 February	Trial of Sacheverell opens; rioting breaks out on 1–2 March
	8 August	Godolphin dismissed as Lord Treasurer
	October	General election: Tories win large majority
	25 November–12 June 1711	First session of Anne's fourth Parliament
	9 December	Allies defeated at Brihuega, near Madrid
1711	29 March	Sir Robert Harley appointed Lord Treasurer
	7 December–8 July 1712	Second session of Anne's fourth Parliament
	31 December	Marlborough dismissed as Captain-General
	December	Fourth occasional conformity bill passed
1713	31 March, 2 July	Treaties of Utrecht end War of the Spanish Succession

1 The Context of War

William's primary motive for invading England had been to draw the nation into the European coalition against France, and his arrival produced a dramatic transformation of British foreign policy. Whereas England had been involved in continental warfare for barely thirteen of the eighty-five years between 1603 and 1688, during the twenty-five years from 1689 to 1714 it was at war for all but five, thus reverting to a level of direct military activity on the Continent unknown since the Middle Ages. Furthermore, these years saw a remarkable mobilization of fiscal and human resources that enabled Britain to emerge, in less than two decades, as a leading military and maritime power with a radically changed perception of her place within Europe and the world. Although space does not permit more than the briefest outline of the wars fought under William and Anne, it is essential to gain some sense of their course and heavy cost, for this became the context for profound political, constitutional and administrative change at home.

The Dutch declared war on France in February 1689, and the following May a Grand Alliance was signed between the Republic, England, Spain, Sweden, Savoy and the Emperor, pledged to containing France within her frontiers of 1684. That same month, England – followed shortly afterwards by Scotland – entered the war against Louis. An austere, reserved and somewhat humourless man, William was driven above all by a vision of European harmony and collective security and a wish to protect Protestantism from the Catholic monarchy of France. There was initially some reluctance in England to participate in a war that appeared to be fought mainly in Dutch interests, but William's propagandists, led by Gilbert Burnet, carefully portrayed the new King as a godly ruler wedded to the cause of international Protestantism. As Tony Claydon has recently argued, the cultivation of William's image as a religious reformer helped considerably to overcome anti-Dutch xenophobia, to smooth the King's relations with Parliament, and to disarm opposition to the idea of fighting France.[1] James's landing in Ireland in March 1689 also served to rally support for the war. The fact that James enjoyed Louis's support persuaded most people on the mainland that the Revolution Settlement, the Protestant succession, and indeed Britain's territorial independence, could only be preserved by joining the international coalition against France.

The war got off to a very bad start for Britain. On 30 June 1690 – the day before William's victory at the Boyne – the French roundly defeated a combined Anglo-Dutch fleet off Beachy Head. Although Louis was so preoccupied on the Continent that he failed to follow up this success, the danger of a French-backed Jacobite invasion remained very real until the English and Dutch managed to defeat the French fleet in the Bay of La Hogue in May 1692. However, the following year Admiral Tourville destroyed part of the Anglo-Dutch merchant fleet off the south coast of Portugal as it was bound for the Levant, inflicting losses estimated at £1 million. In all, between 1689 and 1697, about 4,000 British merchant vessels were captured by France. But this dispiriting naval war did at least have one important long-term benefit. By

Plate 19 *William III*, by Godfried Schalcken, 1692. This haunting portrait catches something of William's reserved, solitary and driven personality. He never felt entirely at ease among his English subjects, and his natural austerity and loneliness were exacerbated by indifferent health and the burdens of ruling in an era of almost incessant warfare. He had invaded England primarily in order to bring it into the international coalition against France, and here he is appropriately depicted wearing armour.

Source: National Trust Photographic Library/John Bethell

revealing the inadequacy of the fleet it precipitated a massive ship-building programme that laid the foundations for Britain's subsequent naval dominance and imperial expansion. The navy, which had comprised 156 ships in 1660 and 173 in 1688, grew to 224 in 1702 and 313 by 1710. By 1713 the British navy was the largest and strongest in the world.

In the meantime the land war went badly for William. He suffered serious defeats in the set-piece battles at Steenkirk (July 1692) and Neerwinden (July 1693). Much of the war consisted of prolonged sieges of strategically significant garrisons, and the French got the better of this struggle, capturing Mons (April 1691), Namur (June 1692), Huy (July 1693) and Charleroi (October 1693). The one moment of brightness for the Grand Alliance came in August 1695 when William recaptured Namur. He doggedly managed to prevent the French from overrunning the Spanish Netherlands, but by the mid-1690s the Alliance was beset by mutual suspicion. The Habsburgs felt uneasy about allying with the Protestant English and Dutch, and the Emperor Leopold I had begun secret negotiations with Louis as early as 1692. The Alliance's survival owed much to the personal diplomacy of William, who shuttled constantly between London and The Hague throughout these years. Eventually, their economies disrupted by what had become a war of attrition, the two sides fought themselves into a state of financial exhaustion. The stalemate was finally resolved in September 1697 by the Treaty of Ryswick. Louis renounced all his gains in the Netherlands and the Rhineland since 1688 and recognized William as 'King of Great Britain by the grace of God'. The treaty promised 'perpetual peace and friendship' between Louis and William and their successors, which was regarded in England as a French guarantee of the Protestant succession. It was subsequently agreed that the Dutch would establish eight 'barrier fortresses' in the Spanish Netherlands as further protection against French attack.[2]

This was a welcome outcome to what had been an unprecedentedly expensive war. Between 1689 and 1697, England supported a navy of over 40,000 men and an army of more than 70,000 (of whom about 20,000 were foreign hirelings). Average expenditure on the armed forces reached about £2.5 million a year, and the war thus cost three times as much each year as the entire second Anglo-Dutch War of 1665–7. How these vast sums were raised will be examined in the next section; here we should just note that by the end of the war the prevailing mood was understandably one of pacifism and intense aversion to any further conflict. In December 1697 Parliament, terrified of the danger posed by a standing army, voted to disband most of the forces and reduce the army in England to 8,000. Lord Chancellor Somers discerned in 1698 'a deadness and want of spirit in the nation universally'. To William, whose outlook remained emphatically European, this quietism and isolationism were extremely frustrating. He complained bitterly to the Grand Pensionary of Holland that 'the people here are now so foolishly engrossed with themselves that they do not pay the least attention to what is going on in foreign countries', adding that it was as if 'this island is the only thing on the face of the earth'. To William, on the other hand, the struggle against France was far from over.

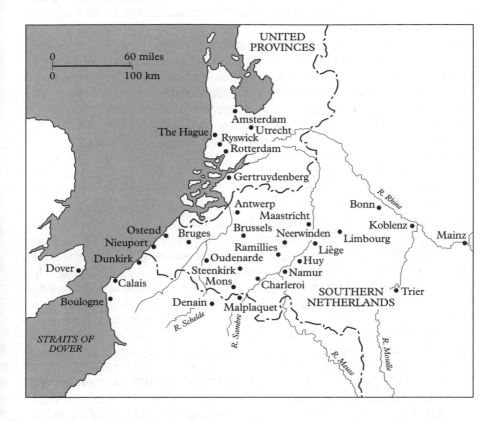

Map 7 The Low Countries during the Nine Years' War (1689–97) and the War of the Spanish Succession (1702–13).

The Treaty of Ryswick had failed to resolve an issue that potentially posed an even greater threat to the balance of power within Europe than French aggression on its northeastern frontier. European diplomacy in the closing decades of the seventeenth century was dominated by the uncertainty that hung over the Spanish Succession. King Carlos II of Spain, a sickly and feeble-minded invalid, had no heir and was not expected to live much longer. There were three main contenders for the Spanish throne, all of whom had a legitimate claim: the Archduke Charles, son of the Emperor, Joseph Ferdinand, son of the Elector of Bavaria, and Louis XIV's own son, the Dauphin (see page xviii). William, committed to a balance of power between the Bourbons and the Habsburgs, was anxious that the same person should not rule both France and Spain. Louis, while keen to defend the dynastic interests of his family, did not wish to precipitate another war, and in the early summer of 1698 opened talks with William. The result was the First Partition Treaty, signed in October 1698 by France, Britain and the Dutch. This stipulated that on Carlos II's death the bulk of the Spanish Empire should go to Joseph Ferdinand, while the

Archduke Charles would receive the Duchy of Milan and the Dauphin Naples, Sicily and Tuscany. It seemed that a settlement acceptable to all had been achieved.

Unfortunately, in January 1699 Joseph Ferdinand died of smallpox. After further negotiations, the three powers signed the Second Partition Treaty of March 1700 whereby the Dauphin would inherit Naples, Sicily, Tuscany and the Duchy of Lorraine, while the rest of the Spanish Empire would pass to the Archduke Charles. Throughout these lengthy talks, nobody bothered to consult Carlos II. The dying King abhorred the projected partition of his Empire, and in September 1700 he made a will leaving the entire inheritance to Louis's grandson, the Duke of Anjou, with the proviso that the Duke accepted it intact and that he should never become King of France as well. Thus, when Carlos died on 21 October, Louis's grandson stood to inherit the whole Spanish Empire. After brief hesitation, Louis decided to uphold Carlos II's will even though this violated the Second Partition Treaty, which he had himself signed. Most people in Britain were so sick of war that they felt no desire to object, but William wanted to uphold the treaty and sought to mobilize international resistance to France. Louis played into his hands by insisting that the Duke of Anjou should retain his claim to the French throne as well, thereby flouting Carlos II's will and creating the prospect of a Franco-Spanish union. To back up his demands, Louis occupied the Dutch barrier fortresses, despatched French troops to Spain, and imposed restrictions on Anglo-Dutch trade with France and Spain. In the spring of 1701 documents such as a Kentish petition and Daniel Defoe's *Legion Memorial* revealed that opinion was turning strongly in favour of war, and on 27 August William concluded a second Grand Alliance with the Emperor pledged to securing a French withdrawal from Spanish territory. Louis flatly refused and added insult to injury in September when, on James VII and II's death, he officially recognized his son as James VIII and III in direct contravention of the Treaty of Ryswick. On 8 March 1702, as Britain teetered on the brink of war, William died following a riding accident. He was succeeded by Anne, a devout Protestant and staunch enemy of Louis XIV. Thus, when war was finally declared on France in May 1702, it was with the express purpose not only of thwarting French aggrandizement, but also of defending the Protestant line of succession.

The War of the Spanish Succession lasted until 1713 and proved even more costly than the Nine Years' War. This was mainly because the fighting ranged more widely, encompassing lengthy campaigns in the Iberian peninsula as well as in the Spanish Netherlands and the Empire. In 1703 the Methuen Treaties brought Portugal into the Grand Alliance in support of the Archduke Charles's claim to the Spanish throne. Allied forces took Gibraltar the following year, and in October 1705 captured Barcelona. In June 1706 they occupied Madrid, but by this time local nationalists, especially within Castile, were becoming increasingly resentful of the Allied military presence in Spain. Louis was able to harness such feelings in the defence of his grandson's claim and the war reached deadlock. There was growing criticism at home of the Crown's policy of 'no peace without Spain', especially after the Allies suffered disastrous defeats at Almanza (April 1707) and at Brihuega near Madrid (December

1710). The conflict dragged on until 1713, when the Allies recognized the Duke of Anjou as Philip V of Spain on condition that he renounced his claim to the French throne, and Gibraltar and Minorca were ceded to Britain, thereby giving her naval control of the Mediterranean.

It was, however, in the Spanish Netherlands and the German territories that the most decisive campaigns of the war were fought. Here the Allies were fortunate to find a military leader of genius in John Churchill, who was created Duke of Marlborough and Captain-General of the Forces in 1702. Marlborough combined rare organizational ability and a flair for diplomacy with supreme talent as a military strategist. Initially, in 1702–3, he was rather held back by the extreme caution of the Dutch generals. However, in the spring of 1704 the French general Tallard launched a dramatic advance into the heart of the Empire, aiming straight for Vienna. Marlborough led 40,000 troops on an epic six-week march from the Netherlands to Bavaria, linked up with the imperial forces commanded by Prince Eugène of Savoy, and together they inflicted a crushing defeat on Tallard's army at Blenheim on 2 August. This battle deflected the French advance and ensured the protection of the Empire.

However, even this great victory did not give Marlborough complete authority over the Allies, and in 1705 he failed to secure Dutch and imperial support for his planned invasion of France up the Moselle. The Dutch preferred a defensive war concentrated on the Low Countries, and it was in that theatre that Marlborough scored further important victories over the French at Ramillies (12 May 1706) and Oudenarde (30 June 1708). The latter conclusively dispelled the threat of a French invasion of the Dutch Republic. By this stage the Emperor – encouraged by Louis XIV – wished to end the war as soon as possible, and Louis formally sued for peace in 1709. Negotiations broke down over the future of Spain, and Marlborough and his Whig allies, especially the Lord Treasurer Sidney Godolphin, held to the fruitless principle of 'no peace without Spain'. Marlborough won another victory over the French at Malplaquet on 31 August 1709, but at the severe price of 24,000 Allied troops killed and wounded. As war-weariness spread at home Marlborough's stock began to wane: the close friendship between his wife and Queen Anne came to a tempestuous end, and the Tories – who sought peace at the first opportunity – won a large majority in the general election of October 1710. Marlborough was dismissed on trumped-up charges of corruption at the end of 1711, and the war was finally concluded by the Treaties of Utrecht (March and July 1713). Apart from the fact that Philip V became King of Spain, Britain secured all her war aims. Her possession of Gibraltar and Minorca was confirmed, and she also gained Newfoundland in Canada and St Kitts in the West Indies. Louis XIV agreed never to support the Jacobite cause again and surrendered any prospect of the French and Spanish crowns being united. Spanish lands in the Netherlands and Italy were ceded to the Emperor, while further Barrier Treaties in 1713 and 1715 restored the barrier fortresses to the Dutch, with Britain acting as their guarantor against attack. This settlement marked the culmination of the conflicts against France into which William had drawn Britain: it embodied her new status as a leading military State within Europe and gave her overseas

Map 8   Western Europe during the Nine Years' War (1689–97) and the War of the Spanish Succession (1702–13).

possessions that helped to make her the greatest maritime power in the world.

But that success was achieved at a very heavy price. The war cost Britain an average of more than £4 million a year in supporting combined armies of over 90,000 men and a navy of about 40,000. The total cost of the Nine Years' War and the War of the Spanish Succession was in excess of £72 million. By 1710–11 Anne was spending as much on the war each year as Charles II had raised in revenue for the entire first decade of his reign. The provision of such sums represented a spectacularly successful mobilization of national resources. It also necessarily entailed a radical overhaul of Britain's fiscal machinery, which in turn had profound implications for the development of the constitution and the relationship between the Crown and Parliament.

2 Government and the Constitution

The reign of William III was of crucial importance in the emergence of Britain as a major fiscal–military state. At the root of this transformation lay a fundamental recasting of the nation's financial administration. Until the 1690s the medieval distinction between the Crown's ordinary and extraordinary revenue had survived. The monarch had been expected to live off the ordinary revenue during peacetime and only to need extraordinary (parliamentary) revenue in time of war.[3] The Revolution Settlement had deliberately left the Crown in a weak financial position, and this – together with the enormous cost of the wars that followed – rendered the existing system obsolete.

By 1689 it had become glaringly obvious that the Crown could only survive, in peacetime as well as during a war, on the basis of revenues voted by Parliament. The proportion of national revenues derived from non-parliamentary sources shrank from 76 per cent in 1626–40 to 10 per cent in 1661–85, and then to a mere 3 per cent in 1689–1714. The remainder all came from direct or indirect taxation raised with Parliament's consent and mainly collected not (as in most of the continental monarchies) by tax farmers but by members of the local elites. Of the direct taxes, the most important in this period was the land tax. Introduced in 1693, this tax resembled earlier taxes such as the parliamentary subsidy or the assessment of the 1640s and 1650s, and it yielded £46 million of the total revenue of £122 million raised between 1688 and 1714. The other two most important taxes were both indirect: customs duties on imports, which raised around £35 million; and the excise, initially levied on 'beer, ale and other liquors' and ultimately expanded to cover most popular consumer goods, which yielded about another £30 million. In addition, there were experiments with various other parliamentary taxes, such as the window tax, introduced in 1696, and even taxes on births, marriages and deaths, and on bachelors and widowers. Between them, these taxes produced a spectacular mobilization of national resources and created a situation in which Britain's population was generating a level of revenue per capita exceeded only by the Dutch Republic.

The Crown's desperate need for tax revenues transformed Parliament from an occasional event into a permanent institution of government. It is a remarkable fact that the English Parliament has met every year since 1689. This trend was reinforced by the Triennial Act of 1694,[4] but the really binding guarantee of Parliament's continuous existence was the monarch's abject dependence on its taxes. The huge financial demands of war ensured that annual sessions of Parliament became an absolute necessity. Parliament was in a position not only to withhold its consent to taxation, but also to dictate how tax revenue was spent and to scrutinize the fiscal propriety of the government: without its active co-operation, public confidence in the legitimacy of the tax system – and with it the readiness to pay such high levels of taxation – would have collapsed.

Parliament exploited this opportunity to the full. During the 1690s the principle of 'appropriation' was established, whereby parliamentary grants could only be used for the purpose for which they had been voted. The 'power of the purse' became much greater than ever before, and Parliament made increasingly frequent and ferocious use of it, not least by 'tacking' clauses redressing constitutional grievances onto revenue bills that the Crown simply could not afford to veto. From 1690 a Commons Commission of Public Accounts carefully monitored government spending and investigated financial mismanagement. Two developments above all symbolized this major transfer of fiscal power from the Crown to the legislature. First, in 1698 Parliament voted the Crown tax revenues worth approximately £700,000 per annum 'to meet the costs of the civil government and the royal establishments'. Any surplus yield on the taxes allocated for this purpose was not to be retained by the Crown 'without the authority of Parliament'. This grant, known as the Civil List, marked the final end of the belief that the monarch should live off the ordinary, non-parliamentary revenues, and established the principle that the costs of civil government were paid from parliamentary revenue. Second, the government's fiscal credit became dependent upon parliamentary guarantees. Money was raised from long-term public loans which led to the establishment in 1693 of a new 'National Debt' that grew from £16.7 million in 1696 to £36.2 million by 1713. For the first time, the monarch's personal debts gave way to a funded National Debt, underwritten by Parliament. The foundation of the Bank of England in 1694 was part of this process. The Bank was a joint-stock company whose subscribers lent a total of £1.2 million to the government at a rate of interest of 8 per cent in return for incorporation as a bank and the authority to issue notes and discount bills on the security of parliamentary taxation. The following year the Bank of Scotland was formed along similar lines. In this way, parliamentary guarantees became the basis of public credit, thereby enabling William and Anne to borrow far more extensively than any of their predecessors.

Neither monarch was in any position to resist these developments. Furthermore, the 'financial revolution' was only part of a wider redefinition of the relationship between Crown and Parliament. William's reign saw a remarkable series of statutes that permanently diminished the powers of the Crown and established the principle that the legislature could monitor and constrain the behaviour of the executive. The King did not go down without a fight: he vetoed some of these bills more than once before financial need obliged him to accept them; others were 'tacked' onto revenue bills that he could ill afford to lose. The Triennial Act of 1694, for example, was vetoed twice before it received the royal assent. The act stipulated that a new Parliament should be held within three years of the dissolution of the last and that no Parliament should last longer than three years: it thus circumscribed the royal prerogative of summoning and dissolving Parliament at will in a way that the much weaker act of 1664 had not. Between 1694 and 1706, the demarcation between executive and legislature was sharpened by a number of Place Acts or clauses that excluded several thousand office-holders from Parliament. This ensured, in particular, that no revenue official could sit in either House and thereby influence parliamentary appraisal of the government's fiscal probity. The Crown's hold over the judiciary was also weakened. Although a bill requiring judges to be appointed *quamdiu se bene gesserint* was vetoed in 1692, William in practice never violated this principle. In 1696 a new Trial of Treasons Act strengthened the position of the accused in such cases (or at least ensured that the scales were less heavily weighted against them) by stipulating that they were to receive a copy of the indictment at least five days before the trial, that they could swear witnesses in their own defence, and that a conviction needed more than one witness for the prosecution. In this way, the boundaries of the royal prerogative were defined with greater precision than ever before, and thereby diminished.

This process culminated in the 1701 Act of Settlement, or to use its official title, 'an Act for the further limitation of the Crown, and better securing the rights and liberties of the subject'. It was prompted by the death in July 1700 of Princess Anne's last surviving child, William, Duke of Gloucester, which plunged the future of the succession into uncertainty. The resultant act not only excluded fifty-seven Catholic heirs to the throne in favour of the Protestant Electress Sophia of Hanover and her descendants, but imposed several important constraints on the Crown to take effect on Anne's death. These reflected unhappiness with William's style of government as much as fear for the future. There had been growing resentment of William's secretive conduct of foreign policy (Parliament, for example, only found out about the two Partition Treaties after the second had been concluded), especially because of his reliance on Dutch advisers such as Hans Willem Bentinck, whom he created Duke of Portland in April 1689. The Act of Settlement insisted that any future monarch who was not a native of England could not declare war in 'defence of any dominions or territories which do not belong to the Crown of England, without the consent of Parliament'. In another bid to thwart the influence of hidden advisers, 'all matters and things relating to the well governing of this kingdom' were to be transacted in the Privy Council. The act also enshrined the principles that 'no person who has an office or place of profit under the King, or receives a pension from the Crown, shall be capable of serving as a member of the House of Commons', and that judges should be appointed *quamdiu se bene gesserint*. Above all, the act debarred Catholics from the throne and obliged the monarch to be 'in communion with the Church of England'. This requirement – already adumbrated in the Declaration of Rights – really marked the beginning of a new era. For it removed at a stroke one of the principal sources of political instability in seventeenth-century Britain. No longer would fears about a monarch's dubious Protestant credentials generate mistrust and disrupt national life.

This remarkable denial of the monarch's freedom to choose his or her own religion was a complete negation of the principle of *cuius regio, eius religio*. It epitomized a pronounced shift during these years away from personal monarchy towards greater constitutional regulation. Among the most significant developments of the reigns of William and Anne was the emergence of Cabinet government. The particular context of incessant warfare was again crucial here. During William's frequent absences on the Continent, Mary governed by herself until her death from smallpox in December 1694: at these times she badly needed systematic advice from an inner group of officers of state and Privy Councillors. William accepted the 'necessity of a Cabinet

Council' in such circumstances, not least because effective co-ordination of the financial, military and diplomatic aspects of the war by a relatively small and efficient group of advisers was vital. By the time of Anne's accession, the Cabinet, usually numbering between about nine and sixteen, was a well-established feature of government and an important linchpin between the Crown and Parliament. Anne's own tireless use of the Cabinet – she attended an average of more than one meeting a week throughout her reign – further confirmed this trend.

The growth of Cabinet government was accompanied by a parallel decline in the political significance of the Court. Although the influence of those with personal access to the monarch remained considerable – notably Anne's close friends Sarah Churchill, Duchess of Marlborough, and Abigail Masham – the principal arenas for political debate and intrigue lay more and more in the Cabinet and in Parliament. The Crown's straitened financial circumstances reduced the opportunities for patronage available at Court, with the result that ambitious individuals increasingly looked elsewhere for advancement – to Parliament, to the City of London and to the professions. Although Anne realized the ceremonial significance of the Court, and regularly conducted such rituals as touching for scrofula, the focus of cultural and political activity shifted steadily towards the great households of the nobility and the coffee-houses and clubs of polite London society. Anne was anxious to stand aloof, above the 'rage of party'; but the result was that by the time of her death the Court was becoming ever more politically marginalized.

The corollary of this was that ministers needed to cultivate political support more and more widely. Anne's limited abilities, weak eyesight and precarious health left her more dependent on a chief minister than any of her seventeenth-century predecessors, and after 1702 the Whig Lord Treasurer Godolphin wielded powers similar to those later associated with the office of Prime Minister. By the latter part of her reign the position of such a minister increasingly rested on a capacity to command support in the Houses of Parliament as well as the enjoyment of royal favour. In 1710 Anne dismissed Godolphin and appointed the Tory Sir Robert Harley because she fell out with the Whig leaders; but this decision was subsequently confirmed by the large majority that the Tories secured in the general election of that year. The basis of political ascendancy had changed since the days of Buckingham or even Clarendon.

In constitutional terms the reigns of William and Anne were thus of immense significance. They saw the resolution of many of the knotty issues that had generated political tensions under the Stuarts. The fact that the monarch was now compelled to be in communion with the Church of England; that the distinction between the ordinary and extraordinary revenue had been swept away and replaced by a system in which parliamentary taxation funded the Crown and underwrote a National Debt; that the permanence of Parliament was guaranteed by the Crown's financial dependence as well as by statute; that judges possessed security of tenure during good behaviour and could not be removed at the monarch's whim; and that the monarch had to conduct foreign policy in collaboration with Parliament: all these developments marked important steps away from the personal monarchy that existed in 1603 and towards the more balanced constitution of the eighteenth century and after. It would be anachronistic to exaggerate the magnitude of these shifts, or to underestimate the continuing power of the Crown. But they did ensure that some of the problems that had most clearly defined the seventeenth century either disappeared or became much less prominent thereafter.

3 Parties and Political Culture

Another area in which the reigns of William and Anne witnessed a major transformation was the growth of a political culture characterized by the existence of parties. Although the terms Whig and Tory had appeared during the latter stages of the Exclusion Crisis, the actual crystallization of two 'parties' was really a consequence of the Revolution of 1688–9. The emergence of Whig/Tory as the principal dichotomy in political life reflected the fact that people accepted the Revolution Settlement for a range of reasons and henceforth wished to see it develop in contrasting directions. Many of the differences between Whigs and Tories stemmed from the divergent interpretations of the Revolution that they each espoused: whereas Whigs insisted that the political nation had actively resisted James, Tories found this unthinkable and argued that he had simply abdicated the throne. From this premise, the parties developed clearly identifiable ideological positions on all the crucial issues of the day: the powers of the Crown and its relationship with Parliament; the future of the succession; religion and the Church; and the conduct of the war. During the reigns of William and Anne these issues came to dominate political culture, with the result that by the early eighteenth century the 'rage of party' pervaded not only national and local politics, but also many other areas of religious, social and economic life.

Although the two parties were never monolithic and embraced a spectrum of opinions, their characteristic outlooks can be delineated fairly clearly. Few Whigs were fully-fledged Lockeians, but most did believe in a contract between monarch and subject, and asserted that monarchs who breached this contract could legitimately be resisted. Parliament provided an essential bulwark against any extension of the royal prerogative or infringement of the rule of law. By contrast, most Tories continued to espouse the doctrine of monarchy by divine right and abhorred the idea of resisting or deposing a sovereign: passive obedience and non-resistance remained their watchwords. A minority of Tories (never as many as Whigs alleged) were Jacobites in that they supported a restoration of James and his descendants, although very few actively pursued such a goal. Most Tories, however, were at least prepared to accept William and Anne as *de facto* sovereigns. The fundamental divergence of opinion nevertheless surfaced from time to time, most notably in February 1696 when the revelation of a Jacobite plot to assassinate William led the Whigs to propose an oath of association by which all office-holders and members of Parliament acknowledged the King as their 'rightful and lawful' monarch. This was precisely the formula that the Revolution Settlement had studiously avoided, and for some Tory consciences it proved acutely embarrassing. Nearly twenty

Tories in the Lords and more than ninety in the Commons declined to take the oath. The Whigs exploited this to strengthen their own position, and ensured that Tory non-subscribers were purged from the lieutenancy and the commission of the peace and replaced by Whigs.

These contrasted ideologies of monarchy were closely connected to the issue of the succession. The Whigs were strongly committed to a Protestant succession and abominated the prospect of a Catholic ever regaining the throne. They were the leading architects of the 1701 Act of Settlement, and early the following year they pushed through an Abjuration Act that compelled all office-holders and members of Parliament to take an oath forswearing allegiance to 'the pretended Prince of Wales'. Many Tories came to accept the Hanoverian succession as a political and religious necessity, and virtually all of them supported the Act of Settlement. On the other hand, although few Tories ever contemplated dislodging William or Anne, many still clung to the principle of an indefeasible hereditary line of succession. They went along with measures designed to safeguard a Protestant succession, not least for fear of being branded Jacobites; but they were never as zealously and ideologically committed to them as the Whigs.

A more intractable source of disagreement between Whigs and Tories was religion. The latter retained a strong attachment to the established Church and were deeply mistrustful of any concessions to dissenters. The Whigs, on the other hand, sought greater religious toleration and were anxious to support the cause of international Protestantism. They warmly welcomed William as a Calvinist hero, and were delighted when his episcopal appointments consistently favoured Latitudinarians. John Tillotson, who became Archbishop of Canterbury in 1691, and Thomas Tenison who succeeded him in 1694, together with other leading bishops like Gilbert Burnet of Salisbury and Edward Stillingfleet of Worcester, were all divines of that persuasion. These years also saw significant evangelical initiatives of a kind that Latitudinarians and dissenters welcomed, including the Society for the Promotion of Christian Knowledge, founded in 1699.

Tories viewed such developments with alarm, and they were appalled at the rapid expansion of the main nonconformist sects, especially the Quakers, in the wake of the 1689 Toleration Act. No fewer than 3,614 dissenter meeting houses were licensed between 1689 and 1710 under the terms of the act. During the 1690s and early 1700s the Church became more and more sharply divided between the liberals – Latitudinarians who advocated a broad, comprehensive Church that imposed the minimum of demands on nonconformist consciences – and those traditionalists who staunchly defended the established Church and urged Parliament and Convocation to safeguard its authority by strictly enforcing and extending the laws against dissenters. The liberals were mainly Low Churchmen and they were sympathetic towards dissenters and Whigs, whereas the traditionalists were predominantly High Churchmen who found natural allies among the Tories. The latter rallied to the slogan of 'the Church in danger', and as a flood of nonconformist publications appeared following the expiry of the Licensing Act in 1695, High Church Tories became increasingly vociferous in their calls for more effective protection of the

Church. The classic polemical expression of these attitudes was *A Letter to a Convocation Man* (1696), by Francis Atterbury, later Bishop of Rochester, in which he called on Convocation to stem the 'deluge' of 'heresies of all kinds' that were fomenting 'a settled contempt of religion and the priesthood'.[5] Tories were perhaps most alarmed by the growing practice of 'occasional conformity', whereby nonconformists could evade the penal laws by taking Anglican communion once a year and then standing for public office. To Tories this was an 'abominable hypocrisy', and between 1702 and 1704 they introduced no fewer than three bills to stamp it out. Each was defeated in the Lords, where the Whigs combined with the Low Church bishops to form a majority.

All these tensions came to a head in November 1709 when High Church cleric Dr Henry Sacheverell preached a sermon in St Paul's Cathedral in which he denounced Low Churchmen and occasional conformists as 'a brood of vipers'. He also robustly defended the principles of passive obedience and non-resistance. The Whig ministry led by Godolphin attempted to impeach him for a 'malicious, scandalous and seditious libel', but his trial triggered off violent demonstrations in support of 'High Church and Sacheverell'. These disorders were the worst of the entire eighteenth century apart from the Gordon Riots of 1780, and in their wake Sacheverell received the fairly mild sentence of three years' suspension from preaching. Public opinion – although not unanimous – rallied so enthusiastically to the defence of the Church that the Tories decisively won the general election of October 1710. They seized the opportunity to push home their campaign against dissent, and in December 1711 a fourth occasional conformity bill finally became law. But the legacy of mistrust between Anglicans and dissenters would continue to dog the Church for decades to come.

These contrasting religious attitudes help to explain why Whigs and Tories were also deeply divided over the conduct of the wars. The Whigs were vehemently committed to the cause of European Protestantism and wanted Britain to engage in a full-scale continental campaign against the popish enemy. The Tories, although sympathetic to the wars against France, were fundamentally more isolationist in their outlook. Reluctant to launch campaigns unless they directly served Britain's strategic and commercial interests, they favoured a 'blue-water' policy that emphasized the maritime and colonial theatres. They criticized the Whigs for excessive expenditure on continental fighting, while the Whigs countered by accusing the Tories of being soft on France and too ready to seek peace. Indeed, it was a Tory ministry, led by Harley, that finally brought the War of the Spanish Succession to a close in 1713.

The characteristic Whig and Tory positions on each of these issues fitted together to form two coherent ideological platforms, each closely associated with a corresponding account of the seventeenth century past. Tories regarded themselves as the descendants of the Royalists of the Civil War and every year commemorated 30 January as the anniversary of the execution of 'Charles, King and Martyr'. The Whigs, on the other hand, admired those who had stood up against 'popery and arbitrary government', from the Parliamentarians of the 1640s to the exclusionists and the 'Immortal Seven': their hallowed day was 5 November, the date of William's landing at Torbay as well as of the Gunpowder Plot. Many people remembered both dates, but the relative priority that they gave them was directly linked to party allegiance. Certainly there was a variety of opinion within each party, and they merged into each other almost imperceptibly. Nevertheless, especially during Anne's reign, the broad outlines of a two-party system can be discerned. Geoffrey Holmes's seminal work on poll-books and division lists has revealed that the voting patterns of most members of Parliament generally followed party alignments, and the vast majority of those active in politics in this period can be identified as either Whig or Tory.[6] The polarity became more and more dominant, with normally less than 20 per cent of members voting across party lines. The Whigs were probably the more tightly organized of the two parties, and the Tories followed their lead in co-ordinating their activities and developing a system of 'whips' and circular letters to maximize their voting strength.

These political machinations were frequently conducted in clubs and coffee-houses, and the Whig/Tory dichotomy soon permeated many aspects of political culture and social life. Whereas Whigs frequented the Kit-Cat Club and the St James's Coffee House, Tories went to such venues as Ouzinda's Chocolate House in St James's Street, and the Society of Brothers, and there was remarkably little overlap between the two groups. Partisan loyalties also spilled over into charitable and educational activities, so that the governors and staff of charity schools and hospitals tended to be predominantly Whig or Tory. Thus St Thomas's was a distinctively Whig hospital, whereas St Bart's was known to be Tory. Party alignments ran through the worlds of business and the professions, shaping transactions and patronage networks, and they exercised a significant influence on the marriage market. After the Licensing Act lapsed in 1695, pamphlets, newspapers and periodicals proliferated, and these too had allegiances to one or other party. Whigs wrote for such papers as John Tutchin's *Observator*, which appeared twice a week between 1702 and 1707, while Tories supported Charles Leslie's *Rehearsal*, published weekly and then twice weekly from 1704 to 1709. In 1704 nine newspapers appeared in London, generating between them a total of 44,000 copies a week; by the following year there were twelve newspapers appearing regularly. They catered for a mass political culture that became rapidly larger and more sophisticated during these years.

As the electorate engaged more and more actively with national issues and debates, so party alignments came to the fore in local politics as well. The annual elections of town magistrates, sheriffs and parish officials often became disputes between Whigs and Tories, and some towns – including Marlborough and Portsmouth – even had rival Whig and Tory corporations. The electorate expanded steadily throughout this period, with the result that by Anne's reign approximately one in four adult males in England and Wales (about 300,000) had the right to vote. Following the Triennial Act of 1694, ten general elections were held between 1695 and 1715, and only nineteen of the 269 constituencies in England and Wales had no election at any stage in this twenty-year period. Before the Civil War many MPs had been *selected* by informal negotiation and contested elections were very much the exception. In general elections between 1660 and 1689 there were normally about sixty or seventy contests, and by the end of the century such contested elections between Whigs and Tories had become the norm. These occasions generated considerable passions and even at times degenerated into violent scenes. Demonstrations and disorders at election-time were far from uncommon, and regularly included women, who were just as politically informed and committed as men even though they did not possess the vote. Few remained unaware of the political controversies and party struggles of the day.

This prompts the question of whether there were any marked social differences between those who typically became Whigs or Tories. There was some substance to the contemporary stereotypes that identified the Whigs with monied, commercial interests and the Tories with landed interests. For example, between 1694 and 1714, of those Directors of the Bank of England, the Million Bank, and the New and United East India Companies who were involved in City of London affairs, seventy-three were Whigs and only thirteen Tories. But although the Whigs dominated the London mercantile elite, by the opening years of the eighteenth century the Tories arguably possessed the larger popular following. Ironically, this was partly because the Revolution and the arrival of William had transformed the Tories from the loyalists of the Exclusion Crisis into an opposition party. Sceptical about William's legitimacy as monarch, his conduct of foreign policy and his religious credentials, they became the Crown's natural opponents: war weariness, resentment of taxation and fears for 'the Church in danger' all worked to their advantage.

This shift helps to explain the relationship between the Whig/Tory axis and another polarity, that of Court versus Country. Unlike Whig and Tory, which had consistent ideological coherence and increasingly effective party organization, Court and Country were far more inchoate, temporary alignments in which individuals briefly made common cause on particular issues and then fragmented again. They did not have continuous existence, but came to prominence at certain times, most notably in 1690–3 and 1697–1700. Both the Whig and Tory parties had their own Court and Country wings, but by the mid-1690s Whigs were more commonly associated with the Court, Tories with the Country. The specific issues which tended to open up the Court/Country divide were usually related to the accountability of the executive (especially regarding its fiscal probity), the role of placemen, levels of taxation and the conduct of the war. People's views on these particular questions did not necessarily synchronize with their allegiances to the Whig or Tory parties, and they were therefore much more transient and shifting. Furthermore, the constitutional reforms of William's reign introduced safeguards against many of the grievances that had most exercised Country members, with the result that under Anne the duality of Court and Country gave way almost entirely to that of Whig and Tory.

The monarchs themselves found the 'rage of party' highly distasteful and tried very hard to stand above it. William was thoroughly confused about who his real friends were and was anxious not to become the prisoner of either party. He once told Sunderland that 'he believed the Whigs loved him best, but they did not love monarchy, and although the Tories did not like him so well as the others, yet as they were zealous for monarchy he thought they would serve his government the best.' The Earl replied that 'it was very true that the Tories were better friends to monarchy than the Whigs were, but then His Majesty was to consider that he was not their monarch.' William retained his preference for the Tories, but he was prepared to work with the Whigs – for example the 'Junto' led by Somers, Wharton, Montagu and Russell between 1694 and 1699 – when that suited the needs of his wider European strategy. Anne deeply disliked 'the merciless men of both parties' and once remarked: 'I pray God keep me out of the hands of both of them'. Yet she managed to retain the support of Whigs and Tories alike: the former welcomed her acceptance of the Protestant succession, while the latter applauded her unwavering commitment to the Church of England. However, by standing aloof from party conflict Anne only accelerated the political marginalization of the Crown. By the autumn of 1710, when a general election confirmed one party's supplanting of the other in government, the outlines of the modern two-party system were clearly apparent. Party struggles within Parliament had replaced factional struggles at Court as the crux of political life, and in the process the power and patronage of the Crown had been significantly reduced.

4 The Augustan Age

The term 'Augustan age' was originally coined by literary scholars to describe the years between about 1680 and 1730: roughly the period in literature that runs from John Dryden to Alexander Pope. More recently, historians have recognized that these decades, and especially the reigns of William and Anne, witnessed a remarkable range of intellectual and cultural achievement. Military success in the continental wars not only transformed Britain's place within Europe and the wider world; it also generated a national mood of much greater self-confidence that fostered a spirit of energy and enquiry. In such a positive climate emerged not only distinguished works of 'natural philosophy' (science) and political thought, drama and music, but also fine architectural and artistic achievements, a major growth in the professions, and the rapid development of 'polite' society.

In terms of intellectual distinction, the two greatest figures of the age were John Locke and Isaac Newton. In addition to his *Two Treatises of Government*, discussed above,[7] Locke wrote on a wide variety of political, ethical and epistemological themes. He followed his friend and ally Shaftesbury to Holland in 1683 and did not return until after the Glorious Revolution. While in exile he composed *A Letter Concerning Toleration* (published 1689) which argued that, within certain limits, no one should dictate the form of another's religion. Underpinning this thesis was an essentially rationalistic view of religious belief which Locke developed fully in *The Reasonableness of Christianity* (1695). This idea was linked to a more general theory of knowledge advanced in the *Essay Concerning Human Understanding* (1690) in which Locke suggested that human knowledge was not innate but derived empirically through experience. At one level, he was trying to formulate a theory of knowledge consistent with the scientific findings of Newton, who was also at the height of his powers in this period. Widely regarded as the founder of modern Physics and Mathematics, Newton applied his laws of mechanics to develop the theory of universal gravity set out in his *Principia* (1687). He then went on to make fundamental break-throughs in the field of optics, published in his *Optics* of 1704. He was appointed Master of the Royal Mint in 1699, and from 1703 until his death in 1727 he was President of the Royal Society. The Society enjoyed a halcyon period during his presidency, and among its most distinguished Fellows were the astronomers Edmund Halley and John Flamsteed, and the physicians Sir Hans Sloane and William Cockburn.

In literature too the reigns of William and Anne marked the opening of a golden age. Some of the greatest works, such as Defoe's *Robinson Crusoe* (1719) or Swift's *Gulliver's Travels* (1726), appeared after the end of the period covered by this book, but the last decade of the seventeenth century and the first of the eighteenth witnessed the opening performances of some of the finest Restoration comedies. In plays such as *The Double Dealer* (1693), *Love for Love* (1695) and above all *The Way of the World* (1700), William Congreve perfected a sophisticated comic style in which brilliant verbal wit concealed darker and more cynical undertones. He combined an urbane comedy of manners with merciless satire of human foibles and moral failings. Much the same was true also of George Farquhar, an Irish-born dramatist and actor whose two come-dies *The Recruiting Officer* (1706) and *The Beaux's Stratagem* (1707) – the latter completed just before his tragically early death at the age of twenty-nine – extended the genre of Restoration comedy by being set in the provinces rather than in London. An increasingly rational approach to religion and to natural philosophy thus coexisted alongside theatrical productions that nourished few illusions about human nature.

Dramatic forms were further exploited in the operas and masques that formed part of the vast output of Henry Purcell, the greatest British composer until Elgar. Purcell, who became organist of Westminster Abbey in 1679 and of the Chapel Royal in 1682, composed in an extraordinary variety of genres. His *Dido and Aeneas* (1689) is often regarded as the first English opera, and revealed an instinctive capacity not only to transform a genre that originated in Italy, but also to develop and transcend the theatrical conventions of the time. In addition, Purcell wrote an immense amount of church music – organ volun-taries, services, motets and anthems – as well as more than a hundred solo songs. His music to accompany royal weddings and funerals, and his occasional pieces to mark the arrival, birthday or marriage of members of the royal family or the nobility, were often particularly effective: the Birthday Ode which he composed for Queen Mary's last birthday in 1694, and the music for her funeral in March 1695 (the year of Purcell's own death), are masterpieces of their kind.

Purcell's Court music was frequently performed in physical settings that became much more imposing during these years. Sir Christopher Wren was at his most productive in the twenty years after the Revolution, when his designs included the south and east fronts of Hampton Court (1689–1702), Kensington Palace (1689–96) and the Royal Hospital for Seamen at Greenwich (1695–1707). Like St Paul's Cathedral and his City churches, these buildings proved highly influential in introducing Renaissance and Baroque forms into English architecture. Continental patterns were also evident in the remarkable series of palaces and prodigy houses for the nobility which sprang up in the decades after the Revolution. Among the earliest of these were Chatsworth, designed by William Talman for the Duke of Devonshire, and Blenheim Palace, built by Sir John Vanbrugh as a symbol of the nation's gratitude to the Duke of Marlborough. But it was not just on this palatial scale that the reigns of William and Anne saw a surge of building. All over the country, towns expanded and new houses were built of stone and brick with tall windows, large doorways and spacious interiors. These houses assimilated classical forms into a more distinctively indigenous style, and even today Queen Anne houses are synonymous with gracious elegance.

The decoration and furnishing of these houses, both great and small, called forth an impressive array of artists and craftsmen. Here again, continental influences were accepted far more readily than before, and were less widely perceived as the accoutrements of Europe's authoritarian monarchies. Possibly because Britain's position within Europe was becoming rapidly stronger, it felt less threatened by the cultural influences of the Continent. The Frenchman Jean Tijou introduced Baroque wrought ironwork to Britain, and examples of his exquisite work can still be seen at Hampton Court and in St Paul's Cathedral. William and Anne employed painters such as the Frenchman Louis Laguerre and the Italian Antonio Verrio to decorate the ceilings, halls and staircases of Windsor Castle and Hampton Court. Soon they were in great demand among the nobility and worked, in particular, at Burghley House, Blenheim Palace and Chatsworth. Native painters, most notably James Thornhill, took up their example and worked alongside them, especially at Hampton Court. Thornhill's work culminated in the Painted Hall of Wren's Royal Hospital at Greenwich, and was crucial in fostering a distinctively native tradition of painting. The same was true of Sir Godfrey Kneller, the foremost portrait painter of his day, who was appointed principal painter to William III in 1691. Kneller's portraits present a wonderful gallery of the leaders of Augustan society, especially members of the royal family and the Whig grandees. William brought many Old Masters and other works of art across from Holland and thus set a new trend in Britain for collecting continental paintings, porcelain and furniture. Nor was this fashion confined to the social elite: one contemporary described the prevailing 'humour . . . of furnishing houses with china ware', and even relatively humble houses were adorned with decorated ceilings, plasterwork and wooden panelling. The desire to build, ornament and adorn was seemingly insatiable.

This vigorous burst of urban building was accompanied by the development of the hallmarks of 'polite society' that would characterize the eighteenth century. The proliferation of newspapers and periodicals has already been discussed, as has the rapid growth of clubs and coffee-houses. Towns and cities all over the country followed the lead set by London, which had over 650 coffee-houses by 1714. Channels of communication and political networks became ever-more efficient and sophisticated. Another striking trend of the period was the expansion and commercialization of leisure activities. One of

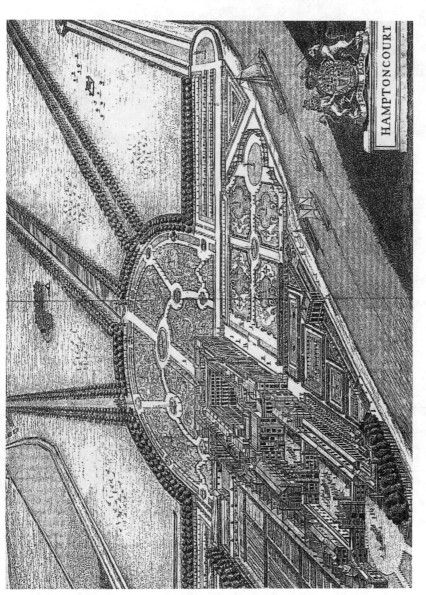

Plate 20   An engraving of Hampton Court from the southwest, by Johannes Kip after Leonard Knyff, published in *Britannia Illustrata*, 1707. The south and east fronts, built to designs by Sir Christopher Wren between 1689 and 1702, are visible beyond the original Tudor palace. Wren's elegant façades of brick faced with Portland stone consciously emulated continental models, especially Versailles. Similarly, the vast ornamental gardens designed by Wren's deputy William Talman and the Huguenot designer Daniel Marot, and also constructed between 1689 and 1702, were a blend of English, French and Dutch influences. The Privy Garden on the south side of the palace – recently restored to its Baroque splendour – was enclosed by a screen of wrought-iron gates by another Huguenot refugee, Jean Tijou (see plate 21, below).
Source: Bodleian Library Oxford

Plate 21 Wrought-iron gates in St Paul's Cathedral, by Jean Tijou, *c.* 1698. A Huguenot refugee, Tijou was responsible for bringing the craft of wrought ironwork from France to England. With his *New Book of Drawings* (1693), and through pupils such as Thomas Robinson and Robert Bakewell, Tijou established this as a new and important skill, and exercised an important influence on the development of English metal-working.

Source: Unichrome Ltd

the most popular pastimes was horse-racing: Queen Anne founded the famous Ascot Races, and there were over a hundred recognized race-courses in England by 1714. Also very fashionable among the leisured classes of this period were bowling greens. Bath, Scarborough and Tunbridge Wells led the way among the newly fashionable spa towns where it was possible to 'take the waters' as widely recommended by the rapidly expanding medical profession. The number of apothecaries in London grew from 104 in 1617 to nearly a thousand by 1704, and by the beginning of the eighteenth century they – along with increasing numbers of licensed surgeons – were accepted as fully-fledged members of the medical profession. The great take-off in the practice of Medicine from the 1720s onwards had its origins in the reigns of William and Anne. A similar trend was evident in the legal profession, which numbered at least 10,000 in 1688 and continued to grow relentlessly thereafter. Such professional growth was made possible and necessary by a swiftly changing society and economy, which will be examined more fully in the following chapter.[8]

The diversity and excitement of these intellectual, cultural and social developments all helped to give the Augustan age much of its distinctive colour and vitality. Together with the fundamental reforms in the constitution and the dramatic transformation of Britain's place within Europe and the world, they undoubtedly made this a period of profound and vigorous change. By the opening decade of the eighteenth century we have clearly entered a world far removed from that inhabited by James VI and I, with significantly different structures of government, society and economy. The next and final chapter will take stock of where Britain stood in 1707 – of what had changed over the preceding 104 years, and what remained largely the same. But first, we must examine a further major reform of the Augustan age, and one of the most important constitutional landmarks in British history, namely the Union of the Kingdoms of England and Scotland in 1707. That Union makes 1707 a fitting date at which to draw this book to a close, for it was only then that the Double Crown created in 1603 was finally transformed into the United Kingdom that still exists today.

13   1707: Union of the Kingdoms

1 The Path to Union

The thrust of most recent writings on the Anglo-Scottish Union of 1707 has been to argue that such a development was far from inevitable. The Union of the Crowns that lasted from 1603 until 1707 should not be seen as an unstable and necessarily temporary arrangement, as a mere staging-post to Union of the Kingdoms. Although, as we have seen throughout this book, the regal union brought problems of its own, they were not insuperable and such a polity was not doomed to collapse. Far from being a natural end-point, the 1707 Union was the result of a complex combination of short-term factors. An assessment of Scotland's long-term interests and identity undoubtedly affected contemporary attitudes towards the issue of union, but the nature and timing of the event grew out of a very specific set of historical circumstances, and as late as 1704–5 the balance of probability appeared to lie against it. It is essential to avoid teleological explanations in which the fact of the union's survival to the present day makes it appear the destined outcome to which events inexorably led.

Indeed, in the wake of the Revolution of 1688–9 the two kingdoms seemed to be growing further apart rather than closer together. The Revolution Settlement took quite different forms in England and Scotland, with the latter embracing a far more aggressively contractual idea of monarchy. Similarly, the Scottish Church Settlement safeguarded the Presbyterian Church and repudiated episcopalian structures. In a firm rebuff to Anglican notions of a royal supremacy, in 1698 the General Assembly reaffirmed the separation of Church and State and asserted that 'Jesus Christ is the only Head and King of his Church'. These political and religious beliefs proved deeply divisive within England: although Whigs were quite sympathetic, High Church Tories abominated the endorsement of contractual monarchy and a Presbyterian Kirk, and strenuously opposed any suggestion of closer ties with a kingdom that had espoused them.

Relations between the two kingdoms worsened steadily during the 1690s. William experienced great difficulty in controlling the Highlands, where the Jacobite magnates formed an intractable core of resistance. In 1690 he established a garrison at Fort William, and in August 1691 all Highland chiefs were promised an indemnity provided that they took the oath of allegiance by 1 January 1692. Through a mixture of truculence and bad weather, the MacDonalds of Glencoe failed to meet this deadline. The Lord Advocate, James Dalrymple of Stair, ordered a body of government soldiers led by Captain Robert Campbell to bring the MacDonalds into line, but the operation was botched, the ancient enmity between the Campbells and MacDonalds flared up, and on 13 February thirty-eight MacDonalds were treacherously murdered in the notorious 'Massacre of Glencoe'. This was a catastrophe for the Crown: William's regime was shown to have lost control of the Highlands, and Jacobite sympathies gained renewed strength, especially in the West. The dismissal of Dalrymple could not dispel the impression of an incompetent and callous regime.

This image was reinforced by the economic setbacks that befell Scotland over the next few years. The country suffered badly from England's closure of the French trade after the outbreak of war in 1689. During the later seventeenth century, over 50 per cent of Scottish exports went to England, mainly in the form of linen and black cattle. The war undermined this trade, and its effects were aggravated by the consistently poor harvests that Scotland experienced during the 'seven ill years' between 1692 and 1698: these caused prices to rise steeply and over 5 per cent of the population to die of starvation. In a bid to break into overseas markets, the Scottish Parliament passed an Act for Encouraging of Foreign Trade in 1693, and two years later the Company of Scotland was founded. This company sent two expeditions, in 1698 and 1699, to establish a trading colony at Darien, on the narrow isthmus of Panama, but the scheme went disastrously wrong. The Spaniards resented the colony and William, realizing that friendship with Spain was an essential part of the international alliance against France, disowned it. A combination of disease and Spanish attacks was responsible for the deaths of over 2,000 Scottish colonists: the venture collapsed and Scotland lost around £153,000 (1.8 million pounds Scots), nearly a quarter of her liquid capital. The Scots understandably felt utterly betrayed by England.

William's handling of Darien illustrated plainly how his European strategy dictated his British policy. Throughout the war years his principal concern was that his northern kingdom, with its persistent Jacobite sympathies, should not provide a base for a French invasion. This hazard became all the greater when the Duke of Gloucester's death in 1700 raised the issue of the succession. The Scots did not immediately follow England in recognizing the Hanoverian succession and thus created the possibility that the Scottish Crown might once again be separated from the English. In an attempt to forestall this, William made overtures for a 'firm and entire union' between the two kingdoms in 1700 and 1702, and was deeply exercised by this question at the time of his death. But the Scots refused to be browbeaten, and the 1703 Parliament passed three defiant measures. The Wine Act asserted Scotland's commercial independence and attempted to restore the old trading links with France despite the wartime blockade. The Act Anent Peace and War required that Scotland's Parliament should control her foreign policy regardless of who sat on the throne. Finally, the Act of Security threatened to dissolve the union of the crowns unless

England offered guarantees of Scotland's sovereignty, and the freedom of its Parliament, religion and commerce: only on these terms would Scotland accept the 1701 Act of Settlement. When the royal assent was withheld from this last act, the Scottish Parliament bluntly refused to vote supply for the war.

The English retaliated by passing the Alien Act (March 1705), which stipulated that if the Scots did break the regal union they would henceforth be regarded as a foreign nation, with no rights of English citizenship or opportunity to trade with England. This was the crucial turning-point for many Scots. The more realistic accepted that an independent Scotland was simply not economically viable. The country remained relatively impoverished – was if anything becoming poorer – and unemployment was on the increase. The Scottish economy was still overwhelmingly rural and agrarian: even as a pre-industrial economy it remained considerably more underdeveloped than her southern neighbour. There seemed no way to alleviate that predicament except for Scotland to trade with England and secure her acquiescence to Scottish involvement in colonial trade. As William Seton of Pitmedden later put it, 'this nation, being poor and without force to protect its commerce, cannot reap great advantages by it, till it partake of the trade and protection of some powerful neighbour nation, that can communicate both these.' By the summer of 1705 a growing number of the Scottish nobility were coming round to the view that both they and the nation as a whole would benefit from a closer union. As the Earl of Cromarty put it, 'may we be Britons, and down go the old ignominious names of Scotland and England'. On 1 September the Duke of Hamilton, the unofficial leader of the loose-knit Country opposition, came out in favour of allowing Queen Anne to appoint Union commissioners – a crucial 'defection' which generated a gathering momentum towards union. The following year the Queen appointed thirty-one commissioners from each nation: they began their deliberations at Whitehall on 16 April, and by 22 July a draft treaty was complete.

The terms of the treaty were sufficiently conciliatory to make them acceptable to a wide range of Scottish opinion. England and Scotland were to form a single United Kingdom of Great Britain, and the Hanoverian succession to the throne was guaranteed. There was to be a single Parliament of Great Britain, in which Scotland would have sixteen representatives in the Lords and forty-five in the Commons. One in twelve members of the Commons would thus be Scots. This proportion seems miserly given the relative populations of the two nations (roughly one million as against five million), but decidedly generous when it is remembered that the ratio of Scotland's land tax assessment to England's was one to forty-five. The prime importance of economic and financial considerations was reflected in the fact that fifteen of the twenty-five articles in the treaty related to such matters. There was to be 'full freedom and intercourse of trade and navigation' throughout the United Kingdom, thereby creating the largest free-trade zone in Europe up to that date. A single coinage and a single system of weights and measures were established. These measures, together with the creation of a single British peerage, offered sufficient advantages and opportunities to win most Scottish nobles over to the idea of union. Furthermore, the independent integrity of the Scottish legal system was explicitly safeguarded, thus protecting not only existing courts and patterns of law but also the heritable jurisdictions of landlords. The rights and privileges of Scotland's royal burghs likewise remained intact. Above all, the union was accompanied by an 'Act for securing the Protestant Religion and Presbyterian Church Government' which stipulated that the Scottish Kirk would 'remain and continue unalterable' and obliged any new monarch to 'maintain and preserve' it. The union thus presented no threat to the distinctive reformed Church that so many Scots had passionately defended – and at times even wished to export – during the seventeenth century.

In England, despite some Tory misgivings about closer ties with Scotland, the union was approved relatively easily. It did, after all, resolve the issue of the succession and also help to defuse the danger of a French or Jacobite invasion through Scotland. An abortive Jacobite revolt in 1708 – like the further rebellions of 1715 and 1745 – proved easier to suppress within the context of a United Kingdom. It is also worth stressing that the Jacobites were just as unionist in their outlook as the Hanoverians, and Jacobitism was never associated with Scottish separatism. The union did encounter resistance when it was debated in the Scottish Parliament between 3 October 1706 and 16 January 1707. Some passionate voices were raised against it, as in Lord Belhaven's emotional speech about 'Mother Caledonia', but in the end the treaty was passed with only minor amendments by 110 votes to 67. Nor was this outcome unrepresentative of sentiments throughout the nation as a whole: only one quarter of the shires and one third of the burghs submitted petitions to Parliament protesting against the union. Some historians have followed Robert Burns's memorable view that Scotland's leaders were 'bought and sold for English gold', and certainly the financial inducements that accompanied the union cannot be ignored. The 'Equivalent', a sum of £398,085 10s., was voted to compensate all private losses incurred through the standardization of the coinage or investment in the Darien scheme. Furthermore, Godolphin entrusted the Queen's Commissioner in Scotland, the Duke of Queensberry, with £20,000 in cash to cover 'expenses' and the arrears of office-holders. There is evidence that some key individuals, such as Hamilton, voted for union because they received 'bribes'.

On the other hand, it is important not to underestimate the growth of principled support for the union in Scotland. A significant number of those who voted for the union did so without any rewards in the form of money or preferment. Some of the union commissioners, such as Sir John Clerk, genuinely felt that union was 'the best expedient to preserve the honour and liberties of Scotland'. Rather more numerous were those who recognized the powerful economic case in favour of union. The Earl of Roxburghe placed particular emphasis on this consideration in his assessment of why a majority of the Scottish Parliament voted for union:

> The motives will be, trade with most, Hanover with some, ease and security with others, together with a general aversion at civil discords, intolerable poverty, and the constant oppression of a bad ministry, from generation to generation, without the least regard to the good of the country.

In the end, although the arguments of patriots such as Andrew Fletcher of Saltoun, who urged Scotland to free herself from 'perpetual dependence upon another nation', exercised a strong emotional appeal, more and more Scots reluctantly recognized that the stark choice lay, in the words of the English propagandist Daniel Defoe, between 'peace and plenty' on the one hand and 'slavery and poverty' on the other. In particular, the economic, social and legal interests of the Scottish elite were sufficiently secured to make most of them amenable to union. In a country that was still so dominated by a relatively small clique of nobles and lairds, this was enough to persuade the majority of shires and burghs that further opposition was futile. The most common reaction was neither a hankering after independence nor indignation that Scotland had been trapped into union, but rather a wearily realistic acceptance that a brighter future existed for Scotland within a British State than outside it.

Scotland thus surrendered parliamentary independence in return for free trade. Her distinctive legal and religious structures were preserved, and her educational system grew up independently of England. Although the use of the Gaelic language declined quite rapidly, Scotland's native culture was impressively resilient, and the eighteenth century witnessed the seminal intellectual achievements of the Scottish Enlightenment. When the Scottish Parliament was finally dissolved on 28 April 1707, and the union came into effect three days later, a United Kingdom was established that is still in existence today. Whatever uncertainties currently surround its future, by the standards of most political or constitutional structures it has proved remarkably durable. Union of the kingdoms has already lasted nearly three times longer than the union of the crowns that it superseded. As its exponents recognized at the time, such an arrangement had much to commend it. Nor was this realization confined to Scotland, for the union was viewed with considerable envy from across the St George's Channel, in Ireland.

2 Ireland

The belief that a union of the kingdoms along Anglo-Scottish lines would benefit Ireland was perhaps most eloquently expressed by the Ulster MP Henry Maxwell in his *Essay towards a Union of Ireland with England* (1703). Maxwell argued that such a union would 'greatly increase the manufactures, trade and supply of each nation . . . and will be the common interest of manufacturer, merchant, landlord and of the monarchy'. That same year, the Irish House of Commons presented an address to Queen Anne explicitly requesting union. Others thought union very much the second best solution, and would have preferred a full recognition of the Irish Parliament's constitutional autonomy. This was the claim advocated in William Molyneux's celebrated *Case of Ireland's being bound by Acts of Parliament in England, stated* (1698). He insisted that Ireland was 'a complete kingdom within itself', with a Parliament of its own, and that the English Parliament therefore had no right to legislate for Ireland. To an assertion of Ireland's ancient parliamentary rights Molyneux added the Lockeian claim that 'all men are by nature in a state of equality', and were therefore 'free from all subjection to positive laws till by their own consent they give up their freedom by entering into civil societies'. The vast majority of people in Ireland wanted either parliamentary independence or full-scale union. What they actually got was an uncompromising English assertion that Ireland was 'a dependent and subordinate kingdom'. Ireland's status as a colonial dependency became more glaring than ever during the two decades after the Treaty of Limerick. These years saw the institutionalization of the Protestant ascendancy through a series of penal laws that enshrined the exclusion of Catholics from political, social and territorial power.

The penal laws stemmed primarily from the deep anxiety of an embattled Protestant minority – overwhelmingly of English or Scottish descent – that by 1703 comprised less than 20 per cent of the population but owned 86 per cent of the land. An English statute of December 1691 had given the Protestants a stranglehold on the Irish Parliament by requiring all MPs to take an oath repudiating the pope's authority to depose any monarch and denying Catholic doctrines such as transubstantiation. This allowed the Protestant Parliament to pass wide-ranging penal legislation against Catholics between 1695 and 1709. William, Anne and their ministers were only too happy to support such measures because Catholic Ireland appeared to pose a standing threat to security throughout the wars against Louis XIV.

The penal laws – or the 'popery laws', as Protestants called them – were never designed as a coherent package, but rather grew up piecemeal over a decade and a half. The first two, enacted in 1695, were the 'Act to restrain foreign education', which stipulated that no Catholic could teach or run a school, and another act which forbade Catholics to keep weapons or to own a horse worth more than £5. These were followed two years later by the Marriage Act, which insisted that Protestants who married a Catholic would themselves be regarded as Catholics 'for all intents and purposes'; and the Bishops' Banishment Act, which banished all Catholic bishops and regular clergy. The penal laws culminated in the 1704 'Act to prevent the further growth of popery'. This reaffirmed earlier penal legislation and required all holders of public office to take an 'oath of abjuration' repudiating the doctrine of transubstantiation, and an oath swearing allegiance to Queen Anne as the 'lawful and rightful Queen of the realm'. They were also obliged to take communion 'according to the usage of the Church of Ireland', a form of words that excluded Protestant dissenters from public office as well. All those seeking to vote in parliamentary elections were required to take the same oaths (though not the sacramental test), thereby disenfranchising the entire Catholic population. These clauses show very clearly how Catholicism and Jacobitism were perceived as synonymous, and how the steps taken against them were inseparably linked. A further act of 1707 established a national registry of deeds to prevent fraudulent land transactions by Catholics. Finally, in 1709 all Catholic clergy were required to take the oaths of abjuration and allegiance, although only thirty-three are definitely known to have done so.

In practice, the enforcement of the penal laws was patchy, and those regulating property were implemented far more stringently than those concerning clerics and religious practices. While it is possible, as Sean Connolly has argued,[1] that the direct impact of the penal laws against Catholics in this period has been overestimated, their psychological effect must have been profound, for they marked the institutionalization of the surrender of Catholic Ireland at Limerick in 1691, and the foundation of a 'Protestant nation' that endured for the next two centuries. During these years the legal machinery was constructed to give Protestants a monopoly of public office and a virtual monopoly of many other rights of citizenship. The fundamental division between Protestants and Catholics, drawn around the twin issues of land ownership and religion, was henceforth the dominant characteristic of Irish national life. One of the lasting legacies of the seventeenth century was thus the recasting of the Irish problem in its modern form.

The two most significant changes in the conduct of politics within the Protestant elite during the reigns of William and Anne closely paralleled developments on the mainland. First, the demands of war finance ensured regular meetings of Parliament, in 1692, 1695, 1698, 1703, 1705, 1707, 1709, 1710, 1711 and 1713. These Parliaments became directly dependent upon Westminster to a much greater degree than before, and this made it increasingly difficult to sustain Molyneux's claim that Ireland was a separate kingdom. Second, by 1703–4 the terms Whig and Tory had made their way from the mainland to Ireland. The fundamental differences of principle were much the same, but translated to a specifically Irish context. Tories were generally committed to the Church of Ireland, whereas the Whigs were more sympathetic to Protestant dissenters, and the two parties disagreed over whether Catholics or dissenters posed the greater threat to the Church of Ireland. They also espoused contrasting interpretations of the events of 1688–9, and although Irish Tories were largely untainted by Jacobitism, they shied away from the account of resistance against James II advanced by the Whigs. Here again, Irish politics, restricted to the Protestant nation, became more and more a spin-off of Westminster.

The vast majority of the inhabitants remained wedded to Catholicism and excluded from political life. Catholics comprised between 80 and 90 per cent of a total population that rose from about 2.2 million in 1687 to 2.8 million by 1712. Although the Catholic Church in Ireland was relatively thinly staffed by clergy compared with the Counter-Reformation churches of the Continent, with perhaps one priest for every thousand laity, standards of devotion and observance remained quite high. The same was true at the opposite end of the religious spectrum, among the Protestant dissenters. The Ulster Presbyterians formed the largest single group, and they were increasingly tightly organized after the Synod of Ulster was established in 1691. Their numbers received a major boost from the 50,000 or so Scottish immigrants who crossed to Ireland during the famine of the 1690s. To members of the Church of Ireland, who were probably slightly outnumbered by Protestant dissenters, these developments were profoundly alarming. The Williamite war had left the Church of Ireland in a dreadful condition: Queen Mary called it 'the worst in Christendom' in 1690. Everywhere churches lay in ruins – only 43 of 197 parish churches in the diocese of Meath were in repair in 1697, for example – and among the clergy pluralism and non-residence were rife. Adherence to the

Church was further limited by its reluctance to make any use of the Irish language. The vitality of Protestant nonconformity merely fuelled the anxieties of members of the Church, prompting a savage attack from Bishop William King of Londonderry in his *Discourse concerning the inventions of men in the worship of God* (1694), and, a decade later, the clauses against dissenters in the 1704 Popery Act. The Church of Ireland thus remained a misnomer: the Church of the political elite and of most landowners, it was dependent upon England for money and clergy, and utterly incapable of making serious inroads into the entrenched Catholicism of the majority of the population.

The Irish economy was still poorly developed and only began to expand significantly after the middle of the eighteenth century. Although Ireland did not suffer the famine that afflicted Scotland during the 1690s, the war of 1689–91 caused extensive damage to livestock, with the result that Irish exports of beef, butter and pork declined. By 1695 the value of exports stood at only half that of 1681. However, Ireland's principal export, woollen cloth, held up remarkably well, and more than doubled in value in 1696, 1697 and 1698. English merchants and clothiers were alarmed at this competition, and secured the passing of a Woollen Act in 1699 that banned the export of Irish woollen cloth to any destination other than England. This restriction further stymied the growth of the Irish economy. Dublin was Ireland's only sizeable city, and its social and political dominance, together with its significance in the linen industry (over three-quarters of linen exports were shipped from the city) led to a rapid expansion, from about 45,000 inhabitants in 1685 to over 90,000 by 1725. However, the vast majority of the population continued to live and work on the land: oats and barley were their staple foods, and they engaged in a barter-orientated subsistence economy. The lack of technical development in agriculture and manufacturing ensured that levels of wealth remained very low. The English visitor John Dunton wrote in 1699: 'If you peep into forty cabins, they are as spacious as our English hogsties, but not so clean; you will scarcely find a woman with a petticoat can touch her knee; and of ten children not one has a shoe to his foot.' William King, who became Archbishop of Dublin in 1703, described Ireland at the close of the seventeenth century as 'a miserable enslaved country without money or trade'.

Small wonder, then, that a strong lobby asserted that Ireland's plight could only be remedied by closer union with England. In 1707, as the kingdoms of England and Scotland were united, Jonathan Swift wrote (but did not publish) a pamphlet entitled 'The Story of the Injured Lady' which protested at Ireland's exclusion from the union. He insisted on Ireland's equality with England, and asserted the rights of the Irish Parliament, the iniquity of Poynings' Law and the need for free trade. A staunch defender of the Church of Ireland, he denounced dissenters and was appalled to see Presbyterian Scotland achieving a union of equals with England while Ireland remained a 'dependent kingdom'. But Swift's words fell on deaf ears. Crucially, in England there was strong support for union with Scotland but virtually none for union with Ireland. Whereas England's rulers regarded union with Scotland as essential to protect security and safeguard the succession, they had other – equally effective – methods to ensure control over Ireland. The expropriation of

Catholic landowners, the emergence of a Protestant ascendancy, and in the last resort an army of 12,000 troops, meant that a union of the kingdoms was not needed to maintain Ireland's subjugation. But such a situation could not be sustained indefinitely, and when it eventually disintegrated the results were to be catastrophic.

3 Wales

The principality of Wales presented a picture that was different again from either Scotland or Ireland. The fact that they had been united since 1536 ensured that there was a much lengthier and deeper history of intermingling between England and Wales than was the case with the other kingdoms. Many English visitors to Wales felt less sense of 'otherness' than they did when they journeyed to Scotland or Ireland. Indeed, much that has been said about England during the course of this book would be applicable also to Wales in a way that it would not to the other two kingdoms. Economic, social, political and religious developments in England and Wales were all closely intertwined, and yet at the same time Wales remained, in Philip Jenkins' words, 'a Celtic society with a distinctive hierarchy, language and customs'.

Wales was still an overwhelmingly rural country at the beginning of the eighteenth century. Its population stagnated from about 1640 onwards: it stood at around 350,000 in 1670 and had barely risen by 1700. Far more people lived in London at this time than in the whole of Wales. Only about a tenth of the Welsh population lived in towns, and the remainder worked on the land, inhabiting a terrain that was often bleak and inhospitable, especially in the north. Husbandmen and hill farmers comprised the largest single group in Welsh society: their farms were generally quite small – commonly between ten and sixty acres – and improvements in farming techniques were still very limited. By the beginning of the eighteenth century there were some signs of industrial activity, albeit on a small scale, notably coal-mining (especially in the south and northeast), slate quarrying in Carmarthenshire, and iron-working, for example in Pontypool and Wrexham. But these industries only really developed significantly during the second half of the eighteenth century, and in 1700 the Welsh economy continued to be predominantly agrarian, dependent above all on arable and cattle farming.

Society retained its hierarchical structure, and the attitudes of the nobility and gentry exerted a powerful influence on their local communities. Magnates such as the Earl of Worcester had ensured that Wales was mostly Royalist during the 1640s, and particular noble 'interests' – like that of the Earls of Carbery in Carmarthenshire – did much to colour later seventeenth-century Welsh politics. Loyalty to the Crown was deeply entrenched: the Restoration was warmly welcomed in Wales and Toryism emerged as a major political force after 1689. Welsh and English party politics became ever more closely enmeshed, and the Welsh MPs ceased to form a separate or coherent interest group at Westminster from the 1660s onwards. The strength of Welsh Royalism and later Toryism was closely associated with a widespread commitment to the established Church. In the absence of a Welsh university, Oxford – and particularly Jesus College – became the nearest equivalent to a 'university college' for Wales. The influence of Oxford served to strengthen the High Church clergy and laity, and by 1700 they were in a commanding position, as the rapturous reception accorded to Dr Sacheverell on his tour of Wales demonstrated. Although the Church in Wales suffered constantly from insufficient funds, its clergy were generally effective and the Society for the Promotion of Christian Knowledge, founded in 1699, enjoyed considerable success in setting up schools, especially in the south. Welsh Anglicanism was allied to virulent anti-popery that surfaced most forcefully during the 'Popish Plot' crisis, but in fact Welsh Catholics numbered fewer than 2,000 and they never posed any serious threat. A greater danger to the Church (although much less potent than it later became) was Wales's resilient tradition of religious dissent. Nonconformists made up a mere 5 or 6 per cent of the Welsh population, concentrated in the south, but they proved ineradicable.

Because of the union with England, Welsh patriotism could not be embodied in a flag, or an army, or the institutions of government. It was, however, expressed linguistically and culturally. Although some of the semi-pagan rural customs in Wales (such as maypoles or sacred wells) were little different from those found in western or upland England, there was a distinctive and vibrant Welsh culture. Gentry and noble patronage of the bardic poets declined during the later seventeenth century as the Welsh elite increasingly emulated the language and mores of their English counterparts. Yet Welsh culture found other patrons further down the social ladder, among the humbler folk who bought vernacular almanacs or imbibed Welsh poetry. The clergy also helped to preserve the use of the Welsh language and fostered an interest in Welsh history, as did antiquarians and genealogists such as Edward Lhuyd, whose *Archaeologia Britannica* (1707) confirmed that Welsh was one of a family of Celtic languages.

Remarkably, the Welsh language remained the everyday medium of communication for about 90 per cent of the population. Certainly the proportion of those who spoke *only* Welsh declined, and the nobility and gentry were coming to regard use of the vernacular as incompatible with social status or pretensions. Nevertheless, the translation of the Bible and Prayer Book into Welsh during the 1580s and the willingness of most clergy to use the vernacular rescued the language from any association with political sedition. By contrast, in Ireland and Scotland, where the established churches avoided the vernacular as much as possible, the Celtic languages suffered a more rapid decline and became tainted with subversion and Catholicism. By 1700 only 60 per cent of people in Ireland spoke Gaelic; in Scotland it was well below half. Paradoxically, Wales, the nation that was administratively, socially, economically and ecclesiastically most fully integrated with England, was also the one whose indigenous language remained the most widely spoken. The relentless spread of the English language during the early modern period – the total proportion of English speakers in Britain and Ireland rose from around 65 per cent in 1500 to about 85 per cent in 1700 – makes the survival of the Welsh language all the more significant. Ironically, it was probably precisely because

Wales was so assimilated into England that its language and culture were not perceived as a political threat. This in turn helps to explain why the Welsh cultural revival that took place during the late eighteenth and nineteenth centuries was much less politically aggressive than the equivalent movements in Ireland and Scotland.

4 England: Society and Economy

In many ways the social structure of Ireland, Scotland and Wales, in which a small elite dominated a large group of small farmers, was much closer to the typical continental pattern than it was to the situation in England, where beneath the nobility and gentry there was a considerable number of sizeable tenant farmers and then a mass of landless labourers. We have seen that the expansion of the gentry and yeomanry was one of the most marked features of English society during the century before 1640. By the end of the seventeenth century, a complicated mixture of change and continuity was evident. Hierarchy and inequality of wealth remained entrenched, and Gregory King's 'Scheme of the income and expense of the several families of England . . . for the year 1688' divided society into categories that were little different in essentials from those used by William Harrison in his *Description* of 1577. But these structural continuities belied a rapidly changing economic context which had far-reaching implications for the nature of English society.

Particularly significant was the fact that over a century of sustained demographic growth came to an end after the mid-seventeenth century. The population of England actually fell from just over 5.2 million in the 1650s to 5.05 million by 1701. This was partly due to increased mortality levels which remained high until the 1690s because of epidemic disease – typhus, smallpox and influenza more than bubonic plague – but it probably owed more to declining fertility rates as couples married later (often in their late twenties) and had fewer children. This behaviour may well reflect a conscious attempt to protect standards of living by having smaller families. At any rate, the effect was to reduce much of the pressure on agricultural resources that had afflicted England at the start of the century, with the result that prices stagnated until the early eighteenth century. At the same time the lack of population growth made labour more valuable and produced a steady increase in real wages. The long-term consequence of this was to improve the disposable income of wage-earners and thus diffuse wealth more widely within society, a development which probate inventories of the period clearly illustrate.

On the other hand, the stagnation in prices and the enhancement of wages worked to the disadvantage of smaller landowners. Bigger estates were better placed to withstand these developments, and this produced a marked trend towards fewer, larger farms by the closing years of the century. Although the scale of its use has probably been overestimated, the strict settlement provided a useful legal device to prevent the break-up of large estates.[2] In contrast to most of Europe, smaller farms declined, and those with profit margins of £3–5 a year often ceased to be viable. Overall, by the end of the seventeenth century England's agricultural productivity was increasing far more vigorously than in Scotland or Ireland as more land was cleared or drained, and as improvements in farming techniques became more widely practised, not least because of publications like John Houghton's *Letters for the Improvement of Husbandry and Trade*, which appeared throughout the 1690s. Among the most important of these improvements was the use of fodder crops, such as turnips, and artificial grasses like clover, lucerne and sainfoin, which were sown instead of a fallow year. The practice of floating water meadows, increasingly common in the south and west, also served to improve agricultural yields. As a result, England became, for the first time, a net grain exporter, from a mere 2,000 quarters a year in the 1660s to 300,000 quarters a year by 1675–7.

These developments, together with the improvement of England's communication network of roads and navigable waterways into one of the most efficient in Europe, stimulated internal and coastal trade and accelerated the growth of regional specialization. Areas with lighter soils, such as Norfolk, Suffolk, Wiltshire, Kent and Sussex, were especially well suited to the new fodder crops, and tended to move towards mixed sheep-corn husbandry. On the other hand, heavier soils, as in Leicestershire, Northamptonshire and Lincolnshire, lent themselves to more exclusively pasture farming. Existing forms of specialization were further expanded: market-gardening thrived in Kent and the Thames Valley, while hop-growing was a staple activity in Kent, Sussex, Herefordshire and Worcestershire. A similar trend towards specialization was also evident in manufacturing and industry. Textiles remained England's largest single export and accounted for over half of all exports in 1700. The later seventeenth century saw considerable growth in the 'new draperies' – lighter, cheaper and more colourful forms of cloth – and the rise of regional specialities: 'medley' cloths in Somerset and Wiltshire, 'stuffs' in Norfolk, 'serges' in Devon. Non-woollen textiles, including silk, linen and ribbons, also proliferated. By the beginning of the eighteenth century the coal-mining and metal industries were expanding as well. The introduction of steam pumping engines in the late 1690s and 1700s facilitated the development of coal fields in south Wales, southwest Lancashire and especially in the area between the Tyne and the Wear. The manufacture of metal implements, like nails and axes, often grew up in close association with coal fields, and this led to the transfer of iron-smelting from the Sussex Weald to south Wales, the Forest of Dean and south Yorkshire. If much of this industry remained organized on a domestic system, the foundations were gradually being laid for England's rapid industrialization during the later eighteenth century.

One of the most striking shifts in this period was the rapid expansion of England's overseas trade. During the second half of the seventeenth century the English overtook the Dutch in dominating the colonial slave trade and the European carrying trade, and by the early 1700s England was fast emerging as the leading commercial power in Europe. New trade routes with the Americas, Africa and the Far East were being swiftly opened up. The reduction of export duties on corn, cloth, iron and copper during the 1690s greatly encouraged trade. The value of trade handled by the East India Company, for example, increased from barely £100,000 a year before 1640 to £703,497 by 1700–1, while the abolition of many trading monopolies from 1689 onwards enabled the foundation of new companies, such as the New East India Company in 1698, which stimulated healthy competition between traders. England quickly cornered the market in the re-export of commodities imported from the Americas or India, such as tobacco from Virginia, sugar from the West Indies and calicoes from India: between them, these items made up 30 per cent of exports by the early 1700s. The wars against France also served to strengthen England's existing Mediterranean trade routes, especially with Portugal. England's principal trading competitor, the Dutch Republic, gradually lost its primacy, and by 1710 the growth of insurance and credit facilities in London meant that it was coming to replace Amsterdam as the centre of the commercial world.

This economic and commercial growth had important social implications. By the turn of the century contemporaries were increasingly worried about the 'conflict of interests' between the 'landed interest' and the new mercantile and business elite who were labelled the 'monied interest'. The high level of the land tax, which took four shillings in the pound (20 per cent) off the real value of landed estates during the war years, fuelled fears that landowners were bearing a disproportionate share of the costs of the conflict. Such anxieties were reinforced by the fact that so many of the rising merchants and businessmen did not come from traditional landowning families but included instead large numbers of Jews, French and Dutch immigrants, and dissenters. The issue became politicized because this 'monied interest' was predominantly Whig in sympathy, sparking the Tory alarm so forcefully expressed in some of Dr Sacheverell's sermons. At first, members of the 'monied interest' were understandably reluctant to invest their fortunes in land only to lose it in tax, although once the wars ended and the land tax was reduced they began to enter the ranks of the landowners. Nevertheless, the tension between old land and new money became one of the central themes of English society during the decades that followed.

It was not only merchants and businessmen who benefited: increasing prosperity was accompanied by the growth of a range of professions, including clerics, lawyers, doctors, schoolteachers, civil servants, architects, land agents and stewards. As wealth became diffused more widely there was a spate of building activity, and although three-quarters of the population still lived on the land or in small villages, many towns were expanding rapidly. London's population grew from about 400,000 in 1650 to over 575,000 by 1700. That rate of growth was equalled by a number of provincial towns, such as Newcastle, whose population rose from 12,000 in the 1600s to 16,000 at the end of the century. By 1700 there were about fifteen English towns with a population of over 10,000. London remained the pre-eminent political, social and cultural centre, and set the lead in the development of an urban culture characterized by artistic, literary and other leisure activities. As more people gained more disposable income, the beginnings of a 'consumer society' were apparent, catered for by the rising number of retail shops, and the opening years of the eighteenth century have justly been seen as a time of 'urban renaissance'.

Burgeoning economic opportunities gave many people a greater incentive to become literate. The provision of school education was steadily improving: over eighty grammar schools were founded during Charles II's reign, and the Society for the Promotion of Christian Knowledge set up a significant number of charity schools after 1699. Dissenting academies also began to spring up. Newspapers were being widely read by 1700, as were pamphlets, small books, ballads and almanacs. Yet literacy spread far more rapidly among men than women, and the educational gulf between the sexes probably widened during the later seventeenth century. In her *Defence of the Female Sex* (1697), Mary Astell lamented that 'they have endeavoured to train us up altogether to ease and ignorance'. The traumatic upheavals of the mid-seventeenth century had led to women taking on extra responsibilities and had challenged existing gender roles, yet – possibly for this very reason – after the Restoration there was a concerted male attempt to reassert the traditional subordination of women. The deaths of so many males during the Civil Wars meant that more women remained single in the latter part of the century, and a variety of possible occupations lay open to them: in industries, especially textiles (hence 'spinsters'), in domestic service, even as courtesans or actresses. But it would be misleading, in a period that saw the publication in 1683 of Robert Gould's *A Late Satyr Against the Pride, Lust and Inconstancy of Women*, to suggest that there had been any dramatic or uniform improvement in the position of women in England during the seventeenth century. As an anonymous verse put it in 1733:

> How wretched is a woman's fate,
> No happy change her fortune knows;
> Subject to man in every state,
> How can she then be free from woes?

It is, however, difficult to generalize when the experiences of individual women varied so widely. Many marriages were characterized by mutual love and respect, and it is possible that the trend towards smaller families tended to strengthen the bonds between family members.

It is worth stressing that whatever tensions existed within society, the incidence of public violence and disorder in England seemed to be steadily declining at the end of the seventeenth century. Grain riots did occur in 1693–5 and 1708–9, but they were on a small scale and largely confined to those areas, such as the Thames Valley or the cloth towns of the West Country, where there was a sizeable non-agrarian population. John Stevenson has observed that these riots displayed a vital 'element of ritual and restraint': the participants wished to alert those in authority to their suffering and to make the existing system of provision work more effectively rather than to overthrow it completely. Although poverty remained widespread, the rise in wages and the stagnation in prices helped to alleviate the plight of the poor and eased the relationships between different social groups. In general, the poor law functioned reasonably well, and the total sums raised by compulsory poor rates increased from £250,000 in about 1650 to over £700,000 by 1700. The restrained and limited nature of English disorders contrasted sharply with the pattern that prevailed in much of Europe – where the living standards of the lower orders were often much poorer – and it raises the question of how the country was able to support such a costly war effort and to shoulder such a massive tax burden without significant protest. To answer that, we need to explore another area of marked contrast with the Continent, namely politics and government.

5 England: Politics and Government

English government at the beginning of the eighteenth century bore only a superficial resemblance to the position in 1603. The principal institutions remained the same – monarch, Privy Council, Great Council (Parliament) – and yet the relationships between them had altered significantly. Reforms in the decade or so after the Revolution of 1688–9, enacted against the background of almost constant war, enhanced Parliament's powers considerably and established it as a permanent institution of government. These changes removed many of the most fundamental sources of instability that had dogged seventeenth-century England and heralded a new era in the nation's constitutional development. In so doing, they laid the foundations for a period of political stability at home that provided the springboard for England's (and Britain's) dramatically enhanced role in Europe and the world. Closely associated with this was a profound change in the way in which the English viewed their system of government – and themselves – in comparison with other nations.

In 1603 it had been generally held that the Crown possessed discretionary powers, known as the royal prerogative, which could be divided into two branches: the absolute or 'extraordinary' prerogative (which supplemented rather than contravened the common law) and the legal or 'ordinary' prerogative (which the monarch exercised through Parliament and the law). It was thus possible to argue that royal powers were both absolute and legally limited without any sense of paradox. This concept was by no means unique to England. A very similar idea could be found, for example, in the work of French theorists such as Claude de Seyssel or Jean Bodin, and this helps to explain why the latter's works received a sympathetic reception in early seventeenth-century England.

During the course of the century, however, this ideal began to break down in England. The personality and policies of Charles I raised profound questions about the boundaries of royal power and its relationship with Parliament and the rule of law. During the 1640s and 1650s, theorists as different as Sir Robert Filmer, Henry Parker and Thomas Hobbes contended that the idea of power as both absolute and limited was a contradiction in terms. In later seventeenth-century England, absolute monarchy became more and more a term of opprobrium, associated with tyranny and despotism. On the other hand, French political theorists during the reign of Louis XIV, most notably

Bossuet, continued to endorse the idea of absolute monarchy and distinguished it sharply from arbitrary government. Bossuet insisted that the monarch was absolute in the sense that he was 'independent of all human authority', but he was not arbitrary, for his will was constrained by the dictates of natural and divine law, although not by positive human law.

In England, by contrast, absolute and arbitrary power came to be seen as inseparable, especially after the Revolution of 1688–9. In his defence of the Bill of Rights, the Lord Chancellor, John Lord Somers, denounced 'absolute, arbitrary and tyrannical government' in a single breath as 'the ruin of the nation'. He contended that the English monarchy was not absolute precisely because it was legally limited:

> Our kings must act by law and not absolutely ... So that our government not being arbitrary, but legal, not absolute, but political, our princes can never become arbitrary, absolute, or tyrants without forfeiting at the same time their royal character, by the breach of the essential customs of their regal power, which are to act according to the ancient customs and standing laws of the nation.

This account was self-consciously worked out in contradistinction to what Somers called 'the slavery of the French nation', a gross caricature doubtless sharpened by the grim mood of war. It nevertheless remains true that Louis XIV could still levy taxes without his subjects' consent, could imprison without trial by issuing *lettres de cachet*, and did oblige the parlements to register royal edicts before remonstrating against them. All this stood in marked contrast to the powers of the English Crown in the opening years of the eighteenth century.

English claims about the limitations that existed upon their sovereigns were not mere rhetoric. The Revolution of 1688–9, and more importantly the reforms that followed in the wake of it, marked a dramatic divergence away from both continental patterns and the situation that had existed in earlier seventeenth-century England. Faced with unprecedentedly costly wars, the Crown was in no position to resist these changes. In the first place, the antiquated fiscal system, hitherto based on the medieval distinction between 'ordinary' and 'extraordinary' revenues, proved hopelessly inadequate and was superseded by one based on annual parliamentary grants. This meant that it became possible for the government to wage a war without endlessly antagonizing Parliament or trying to bypass it altogether. The fact that Parliament endorsed these grants, and monitored the financial probity of those responsible for spending them, also ensured that the subjects were prepared to pay a level of taxation per head twice that of the French, and surpassed only in the Dutch Republic. The 1690s and 1700s saw a mobilization of national resources equalled perhaps only by the Parliamentarian levies of the 1640s and 1650s, and quite unlike them in the fact that they were almost universally perceived as legitimate. The enhanced role of Parliament ensured that England's financial base as a major fiscal–military state was created with the consent of the leading subjects, a remarkable achievement that allowed the government to benefit from a period of sustained economic growth. England's war effort against France thus achieved all the benefits of a centralized harnessing of economic resources without any of the drawbacks of royal authoritarianism.

The Crown's financial needs guaranteed Parliament's permanence as an institution of government more securely than the Triennial Act of 1694 ever could. They also enabled Parliament to insist on the principle of 'appropriation' whereby taxes had to be spent on the purposes for which the Houses had voted them. This left Parliament in a very strong position to demand that it be fully involved in foreign policy decisions. Such developments were a far cry from the world of earlier Stuart monarchs, where Parliament was an event rather than an institution, constantly fearful of any threat to its existence, and where its right to advise on foreign policy was a source of frequent dispute. Parliament's newly acquired permanence as an institution enabled it gradually to displace the Court as a centre of political life, while the frequency of general elections ensured that the dichotomy between the Whig and Tory parties had become the defining feature of English politics by the end of Anne's reign. Political ascendancy came to depend less on royal favour and acceptance by Court factions than on the capacity to command a majority in the Houses of Parliament. This subsequently became the basis of the office of Prime Minister, and the rough outlines of the modern party system, focused on Parliament, were beginning to emerge. Likewise, it was during the reigns of William and Anne that the 'Cabinet', an inner circle of officers of state and Privy Councillors, started to develop as the crucial link between the Crown and Parliament.

Another area that was very poorly defined within the 'ancient constitution', and had the potential to provoke conflict, was the relationship between the Crown and the rule of law. The distinction between the 'absolute' and 'legal' prerogative did not specify which royal powers fell under each heading; nor did it offer any means of redress if a monarch exercised particular powers in what were perceived as inappropriate circumstances. By the close of the seventeenth century the position was greatly clarified. It was established after the Restoration that non-parliamentary taxation was not under any circumstances legal. The Revolution Settlement and subsequent legislation defined the monarch's powers in relation to due process of law: the Crown could neither imprison for no 'known cause' nor impose 'excessive bail', while the 1696 Trial of Treasons Act reformed procedure in treason trials in ways that strengthened the position of the accused and made it more difficult for the Crown to secure a favourable verdict. Finally, the principle was established that judges were appointed *quamdiu se bene gesserint* and could only be dismissed for gross moral turpitude or incompetence. The relationship between the Crown and the legal system was thus delineated more clearly than ever before.

But perhaps the most important single change, in terms of fostering stability, was the stipulation – adumbrated in the Bill of Rights and enshrined in the Act of Settlement – that the monarch had to be in communion with the Church of England. When we consider the amount of conflict and mistrust generated throughout the seventeenth century by fears over successive monarchs' religious beliefs – by doubts about their commitment to the Church of England or even to Protestantism – the momentous importance of this reform is clear. It marked a complete reversal of the principle, established at the Peace of

Augsburg in 1555 and thereafter normative in most of early modern Europe, that the faith of the monarch determined that of the nation. At a stroke it defused one of the most besetting problems of seventeenth-century Britain, and although religious controversy continued, especially over the nature of the Church and the rights of nonconformists, much of the political sting was taken out of the issue by the controls that now existed on the monarch's own faith. Here again, these reforms drastically reduced those grey areas where stability depended on personal trust between monarch and subjects, and thereby diminished the scope for mistrust of individual monarchs. Overall, during the years that followed the Revolution of 1688–9, the polity thus gained statutory safeguards against the foibles of particular sovereigns that marked a fundamental shift away from the personal monarchy of the early seventeenth century towards the more constitutional monarchy of the centuries that followed.

This period also witnessed a significant growth in the machinery and personnel of government. Once again, the manifold demands of war were a crucial catalyst of change. The permanent staff of the Admiralty increased from 147 in 1692 to 211 in 1716, that of the diplomatic service from 80 under William to 136 during Anne's reign. In the financial departments, of which the Treasury became the most powerful, the expansion was even more dramatic, from 2,524 in 1690 to 5,947 by 1716. At Anne's death the total number of permanent bureaucrats in government service stood at over 10,000, roughly a sixfold increase since the days of Charles I. The fact that those holding Court offices shrank from nearly 1,500 under Charles I to less than 1,000 in 1700 indicated the corresponding decline in the scale and significance of the Court. It was also during the later seventeenth century that the earliest signs of a nonpolitical civil service can be discerned, staffed by career bureaucrats of whom William Blathwayt (secretary-at-war, 1683–1704) was a notable example. The face of local government, however, was much less changed. The government remained heavily dependent upon the co-operation of local elites for the collection of taxes, the enforcement of laws and the administration of justice through the assizes and quarter sessions. But though fundamentally unchanged, the machinery of local government probably worked more effectively than earlier in the century because the leading subjects represented in Parliament were more directly and constantly involved in the formulation of policy than hitherto. This meant that there became progressively less scope for the formation of a 'country' opposition.

It is important, of course, not to underestimate the elements of continuity that persisted after 1707. The powers of the Crown remained considerable, the Church and landed elite retained formidable strength, and the two-party system was arguably more evident under Anne than during most of the remainder of the eighteenth century. Nevertheless, the extent to which England differed from much of Europe at the end of the seventeenth century, as well as from itself earlier in the century, is striking. To suggest that many of the most durable changes were crowded into the years after 1688–9 is not to ignore the profound legacy of the 1640s and 1650s. The mid-century Revolution was indelibly imprinted on the nation's collective memory, and it engendered a deep desire to avoid further bloodshed and to achieve political change peacefully. This is crucial in explaining the pragmatic attitude towards constitutional development so characteristic of England after the mid-seventeenth century. The Marquis of Halifax remarked in the 1680s that the life of a constitution 'is prolonged by changing seasonably the several parts of it at several times', while in 1733 Alexander Pope declared:

> For forms of government let fools contest.
> Whate'er is best administer'd is best.

A mistrust of political and religious zeal, and a preference for gradual rather than cataclysmic change, owed much to the searing experiences of the English Revolution. Many of the problems that lay behind that revolution had been resolved by the early eighteenth century; others, such as the Irish question, had been cast into a radically different form. In 1707 a new polity was created, the United Kingdom of Great Britain and Ireland, that marked the end of the period of regal union. With the union of the kingdoms of England and Scotland, and the moves towards a more constitutional, less personal, monarchy during the two decades or so that preceded it, 1707 is an appropriate date at which to draw the story of the 'Double Crown' to a close. The State created in that year has lasted into the twentieth century, and along the way it gained dominion over a worldwide empire and led the field in the process of industrialization. The United Kingdom emerged with enough confidence in its own institutions and way of life, and sufficient political stability at home, to turn its energies outwards into the wider world. In 1707 all those remarkable developments lay far in the future. But as the dust slowly settled after the extraordinary turmoil and upheaval of the seventeenth century, it became apparent that their foundations had been set in place.

Notes

1 *1603: Union of the Crowns*

1 See especially Christopher W. Marsh, *The Family of Love in English Society, 1550–1630* (Cambridge, 1993).
2 This thesis was presented in Lawrence Stone, *The Crisis of the Aristocracy, 1558–1641* (Oxford, 1965). For cogent critiques, see in particular the articles by Conrad Russell and Christopher Thompson, together with Stone's replies, in *EcHR*, 2nd series, 25 (1972), 117–36.
3 See below, pp. 151–2.
4 They especially applauded the fact that Geoffrey of Monmouth's *Historia Regum Britanniae* enshrined the position of the Welsh nation among the ancient Britons. A British identity thus offered some defence against the forces of Anglicization. The Welsh much preferred Geoffrey's account to the altogether more Anglocentric vision found in Polydore Vergil's *Anglica Historia*.
5 'Great Britain' was used here as a geographical term, intended to distinguish James's kingdoms from Lesser Britain, the name applied at this time to Brittany.
6 See Jenny Wormald, 'James VI, James I and the Identity of Britain', in *The British Problem, c. 1534–1707: State Formation in the Atlantic Archipelago*, ed. Brendan Bradshaw and John Morrill (London, 1996), pp.148–71.

2 *Great Britain's Solomon*

1 Jenny Wormald, 'James VI and I: Two Kings or One?', *History*, 68 (1983), 187–209. This seminal article really marked the beginning of scholarly reappraisal of the King's reputation.
2 See G. R. Elton, 'A high road to civil war?' in his *Studies in Tudor and Stuart Politics and Government* (4 vols, Cambridge, 1974–92), II, 164–82. For the role of Court politics in stirring up the Commons, see especially R. C. Munden, 'The defeat of Sir John Fortescue: Court versus Country at the Hustings?', *EHR*, 93 (1978), 811–16.
3 See below, p. 38.
4 The Gunpowder Plot is discussed more fully below, pp. 34, 40–1.
5 Robert Cecil had been created Earl of Salisbury in May 1605.
6 These developments at Court are examined below, pp. 41–4.
7 Mark H. Curtis, 'The Hampton Court Conference and its Aftermath', *History*, 46 (1961), 1–16; Frederick Shriver, 'Hampton Court Re-visited: James I and the

Puritans', *JEH*, 33 (1982), 48–71; Patrick Collinson, 'The Jacobean Religious Settlement: the Hampton Court Conference', in *Before the English Civil War*, ed. Howard Tomlinson (London, 1983), pp. 27–51. For a counter-argument, see Peter White, *Predestination, Policy and Polemic: Conflict and Consensus in the English Church from the Reformation to the Civil War* (Cambridge, 1992), pp. 140–52. White demonstrates that the area where James gave least ground was in matters of doctrine. However, this does not so much indicate that Hampton Court was a 'decisive defeat' for the Puritans as offer another illustration of the King's church-manship. For to please the Puritans more on doctrinal matters would necessarily have meant pleasing many others less, and would thus have jeopardized James's ideal of a broad, comprehensive Church. His policies were carefully calculated to draw as many into the fold as possible.

8   There is not a shred of evidence that Cecil connived in this plot to discredit English Catholics and stir up anti-popish feeling: Mark Nicholls, *Investigating Gunpowder Plot* (Manchester, 1991). On the role of anti-Scottish sentiment, see Jenny Wormald, 'Gunpowder, Treason, and Scots', *JBS*, 24 (1985), 141–68.

9   The Earl and Countess of Somerset remained in the Tower until 1622 when they were released on condition that they lived quietly in the country. She died in 1632; he in 1645.

10   This was the so-called *commendams* affair. The Crown had an ancient right to grant a clergyman an additional benefice (or *commendam*). James wanted to be consulted on cases involving this right, but Coke felt that this encroached upon the independence of the judiciary. Ellesmere sided with the King.

11   John Morrill, 'A British patriarchy? Ecclesiastical imperialism under the early Stuarts', in *Religion, Culture and Society in Early Modern Britain: Essays in Honour of Patrick Collinson*, ed. Anthony Fletcher and Peter Roberts (Cambridge, 1994), pp. 209–37. Much of the next two paragraphs is indebted to this essay.

3 The Ascendancy of Buckingham

1   The Wardrobe was the department of the King's Household responsible for looking after the royal apparel.

2   Impeachment had not been used since the trial of Lord Stanley in 1459. Its revival from 1621 onwards is examined in Colin G. C. Tite, *Impeachment and Parliamentary Judicature in Early Stuart England* (London, 1974).

3   The complex reasons for this misunderstanding are unravelled in Conrad Russell, *Unrevolutionary England, 1603–1642* (London, 1990), chapter 3; and in his *Parliaments and English Politics, 1621–1629* (Oxford, 1979), pp. 121–44.

4   'Infanta' was the title traditionally accorded to the eldest daughter of the King of Spain.

5   Cranfield was also obliged to forfeit his London house at Chelsea. After his fall, he retired to his country seat at Copt Hall in Essex, and lived there in seclusion until his death in August 1645.

6   Jacobus Arminius (1560–1609) was a Dutch theologian who challenged the Calvinist doctrine of double predestination and asserted instead that human beings possessed free will to attain or forfeit salvation by their own actions. The term 'Arminian' is often used rather loosely as a label for anti-Calvinists.

7   Much the fullest study of the Forced Loan and reactions to it is Richard Cust, *The Forced Loan and English Politics, 1626–1628* (Oxford, 1987), to which the following account is greatly indebted.

8 However, only about £160,000 actually reached the Exchequer: the remainder was paid out in various concessions – such as the reimbursement of billeting charges – designed to foster local co-operation and encourage further payments of the Loan.

9 The Five Knights' Case and Charles's intervention are examined in J. A. Guy, 'The Origins of the Petition of Right Reconsidered', *HJ*, 25 (1982), 289–312.

10 The King's treatment of these prisoners is discussed in detail in L. J. Reeve, *Charles I and the Road to Personal Rule* (Cambridge, 1989), chapter 5.

4 The Personal Rule of Charles I

1 At any rate in England: Parliaments were called in Scotland in 1633 and 1639, and in Ireland in 1634.

2 Kevin Sharpe, *The Personal Rule of Charles I* (New Haven and London, 1992).

3 This point is also persuasively made in Conrad Russell, *The Fall of the British Monarchies, 1637–1642* (Oxford, 1991), chapter 1.

4 For some examples, see below, pp. 91, 97–8.

5 For a sample of recent works which advance this general line of argument, see Esther S. Cope, *Politics without Parliaments, 1629–1640* (London, 1987); Glenn Burgess, *The Politics of the Ancient Constitution: An Introduction to English Political Thought, 1603–1642* (London, 1992); L. J. Reeve, *Charles I and the Road to Personal Rule* (Cambridge, 1989); and *Conflict in Early Stuart England: Studies in Religion and Politics, 1603–1642*, ed. Richard Cust and Ann Hughes (Harlow, 1989).

6 See above, pp. 35–6, 58.

7 The King's Evil was the name given to scrofula, the tubercular inflammation of the lymph glands in the neck. From the reign of Edward the Confessor it was widely believed that English monarchs had the ability to heal this affliction by touch. Since the symptoms associated with scrofula were sometimes psychogenic, and therefore more likely to recede if the sufferer were convinced of the efficacy of the remedy, there were enough cases of apparent cures to perpetuate the belief. Doctors continued to prescribe the cure by royal touch until the early eighteenth century, and the last monarch to touch the scrofulous was Queen Anne. For a judicious discussion of this phenomenon, see Keith Thomas, *Religion and the Decline of Magic: Studies in Popular Beliefs in Sixteenth- and Seventeenth-Century England* (London, 1971), chapter 7. Charles's curtailing of the practice is analysed in Judith Richards, '"His Nowe Majestie" and the English Monarchy: The Kingship of Charles I before 1640', *PP*, 113 (1986), 70–96.

8 The Mantua collection consisted of about 175 paintings, including nineteen Titians, twelve Mantegnas and ten Brueghels. Some of these works are still among the Royal Collections today, and many of them were inspired by the Catholic Counter-Reformation. The sum of £18,000 represented almost 5 per cent of an annual income that was already overstretched.

9 These exploited a loophole in the 1624 Monopolies Act, which had only outlawed such grants to individuals. The various grants during the Personal Rule were always made to syndicates or corporations.

10 This rough estimate of the national position does however conceal some striking regional variations. In Somerset, for example, it seems that only about a quarter of parishes had followed Laud's injunctions.

11 The studies referred to in this paragraph are: Ann Hughes, 'Thomas Dugard and his Circle in the 1630s – a "parliamentary-puritan" connexion?', *HJ*, 29 (1986),

771–93; S. P. Salt, 'The Origins of Sir Edward Dering's Attack on the Ecclesiastical Hierarchy, *c.* 1625–1640', *HJ*, 30 (1987), 21–52; and John Fielding, 'Opposition to the Personal Rule of Charles I: the Diary of Robert Woodford, 1637–1641', *HJ*, 31 (1988), 769–88.

12 See below, p. 102.
13 For Charles's assault on security of property in Scotland see below, pp. 101–2.
14 See above, pp. 23, 45.

5 The Collapse of Multiple Monarchies

1 For these contacts, see especially Peter Donald, *An Uncounselled King: Charles I and the Scottish Troubles, 1637–1641* (Cambridge, 1990), pp. 135–6, 184–5, 244–7; idem, 'New light on the Anglo-Scottish contacts of 1640', *HR*, 62 (1989), 221–9; and Conrad Russell, *The Fall of the British Monarchies, 1637–1642* (Oxford, 1991), pp. 60–4, 68–70, 151–3. The existence of these links can be clearly established by the summer of 1639, but they may have begun to develop even earlier: see John Morrill, *The Nature of the English Revolution* (Harlow, 1993), pp. 109–111.

2 The phrase 'both of your realms' is highly significant. It not only indicates the extent to which the authors of the Petition were thinking in Anglo-Scottish terms, but also offers another illustration of the contemporary perception of Ireland as a colony rather than a kingdom. The implications of this were not lost on the Irish: see below, pp. 120–2.

3 Russell, *Fall of the British Monarchies*, pp. 291–4, 330–7; idem, *Unrevolutionary England, 1603–1642* (London, 1990), chapter 16.

4 See below, p. 118.

5 Russell, *Fall of the British Monarchies*, pp. 322–8, 405, 408–9; Donald, *An Uncounselled King*, pp. 297, 312–24, 316.

6 See above, pp. 112–13.

7 See especially Jane Ohlmeyer, 'The "Antrim plot" of 1641 – a myth?', *HJ*, 35 (1992), 905–19; and the subsequent debate between Ohlmeyer and Perceval-Maxwell in *ibid.*, 37 (1994), 421–37.

8 John Morrill, *The Revolt of the Provinces: Conservatives and Radicals in the English Civil War, 1630–1650* (revised edition, Harlow, 1980), pp. 36–42.

9 This point is strikingly demonstrated in Conrad Russell, *The Causes of the English Civil War* (Oxford, 1990), pp. 19–22, 222–4. See also Morrill, *Nature of the English Revolution*, especially pp. 60–8, 118–47.

10 Cf. Morrill, *Nature of the English Revolution*, p. 68; Morrill, *Revolt of the Provinces*, pp. 25, 48–9.

11 John Morrill, 'William Davenport and the "silent majority" of early Stuart England', *Journal of the Chester and North Wales Archaeological Society*, 58 (1975), 115–29.

12 The issues discussed in this paragraph may be explored further in Brian Manning, *The English People and the English Revolution* (London, 1976); David Underdown, *Revel, Riot and Rebellion: Popular Politics and Culture in England, 1603–1660* (Oxford, 1985); and Morrill, *Nature of the English Revolution*, pp. 214–41.

13 See below, chapter 11.

6 War in Three Kingdoms

1 See below, pp. 144–6.

2   The issue between Independents and Presbyterians revolved around what should replace the old Church of England, which Parliament was in the process of dismantling (see below, p. 150). Independents initially favoured 'the New England way': mandatory attendance at local ('parish') churches with full membership for the covenanted only. However, the experience of exclusion from the established Church led many of them to support a wide measure of toleration for religious radicals: they opposed a coercive national Church, and believed that each congregation should be independent and free to organize its own style of worship. Presbyterians, by contrast, saw the national Churches of Scotland or Geneva as models for what they hoped to introduce in England. They envisaged a rigid hierarchical structure based on the Calvinist institutions of a national synod, regional assemblies, and local groupings of parishes ('classes', the equivalent of the Scottish 'presbyteries'). Their attempts to establish such a system are discussed below, p. 150.

3   The fullest studies of the New Model Army are Mark A. Kishlansky, *The Rise of the New Model Army* (Cambridge, 1979); and Ian Gentles, *The New Model Army in England, Ireland and Scotland, 1645–1653* (Oxford, 1992).

4   After this defeat Montrose disbanded his remaining forces and escaped into hiding. He eventually sailed for Norway in September 1646. For his subsequent career, see below, p. 175.

5   See below, p. 155.

6   Christopher Durston, *The Family in the English Revolution* (Oxford, 1989).

7   For Spenser, see above, pp. 23, 100.

8   John Morrill has recently suggested that the contemporary interchangeability of the terms 'agitator' and 'adjutator' ('helper' or 'assistant') may indicate that these people were not 'elected' by the rank and file but co-opted by their officers: John Morrill, *The Nature of the English Revolution* (Harlow, 1993), pp. 248–9. See also Austin Woolrych, *Soldiers and Statesmen: The General Council of the Army and its Debates, 1647–1648* (Oxford, 1987), especially pp. 59–90.

9   Leveller influence within the army is discussed more fully below, pp. 155–6, 173–4.

10 Cf. above, pp. 101–4, 141–2.

11 The Vote was subsequently passed by the Lords on 17 January.

12 On doctrines of blood-guilt and their importance in 1648–9, see especially Patricia Crawford, 'Charles Stuart, that Man of Blood', *JBS*, 16 (1977), 41–61; Stephen Baskerville, *Not Peace but a Sword: The Political Theology of the English Revolution* (London, 1993), pp. 82–95, 101–4, 126–30.

13 With Cromwell absent in Yorkshire, the key army grandee in engineering this compromise was Henry Ireton, himself an MP since 1645. The other MPs almost certainly included Edmund Ludlow and Henry Marten. These manoeuvres are brilliantly unravelled in David Underdown, *Pride's Purge: Politics in the Puritan Revolution* (Oxford, 1971), especially pp. 106–42.

14 Several 'regicides' later alleged that Cromwell had forced them to sign the death warrant. However, such stories must be treated with caution because they mostly date from after the Restoration when Cromwell, who was no longer alive to defend himself, made an easy scapegoat. But it does seem that by January 1649 Cromwell had become a vigorous supporter of the King's execution on the grounds that it was 'necessary' to fulfil God's will. The legend that on the evening of 30 January he returned secretly to Whitehall Palace, opened the King's coffin, and after looking for some time at the corpse with its severed head muttered the words 'cruel necessity', has a certain plausibility.

7 The British Republic

1 For Scottish reactions to the Regicide, see below, pp. 174–6.

2 On 3 February a special High Court of Justice had been established to try Hamilton (under his English title of Earl of Cambridge), the Earls of Holland and Norwich, Lord Capel and Sir John Owen for their part in fomenting the second Civil War. All five were sentenced to death on 6 March. Owen and Norwich were reprieved on 8 March; the other three were beheaded outside Westminster Hall the next day.

3 See J. C. Davis, *Fear, Myth and History: The Ranters and the Historians* (Cambridge, 1986); and also Davis's response to his critics: 'Fear, Myth and Furore: Reappraising the "Ranters"', *PP*, 129 (1990), 79–103.

4 See below, pp. 180–93.

5 In practice, however, the majority of MPs 'elected' in both Scotland and Ireland were nominated by the English commissioners appointed to administer each country. Apart from the Nominated Assembly (for which see pp. 183–4, below), the Protectorate Parliaments were the only occasions before 1707 when Scottish and English members formed a single Parliament, and the only time until 1801 that British and Irish members sat together.

6 The fullest account of English republican thought during the Interregnum can be found in Blair Worden's contributions to *Republicanism, Liberty, and Commercial Society, 1649–1776*, ed. David Wootton (Stanford, 1994), pp. 45–193. For useful overviews, see Jonathan Scott, 'The English Republican Imagination', in *Revolution and Restoration: England in the 1650s*, ed. John Morrill (London, 1992), pp. 35–54; and Blair Worden, 'English republicanism', in *The Cambridge History of Political Thought, 1450–1700*, ed. J. H. Burns and Mark Goldie (Cambridge, 1991), pp. 443–75.

7 This assembly is also sometimes known as 'Barebone's Parliament' (after one of its members, Praise-God Barebone) or as the 'Little Parliament'.

8 These 139 included six from Wales, five from Scotland and six from Ireland.

9 Cromwell's life up to 1640 is brilliantly reconstructed in John Morrill, *The Nature of the English Revolution* (Harlow, 1993), pp. 118–47.

10 In this passage, 'the firstborn' means the firstborn of God the Father (i.e. Christ), while 'the congregation' refers to the elect, those predestined to attain salvation.

11 Throughout Cromwell's career, a belief in God's mission for England is easier to discern than any sense of a British destiny. His vision of an elect nation was generally couched in Anglocentric terms, and in so far as it extended to Scotland and Ireland it involved incorporating them into a greater English Commonwealth, making them 'little Englands'. On this point, see *Oliver Cromwell and the English Revolution*, ed. John Morrill (Harlow, 1990), especially pp. 149–80, 281.

12 By an irony, Lord Chief Justice Henry Rolle was the elder brother of John Rolle, one of the London merchants whose goods had been confiscated in 1628 after they refused to pay tonnage and poundage without Parliament's consent. This must have given the Lord Chief Justice a particularly acute appreciation of Cromwell's capacity to act in disturbingly similar ways to Charles I.

13 Cromwell later disowned this purge, yet made no attempt to undo it. It seems that – as perhaps also at the time of Pride's Purge – he was anxious not to be associated with the exclusion of elected members of Parliament. However, he may well have approved of the motives that lay behind the purge, and the Council was acting within the powers vested in it by the Instrument of Government.

14 Cromwell insisted that the Instrument of Government 'was never intended to maintain and protect blasphemers', but in order to avoid an embarrassing test case

on this point he ensured that Biddle was imprisoned on the Scilly Isles, outside the jurisdiction of the Westminster courts and of *habeas corpus*. It is not impossible that this move was partly intended to protect Biddle: certainly Cromwell provided him with a weekly allowance of ten shillings, apparently out of his own pocket.

15 The circumstances surrounding this nomination remain mysterious. Eyewitnesses claimed that Cromwell did not name a successor on his deathbed. He had previously stated that he had made a written nomination, but the Secretary of the Council, John Thurloe, said that this could not be found. It is possible that Cromwell had nominated John Lambert but that the Council, horrified by the prospect of such an ambitious army officer becoming Lord Protector, decided to back the more malleable Richard Cromwell instead. For a discussion of this episode, see W. H. Dawson, *Cromwell's Understudy: The Life and Times of General John Lambert and the Rise and Fall of the Protectorate* (London, 1938), pp. 287–96.

8 The Restoration of the British Monarchies

1 For an explanation of this custom, see above, p. 351. Charles II's revival of it is discussed in Keith Thomas, *Religion and the Decline of Magic: Studies in Popular Beliefs in Sixteenth- and Seventeenth-Century England* (London, 1971), pp. 228, 231; and in Ronald Hutton, *Charles II: King of England, Scotland, and Ireland* (Oxford, 1989), pp. 134, 403.

2 Charles confided to Clarendon in late 1661: 'rebel for rebel, I had rather trust a papist rebel than a presbyterian one'. In seeking to justify religious toleration for Catholics, Charles later expressed his 'due sense ... of the greatest part of our Roman Catholic subjects of this kingdom having deserved well from our father of blessed memory, and from us, and even from the Protestant religion itself, in adhering to us with their lives and fortunes for the maintenance of our Crown in the religion established against those who under the name of zealous Protestants employed both fire and sword to overthrow them both.' This passage appears in the Declaration of Indulgence, 26 December 1662, quoted in *The Stuart Constitution: Documents and Commentary*, ed. J. P. Kenyon (2nd edition, Cambridge, 1986), p. 381.

3 See below, pp. 290–1, 313–14, 344–5.

4 For studies of the Restoration land settlement, see especially H. J. Habbakuk, 'The Land Settlement and the Restoration of Charles II', *TRHS*, 5th series, 28 (1978), 201–22; Joan Thirsk, 'The Restoration Land Settlement', *JMH*, 26 (1954), 315–28; and idem, *The Restoration* (London, 1976), pp. 81–109.

5 Some historians have suggested that Charles and Clarendon actually wanted a narrow, intolerant Church settlement all along and were simply biding their time: Robert S. Bosher, *The Making of the Restoration Settlement* (London, 1951); I. M. Green, *The Re-establishment of the Church of England, 1660–1663* (Oxford, 1978). But for persuasive counter-arguments, suggesting that their preferences were thwarted by the intolerance of the Cavalier Parliament, see in particular Anne Whiteman, 'The Restoration of the Church of England', in *From Uniformity to Unity, 1662–1962*, ed. Geoffrey F. Nuttall and Owen Chadwick (London, 1962), pp. 21–88; G. R. Abernathy, *The English Presbyterians and the Stuart Restoration, 1648–1663* (Transactions of the American Philosophical Society, new series, 55, Part 2, Philadelphia, 1965); D. T. Witcombe, *Charles II and the Cavalier House of Commons, 1663–74* (Manchester, 1966), pp. 4–10; and Ronald Hutton, *The Restoration: A Political and Religious History of England and Wales, 1658–1667*

(Oxford, 1985), pp. 166–80. Support in the Lords for a broad, tolerant Church is examined in Andrew Swatland, *The House of Lords in the Reign of Charles II* (Cambridge, 1996).

6 For Morley's hostility towards the Laudians, see above, p. 92. A few Laudians did receive bishoprics in 1660, notably John Cosin at Durham, and William Juxon who became Archbishop of Canterbury. But the latter's appointment owed much to his personal loyalty to Charles and his father, and by 1660 he was so elderly and ailing that the more moderate Sheldon effectively exercised the role of primate. Sheldon became Archbishop of Canterbury on Juxon's death in 1663.

7 For this, see especially Richard L. Greaves's trilogy: *Deliver us from Evil: The Radical Underground in Britain, 1660–1663* (Oxford, 1986); *Enemies under his Feet: Radicals and Nonconformists in Britain, 1664–1677* (Stanford, 1990); and *Secrets of the Kingdom: British Radicals from the Popish Plot to the Revolution of 1688–89* (Stanford, 1992). See also below, pp. 236–8.

8 See below, pp. 216–18.

9 See above, pp. 208–10.

10 The Plague's greatest impact was among the poor and many deaths – perhaps as many as 30,000 – were not recorded in the London Bills of Mortality. The total number of victims may thus have been approaching 100,000, about a quarter of the city's population.

9 Court and Country

1 Charles's motives, and the various interpretations of them, are discussed in Ronald Hutton, 'The Making of the Secret Treaty of Dover, 1668–1670', *HJ*, 29 (1986), 297–318. See also Hutton's *Charles II: King of England, Scotland, and Ireland* (Oxford, 1989), pp. 263–73; and his 'The Religion of Charles II', in *The Stuart Court and Europe: Essays in Politics and Political Culture*, ed. R. Malcolm Smuts (Cambridge, 1996), pp. 228–46; and John Miller, *Charles II* (London, 1991), pp. 142–82.

2 James's first wife, Anne Hyde, had died in 1671. The daughter of Clarendon, she was a Protestant for most of her life, but in 1670 she was secretly received into the Catholic Church. She and James had two surviving Protestant children, Mary and Anne.

3 This was Arthur Capel, who had been created Earl of Essex in April 1661. He was no relative of Robert Devereux, third Earl of Essex, whose title had lapsed when he died without an heir in September 1646.

4 By the same token, the Compton Census also dramatically underestimated the number of Catholics in England and Wales, placing at 14,000 a total that was almost certainly in the region of 60,000. For an edition of the Census, with an excellent introduction, see *The Compton Census of 1676*, ed. Anne Whiteman (London, 1986).

5 See especially John Spurr, '"Latitudinarianism" and the Restoration Church', *HJ*, 31 (1988), 61–82; and Spurr's *The Restoration Church of England, 1646–1689* (New Haven and London, 1991).

6 Basset was a type of card game that originated in Venice.

7 For a fuller discussion of the King's Evil, see above, p. 202.

10 Exclusion and Reaction

1   See above, pp. 235–6.
2   Jonathan Scott, *Algernon Sidney and the Restoration Crisis, 1677–1683* (Cambridge, 1991); Mark Knights, *Politics and Opinion in Crisis, 1678–81* (Cambridge, 1994).
3   These further prorogations were issued on 26 January, 15 April, 17 May, 1 July, 22 July and 23 August 1680.
4   See below, p. 264.
5   See below, pp. 259–61.
6   Although they were not labelled 'Whig' and 'Tory', the origins of these 'parties' can be discerned rather sooner in the Lords than in the Commons, possibly from as early as 1675: see Andrew Swatland, *The House of Lords in the Reign of Charles II* (Cambridge, 1996).
7   The fullest discussion of the granting of new borough charters during this period is John Miller, 'The Crown and the Borough Charters in the reign of Charles II', *EHR*, 100 (1985), 53–84.
8   Laurence Hyde had been appointed First Lord of the Treasury in November 1679; he was created Earl of Rochester in November 1682.
9   Originally an exclusionist, the wily Sunderland had recanted in February 1681 and made an abject submission to James, who thereafter regarded him as an ally. He was appointed Secretary of State in January 1683. Jeffreys became Lord Chief Justice in 1682 and a Privy Councillor the following year.
10 Rochester however declined the post, as did Sunderland. Eventually, in October 1685, Rochester's elder brother, Henry Hyde, second Earl of Clarendon, became Lord Lieutenant.
11 The exact nature of the King's illness is not certain. Some accounts of the symptoms are consistent with a chronic form of kidney disease, whereas others suggest that he may have suffered a stroke.

11 A Glorious Revolution?

1   James rewarded Jeffreys by appointing him Lord Chancellor on 28 September.
2   Parker's motives for supporting the Declaration are difficult to unravel. Some historians have suggested that he was a time-server who was mindful of the fact that he owed his appointment as Bishop of Oxford in 1686 to James. On the other hand, part of the reason why James favoured him was that Parker consistently adopted an Erastian position which upheld the authority of the civil magistrate to order outward forms of religion. Support for the Declaration would be entirely in line with this. There is even a third, perhaps less plausible, theory that Parker was a closet Catholic. I am most grateful to Jon Parkin for his helpful advice about Parker.
3   In addition to Sancroft, the other six were Bishops Trelawny of Bristol, Lloyd of St Asaph, Turner of Ely, White of Peterborough, Ken of Bath and Wells, and Lake of Chichester.
4   These 'Immortal Seven', as they came to be called, were Bishop Compton of London, the Earl of Danby, Lord Lumley, Edward Russell, Henry Sidney, and the Earls of Devonshire and Shrewsbury.
5   The number of troops has usually been estimated at around 14–15,000, but Jonathan Israel and Geoffrey Parker have shown that the overall total, including the crews of the vessels, was much higher than this: see *The Anglo-Dutch Moment:*

Essays on the Glorious Revolution and its World Impact, ed. J. I. Israel (Cambridge, 1991), chapters 3 and 10.

6   These words remained highly controversial in the Upper House, however: a lively debate preceded the vote, and it was only passed by a majority of sixty-five to forty-five.

7   Poynings' Law (1494) stipulated that the Irish Parliament could neither be summoned nor legislate without the King's prior approval (see above, p. 20). Thus James, although amenable to the idea that the English *Parliament* could not bind Ireland, was reluctant to end Irish subordination to the English *Crown*. This is another instance of his staunch defence of the rights and powers of the Crown.

8   King became Bishop of Londonderry in 1691 and Archbishop of Dublin in 1703; Dopping was Bishop of Meath from 1682. Their writings are emblematic of Irish Protestant opinion in this period: see, especially, William King, *The State of the Protestants under the late King James Government* (1691), and the various printed sermons of Anthony Dopping. Although, thanks to William's effective military intervention, the Protestants emerged victorious in the war, they never felt entirely secure and continued to exhibit an edgy siege mentality thereafter.

9   For Jacobitism after 1690, see below, pp. 317, 329–30, 332.

12 Britain under William and Anne

1   See Tony Claydon, *William III and the Godly Revolution* (Cambridge, 1996).

2   These 'barrier fortresses' were Niewport, Courtrai, Oudenarde, Ath, Mons, Charleroi, Namur and Luxembourg.

3   See above, p. 7.

4   See below, p. 314.

5   G. V. Bennett, *The Tory Crisis in Church and State, 1688–1730: The Career of Francis Atterbury, Bishop of Rochester* (Oxford, 1975) is a splendid account not only of Atterbury's career but also of the High Church Tory principles that he upheld.

6   Geoffrey Holmes, *British Politics in the Age of Anne* (revised edition, London, 1987).

7   See above, pp. 257, 260.

8   See below, pp. 339–43.

13 1707: Union of the Kingdoms

1   See S. J. Connolly, *Religion, Law, and Power: The Making of Protestant Ireland, 1660–1760* (Oxford, 1992).

2   For the development of the strict settlement, see especially Lloyd Bonfield, *Marriage Settlements, 1601–1740: The Adoption of the Strict Settlement* (Cambridge, 1983).

Bibliographical Essay

It has long since proved quite impossible to offer anything resembling a comprehensive bibliography of seventeenth-century British history in a book of this kind. What follows makes no claim to completeness, nor even to indicate those works to which I am indebted, but rather to give a brief, personal guide to selected books and (more sparingly) articles in which the subject may be pursued further. The allocation of items to particular sections is inevitably somewhat arbitrary at times: cross-references are employed where necessary, and whenever a work is cited more than once a shortened version of the title is used. Works referred to in the endnotes are not invariably mentioned here as well, and this bibliographical essay should therefore be used in conjunction with the endnotes. It contains no work published after the end of March 1997.

1 General

Bibliographies

By far the fullest bibliography relating to British history in this period is found in the Royal Historical Society British Bibliographies Project, Volume 3 (1500–1700), ed. John Guy, Linda Levy Peck and David L. Smith. This is available on CD-ROM. The older *Bibliography of British History: Stuart Period, 1603–1714*, ed. G. Davies and M. F. Keeler (Oxford, 1970), is still worth consulting as it also identifies some of the more easily accessible primary sources. Two other bibliographies retain value because of their lively critical comments: G. R. Elton, *Modern Historians on British History, 1485–1945: A Critical Bibliography, 1945–1969* (New York, 1970); and J. S. Morrill, *Seventeenth-Century Britain, 1603–1714* (Folkestone, 1980).

Survey works

The most up-to-date single-volume surveys of seventeenth-century England are Barry Coward, *The Stuart Age: England, 1603–1714* (2nd edition, Harlow, 1994), a clear and judicious introduction, and Mark Kishlansky, *A Monarchy*

Transformed: Britain, 1603–1714 (Harmondsworth, 1996), a vivid and lively narrative. J. P. Kenyon, *Stuart England* (2nd edition, London, 1985), is elegant, intuitive and mildly idiosyncratic. *The Oxford Illustrated History of Tudor and Stuart Britain*, ed. John Morrill (Oxford, 1996), makes a great deal of recent research and debate easily accessible in a beautifully presented volume. Two books in Longman's Foundations of Modern Britain series cover this period and are especially helpful because of their full date-charts and compendia of information: A. G. R. Smith, *The Emergence of a Nation State: The Commonwealth of England, 1529–1660* (2nd edition, Harlow, 1997); and Geoffrey Holmes, *The Making of a Great Power: Late Stuart and Early Georgian Britain, 1660–1722* (Harlow, 1993). A subtle and sophisticated account of the first part of the century is found in Derek Hirst, *Authority and Conflict: England, 1603–1658* (London, 1986). This book's successor in Arnold's New History of England series, J. R. Jones, *Country and Court: England, 1658–1714* (London, 1978), is notable for its judiciousness and balance, although subsequent research has challenged much of its interpretative framework.

Collections of essays

Collections relating to specific themes and/or parts of the period will be covered in the relevant section below: here I will confine myself to a few works covering large portions of the period. These can be divided into two categories. First, several distinguished scholars have published collections of their own essays. The most prolific of these is Christopher Hill, whose immense output was seminal between the early 1950s and late 1970s but is now too often neglected. His *Collected Essays* (3 vols, Brighton, 1985–6) serve to remind us how much subsequent work, particularly on the history of society, religion and radicalism, owes to him. Another Oxford historian of staggering range and erudition was J. P. Cooper, and many of his essays, covering political, social and economic themes, were assembled in a posthumous collection, *Land, Men and Beliefs: Studies in Early-Modern History*, ed. G. E. Aylmer and J. S. Morrill (London, 1983). John Morrill's *The Nature of the English Revolution* (Harlow, 1993) presents a selection of his most important work which has proved highly influential in exploring the relationship between national and provincial politics; in seeing religious tensions as the single most important cause of the crisis that befell mid-seventeenth century Britain; and in urging the study of *British* – as distinct from *English* – history. A subtly different approach to the British dimension and to the significance of religion has characterized many of Conrad Russell's recent essays, collected in his *Unrevolutionary England, 1603–1642* (London, 1990). This volume also contains Russell's earlier pioneering pieces on the nature of politics, Parliaments and fiscal administration under the early Stuarts. Finally, there are many stimulating essays that challenge old orthodoxies and open up new interdisciplinary perspectives in Kevin Sharpe, *Politics and Ideas in Early Stuart England* (London, 1989).

Second, there are the *festschriften*, volumes of essays presented to leading scholars on their retirement. Christopher Hill's remarkable capacity to transcend traditional boundaries between political, religious, social and intellectual history was honoured in an appropriately diverse collection, *Puritans and Revolutionaries: Essays in Seventeenth-Century History presented to Christopher Hill*, ed. Donald Pennington and Keith Thomas (Oxford, 1978). Also valuable is *History and Imagination: Essays in Honour of H. R. Trevor-Roper*, ed. Hugh Lloyd-Jones, Valerie Pearl and Blair Worden (London, 1981) (especially the contributions by Kevin Sharpe and Blair Worden). Of more recent *festschriften*, perhaps the most important are *Public Duty and Private Conscience in Seventeenth-Century England: Essays presented to Gerald Aylmer*, ed. John Morrill, Paul Slack and Daniel Woolf (Oxford, 1993), particularly the essays by Keith Thomas, Kevin Sharpe, Conrad Russell and John Morrill; and *Political Culture and Cultural Politics in Early Modern England: Essays presented to David Underdown*, ed. Susan D. Amussen and Mark A. Kishlansky (Manchester, 1995), which includes a major reappraisal of Pym's role in the Long Parliament by John Morrill.

Printed primary sources

Again, more specific works will be discussed in the appropriate section below. Of those that cover longer periods, much the best starting-point is J. P. Kenyon, *The Stuart Constitution* (2nd edition, Cambridge, 1986), in which nearly 150 extracts of central importance are accompanied by a crisp and illuminating commentary. In addition, three older collections of political and constitutional documents remain very valuable: *Select Statutes and other Constitutional Documents illustrative of the Reigns of Elizabeth I and James I*, ed. G. W. Prothero (4th edition, Oxford, 1913); *Constitutional Documents of the Reign of James I*, ed. J. R. Tanner (Cambridge, 1930); and *The Constitutional Documents of the Puritan Revolution, 1625–1660*, ed. S. R. Gardiner (3rd edition, Oxford, 1906). For the latter part of the period *English Historical Documents, Volume 8: 1660–1714*, ed. Andrew Browning (London, 1953) is full and wide-ranging. Drier, but still useful, especially for statutes and judicial proceedings, is *The Law and Working of the Constitution: Documents, 1660–1914*, ed. W. C. Costin and J. Steven Watson, vol. 1 (London, 1952). *Divine Right and Democracy*, ed. David Wootton (Harmondsworth, 1986) is a lively anthology of English political writings throughout the century. It helpfully juxtaposes political thought in the strict sense with some key documents generated by the actual processes of politics.

Ann Hughes, *Seventeenth-Century England: A Changing Culture*, vol. 1 (London, 1980) offers a varied selection of extracts spanning political, religious and social themes. On religion and the Church, *Religion and Society in Early Modern England: A Sourcebook*, ed. David Cressy and Lori Anne Ferrell (London, 1996) is very useful. For economic history, *Seventeenth-Century Economic Documents*, ed. Joan Thirsk and J. P. Cooper (Oxford, 1972) is an extensive collection of sources, organized by topic.

A number of contemporary diaries and memoirs that give the flavour of the period are now conveniently available in abridged paperback editions. The following are especially recommended and afford a range of political, religious and social perspectives: *Clarendon: Selections from The History of the Rebellion and The Life by Himself*, ed. G. Huehns (Oxford, 1978); *The Autobiography of Richard Baxter*, ed. N. H. Keeble (London, 1931; revised edition, 1985); *The Diary of John Evelyn*, ed. John Bowle (Oxford, 1985); *The Illustrated Pepys*, ed. Robert Latham (London, 1978); and Bishop Gilbert Burnet, *History of His Own Time*, ed. Thomas Stackhouse (London, 1906; paperback edition, 1991). Richard Gough, *The History of Myddle*, ed. David Hey (Harmondsworth, 1981) presents an intimate portrait of a Shropshire parish written by a yeoman who lived there.

2 Government and Administration

Much the most authoritative introduction to Stuart government at both national and local levels is found in J. P. Kenyon's *The Stuart Constitution*, noted above. The monographic literature in this area is often very illuminating but also somewhat uneven in its coverage. The office-holders of central government are analysed in two magisterial books by Gerald Aylmer: *The King's Servants: The Civil Service of Charles I, 1625–1642* (London, 1961) and *The State's Servants: The Civil Service of the English Republic, 1649–1660* (London, 1973). On the central law courts and the legal profession, see W. J. Jones, *Politics and the Bench: The Judges and the Origins of the English Civil War* (London, 1971) and Wilfrid R. Prest, *The Rise of the Barristers: A Social History of the English Bar, 1590–1640* (Oxford, 1986).

We urgently need a general institutional study of Parliament during the seventeenth century. The existing literature is quite specialized and can mostly be divided into two categories. First, there is a lively debate over how members secured their seats in the Commons. Derek Hirst, *The Representative of the People? Voters and Voting in England under the Early Stuarts* (Cambridge, 1975) suggests that the electorate became steadily more difficult to control in parliamentary elections under the early Stuarts. Mark A. Kishlansky has advanced a cogent critique of Hirst in *Parliamentary Selection: Social and Political Choice in Early Modern England* (Cambridge, 1986), arguing that most members of the early seventeenth-century Commons were *selected* rather than elected, and that elections were very much the exception until the latter part of the century. Second, we have several excellent studies of specific aspects of parliamentary procedure, notably Sheila Lambert, 'Procedure in the House of Commons in the early Stuart period', *EHR*, 95 (1980); Colin G. C. Tite, *Impeachment and Parliamentary Judicature in Early Stuart England* (London, 1974); and E. R. Foster, *The House of Lords, 1603–1649: Structure, Procedure, and the Nature of its Business* (Chapel Hill, 1983). This last work demonstrates that the Lords were at least as important as the Commons in this period, a theme that is also central to James S. Hart's ground-breaking book *Justice upon Petition: The House of Lords and the Reformation of Justice, 1621–1675* (London, 1991) and Andrew Swatland's study *The House of Lords in the Reign of Charles II* (Cambridge, 1996).

On the financial aspects of government, the most significant developments are two books by M. J. Braddick: *Parliamentary Taxation in Seventeenth-Century*

England: Local Administration and Response (Woodbridge, 1994) and *The Nerves of State: Taxation and the Financing of the English State, 1558–1714* (Manchester and New York, 1996). Braddick shows how the English state was able gradually to increase the yield of public revenue during the course of the century, with the result that by 1700 parliamentary taxation had become the basis for public finance. In general, the workings of fiscal administration are more readily accessible for the years after 1660, thanks to the invaluable overview in Henry Roseveare, *The Financial Revolution, 1660–1760* (Harlow, 1991). Also fundamental are Roseveare's *The Treasury, 1660–1870: The Foundations of Control* (London, 1973), C. D. Chandaman, *The English Public Revenue, 1660–1688* (Oxford, 1975) and P. K. O'Brien and P. A. Hunt, 'The Rise of a Fiscal State in England, 1485–1815', *HR*, 66 (1993).

By far the fullest study of local government is Anthony Fletcher, *Reform in the Provinces: The Government of Stuart England* (New Haven and London, 1986). Much valuable information on this subject can also be gleaned from the numerous county studies: for a sample of some of the most important, see Andrew Coleby, *Central Government and the Localities: Hampshire, 1649–1689* (Cambridge, 1987); Anthony Fletcher, *Sussex, 1600–1660: A County Community in Peace and War* (London, 1975); Ann Hughes, *Politics, Society and the Civil War in Warwickshire, 1620–1660* (Cambridge, 1987); and J. S. Morrill, *Cheshire, 1630–1660: County Government and Society during the English Revolution* (Oxford, 1974).

3 Politics and Personalities

The most detailed history of English politics from 1603 to 1656 remains S. R. Gardiner's *History of England from the Accession of James I to the Outbreak of the Civil War, 1603–1642* (10 vols, London, 1883–4), *History of the Great Civil War, 1642–1649* (4 vols, London, 1893; reprinted 1987) and *History of the Commonwealth and Protectorate, 1649–1656* (4 vols, London, 1903; reprinted 1989). It has become conventional to criticize Gardiner for his 'Whig' perspective, but this is actually far less obtrusive than is often suggested. Much more striking is his astonishing gift for sustained narrative history, and the sheer depth and thoroughness of his great sequence of volumes give them enduring importance. The story was subsequently taken up to 1660 in C. H. Firth, *The Last Years of the Protectorate, 1656–1658* (2 vols, London, 1909) and Godfrey Davies, *The Restoration of Charles II* (London, 1955).

The political history of England before the Civil War continues to generate lively debate. Roger Lockyer's *The Early Stuarts: A Political History of England, 1603–1642* (Harlow, 1989) is a careful and lucid overview, although the sequence of the chapters is slightly confusing. A more thematic approach is adopted in Ann Hughes, *The Causes of the English Civil War* (London, 1991), which is useful for its interweaving of political, social and cultural issues. The diversity and complexity of recent research on this period is well illustrated by two collections of essays, both of which begin with valuable historiographical surveys: *Before the English Civil War*, ed. Howard Tomlinson (London, 1983) and *Conflict in Early Stuart England: Studies in Religion and Politics, 1603–1642*, ed. Richard Cust and Ann Hughes (Harlow, 1989).

We still lack a really authoritative biography of James VI and I. Of those currently available, the best is Maurice Lee, *Great Britain's Solomon: James VI and I in his Three Kingdoms* (Urbana, 1990), while S. J. Houston, *James I* (2nd edition, Harlow, 1995) and Christopher Durston, *James I* (London, 1993) both provide good introductions. James's reputation is at present undergoing considerable – though not uncritical – rehabilitation. A number of articles by Jenny Wormald have proved seminal in this respect, including 'James VI and I: Two Kings or One?', *History*, 68 (1983); 'Gunpowder, Treason and Scots', *JBS*, 24 (1985); and her chapters in *Uniting the Kingdom? The Making of British History*, ed. Alexander Grant and Keith J. Stringer (London, 1995); and *The British Problem, c. 1534–1707: State Formation in the Atlantic Archipelago*, ed. Brendan Bradshaw and John Morrill (London, 1996). Wormald is currently working on a major biography of the King. The vibrancy, eclecticism and essential tolerance of James's Court are captured in *The Mental World of the Jacobean Court*, ed. Linda Levy Peck (Cambridge, 1991). Also useful on the Court are *The English Court from the Wars of the Roses to the Civil War*, ed. David Starkey (London, 1987) and Neil Cuddy, 'Anglo-Scottish Union and the Court of James I, 1603–1625', *TRHS*, 5th series, 39 (1989). For other works on James's abortive attempts to secure a union of the kingdoms, see 'The British Problem: Scotland', below.

Much of the recent controversy surrounding early Stuart politics, particularly during the 1620s, has engaged with the work of Conrad Russell, especially his *Parliaments and English Politics, 1621–1629* (Oxford, 1979). His placing of Parliament within the wider political world, and his argument that it was a working institution which required a reasonable level of agreement in order to transact business, have set the terms of the debate. Some critics have argued, however, that such 'revisionism' underestimates the amount of principled conflict evident in the Parliaments of James VI and I and Charles I. Interpretations that, in varying degrees, run counter to some of Russell's original assertions may be found in the collection edited by Cust and Hughes, noted above; and also in such works as *Parliament and Liberty from the Reign of Elizabeth to the English Civil War*, ed. J. H. Hexter (Stanford, 1992) (particularly the essays by Clive Holmes and Thomas Cogswell); Richard Cust, *The Forced Loan and English Politics, 1626–1628* (Oxford, 1987); Thomas Cogswell, *The Blessed Revolution: English Politics and the Coming of War, 1621–1624* (Cambridge, 1989), and also Cogswell's article 'A Low Road to Extinction? Supply and Redress of Grievances in the Parliaments of the 1620s', *HJ*, 33 (1990) (the forerunner of a major book); and L. J. Reeve, *Charles I and the Road to Personal Rule* (Cambridge, 1989). Many of these contributions, by Russell and others alike, present Charles I as a less effective monarch than his father, and suggest that 1625 marked a significant shift in English (and British) political history.

Charles himself has eluded his biographers. Charles Carlton's *Charles I: the Personal Monarch* (2nd edition, London, 1995) is certainly the most successful biography, but the discussions of Charles's political persona in chapter six of

Reeve's *Charles I and the Road to Personal Rule*, noted above, and in the final chapter of Conrad Russell, *The Causes of the English Civil War* (Oxford, 1990) are probably more penetrating. Christopher W. Daniels and John Morrill, *Charles I* (Cambridge, 1988) provides a helpful introduction, built around a valuable selection of documents. Other recent and effective overviews are Brian Quintrell, *Charles I, 1625–1640* (Harlow, 1993) and Michael B. Young, *Charles I* (London, 1997). Roger Lockyer, *Buckingham* (London, 1981) paints a full but perhaps too sympathetic portrait of its subject. Kevin Sharpe, *The Personal Rule of Charles I* (New Haven and London, 1992) offers a massively researched and beautifully sustained panorama of England during the 1630s. Its great strength lies in presenting developments from Charles I's perspective; it is less effective in explaining why royal policies proved offensive to so many people and as a result it almost certainly underestimates the level of latent tension that existed by the end of the decade.

There are several first-rate surveys of the period 1640–60, of which the finest are probably G. E. Aylmer, *Rebellion or Revolution? England 1640–1660* (Oxford, 1986) and Ivan Roots, *The Great Rebellion, 1642–1660* (2nd edition, Stroud, 1995). Also excellent on the origins and course of the Civil War is Robert Ashton, *The English Civil War: Conservatism and Revolution, 1603–1649* (2nd edition, London, 1989). Howard Tomlinson and David Gregg, *Politics, Religion and Society in Revolutionary England, 1640–1660* (London, 1989) is a varied collection of documents with a good commentary.

There is a very helpful examination of the complex historiography relating to the outbreak of the Civil War in Glenn Burgess, 'On Revisionism: An Analysis of Early Stuart Historiography in the 1970s and 1980s', *HJ*, 33 (1990), a most judicious article that has the great merit of demonstrating that the competing interpretations are not necessarily mutually exclusive. Conrad Russell, *The Fall of the British Monarchies, 1637–1642* (Oxford, 1991), and Anthony Fletcher, *The Outbreak of the English Civil War* (London, 1981) give immensely detailed accounts of the crisis leading to Civil War: they are complementary and should be read alongside each other. Fletcher's book is especially effective on the years 1641–2, and on the relationship between national and provincial developments. Russell is stronger on 1638–41 and his arguments, which emphasize the importance of religious differences and of the British dimension, are synthesized in his *Causes of the English Civil War*. The themes of religious dysfunction and the British context are also perceptively explored in John Morrill's work, most readily accessible in *The Nature of the English Revolution*. A rather different approach, drawing out the role and attitudes of the nobility, is offered in J. S. A. Adamson, 'The Baronial Context of the English Civil War', *TRHS*, 5th series, 40 (1990). The contribution of social tensions in fuelling the conflict is explored in Brian Manning's *The English People and the English Revolution* (London, 1976) and *Aristocrats, Plebeians and Revolution in England, 1640–1660* (London, 1996); and also in David Underdown's *Revel, Riot and Rebellion: Popular Politics and Culture in England, 1603–1660* (Oxford, 1985) (for which see also the debate between Underdown and Morrill in *JBS*, 26 (1987)). It has to be said, however, that their persuasive evidence of cultural and social hostilities does not necessarily prove that these were a significant cause of *political* rifts or that they actually *determined* allegiances in the Civil War.

The impact of the war and the variety of responses to it are surveyed in two collections of essays edited by John Morrill: *Reactions to the English Civil War, 1642–1649* (London, 1982) and *The Impact of the English Civil War* (London, 1991). Morrill's *The Revolt of the Provinces: Conservatives and Radicals in the English Civil War, 1630–1650* (revised edition, Harlow, 1980) is still the most vivid analysis of how the two contrasting war efforts impinged upon the provinces. The experience of war in individual counties can also be traced in the many local studies, some of which are listed in section 2, above. Contrasting interpretations of the creation and political involvement of the New Model Army are presented in Mark Kishlansky, *The Rise of the New Model Army* (Cambridge, 1979) and Ian Gentles, *The New Model Army in England, Ireland and Scotland, 1645–1653* (Oxford, 1992). On the Royalist side, the recruitment and organization of the armies are analysed in Ronald Hutton, *The Royalist War Effort, 1642–1646* (Harlow, 1982). P. R. Newman, *The Old Service: Royalist Regimental Colonels and the Civil War, 1642–46* (Manchester, 1993) investigates the backgrounds and beliefs of the Royalist colonels, while David L. Smith, *Constitutional Royalism and the Search for Settlement, c. 1640–1649* (Cambridge, 1994) examines the political careers and ideological context of those moderate Royalists who urged the King to reach an 'accommodation' with Parliament. The finest account of the politics of the later 1640s – masterly in its integration of the worlds of Westminster, the army and the provinces – is David Underdown, *Pride's Purge: Politics in the Puritan Revolution* (Oxford, 1971). Austin Woolrych, *Soldiers and Statesmen: The General Council of the Army and its Debates, 1647–1648* (Oxford, 1987) is an excellent analysis of the Army's increasingly radical involvement in politics, while Robert Ashton, *Counter-Revolution: The Second Civil War and its Origins, 1646–8* (New Haven and London, 1994) provides a complementary perspective by focusing on the resurgence of provincial conservatism. These books, together with Patricia Crawford, 'Charles Stuart, that Man of Blood', *JBS*, 16 (1977), are essential for understanding the origins of the Regicide.

The following offer helpful and accessible introductions to the political history of the Interregnum: Austin Woolrych, *England without a King, 1649–1660* (London, 1983); Toby Barnard, *The English Republic* (Harlow, 1982); and Ronald Hutton, *The British Republic, 1649–1660* (London, 1990). There are many valuable essays on diverse aspects of the 1650s in *Revolution and Restoration: England in the 1650s*, ed. John Morrill (London, 1992) and *The Interregnum: The Quest for Settlement, 1646–1660*, ed. G. E. Aylmer (London, 1972). In general, the Protectorate has been less exhaustively researched than the Commonwealth, which is illuminated by two outstanding monographs: Blair Worden, *The Rump Parliament, 1648–53* (Cambridge, 1974) and Austin Woolrych, *Commonwealth to Protectorate* (Oxford, 1982).

The complex and enigmatic personality of Oliver Cromwell dominates this decade and has been the subject of innumerable biographies. The best recent studies are Barry Coward, *Oliver Cromwell* (Harlow, 1991) and Peter Gaunt, *Oliver Cromwell* (Oxford, 1996), although C. H. Firth, *Oliver Cromwell and the*

Rule of the Puritans in England (Oxford, 1900) retains considerable value as a narrative, and there are many perceptive insights in Christopher Hill, *God's Englishman: Oliver Cromwell and the English Revolution* (Penguin edition, Harmondsworth, 1972). The essays in *Oliver Cromwell and the English Revolution*, ed. John Morrill (Harlow, 1990) present a lively and penetrating reassessment of his personality. Three essays by Blair Worden are also of fundamental importance: 'Toleration and the Cromwellian Protectorate', in *Persecution and Toleration: Studies in Church History*, 21, ed. W. Shiels (Oxford, 1984); 'Oliver Cromwell and the Sin of Achan', in *History, Society and the Churches: Essays in Honour of Owen Chadwick*, ed. Derek Beales and Geoffrey Best (Cambridge, 1985); and 'Providence and Politics in Cromwellian England', *PP*, 109 (1985). Finally, two books offer convenient selections of primary sources: David L. Smith, *Oliver Cromwell: Politics and Religion in the English Revolution, 1640–1658* (Cambridge, 1991) prints 130 extracts from Cromwell and his contemporaries, together with an introduction and commentary, while his most important speeches and several intriguing conversations are handily available in *Speeches of Oliver Cromwell*, ed. Ivan Roots (London, 1989).

The fullest accounts of the disintegration of the Republic and the Restoration of Charles II are Austin Woolrych's book-length introduction to *The Complete Prose Works of John Milton*, vol. 7 (New Haven and London, 1980), and Ronald Hutton, *The Restoration: A Political and Religious History of England and Wales, 1658–1667* (Oxford, 1985). The best starting-points for the reign of Charles II as a whole are Robert W. Bliss, *Restoration England, 1660–1688* (London, 1985); John Miller, *Restoration England: The Reign of Charles II* (Harlow, 1985); and K. H. D. Haley, *Politics in the Reign of Charles II* (Oxford, 1985). *The Reigns of Charles II and James VII & II*, ed. Lionel K. J. Glassey (London, 1997) is an admirable collection. A more detailed introduction to the themes of Restoration politics can be found in Paul Seaward, *The Restoration, 1660–1688* (London, 1991). Tim Harris, *Politics under the Later Stuarts: Party Conflict in a Divided Society, 1660–1715* (London, 1993) is a stimulating investigation of Restoration politics and political culture. This is also true of the essays in *The Politics of Religion in Restoration England*, ed. Tim Harris, Paul Seaward and Mark Goldie (Oxford, 1990). Together, these last three books point towards a fundamental reinterpretation which integrates constitutional and religious issues and bridges the traditional gulf between elite and popular politics in the later Stuart period.

Charles II is in many ways as elusive a personality as his father. The most effective biographies are Ronald Hutton, *Charles II: King of England, Scotland and Ireland* (Oxford, 1989) and John Miller, *Charles II* (London, 1991). Two important articles by John Miller examine his political behaviour and conclude that he lacked the energy and single-mindedness needed to create anything resembling 'absolutism': 'Charles II and his Parliaments', *TRHS*, 5th series, 32 (1982); and 'The Potential for "Absolutism" in later Stuart England', *History*, 69 (1984). Paul Seaward, *The Cavalier Parliament and the Reconstruction of the Old Regime, 1661–1667* (Cambridge, 1989) is a fine study of the opening years of the reign, while the most detailed treatment of the period immediately afterwards remains Maurice Lee, *The Cabal* (Urbana, 1965). Our understanding of the Popish Plot and the Exclusion Crisis has been transformed by the work of Jonathan Scott, particularly *Algernon Sidney and the Restoration Crisis, 1677–1683* (Cambridge, 1991), 'Radicalism and Restoration', *HJ*, 31 (1988) and his essay in *The Politics of Religion in Restoration England*, ed. Harris et al. Scott sees the crisis as one of three 'crises of popery and arbitrary government' (the others being the Civil War and the Glorious Revolution), and argues that its strong affinities with the events of 1637–42 have been obscured by the supposed emergence of Whig and Tory 'parties'. This is an original and provocative thesis that sets the agenda for future debate, as the contributions in *Albion*, 25 (1993) have already demonstrated. Another important treatment of the Exclusion Crisis, which partially qualifies Scott's arguments, especially regarding the emergence of political 'parties', is Mark Knights, *Politics and Opinion in Crisis, 1678–81* (Cambridge, 1994).

On the reign of James VII and II, John Miller, *The Glorious Revolution* (Harlow, 1983), and Michael Mullett, *James II and English Politics, 1678–1688* (London, 1984) are good, clear introductions. Of the more detailed accounts, the finest is W. A. Speck, *Reluctant Revolutionaries: Englishmen and the Revolution of 1688–9* (Oxford, 1989). Speck's was one of many works spawned by the tercentenary of the Revolution of 1688–9 which have transformed the scholarly landscape in this area. A panorama of recent research can be gained from the essays in *Liberty Secured? Britain before and after 1688*, ed. J. R. Jones (Stanford, 1992); *The Revolution of 1688–89: Changing Perspectives*, ed. L. G. Schwoerer (Cambridge, 1992); *The Revolutions of 1688*, ed. R. Beddard (Oxford, 1991); *The Anglo-Dutch Moment: Essays on the Glorious Revolution and its World Impact*, ed. J. I. Israel (Cambridge, 1991); and *The World of William and Mary: Anglo-Dutch Perspectives on the Revolution of 1688–89*, ed. D. Hoak and M. Feingold (Stanford, 1996). The last two of these collections are valuable for placing the revolution in a European context. Among older works, J. R. Western, *Monarchy and Revolution: The English State in the 1680s* (London, 1972) is still worth reading, although its argument that royal policies of the 1680s formed a unified whole and that the revolution was the climax of a crisis that had begun with the Tory Reaction has been challenged by more recent work. The best biographies of James are F. C. Turner, *James II* (London, 1948), and John Miller, *James II: A Study in Kingship* (Hove, 1978). J. P. Kenyon, *Robert Spencer, Earl of Sunderland, 1641–1702* (London, 1958) is an outstanding life of a wily political survivor whose career spanned the reigns of Charles II, James II and William III.

Several of the works noted above also examine the years following the revolution – especially those edited by Jones and Schwoerer – but in recent years the political history of the Augustan Age has been less intensively worked on than the rest of the century. *Britain after the Glorious Revolution, 1689–1714*, ed. Geoffrey Holmes (London, 1969) remains an effective overview. A rich and colourful portrait of the age is found in Geoffrey Holmes, *Augustan England: Professions, State and Society, 1680–1730* (London, 1982). On the 1690s, the fullest (though not very readable) narrative is Henry Horwitz, *Parliament, Policy and Politics in the Reign of William III* (Manchester, 1977). A forthcoming account of this decade by Craig Rose is eagerly awaited. Tony Claydon, *William III and the Godly Revolution* (Cambridge, 1996) is an important and persuasive monograph that shows how Williamite propagandists used the theme of 'courtly reformation' to foster political unity and reinforce support for the wars against France. S. B. Baxter, *William III* (London, 1966) is still useful as a biography of William. A fresh evaluation of parliamentary politics is found in David Hayton, 'Moral reform and country politics in the late seventeenth century House of Commons', *PP*, 128 (1990). Angus McInnes, 'When was the English Revolution?', *History*, 67 (1982) is an interesting article that sees the 1690s as a political and constitutional watershed. The financial and economic impact of war is analysed in John Brewer, *The Sinews of Power: War, Money and the English State, 1688–1783* (London, 1989) and D. W. Jones, *War and Economy in the Age of William III and Marlborough* (Oxford, 1988).

On Anne's reign, the outstanding work is still Geoffrey Holmes, *British Politics in the Age of Anne* (revised edition, London, 1987), a magisterial study that sees the Whig–Tory dichotomy as the central feature of political life in the opening years of the eighteenth century. W. A. Speck, *Tory and Whig* (London, 1970) observes the same divide at work in local politics and elections. Speck has also given us a detailed overview of the decade in *The Birth of Britain: A New Nation, 1700–1710* (Oxford, 1994). Edward Gregg, *Queen Anne* (London, 1980) is a good, scholarly biography of the queen, while R. O. Bucholz, *The Augustan Court: Queen Anne and the Decline of Court Culture* (Stanford, 1993) charts the diminishing political significance of the later Stuart Court, despite Anne's efforts. The best overview of Jacobitism is Daniel Szechi, *The Jacobites, Britain and Europe, 1688–1788* (Manchester, 1994). Lastly, for works on the Anglo-Scottish Union of 1707 and its background, see 'The British Problem: Scotland', below.

4 Religion and the Church

Two good, up-to-date introductions are S. Doran and C. Durston, *Princes, Pastors and People: The Church and Religion in England, 1529–1689* (London, 1991) and Andrew Foster, *The Church of England, 1570–1640* (Harlow, 1994).

The history of the early Stuart Church has proved particularly controversial in recent years. *The Early Stuart Church, 1603–1642*, ed. Kenneth Fincham (London, 1993) provides a helpful guide to current views. The essay in this volume by Fincham and Peter Lake – together with their earlier article 'The Ecclesiastical Policy of King James I', *JBS*, 24 (1985) and Fincham's *Prelate as Pastor: The Episcopate of James I* (Oxford, 1990) – form the basis of a radical rehabilitation of James I's achievements as Supreme Governor, suggesting that he displayed considerable wisdom and skill in balancing the various strands of opinion within the Church and effectively defused religious debate for most of his reign. Also of central importance here are Patrick Collinson, *The Religion of Protestants: The Church in English Society, 1559–1625* (Oxford, 1982), and Peter Lake, *Anglicans and Puritans? Presbyterianism and English Conformist Thought from Whitgift to Hooker* (London, 1988).

Conversely, much recent research has emphasized how Charles I's backing of the Laudian programme disrupted this essentially stable situation. Nicholas Tyacke, *Anti-Calvinists: The Rise of English Arminianism, c. 1590–1640* (2nd edition, Oxford, 1990) has proved highly influential in this respect. Similar lines of argument are advanced in, for example, Peter Lake, 'Calvinism and the English Church, 1570–1635', *PP*, 114 (1987); in the essays by Tyacke and by Lake in the Fincham collection; in Andrew Foster's contribution to *Conflict in Early Stuart England*, ed. Cust and Hughes; and in J. S. McGee's essay in *Leaders of the Reformation*, ed. R. L. DeMolen (London and Toronto, 1984). Also indispensable, particularly on the distinction between Laudianism and Arminianism, is Hugh Trevor-Roper's essay on 'Laudianism and Political Power' in his *Catholics, Anglicans and Puritans* (London, 1987).

There have, however, been several vigorous challenges to this 'Tyackian consensus'. Julian Davies, *The Caroline Captivity of the Church: Charles I and the Remoulding of Anglicanism* (Oxford, 1992) is a provocative and not wholly convincing attempt to give the King primary responsibility for the religious policies of the 1630s and their destabilizing effects. In *The Personal Rule of Charles I*, Kevin Sharpe takes a similar view of Charles's role, but argues cogently that the Personal Rule was a period of creative reform in the Church and that Laudianism had a less polarizing effect than has often been supposed. Several other scholars have also stressed that the continuities before and after 1625 should not be underestimated, notably G. W. Bernard, 'The Church of England, *c.* 1529–*c.* 1642', *History*, 75 (1990); Peter White, 'The Rise of Arminianism Reconsidered', *PP*, 101 (1983); and also White's *Predestination, Policy and Polemic: Conflict and Consensus in the English Church from the Reformation to the Civil War* (Cambridge, 1992). Yet such arguments do not take full account of the growing body of evidence that Laudianism caused deep divisions and resentments, even if these were not always openly expressed. For this, see in particular the case studies cited on page 351–2, above. Anthony Milton, *Catholic and Reformed: The Roman and Protestant Churches in English Protestant Thought, 1600–1640* (Cambridge, 1995) is a subtle and intricate exploration of how the Roman and continental reformed Churches were perceived in early Stuart England that takes the debate to a new level of sophistication.

To emphasize the success of Laud's programme undoubtedly makes it very difficult to explain the intense hostility voiced against him when the Personal Rule collapsed. Much recent research has argued for the importance of religious tensions in precipitating the demise of the Stuart monarchies: see especially John Morrill, *The Nature of the English Revolution* and Conrad Russell, *Causes of the English Civil War* and *Fall of the British Monarchies*. Although this approach has not convinced everyone (see section 3, above), it has crucially shaped the terms of current debate. On the war years, chapter seven of Morrill's volume is much the fullest account of the resilience of the Church and the survival of 'folk Anglicanism', while Claire Cross's article in *The Interregnum*, ed. G. E. Aylmer, carries the story up to the Restoration. On the growth of religious radicalism during the 1640s and 1650s, F. D. Dow,

Radicalism in the English Revolution, 1640–1660 (Oxford, 1985) and *Radical Religion in the English Revolution*, ed. J. F. McGregor and B. Reay (Oxford, 1984) provide good introductions to recent research. The following studies are also important: J. C. Davis, *Fear, Myth and History: The Ranters and the Historians* (Cambridge, 1986) (for which see also the debate in *PP*, 129 (1990) and 140 (1993)); A. Morton, *The World of the Ranters* (London, 1970); Christopher Hill, *The World Turned Upside Down: Radical Ideas during the English Revolution* (London, 1972); and William Lamont, 'The Muggletonians, 1652–1979: A "Vertical" Approach', *PP*, 99 (1983).

The controversy surrounding the Restoration Church Settlement can be explored in the various works cited on pages 355–6. On the Restoration Church see John Spurr, *The Restoration Church of England, 1646–1689* (New Haven and London, 1991); I. M. Green, *The Re-establishment of the Church of England, 1660–1663* (Oxford, 1978); and *From Uniformity to Unity, 1662–1962*, ed. Geoffrey F. Nuttall and Owen Chadwick (London, 1962). The best introduction to the history of dissent is N. H. Keeble, *The Literary Culture of Nonconformity in Later Seventeenth-Century England* (Leicester, 1987). *Philosophy, Science and Religion in England, 1640–1700*, ed. Richard Kroll, Richard Ashcraft and Perez Zagorin (Cambridge, 1992) adopts a fruitful interdisciplinary approach to latitudinarianism, and locates that outlook in a long context that reaches back to the so-called Cambridge Platonists.

For the Church and religious life in the wake of the Glorious Revolution, see in particular Gordon Rupp, *Religion in England, 1688–1791* (Oxford, 1986); *From Persecution to Toleration: The Glorious Revolution and Religion in England*, ed. O. P. Grell, J. I. Israel and N. Tyacke (Oxford, 1991); and *The Church of England, c. 1689–c. 1833: From Toleration to Tractarianism*, ed. John Walsh, Colin Haydon and Stephen Taylor (Cambridge, 1993). The finest study of Tory Anglicanism remains G. V. Bennett, *The Tory Crisis in Church and State, 1688–1730: The Career of Francis Atterbury, Bishop of Rochester* (Oxford, 1975), while for the relationship between religious attitudes and party alignments between 1689 and 1714, see chapter eight of Geoffrey Holmes, *Politics, Religion and Society in England, 1679–1742* (London, 1986).

On popular religion, the outstanding work is Keith Thomas, *Religion and the Decline of Magic: Studies in Popular Beliefs in Sixteenth- and Seventeenth-Century England* (London, 1971). Also valuable is Patricia Crawford, *Women and Religion in England, 1500–1720* (London, 1993), a path-breaking reconstruction of the religious experiences and contributions of women in early modern England.

5 Society and Economy

Three helpful and complementary introductions to the social history of this period are Barry Coward, *Social Change and Continuity in Early Modern England, 1550–1750* (London, 1988); Keith Wrightson, *English Society, 1580–1680* (London, 1982); and J. A. Sharpe, *Early Modern England: A Social History, 1550–1760* (London, 1987).

On the social order, Lawrence Stone, *An Open Elite? England, 1540–1880* (Oxford, 1984) has proved both influential and controversial. Two more recent books provide excellent studies of particular social groups: *The Middling Sort of People: Culture, Society and Politics in England, 1550–1800*, ed. Jonathan Barry and Christopher Brooks (London, 1994) and Felicity Heal and Clive Holmes, *The Gentry in England and Wales, 1500–1700* (London, 1994).

The definitive history of English demographic patterns is E. A. Wrigley and R. S. Schofield, *The Population History of England, 1541–1871* (2nd edition, Cambridge, 1989). For a briefer and more accessible alternative which extends beyond England, see R. A. Houston, *The Population History of Britain and Ireland, 1550–1750* (2nd edition, Cambridge, 1995). Other useful studies, especially of the various factors that held population growth in check, are: A. B. Appleby, *Famine in Tudor and Stuart England* (Stanford, 1978); P. Slack, *The Impact of Plague in Tudor and Stuart England* (London, 1985); and *Famine, Disease and the Social Order in Early Modern Society*, ed. J. Walter and R. Schofield (Cambridge, 1989).

On the history of marriage, families and households, much recent debate has engaged with Lawrence Stone, *The Family, Sex and Marriage in England, 1500–1800* (London, 1977), a seminal book that argued that the early modern period saw a crucial shift from larger, loose-knit families to small, closely bonded, nuclear units. For a cross-section of works that in varying degrees challenge Stone's thesis, see *Marriage and Society: Studies in the Social History of Marriage*, ed. R. B. Outhwaite (London, 1981); R. A. Houlbrooke, *The English Family, 1450–1700* (Harlow, 1984); A. Macfarlane, *Marriage and Love in England: Modes of Reproduction, 1300–1840* (Oxford, 1986); and R. B. Outhwaite, *Clandestine Marriage in England, 1500–1850* (London, 1995).

There are several outstanding recent works on the position of – and attitudes towards – women, notably Amy Louise Erickson, *Women and Property in Early Modern England* (London, 1993); Anne Laurence, *Women in England, 1500–1760: A Social History* (London, 1994); *Women, Crime and the Courts in Early Modern England*, ed. J. Kermode and G. Walker (London, 1994); and Anthony Fletcher, *Gender, Sex and Subordination in England, 1500–1800* (New Haven and London, 1995). Between them, these books synthesize much disparate research and transform our understanding of gender roles and of women's experiences in this period.

There is a good general introduction to crime and punishment in J. A. Sharpe, *Crime in Early Modern England, 1550–1750* (Harlow, 1984). C. B. Herrup, *The Common Peace: Participation and the Criminal Law in Seventeenth-Century England* (Cambridge, 1986) examines attitudes towards law enforcement and the ways in which property holders participated in the legal process. On popular disturbances and uprisings, two collections of essays are important: *Rebellion, Popular Protest and the Social Order in Early Modern England*, ed. Paul Slack (Cambridge, 1984) and *Order and Disorder in Early Modern England*, ed. A. Fletcher and J. Stevenson (Cambridge, 1985). Keith Lindley, *Fenland Riots and the English Revolution* (London, 1982) is a valuable local study of popular disorder. An important and wide-ranging collection that explores how different social groups received and mediated ideas of authority is *The Experience of Authority in Early Modern England*, ed. Paul Griffiths, Adam Fox and Steve Hindle (London, 1996).

On popular culture, Keith Thomas, *Religion and the Decline of Magic* remains the classic work. *Popular Culture in Seventeenth-Century England*, ed. B. Reay (London, 1985) and *Popular Culture in England, c. 1500–1850*, ed. Tim Harris (London, 1995) give a good sense of the variety of more recent trends in research. Much the fullest treatment of witchcraft in this period is James Sharpe, *Instruments of Darkness: Witchcraft in England, 1550–1750* (London, 1996). There is a ground-breaking study of the religious and secular rituals that marked the passage of the year in Ronald Hutton, *The Rise and Fall of Merry England: The Ritual Year, 1400–1700* (Oxford, 1994); while Tessa Watt, *Cheap Print and Popular Piety, 1550–1640* (Cambridge, 1991) uses cheaply printed material to reconstruct popular culture. The clearest overview of the problem of poverty and provisions for the poor is Paul Slack, *Poverty and Policy in Tudor and Stuart England* (Harlow, 1988). R. B. Outhwaite, *Dearth, Public Policy and Social Disturbance in England, 1550–1800* (2nd edition, Cambridge, 1995) is a clear and authoritative introduction to government attempts to regulate economic and social life.

Much the best starting-points for the economic history of Stuart England are D. C. Coleman, *The Economy of England, 1450–1750* (Oxford, 1977) and C. G. A. Clay, *Economic Expansion and Social Change: England 1500–1700* (2 vols, Cambridge, 1984). On trends in wages and prices, R. B. Outhwaite, *Inflation in Tudor and Early Stuart England* (2nd edition, London, 1982) is invaluable. Joan Thirsk, *England's Agricultural Regions and Agrarian History, 1500–1750* (London, 1987) offers an excellent introduction to agrarian history, a subject that may be pursued more fully in volumes 4 and 5 of *The Agrarian History of England and Wales*, ed. Joan Thirsk (Cambridge, 1967–85). Some sense of the diversity of regional patterns and structures can be gained from two fine local studies by Keith Wrightson and David Levine: *Poverty and Piety in an English Village: Terling, 1525–1700* (2nd edition, Oxford, 1995), and *The Making of an Industrial Society: Whickham, 1560–1765* (Oxford, 1991). Helpful overviews of how domestic and overseas trade developed in this period are found in J. A. Chartres, *Internal Trade in England, 1500–1700* (London, 1977) and Ralph Davis, *English Overseas Trade, 1500–1700* (London, 1973). Robert Brenner, *Merchants and Revolution: Commercial Change, Political Conflict and London's Overseas Trade, 1550–1653* (Cambridge, 1993) is a bold but not entirely persuasive attempt to create a new social interpretation of the English Revolution couched in Marxist terms.

A fine introduction to urban history can be found in Sybil M. Jack, *Towns in Tudor and Stuart Britain* (London, 1996). Other helpful works on the social and economic development of towns are P. Clark and P. Slack, *English Towns in Transition, 1500–1700* (Oxford, 1976); *The Tudor and Stuart Town: A Reader in English Urban History, 1530–1688*, ed. Jonathan Barry (Harlow, 1990); and *The Transformation of English Provincial Towns, 1600–1800*, ed. Peter Clark (London, 1984). On the growing economic dominance of London, F. J. Fisher, *London and the English Economy, 1500–1700*, ed. P. J. Corfield and N. B. Harte (London, 1990) is invaluable. Also very useful is *London, 1500–1700: The*

Making of the Metropolis, ed. A. L. Beier and Roger Finlay (London, 1986).

Two lucid surveys of the development of industry in seventeenth-century England are D. C. Coleman, *Industry in Tudor and Stuart England* (London, 1975) and L. A. Clarkson, *Proto-Industrialization: The First Phase of Industrialization* (London, 1985). Finally, changing patterns of consumption and the growth of a 'consumer society' are charted in Joan Thirsk, *Economic Policy and Projects: The Development of a Consumer Society in Early Modern England* (Oxford, 1978) and *Consumption and the World of Goods*, ed. John Brewer and Roy Porter (London, 1993).

6 Intellectual and Cultural Life

There is a magisterial survey of political thought in this period in *The Cambridge History of Political Thought, 1450–1700*, ed. J. H. Burns and Mark Goldie (Cambridge, 1991), complete with a full bibliography and short biographies of the major theorists. *Political Discourse in Early Modern Britain*, ed. Nicholas Phillipson and Quentin Skinner (Cambridge, 1993) contains some very important essays. On the period prior to the Civil War, J. P. Sommerville, *Politics and Ideology in England, 1603–1640* (Harlow, 1986) is a masterly analysis of the relationship between political theory and practice. It should, however, be read in conjunction with two books by Glenn Burgess: *The Politics of the Ancient Constitution: An Introduction to English Political Thought, 1603–1642* (London, 1992) and *Absolute Monarchy and the Stuart Constitution* (New Haven and London, 1996). These are both subtle and nuanced studies which unravel how Charles I's policies disrupted the 'ideological consensus' that had existed before 1625. Burgess's discussion of the common law complements and extends that in J. G. A. Pocock's classic *The Ancient Constitution and the Feudal Law* (2nd edition, Cambridge, 1987). Many insights and interpretations that have since become normative were adumbrated in another seminal work: Margaret A. Judson, *The Crisis of the Constitution: An Essay in Constitutional and Political Thought in England, 1603–1645* (New Brunswick, 1949). Two books by Richard Tuck are valuable for locating English ideas within the context of European political theory: *Natural Rights Theories: Their Origin and Development* (Cambridge, 1979) and *Philosophy and Government, 1572–1651* (Cambridge, 1993).

There is a good introduction to the political thought of the 1640s in John Sanderson, *'But the People's Creatures': The Philosophical Basis of the English Civil War* (Manchester, 1989). Andrew Sharp, *Political Ideas of the English Civil Wars, 1641–1649* (Harlow, 1983) gives representative examples of the main strands of political theory that emerged during the decade of civil war, together with a commentary. An older survey that has still not been completely superseded is Perez Zagorin, *A History of Political Thought in the English Revolution* (London, 1954). More specific studies of contrasting strains of Parliamentarian thought and the variety of Royalist responses may be found in the chapters by Sommerville and Weston in *The Cambridge History of Political Thought*, ed. Burns and Goldie; C. C. Weston, *English Constitutional Theory and the House of*

Lords, 1556–1832 (London, 1965); Michael Mendle's essay in *Political Discourse*, ed. Phillipson and Skinner; and chapter seven of David L. Smith, *Constitutional Royalism and the Search for Settlement*. Good overviews of the political thought of the Levellers are G. E. Aylmer, *The Levellers in the English Revolution* (London, 1975) and David Wootton's essay in *The Cambridge History of Political Thought*, ed. Burns and Goldie.

The development of republican thought after the Regicide is best approached through Jonathan Scott's contributions to *Revolution and Restoration*, ed. Morrill, and *Political Discourse*, ed. Phillipson and Skinner; together with Blair Worden's essays in *Republicanism, Liberty, and Commercial Society, 1649–1776*, ed. David Wootton (Stanford, 1994). A vast literature surrounds the life and thought of Thomas Hobbes: perhaps the most accessible introductions – all with full bibliographies – are Richard Tuck, *Hobbes* (Oxford, 1989); Johann P. Sommerville, *Thomas Hobbes: Political Ideas in Historical Context* (London, 1992); *The Cambridge Companion to Hobbes*, ed. Tom Sorell (Cambridge, 1996); and Quentin Skinner, *Reason and Rhetoric in the Philosophy of Hobbes* (Cambridge, 1996).

The reception of Hobbes, and the range of Restoration political thought in general, is surveyed in Mark Goldie's chapters in *The Cambridge History of Political Thought*, ed. Burns and Goldie, and *The Reigns of Charles II and James VII & II*, ed. Glassey. Jonathan Scott's two books, *Algernon Sidney and the English Republic, 1623–1677* (Cambridge, 1988) and *Algernon Sidney and the Restoration Crisis* are crucial not only on the survival of the republican tradition but also on the nature of early Whig and Tory ideologies. The political thought of the closing decades of the century is dominated by the figure of John Locke, on whom good starting-points are James Tully's chapter in *The Cambridge History of Political Thought*, ed. Burns and Goldie; *The Cambridge Companion to Locke*, ed. Vere Chappell (Cambridge, 1994); *Locke's Philosophy*, ed. G. A. J. Rogers (Oxford, 1996); and Richard Ashcraft, *Revolutionary Politics and Locke's 'Two Treatises of Government'* (Princeton, 1986). Among recent monographs on Locke, possibly the most significant is John Marshall, *John Locke: Resistance, Religion and Responsibility* (Cambridge, 1994), which places his political, religious, social and moral ideas in their historical context.

The political thought directly associated with the events of 1688–9 and its aftermath is examined in many of the recent works on the revolution noted in section 3, above. Also of crucial importance are a number of other essays by Mark Goldie, most notably 'The Revolution of 1689 and the Structure of Political Argument', *Bulletin of Research in the Humanities*, 83 (1980); 'The Roots of True Whiggism, 1688–94', *History of Political Thought*, 1 (1980); and 'John Locke's Circle and James II', *HJ*, 35 (1992).

Several excellent works exist on science in seventeenth-century England. Charles Webster, *The Great Instauration: Science, Medicine and Reform, 1626–1660* (London, 1975) contextualizes medical and scientific ideas among a range of reforming projects intended to advance learning and extend humanity's control over the natural world. Some of Webster's arguments have been challenged, notably in A. R. Hall, *The Revolution in Science, 1500–1750* (London, 1983). The story after 1660 is told in Michael Hunter, *Science and*

Society in Restoration England (Cambridge, 1981). Several of the essays in *The Intellectual Revolution of the Seventeenth Century*, ed. Charles Webster (London, 1974) discuss the relationship between science and religion.

For cultural history, *The Cambridge Cultural History, vol. 4: Seventeenth-Century Britain*, ed. Boris Ford (Cambridge, 1992) provides a comprehensive introduction, including a very full bibliographical guide to all branches of the arts. Some of the most interesting research of recent years has explored the inter-relationship between cultural developments (especially in literature and the visual arts) and wider political, religious and social trends. Several collections of essays show how illuminating such an interdisciplinary approach can be, for example *Politics of Discourse: The Literature and History of Seventeenth-Century England*, ed. Kevin Sharpe and Steven N. Zwicker (Berkeley, 1987); *Culture and Politics in Early Stuart England*, ed. Kevin Sharpe and Peter Lake (London, 1994); *The Theatrical City: Culture, Theatre and Politics in London, 1576–1649*, ed. David L. Smith, Richard Strier and David Bevington (Cambridge, 1995); *Religion, Literature and Politics in Post-Reformation England, 1540–1688*, ed. Donna B. Hamilton and Richard Strier (Cambridge, 1996); and *The Stuart Court and Europe: Essays in Politics and Political Culture*, ed. R. Malcolm Smuts (Cambridge, 1996). A good example of the lively and fruitful debates that can ensue is the controversy over the plays, poems and masques produced during Charles I's Personal Rule, for which see Martin Butler, *Theatre and Crisis, 1632–1642* (Cambridge, 1984); Kevin Sharpe, *Criticism and Compliment: The Politics of Literature in the England of Charles I* (Cambridge, 1987); and *Theatre and Government under the Early Stuarts*, ed. J. R. Mulryne and M. Shewring (Cambridge, 1993). This area – and the relationship between politics and culture in general – will probably stimulate much further research in the years ahead.

7 Foreign Policy and War

Two books by J. R. Jones provide lucid introductions to British foreign policy in this period: *Britain and Europe in the Seventeenth Century* (London, 1966) and *Britain and the World, 1649–1815* (Brighton, 1980). The most important recent work in this area has focused on the Interregnum and early years of Charles II. In particular, three books have revised older interpretations of the three Anglo-Dutch wars by placing less emphasis on economic motives than on political attitudes and divisions within both Britain and the Dutch Republic: see Timothy Venning, *Cromwellian Foreign Policy* (London, 1995); Steven C. A. Pincus, *Protestantism and Patriotism: Ideologies and the Making of English Foreign Policy, 1650–1668* (Cambridge, 1996); and J. R. Jones, *The Anglo-Dutch Wars of the Seventeenth-Century* (London and New York, 1996).

The latter part of the century is examined in Jeremy Black, *A System of Ambition? British Foreign Policy, 1660–1793* (Harlow, 1991); and for the last part of the period there are some important essays in *William III and Louis XIV: Essays 1680–1720 by and for Mark A. Thomson*, ed. Ragnhild Hatton and J. S. Bromley (Liverpool, 1968).

On military affairs, the pre-Civil War militia is analysed in chapter nine of Fletcher, *Reform in the Provinces*. The finest military histories of the Civil Wars are John Kenyon, *The Civil Wars of England* (London, 1988) and P. Young and R. Holmes, *The English Civil War: A Military History of the Three Civil Wars, 1642–1651* (London, 1974). The experiences of ordinary soldiers in battle are vividly evoked in Charles Carlton, *Going to the Wars: The Experience of the British Civil Wars, 1638–1651* (London, 1992). John Childs examines the development of the army after 1660 in three very sound volumes that also contain much of value on war and diplomacy: *The Army of Charles II* (London, 1976), *The Army, James II and the Glorious Revolution* (Manchester, 1980) and *The British Army of William III, 1689–1702* (Manchester, 1987). J. R. Jones, *Marlborough* (Cambridge, 1993) places a distinguished military career in its social, political and international contexts. On naval affairs, Paul Kennedy, *The Rise and Fall of British Naval Mastery* (London, 1976) remains unsurpassed.

8 The British Problem

General

Among the most significant historiographical developments of the last few years has been the recognition that England formed part of a composite monarchy, and that English developments can only be fully understood within a wider British context. For too long, the historiographies of Wales, Ireland and Scotland have remained discrete, and even now the construction of a genuinely British history is still in its early stages. However, five recent collections of essays point the way towards a more integrated approach for this period as a whole: *Three Nations – a Common History? England, Scotland, Ireland and British History, c. 1600–1920*, ed. Ronald G. Asch (Bochum, 1993); *Conquest and Union: Fashioning a British State 1485–1725*, ed. Steven G. Ellis and Sarah Barber (Harlow, 1995); *Uniting the Kingdom? The Making of British History*, ed. Alexander Grant and Keith J. Stringer (London, 1995); *The British Problem, c. 1534–1707: State Formation in the Atlantic Archipelago*, ed. Brendan Bradshaw and John Morrill (London, 1996); and *Celtic Dimensions of the British Civil Wars*, ed. John R. Young (Edinburgh, 1997).

Wales

The history of Wales remains seriously understudied. Good introductions to the present state of knowledge are found in Philip Jenkins, *A History of Modern Wales, 1536–1990* (Harlow, 1992) and J. Gwynfor Jones, *Early Modern Wales, c. 1525–1640* (London, 1994). Two excellent volumes in the Oxford History of Wales provide more detailed accounts: Glanmor Williams, *Recovery, Reorientation and Reformation, c. 1415–1642* (Oxford, 1987) and Geraint H. Jenkins, *The Foundations of Modern Wales: Wales, 1642–1780* (Oxford, 1987). There is a useful survey of Wales in the opening decades of the seventeenth century in G. Dynfallt Owen, *Wales in the Reign of James I* (Woodbridge, 1988). We badly need more local studies, especially on central and northern Wales: the finest of those currently available are Howell A. Lloyd, *The Gentry of South-West Wales, 1540–1640* (Cardiff, 1968) and Philip Jenkins, *The Making of a Ruling Class: The Glamorgan Gentry, 1640–1790* (Cambridge, 1983).

Scotland

Michael Lynch, *Scotland: A New History* (London, 1991) provides an efficient single-volume history. There are clear and straightforward introductions to this period in Jenny Wormald, *Court, Kirk and Community: Scotland 1460–1625* (London, 1981) and Rosalind Mitchison, *Lordship to Patronage: Scotland 1603–1745* (London, 1983). Keith Brown, *Kingdom or Province? Scotland and the Regal Union, 1603–1715* (London, 1992) is a lively, challenging and up-to-date account. Older, but still informative, is Gordon Donaldson, *Scotland: James V to James VII* (Edinburgh, 1965).

On the reign of James VI and I, Maurice Lee, *Government by Pen: Scotland under James VI and I* (Urbana, 1980) offers a detailed and readable narrative. All previous accounts of James's attempt to secure a union of the kingdoms have been superseded by Bruce Galloway, *The Union of England and Scotland, 1603–1608* (Edinburgh, 1986). Three articles by Jenny Wormald are also valuable: her essays in *The British Problem*, ed. Bradshaw and Morrill, and *Uniting the Kingdom?*, ed. Grant and Stringer; and 'The Creation of Britain: Multiple Kingdoms or Core and Colonies?', *TRHS*, 6th series, 2 (1992). *Scots and Britons: Scottish Political Thought and the Union of 1603*, ed. Roger A. Mason (Cambridge, 1994) is an important collection that locates attitudes towards the union of 1603 in the context of late sixteenth and early seventeenth-century Scottish political thought and also explores Scotland's subsequent problems of identity and self-definition within the regal union. Brian P. Levack, *The Formation of the British State: England, Scotland and the Union, 1603–1707* (Oxford, 1987) analyses different aspects of union (political union, religious union, economic union, etc.) and considers changing attitudes towards them during the course of the century.

Maurice Lee, *The Road to Revolution: Scotland under Charles I, 1625–1637* (Urbana, 1985) is a full and reliable narrative of the reign of Charles I. The contrasts between Charles's rule and that of his father are discussed in the articles by John Morrill and Conrad Russell in *Religion, Culture and Society in Early Modern Britain: Essays in Honour of Patrick Collinson*, ed. A. Fletcher and P. Roberts (Cambridge, 1994). Charles's Scottish policies and the growth of opposition to them form the subject of Allan I. MacInnes, *Charles I and the Making of the Covenanting Movement, 1625–1641* (Edinburgh, 1991). The collapse of Charles's rule in Scotland has been persuasively set within a British context in such recent works as Russell's *Causes of the English Civil War* and *Fall of the British Monarchies*, and *The Scottish National Covenant in its British Context*, ed. John Morrill (Edinburgh, 1990). Scottish history during the 'war of the three kingdoms' is recounted in David Stevenson's *The Scottish Revolution, 1637–1644* (Newton Abbott, 1973) and *Revolution and Counter-*

Revolution in Scotland, 1644–1651 (London, 1977). Two other books by Stevenson are useful for their exploration of Scottish–Irish relations in the mid-seventeenth century: *Alasdair MacColla and the Highland Problem in the Seventeenth Century* (Edinburgh, 1980) and *Scottish Covenanters and Irish Confederates: Scottish-Irish Relations in the Mid-Seventeenth Century* (Belfast, 1981). Much the most detailed account of Scotland during the Interregnum is F. D. Dow, *Cromwellian Scotland, 1651–1660* (Edinburgh, 1979).

A good introduction to Scottish history from the Restoration to the Union of 1707 is provided by Mark Goldie's essay in *The British Problem*, ed. Bradshaw and Morrill. Two books by Julia Buckroyd, *The Life of James Sharp, Archbishop of St Andrews, 1618–1679* (Edinburgh, 1987) and *Church and State in Scotland, 1660–1681* (Edinburgh, 1980), are illuminating on political as well as religious affairs, while the experience of Scottish dissenters is persuasively reconstructed in Ian B. Cowan, *The Scottish Covenanters, 1660–1688* (London, 1976). On the revolution of 1688–89 in Scotland, Cowan's essays in *The Anglo-Dutch Moment*, ed. Israel, and *By Force or by Default? The Revolution of 1688–1689*, ed. E. Cruickshanks (Edinburgh, 1989) are indispensable, as are Bruce Lenman's contributions to *The Revolution of 1688–89*, ed. Schwoerer, and *The Revolutions of 1688*, ed. Beddard. C. Halliday, 'The Club and the Revolution in Scotland, 1689–90', *ScHR*, 45 (1966) is still of value.

The thrust of recent research on the Union of 1707 has been to stress that the final outcome was far from inevitable. An excellent overview of the historiography can be found in Christopher A. Whatley, *'Bought and Sold for English Gold'? Explaining the Union of 1707* (Glasgow, 1994). Particularly important contributions are P. W. J. Riley, *The Union of England and Scotland: A Study of Anglo-Scottish Politics in the Early Eighteenth Century* (Manchester, 1978); T. C. Smout's essay in *Britain after the Glorious Revolution*, ed. Holmes; and Paul Henderson Scott, *Andrew Fletcher and the Treaty of Union* (Edinburgh, 1992). The intellectual context of the Union is examined in *A Union for Empire: Political Thought and the British Union of 1707*, ed. John Robertson (Cambridge, 1995), while Colin Kidd, *Subverting Scotland's Past: Scottish Whig Historians and the Creation of an Anglo-British Identity, 1689–c. 1830* (Cambridge, 1993) is an outstanding study of the impact of the Union on Scottish culture and identity.

Ireland

In general, the rich and varied historiography of sixteenth-century Ireland becomes somewhat thinner for the following century. The essays in *A New History of Ireland, Volume 3: Early Modern Ireland, 1534–1691*, ed. T. W. Moody, F. X. Martin and F. J. Byrne (2nd edition, Oxford, 1991) provide an authoritative overview. Briefer, but lucid and informative, is R. F. Foster, *Modern Ireland, 1600–1972* (London, 1988). Brendan Fitzpatrick, *Seventeenth-Century Ireland: The War of Religions* (Dublin, 1988) is penetrating on the religious ideas and tensions of the period. The best introduction to the economic history of early modern Ireland is Raymond Gillespie, *The Transformation of the Irish Economy, 1550–1700* (Dublin, 1991).

The plantation of Ulster during the early seventeenth century is examined in Raymond Gillespie, *Colonial Ulster: The Settlement of East Ulster, 1600–1641* (Cork, 1985) and Philip S. Robinson, *The Plantation of Ulster: British Settlement in an Irish Landscape, 1600–1670* (Dublin, 1984). Alan Ford, *The Protestant Reformation in Ireland, 1590–1641* (Frankfurt, 1985) explores the problems that confronted the Church of a Protestant minority amidst a Catholic majority. *The Political World of Thomas Wentworth, Earl of Strafford, 1621–1641*, ed. J. F. Merritt (Cambridge, 1996) reappraises Strafford's career within an archipelagic context, while two other books on Ireland under Charles I are also fundamental and complementary: Aidan Clarke, *The Old English in Ireland, 1625–1642* (London, 1966) and Hugh Kearney, *Strafford in Ireland, 1633–41: A Study in Absolutism* (2nd edition, Cambridge, 1989).

There is an excellent collection of essays on the period from the 1641 rebellion to the Restoration in *Ireland from Independence to Occupation, 1641–1660*, ed. Jane H. Ohlmeyer (Cambridge, 1995). Contrasting interpretations of the rebellion and its impact on England and Scotland can be found in chapter fifteen of Russell's *Unrevolutionary England*; Aidan Clarke's essay in *Plantation to Partition: Essays in Ulster History in Honour of J. L. McCracken*, ed. P. Roebuck (Belfast, 1981); *Ulster, 1641: Aspects of the Rising*, ed. Brian Mac Cuarta (Belfast, 1993); Michael Perceval-Maxwell, *The Outbreak of the Irish Rebellion of 1641* (Dublin, 1994); Jane H. Ohlmeyer, *Civil War and Restoration in the Three Stuart Kingdoms: The Career of Randal MacDonnell, Marquis of Antrim, 1609–1683* (Cambridge, 1993); and the debate between Perceval-Maxwell and Ohlmeyer cited on page 352, note 7. The effects of the rebellion on the mainland are also analysed in Keith Lindley, 'The Impact of the 1641 Rebellion upon England and Wales, 1641–5', *IHS*, 18 (1972). Further useful material on Ireland during the war of the three kingdoms is found in Michael Perceval-Maxwell's essay in *The Scottish National Covenant in its British Context*, ed. Morrill, and the two books on Scottish–Irish relations by David Stevenson noted above.

Stevenson's essay in *Oliver Cromwell and the English Revolution*, ed. Morrill, is a succinct introduction to Cromwellian policy towards Ireland. Karl S. Bottigheimer, *English Money and Irish Land: The 'Adventurers' in the Cromwellian Settlement of Ireland* (Oxford, 1971) remains much the fullest account of the land transfers of the 1650s; while the regime's largely unsuccessful attempts at ecclesiastical, educational, legal and administrative reform are the subject of T. C. Barnard, *Cromwellian Ireland: English Government and Reform in Ireland, 1649–1660* (Oxford, 1975).

There are concise surveys of Restoration Ireland in Barnard's contribution to *Conquest and Union*, ed. Ellis and Barber, and Smyth's essay in *The British Problem*, ed. Bradshaw and Morrill. For a more detailed account, see Sean Connolly, *Law, Religion and Power: The Making of Protestant Ireland, 1660–1760* (Oxford, 1992). The Settlement itself is assessed in K. Bottigheimer, 'The Restoration Settlement in Ireland: A Structural View', *IHS*, 18 (1972). T. C. Barnard, 'Crises of Identity among Irish Protestants, 1641–1685', *PP*, 127 (1990) reconstructs the development of an Anglo-Irish identity during the later seventeenth century.

Our understanding of the events of 1688–91 in Ireland, and their implications for subsequent Irish history, has benefited greatly from the recent flurry of works marking the tercentenary of the revolution. Of particular importance are the essays by David Hayton in *The Anglo-Dutch Moment*, ed. Israel; Karl Bottigheimer in *The Revolution of 1688–89*, ed. Schwoerer; and Patrick Kelly in *The Revolutions of 1688*, ed. Beddard. The background to the revolution is also investigated in John Miller, 'The Earl of Tyrconnel and James II's Irish Policy, 1685–1688', *HJ*, 20 (1977). The finest treatment of the period after 1691 is provided by the essays in *A New History of Ireland, Volume 4: Eighteenth-Century Ireland, 1691–1800*, ed. T. W. Moody and W. E. Vaughan (Oxford, 1986).

Appendix 1:
Glossary

Note: Words in italics denote terms that are themselves defined in this glossary.

Advowson The right to choose the clergyman to occupy a parish living. Advowsons were usually held by laymen, and were regarded as a form of property that could be bought or sold or rented out.

Anabaptists A sect that originated in Germany and the Low Countries during the sixteenth century. They believed in adult rather than infant baptism and were associated with a fundamentalist form of Protestantism. 'Anabaptist' became a term of abuse used against radical *Puritans*.

Antinomianism The belief that those who were destined to attain salvation could not sin, and were therefore freed from conventional moral law.

Arminians Those accused of espousing the beliefs of the Dutch theologian Jacobus Arminius, who emphasized the role of free will in attaining salvation and opposed the *Calvinist* doctrine of predestination.

Assessment A land tax, introduced by the Houses of Parliament in February 1643. It was levied weekly (later monthly) at a rate roughly equivalent to a parliamentary *subsidy* every fortnight.

Assizes Courts held twice yearly in each county by royal judges travelling in pairs on circuit round England. These courts came to deal with most kinds of *felony*.

Attainder An Act of Parliament declaring an individual guilty of treason or some other *felony* without the requirement of a formal trial.

Baptists A sect whose members believed in adult rather than infant baptism. They separated from the Church of England and preached that only those who joined their Church through adult baptism, and were thus 'born again', could attain salvation.

Benevolences (or Free Gifts) Levies, raised by English monarchs in national emergencies. They were raised under *prerogative* powers and payment was voluntary (although informal pressure was sometimes exerted to persuade subjects to pay). The meagre yield of the Benevolence of 1626 led Charles I to levy a Forced Loan, payment of which was compulsory.

Bond of manrent Form of agreement, common in late medieval and early modern Scotland, whereby lords and their men bound themselves to serve and protect each other.

Books of Orders The monarch and *Privy Council* published these at various times between the 1570s and the 1630s, usually during crises such as dearth or plague. They were issued to *Justices of the Peace* and consisted of sets of instructions about how to resolve particular problems. The 1631 Book of Orders introduced the requirement that the Justices report back to the *Privy Council* about their activities.

Books of Rates These contained the official valuations of items that were liable to *customs* duties. Most goods paid a fixed sum, or a percentage of their nominal value, with the result that customs duties failed to keep pace with inflation. In 1608, Salisbury issued a new Book of Rates – the first since 1558 – which extended *impositions* to most imports and increased the rates of payment. Another Book of Rates increased duties still further in 1635.

Book of Sports Originally issued by James VI and I in 1618 to legalize morris dancing and other sports and recreations after divine service on Sundays. It was reissued by Charles I in 1633 when, especially in the context of *Laudian* reforms, it was widely perceived as an attack on the *Puritan* ideal of the sabbath.

Brehon law Customary form of law and legal practice used among the Gaelic Irish. It was gradually supplanted by the English common law and had largely disappeared by the mid-seventeenth century.

Brownists A group of late Elizabethan *separatists*, led by Robert Browne, who eventually emigrated to the Netherlands. The name was often used as an all-purpose term of abuse for radical *Puritans*.

Calvinism The doctrine based on the ideas of John Calvin, the Genevan theologian. He particularly emphasized predestination, the belief that some people (the 'elect') are chosen by God to attain salvation whereas others (the 'reprobate') are foreordained to be damned. Calvinists also believed that the Bible contained everything needed for salvation, and they vehemently opposed the imagery and ritual associated with Catholicism.

Charivari A festive procession to mock unpopular persons in a local community, such as cuckolds or domineering wives. It was accompanied by a 'serenade' of rough music, made with kettles, pans and other household implements. These rituals were also sometimes called skimmingtons, especially in the south and west of England.

Clarendon Code The name later applied, somewhat misleadingly, to the body of legislation enacted between 1662 and 1665 to penalize those who refused to conform to the Church of England or who attended unauthorized services. In fact, Clarendon initially tried to moderate such penal laws, and only accepted them reluctantly.

Coat-and-conduct Money A levy that the Crown could raise by royal *prerogative* powers in time of war and use to provide clothing and other supplies for soldiers.

Commendam The Crown possessed an ancient right to grant a clergyman an additional benefice (or *commendam*) that happened to fall vacant. James VI and I's determination to be consulted in such cases brought him into conflict with Chief Justice Coke, who saw this as an encroachment on the powers of the *common law* judges.

Commissions of Array A royal commission to raise troops. Originally devised by Edward I and enshrined in a statute of 1405, it fell into disuse under the Tudors. Charles I revived it in the summer of 1642 because it enabled him to raise soldiers by royal *prerogative*.

Common law The system of precedent and custom which formed the basis of English criminal law and much civil law. It could be changed only by Acts of Parliament.

Comprehension The belief that the doctrines and practices of the Church of England should be broad enough to enable as many people as possible to be members of it.

Congregationalists See *Independents*.

Conventicles Illegal religious meetings or assemblies, especially those held by Protestant *nonconformists* after the Restoration.

Convocation An assembly of clergy that met at the same time as Parliament. Within the Church of England there was a convocation for each of the two 'provinces', Canterbury and York. The former was the more important, and was often referred to simply as 'Convocation'.

Court Baron A manorial court comprising *freehold* tenants and held in the presence of the lord of the manor or his steward. The Court Baron could adjudicate cases of debt and trespass, and decide agricultural practices within the manor.

Cuius regio, eius religio The principle, established at the Peace of Augsburg in 1555, that the religion of a particular ruler should determine the religion of the State which he or she ruled.

Customs Duties levied by the Crown on imports according to rates laid down in the *Book of Rates*. Parliament traditionally granted these revenues to the monarch at the beginning of each reign.

Diggers (or True Levellers) An off-shoot of the *Leveller* movement that emerged at the end of the 1640s under the leadership of Gerrard Winstanley. They believed in common ownership of property and set up a number of colonies on waste or common land during 1649–50. However, they never numbered more than a few hundred and their experiments in communal landownership proved to be short-lived.

Dissenters Usually applied to those Protestants who refused to conform to the practices and discipline of the established Church; often also referred to as *Nonconformists*.

Durante bene placito Literally, 'during [the King's] good pleasure'. Commissions issued to judges *durante bene placito* meant that the monarch could dismiss them at will. Such commissions were last issued during the reign of James VII and II.

Enclosure The hedging or fencing off of open or common fields which had been farmed communally during the Middle Ages and dividing them into individual holdings. The practice was usually intended either to consolidate smallholdings or to substitute sheep farming for arable or common grazing rights.

Erastianism The belief that the laity and the secular State should exercise control over matters of religion.

Excise A sales tax, introduced by the Houses of Parliament in July 1643. It was imposed on such vital commodities as beer, meat and salt, and extended to more and more products during the course of the Civil Wars. Although widely unpopular, it was retained after the Restoration.

Extraordinary revenue Tax revenue granted to the Crown by Parliament from time to time to meet a special need, such as a war or some other national emergency. The principal forms of parliamentary taxation were the *Subsidy* and *Fifteenths and Tenths*.

Felonies Crimes that carried the death penalty.

Feoffees for Impropriations A group of laity and clergy established in 1625 to buy back impropriated tithes and use them to augment the stipends of lecturers. Laud regarded them – and the lecturers they supported – as *Puritans*, and secured their abolition by the Court of Exchequer in 1633.

Fifteenths and Tenths A form of parliamentary taxation, first introduced in the fourteenth century. It was levied on land and movable property, and became increasingly burdensome for smaller landowners.

Fifth Monarchists A millenarian sect which emerged in the wake of the Regicide. They believed that the four great empires of Babylon, Persia, Greece and Rome would shortly be followed by the Fifth Monarchy in which King Christ would rule on earth with his saints for a thousand years culminating in the Day of Judgement. They consisted mainly of labourers, servants, apprentices and journeymen in the urban areas of southern England, and they never numbered more than 10,000 at the very most.

Forced Loans Levies, raised from the mid-fifteenth century by English monarchs in national emergencies. They were raised under *prerogative* powers and then retrospectively turned into taxes by Parliament, but Charles I's loan of 1627 proved extremely controversial.

Forest fines As a way of raising revenue, from the summer of 1634 onwards Charles I sought to reassert the medieval boundaries of royal forests, and to fine landowners whose estates had inadvertently encroached upon them.

Freeholders People who held land in freehold. This meant that they held their land for life, paid little or no rent, and were generally free to use or sell it as they pleased.

General Assembly The governing body of the Scottish Kirk. It consisted of ministers and lay elders elected by the local *presbyteries*.

Great Council A term sometimes applied to a full assembly of peers; during the Middle Ages, such assemblies were at times afforced by representatives of the shires and boroughs to form what became known as Parliaments. As a result, 'Great Council' was also sometimes used as an alternative name for Parliament.

Habeas Corpus A writ requiring an imprisoned person to be brought to trial. The Habeas Corpus Amendment Act of 1679 required prisoners to be brought to trial, and the cause of their imprisonment stated, within a specified period of time. The Act also made it illegal to evade writs of *habeas corpus* by moving prisoners from one prison to another, or by detaining them 'beyond the seas', for example in the Channel Islands, or in Scotland or Ireland.

High Commission A court to hear ecclesiastical cases set up during Elizabeth I's reign. This was the only Church court allowed to impose fines or imprisonment. It became unpopular as an instrument for enforcing *Laudian* policies during the 1630s, and was abolished in 1641.

Hostile laws The diffuse body of legislation that restricted trade, aid and communication across the border between England and Scotland. These laws had grown up on an *ad hoc* basis during times of conflict since the Middle Ages, and were repealed in May 1607.

Huguenots French *Calvinists*. King Henri IV of France had granted them extensive civil and religious rights in the Edict of Nantes (1598). When Louis XIV revoked this edict in 1685, somewhere between 50,000 and 80,000 Huguenots fled to England to escape persecution.

Husbandmen Small farmers of similar status to, but less substantial than, *yeomen*. They generally farmed less than fifty acres.

Impeachment A trial in Parliament in which the Commons acted as prosecutors and the Lords as judges. It fell into disuse after 1459 but was revived in 1621.

Impositions Additional duties on imports, imposed by royal *prerogative* powers, and charged over and above the *customs* granted to the Crown at the beginning of each reign. The Crown's right to levy them was upheld in Bate's Case (1606), but remained a cause of controversy.

Independents Those Protestants who opposed a coercive national Church, and believed that each congregation should be independent and free to organize its own style of worship. They advocated a wide measure of toleration for religious radicals. Independents were also sometimes called Congregationalists.

Jacobites Those who supported James VII and II and his descendants after the revolution of 1688–9 and wished to see them restored to the throne.

Justices of the Peace Commissioners appointed by the Crown in each county to administer justice and to implement a wide range of social and economic legislation.

King's Evil The name often given to scrofula, the tubercular inflammation of the lymph glands in the neck. From the reign of Edward the Confessor it was widely believed that English monarchs had the ability to heal this affliction by touch, in a ceremony known as 'touching for the King's Evil'.

Knighthood fines In January 1630 Charles I appointed a commission to fine those who owned *freehold* land worth £40 a year, and were thus eligible for knighthood, but who had ignored the sixteenth-century precedents requiring them to present themselves to be knighted at the King's coronation. The practice was declared illegal in 1641.

Lairds The large and diverse category of Scottish landowners immediately beneath the nobility. They numbered perhaps as many as 10,000, but only around 1,500 owned really extensive estates. The rest, sometimes called 'bonnet lairds', were relatively small landowners who were mostly less substantial than English gentry and more akin to *yeomen*.

Latitudinarians Those churchmen in the later seventeenth century who favoured a broad, comprehensive Church which eschewed dogma, made relatively few demands in terms of doctrine or discipline, and accommodated as many people within it as possible. See also *comprehension*.

Laudian The beliefs and practices associated with Archbishop William Laud, who emphasized clericalism, ceremonialism and the 'beauty of holiness'. His commitment to the priesthood and the sacraments brought him into conflict with *Calvinists* who stressed the importance of the sermon and detested 'idolatry'.

Levellers A group of pamphleteers, of whom the most prominent were John Lilburne, Richard Overton and William Walwyn. Especially active between 1645 and 1649, they advocated radical and wide-ranging reforms including religious toleration, abolition of the monarchy and the Lords, universal male suffrage and a drastic reduction in taxation. Their influence extended to the army, particularly during the years 1647–9.

Lords of the Articles The inner committee, consisting of the chief officers of state and representatives from all the estates, that drew up the agenda of the Scottish Parliament. From 1612 the monarch had effective control over the selection of the committee. It was abolished in 1641, revived in 1663, and finally abolished in 1690.

Lords Lieutenant Royal appointees, nearly all from the peerage, who were responsible for maintaining security and organizing the local militias within each county.

Masque A ritualized blend of dance, drama and fantasy very popular at the Courts of James VI and I and Charles I. Masques were usually performed with elaborate costumes and specially designed sets.

Monopoly A grant by the Crown, to an individual or institution, of the sole right to make or distribute a particular product or commodity. The 1624 Monopolies Act made them illegal except to inventors, boroughs, syndicates or trading companies.

Muggletonians A millenarian sect which emerged after the Regicide. They were the followers of Lodovick Muggleton and John Reeve, who claimed to be the two witnesses foretold in the Book of Revelation, whose arrival would herald the end of the world. They probably numbered several hundred, and were mainly drawn from artisans and shopkeepers in London and the south.

Nonconformists Usually applied to those Protestants who refused to conform to the practices and discipline of the established Church; often also referred to as *dissenters*.

Non-jurors Those who forfeited office in 1689–90 for refusing to swear the oath of allegiance to William and Mary on the grounds that this was inconsistent with their earlier oath to James VII and II. These 'non-jurors' comprised several peers, Archbishop Sancroft, seven bishops, and nearly 400 other clergy.

Occasional conformists Those *dissenters* who took Anglican communion once a year in order to evade the penal laws against *nonconformists* and thereby qualify for appointment or election to public office. The *Tories* were deeply hostile towards occasional conformity and, after several unsuccessful attempts, they secured an act making the practice illegal in 1711.

Ordinance Between 1642 and 1649, the English Houses of Parliament claimed the right, in time of emergency, to pass ordinances which had the force of *statute* law even though they had not received the royal assent. The term was also applied to measures enacted by Cromwell as Lord Protector when Parliament was not sitting.

Ordinary revenue The income that the Crown derived on a regular basis from its lands, from feudal revenues, from the profits of justice, and from a range of duties such as *customs*.

Pale The area of Ireland around Dublin that was under the direct control of officials appointed by the English Crown.

Patent A document, bearing the Great Seal, by which the Crown made a grant to a particular individual. The term was often used especially of patents of *monopoly*.

Pluralism The holding by a clergyman of more than one church living at the same time. The 1604 Canons banned the holding of livings more than thirty miles apart.

Poynings' Law The law of 1494 which stipulated that no Irish Parliament could meet without a licence from the English monarch, and that no bill could be introduced until it had received the approval of the King and *Privy Council* in England.

Prelatist A term of abuse applied to someone who believed that the Church should be governed by bishops. 'Prelacy' was sometimes used as a pejorative term for 'episcopacy'.

Prerogative The general term applied to royal discretionary powers; sometimes sub-divided into the 'ordinary' (or legal) prerogative, exercised through Parliament and the common law, and the 'extraordinary' (or absolute) prerogative which could supplement (but not contravene) the law in order to safeguard the public good.

Presbyterians Those who saw all ministers as equal and opposed clerical hierarchies. They envisaged a rigid structure of discipline based on the *Calvinist* institutions of a national synod, regional assemblies and local groupings of parishes (called 'presbyteries' in Scotland and 'classes' in England). English Presbyterians regarded the churches of Scotland and Geneva as models and tried (unsuccessfully) to introduce a similar system in England.

Primogeniture The principle, well established throughout most of England, that the eldest son inherited by right most of his father's property.

Privy Council The inner body of royal advisers, selected by the monarch, that emerged out of the King's *Great Council* (or Parliament). It usually numbered somewhere between fifteen and forty-five, and discharged a wide range of political, administrative and judicial functions.

Proclamation An edict issued by the King or the King and Council. Proclamations were less powerful than *statutes* in that they could not touch life or limb, or affect *common law* rights of property.

Prophesyings Meetings of clergy, often before a lay audience, to expound and discuss Scripture and to improve preaching skills.

Prorogue The royal right to end a particular parliamentary session without actually dissolving the Parliament, thus keeping it in existence for further sessions.

Puritans Those who regarded the Church of England as 'but halfly reformed', and wished to purify it of the legacies of Catholicism, such as bishops, vestments and the Prayer Book. They were sometimes also called 'the hotter sort of Protestants' or 'the godly'.

Purveyance The traditional royal right to purchase transport, food and other supplies for the royal household at prices well below market level.

Quakers A radical religious sect that emerged in the late 1640s. They rejected an ordained ministry and set forms of worship, and stressed instead the concept of an 'inner light' within people that would bring salvation to those who accepted its guidance. They were hostile to hierarchy and civil authority, and their refusal to swear oaths, to pay *tithes* or to doff their hats was widely regarded as subversive.

Quamdiu se bene gesserint Literally, 'for as long as they shall do good'. Commissions issued to judges *quamdiu se bene gesserint* meant that they in effect had security of tenure, except on evidence of complete incompetence, corruption or gross moral turpitude.

Quarter sessions General courts held four times a year in every county, in which the *Justices of the Peace* would hear and determine matters relating to breaches of the peace, and deal with other legal or administrative business.

Quo warranto Literally, 'by what warrant'. Writs of *quo warranto* called for the legal scrutiny and surrender of a charter of rights, and were used extensively during the reigns of Charles II and James VII and II to rescind borough charters of incorporation.

Ranters In the late 1640s and early 1650s contemporaries lumped together a number of radical writers under the term 'Ranter'. In fact, they never formed an organized group and espoused no coherent ideology, but the general direction of many of their writings pointed towards *Antinomianism*.

Recusants Those, especially Catholics, who refused to attend Church of England services. They were liable to a number of penal laws, extended in 1606, that imposed punishments ranging from increasingly heavy fines to imprisonment or banishment.

Schismatics Another, more pejorative word for *separatists*, sometimes loosely applied as a term of abuse to radical *Puritans*.

Scrofula See *King's Evil*.

Sectaries Another, more pejorative word for *separatists*, sometimes loosely applied as a term of abuse to radical *Puritans*.

Separatists Those who withdrew completely from the established Church and formed their own religious assemblies or sects. They rejected the idea of a national Church and believed that each 'gathered congregation' should organize its own affairs.

Sheriff An officer appointed annually by the Crown in each county to collect royal revenues and to preserve public order. They also acted as returning officers in parliamentary elections, and were therefore debarred from serving as members of Parliament themselves.

Ship Money From Edward III's reign, the Crown had raised money on royal writs from coastal regions during national emergencies to build a fleet. Such levies were normally imposed every few decades, but between 1634 and

1639 Charles raised them every year, and from 1635 he extended Ship Money to the whole of England and Wales. It produced a high financial yield but at heavy political cost, and it was abolished in 1641.

Skimmington See *Charivari*.

Socinianism Named after the sixteenth-century theologian Faustus Socinus, Socinians denied the Trinity and also the divinity of Christ. Often, the term was also loosely used to mean the application of human reason to religious matters.

Star Chamber The *Privy Council* and Judges sitting as a court of law that dealt with criminal offences, especially those involving breaches of public order. It became widely unpopular during the 1630s because of the savage penalties imposed on *Puritan* critics of royal policies, and was abolished in 1641.

Statute An act passed by the Crown and the two Houses of Parliament. Statute was the highest form of human law, and its omnicompetence was definitively established during the Reformation Parliament (1529–36).

Subsidy A form of parliamentary taxation, first introduced in 1523. It was a tax on land and other forms of property, but its yield diminished with time because outdated assessments led to the rich being increasingly under-assessed.

Surplice A white linen robe worn by clergy both before and after the Reformation. Many *Puritans* attacked it as a 'popish rag' and wanted ministers to wear a plain black gown.

Tanistry The system of inheritance practised among the Gaelic Irish whereby the dead lord's land was conferred by election upon the 'eldest and worthiest' of his surviving kinsmen. It was gradually supplanted by the principles of the English *common law*, and was declared illegal in 1608.

Teinds The Scottish word for *tithes*.

Tithes In theory, one tenth of the produce of a parish was supposed to be paid to support the local clergyman. In practice, it was frequently commuted for a fixed sum, and often paid to a lay 'impropriator' who in turn paid the clergyman a stipend, the real value of which declined with inflation.

Tonnage and Poundage Duties imposed on every tun of wine imported, and every pound's worth of goods that was either imported or exported. Traditionally, the first Parliament of each reign granted these duties to a new monarch for life, but the Parliament of 1625 granted them to Charles I for one year only. His continued collection of them without Parliament's consent proved highly controversial.

Tories The name originally given to Irish (Catholic) cattle rustlers. From around 1680 it was applied to those who upheld the principle of divine right monarchy and believed that civil authority derived directly from God. Most Tories strongly defended the established Church and were hostile towards *dissenters* and republicans.

Trained Bands Selected members of local citizen militias who, from Elizabethan times, received special training to prepare them to defend their counties.

Transubstantiation The Roman Catholic belief that during the Mass the bread and wine are literally transformed into the body and blood of Christ.

Unitarians Those who believed in a single godhead and denied the doctrine of the Trinity.

Wardship The monarch's feudal right to assume the guardianship of those of its tenants-in-chief who inherited estates as minors. It involved both the management of the wards' lands and the right to arrange their marriages. This highly profitable right was either administered by the Crown through the Court of Wards or sold off to interested parties.

Whigs A name originally given to Scottish Presbyterian rebels of the late 1640s. From around 1680 it was applied to those who believed that civil authority derived from the people, and that rulers who did not govern for the public good could be resisted. They saw Parliament as an essential safeguard of Protestantism, liberties and property. Most Whigs opposed the intolerance of the Church of England and were sympathetic towards *dissenters*.

Yeomen Moderately substantial *freeholders*, owning up to about a hundred acres, who often discharged the lesser local offices such as constable, elder and juryman at the *quarter sessions*. Yeomen prospered and increased during the late sixteenth and seventeenth centuries, and some ultimately entered the ranks of the gentry.

Appendix 2:
Archbishops of
Canterbury, 1603–1707

Note: Dates in the second column are those of royal nomination. Dates in the third column are those of death unless otherwise indicated.

John Whitgift	14 August 1583	29 February 1604
Richard Bancroft	9 October 1604	2 November 1610
George Abbot	4 March 1611	4 August 1633
William Laud	6 August 1633	10 January 1645 (executed)
William Juxon	2 September 1660	4 June 1663
Gilbert Sheldon	16 June 1663	9 November 1677
William Sancroft	29 December 1677	deprived 1 February 1690; died 24 November 1693
John Tillotson	22 April 1691	22 November 1694
Thomas Tenison	6 December 1694	14 December 1715

Source: E. B. Fryde, D. E. Greenway, S. Porter and I. Roy (eds), *Handbook of British Chronology* (3rd edition, Cambridge, 1996), p. 234.

Appendix 3:
Lord Chancellors and Lord Keepers of the Great Seal of England, 1603–1707

Note: A Lord Keeper (LK) exercised the same authority as a Lord Chancellor (LC), but his office was of less dignity.

Sir Thomas Egerton, later Lord Ellesmere
LK 6 May 1596   LC 24 July 1603   d. 3 March 1617

Sir Francis Bacon, later Lord Verulam
LK 7 March 1617   LC 7 January 1618   dism. 1 May 1621

John Williams, later Bishop of Lincoln
LK 16 July 1621   dism. 25 October 1625

Sir Thomas Coventry, later Lord Coventry
LK 1 November 1625   d. 14 January 1640

Sir John Finch, later Lord Finch
LK 17 January 1640   fled abroad 31 December 1640

Sir Edward Lyttleton, later Lord Lyttleton
LK 18 January 1641   d. 9 August 1645

Sir Richard Lane
LK 30 August 1645   d. April 1650

On 10 November 1643 the Houses of Parliament authorized a new Great Seal which they entrusted to commissioners. In January 1649 a new Commonwealth Seal was created. This was again entrusted to commissioners, who finally ceased to act on 28 May 1660. The Commonwealth Seal was defaced and then broken up.

Sir Edward Herbert
LK 6 April 1653   res. June 1654

Sir Edward Hyde, later Lord Hyde, then Earl of Clarendon
LC 13 January 1658   dism. 30 August 1667

Sir Orlando Bridgeman
LK 30 August 1667   dism. 17 November 1672

Anthony Ashley Cooper, Lord Ashley, later Earl of Shaftesbury
LC 17 November 1672   dism. 9 November 1673

Sir Heneage Finch, later Lord Finch, then Earl of Nottingham
LK 9 November 1673   LC 19 December 1675   d. 18 December 1682

Sir Francis North, later Lord Guilford
LK 20 December 1682   d. 5 September 1685

Sir George Jeffreys, later Lord Jeffreys
LC 28 September 1685   depr. 11 December 1688

The Seal placed in commission   1689–23 March 1693

Sir John Somers, later Lord Somers
LK 23 March 1693   LC 22 April 1697   dism. 17 April 1700

Sir Nathan Wright
LK 21 May 1700   dism. 11 October 1705

William Cowper, later Lord Cowper
LK 11 October 1705   LC of Great Britain 4 May 1707

Main source: E. B. Fryde, D. E. Greenway, S. Porter and I. Roy (eds), *Handbook of British Chronology* (3rd edition, Cambridge, 1996), pp. 89–90.

Appendix 4:
Lord Treasurers of
England, 1603–1707

Note: The office of Lord Treasurer was not always filled, and from time to time it was entrusted to a team of Treasury Commissioners headed by the First Lord of the Treasury.

Thomas Sackville, Lord Buckhurst, later Earl of Dorset
        15 May 1599   d. 19 April 1608

Robert Cecil, Earl of Salisbury
        4 May 1608   d. 24 May 1612

Treasury Commissioners
        17 June 1612   11 July 1614

Thomas Howard, Earl of Suffolk
        11 July 1614   susp. 19 July 1618

Treasury Commissioners
        19 July 1618   14 December 1620

Henry Montagu, Viscount Mandeville, later Earl of Manchester
        14 December 1620   res. 29 September 1621

Lionel Cranfield, later Earl of Middlesex
        29 September 1621   dism. 13 May 1624

James Ley, Lord Ley, later Earl of Marlborough
        11 December 1624   res. 15 July 1628

Richard Weston, Lord Weston, later Earl of Portland
        15 July 1628   d. 13 March 1635

Treasury Commissioners
        15 March 1635   6 March 1636

William Juxon, Bishop of London
        6 March 1636   res. 17 May 1641

Treasury Commissioners
       21 May 1641   3 October 1643

Francis Cottington, Lord Cottington
       3 October 1643   d. 19 June 1652

Treasury Commissioners
       August 1654   May 1659

Thomas Wriothesley, Earl of Southampton
       8 September 1660   d. 16 May 1667

Treasury Commissioners
       1 June 1667   28 November 1672

Thomas Clifford, Lord Clifford
       28 November 1672   res. 18 June 1673

Sir Thomas Osborne, later Earl of Danby
       19 June 1673   res. 26 March 1679

Treasury Commissioners
       26 March 1679   16 February 1685

Laurence Hyde, Earl of Rochester
       16 February 1685   dism. 10 December 1686

Treasury Commissioners
       5 January 1687   8 May 1702

Sidney Godolphin, Lord Godolphin
       8 May 1702   dism. 8 August 1710

Main source: E. B. Fryde, D. E. Greenway, S. Porter and I. Roy (eds), *Handbook of British Chronology* (3rd edition, Cambridge, 1996), pp. 108–9.

Appendix 5: Principal Secretaries of State of England, 1603–1707

Note: From 1540 there were almost always two Principal Secretaries of State in office at any one time. Unless otherwise stated, each continued in post until the date of the appointment of the successor indicated in the same column.

5 July 1596
  Sir Robert Cecil (d. 24 May 1612

10 May 1600
  John Herbert

1612
  Robert Carr, later Earl of Somerset (conducted King's correspondence without title of Sec.)
29 March 1614
  Sir Ralph Winwood (d. October 1617)

13 January 1616
  Sir Thomas Lake

8 January 1618
  Sir Robert Naunton

16 February 1619
  Sir George Calvert, later Lord Baltimore

16 January 1623
  Sir Edward Conway, later Viscount Conway

February 1625
    Sir Albertus Morton
September 1625
    Sir John Coke

17 December 1628
    Sir Dudley Carleton, later
    Viscount Dorchester
15 June 1632
    Sir Francis Windebank (fled
    abroad December 1640)

3 February 1640
    Sir Henry Vane the elder
    (dismissed November 1641)

27 November 1641
    Sir Edward Nicholas

8 January 1642
    Lucius Carey, Viscount Falkland
    (killed at Newbury, 20
    September 1643)

4 October 1643
    George Digby, later Earl of
    Bristol (resigned 1645,
    reappointed 1658)

SECRETARIES OF STATE UNDER THE PROTECTORATE

16 December 1653
    John Thurloe (until April–May 1659)

17 January 1660
    Thomas Scot

27 February 1660
    John Thurloe and John Thompson (jointly)

From 1662 the Secretaries' work became more formally divided, with one responsible for the Northern aspects of foreign affairs (i.e. for Protestant countries) and the other for Southern (i.e. for Catholic countries). The usual pattern was for the Northern Secretary, who was the junior partner, to become Southern Secretary when the latter office fell vacant.

1 June 1660
    Sir Edward Nicholas

27 June 1660
    Sir William Morice

20 October 1662
Sir Henry Bennet, later Lord
Arlington, then Earl of Arlington
(S)

29 September 1668
Sir John Trevor (N)
8 July 1672
Henry Coventry (N till 1674,
then S till 1680)

11 September 1674
Sir Joseph Williamson (N)
20 February 1679
Robert Spencer, Earl of
Sunderland (N till April 1680,
then S till 1681)

26 April 1680
Sir Leoline Jenkins (N till
February 1681, then S till 1684)

2 February 1681
Edward Conway, Earl of
Conway (N)
28 January 1683
Robert Spencer, Earl of
Sunderland (N till April 1684,
then S till 1688)

14 April 1684
Sidney Godolphin, later Lord
Godolphin (N)
24 August 1684
Charles Middleton, Earl of
Middleton (N till 1688, S
October 1688)

28 October 1688
Richard Graham, Viscount
Preston (N)

From 1689 a formal division between the Northern and Southern Departments
was officially established:

Northern   *Southern*

14 February 1689
Charles Talbot, Earl of
Shrewsbury, later Duke of
Shrewsbury

5 March 1689
Daniel Finch, Earl of Nottingham

2 June 1690
Nottingham sole Sec.

Northern

26 December 1690
Henry Sidney, Viscount Sidney,
later Earl of Romney
3 March 1692
Nottingham sole Sec.
23 March 1693
Sir John Trenchard

November 1693
Sir John Trenchard sole Sec.
2 March 1694
Charles Talbot, Duke of
Shrewsbury

3 May 1695
Sir William Trumbull
(vac. 1–2 December 1697)
2 December 1697
James Vernon
12 December 1698
James Vernon sole Sec.
14 May 1699
James Vernon

27 June 1700
James Vernon sole Sec.
5 November 1700
Sir Charles Hedges (dismissed
29 December 1701)
4 January 1702
James Vernon (dismissed
1 May 1702)

2 May 1702
Sir Charles Hedges

Southern

26 December 1690
Earl of Nottingham

23 March 1693
Earl of Nottingham (dismissed
November 1693)

2 March 1694
Sir John Trenchard (d. 27 April
1695)

late April 1695
Charles Talbot, Duke of
Shrewsbury (vac. 12 December
1698)

14 May 1699
Edward Villiers, Earl of Jersey
(dismissed 27 June 1700)

5 November 1700
James Vernon

4 January 1702
Charles Montagu, Earl of
Manchester (dismissed 1 May
1702)

2 May 1702
Earl of Nottingham (vac. April
1704)

18 May 1704	18 May 1704
Robert Harley	Sir Charles Hedges (dismissed
	December 1706)
	3 December 1706
	Charles Spencer, Earl of
	Sunderland

Main sources: E. B. Fryde, D. E. Greenway, S. Porter and I. Roy (eds), *Handbook of British Chronology* (3rd edition, Cambridge, 1996), pp. 117–19; John Wroughton, *The Longman Companion to the Stuart Age, 1603–1714* (Harlow, 1997), pp. 143–5.

Appendix 6:
Chief Governors of
Ireland, 1603–1707

Note: The term 'Chief Governor' is used here to mean those who exercised authority on the Crown's behalf in Ireland. This was usually either a Lord Lieutenant (LL) or Lord Deputy (LD). However, in the absence of such an officer, for example because a new appointee had not yet arrived in Ireland, authority could be exercised by the Lord Chancellor (LC) and/or Lords Justices (LJs) of Ireland. Relatively brief absences when a Lord Lieutenant or Lord Deputy visited England but then resumed office (for example Wentworth's absence from 3 June to 23 November 1636) have been omitted. In each case, the date given is the actual date of appointment, not of arrival in Ireland or of swearing-in.

12 April 1603	Charles Blount, Lord Mountjoy, later Earl of Devonshire (LD; LL from 25 April 1603)
30 May 1603	Sir George Carey (LD)
15 October 1604	Sir Arthur Chichester (LD)
7 February 1614	Archbishop Thomas Jones of Dublin and Sir Richard Wingfield (LJs)
29 November 1615	Archbishop Thomas Jones of Dublin and Sir John Denham (LJs)
2 July 1616	Sir Oliver St John (LD)
4 February 1622	Henry Carey, Viscount Falkland (LD)
18 April 1622	Sir Adam Loftus (LC) and Richard Wingfield (LJ) [until Falkland sworn in on 8 September 1622]
10 August 1629	Adam Loftus, Viscount Loftus (LC) and Richard Boyle, Earl of Cork (LJ)
12 January 1632	Thomas Wentworth, Viscount Wentworth, later Earl of Strafford (LD; LL from 13 January 1640)
30 December 1640	Sir John Borlase and Sir William Parsons (LJs)
14 June 1641	Robert Sidney, Earl of Leicester (LL)
31 March 1643	Sir John Borlase and Sir Henry Tichborne (LJs; appointed by the King)
13 November 1643	James Butler, Marquis of Ormond (LL; appointed by the King)

21 January 1646	Philip Sidney, Viscount Lisle (LL; appointed by Parliament)
19 June 1647	Arthur Annesley, Michael Jones, Sir Robert King, Sir Robert Meredith, John Moore (commissioners of Parliament)
30 September 1648	James Butler, Marquis of Ormond (LL; appointed by the King)
22 June 1649	Oliver Cromwell (LL; appointed by Parliament)
26 May 1650	Henry Ireton (LD; appointed by Parliament)
6 December 1650	Ulick Burke, Marquis of Clanricard (LD; appointed by Charles II in exile)
13 August 1652	Charles Fleetwood, Miles Corbet, Edmund Ludlow, John Jones (commissioners appointed by Parliament); Oliver Cromwell and John Weaver added 25 August 1652
27 August 1654	Charles Fleetwood (LD)
17 November 1657	Henry Cromwell (LD; LL from 6 October 1658)
7 July 1659	John Jones, William Steele, Robert Goodwin, Matthew Tomlinson, Miles Corbet (parliamentary commissioners)
19 January 1660	John Weaver, Robert Goodwin, Sir Charles Coote, William Bury, Sir Hardress Waller, Henry Markham (parliamentary commissioners)
June 1660	George Monck, Baron Monck, later Duke of Albemarle (LL)
25 July 1660	John Robartes, Lord Robartes (LD)
26 October 1660	Sir Maurice Eustace (LC); Roger Boyle, Earl of Orrery, and Charles Coote, Earl of Mountrath (LJs)
21 February 1662	James Butler, Duke of Ormond (LL)
7 February 1668	Thomas Butler, Earl of Ossory (LD)
3 May 1669	John Robartes, Lord Robartes (LL)
4 February 1670	John Berkeley, Lord Berkeley (LL)
21 May 1672	Arthur Capel, Earl of Essex (LL)
24 May 1677	James Butler, Duke of Ormond (LL)
24 February 1685	Archbishop Michael Boyle of Dublin and Arthur Forbes, Earl of Granard (LJs)
1 October 1685	Henry Hyde, Earl of Clarendon (LL)
8 January 1687	Richard Talbot, Earl of Tyrconnell (LD)
12 March 1689– 4 July 1690	James VII and II in Ireland
14 June– 5 September 1690	William III in Ireland
4 September 1690	Henry Sidney, Viscount Sidney, and Thomas Coningsby (LJs); joined by Sir Charles Porter (LC) on 4 December 1690
18 March 1692	Henry Sidney, Viscount Sidney (LL)

13 June 1693	Sir Charles Porter (LC); joined by Henry Capel, Baron Capel, Sir Cyril Wyche and William Dunscombe (LJs) on 26 June 1693
9 May 1695	Henry Capel, Baron Capel (LD)
2 June 1696	Sir Charles Porter (LC); joined by Charles Coote, Earl of Mountrath and Henry Moore, Earl of Drogheda (LJs) on 10 July 1696
21 January 1697	Henry de Massue, Viscount Galway, later Earl of Galway (LJ); joined by Edward Villiers, Viscount Villiers (LJ) on 14 May 1697
29 June 1699	Henry de Massue, Earl of Galway, Charles Berkeley, Earl of Berkeley, Charles Paulet, Duke of Bolton (LJs)
28 December 1700	Laurence Hyde, Earl of Rochester (LL)
19 February 1703	James Butler, 2nd Duke of Ormond (LL)
30 April 1707	Thomas Herbert, Earl of Pembroke and Montgomery (LL)

Main sources: T. W. Moody, F. X. Martin and F. J. Byrne (eds), *A New History of Ireland*, vol. 9 (1984), pp. 487–91; E. B. Fryde, D. E. Greenway, S. Porter and I. Roy (eds), *Handbook of British Chronology* (3rd edition, Cambridge, 1996), pp. 168–70; John Wroughton, *The Longman Companion to the Stuart Age, 1603–1714* (Harlow, 1997), pp. 131–3.

Appendix 7:
Scottish Secretaries,
1603–1707

Note: Unless otherwise stated, each Scottish Secretary continued in post until the date of the appointment of his successor. Sometimes there was more than one Secretary in office at the same time.

19 January 1598	James Elphinstone, Lord Balmerino (forfeited 1 April 1609)
May 1608	Sir Alexander Hay
24 July 1612	Sir Thomas Hamilton, later Earl of Melrose (until 18 October 1627)
8 March 1626	William Alexander, later Earl of Sterling (d. 12 February 1640)
21 October 1627	Sir Archibald Acheson (d. 9 September 1634)
15 March 1640	William Hamilton, Earl of Lanark (dismissed by King January 1644 but confirmed by Parliament July 1644; dismissed 13 February 1649)
26 March 1640	Sir James Galloway (not recognized by Parliament after 1641; finally vacated office 1646)
January 1644	Sir Robert Spottiswoode (not recognized by Parliament; vacated September 1645)
10 March 1649	William Ker, Earl of Lothian (resigned 6 August 1660)
August 1660	John Maitland, Earl of Lauderdale, later Duke of Lauderdale
11 October 1680	Alexander Stewart, Earl of Moray (until 7 December 1688)
26 September 1682	Charles Middleton, Earl of Middleton (until 24 August 1684)
15 September 1684	John Drummond, Viscount Melfort, later Earl of Melfort (until 7 December 1688)
13 May 1689	George Melville, Earl of Melville (until 29 December 1691)

1 January 1691	John Dalrymple, later Earl of Stair (until July 1695)
3 March 1692	James Johnston
15 January 1696	John Murray, Earl of Tullibardine (until 31 March 1698)
5 February 1696	Sir James Ogilvy, later Earl of Seafield (until 21 November 1702)
31 January 1699	John Carmichael, Lord Carmichael
6 May 1702	James Douglas, Duke of Queensberry (until 16 October 1704)
21 November 1702	George Mackenzie, Viscount Tarbat, later Earl of Cromarty (until 17 October 1704)
16 October 1704	John Ker, Earl of Roxburghe (until 5 June 1705)
17 October 1704	James Ogilvy, Earl of Seafield
10 March 1705	William Johnston, Marquis of Annandale (until 29 September 1705)
5 June 1705	Hugh Campbell, Earl of Loudoun (reappointed after Union; resigned 25 May 1708)
29 September 1705	John Erskine, Earl of Mar (reappointed after Union; dismissed February 1709)

Source: E. B. Fryde, D. E. Greenway, S. Porter and I. Roy (eds), *Handbook of British Chronology* (3rd edition, Cambridge, 1996), pp. 194–5.

Appendix 8(A):
English Parliamentary
Sessions, 1604–1707

Parliament	Dates of sessions	Date of dissolution
James VI and I		
1604–11	(1) 19 March–7 July 1604	
	(2) 5 November 1605–27 May 1606	
	(3) 18 November 1606–4 July 1607	
	(4) 9 February–23 July 1610	
	(5) 16 October–6 December 1610	9 February 1611
1614	5 April–7 June 1614	7 June 1614
1621–2	(1) 30 January–4 June 1621	
	(2) 20 November–18 December 1621	6 January 1622
1624–5	19 February–29 May 1624 (automatically dissolved by the King's death)	27 March 1625
Charles I		
1625	(1) 18 June–11 July 1625	
	(2) 1–12 August 1625	12 August 1625
1626	6 February–15 June 1626	15 June 1626
1628–9	(1) 17 March–26 June 1628	
	(2) 20 January–10 March 1629	10 March 1629
1640	13 April–5 May 1640 (Short Parliament)	5 May 1640
1640–53	3 November 1640–20 April 1653 (Long Parliament)	Rump Parliament after Pride's Purge on 6 December 1648
1644	22 January–16 April 1644 (Oxford Parliament)	Never formally dissolved

Parliament	Dates of sessions	Date of dissolution

The Interregnum

1648–53	6 December 1648–20 April 1653 (Rump Parliament)	20 April 1653
1653	4 July–12 December 1653 (Nominated Assembly)	12 December 1653
1654–5	3 September 1654–22 January 1655 (1st Protectorate Parliament)	22 January 1655
1656–8	(1) 17 September 1656–26 June 1657 (2) 20 January–4 February 1658 (2nd Protectorate Parliament)	4 February 1658
1659	27 January–22 April 1659 (3rd Protectorate Parliament)	22 April 1659
1659–60	7 May–13 October 1659 26 December 1659–16 March 1660 (Rump Parliament; Long Parliament from February 1660)	16 March 1660

Charles II

1660	(1) 25 April–13 September 1660 (2) 6 November–29 December 1660 (Convention)	29 December 1660
1661–79	(1) 8 May 1661–19 May 1662 (2) 18 February–27 July 1663 (3) 16 March–17 May 1664 (4) 24 November 1664–2 March 1665 (5) 9–31 October 1665 (6) 18 September 1666–8 February 1667 (7) 25–29 July 1667 (8) 10 October 1667–1 March 1669 (9) 19 October–11 December 1669 (10) 14 February 1670–22 April 1671 (11) 4 February–20 October 1673 (12) 27 October–4 November 1673 (13) 7 January–24 February 1674 (14) 13 April–9 June 1675 (15) 13 October–22 November 1675 (16) 15 February 1677–13 May 1678 (17) 23 May–15 July 1678 (18) 21 October–30 December 1678 (Cavalier Parliament)	24 January 1679
1679	6 March–27 May 1679	12 July 1679
1680–1	21 October 1680–10 January 1681	18 January 1681
1681	21–28 March 1681	28 March 1681

Parliament	Dates of sessions	Date of dissolution

James VII and II

1685–7	(1) 19 May–2 July 1685	
	(2) 9–20 November 1685	2 July 1687
1689–90	(1) 22 January–20 August 1689	
	(Recognized as a Parliament, 23 February 1689)	
	(2) 19 October 1689–27 January 1690	6 February 1690
	(Convention)	

William III and Mary

1690–5	(1) 20 March–23 May 1690	
	(2) 2 October 1690–5 January 1691	
	(3) 22 October 1691–24 February 1692	
	(4) 4 November 1692–14 March 1693	
	(5) 7 November 1693–25 April 1694	
	(6) 12 November 1694–3 May 1695	11 October 1695
1695–8	(1) 22 November 1695–27 April 1696	
	(2) 20 October 1696–16 April 1697	
	(3) 3 December 1697–5 July 1698	7 July 1698
1698–1700	(1) 6 December 1698–4 May 1699	
	(2) 16 November 1699–11 April 1700	19 December 1700
1701	6 February–24 June 1701	11 November 1701
1701–2	30 December 1701–23 May 1702	2 July 1702

Anne

1702–5	(1) 20 October 1702–27 February 1703	
	(2) 9 November 1703–3 April 1704	
	(3) 24 October 1704–14 March 1705	15 April 1705
1705–8	(1) 25 October 1705–21 May 1706	
	(2) 3 December 1706–24 April 1707	
	(3) 23 October 1707–1 April 1708	3 April 1708
	(Declared to be first Parliament of	
	Great Britain, 29 April 1707)	

Main sources: E. B. Fryde, D. E. Greenway, S. Porter and I. Roy (eds), *Handbook of British Chronology* (3rd edition, Cambridge, 1996), pp. 574–7; B. D. Henning (ed.), *The House of Commons, 1660–1690* (3 vols, London, 1983), vol. 1, pp. 85–7.

Appendix 8(B):
Irish Parliamentary
Sessions, 1613–1713

Parliament	Dates of sessions	Date of dissolution
James VI and I		
1613–15	(1) 18 May–5 June 1613	
	(2) 11 October–29 November 1614	
	(3) 18 April–16 May 1615	24 October 1615
Charles I		
1634–5	(1) 14 July–2 August 1634	
	(2) 4 November–14 December 1634	
	(3) 26 January–21 March 1635	
	(4) 24 March–18 April 1635	18 April 1635
1640–9	(1) 16 March–17 June 1640	
	(2) 1 October–12 November 1640	
	(3) 26 January–5 March 1641	
	(4) 11 May–17 November 1641	
	(5) 11 January 1642–9 February 1647	
	(6) 26 March–15 June 1647	30 January 1649
	(Dissolved by King's execution)	
The Interregnum		
Irish representatives were members of the following:		
1653	4 July–12 December 1653	12 December 1653
	(Nominated Assembly)	
1654–5	3 September 1654–22 January 1655	22 January 1655
	(1st Protectorate Parliament)	
1656–8	(1) 17 September 1656–26 June 1657	

Parliament	Dates of sessions	Date of dissolution
	(2) 20 January–4 February 1658 (2nd Protectorate Parliament)	4 February 1658
1659	27 January–22 April 1659 (3rd Protectorate Parliament)	22 April 1659

Charles II

1661–6	(1) 8 May–31 July 1661	
	(2) 6 September 1661–22 March 1662	
	(3) 17 April 1662–16 April 1663	
	(4) 26 October 1665–7 August 1666	7 August 1666

James VII and II

1689	7 May–18 July 1689 ('Patriot Parliament')	18 July 1689

William III and Mary

1692–3	5 October–3 November 1692	26 June 1693
1695–9	(1) 27 August 1695–3 December 1697	
	(2) 27 September 1698–26 January 1699	14 June 1699

Anne

1703–13	(1) 21 September 1703–4 March 1704	
	(2) 10 February–16 June 1705	
	(3) 1 July–30 October 1707	
	(4) 5 May–30 August 1709	
	(5) 19 May–28 August 1710	
	(6) 9 July–9 November 1711	6 May 1713

Source: T. W. Moody, F. X. Martin and F. J. Byrne (eds), *A New History of Ireland*, vol. 9 (Oxford, 1984), pp. 605–6.

Appendix 8(C):
Scottish Parliamentary
Sessions, 1604–1707

Parliament	Dates of sessions	Date of dissolution
James VI		
1604–5	(1) 10 April–11 July 1604	
	(2) 7 June–26 November 1605	26 November 1605
1606	14 January–11 July 1606	11 July 1606
1607–9	(1) 18 March–11 August 1607	
	(2) 10 May 1608–27 January 1609	27 January 1609
1609	12 April–17 June 1609	17 June 1609
1612	12–23 October 1612	23 October 1612
1617	27 May–28 June 1617	28 June 1617
1621	25 July–4 August 1621	4 August 1621
Charles I		
1633	18–28 June 1633	28 June 1633
1639–41	(1) 30 August–18 November 1639	
	(2) 2–11 June 1640	
	(3) 15 July–17 November 1641	17 November 1641
1644–7	(1) 4 June–29 July 1644	
	(2) 7 January–8 March 1645	
	(3) 8–11 July 1645	
	(4) 29 July–7 August 1645	
	(5) 26 November 1645–4 February 1646	
	(6) 3 November 1646–27 March 1647	27 March 1647

Parliament	Dates of sessions	Date of dissolution

Charles I/Charles II

1648–51	(1) 2 March–10 June 1648	
	(2) 4 January–16 March 1649	
	(3) 23 May–7 August 1649	
	(4) 7–8 March 1650	
	(5) 15 May–5 July 1650	
	(6) 26 November–30 December 1650	
	(7) 13–31 March 1651	
	(8) 23 May–6 June 1651	6 June 1651

The Interregnum

Scottish representatives were members of the following:

1653	4 July–12 December 1653 (Nominated Assembly)	12 December 1653
1654–5	3 September 1654–22 January 1655 (1st Protectorate Parliament)	22 January 1655
1656–8	(1) 17 September 1656–26 June 1657	
	(2) 20 January–4 February 1658 (2nd Protectorate Parliament)	4 February 1658
1659	27 January–22 April 1659 (3rd Protectorate Parliament)	22 April 1659

Charles II

1661–3	(1) 1 January–12 July 1661	
	(2) 8 May–9 September 1662	
	(3) 18 June–9 October 1663	9 October 1663
1669–74	(1) 19 October–23 December 1669	
	(2) 22 July–22 August 1670	
	(3) 12 June–11 September 1672	
	(4) 12 November–2 December 1672	3 March 1674
1681	28 July–17 September 1681	17 September 1681

James VII

1685–6	(1) 23 April–16 June 1685	
	(2) 29 April–15 June 1686	15 June 1686

Parliament	Dates of sessions	Date of dissolution

William III and Mary

1689–1702	(1) 14 March–24 May 1689 (Convention)	
	(2) 5 June–2 August 1689 (Recognized as a Parliament, 5 June 1689)	
	(3) 15 April–22 July 1690	
	(4) 3–10 September 1690	
	(5) 18 April–15 June 1693	
	(6) 9 May–17 July 1695	
	(7) 8 September–12 October 1696	
	(8) 19 July–1 September 1698	
	(9) 21–30 May 1700	
	(10) 29 October 1700–1 February 1701	
	(11) 9–30 June 1702	14 August 1702

Anne

1703–7	(1) 6 May–16 September 1703	
	(2) 6 July–28 August 1704	
	(3) 28 June–21 September 1705	
	(4) 3 October 1706–25 March 1707	28 April 1707

Main source: C. Innes and T. Thomson (eds), *The Acts of the Parliaments of Scotland, 1124–1707* (12 vols, Edinburgh, 1814–75), vols 4–11.

Appendix 9(A):
The Population of
England and Wales,
1601–1706

Note: This table gives estimates, rounded to the nearest 1,000, of the populations of England and Wales at five-yearly intervals. The figures for England include Monmouthshire, and have been derived from E. A. Wrigley and R. S. Schofield, *The Population History of England, 1541–1871* (2nd edition, Cambridge, 1989), pp. 208–9. The figures for Wales have been obtained by following Wrigley and Schofield's suggested method of treating the population of Wales as approximately 7 per cent of that of England.

Year	England	Wales	England and Wales
1601	4,110,000	288,000	4,398,000
1606	4,253,000	298,000	4,551,000
1611	4,416,000	309,000	4,725,000
1616	4,510,000	316,000	4,826,000
1621	4,693,000	329,000	5,022,000
1626	4,720,000	330,000	5,050,000
1631	4,893,000	343,000	5,236,000
1636	5,058,000	354,000	5,412,000
1641	5,092,000	356,000	5,448,000
1646	5,177,000	362,000	5,539,000
1651	5,228,000	366,000	5,594,000
1656	5,281,000	370,000	5,651,000
1661	5,141,000	360,000	5,501,000
1666	5,067,000	355,000	5,422,000
1671	4,983,000	348,000	5,331,000
1676	5,003,000	350,000	5,353,000
1681	4,930,000	345,000	5,275,000
1686	4,865,000	341,000	5,206,000
1691	4,931,000	345,000	5,276,000
1696	4,962,000	347,000	5,309,000
1701	5,058,000	354,000	5,412,000
1706	5,182,000	363,000	5,545,000

Appendix 9(B):
The Population of
Ireland, 1603–1712

Note: This table gives estimates, rounded to the nearest 100,000, of the population of Ireland.

Year	Population
1603	1,400,000
1641	2,100,000
1672	1,700,000
1687	2,200,000
1712	2,800,000

Sources: T. W. Moody, F. X. Martin and F. J. Byrne (eds), *A New History of Ireland*, vol. 3 (Oxford, 1976), pp. 388–90; L. M. Cullen, 'Economic Trends in Seventeenth-century Ireland', *The Economic and Social Review*, 6 (1974–5), 149–65.

Appendix 9(C):
The Population of
Scotland, 1603–1707

Note: There are no equivalent estimates for the population of seventeenth-century Scotland of the kind that exist for England and Wales, or even Ireland. Virtually no reliable evidence exists upon which to base such figures prior to the mid-eighteenth century. These estimates are therefore more than usually tentative.

Year	Population
1603	800,000
1691	1,230,000
1707	1,000,000–1,250,000

Main sources: S. G. E. Lythe and J. Butt, *An Economic History of Scotland, 1100–1939* (Glasgow, 1975), pp. 3–4; Michael Flinn (ed.), *Scottish Population History from the Seventeenth Century to the 1930s* (Cambridge, 1977), p. 4; R. A. Houston, *The Population History of Britain and Ireland, 1500–1750* (London, 1992), pp. 29–30.

Appendix 10: Prices in England, 1601–1700

Note: This table gives indexes of (1) the price of a composite unit of foodstuffs, and (2) the price of a sample of industrial products. This is an index rather than a list of actual prices, but it does indicate the scale and rate of the inflation. Figures for 1451–75 and for three decades in the sixteenth century are given for comparison.

Year	*(1)*	*(2)*
1451–75	100	100
1501–10	106	98
1531–40	161	110
1571–80	341	223
1601–10	527	256
1611–20	583	274
1621–30	585	264
1631–40	687	281
1641–50	723	306
1651–60	687	327
1661–70	702	343
1671–80	675	351
1681–90	631	310
1691–1700	737	331

Source: R. B. Outhwaite, *Inflation in Tudor and Early Stuart England* (2nd edition, London, 1982), p. 12.

Appendix 11:
Wage-rates in England,
1580–1710

Note: This table gives estimates of the daily wage in pence of a building craftsman (left-hand columns) and of a labourer (right-hand columns) in southern England between 1580 and 1710. Selected figures from the fifteenth and sixteenth centuries are also given for comparison. Many of the figures indicate the rough range within which wages probably fell rather than anything more precise.

Year	Craftsman	Year	Labourer
1412–1532	6	1412–1545	4
1552–61	from 7 to 10		
1580–1629	12	1580–1626	8
1629–42	from 12 to 16	1626–39	from 8 to 10
1642–55	from 16 to 18	1639–46	from 10 to 12
1655–87	18	1646–93	12
1687–1701	from 18 to 20	1693–1701	from 12 to 14
1701–10	from 20 to 22	1701–10	from 14 to 15

Source: E. H. Phelps Brown and Sheila V. Hopkins, 'Seven Centuries of Building Wages', reprinted in E. M. Carus-Wilson (ed.), *Essays in Economic History*, vol. 2 (London, 1962), pp. 168–78.

Index

Abbot, George, Archbishop of Canterbury, 41, 56, 92
Abjuration Act (1702), 318
Adamson, Patrick, Archbishop of St Andrews, 17
Addled Parliament, 35
Admiralty, 346
advowson, 382
Adwalton Moor, battle of (1643), 140
Agreement of the People, 156, 173
Alford, battle of (1645), 146
Alibone, Sir Richard, 281
Alien Act (1705), 331
Allestree, Richard, *The Whole Duty of Man*, 238
Almanza, battle of (1707), 310
Anabaptists, 189, 382
Andrewes, Lancelot, Bishop of Winchester, 39, 92
Anglican–Royalist theory, 125
Anglicans, 236–40
Anglo-Dutch treaty (1677), 235
Anglo-Dutch Wars, 182, 187, 212, 216–17, 218, 227, 229, 230, 234
Anjou, Duke of, *see* Philip V, King of Spain
Anne, Queen, 288, 310, 311–12, 315–16, 327, 331
Antinomianism, 173, 382
Antrim, Randal MacDonell, Earl of, 110, 122, 141, 144
Antrim plot, 122
Antwerp, 11
Appeals Act (1533), 6
appropriation, principle of, 313–14
architecture, 323–4
Argyll, Archibald Campbell, 8th Earl of, 119, 120, 141, 144, 146, 159
Argyll, Archibald Campbell, 9th Earl of, 276
Arlington, Henry Bennet, Earl of, 216, 225, 226, 228, 229
Arminians, 69, 74, 92, 382
Arms Act (1558), 88
army, 171, 181, 187–8; billeting of, 71–2; reform of, 88; *see also* New Model Army
Army Council, 195
Army Plots, 114, 122, 124
Articles of Grievances, 293
Arundel, Henry, Baron, 280
Arundel, Thomas Howard, Earl of, 70, 80
Ascham, Anthony, 181
Ascot Races, 327

Ashley Cooper, Anthony, *see* Shaftesbury, Earl of
Assessment, 148, 382
Assizes, 149, 192, 346, 382
Astell, Mary, *Defence of the Female Sex*, 342
Aston, Sir Thomas, 118, 129
Atlantic archipelago, 17, 19
Attainder, 382
Atterbury, Francis, Bishop of Rochester, *A Letter to a Convocation Man*, 319
Aughrim, battle of (1691), 296
Augsburg, Peace of (1555), 345–6
Augustan Age, 322–4, 327
Auldearn, battle of (1645), 146

Bacon, Sir Francis, 59
Baillie, Robert, 112, 114, 150, 179
Balfour, Sir James, 101
Balmerino, John Elphinstone, Baron, 102
Bancroft, Richard, Archbishop of Canterbury, 37
Bank of England, 314, 321
Bankes, Sir John, 88
Bankes, Lady Mary, 152
Banqueting House, Whitehall, 41, 83, 163
Baptists, 237, 382
Bargrave, Isaac, 71
Barillon, Paul, French Ambassador, 258
Barlow, Thomas, Bishop of Lincoln, 37
baronets, 35
Barrier Treaties (1713, 1715), 311
Barrington, Lady Joan, 9
Barrowists, 7
Bastwick, John, 97
Bate, John, 33
Baxter, Richard, 183, 208–9
Beachy Head, battle of (1690), 306
Bedford, Francis Russell, Earl of, 95, 117
Bedloe, William, 252
Behn, Aphra: *Sir Patient Fancy*, 243; *The Town Fop*, 243
Belasyse, John, Lord, 276, 280
Belhaven, John Hamilton, Lord, 332
Benburb, battle of (1646), 146
Benevolences, 58, 70, 382
Bentinck, Hans Willem, *see* Portland, Duke of
Berkeley, George, 228, 233–4
Berwick, Pacification of (1639), 110
Biddle, John, 190
Bill of Rights (1689), 289, 345